MW01629085

ROWN INTO THE SEA ONE STANDARD AIR
ORCE DYE MARKER THROWN INTO THE SEA
ONE STANDARD AIR FORCE DYE MARKER T
ROWN INTO THE SEA ONE STANDARD AIR
ORCE DYE MARKER THROWN INTO THE SEA
ONE STANDARD AIR FORCE DYE MARKER T
ROWN INTO THE SEA ONE STANDARD AIR
ORCE DYE MARKER THROWN INTO THE SEA
ONE STANDARD AIR FORCE DYE MARKER T
ROWN INTO THE SEA ONE STANDARD AIR
ORCE DYE MARKER THROWN INTO THE SEA
ONE STANDARD AIR FORCE DYE MARKER T
ROWN INTO THE SEA ONE STANDARD AIR
ORCE DYE MARKER THROWN INTO THE SEA
ONE STANDARD AIR FORCE DYE MARKER T
ROWN INTO THE SEA ONE STANDARD AIR
ORCE DYE MARKER THROWN INTO THE SEA
ONE STANDARD AIR FORCE DYE MARKER T
ROWN INTO THE SEA ONE STANDARD AIR
ORCE DYE MARKER THROWN INTO THE SEA
ONE STANDARD AIR FORCE DYE MARKER T
ROWN INTO THE SEA ONE STANDARD AIR
ORCE DYE MARKER THROWN INTO THE SEA
ONE STANDARD AIR FORCE DYE MARKER T
ROWN INTO THE SEA ONE STANDARD AIR
ORCE DYE MARKER THROWN INTO THE SEA
ONE STANDARD AIR FORCE DYE MARKER T
ROWN INTO THE SEA ONE STANDARD AIR
ORCE DYE MARKER THROWN INTO THE SEA
ONE STANDARD AIR FORCE DYE MARKER T
ROWN INTO THE SEA ONE STANDARD AIR
ORCE DYE MARKER THROWN INTO THE SEA
ONE STANDARD AIR FORCE DYE MARKER T
ROWN INTO THE SEA ONE STANDARD AIR
ORCE DYE MARKER THROWN INTO THE SEA
ONE STANDARD AIR FORCE DYE MARKER T
ROWN INTO THE SEA ONE STANDARD AIR
ORCE DYE MARKER THROWN INTO THE SEA
ONE STANDARD AIR FORCE DYE MARKER T
ROWN INTO THE SEA ONE STANDARD AIR
ORCE DYE MARKER THROWN INTO THE SEA

DWAN GALLERY

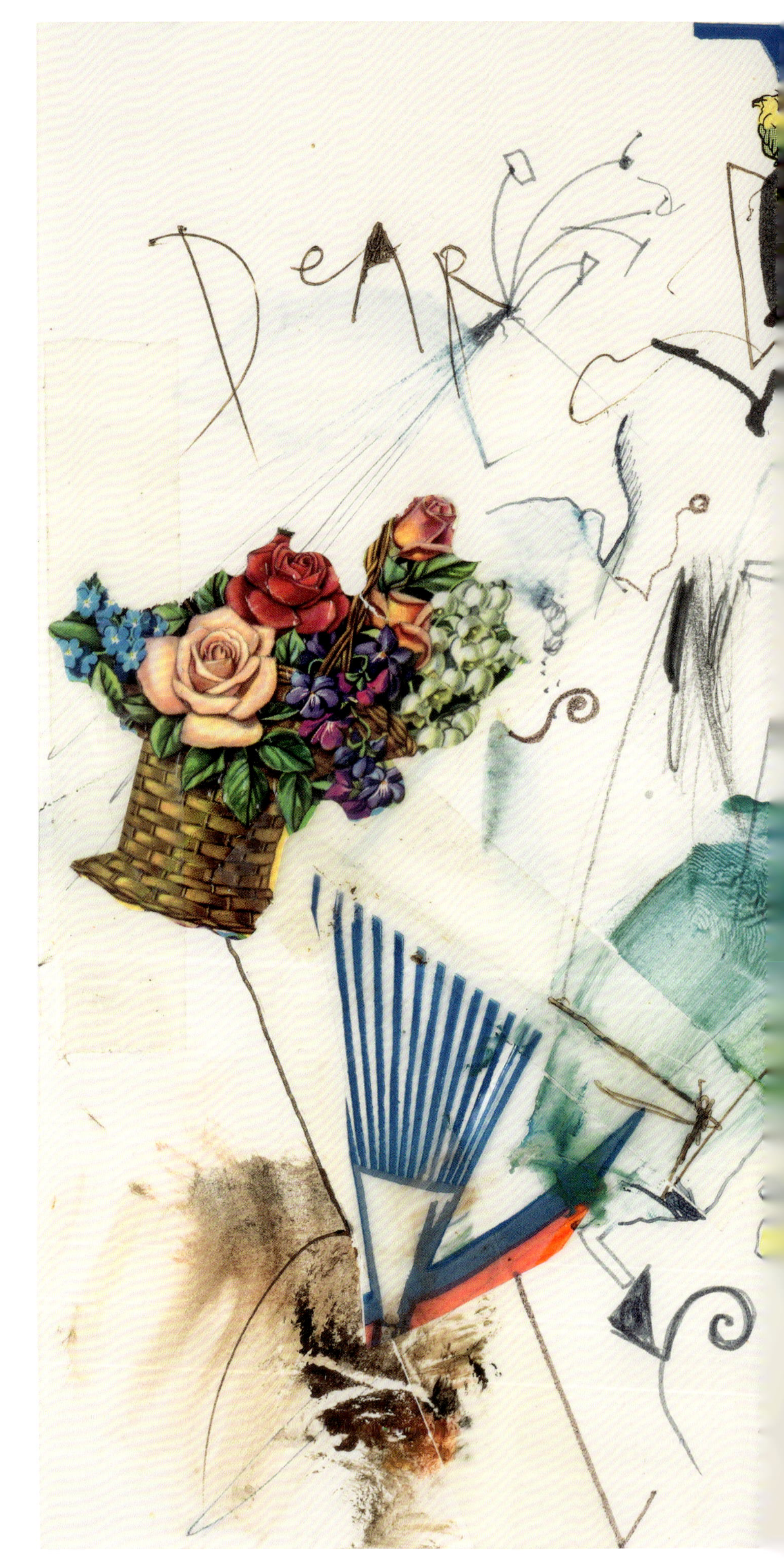
DeAR

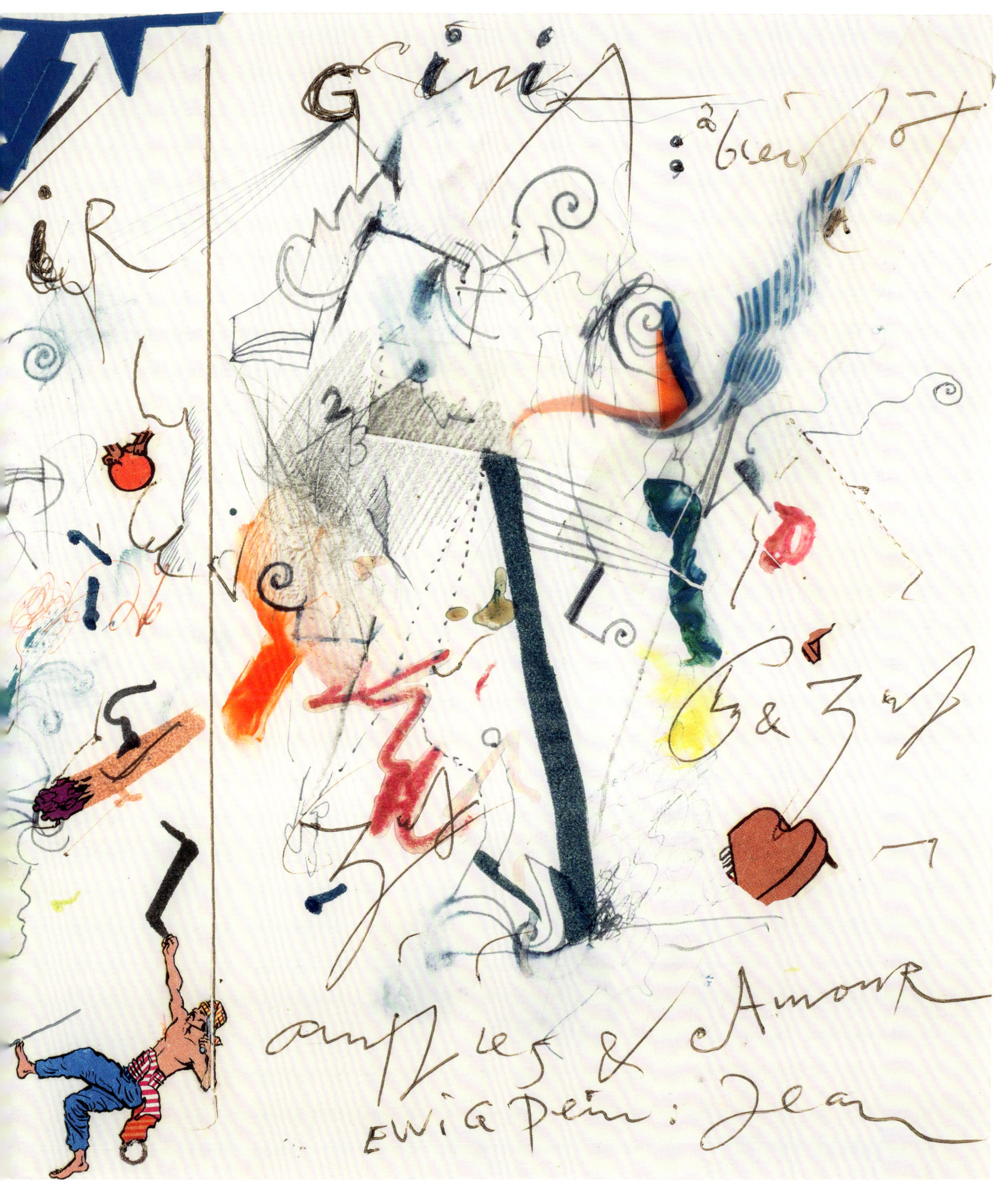
à bientôt
& Amour
EWiG Dein : Jean

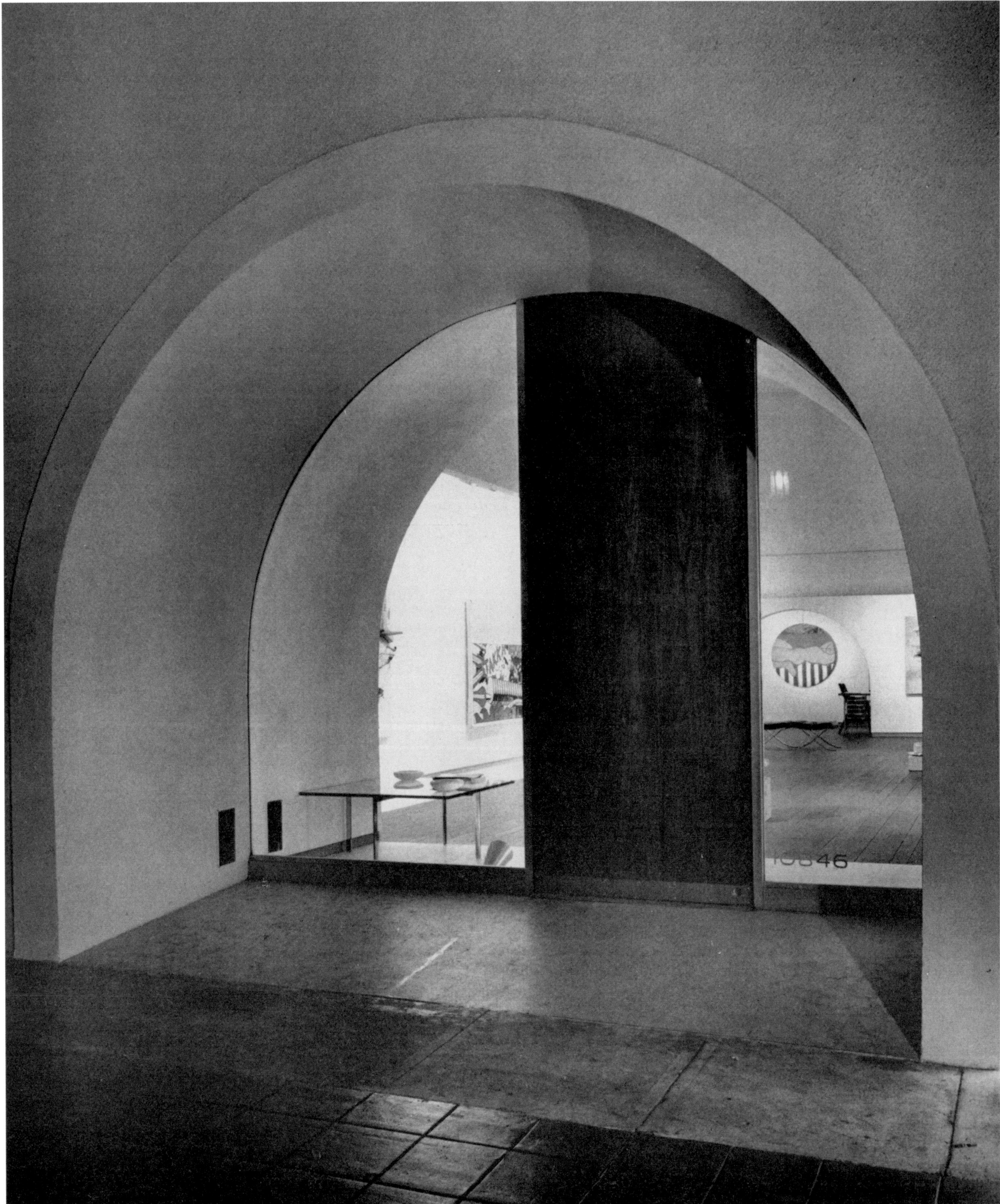

Los Angeles to New York DWAN GALLERY *1959–1971*

JAMES MEYER
WITH PAIGE ROZANSKI
AND VIRGINIA DWAN

NATIONAL GALLERY OF ART
WASHINGTON

IN ASSOCIATION WITH
THE UNIVERSITY OF CHICAGO PRESS
CHICAGO AND LONDON

The exhibition *Los Angeles to New York: Dwan Gallery, 1959–1971* is organized by the National Gallery of Art, Washington.

It is made possible through the generous support of the Robert and Mercedes Eichholz Foundation.

Exhibition dates:

National Gallery of Art
September 30, 2016–January 29, 2017

Los Angeles County Museum of Art
March 19–September 10, 2017

Produced by the Publishing Office,
National Gallery of Art, Washington
www.nga.gov

Judy Metro, editor in chief
Chris Vogel, deputy publisher and production manager
Wendy Schleicher, design manager

Designed by Margaret Bauer, Washington, DC

Sara Sanders-Buell, photography rights coordinator
John Long, print and digital production associate
Mariah Shay, production assistant
Katie Brennan, program assistant

Typeset in Sabon and Zwo Pro and printed on 150 gsm Arctic Volume White by Graphicom, Vicenza, Italy

Hardcover edition copublished by
The University of Chicago Press
1427 East 60th Street
Chicago, IL 60637
www.press.uchicago. edu

ISBN-13: 978-0-226-42510-8 (cloth)

10 9 8 7 6 5 4 3 2 1

Library of Congress Cataloging-in-Publication Data

Names: Meyer, James Sampson, author / Dwan Virginia. / Rozanski, Paige. / National Gallery of Art (U.S.). Publishing Office. / National Gallery of Art (U.S.), issuing body. / University of Chicago Press.

Title: *Dwan Gallery: Los Angeles to New York, 1959–1971* / James Meyer, with Paige Rozanski and Virginia Dwan.

Description: 1st edition. / Washington, D.C.: National Gallery of Art; Chicago; London: University of Chicago Press, 2016. / "The exhibition *Los Angeles to New York: Dwan Gallery, 1959–1971* is organized by the National Gallery of Art, Washington." / Includes bibliographical references and index.

Identifiers: LCCN 2016028114 <tel:2016028114> / ISBN 9780226425108 (cloth) / ISBN 022642510X (cloth)

Subjects: LCSH: Dwan Gallery (Los Angeles, Calif.)—History. / Dwan Gallery (New York, N.Y.)—History. / Dwan, Virginia. / Art, Modern—20th century—Exhibitions.

Classification: LCC N8660.D87 M49 2016 / DDC 709.2—dc23 / SUDOC SI 8.2:D 96
LC record available at *https://lccn.loc.gov/2016028114*

Display images:

pp. 2–3: Jean Tinguely with Niki de Saint Phalle, *Dear Virginia: a bientôt* (cat. 29); p. 4: Dwan Gallery Los Angeles, entrance, 10846 Lindbrook Drive; p. 8: Larry Rivers, *Maquette for Larry Rivers Exhibition at Dwan Gallery* (cat. 3, detail); p. 14: Virginia Dwan preparing *Boxes* exhibition, Dwan Gallery Los Angeles, 1964; p. 16: Robert Smithson's *Second Upside-Down Tree*, 1969; p. 98: Franz Kline, *Pittston* (cat. 9, detail); p. 240: Virginia Dwan, Dwan Gallery New York, c. 1967; p. 284: Robert Smithson, Nancy Holt, and Virginia Dwan on New Jersey site search, spring 1967; p. 318: Installation view of Carl Andre's *Cuts* at Dwan Gallery Los Angeles, 1967 (detail); p. 368: Robert Rauschenberg, *Coexistence* (cat. 19, detail); p. 376: Jean Tinguely, *Odessa* (cat. 25, detail); front endsheets: Agnes Martin, *The Cliff* (cat. 61, detail); Lawrence Weiner, *Structure Poem* (cat. 82, detail); back endsheets: Agnes Martin, *The Cliff* (cat. 61, detail); Jean Tinguely with Niki de Saint Phalle, *Chère Virginia: come sta?* (cat. 30, detail)

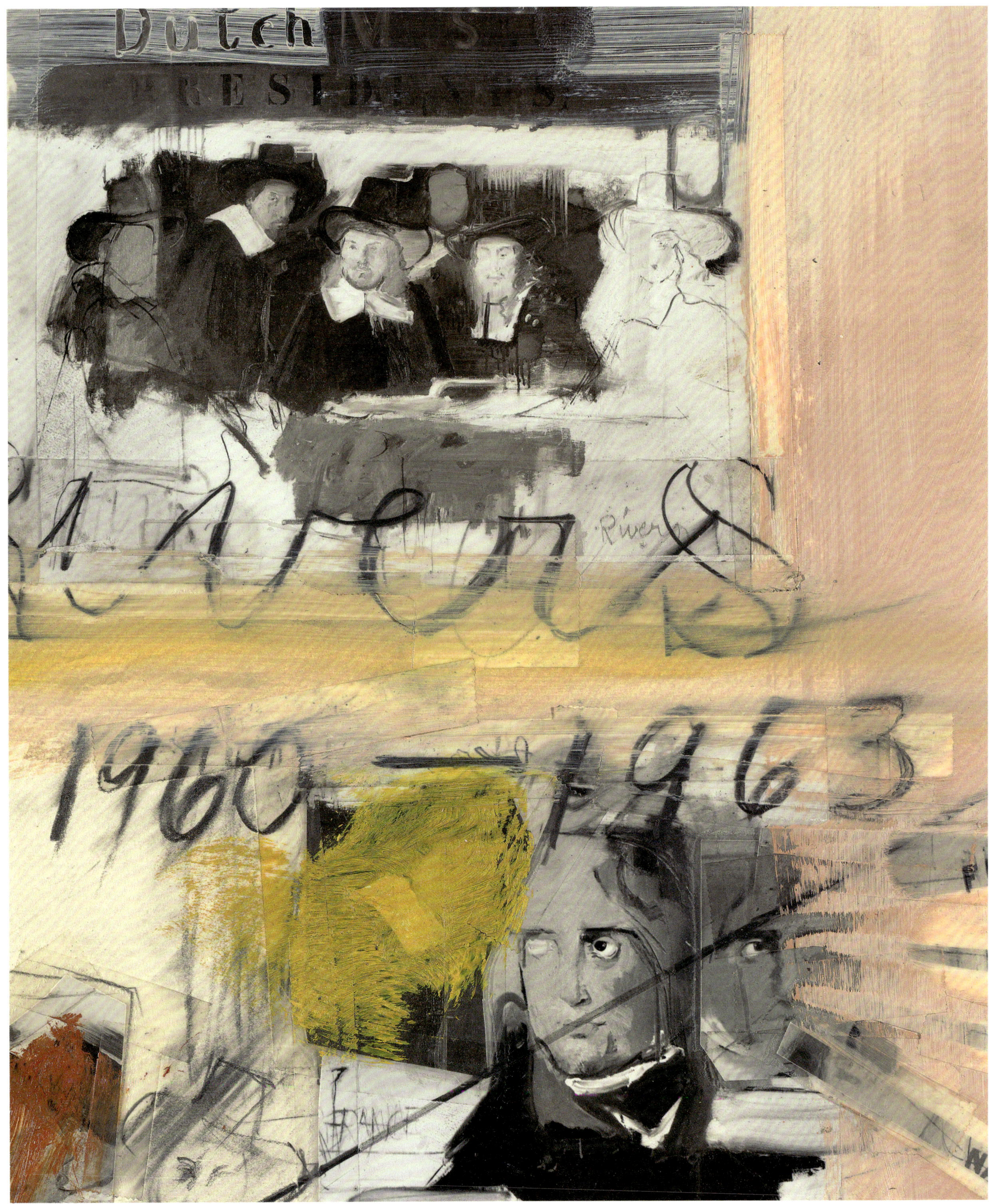

Dutch
PRESIDENTS
1960 — 1963

The run of the Dwan Gallery was brief yet momentous. During its eleven years, Virginia Dwan mounted 134 shows, introducing viewers in Los Angeles and New York to the most challenging art practices of the time. This exhibition traces the history of Dwan's storied gallery and—after it closed in 1971—her patronage of some of the great monuments of land art.

The initial inspiration for the exhibition was Virginia Dwan's promised gift of 250 works from her collection to the National Gallery of Art in 2013. Comprising paintings, sculptures, works on paper, photographs, and artists' books of extraordinary quality, the vast majority acquired directly from the artists, Dwan's generous gift is among the most historically significant ever received by the National Gallery. Including major examples of postwar abstraction, nouveau réalisme, minimalism, conceptualism, and land art heretofore unrepresented in the national collection, the gift will extend and redefine the Gallery's modern collection. Our gratitude to Virginia Dwan is immense.

The National Gallery is a collection of great collections. What makes the Dwan gift unique is Dwan's involvement in the creation of the works in her collection as both the dealer and patron of the artists. This exhibition, conceived by James Meyer, former associate curator of modern art at the National Gallery and currently deputy director and chief curator of the Dia Art Foundation, draws works from both the Dwan Collection and elsewhere, telling Dwan's remarkable story for the first time.

We have been joined in this effort by the Los Angeles County Museum of Art, led by the museum's director, Michael Govan, and its senior curator of modern art, Stephanie Barron. As a result of our partnership, Dwan's groundbreaking shows and the impact of her gallery on both the Los Angeles and New York art scenes during the sixties are finally being fully explored. Our gratitude extends as well to the Robert and Mercedes Eichholz Foundation for its benevolent support of the exhibition. We are grateful to the many museums and collectors whose loans have made the exhibition possible. Thanks to these generous institutions and individuals, we have been able to bring together works that highlight well over 40 seminal shows that Dwan installed in her Los Angeles and New York galleries. We thank Virginia Dwan and her daughter, Candace Dwan, in particular for sharing works in the Dwan Collection for the entire run of the exhibition.

The Dwan Gallery emerged during a period of unprecedented mobility linking the East and West Coast art worlds as never before and inducing artists to forsake the fine art "object" for conceptual and land-based projects, many of which Dwan sponsored personally. Meyer explores this subject—indeed, the thesis of our exhibition—in detail in his essay for the catalog, which is also enriched by Dwan's own voice. We thank Virginia Dwan for allowing us to gather for the first time some of her recollections and firsthand accounts of her encounters and journeys with several of her artists. An exhaustive chronology of Dwan's life and professional activities and a separate exhibition history prepared by Paige Rozanski, curatorial assistant in the department of modern art at the National Gallery, round out the volume, supplementing the art historical and personal narratives of Meyer and Dwan with intensive archival research.

We are delighted to recognize Virginia Dwan's significant contributions to postwar art in the United States and France—offering visitors to the exhibition and readers of this volume one iconic artwork after the other, almost all of them originally shown at her gallery. We are grateful to Dwan for her magnificent gift, and we hope that she is pleased with this exhibition.

EARL A. POWELL III, *Director, National Gallery of Art*

FOREWORD (LOS ANGELES)

Writing an accurate history of contemporary art in Los Angeles during the 1950s and 1960s is impossible without recognizing the role that several leading galleries and art dealers played in introducing artworks and artists to a local audience as well as presenting them nationally and internationally. While recent publications and exhibitions have focused on the activities of the Ferus Gallery (1957–1966), the story of the Dwan Gallery—founded and run by Virginia Dwan, first in the Westwood area of Los Angeles between 1959 and 1967 and then in New York between 1965 and 1971—is largely untold. Yet for a number of artists and collectors, the Dwan Gallery was an incredibly important place where they first encountered works by postwar French artists, in addition to the numerous minimal, conceptual, and earthwork artists who had their first exhibitions there. Virginia Dwan, along with her long-time gallery director John Weber, maintained a close and personal relationship with many of the gallery artists. Dwan provided generous stipends to gallery artists and invited them to spend time at her home in Malibu, often accompanying them on forays to find objects to incorporate into their works or to explore remote locations to create earthworks.

When the National Gallery of Art began to organize this exhibition on the occasion of Virginia's generous gift to the Gallery, it made sense that the show should be seen in Los Angeles as well. It has been a pleasure to work with exhibition curator James Meyer and curatorial assistant Paige Rozanski at the National Gallery on all aspects of the exhibition and publication. At the Los Angeles County Museum of Art (LACMA), we have augmented the scope of artists presented by including many works that entered area collections and museums, having been either exhibited or sold by the Dwan Gallery. Two former LACMA trustees, Michael Blankfort and Robert Halff, both acquired many works through the Dwan Gallery and subsequently donated their collections to the museum. Numerous works still remain with the families of the original collectors or are in the collections of other museums. We are indebted to those lenders who agreed to enhance the LACMA presentation; in particular we thank colleagues Carol Togneri at the Norton Simon Museum in Pasadena; Philippe Vergne, Helen Molesworth, and Bennett Simpson at the Museum of Contemporary Art, Los Angeles; Susan Guadamuz at the California African American Museum; Erik H. Neil at the Chrysler Museum of Art; collectors Susan and David Gersh; and artist Ronald Miyashiro for their generous loans.

We are grateful to Jamin An, the Yvonne Lenart UCLA Fellow during summer 2015 for his excellent sleuthing, which enabled us to locate a number of works that we have added to the checklist. Our museum archivist Jessica Gambling and the staff of our Balch Art Research Library have been resourceful in finding ephemeral materials to enrich our presentation. Tiffany Daneshgar, senior curatorial administrator in modern art, has assumed the responsibility of working closely with us on all of the administrative details of the exhibition and has been the liaison with both the National Gallery and many of our lenders. We are extremely grateful to her for willingly undertaking these responsibilities with her customary efficiency, graciousness, and enthusiasm. Our exhibitions team, led by Zoe Kahr, has worked with us to ensure that the show is presented at LACMA in the best possible manner. The Los Angeles presentation benefited enormously from conversations over the years with Betty Asher, John Baldessari, Michael and Dorothy Blankfort, Virginia Dwan, Stanley and Elyse Grinstein, Bob Halff, Michael Heizer, Pauli Hirsh, Richard Jackson, Lyn Kienholz, Nancy Reddin Kienholz, Paul McCarthy, Maurice Tuchman, and John Weber, all of whom affirmed and elucidated the remarkable achievements of Dwan Gallery's early days in Westwood.

It is a true honor to bring the activities of the Dwan Gallery to Los Angeles audiences. Most importantly we thank Virginia Dwan for her commitment to the art and artists she presented and for her generosity in sharing these works with the public.

MICHAEL GOVAN, *CEO and Wallis Annenberg Director, LACMA*
STEPHANIE BARRON, *Senior Curator of Modern Art, LACMA*

Much of the exhibition history, correspondence, and visual documentation pertaining to Dwan Gallery in its Los Angeles and New York locations is housed in the Dwan Gallery Archives and the Virginia Dwan Archives in New York. While the research for this volume draws from many sources, this account of Dwan Gallery's history could not have been constructed without full and open access to these archives. The authors are grateful to Virginia Dwan and Anne Kovach for sharing these records and allowing them to become part of the published history of Dwan Gallery.

Exhibition History: Aside from the addition of punctuation for clarity and the silent correction of obvious typos or misspelled names, no changes or annotations have been made in the titling or dating of artworks or in their order of appearance in the Dwan Gallery checklists. The treatment of titles in these checklists slavishly reflects the original record with regard to capitalization and italicization, and no attempt has been made to normalize titling styles, to verify the distinction between descriptive titles in roman type and actual titles in italic type, or to reconcile the checklist titles and dates with the titles and dates by which the same works have become known today. The reviews and mentions in this section have been gathered and selected by the author.

Essay, Writings, and Chronology: In these sections the titles and dates of artworks reflect those by which the works are known today and do not necessarily correspond to the information in the Dwan Gallery checklists in the Exhibition History.

Plates: With just a few exceptions the works in the plate section were originally shown at or sold by Dwan Gallery or are from the Collection of Virginia Dwan. These works are privileged in the essay discussion because the provenance of many is a direct line between the artists and Dwan.

Artists: The nationalities and life dates of the Dwan Gallery artists highlighted in this catalog and exhibition appear in the index listings for each artist.

Abbreviations: The abbreviations (DGLA) and (DGNY) have been used in the Chronology and Exhibition History to distinguish between exhibitions in the Los Angeles and New York galleries.

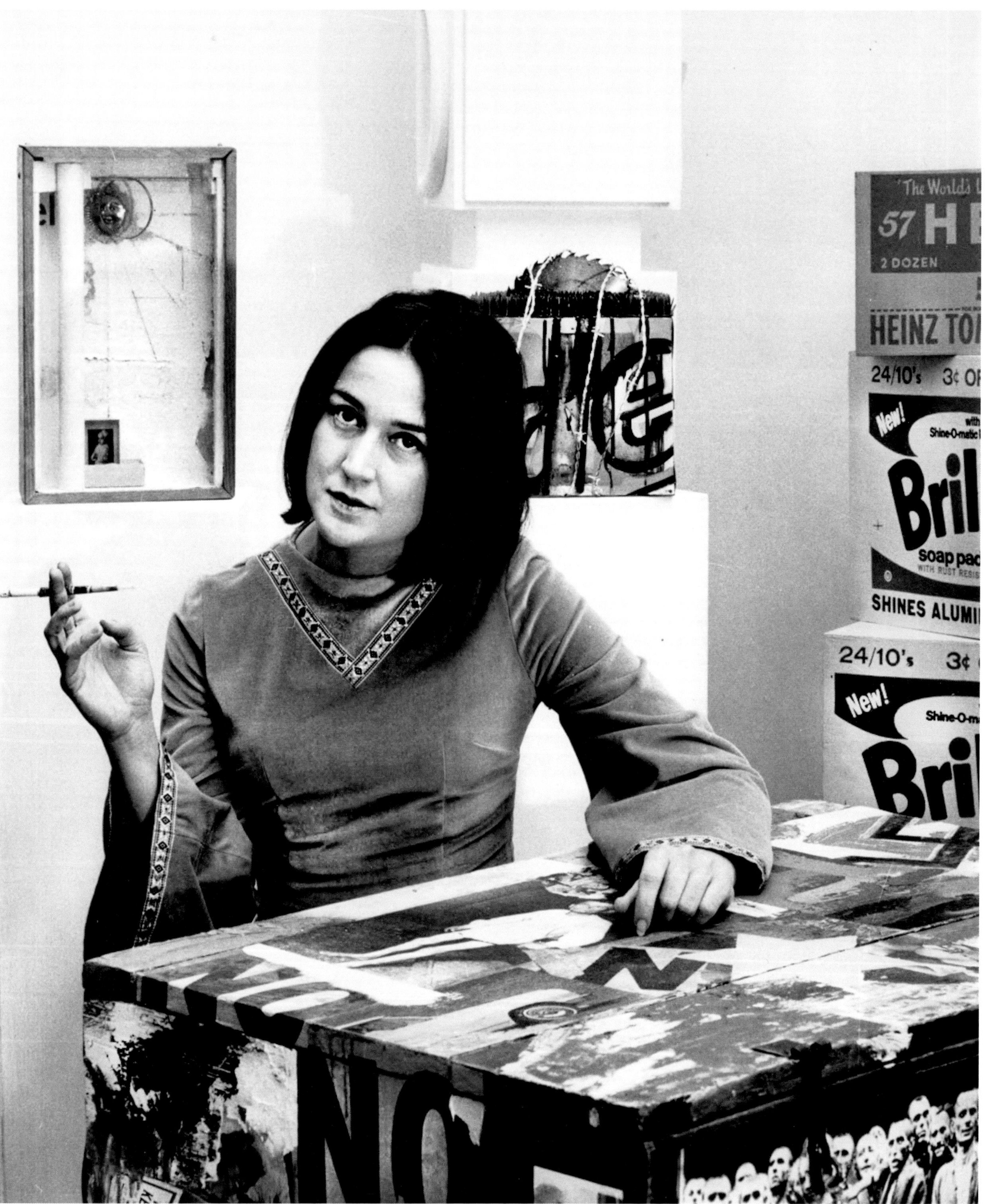
'The World's
57 HE
2 DOZEN
HEINZ TO
24/10's 3¢ OF
New!
Shine-O-matic
Bril
soap pac
SHINES ALUMI
24/10's 3¢
New!
Shine-O-m
Bril
NO

LENDERS TO THE EXHIBITION

California African American Museum
Broadway 1602 Uptown & Harlem
Castelli Gallery
Estate of Rosemarie Castoro
Centre Pompidou, Musée national d'art moderne, Paris
Chrysler Museum of Art
Virginia Dwan
Fine Arts Museums of San Francisco
Susan and David Gersh
Hirshhorn Museum and Sculpture Garden
Estate of Nancy Holt
Nancy Reddin Kienholz
Joseph Kosuth
L.A. Louver, Venice, California
Jeanne and Richard Levitt
LeWitt Collection
Los Angeles County Museum of Art
Ronald Miyashiro
Robert Morris
The Museum of Contemporary Art, Los Angeles
Museum of Contemporary Art Chicago
The Museum of Modern Art
National Gallery of Art
Norton Simon Museum
Private Collectors
Sean Kelly Gallery
Seattle Art Museum
Tate
Lynn and Allen Turner
Virginia Museum of Fine Arts
Wadsworth Atheneum Museum of Art
Frederick R. Weisman Art Foundation
Whitney Museum of American Art

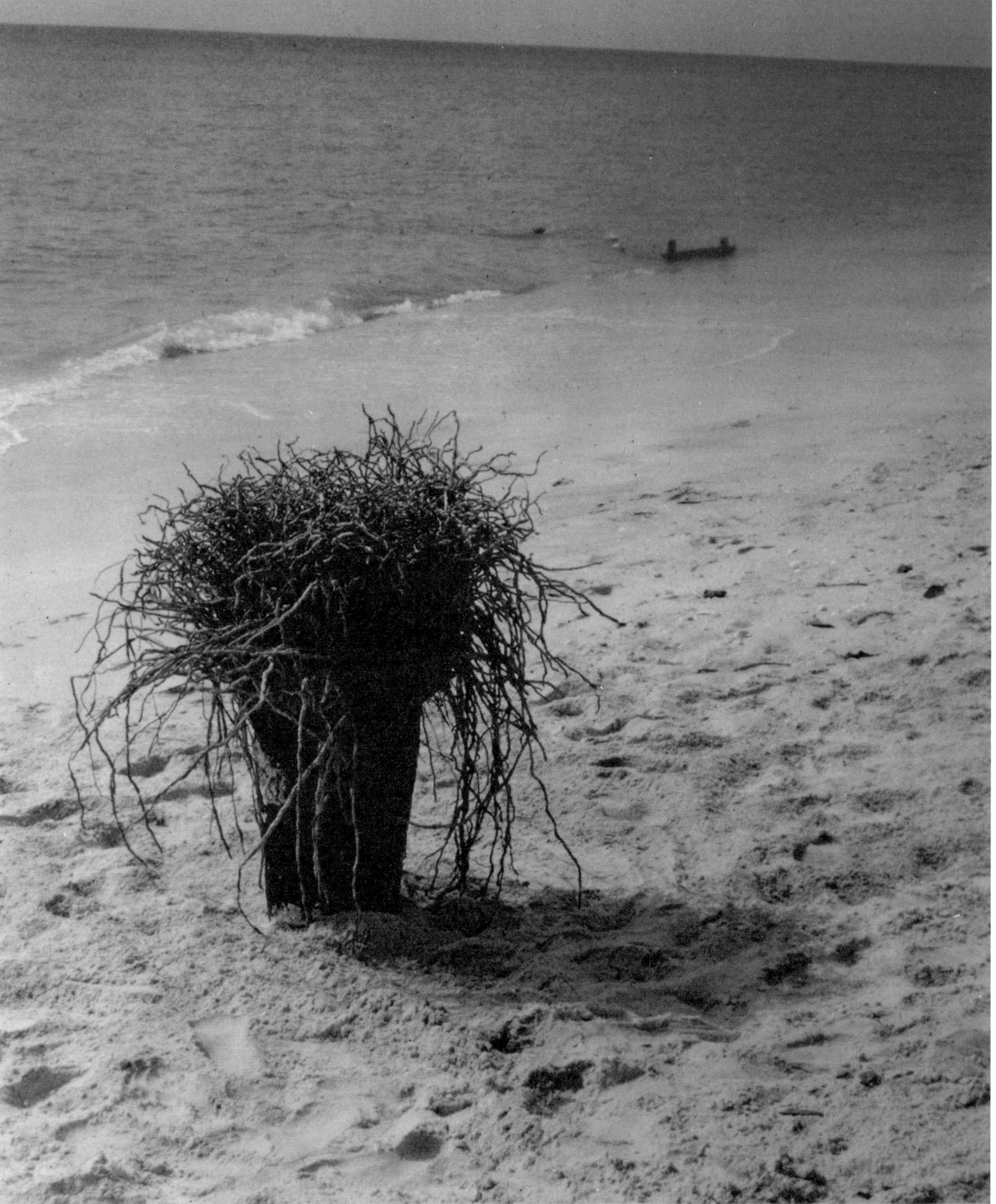

JAMES MEYER

THE ART GALLERY IN AN ERA OF MOBILITY

The experience of the place was a large part of the aesthetic experience of the work itself. It wasn't the object; it was getting to the object that was part of the art experience.

—Virginia Dwan[1]

This time tomorrow, where will we be?
On a spaceship somewhere sailing across an empty sea.

—The Kinks[2]

QUICKSAND

On April 15, 1969, Virginia Dwan started out on a journey that has entered the annals of art historical myth. Joining the artists Robert Smithson and Nancy Holt at Kennedy Airport in New York, Dwan boarded a Pan Am flight to Fort Myers on Florida's Gulf Coast.[3] Smithson, as an only child growing up in suburban New Jersey, had planned the itineraries of family trips to places of natural wonder. They had visited Sanibel, an island known for the rich bounty of shells that wash up on its shores; he led Dwan and Holt there now.[4]

On the island's southern shore the trio gathered sand dollars and conch, whelk, cockle, and Junonia shells to construct Smithson's *Hypothetical Continent (Lemuria)*, an earthwork in the kidney shape of a "lost" continent once thought to have existed off the coast of East Africa. At the water's edge Smithson arranged eleven one-foot-square mirrors in a parallel line. *Mirror Shore* reflected sunrays and aqueous reflections onto the sand and sea. The reflections lengthened and slanted and dissolved as the earth turned.[5]

The planning of the trip was a collaborative affair. At Dwan's instigation the group paid a visit to Robert Rauschenberg on nearby Captiva Island.[6] Conversation between the men was lively; ideas flew about the room; a work was proposed. Down the beach Smithson spied a dead date-palm tree. The artists swam the massive stump to the strand in front of Rauschenberg's house and buried it upside down.[7] In Smithson's photograph of the work, Rauschenberg, Holt, Dwan, and an unidentified friend gather around the overturned tree. The slender Dwan, in bathing suit, hat, and sunglasses; Holt smiling behind her matching hat; Rauschenberg, bare-chested, bronzed, his hair matted from the swim; and his muscular companion are a vision of vitality (figs. 1 and 2). The palm is a dark trophy, its roots tangled and pendulous and vaguely threatening. To bury a tree upside down is a violent reversal of its natural state, an upending

FIG. 1

ROBERT SMITHSON AND ROBERT RAUSCHENBERG ROLLING TREE STUMP ASHORE, CAPTIVA ISLAND, APRIL 1969

FIG. 2

RAUSCHENBERG, NANCY HOLT, DWAN, AND UNIDENTIFIED FRIEND WITH *SECOND UPSIDE-DOWN TREE*, CAPTIVA ISLAND, APRIL 1969

of its vitalist associations. In Smithson's ink drawing *Inverted Tree* (cat. 98), the gnarly roots evoke jellyfish tendrils and serpents, amplifying its medusan associations. Inverted, the "tree of life" has been transfigured into an infernal image, an emblem of death.[8] This and Smithson's other toppled trees subvert organicist models of growth and renewal; they thwart anthropocentric conceptions of linear time and Enlightenment dreams of "progress" predicated on biological metaphors. On the sunny beach at Captiva the *Second Upside-Down Tree* announced an entropic eternity devoid of human history and organic life, an earth sheathed in crystals and sheets of ice.[9]

An ancient myth holds that Sanibel and Captiva exist at the end point of a "lost" land bridge connecting Florida to the Yucatán peninsula.[10] The three travelers, ever mindful of such histories, now flew to Mérida across the gulf, where they rented a car. Smithson completed nine *Mirror Displacements* during the trip; his photo-essay "Incidents of Mirror-Travel in the Yucatan" documents these works (fig. 3). It has often been remarked about this essay that Smithson does not depict the Maya sites that they visited. Nor does he refer to himself or his companions; the pronouns *I* and *we* are missing.[11] The images that Dwan took with her Hasselblad and Super 8 mm cameras during the trip supplement Smithson's celebrated account. She photographed the ruins at Uxmal, Palenque, and Yaxchilan; she photographed her friends and their guide.[12] She photographed Smithson's *Mirror Displacements* differently from the way Smithson

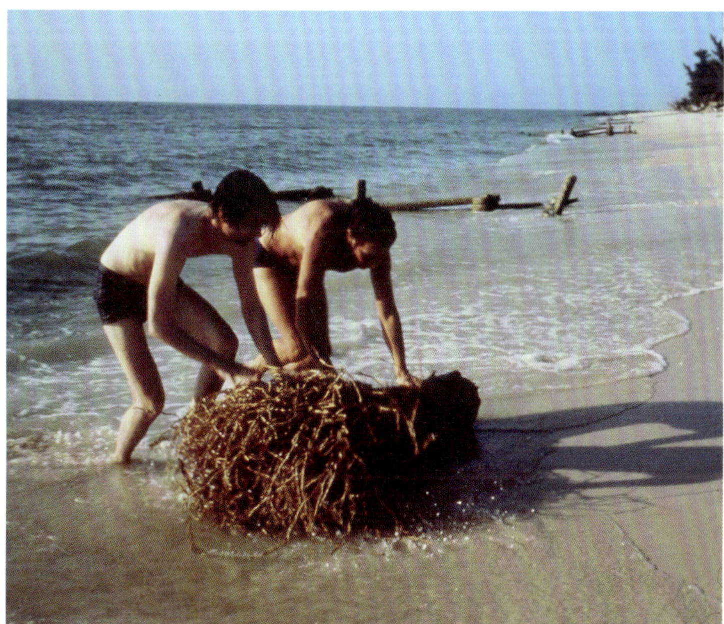

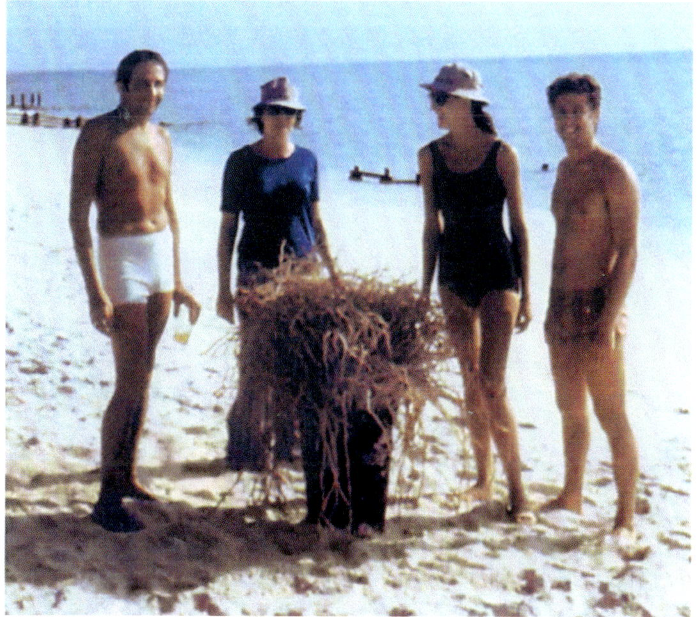

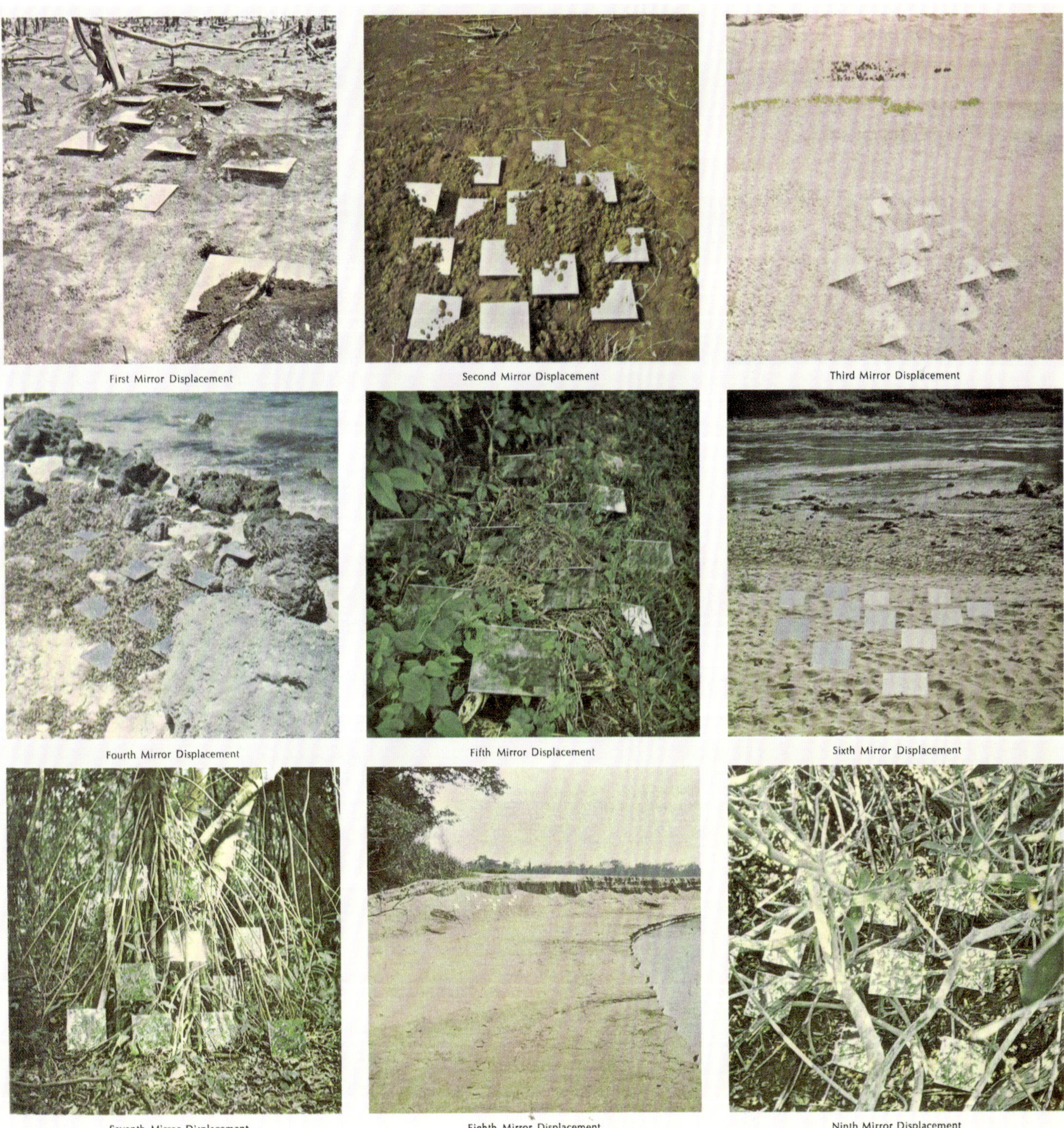

First Mirror Displacement

Second Mirror Displacement

Third Mirror Displacement

Fourth Mirror Displacement

Fifth Mirror Displacement

Sixth Mirror Displacement

Seventh Mirror Displacement

Eighth Mirror Displacement

Ninth Mirror Displacement

FIG. 3

COMPOSITE OF SMITHSON'S NINE *MIRROR DISPLACEMENTS* PHOTOGRAPHED BY THE ARTIST IN THE YUCATÁN, APRIL 1969

FIG. 4

DWAN'S PHOTOGRAPH OF SMITHSON INSTALLING *FIRST MIRROR DISPLACEMENT*, APRIL 1969

FIG. 5

SMITHSON AND HOLT BENEATH AN ARCHWAY IN UXMAL, MEXICO, APRIL 1969

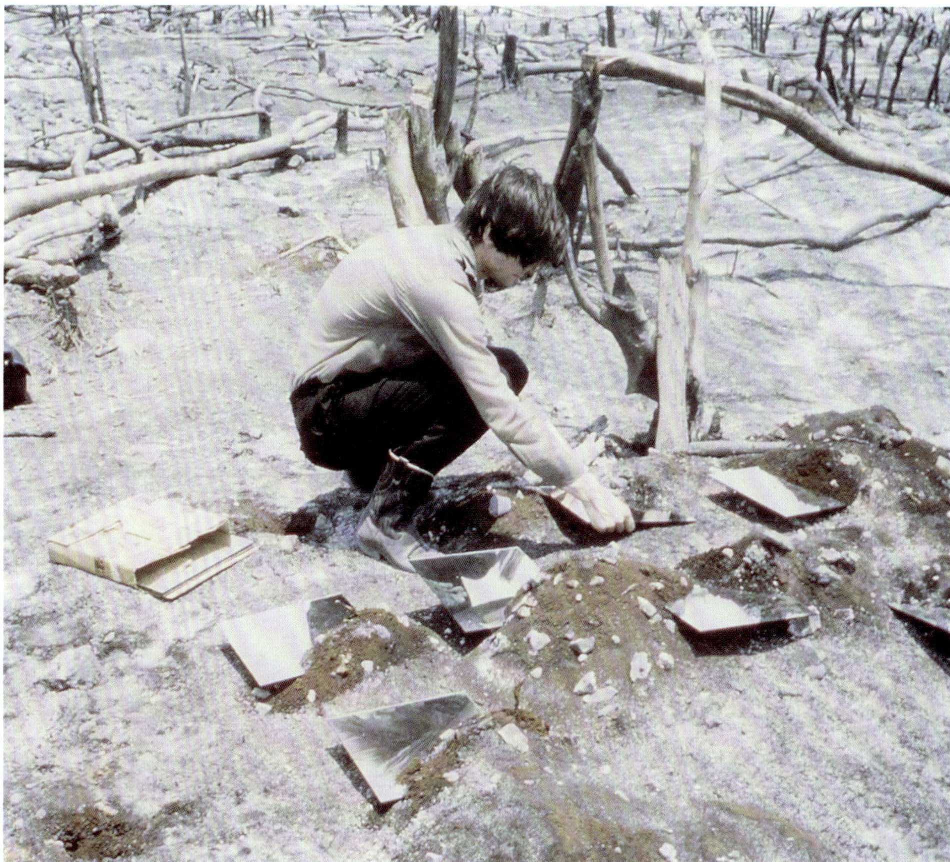

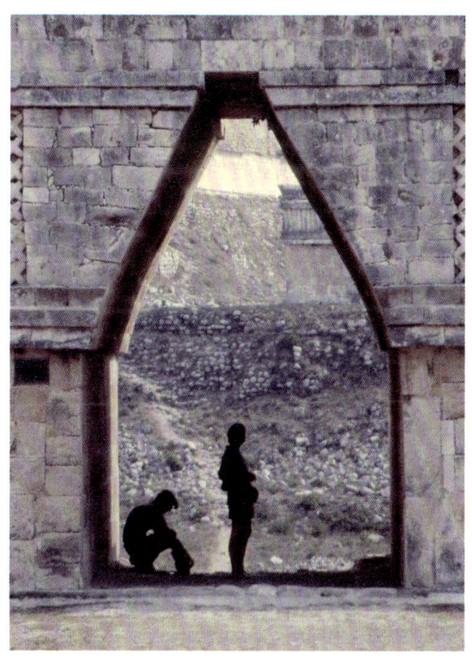

did. In her photo of the first of these works, executed in a forest recently cleared by burning, Smithson hunches over the charred site, inserting the mirrors into the ashen soil (fig. 4). Smithson's depiction shows the work alone. After he photographed the sculpture he returned the mirrors to their carrying box, and the party drove on.

At Uxmal Dwan captured Holt and Smithson in silhouette standing in an ancient portal (fig. 5). Smithson made another *Mirror Displacement* and a limestone map of another "lost continent," Gondwanaland, whose name encompassed Dwan's own. Near the town of Bolonchén, they drove into a swarm of thousands of butterflies that flew past their car in "erratic, jerky flight patterns" and smashed against the car radio antenna.[13] Smithson made the *Third Mirror Displacement* here. In his shot of this work kaleidoscopes of swallowtails appear at the top edge of the image, at a distance from the twelve mirrors in the foreground. Smithson's photo is staid compared with his lively description of the swarm: "For brief moments flying butterflies were reflected. They seemed to

FIG. 6

DWAN'S PHOTOGRAPH OF SMITHSON'S *SEVENTH MIRROR DISPLACEMENT*, 1969

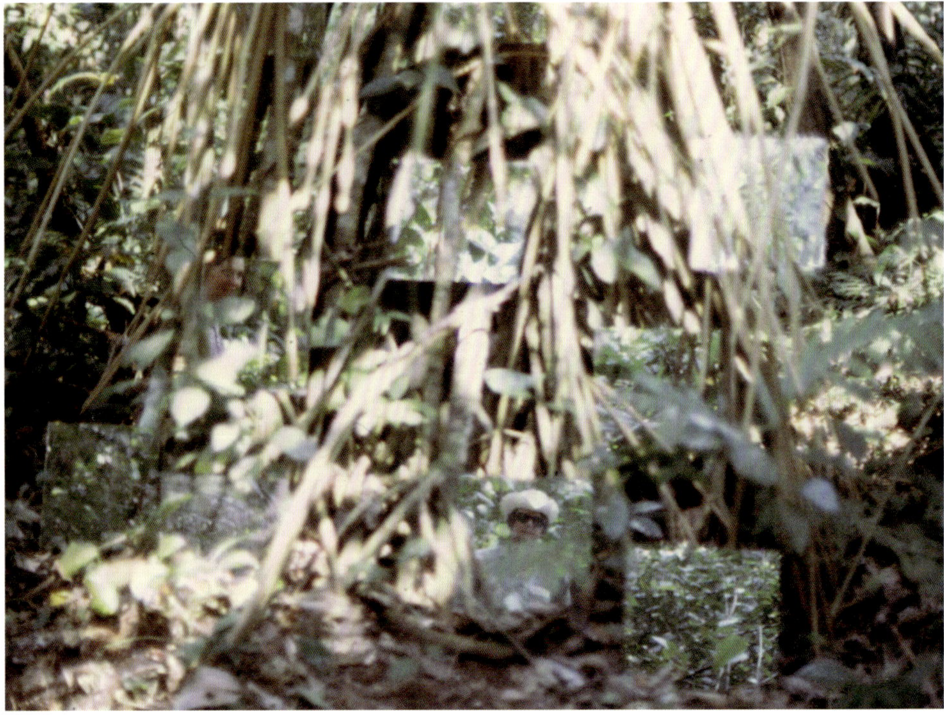

fly through a sky of gravel. Shadows cast by the mirrors contrasted with those seconds of color."[14] Dwan's film clip of the Bolonchén stop, one of the few portions of her film to survive the journey, evokes this hallucinatory scene. Black swallowtails infest the sky like locusts. Green and yellow ones hover above the gravelly soil like clumps of leaves swaying in a lazy breeze.[15]

From Palenque—where Coatlicue, Maya Serpent Lady and earth goddess (and Dwan's avatar during the trip), emerged from the tangle of roots and leaves of the *Fifth Mirror Displacement*[16]—the party flew to Bonampak, where they viewed the frescoes of warriors and captives, and onto Agua Azul. They reached Yaxchilan, a site on the Usumacinta River, by boat, a journey Dwan filmed. Smithson made his *Third Upside-Down Tree* here and another *Mirror Displacement*, a distribution of mirrors in a small tree. His photograph of this work records a densely saturated pattern of emerald greens, sunrays, and reflections. Distinctions between leaves and branches, between what is actual and mirrored—and what is "up" and "down," in front and behind—are difficult to discern. Dwan's photo embeds the travelers *inside* Smithson's work. Smithson's face is reflected in one mirror. Holt appears in another. The other mirrors reflect the dense jungle, its dappled sunlight. Dwan is invisible—an absent presence in the dead center of the image (fig. 6).

Their dugout moved ponderously upriver during their return trip. I quote Dwan's recollection of this moment at length:

> The sun was absolutely blazing and there were no proper seats in the boat; so finally I found that squatting was one position that I could tolerate. And we had several hours' travel this way — it was truly a kind of torture; but the funniest part of it was, when we were about halfway along, Bob announced that he had to get out and make a work of art. This is the first time I ever rebelled about an artist making a work of art, because we actually got off on a spit of sand and climbed out on this blazing, absolutely relentless white sand and he went off and did another *Mirror Displacement* piece. I in the meantime was sort of trailing behind, and as I got out of the boat I realized I was in quicksand, and I'm calling behind to them, to Bob and Nancy, "I'm in quicksand!" And they didn't look back. . . . Contrary to the world's opinion of [artists'] being lazy creatures, they will force themselves into the most impossible situations to continue their work because — he had to do it; he *had* to make a work of art at that point.[17]

In "Incidents of Mirror-Travel in the Yucatan" Smithson calls this sandy spit the Island of Blue Waters:

> Against the current of the Usumacinta the dug-out headed for the Island of Blue Waters. The island annihilates itself in the presence of the river, both in fact and mind. Small bits of sediment dropped away from the sand flats into the river. Small bits of perception dropped away from the edges of eyesight. Where is the island? The unknowable zero island.[18]

Like *Mirror Shore* at Sanibel, all of the *Mirror Displacements* complicate and invert binocular vision.[19] In Smithson's account, the unstable ground where Dwan's legs plunged into the soggy sand is a place of *perceptual* oblivion. The island "annihilates itself" as it erodes. "Bits of perception" drop away as "bits of sediment" drop away. Smithson distributed the mirrors of the *Eighth Mirror Displacement* over a span of several feet and photographed the work at a distance. On the "relentless white" sand of the river island his mirrors practically disappear. If a viewer did not know what to look for she could easily miss them. This loose arrangement induced an unfocused scanning of the mirrors and their environment—the soggy terrain, river, and sky.[20] It was this work that Smithson made and photographed as Dwan waited impatiently in the blinding sun.

She had come this far. She had gathered sand and shells for earthworks; she had slept in hammocks in thatched huts and fallen asleep to the squeals of pigs; she had been exposed to chiggers, to mosquitoes, to scalding heat. The adventure that Dwan had embarked on when she opened her first storefront gallery with a show of conventional easel paintings had inspired a new kind of gallery. Displaying such radical tendencies as abstract expressionism, pop art, and nouveau réalisme, minimalism, and language art, Dwan began to exhibit plans and photos of projects that existed at a far distance from the gallery. Art could be made anywhere, and so the artist and viewer were compelled to travel to remote places, inconvenient places, even dangerous places, to experience it. The adventure on which she had set out ten years earlier—this "search," as she has described it[21]—had brought Dwan *here*. It had led her to a quicksand spit on a jungle river in the middle of nowhere. To Smithson's "unknowable zero island."

THE DIALECTIC OF MOBILITY AND PLACE

When it first appeared on the cover of the September 1969 *Artforum*, Smithson's *First Mirror Displacement* announced an aesthetic turn that Dwan actively supported and brought to awareness (p. 313, fig. 33). It heralded a sculpture that was located *in a place*, that made "place" the pretext of a work's arrangement and meaning, and so this sculpture came to be called site-specific.[22] (Recall Dwan's remark that Smithson "had" to make his work "at that point.") The improbable setting of the penultimate *Mirror Displacement* is a place that would strike most of us as no place at all. The quicksand shore is one of countless peripheral locations explored by land artists. Often at a remove from the gallery, the site-specific work eschewed the rigid protocols of the late modernist gallery known as the "white cube"—its parquet floors and gray carpeting, its white walls and track lighting, its scalar limitations.[23] Or it turned its attention *to* the gallery, exposing its strictures and conventions.[24] But the gallery alone is not its sole concern. Perhaps the great target of site-specificity is the studio—the "*stationary* place where *portable* objects are produced," as Daniel Buren once described the artist's traditional workplace.[25] Studio works (paintings and sculptures) are "portable objects," exchangeable commodities, made to be sold. For the ultimate destination of the object is not the gallery—a mere transit point after all—but a collector's home, or (to update the analysis) the anonymous Swiss "freeports" where art investors increasingly sequester their treasures.[26]

In the tropical jungle the studio work and white cube were gleefully abandoned. "Oh for the happy days of pure walls and pure floors!" Smithson writes with mock regret. "Flatness was nowhere to be found. Walls of collapsed mud, and floors of bleached detritus replaced the flatness of rooms."[27] What could be more unlike a gallery than Smithson's "zero island"? The *Eighth Mirror Displacement* reflected place back onto itself in a dizzying tautology, blending almost imperceptibly into its sun-blasted terrain. With the merging of work and site the object has all but disappeared, which is to say not entirely. (A photograph of one of Smithson's dismantled arrangements, reproduced in the pages of a widely circulated art magazine, is an "object" of a different kind.)

What is often neglected in discussions of site-specificity is the journey *to* the site. "The experience of the place was a large part of the aesthetic experience," Dwan recalled to her interviewer Charles Stuckey. The site-contingent work forces us to be in a place—to walk around it, to know it for oneself. But this is not all it does. As Dwan noted, "getting to" the work was "part of the art experience" as well.[28] The earthwork demanded a different kind of perceiver: a viewer who is willing to fly long distances and drive to obscure destinations; who is able to trudge, to climb, to descend; who moves through a place and leaves. And so site itself was vectored, transversal. A place of destination was a place of departure.

Mobility and site-specificity: one presupposes the other. The *Mirror Displacements* reflect the site where they are embedded *and* they speak of their own peripatetic nature, of past and future *Mirror Displacements*. They embody a productive tension, a dialectic, of literal and mobile placement that remains influential to this day.[29] All this did not come about in a vacuum. The opening of the first Dwan Gallery in October 1959 occurred during a revolution in transportation technology as profound in its effects as the invention of the electric trolley car, the automobile, and the propeller plane a half-century before.[30] I refer to two innovations in particular. The creation of the interstate highway system by Congress and President Eisenhower in 1956 unleashed a frenzy of freeway construction lasting into the 1970s.[31] Among the most ambitious public works projects in the country's history, the interstate linked the most distant locations in a grid of unary design and signage, dramatically quickening the pace of travel and transforming human relationships to distance and speed.[32] The second of these innovations, the commercial jet, had a profound impact. Developed for military use during and after World War II, the jet propulsion engine had considerable advantages over the propeller kind.[33] Less prone to failure, it reduced the drone of multiple propellers to a soothing white noise and reached speeds of up to six hundred miles per hour, cutting flying time almost in half: the journey between Los Angeles and New York, of particular interest to this study, that had previously taken nearly eight hours now took four and a half hours.[34] The first transcontinental jet flight between these two coastal capitals, on American Airlines, departed on January 9, 1959, the winter before Dwan opened her gallery.[35]

The "jet age," they called it. As a result of jet service (and another invention, computerized ticketing) and aggressive advertising campaigns, the number of flyers grew by leaps and bounds from 1959 to 1970.[36] Equally germane for my argument, the jet was as efficient in transporting goods as people; the volume of domestic and international airfreight greatly increased.[37] With the opening of a vastly expanded Los Angeles International Airport (LAX) in 1961, the metropolis—home of the ultimate tourist destination (Disneyland), the Jet Propulsion Laboratory at Caltech, and the aerospace industry—was itself a symbol of the new mobility, as expressed by the iconic Theme Building at the refurbished airport, a flying saucer–like structure suspended between crossed parabolas (fig. 7).[38]

The impact of such innovations on the making and distribution of art cannot be overstated. Informal networks emerged, linking galleries in Los Angeles and New York. Artists and dealers traveled between the coasts with greater regularity. As the two art scenes came into regular contact, the alleged differences between East and West Coast style and "sensibility" were enunciated in reviews and articles summoning warmed-over stereotypes of place and lifestyle, often to the detriment of California work; even now this binary is rehearsed.[39] The situation was far more fluid, as the history of the Dwan Gallery shows. Artists and artworks moved more swiftly than ever before between the coasts and Europe. Ideas, forms, and techniques were circulated and exchanged.[40] Dwan was a central player in this process of "bicoastalization," and hers was arguably the first bicoastal gallery, a common enough scenario now, altogether uncommon then. Importing works on consignment from galleries in New York and Paris, and eventually works by East Coast artists affiliated with her gallery to her Los Angeles space, Dwan facilitated dialogues across regional and national lines. Like the Castelli and Green Galleries in New York, Rive Droite and Sonnabend in Paris, and Konrad Fischer in Düsseldorf, Dwan existed in a strikingly different milieu at the origins of today's global art industry.[41] Even then, the example of Dwan was unique. It sets before us an image of unbounded creativity catalyzed by the gallerist's largesse and curiosity—her openness to radical aesthetic departures disconnected from market imperatives. Possessing a private income, Dwan was able to offer monthly stipends to artists she believed in, and to sponsor projects of ambitious scale and cost. The first business of Dwan's operation was the cultivation of "ideas," as she described these projects—ensuring that the works were made and put out

FIG. 7

THEME BUILDING AT LOS ANGELES INTERNATIONAL AIRPORT, PEREIRA & LUCKMAN ARCHITECTS, 1961

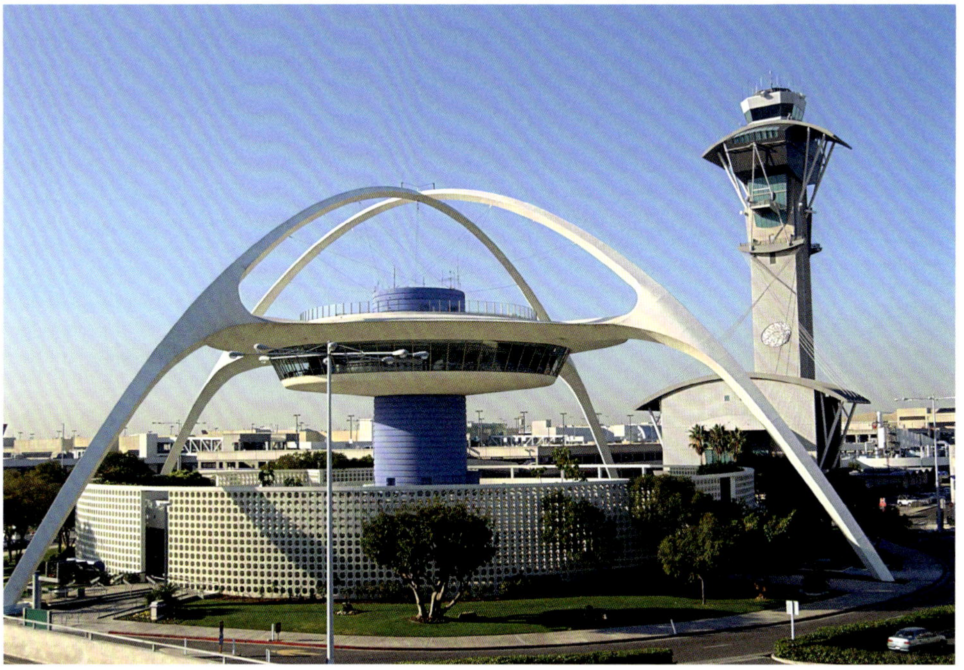

into the world.[42] Sales, sporadic at best, supported the artists and gallery. Sales mattered, but as a secondary concern. Dwan could adopt an idealistic point of view knowing that she would be able to "keep the doors open."[43] She could take risks that most of her peers could not. And she took them again and again. Dwan's fearlessness set her apart, but her attitude is of its time; it speaks of the sixties and early seventies, a period of extreme aesthetic daring. That a gallery of such momentous importance ran at a loss during its entire existence could not seem more at odds with the profit-driven obsessions of our own moment.

The contemporary art gallery is a relatively understudied subject.[44] Dwan Gallery must be counted among the most paradigmatic of its time, but its brief history has yet to be examined in depth.[45] This account of the gallery's short but storied eleven-year run is also a case study of the art gallery as a form during this seminal era. Tracing a succession of tendencies that Dwan brought to visibility, it presents a narrative of vanguard art in the United States and France, highlighting a selection of the 134 exhibitions staged at the gallery between 1959 and 1971. But the Dwan story has still other dimensions. It moves from Los Angeles to New York and on to Paris, from New York to the American West; from art centers to obscure places; from displays of paintings and sculpture to environments and conceptual activities that unsettled definitions of medium and object. It concludes with sited and itinerant endeavors that exposed the conventions and perceptual limitations of the gallery frame. By the time Dwan closed her New York space in June 1971, the most adventuresome of her artists had brought the white cube—the pristine, "neutral" aesthetic container—to the brink of irrelevance.

LOS ANGELES: THE FIRST DWAN GALLERY

In Los Angeles I felt that I had to defend [laughs] just about everything I showed to everyone. —Virginia Dwan[46]

How did the Dwan Gallery come about? Dwan has spoken of her "naiveté" in opening a gallery at age twenty-eight.[47] Apart from an occasional Saturday at the front desk of the gallery of Frank Perls in Beverly Hills, a specialist in School of Paris painting, she had no experience in exhibiting and selling art. But her decision was hardly rash. She had pondered becoming an artist and taken courses in art history, psychology, and philosophy. She had already met a number of Los Angeles artists (Ed Moses, Craig Kauffman, and Edward Kienholz) and the brilliant gallerist and curator Walter Hopps. Two other factors were decisive. At twenty-one she had come into her inheritance from the Minnesota Mining and Manufacturing Company (3M). And in 1958 she married a French-born medical student named Vadim Philippe Kondratief, whose mother, Vera Lazuk, owned a gallery on Long Island in New York. Kondratief's sister, Eugenie Thompson, had worked at the gallery and moved to Los Angeles. Kondratief encouraged Dwan to pursue her dream of owning a gallery; Thompson agreed to serve as codirector. Dwan signed a lease on a storefront space at 1091 Broxton Avenue in Westwood in summer 1959 (p. 289, fig. 6). She opened the gallery that September with a presentation of watercolors by the artist Shim Grudin, one of three initial shows borrowed from Lazuk to jump-start her program.

The location of the Dwan Gallery was crucial. Ostensibly chosen for its convenience to UCLA where Kondratief was studying and to their house in Malibu, Westwood had other benefits, Dwan reasoned: proximity to collectors in the wealthy neighborhoods of Bel Air, Brentwood, and Beverly Hills and to the UCLA art and art history departments. The gallery would not only sell art; it would play a pedagogical role.[48] But Westwood was far afield from the central gallery district of the day, the stretch of North La Cienega Boulevard in West Hollywood where some thirty galleries lined both sides of the avenue and monthly "art walks" attracted collectors and artists from all around the

FIG. 8

POSTER FOR *THE STUDS* GROUP EXHIBITION AT THE FERUS GALLERY, 1964

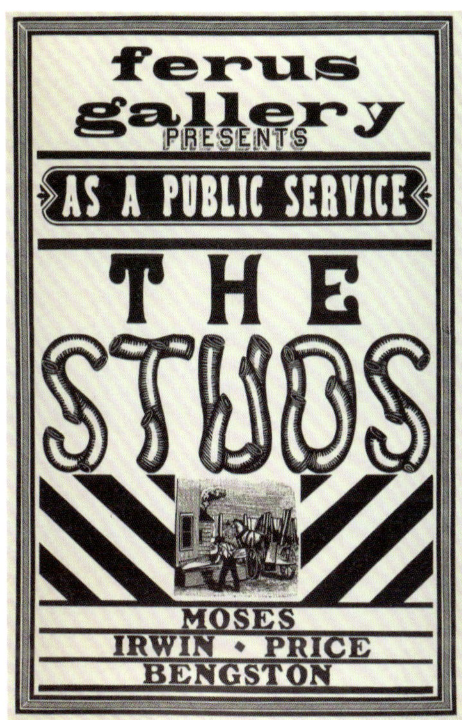

county. "Off the beaten track," the Dwan Gallery did not enjoy the foot traffic of the La Cienega galleries. Even after she learned that some of these competitors discouraged out-of-town visitors from visiting her "far-away" space, Dwan did not leave Westwood.[49] I interpret her choice to remain there (indeed, taking a larger space in 1962) as a sign of stubborn independence. Along with its increasingly audacious program, the gallery's unusual location affected how it would be perceived: from the very beginning Dwan stood slightly apart.

The most visible of the La Cienega galleries, Ferus, was founded by Kienholz and Hopps in the back of an antiques store in 1957. In 1958 Kienholz sold his share to the dealer Irving Blum, a recent arrival from New York, who moved the gallery to a more elegant space across the street and "professionalized" its program.[50] The history of Ferus has been much rehearsed. The Ferus legend—burnished by the media-savvy Blum, and by Philip Leider and John Coplans of *Artforum*, who relocated the magazine from San Francisco in 1964 to an office upstairs from Ferus—has long dominated discussion of the Los Angeles art scene of the fifties and sixties, occluding all other galleries combined.[51] As a consequence, the position of Dwan—"the gallery that was the most competition," according to Blum—has been overlooked.[52]

Ferus took a divergent path. Whereas more established gallerists Paul Kantor and Felix Landau focused on modernist masters, Hopps and Kienholz featured younger, local artists (the gestural abstract painters John Altoon, Hassel Smith, Jay DeFeo, and Sonia Gechtoff, and the mystical figure Wallace Berman). Under Blum's direction, Ferus became increasingly associated with the so-called Finish Fetish aesthetic of Craig Kauffman, Billy Al Bengston, Ken Price, and Larry Bell; Robert Irwin's minimalism; and the pop art of Ed Ruscha. Drawing on the beatnik, hot-rod, and surfer profiles of the gallery's artists—some of whom inflected their work with the production techniques of automobile and surfboard finishing, inviting Coplans's "Finish Fetish" sobriquet—the image of Ferus is a stew of stereotypes: romantic, "West Coast," masculinist. A passage from a text by Coplans is typical: "What these artists have developed is an aggressive and high-spirited arrogance that only young and talented men can have. It is a frontier sensibility—anything a man can stake out for himself is his own."[53] The image was sealed by *The Studs*, a group show of Irwin, Bengston, Price, and Moses promoted with an Old West scene of a stud horse feeding at a trough (fig. 8), copious photos of the Ferus "boys" clowning around, and most notoriously, an advertisement depicting Blum on a motorboat in a spiffy sport coat and pocket square surrounded by female models in bathing suits, the name "Ferus Gallery" appended to the stern.

What was the position of the Dwan Gallery in this ecosphere? It would seem as if Dwan and Ferus were total opposites. Where Ferus initially focused on California artists, Dwan showed precious few (Kienholz was the notable exception). The aim was to bring information from one place to another—from New York and Paris to Los Angeles, and from Los Angeles to New York. "[Dwan] was bringing artists from New York and Europe to L.A.," the artist Ed Bereal noted. "She was getting people straight off the streets of New York and giving us a chance to look at them, which was crucial." Dwan, recalled Kienholz, "was responsible for the whole influence of Europeans into the West Coast. . . . She brought a whole cultural dimension to Los Angeles that no one else did."[54]

Where the Ferus aesthetic evoked the atmosphere and climate of Southern California, the Dwan program was polyglot, cosmopolitan: no single look, no single tendency, prevailed. (This would change when the gallery relocated to New York and became associated with minimalism and land art.) Where Blum, a former salesman at Knoll, was an effective marketer, Dwan took less of an interest in financial matters. (The fact that Kienholz left Ferus for Dwan in 1960 as a protest against Blum's commercialism is telling.) And if the role of women in the Ferus milieu was "to service the men," as Shirley Nielson, who was married to Hopps and Blum at different times, later recalled, at Dwan a woman—a young woman no less—was in charge.[55]

Blum's remark that Dwan's gallery "was the most competition" complicates what might otherwise be a facile narrative of Ferus as a foil for Dwan.[56] He puts Dwan on an equal footing with Ferus and suggests the two galleries shared certain aims. Dwan recalled her relationship with Blum this way:

> We sort of pulled together; Irving would come and visit and discuss what was happening in the so-called art world in Los Angeles, because really the collectors were not that open to the things that I wanted to show and was showing and things Irving was showing. So we sort of gave each other strength and commiserated with each other and joked with each other about the whole thing.[57]

Both dealers showed daring work; they courted the same small group of collectors; in certain instances they competed for the same artists.[58] For Ferus was also an important reception point of East Coast work.[59] And where Blum exhibited artists associated with the influential Castelli Gallery almost exclusively, Dwan, who took regular trips to New York to scout out talent, worked with numerous galleries including Castelli.[60] She presented a more nuanced vision of recent practice in New York; her commitment to showing the latest work from Paris was unmatched.

Let us return to the Broxton space. The location of the first Dwan gallery, a three-story structure at the corner of Broxton and Kinross Avenues, was one of the original blocks of the Westwood neighborhood.[61] The University Office Building, as it was initially known, was decorated with wrought-iron balconies, a red-tiled roof, and glazed tiles typical of the Spanish Colonial Revival style of the 1920s. Two grand arches facing Broxton and Kinross led a visitor to an interior courtyard with smaller shops.

The space of the first Dwan gallery created an impression of depth and volume that exceeded its footprint.[62] Reaching up two stories, with a white wall floating below the ceiling, the exhibition space was tall and airy. A clerestory window brought in natural light.[63] A slight arch and, to the right, an open screen divided the front space from the office. The gallery was by no means a white cube: the developer of the building, Janss, had installed a bank of vitrine windows at front and a lattice grid of Spanish-style wooden beams beneath the ceiling (p. 327, fig. 19). Though handsome, such details hinted at the space's commercial origins (the original tenant was a haberdasher).[64] Well-designed for the display of men's clothing, the vitrines would ultimately prove inadequate for the expansive paintings and sculptures that Dwan began to show.

From the outset, the gallery was oriented to the opposite coast. Abstract expressionist painting dominated Dwan's program during the first year and a half. When Dwan opened the 1960 season with an exhibition of paintings by Matsumi ("Mike") Kanemitsu, gestural abstraction was at its apogee and beginning to wane.[65] The Museum of Modern Art's famous *New American Painting* exhibition, curated by Dorothy Miller, with works by seventeen New York School painters, had just completed its tour of several European venues.[66] Exhibitions of younger abstract expressionists filled the storefront galleries along East 10th Street in the East Village; the phrase "10th Street style" or "10th Street touch" implied an exhausted New York School manner.[67] Apart from the occasional show at Kantor Gallery, New York School painting was rarely exhibited in Los Angeles. Dwan changed this.

Kanemitsu worked in a gestural idiom reminiscent of the work of his friends Franz Kline and Willem de Kooning, but within the tradition of sumi ink painting that he had explored for much of his career. (A reviewer praised the "affinity" between the artist's "Japanese sensibility" and "modern American" technique.[68]) Kanemitsu's paintings of this period are abstract, contained arrangements of vividly hued interlocking forms. In his first show at Dwan, the arresting *Wes Hardin*, a composition in red, ocher, violet, and black with occasional drips spilling out of the erratic shapes, recalls the violent exploits of John Wesley Hardin (1853–1895), a Wild West outlaw and mass murderer, through abstract means (cat. 4). Another abstract expressionist painter, Robert Goodnough, installed a selection of his works at the gallery a few months after Kanemitsu's show closed. Large-scaled, intricately composed, Goodnough's works were warmly received (the lead art critic for the *Los Angeles Times*, Henry Seldis, lauded the "extraordinary gift for color" of the gallery's "latest and most promising import from New York").[69] The fledgling gallery was beginning to be noticed. Although the critic singled out Goodnough's brightest canvases for praise, Dwan showed works of more sober coloration, such as *Abstract No. 4 "Pipes,"* a dense web of black-and-white lines and occasional stick figures and pentimenti on a milky ground. The painting was one of the rare works to sell during the gallery's opening season (cat. 5).[70]

A group show of the following autumn, *15 of New York*, formalized these commitments. Dwan showed Kanemitsu, Goodnough, and other abstract painters, many of the younger generation, several of whom she would come to represent.[71] She managed to procure works by four major figures, too—an oil on board by Willem de Kooning, a drawing by Jackson Pollock, and large paintings by Franz Kline and Philip Guston. *15 of New York* marked a level of ambition on a par with Ferus, which held a show with a similar theme earlier in the year.[72] Dwan eventually bought two major paintings from her show, Guston's *The Room* (cat. 6) and Kline's *Garcia*, for her private collection—as she did on many occasions when works did not sell. Many of these works have entered museums as a result of Dwan's generosity. In fact, Dwan *withheld* certain works from collectors with the express intention of placing them in public collections (see Chronology, p. 296). Among the works Dwan acquired in the early years, *Garcia* took on a talismanic significance, appearing in photographs of Dwan and her artists, such as the glamorous portrait of the dealer in mod sunglasses by Dennis Hopper or the image of Smithson and Carl Andre in her New York apartment arm wrestling in front of Kline's canvas, their limbs clasped in humorous reference to the painter's muscular brushwork (fig. 9). That Dwan acquired major works by Kline and Guston indicates the centrality of these painters during the gallery's early years; the connection was cemented by a two-person show that she organized in April 1961.[73]

In *15 of New York* Dwan presented an earlier Guston. *The Room*—a composition in rose, red, orange, lavender, charcoal, and pale gray—exemplified Guston's so-called pink style of the mid-1950s. Its pleasing palette is misleading: on closer view *The Room* is both harmonious and raw, lyrical and

FIG. 9

CARL ANDRE AND SMITHSON ARM WRESTLING IN FRONT OF FRANZ KLINE'S *GARCIA*, C. 1968

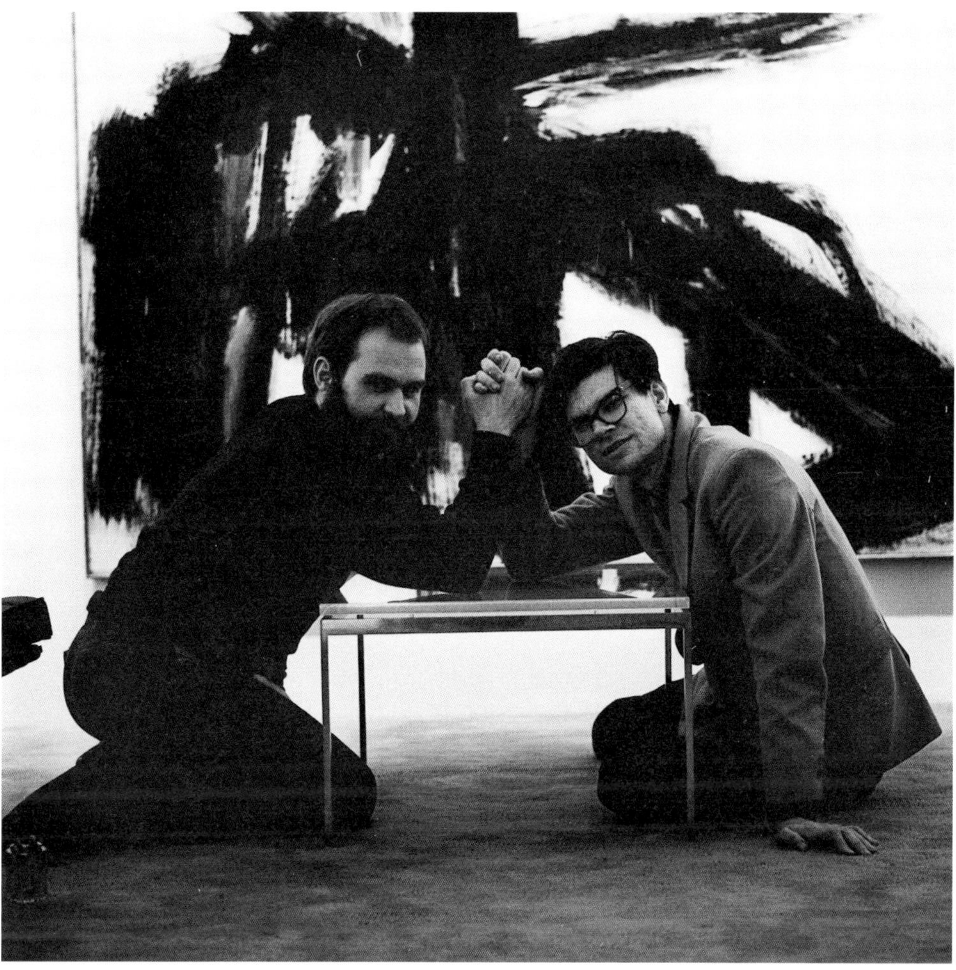

aggressive, as Guston's works of this period typically are.[74] The pinks may evoke flesh or scars; the dark reds, bloody wounds or violent emotions. Guston's "room" is not a happy place to be. The works in Dwan's double show, dating from 1958 to 1960, represented the painter's most recent style. In *Sleeper II*, which was illustrated in the handout for the show, a black shape (apparently inspired by the homburg worn by Mark Rothko) sits precariously amidst a jumble of orange, scarlet, royal blue, and milky gray brushstrokes, as if the vertical and rectangular elements that hold the "hat" up are about to collapse (cat. 7).[75] The brooding tonality and restless energy of Guston's works found their match in Kline's black-and-white paintings on the facing wall, such as *Garcia* and *Black Sienna*, and the midsized *Torres*, an arrangement of thick vertical and horizontal black brushstrokes clustered in a spindly knot (cat. 8). The horizontal band at the bottom pulls the thicker vertical downward, counterpointing the upward thrust of the image and stressing the horizontality of the support. A diagonal of thinner width extends to the right edge of the canvas, activating the rectilinear image and implying that Kline's little world of black bands extends well beyond the canvas into a spatial infinitude that we can only imagine. Unlike the larger works in the show that Kline sized to a viewer's body, the scale of *Torres* far exceeds its size.[76]

The gallery was quickly becoming an outpost of New York School work: a double show of Guston and Kline; solo presentations of Kanemitsu, Goodnough, and other young abstract expressionists (such as Joan Mitchell and Paul Brach). An introduction by Kanemitsu to Larry Rivers, also a participant in *15 of New York*, pointed another way. The entrance of Rivers into our story is important, ushering in an aspect of Dwan's program that ultimately supplanted the abstract formats of Kanemitsu and his peers. In Larry Rivers, Dwan discovered a younger abstract expressionist who irreverently crossed nonobjective and mimetic imagery, and high and low subject matter. The painter's first show at the Westwood gallery, in February 1961, announced a tilt in Dwan's program toward a contemporary form of realism known as pop.

In his memoir *What Did I Do?* Rivers describes the road trip he took from New York to Los Angeles in advance of his show, and his arrival at Dwan's "modest little palace" on the Malibu coast.[77] A stay at the dealer's guesthouse and access to a nearby studio that she owned were among the pleasures enjoyed by Dwan's artist guests. Rivers's charcoal portrait of Dwan with an elaborate sixties bob, dedicated "to my Great Dealer + her sun + surf," is a memento of that balmy sojourn (cat. 1). In preparing his show Rivers transformed the entrance to the Broxton gallery into a great collage, applying copies of the poster he had made to the large windows with swaths of paint and hints of figures, and his own signature (p. 323, fig. 9). The poster, too, was a collage (cat. 2). Letters cut from newspapers and magazines indicate the show's location and dates. Rivers's signature partially covers a photo of the artist at work. A large canvas—*U.N. Painting* (1959), a scene of Soviet leader Nikita Khrushchev and other world leaders in the U.N. General Assembly—leans against the wall. Stepping forward in a dancelike motion, paper in each hand, Rivers in this striking image summons the memory of Hans Namuth's famous photographs of Jackson Pollock in his East Hampton barn in 1950, which did much to inspire the romantic image of the New York School artist as an "action" painter.[78] And though the Dwan show included a number of quasi-figurative canvases, the general look of the show was abstract expressionist: the faintly skeined figures disappeared in a morass of painterly gestures.[79]

The impression of Rivers as a belated abstract expressionist would be dispelled in the artist's second show at Dwan in April 1963, which featured paintings of human figures with labeled body parts (Rivers called them his "French vocabulary lesson" paintings) as well as blatantly referential imagery appropriated from advertising and other sources. In the collage the artist made for the show's announcement, a Dutch Masters cigar-box cover, a Lucky Strike package, and a 100 franc note depicting Napoleon coexist in a shallow space (cat. 3). As in the "Parts of the Body" paintings exhibited in the show, stenciled words identify the emperor's facial features, such as *front* (forehead), *oeil* (eye), and *nez* (nose), alluding to Rivers's recent stay in Paris and his efforts to master spoken French.[80] Eschewing the ambiguity of Jasper Johns's contemporaneous paintings of things and their signifiers (the obvious source of this operation), Rivers proposes a nominative view of language: the words we use to describe our bodies are not opaque but fundamental to our experience of ourselves as living beings.

Another turn in Dwan's program became apparent in 1961–1962. A shift from the abstract expressionist mode to an art of noncomposition, of the grid and monochrome, was an art of reduction. Two pivotal figures concern us: Ad Reinhardt, who had appeared in the famous *Life* magazine group portrait "The Irascibles" in 1951, and Yves Klein. A contemporary of the first generation abstract expressionists, Reinhardt boldly rejected many of the tenets of his peers. Adamantly abstract and nongestural, purged of subject matter and markers of feeling, the artist's monochrome paintings—first red, then blue, then various "shades" of black—posed a powerful alternative to the dominant expressionist mode. As a consequence, Reinhardt was shunted to the margins of the abstract expressionist canon.[81] His fortunes turned belatedly as younger artists, curators, and critics took an interest in his work and writings during the years before his death in 1967.[82] In her support for Reinhardt, Dwan was ahead of the curve; her encounter with the older painter early in her career had a decisive effect on her program. Reinhardt paid a visit to Dwan and Kondratief in Malibu during the winter of 1960; his first show at the gallery two years later consisted of "black," mainly vertical canvases of different heights and widths.[83] *Abstract Painting (A)*, at 108 × 40 inches one of the tallest paintings in the show, was another of the works Dwan acquired in the early sixties that I consider talismanic (cat. 10). Its entrance into her collection marks her embrace of a reductive aesthetic that would eventually be identified with her gallery, a "Dwan look." But for Dwan, the minimalist impulse of negation, a purgation of all that had heretofore been deemed essential to the work of art—all that is "not art," as Reinhardt put it (subject matter, narrative, the artist's subjectivity)—had in fact yielded an art of such powerful presence that it appeared to *transcend* its materiality, as the great canvases of Reinhardt's antagonists Barnett Newman and Mark Rothko sought to do.[84] The Broxton show aimed to make this point—to bear out Dwan's view that "the experience of a Reinhardt painting has always been of a spiritual nature."[85] Rather daringly, and for the first and only time, she hung another vertical work, the slightly shorter *Abstract Painting (C),* above the arch in the clerestory dividing the front gallery and the office (fig. 10). Suspended above the other works, the isolated canvas enhanced the sacral feeling of the all-black installation, calling to mind a retable installed above an altar or (I suspect the reference was unknown to Dwan at the time) Kazimir Malevich's famous hang of the *Black Square* (1913)—the first black painting in the annals of twentieth-century art—in a high corner in the *0.10* exhibition in Petrograd in 1915, itself inspired by the Eastern Orthodox tradition of installing icons high above the beholder (fig. 11).

It is often noted that Reinhardt's works challenge our perception. ("With these paintings, one is forced to make an effort in order to be able to see anything at all," a reviewer wrote of the Dwan show.[86]) The matte surfaces of his canvases, divided into barely perceptible rectangles and squares of proximate value and hue, arrest our vision, causing us to become highly conscious of seeing. Retaining a slight perceptual oscillation (the result of the painter's painstaking process of putting down paint in layers), Reinhardt's works are not "really" black; they are not true but "almost" monochromes.[87]

Now the truly monochromatic works that the French artist Yves Klein showed at Dwan in May 1961 proposed an even more drastic reduction of technique; more "minimal" than even Reinhardt's black pictures, they would elicit an astonished reaction in Los Angeles. Dwan had been riveted by her first sighting of Klein's work in the window of a Parisian gallery the previous year (see Writings, p. 243 and Chronology, p. 289). The author of the electrifying blue canvas in the window had caused a sensation three years earlier with a double exhibition at two galleries in different parts of Paris. At the Iris Clert Gallery on the Left Bank, Klein installed a suite of virtually identical blue monochromes, a decision that challenged a viewer to perceive differences between works that appeared the same but were, of course, not.[88] At the Colette Allendy Gallery, near the Bois de Boulogne, he presented an ensemble of motley objects including sponge reliefs and sculptures and his first *tableau de feu* ("fire painting"). He celebrated the Clert opening with the release of 1,001 blue balloons bunched together like enormous grapes.[89] The following

FIG. 10

INSTALLATION VIEW, *AD REINHARDT*, DWAN GALLERY LOS ANGELES, FEBRUARY 1962

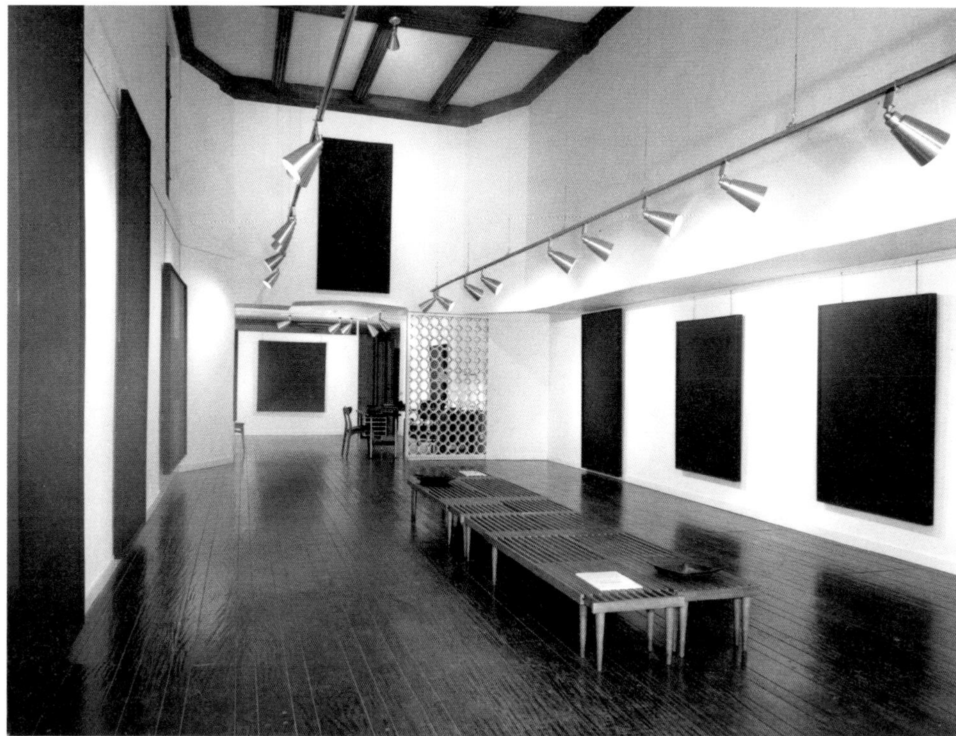

FIG. 11

SUPREMATIST WORKS BY KAZIMIR MALEVICH, *LAST FUTURIST EXHIBITION OF PAINTING 0.10*, PETROGRAD, 1915

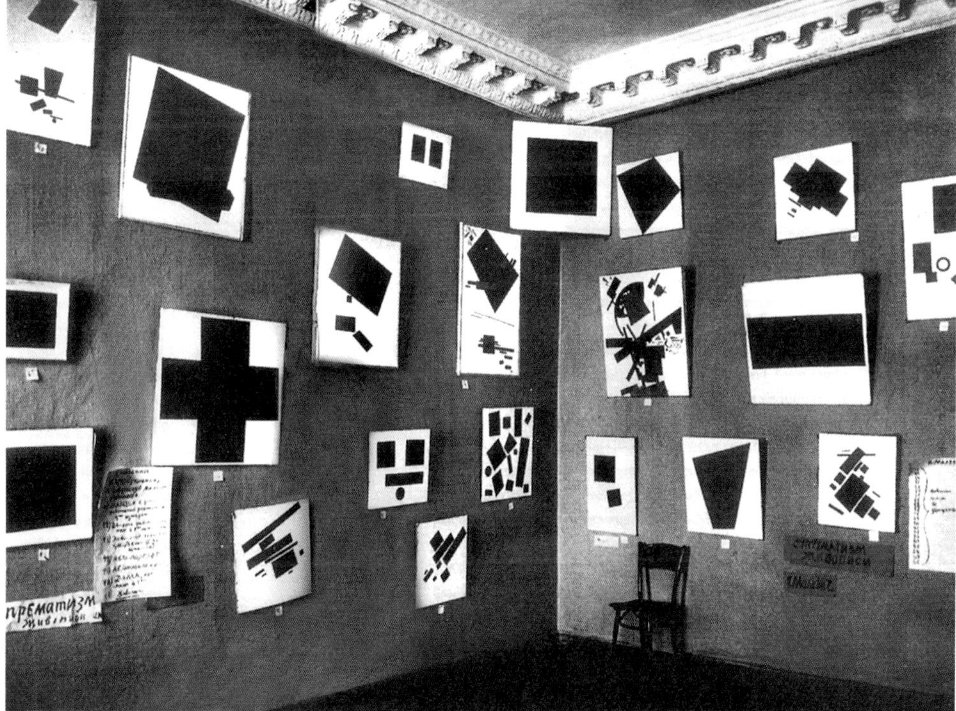

FIG. 12

YVES KLEIN, PERFORMANCE OF *ANTHROPOMETRIES OF THE BLUE PERIOD*, MARCH 1960

year Klein staged the notorious *Le Vide* ("The Void")—an exhibition of Clert's space emptied of objects: a revelation of the gallery as itself.[90] And on March 9, 1960, Klein orchestrated an event of possibly greater notoriety, *Anthropometries of the Blue Period*. Three undressed models appeared before an audience that had been selected by the artist. At Klein's direction the women poured cans of his patented ultramarine paint, IKB (International Klein Blue), over their naked bodies, which they imprinted on sheets of paper as Klein, in white tie, directed their balletic movements and a chamber orchestra played a single note for twenty minutes and then fell silent (fig. 12).

This was the young artist whom Dwan invited to show in Westwood. The New York dealer Leo Castelli had also taken an interest in Klein, and so he and Dwan arranged to exhibit the artist's work in successive presentations in spring 1961.[91] Just as Klein's Clert and Allendy shows followed one another in spaces located on opposite sides of Paris, so the Dwan and Castelli Galleries showed his monochromes in sequence at antipodal locations on the American continent.[92] Klein gave both shows the same name, but just as the contents of the French shows were distinct, the Castelli and Dwan exhibitions were notably

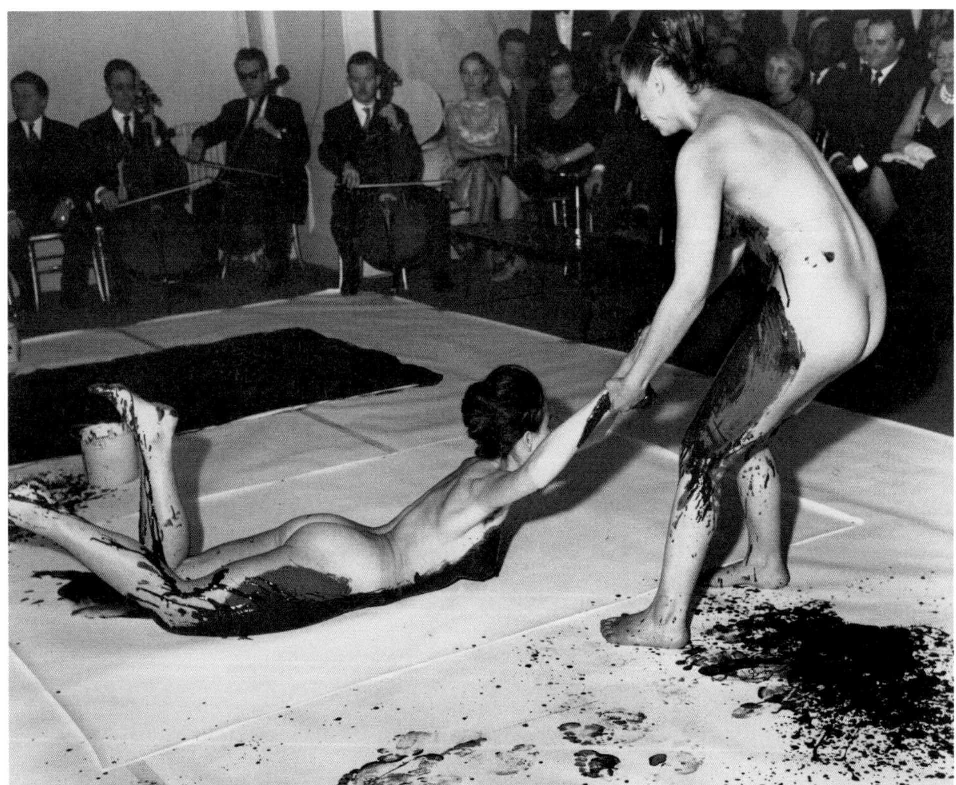

different.[93] The Castelli show consisted of several vertical IKB monochromes of identical size and a large horizontal IKB painting.[94] Whether Klein elected to present himself as a monochrome painter, as he had at Clert, or Castelli persuaded him (which appears more likely) is unclear.[95] Suffice it to say the installation did Klein no favors; he was perceived—he was dismissed—as a maker of all-blue paintings, paintings without variation, image, or expression; paintings that occupied the blurry zone between "art" in the exalted sense and an art that sought merely to provoke, to shock: a neo-Dada endeavor of distinctly French flavor. (A critic's dismissal of Klein as "the latest Sugar-Dada to jet in from the Parisian common market" is typical.[96]) The transcendental aims of Klein's paintings—to give physical form to an experience that "exists beyond our being and yet belongs in our sphere"—were illegible. His visionary rhetoric, as ecstatic as it is imprecise, fell on deaf ears.

Klein's disappointment was keen.[97] He recalled his stay in Malibu more favorably, with good reason. In sunny Southern California the Niçoise artist felt instantly at home.[98] As well, Klein was under no restrictions with regard to the presentation of his work as at Castelli. In the Westwood space the full range of his activity was revealed at Dwan's insistence.[99] Not only did Dwan show several of the large blue monochromes that had failed to sell in New York. In the Broxton gallery a viewer also encountered a pink monochrome; sponge reliefs in pink, gold, and blue (which, unlike his monochromes that were made in a workmanlike manner with rollers instead of brushes, introduced a degree of relational arrangement in the painter's process);[100] and two "fire" paintings, also "composed" to a degree (Klein determined where to apply a torch and water to the pretreated cardboard). Sculpture, incidental at Castelli, was also prominent. A most arresting work greeted visitors, *Blue Rain (pluie)*, its branches dipped in IKB paint and hanging from the ceiling above a tray of IKB pigment.[101] But the most dramatic works were indubitably the two large Anthropometries (*empreintes,* or body prints) that hung prominently on the back walls between the office and the gallery (fig. 13). Even today, the five works by Klein that remain in Dwan's possession—two blue monochromes, a pink monochrome, a gold monochrome, and a "fire" painting—speak of the chromatic and technical variety of Klein's project so apparent in the Broxton show (cats. 12–15 and 17).

In truth, Los Angeles was no more enthusiastic about Klein than New York. The Dwan exhibition also met with "outrage, befuddlement and scurrility."[102] Henry Seldis, who had praised Dwan's other shows, dismissed the French artist as a "flippant opportunist."[103] During a screening of Klein's film

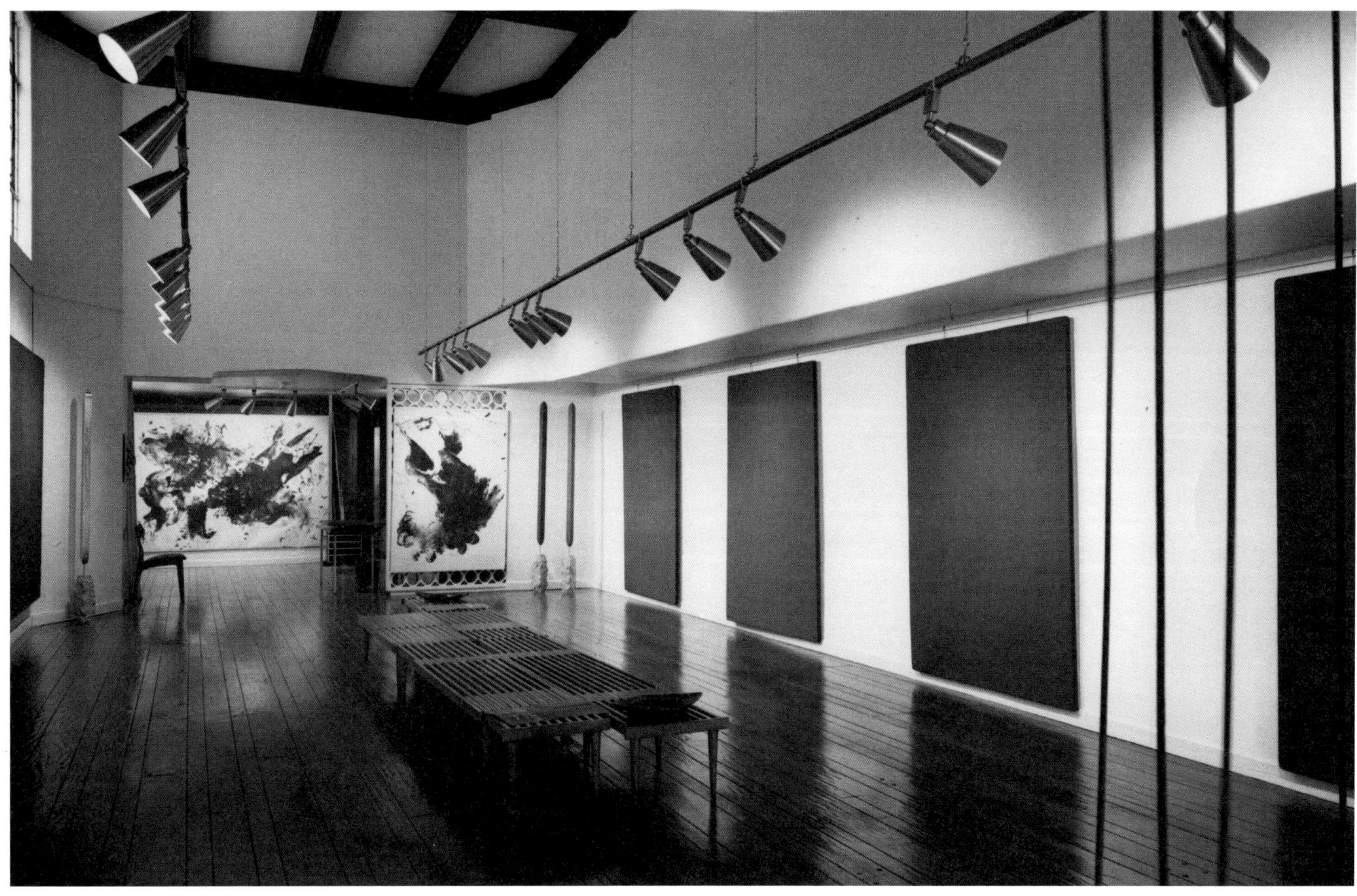

of the performance *Anthropométries de l'époque bleue* (*Anthropometries of the Blue Period*) at the Westwood space this hostility became overt. (Dwan recalled the "anger, jealously, and rivalry" of the audience, largely comprised of artists.[104]) On one hand, the new mobility fostered transnational connections and collaborations (between Rivers and Jean Tinguely, Tinguely and Edward Kienholz, Tinguely and Rauschenberg, and Niki de Saint Phalle and Rauschenberg, to name a few). Rivers served as an informal guide to Klein and his fiancée Rotraut Uecker in New York; in Los Angeles, Kienholz played this role. But mobility inspired a blinkered chauvinism as much as it dispelled it: traditional French condescension was more than equaled by the xenophobic responses to Klein in particular, such as the artist-critic Donald Judd's vulgar description of Klein as "the biggest frog" in the "rather stagnant pond" of French art (a viewpoint that did not preclude Judd's adoption of the nubbed, rolled surfaces of

FIG. 13

INSTALLATION VIEW, *YVES KLEIN—LE MONOCHROME*, AT DWAN GALLERY LOS ANGELES, MAY 1961

the Frenchman's monochromes in his early reliefs, to very different effect), or the acerbic reactions of the artists who attended the film screening and who wondered to Dwan who "this Parisian artist" was and "what the hell is he doing here?"[105]

An emerging network linked the vanguard scenes in America and France. This was far less developed and more informal than our present global system of exchange—an "art world" that grows ever larger and more interconnected with every passing year. The shipping costs of Klein's works from Paris to New York to Los Angeles were exorbitant. Even more, at the dawn of the jet age the crating and shipping of fragile works by air or sea over long distances was risky.[106] It was worth it, though. Dwan relished these "intoxicating" exchanges with visiting artists; the visitors appreciated Dwan's hospitality in turn.[107] Two works by Klein in the Dwan collection were presented by the artist to Dwan and Kondratief with dedications inscribed on the backs (cats. 12 and 15).[108] Mementos of friendship, the portable paintings suggest the nomadic character of Klein's practice.[109] A striking instance of this is the pair of sponge reliefs, one gold, the other blue, that Klein completed on the beach at Malibu (Writings, p. 243). These reliefs are indeed "post-studio" works, not unlike Smithson's interventions at Sanibel and in the Yucatán, even if the destiny of these works could not be more distinct: where Smithson's buried tree washed away long ago, and we know of it and his mirror displacements from their graphic and photographic depictions, the sponge reliefs are more conventional aesthetic objects intended for exhibition and sale. And in fact Dwan sold Klein's *Gold Sponge Relief* out of her office shortly after Klein completed it.

It was Kienholz who captured the itinerant aspect of Klein's project most perceptively. To make *Traveling Art Show Kit* (cat. 18), a souvenir of Klein's visit, Kienholz collected every item that Klein would conceivably need to make a monochrome: a spray can of IKB paint, a page of instructions, a jar labeled "grit," a painter's cloth, a toothbrush, and even a can of air freshener. He also enclosed a press release, a calendar of Klein's visit to California, and other curious things, such as an old doll and a picture album containing a photo of Klein directing his "human paintbrushes" imprinting sheets of paper with IKB. The hang tag lists Klein as the owner of the valise, his place of residence as "The Universe." Klein sought an art without boundaries, a state of limitlessness; he once "signed" the blue sky above the beach at Nice as his greatest work. But as Kienholz implies, this pursuit of the immaterial was tethered to the movements and gestures of a mortal body—a restless peripateticism that came to an abrupt conclusion the following June with Klein's untimely death.

A final episode in the remarkable interaction of Klein and Dwan loops our story back to Paris. On a sunny day in February 1962 a group gathered on a stairwell on the embankment next to Notre Dame. The Hollywood screenwriter Michael Blankfort and his wife, Dorothy, had met Klein during his show in Los Angeles; they had come to Paris to witness a work that Blankfort had commissioned and that Klein would now perform. Among the invited guests were two curators, a critic, and several gallerists including Dwan, a representation in miniature of the art world—the community that defines art as a class of objects distinct from other objects, as a thing of aesthetic and financial value and epistemological form.[110] Blankfort handed Klein sixteen ingots of gold he had acquired at the artist's request. At Klein's instruction the screenwriter gathered some of the ingots and hurled them into the Seine. Blankfort recalled:

> The act of throwing money away was not consonant either with my upbringing or my character. . . . Slowly, my hand lifted itself high in order to reach the Seine some yards away, and in a surge of ecstasy I threw the gold pieces toward the river. I followed the course of their rise, shining in the sun and then disappearing with modest splashes in the water. I felt purged; it was as if I had flown with them, leaving behind the baggage of daily living.[111]

Klein retained the remaining ingots as payment for his work and signed the receipt for the sale of the work. Blankfort lit a match, and Klein lifted up the burning slip in the air as the ashes scattered in the breeze. The exchange of gold for air, of matter for art, had yielded the state of "pure immateriality" that Klein established as the telos of his practice as a young man. Only the photographs of the action remain (cat. 16 a–d).

The Klein show exposed an attitude present in the work of many artists in New York and Los Angeles: that an artist was not restricted to working in a single medium. One could paint, sculpt, perform, *do*. And it made apparent that the rigid distinctions among mediums valorized by influential modernist critics like Clement Greenberg had begun to dissolve. The increasing prevalence of the relief, which combined painterly and sculptural formats (or which could be seen to suggest an altogether new category of art that negated medium outright, as Donald Judd claimed) was evident in Dwan's one-person show of painting-reliefs by Salvatore Scarpitta that succeeded the Klein exhibit, and in the work of the New York artist Lee Bontecou in the group show *Six Sculptors* of October 1961.[112] Bontecou's *Untitled* (1960) (cat. 11), a construction of welded metal, canvas, and wire punctured by holes revealing a black background, combines painterly materials and conventions such as the grid, an inheritance of

FIG. 14

INSTALLATION VIEW, *SIX SCULPTORS*, DWAN GALLERY LOS ANGELES, OCTOBER 1961 (LEE BONTECOU ON WALL AT RIGHT)

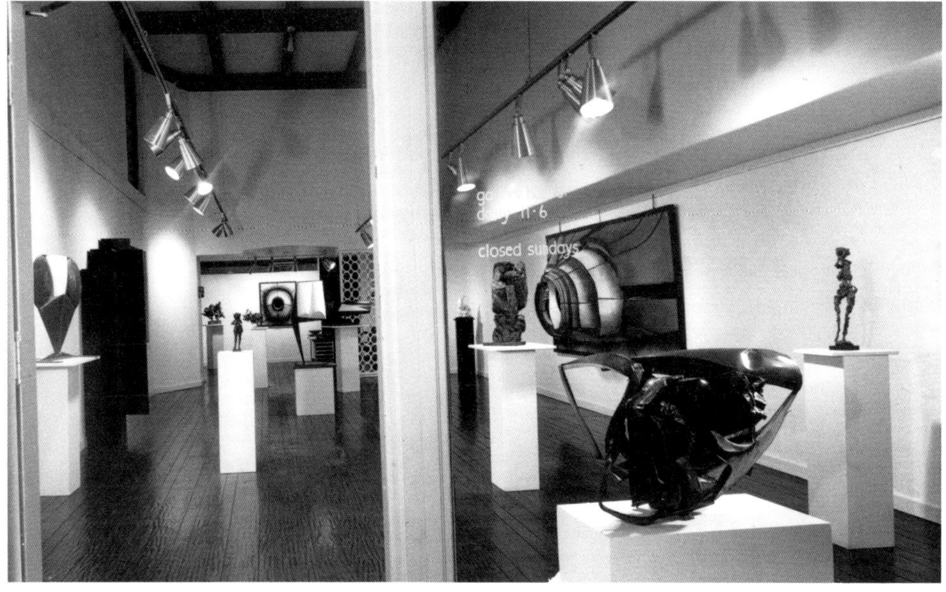

modernist painting (fig. 14). Rather than suggest a shallow illusionistic space, Bontecou's relief projects itself forward into a viewer's space—the space that Judd described as "real." Then it draws vision inside its dark cavity.[113] Where Judd observed that Bontecou and other young artists had invented an art that was "neither painting nor sculpture," that rejected medium tout court, Rauschenberg synthesized aspects of both mediums: his "combines" retained the dynamic brushwork and compositional design of the action painter while incorporating found objects and other elements, as evidenced in the works he exhibited at Dwan in March 1962, many for the first time.

In fact, the works that Rauschenberg shipped to Los Angeles were almost entirely combines.[114] Occupying the wall and extending to the floor (the traditional zones of the pictorial and sculptural), Rauschenberg's works upended a conventional understanding of painting as a homogeneous surface covered with paint. *First Landing Jump*, a board wrapped in a black tarp and covered in glued sheets of paper punctured by a lit bulb, appeared to be "held up" by a battered traffic barrier and a rubber tire, while *Black Market*'s one-way street sign, four clipboards, and license plate clung to a canvas connected by a cord to a suitcase resting on the floor. For this, the work's first presentation, Rauschenberg placed four objects in the suitcase along with instructions inviting a viewer to exchange one of these items for something else. Next the visitor was asked to draw an image of the replacement object on one of the clipboards and stamp the object with one of four numbered and signed stamps, yet another record of the

FIG. 15

INSTALLATION VIEW, *ROBERT RAUSCHENBERG*, DWAN GALLERY LOS ANGELES, MARCH 1962

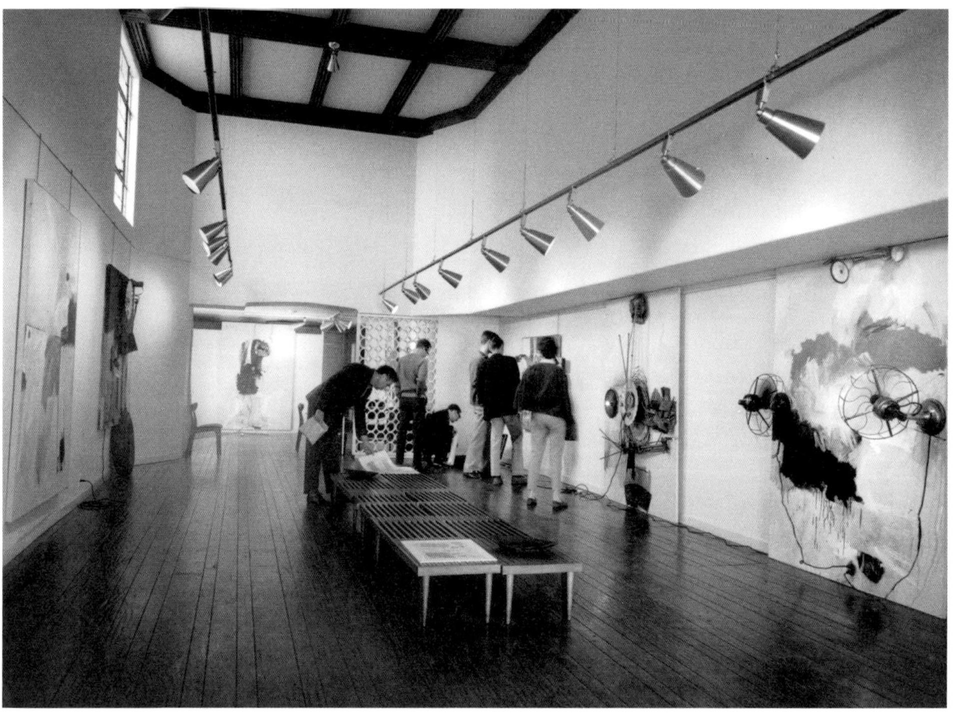

transaction.[115] *Black Market* elicited a degree of viewer involvement unknown at Dwan and anticipated the many participatory works to come. It catalyzed an exchange of information and objects that transpired along the vertical axis of painting and the horizontal plane of sculpture simultaneously, forcing a spectator to bend and stand, to look and read, in order to experience the work in its entirety.[116] In an installation shot, a young man crouches to inspect Rauschenberg's offerings and read his instructions, as other viewers lift up the pages of the clipboard mounted on the canvas to view the drawings of previous visitors (fig. 15).

Coexistence was as little a painting (categorically speaking) as a painting could be (cat. 19). It hung on the wall, as paintings do; it was executed on canvas. The small patch of dripping yellow ocher paint at top left, a few splatters of this hue and the white ground at bottom, and straggling passages of pale pink are vestiges of a once energetic medium, the exhausted bravura gestures of the action painter. The all-but-blank canvas is instead a hanger or support for all the *things* that Rauschenberg has improbably attached to it: rusted sheets of metal, wire brackets, a cooking grill, the splintered sections of a yellow NYPD traffic barrier, a rust-encrusted baton with a rubber ball, a medal painted red, white, and blue. A dirty cloth smudged with blue and white paint hangs at the bottom, and at the top left a rubber element, perhaps a piece of boot, hangs from a wooden plank nailed to the support. Rauschenberg has affixed a stamped metal medallion to the longest piece of the traffic barrier. Inside a glazed oval compartment at its center, surrounded by red beads, is a large tooth. The baton and rubber hose are held up magically by the ends of the wire bracket; this element, with its contorted twists, supports the grill that sustains the cord that holds up the filthy rag. Projecting out from the work several inches, the elements cast a web of shadows onto the support and wall. *Coexistence* has been stuffed with objects so copious and so absurdly weighty we can easily imagine the canvas suddenly ripping apart and collapsing to the floor. Rauschenberg's work is both a material demonstration and an allegory of fragile contingency.

Rauschenberg built *Coexistence* and the other combines he showed at Dwan out of the detritus of construction sites and urban dumps in Lower Manhattan, an area that was then undergoing a dramatic transformation. The old loft and light manufacturing buildings of nineteenth-century vintage, such as the one in which he lived with Jasper Johns at the time, were being replaced by modern office towers and banks, and the narrow streets of the colonial city were being widened and rerouted to facilitate traffic flow.[117] If Rauschenberg's combines spoke of a changing East Coast urbanity, a late addition to the show, *Wooden Gallop,* evoked a local ambience (cat. 20).[118] Created at Malibu, *Wooden Gallop* is a display of souvenirs harvested on Dwan's beach: a deflated yellow rubber life raft, a paddle, collaged bits of paper, wood and metal fragments, and a flattened cola can. Literally built from the flotsam and jetsam of the California coast, Rauschenberg's relief is inextricably bound to the place of its making.

The Dwan show was among Rauschenberg's last installations of combines, a format he had first explored in 1954 and 1955. To prepare the announcement for the show, a collage and "transfer" drawing, the artist soaked a text or image in solvent and rubbed it on a sheet of paper.[119] Like *Coexistence*, the announcement is divided into quadrants (cat. 21). It presents a cacophony of information: two crossword puzzles, one collaged from a newspaper, the other a reverse transfer of a completed puzzle; a strip of paper typed "Mr. Robt. Rauschenberg"; the words *Blue*, *Beer*, and *Bier* (German for "beer"); and the Dwan Gallery logo (a hooked "D" and "G") and date of the opening doubled and reversed. A telegram addressed to Rauschenberg c/o the Dwan Gallery appears not to have arrived.[120] The presence of the telegram—the medium of his *This is a portrait of Iris Clert if I say so* (1961), a famous instance of a conceptualist art of nomination—evokes the itinerant existence of Rauschenberg himself, who had driven across the country with an entourage and was often in transit to Europe during this period.[121] In fact, the opening of Rauschenberg's show coincided with other events in Los Angeles, suggesting a cross-pollination among East Coast, West Coast, and French avant-garde tendencies. Dwan organized the opening to occur concurrently with an exhibition of Jean Tinguely at the Everett Ellin Gallery and a *tir* (shooting) by Niki de Saint Phalle in a parking lot above Sunset Boulevard.[122] Kienholz's breakthrough installation at Ferus, a fantasy of a bordello called *Roxys*, opened there the same week. Merce Cunningham and his dance troupe performed then. John Cage lectured at art schools. Amidst this flurry of activity, Rauschenberg's show was poorly reviewed.[123] And though Dwan kept his works on consignment for more than a year, a whole gallery of combines, many now considered treasures of late twentieth-century art, went unsold.[124] The inverted dollar sign in *Untitled (For Virginia with Hook)* (cat. 22), a portable collage given to Dwan at the time of the artist's second show at the gallery in 1965, is perhaps a wry allusion to his work's unsalability—or a refusal of the very assumption that the aesthetic merit of a work of art is reflected in its price. The growing notoriety of the little gallery on Broxton Avenue was unmatched by pecuniary gain.

LOS ANGELES: THE SECOND DWAN GALLERY

The storefront gallery had begun to outgrow itself. The somatic scale of the new painting and sculpture demanded a more expansive space, Dwan discovered, and she set about finding another location where she could present it. The second Dwan Gallery, at 10846 Lindbrook Drive in Westwood, was wider and more open in feeling than the Broxton space and also had a two-story ceiling. Dwan and her architect, Morris Verger, installed white marble panels underneath the walls in order to reflect light onto the art above; the addition of a deep arched passageway at the entrance effectively separated the exhibition space from the noisy street, establishing the gallery as a place consecrated to the unimpeded experience of works of art. Where in the old space the quality and intensity of light shifted with the sun's movement, here the lighting was entirely artificial and highly controlled. And where previously the track lighting was exposed, here the lamps were hidden within the soffits of the upper walls. A second arch, reiterating the first, separated the gallery from the office, dividing the spaces of commerce and display so as to distinguish the experience of buying art from other retail experiences.[125]

The second Dwan Gallery was an exemplary "white cube." In fact, Dwan determined the proportions of the walls to accommodate Reinhardt's *Abstract Painting (A)*, one of the tallest works in her first Reinhardt show (cat. 10). The merit of that decision was evident in her fall 1963 exhibition of Reinhardt's seven seemingly (but not at all) identical cruciform "black" square works, including Dwan's own *Ultimate Painting* (cat. 60 and p. 333, fig. 38).[126] And it was evident in the striking Franz Kline show that she organized in March 1963 as a memorial to the painter, who had died the previous year (p. 331, fig. 29). The Kline show was a mini-retrospective spanning eleven years of the painter's production, from easel-scale pictures such as *Clock Face* (1950) to the grand black-and-white canvases of 1957–1960 (*Garcia*, *Black Sienna*, *Torres*), to the late, polychromatic *Andrus* (1961). In many of these works a "figure" straddles the ground underneath (as we find in *Torres*, cat. 8, for example). In *Pittston*, named for the Pennsylvania coal town near Kline's place of birth, large passages of white paint edge up against, put pressure on, the thick black brushstrokes we think of as the salient imagery of Kline's mature art, jockeying for dominance (cat. 9). For Kline has laid down white on different tones of black and gray in such a way that we are unable to decide whether white sits on black, or black on white, and thus unable to discern figure from ground. Kline adds and subtracts. His horsehair brushes leave feathery traces, yet he enlists the back ends of these implements to scrape away pigment, exposing raw canvas. An intuitive geometry of almost-rectangles and not-quite-triangles is implied where the black brush-strokes meet off-center, until Kline effaces these vestiges of cubist structure beneath a lather of brushwork.

I interpret this memorial show as an elegy not only to Kline but to abstract expressionism. The tendency that had dominated Dwan's program so far was being superseded by fresher impulses, as suggested by the opening show in the highly anticipated Lindbrook space in May 1962. Yves Klein had spoken to Dwan of his childhood friend Arman and other members of l'École de Nice, a school also known as "nouveau réalisme."[127] During a visit to Arman's studio Dwan had been struck by his "Accumulations," discarded objects displayed in vitrines.[128] She selected some of these works for her opening show and had other Arman works sent to Los Angeles by the artist's New York dealer, Daniel Cordier. But Arman built at least half of the works *after* his arrival in Los Angeles, where he stayed at Dwan's guesthouse for a full three months.[129] The new mobility fostered new approaches and techniques, as we have seen. Rather than complete his or her works in advance and have them shipped to a gallery, an artist could fabricate them near or at the place of exhibition, enlisting local materials. Not exactly site-specific, the "post-studio" work could be installed anywhere. Above all, the new mode of production was eminently practical, making it possible for Dwan to exhibit the work of artists who typically lived elsewhere. "It saved me a certain outlay to be able to have the works made on the spot. Shipping them was far more expensive than having them made there."[130]

Arman presented all manner of things, from doorbells and coffee mills to locks, pots, and radio tubes to shoes, typewriters, and musical instruments he cut up and rearranged. But it was the works made with the "old objects of Europe" sent over from Nice that most impressed Dwan, who chose the artist's *Alarm Clocks* (*Reveils*), a glass-front box filled with old French and Italian alarm clocks, to appear on the show's invitation (cat. 23). In the paintings of Salvador Dali timepieces melt; in Arman's sculpture they repeat. Fifty-two clocks line up haphazardly in five rows. They tilt left and right, some are even upside down. All show wear. They have corroded, their glass faces are broken, their paper dials are torn. Many are missing second hands. The tiny wheels inside have been exposed. Arman is an agent of the clocks' destruction, nailing them crudely to the support and even defacing them with his signature (three of the clocks are signed). And he is the angel of their redemption: salvaging the abandoned timekeepers from the junkman, he has elevated them into the "timeless" condition of art, altering the nature of their existence *in* time.

The work's title (*Reveils,* French for "dreams") is surely ironic: the alarm clock is the shrill martinet that interrupts our dreams, uprooting us from the warm comfort of our beds every morning and marching us off to work.[131] Consider the history of these particular clocks: stamped with the brand names of defunct *horlogères* and *fabbriche* in the vicinity of the artist's native Nice,[132] the clocks bear the memory of an outmoded system of production, a previous capitalist formation. They are the battered survivors of a prewar regional industrial economy superseded by the postindustrial consumer economy that emerged after World War II, when mass-produced electronic timekeepers rendered the wind-up clock obsolete. Now consider the owners of these alarms—all the hands that wound the mechanisms. Consider all the factory workers and laundresses, all the petit-bourgeois shopkeepers and clerks whose livelihoods depended on the punctual ringing of these devices. Consider Kafka's traveling salesman, Gregor Samsa, who wakes up one morning to discover that he has missed his train. As a divine retribution for his tardiness, Samsa has been transformed into a giant insect. He has countless little legs, a hard shell. He is unable to lift himself out of bed. His bedside clock has failed him:

He looked at the alarm clock ticking on the chest. Heavenly Father! he thought. It was half-past six o'clock, and the hands were quietly moving on . . . Could the alarm clock have not gone off?[133]

In *The Metamorphosis*, reality is far worse than the most unsettling dreams. The clock ticks on indifferently as Samsa's time runs out. Arman's clocks are memento mori, souvenirs of lives forgotten and extinguished. The promise of death lurks beneath each one of the discarded objects displayed in his strange vitrines.

An introduction to the Swiss kinetic sculptor Jean Tinguely and the French American artist Niki de Saint Phalle led Dwan to collaborations with both artists, who flew to Los Angeles from Toyko in March 1963. A collage of snapshots of the artist and dealer generated the announcement for Tinguely's show at Dwan Gallery later that spring (cat. 24).[134] As he did for Arman and Martial Raysse, another member of the nouveaux réalistes, Kienholz served as an informal guide to the artist couple, introducing them to local supply stores and junk shops, which he knew intimately.[135] Like his friend Arman, Tinguely fabricated much of his show "on the scene" with Dwan's support. The Swiss artist worked well in Los Angeles. The sculptures he made were more solidly built than previously; and for the first time he covered his works in matte black paint, unifying these disparate works into an ensemble.[136] A viewer could compare the moving sculptures of different type, size, and placement—works on pedestals, on the floor, and installed on a shelf with a large horizontal canvas mounted with two interconnected machines (p. 331, figs. 31, 32).[137]

In the art of Tinguely, comparison is both a bodily and cognitive action triggered by our participation. At the Westwood gallery a visitor turned the works on and off with the flick of a switch: without viewer involvement, the work remained incomplete. In order to experience *Odessa* (cat. 25), the viewer presses a floor switch attached to an electrical cord. An engine mounted on a low metal pedestal causes a rubber belt on a tire rim to rotate. A second rubber belt connected to the rim causes a small wheel at top to spin. The tire rim evokes an engorged belly, the wheel a head, the pedestal a person's feet. The wheels turn erratically. The sculpture sputters, as if we are in the presence of a drunken man. A witty anthropomorphism also animates Tinguely's sculptural portrait of Dwan, a delicate construction of "feminine" appearance incorporating part of an andiron, wires, and a transistor, a work that is meant to project the static sounds of a dysfunctional radio dial (cat. 26).[138] And it was indubitably felt in the series of mechanical fountains that Tinguely installed in the yards of several Los Angeles collectors one evening, which throbbed and shook

FIG. 16

NIKI DE SAINT PHALLE, *KING KONG*, 1963, MODERNA MUSEET, STOCKHOLM, GIFT OF THE ARTIST

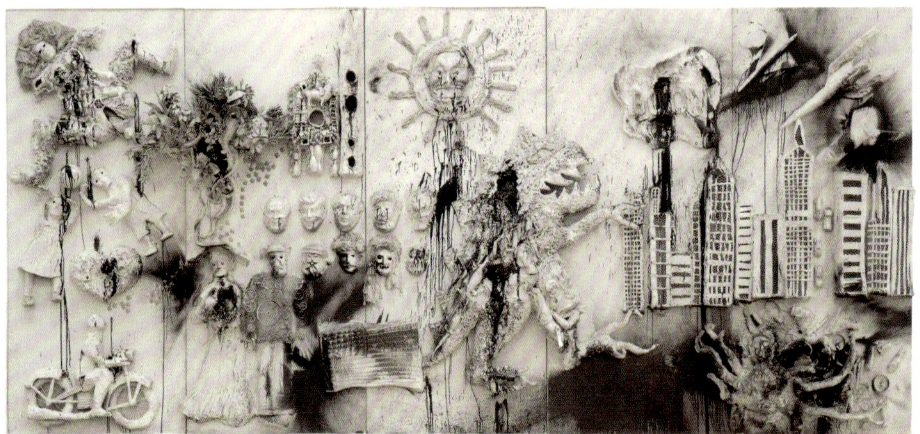

as they ejaculated streams of water onto the patrons' well-tended lawns (p. 297, fig. 15).[139] In a working drawing for one of these works, the rubber wheels that transport the sculpture evoke feet; tubes extend from the sculpture's posterior like legs. The other wheels suggest a head, arms, and stomach. In the background another fountain with outstretched "arms" struggles to stay up (cat. 28).

Where Tinguely populated the gallery with mechanized creatures, Saint Phalle exhibited a grotesque menagerie. The dominant image in her Dwan show was a relief nine feet tall by twenty feet wide, the result of one of her *tirs*, or shootings (examples on pp. 246 and 293, fig. 11). From her perch on a low ladder, Saint Phalle would take aim at a plaster relief with a rifle. *King Kong* (1963) was a stinging allegory of the Cuban Missile Crisis of the preceding October. It depicts a pregnant woman giving birth, a prototype of Saint Phalle's signature female figure, "Nana"; a bride and lovers; a tree of knowledge and serpent; and an apocalyptic rider and a church. Unflattering portraits of world leaders (Nikita Khrushchev, John F. Kennedy, Charles de Gaulle, Fidel Castro, and Abraham Lincoln) float above a Greek tragedy chorus and a US flag. The Godzilla dinosaur marches toward Gotham, undeterred by fighter jets and missiles. A huge octopus with a death's head lurks beneath the city. When Saint Phalle pulled the trigger and fired, rivulets of paint poured down the relief. The church exploded, the monster bled. The sun wept dark tears (fig. 16).

Half of the works that Arman showed were made in Los Angeles; all of Tinguely's and Saint Phalle's were. (*King Kong* remained with Dwan until she was able to exhibit it.[140]) Mobility affected these artists' practices in another way. Back in Paris, Tinguely and Saint Phalle developed an epistolary art. In the letter-drawings of these artists we observe private correspondence constantly giving way to works of visual imagination; more precisely, these works enact a crossing of linguistic and perceptual recognition.[141] In an undated letter to Dwan written in advance of Saint Phalle's visit, she describes her drawing of a tyrannosaurus rex (cat. 31) as a study for a "sculpture relief" (itself a study for the monumental *King Kong*).[142] The red snake strangling the dinosaur is made of smooth plaster (*plâtre lisse*). Their bellies are "stuffed with objects" (*farci d'objets*). But what appears to be an enchanting preparatory drawing is at the same time a letter written in response to one from Dwan. The dragon is filled with writing. The letter begins on its back ("Dear Virginia. Thank you for your leter. [*sic*]"], proceeds to its tail (Saint Phalle proposes a trip to Los Angeles to make the works for her show while Tinguely is there—"I will pay my ticket over"), and continues in a speech bubble from the creature's mouth ("*Bonjour à Philippe. Bonjour à Ed. Bonjour à toi...*"). The image of the snake asphyxiating the monster has a personal meaning. Dwan's letter arrived "the right day," Saint Phalle writes. "I was very depressed. And also I have a sore throat." Even the scaly cobra is made to speak: "Please answer express." Such exchanges continued long after Dwan, a lucky recipient of these bursts of whimsy, closed her gallery. They were often collaborative efforts. In their letter-drawings *Dear Virginia: à bientôt* and *Chère Virginia: come sta?* (cats. 29, 30) personal salutations, drawings, and collaged imagery cohabitate freely, even joyously. In the second drawing, one of Saint Phalle's Nanas waves hello to the gallerist.

Far more than Arman, Tinguely, and Saint Phalle, the work of Martial Raysse, the last of the nouveaux réalistes Dwan represented, drew from the commercial imagery then being explored by American pop artists, and it was within the critical discourse of international pop that Raysse's practice was now received. Dwan had organized *My Country 'Tis of Thee*, one of the earliest shows of the pop movement, in November 1962 (p. 329, figs. 24, 25).[143] A new director, John Weber, helped Dwan install the exhibition, which she conceived after a recent visit to New York.[144] Apart from John Chamberlain's *Rayvredd* (cat. 35), a crushed remnant of an automobile (a deliberate choice on Dwan's part),[145] most of the works in *My Country 'Tis of Thee* were blatantly representational, now iconic examples of proto- or full-blown American pop: Jasper Johns's *Flag on Orange Field* and *Bronze Flag*; Robert Indiana's "sign painting" *The American Reaping Company*; Roy Lichtenstein's *Takka Takka*, a depiction of a comic-strip machine gun; Warhol's portrait of Marilyn Monroe, who had died in Los Angeles that summer; James Rosenquist's *Hey! Let's Go For a Ride*, a cropped image of a woman's face and beer bottle (fig. 17); and one of Tom Wesselmann's *Great American Nudes*, a tondo, hung in the office. (Although Wesselmann was never represented by Dwan, his work was a sporadic presence:

FIG. 17

JAMES ROSENQUIST, *HEY! LET'S GO FOR A RIDE*, 1961, FROM *MY COUNTRY 'TIS OF THEE*, DWAN GALLERY LOS ANGELES, NOVEMBER 1962

his painting and collage *Still Life #2*, a Matissean composition of a flattened tabletop and chair, vase of flowers, oversized pear, Salem cigarette package, and an ad for Four Roses bourbon, was sold by the gallerist even though it was never publicly shown [cat. 42].)

Marisol Escobar's carved and painted portrait of the First Family, *The Kennedys*, stood at the entrance; Claes Oldenburg's *Floorburger*, an eight-foot-wide depiction of a hamburger built from awning cloth stuffed with rubber foam and cardboard, and his charming, paint-splattered, oversized *Coffee Cup* were installed on the floor (cat. 39). And there were other, less emblematic works: Kienholz's *Untitled American President*, a milk can inscribed with a US flag topped by a bicycle seat. Or a tall, narrow relief by Charles Frazier entitled *Albion*, the ancient name for Britain, a representation of a window with finials and lunette inset in wooden siding (cat. 36). Bare canvas stretches across the elongated window sashes, revealing four small protrusions shaped like a

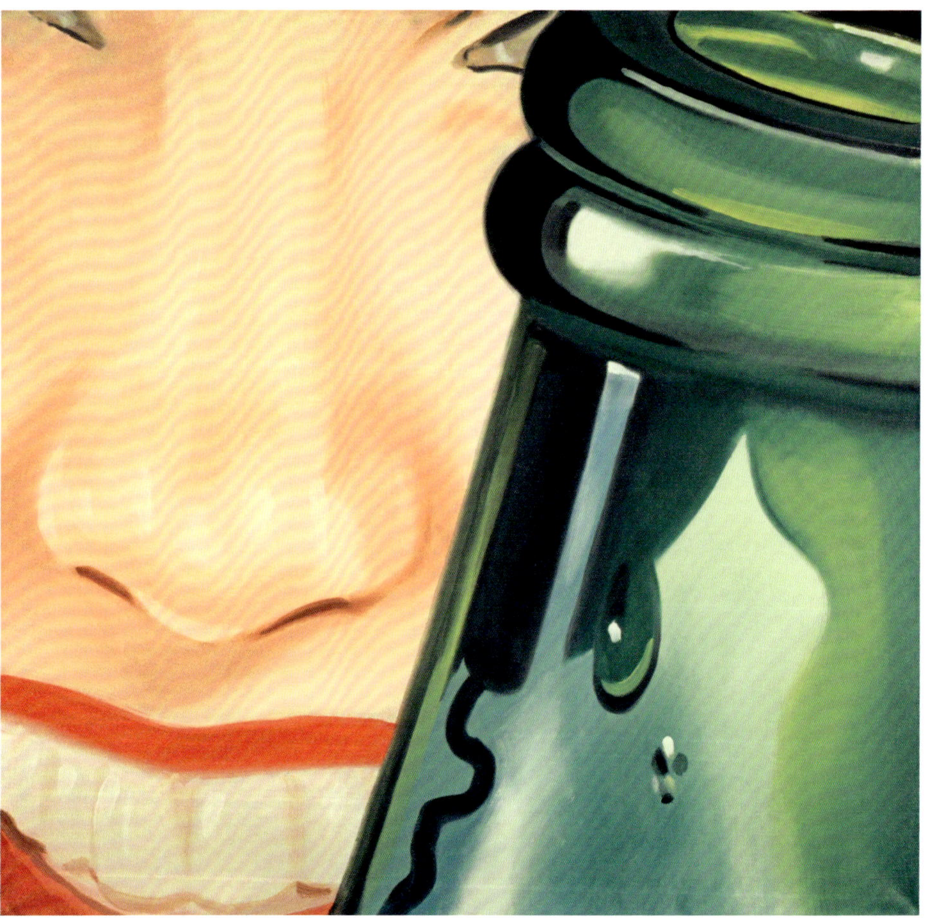

crucifix in the upper sash. The lumps in the lower sash resemble breasts, and farther down a belly—a body confined and headless. A possible reference to the old Victorian houses of downtown neighborhoods imperiled in the sixties by freeway construction and corporate growth combined with hermetic spiritual allusions, *Albion* eschewed the crass blatancy of East Coast pop for an occult and perverse imagery of distinctly Californian flavor such as we find in the symbol-laden reliefs of Billy Al Bengston and the films of Kenneth Anger.

Critics found little to like in *My Country 'Tis of Thee.* Henry Seldis and Jules Langsner chafed at pop levity, denouncing the "sophomoric" depictions of "tarnished idols" by Dwan's artists, their "overt search for novelty."[146] Curiously, the "furor" caused by the show (as Langsner described it) had little impact on sales. To the contrary, from a commercial standpoint the pop show was a resounding success.[147] Taking note of a checklist covered with red dots, Seldis chided the buyers of these "cynical" works. Here was an art without distinction, destined for the homes of Los Angeles's "overly affluent novice" collectors: the entertainment industry nouveaux riches.

This, then, was the milieu that greeted Raysse, whose first exhibition at Dwan opened a month after the pop show closed (p. 330, fig. 27). The show featured blown-up photo-silkscreens of models and starlets cropped and transferred to canvases stained red and blue, emerald and acid orange. Ready-made and collaged elements—sequins, sunglasses, mirrors, powder puffs, false eyelashes, and plastic flowers—evoked a world of suburban shopping centers and dime stores, of beauty shops and drugstore makeup counters, and the highly coded gendering of the Hollywood entertainment industry and ads that would prove equally germane in Raysse's rarer depictions of men.[148] The tiny *Pablo* (1965) presents a cropped image of Picasso's iconic eyes peering out beneath a row of polychrome letters from a child's spelling game (cat. 33), while Raysse's 1964 self-portrait depicts the artist as a mysterious, contemplative, and above all divided figure, whose face has been inverted upside down on one side and appears right side up on the other, and who veils his eyes behind a pair of actual sunglasses and presses his fingers inscrutably to his lips (cat. 32). The title, *C'est Moi* ("It's Me"), is ironic. In this strange, remote image, the artist is as opaque, as unknowable, as the made-up models and starlets that populate so much of his art.

Notable, too, was Raysse's first neon sculpture, a totemic "body" with glowing nose, lips, and Plexiglas "arms" emblazoned with flickering arrows pointing in opposite directions, as street signs do, a work that Raysse named *Homage to Los Angeles* after the city that inspired its making. And in fact neon sculptures dominated his second show at Dwan in 1964. In this and other images such as *Obelisk* and *Oasis* (a stand with colored lights holding up a disk with an image of Brigitte Bardot on one side and another actress on the other), Raysse combined images of mass culture icons and mundane objects with riffs on Old Master paintings. *Made in Japan* (cat. 34), another purchase of Dwan's I consider totemic, is a direct appropriation of a photomechanical reproduction of Ingres's *La Grande Odalisque* (1814). In Raysse's depiction, the flawless skin of Ingres's nude is a sickly green. A plastic fly rests on her arm. The peacock feathers of her fan are not depicted but real. The silvery floral-patterned curtain is actual wallpaper. Placing Ingres's masterpiece in a gallery of flashing neon depictions of movie stars and objects of the most extreme banality, Raysse put these images on an equal footing.

Raysse's blurring of high and low struck a chord. Seldis questioned whether the French artist was an artist after all—and whether his art was describable as "art."[149] Raysse was an entertainer, a trader in "fun and games." Like Warhol and Lichtenstein, he would do well in a city of parvenus. ("The movie capital of the world should be a likely market place for these amusements."[150]) The snobbish critic was not alone in his disdain, and in his manner of expressing it. No less than Kanemitsu decried the shift in Dwan's program from high abstraction to the seemingly superficial activities of "your French [and American] clowns," as he wrote in a scathing missive to the gallerist.[151] Such objections made little impression on Dwan. She had thrown in her lot with her French and American "clowns" and would take on a few more: Oldenburg and Rosenquist now joined the gallery.[152] One of the original Dwan artists, Kanemitsu shot himself in the foot: his next show at the gallery was his last.

Oldenburg's Dwan show, which opened in October 1963, was an extension of, and a significant departure from, his seminal show at Green Gallery in New York the previous fall. Even more than the Green show, the Dwan installation presented a veritable smorgasbord of the prodigious artist's forms and techniques, some developed since Oldenburg's departure from Manhattan with his then-wife and collaborator, Pat Muschinski (also known as Patty Mucha), to Los Angeles, where the disaffected New Yorkers had rented a bungalow and studio in Venice Beach. The Westwood show included works of plaster-soaked muslin dripping with dried enamel paint—similar to the type exhibited at Oldenburg's "Store" on the Lower East Side and at Green, such as the relief *Green Stockings* and *Baked Potato #1*, an oversized spud whose pat of melting "butter" rests on a soft pillow of kapok-filled jersey (cat. 38). It also included stuffed cloth sculptures of things made gigantic and soft, such as the

FIG. 18

CLAES OLDENBURG, *GIANT BLUE SHIRT WITH BROWN TIE,* 1963

eleven-foot-long *Floor Cone* (installed leaning and upside down, as if melting, p. 299, fig. 18) and *Giant Blue Shirt with Brown Tie*, which hung sideways from an actual clothes rack in the back of the Westwood space (fig. 18). Oldenburg and Mucha had presented these or similar works in New York. But now they showed newer confections of plaster and plastic enamel (*Giant Wedge of Pecan Pie*, cat. 40) and vinyl works, some recently fabricated in Venice of colder, more "professional" (and as the art historian Thomas Crow has argued, more "pop") appearance (*Giant BLT Sandwich*, *French Fries with Ketchup*, *Soft Good Humor*, two soft *Pay-Telephones*). Last but not least, they presented brand-new sculptures covered in fake fur (*Leopard Chair in Perspective* and *Four Artificial Fur Good Humors*) inspired by the middle-class domestic interiors and tawdry motel rooms of their temporarily adopted city, an iconography further asserted in Oldenburg's watercolor of Mickey Mouse gazing at a bulbous red heart—lovingly or malignly, depending on how one reads it—that afforded the show its announcement (cat. 37).[153]

Like the downtown Store, Oldenburg's Green Gallery show functioned as both studio and exhibition space. During the course of the exhibition works were made, rearranged, and even removed; the installation never took a definitive form.[154] At Dwan, each work stood out as a unique entity. (Crow has written perceptively of the "consolidation" of Oldenburg's works as "discrete sculptures" at Dwan.[155]) For good reason: the Westwood gallery was considerably larger than the narrow and rather shallow Green Gallery, whose

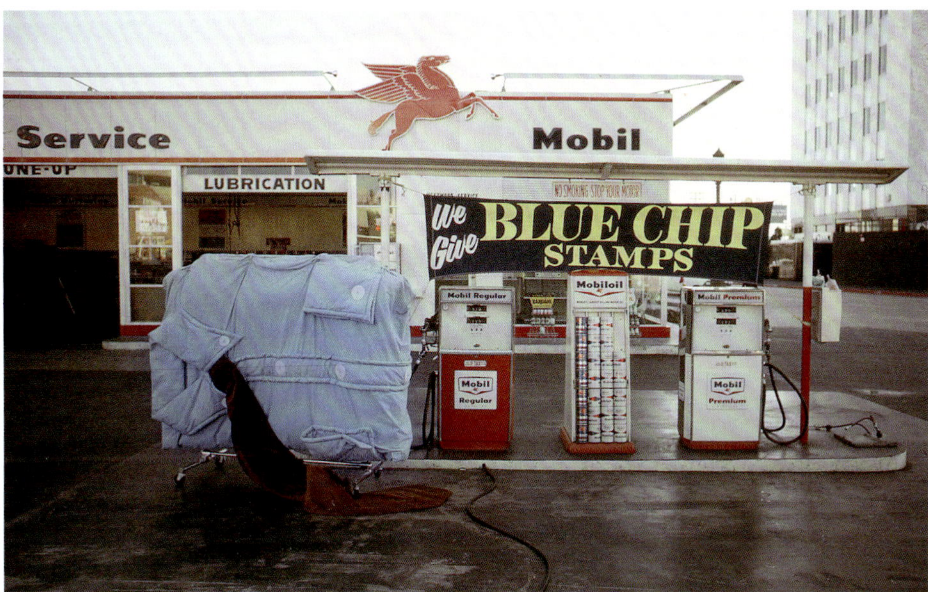

importance far exceeded its size, and which appears larger to us now than it actually was.[156] In Westwood Oldenburg had a grander stage, one that dignified his and Mucha's unconventional objects as viable works of art, as commodities—ironically, an aim the show did not achieve.[157] Never before had the artist shown so many different images, textures, and colors. And because each work had enough ambient room, viewers could relate each sculpture to all the others. "Each piece now stood in all its parameters—form, motif, color, texture, size, and mode of presentation—in a systematic relationship to all the other works in the exhibition."[158] One could begin to grasp the ensemble as a whole by absorbing and comparing its many parts: the baked potato scaled only slightly smaller than the oversized athletic shoes that in actuality are several times a potato's size; or the *Giant Wedge of Pecan Pie*, of comparable size to the pay phones; or the three versions of the pay phone, one the "ghost" of the other on opposite walls, both sagging and soft unlike actual pay phones though arguably the same size as them; and the watercolor of the pay phone on the back wall, an image of an object (as opposed to an object of an object). Oversized to different degrees, hard or soft, hand-painted or industrially finished, matte or shiny, wrinkled or smooth, revealing or resisting gravity, three- or two-dimensional, the works exhibited at Dwan both solicited one's identification with these objects and caused them to appear strange. Things we think we "know" appeared unlike themselves, shorn of their normative associations as in dreams.[159]

In New York Oldenburg organized a performance inside the Green Gallery, the *Sports Happening*, in which his sculptures served as props; in Los Angeles he staged a happening at a distance from Dwan in a parking lot off Beverly Boulevard. In Oldenburg's Los Angeles happening, *Autobodys*, actual things and modes of transportation were put to use (cat. 41 and p. 145). Transpiring over two evenings, the happening imaginatively recast the car-bound reality of daily life in Los Angeles into an event that catalyzed movement without purpose or direction. Viewers were instructed to park their cars in a rectangle on the bare asphalt, leaving openings at four corners, and turn on their headlights.[160] As the event unfolded, automobiles, trucks, and human beings glided past the car-bound spectators, who watched the disconnected actions through their windshields. Drawing upon the palette of his soft pay phones and fake zebra fur sculptures, Oldenburg used black and white cars and trucks exclusively and asked the twenty performers to dress in black and white. The Westwood exhibit confronted visitors with motley shapes, textures, and hues; the parking lot event was a riot of movements, noises, and surprises. Automobile engines revved up. A concrete mixer churned. Horns honked. Flares

FIG. 19

ARMAN, *CAST YOUR BALLOT HERE FOR A CLEANER DWAN GALLERY*, FROM *BOXES*, DWAN GALLERY LOS ANGELES, FEBRUARY 1964

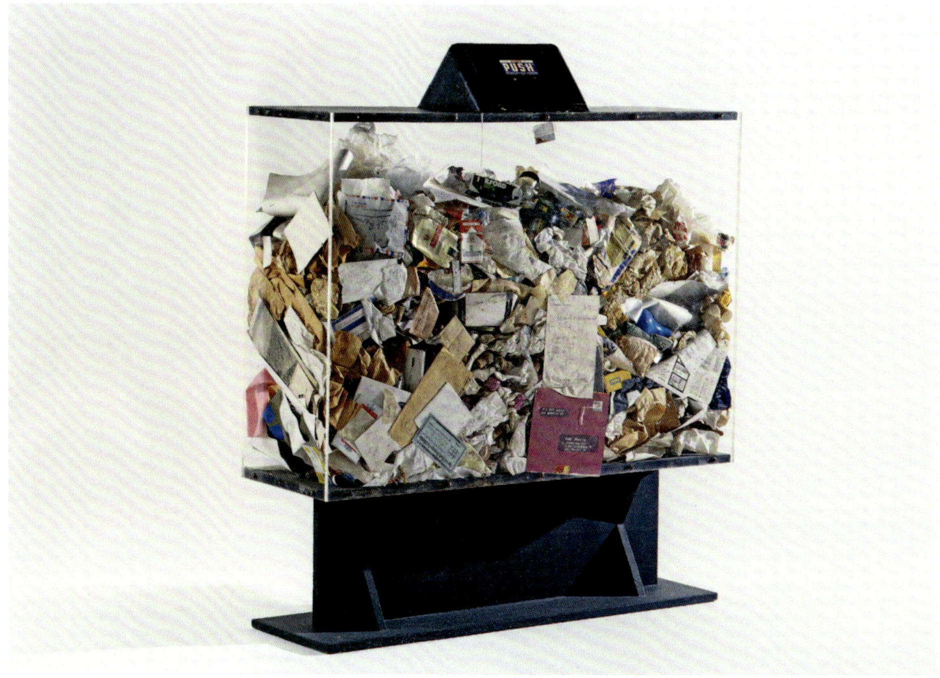

exploded. Radios blared. Milk spilled. Ice melted. Glass broke. And when the action fell silent the performers walked around the parking lot like zombies ("like particles, indifferent to one another," in Oldenburg's words). Like drivers on a freeway, the human beings presented in *Autobodys* are auto-bodies: autonomous, automatic, self-absorbed.[161]

That February the gallery staged an exhibition that reflected one of Weber's curatorial interests. A narrative of the morphology of the box from Dada to Fluxus and pop, *Boxes* was the gallery's most elaborate undertaking so far. Works by "four distinguished elders"—Marcel Duchamp, Kurt Schwitters, Joseph Cornell, and Louise Nevelson—established the show's historical tenor, as did Weber's selection of Walter Hopps as the author of the catalog, which was cleverly presented as an eight-foot scroll in a paper box imprinted with images of the show.[162] The selection of sixty-one works by thirty-nine "heroes, friends and surprising strangers" was productively unrigorous, a "fascinating gerrymander where all sorts of boundaries (of age and origins and style and method and intent) are crossed and intermingled."[163] Dada-surrealist totems—Duchamp's *From or by Marcel Duchamp or Rrose Sélavy (The Box in a Valise)* (cat. 43), boxes by Schwitters and Cornell, and two estimable works by Nevelson—intermixed with works by midcareer and emerging figures. Here were Arman's irreverent *Cast Your Ballot Here for a Cleaner Dwan Gallery* (fig. 19), a plastic container filled with trash from his last show; Raysse's *Supermarket*, an open box of many compartments containing "things bright, shiny, and new"; stacked shelves with two identical pillows by a now-forgotten trader in ready-mades, Aaron Kuriloff; hands-on game sculptures by the Fluxus artist George Brecht (Brecht's *Play Incident* invited a viewer to put a ball in one of two holes at the top of a relief and listen to it fall) and non-interactive ones, such as Robert Watts's *Checkers*, an aquarium containing a goldfish swimming above a checkers board.

In contrast to the proto-conceptual projects of Brecht and Kuriloff (or *Turn Ahead No Stopping*, a deconstruction of a traffic signal by Gerd Stern, a cofounder of the intermedia art collective USCO, fig. 20), other works explored the hermetic iconography of the box form, evoking ossuaries, caskets, and reliquaries, such as an untitled Lucas Samaras sculpture covered with

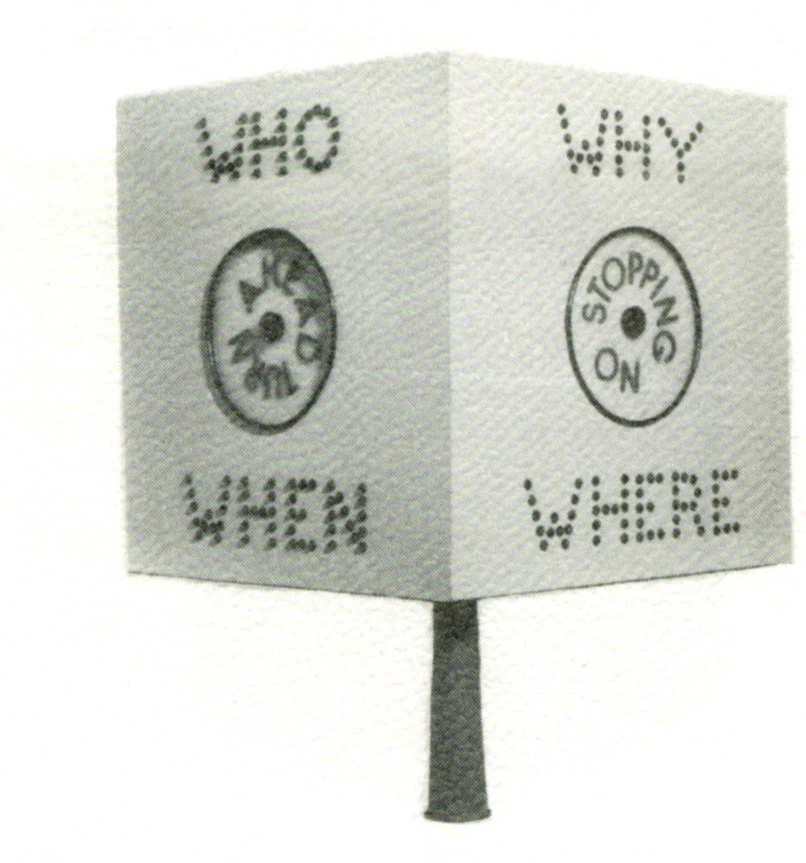

FIG. 20

GERD STERN, *TURN AHEAD NO STOPPING*, 1962, FROM *BOXES*, DWAN GALLERY LOS ANGELES, FEBRUARY 1964

thousands of pins piercing the artist's doubled self-portrait stuffed with colored yarn (cat. 44), or H.C. Westermann's box with an open door surmounted by skull and crossbones, or the *Immigrant No-Box* by the Holocaust survivor and NO!ART movement cofounder Boris Lurie, a trunk-sized container collaged with photos of concentration camp survivors and automobiles defaced with swastikas. The latter is the work that Dwan leans on in Julian Wasser's photograph of the gallerist in the *Boxes* exhibition (p. 14).

There were pop totems, too. Wesselmann sent *Great American Still Life with TV*, an assemblage of a kitchen table with Gilbert Stuart's unfinished portrait of Washington and a TV monitor playing a cartoon. Rosenquist showed the small, effective *Toaster*, a wood frame wrapped in sheer plastic sheeting screened and hand-painted with letters (cat. 45). At first sight, the cropped, blue-edged, transparent letters and inverted number four do not seem to spell anything. Now we notice that the lowercase letters *i*, *d*, and *e* and the vertical capital *T* around the corner spell the word *Tide*. But this is no ordinary box of soap powder, and no ordinary toaster. Sharp-toothed saw blades pop out where toast should be, slicing through the cheap plastic grass. Chrome-plated barbed wire wraps around the delicate box. Rivulets of red paint drip down the sides. Combined, these implements of middle-class orderliness and nourishment—the lawnmower, laundry soap, and toaster—are combustible and dangerous.

More surprising still were the three stacked sculptures of Brillo cartons and one for Heinz ketchup sent by Andy Warhol "with the ink still damp," exhibited for the first time in a gallery (cats. 46–48 and p. 14).[164] It could be claimed—and Weber did claim—that the show's concept inspired the creation of the famous Brillos,[165] whose uncanny resemblance to the originals (a likeness more blatant and unyielding than Rosenquist's creepy Tide box or Oldenburg's witty renditions of food, clothing, and telephones), dignified the most common of common objects, the shipping boxes of soap pads and ketchup bottles, as a subject worthy of our attention because it was art. And how did we know it was art? Not simply by looking at it but judging from the context of its presentation. The Dwan Gallery was this context—the place of the initial staging of the *Brillos* and the voluminous debates they unleashed.[166]

If that were not enough, *Boxes* featured works by local artists who had never shown at the increasingly prestigious gallery, and whose presence hinted at the actual diversity of the Los Angeles scene often unrepresented in the elite precincts of La Cienega and Westwood. On one hand, the show featured "Finish Fetish" artists like Larry Bell, who exhibited one of his fascinating mirror boxes referencing Blum's gallery, *Lux at the Ferus* (cat. 49), and Ken

Price (represented by a skull-shaped clay sculpture of fetishistic beauty installed on a pedestal in a vitrine framed in wood, cat. 50). But *Boxes* included works suggestive of a very different Southern Californian sensibility, such as Ronald Miyashiro's *Concord #9*, a bizarre, black cylindrical construction that revealed a crucifix behind a cage-like protrusion (cat. 51), and Daniel LaRue Johnson's *The Big N*, a sculpture of veiled and disturbing significance (cat. 52). Where Bell's work enticed a viewer to peer inside it in order to take in its internal relay of reflections, Johnson's shiny black box rebuffed one's gaze and denied one's visual pleasure. Inside the open circle is a black doll's hand ensnared in a mouse-trap hidden behind a chain-link fence. The hand is a fragment; its owner is missing. Johnson's work is inarguably an allegory of the violence of black life in America during the centuries prior to and during the civil rights era, when *Boxes* was staged. The focus of this image is the black body—a body confined, viciously beaten, lynched, and torn apart. To some viewers, the doll's hand entrapped in chicken wire surely evoked the bombing of the 16th Street Baptist Church in Birmingham, Alabama, the previous September; the incident left four young girls dead, their dismembered bodies buried under a heap of rubble.[167] Although *Concord #9*, *The Big N*, and other works described here went unremarked in the show's churlish reviews, *Boxes* was a watershed nevertheless: Rosenquist's *Toaster* appeared on the cover of *Artforum*, and the gallery was flooded with requests.[168]

A show by another Los Angeles artist would bring even greater attention. In his first exhibition at Dwan in 1963, Kienholz showed individual sculptures of found objects, not unlike his *Portrait of Virginia* of the same year, a representation of the gallerist as a composite arrangement of an aquarium resting on a rusted metal box supported by the feet of an old table (cat. 53). An upside-down crystal vase inset in a concrete block evokes a face and shoulders, a piece of wire Dwan's coiffure. Kienholz identified one of the works in the 1963 show as a "tableau"—an assemblage depicting a provocative and often timely subject. Consisting of a chair, rickety lamp, bedpan, surgical instruments, stool, hooked rug, and bucket of red paint, *The Illegal Operation* (fig. 21) represented the aftermath of an abortion in the period before the 1973 Supreme Court decision *Roe v. Wade*. His 1964 Dwan show—*Three Tableaux*—featured works on the theme of carnal desire: *While Visions of Sugar Plums Danced in Their Heads*, a tableau of a heterosexual couple in bed who have pillow-like heads that allow us to peer inside their minds at their erotic fantasies; *The Birthday*, a grim depiction of a female mannequin strapped to a physician's exam table in the process of giving birth or being violated as she screams into a plastic bubble with

FIG. 21

EDWARD KIENHOLZ, *THE ILLEGAL OPERATION*, 1962, LOS ANGELES COUNTY MUSEUM OF ART

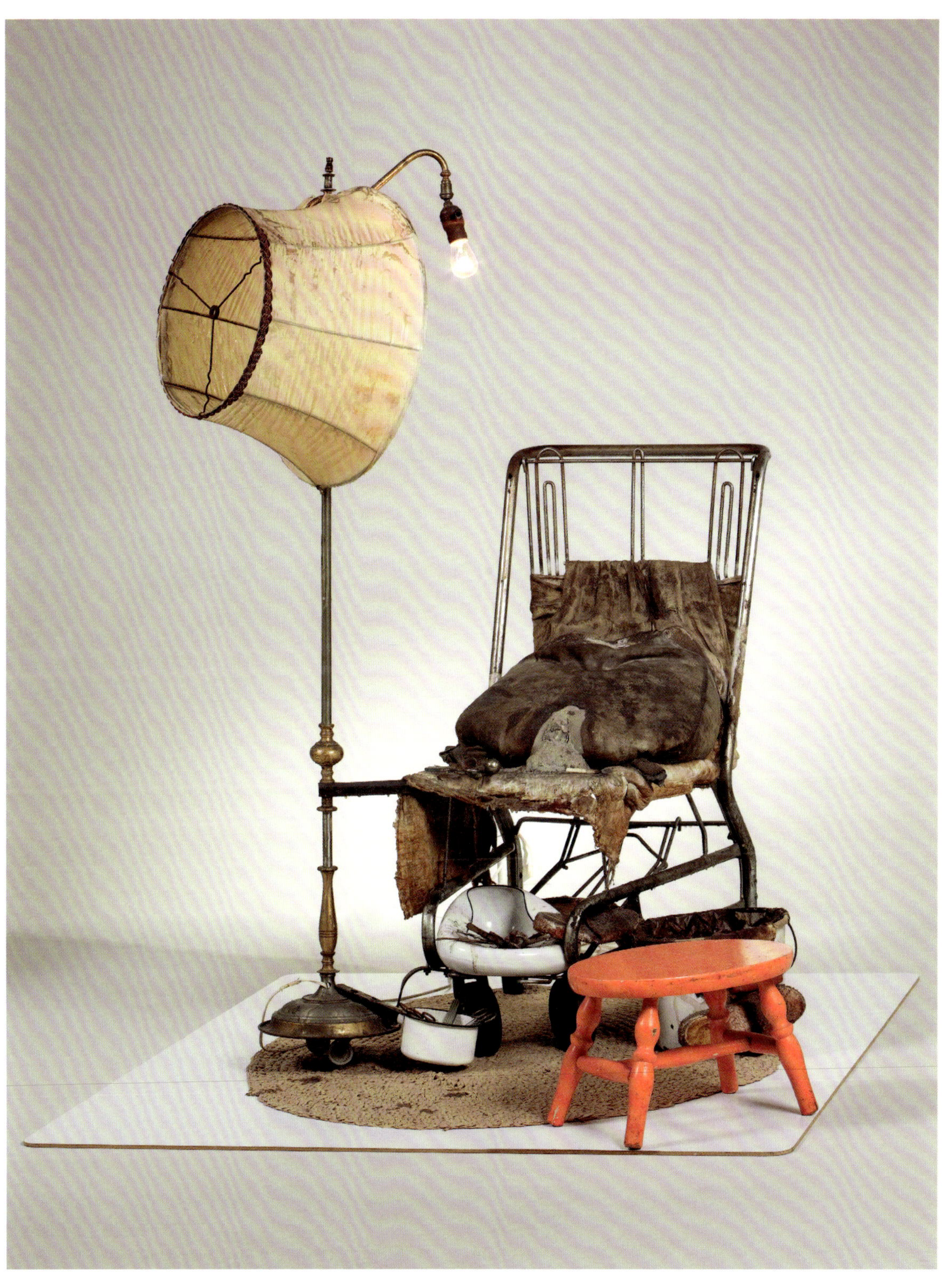

a red rooster's head, her belly sprouting Lucite arrows of pain (p. 301, fig. 20). Last but not least, the remarkable *Back Seat Dodge '38* recalled a late-night tryst from the artist's adolescence in rural Washington State (cat. 54).

A 1938 Dodge sits on a plot of fake grass. Kienholz has removed the wheel system, sliced off a section of the body, and removed the front seat, condensing the arrangement. The blue flocking on the body has the texture of decayed suede, the windows are slathered with gunk, the windshield is chicken wire. The door has swung open, the headlights are on. Jazz plays softly. We approach the old jalopy and peer inside.

A surfeit of details establishes a Barthesian "reality effect"—a scenario so meticulously drawn it projects the illusion that the scene before us is real. A female mannequin cavorts with her chicken-wire beau. A wilted corsage, a cheap pin with the girl's name ("Mildred"), and Hawaiian leis dangling from the mirror suggest the lovers have just come from a high school prom. A crumpled pack of Pall Malls and empty beer bottles (Olympia, a Washington State brand) litter the floor and spill out onto the fake lawn. A bottle dangles tipsily from the girl's hand. Mildred's dress and bra have been removed. Her slip has been thrown carelessly onto the dashboard. One of her shoes has slid to the floor as the heel of the other digs into the boy's shoe. His mannequin hand fumbles with her panties. Their wiry heads merge.

It is hard now to imagine how disturbing the *Three Tableaux* appeared then. I am thinking not only of Seldis's predictable dismissal of Kienholz's "vile images" in his review.[169] An anonymous complaint was registered with the Los Angeles police. Two detectives from the department's vice squad appeared at the gallery while a photographer took close-ups for evaluation. Dwan's support for an art of unflinching realism brought the gallery an unprecedented notoriety—and to the brink of prosecution.[170] In a thoughtful account of the tableaux show, Philip Leider compared Kienholz's incendiary art to Allen Ginsberg's jeremiad *Howl* and the savage humor of the stand-up comedian Lenny Bruce. The common thread of these practices was a disgust with American life, Leider observed—its conventionality, its consumerism, its puritanical attitudes toward sex. The many lawsuits facing Bruce, the threats of show closures for Kienholz, and the obscenity charges leveled at Ginsberg for his poem indicated that these artists had hit a nerve. But their art was controversial (here Leider took an original tack) because it wasn't "obscene." Typically condemned as amoral, Bruce, Kienholz, and Ginsberg were the true *moralists* of a degraded world. They offended because they stared reality in the face:

> It is an art, in the final analysis, of the moralist, and Kienholz, Bruce, Ginsberg and their like link to a tradition that runs from George Orwell back to Isaiah. It is an art of exhortation, and its message is very old: "For all the tables are full of vomit and filthiness, so that there is no place clean."[171]

We conclude our discussion of the early years of the Westwood gallery with a show of a very different kind. The New York sculptor Mark di Suvero had recently returned to Northern California, where he had spent much of his youth. On the shore at Point Reyes north of San Francisco he constructed three sculptures of tree trunks, telegraph poles, railroad ties, steel beams and cables, and ropes, two of which he now exhibited in the Lindbrook space. I should say two *only*. Even the most advanced sculpture previously exhibited at Dwan was sized to a viewer's body. At eighteen-and-a-half-feet tall and twenty-eight-feet long, *Nova Albion*—the title refers to Sir Francis Drake's name for North America—was so gargantuan that a hole had to be cut in Dwan's ceiling to accommodate it.[172] The smaller of the works, *Pre-Columbian*—a construction of a log, an ancient chunk of wood, red-painted steel beams, and a chain and tire pivoting on a cylindrical stump—was eight feet tall by sixteen feet in width and weighed several tons (cat. 57). Where *Nova Albion* punctured Dwan's roof, *Pre-Columbian* put immense pressure on her floor. The gallery was stretched to its limits, literally. Seldis marveled:

> Even the spacious Dwan Gallery can hardly contain the gigantic 'Nova Albion' sculpture by Mark di Suvero. Remarkable for its sheer size, it becomes convincing because of the intricate tensions and balances that this dynamic artist has invented for this astonishing construction. They add up to an unexpected gracefulness emphasized by the easy movement of some of the construction's bulkiest parts.[173]

Di Suvero built "easy movement" into these works, Seldis noted. The sculptor fabricated *Nova Albion* and *Pre-Columbian* on a rustic beach not only for the materials he found there but in order to put these things into motion (fig. 22). Di Suvero's previous works, like *Hankchampion* (1960), did not actually move but appeared to "imitat[e] movement," like Kline's brushstrokes, Judd wrote.[174] The Dwan exhibition—installed just months after Judd published his remarks—was a powerful riposte to such criticisms. The sculptures that di Suvero showed did not evoke movement—they were truly kinetic. At Point Reyes, the blustery wind caused the tire and log on either end of *Pre-Columbian* to pivot and the rubber platform of *Nova Albion* to sway in counterpoint to the beams from which it hung. Inside the gallery was another source of animation

FIG. 22

MARK DI SUVERO'S *NOVA ALBION*, *KNIGHT'S GAMBIT*, AND *PRE-COLUMBIAN* (LEFT TO RIGHT), AT DRAKE'S BAY BEACH, MARIN COUNTY, CALIFORNIA, 1964

FIG. 23

PRE-COLUMBIAN AND *NOVA ALBION*, INSTALLATION VIEW, DWAN GALLERY LOS ANGELES, FALL 1965

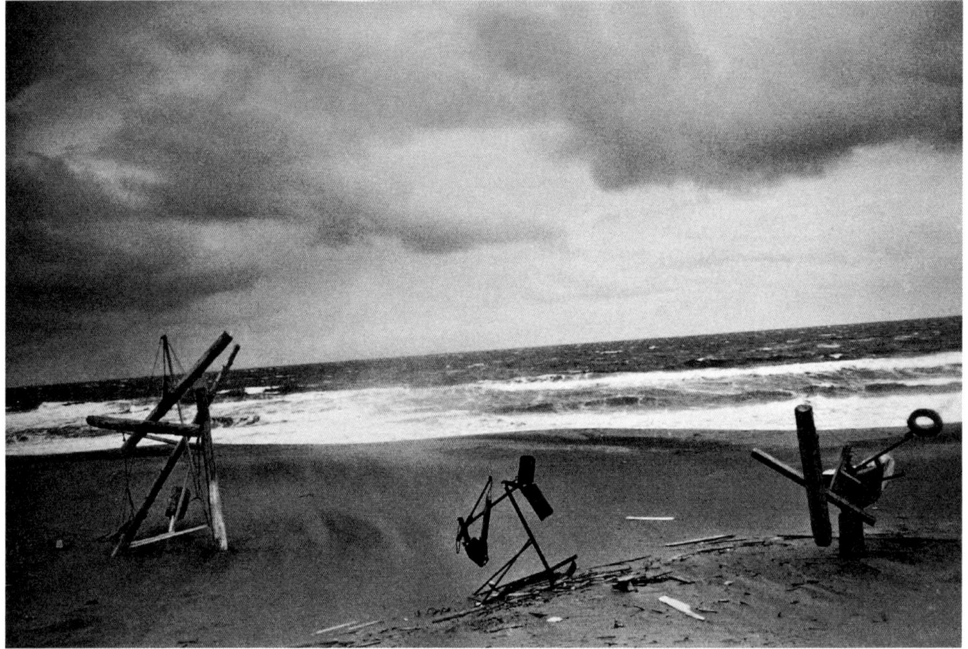

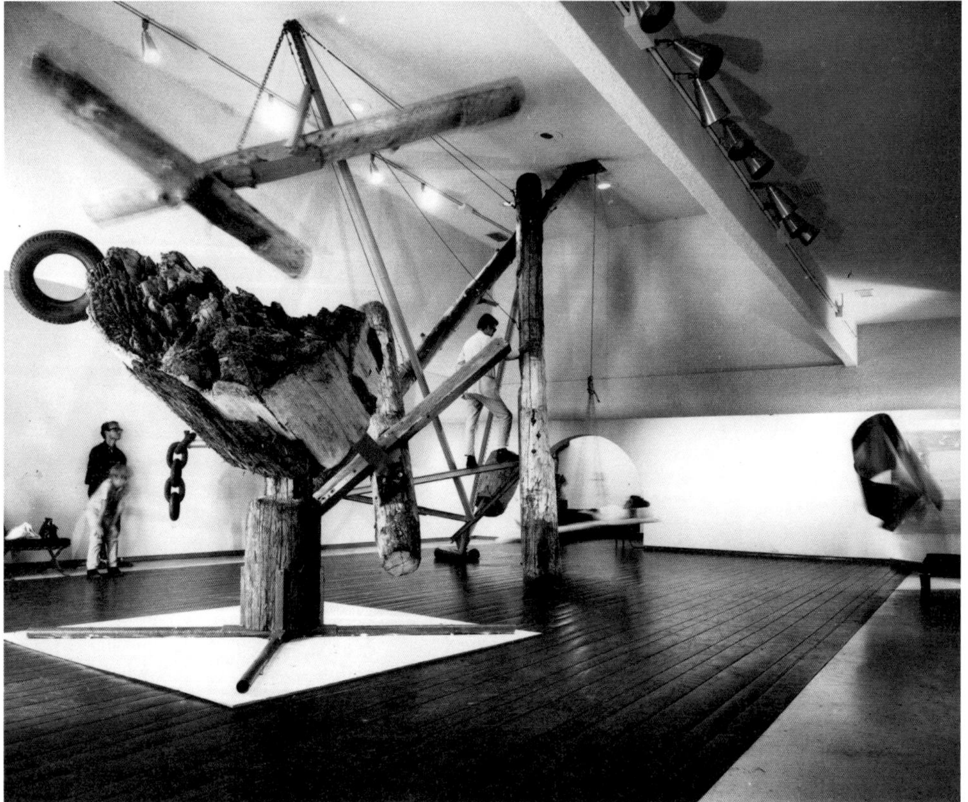

(fig. 23). A viewer caused these works to move—when she lay down on *Nova Albion*'s platform and swung this with her body (and, looking up, saw the moving elements from a supine position), or when she pushed the two ends of *Pre-Columbian* around in circles, or climbing into the tire, tilted the apparatus up and down. Di Suvero's sculptures encouraged a visitor to engage them physically as no works—not even Tinguely's machines or Rauschenberg's combines—had done, anticipating the gallery's exhibitions of the minimalist sculpture of Robert Morris and Carl Andre in the years to come.

THE NEW YORK GALLERY

Dwan moved to New York during the summer of 1964. A frequent visitor to the city, she had long pondered opening a branch of the gallery there—then took the plunge.[175] She would exhibit her artists on both coasts, a novel concept. She would compete with the leading Manhattan gallerists on their own turf. From the beginning, Dwan conceived the New York gallery as something distinct from the Los Angeles space. There she had sited her gallery at a remove from her competitors; here she settled at 29 West 57th Street, the art world's main street.[176] The footprint of the new space was tighter than at Westwood, the ceiling half as tall. The white walls and gray carpeting were not architecturally unique but "anonymous," office-like.[177] These were intentional choices. The New York gallery was austere, cold even: an apposite setting, as it turned out, for the minimalist and conceptual works that Dwan would soon present.

When Dwan signed the lease on this space it was not at all clear whom she would show. Most of the artists she had worked with had New York representation. Kienholz did not, and so Dwan offered her friend the opening spot in her fall 1965 program. He did not disappoint.

Kienholz had spent the last several months constructing a work inspired by a slightly seedy restaurant on Santa Monica Boulevard in West Hollywood. Once frequented by movie stars, Barney's Beanery now drew a different crowd, including artists (Kienholz was a regular). *The Beanery* was a tableau that a viewer could enter—an exacting replica of the intimate bar at a reduced scale (twenty-two by seven-and-one-half by six feet), replete with wood paneling and liquor bottles lining the mirrored shelves. The orchestration of space in this low-ceilinged, narrower Beanery caused a viewer to brush up against the mannequins and plaster-and-chicken-wire figures and barstools and chairs, as if one had entered the claustrophobic bar at a busy hour (fig. 24). The figures themselves—seventeen in all—represented a cross sample of "regulars" and

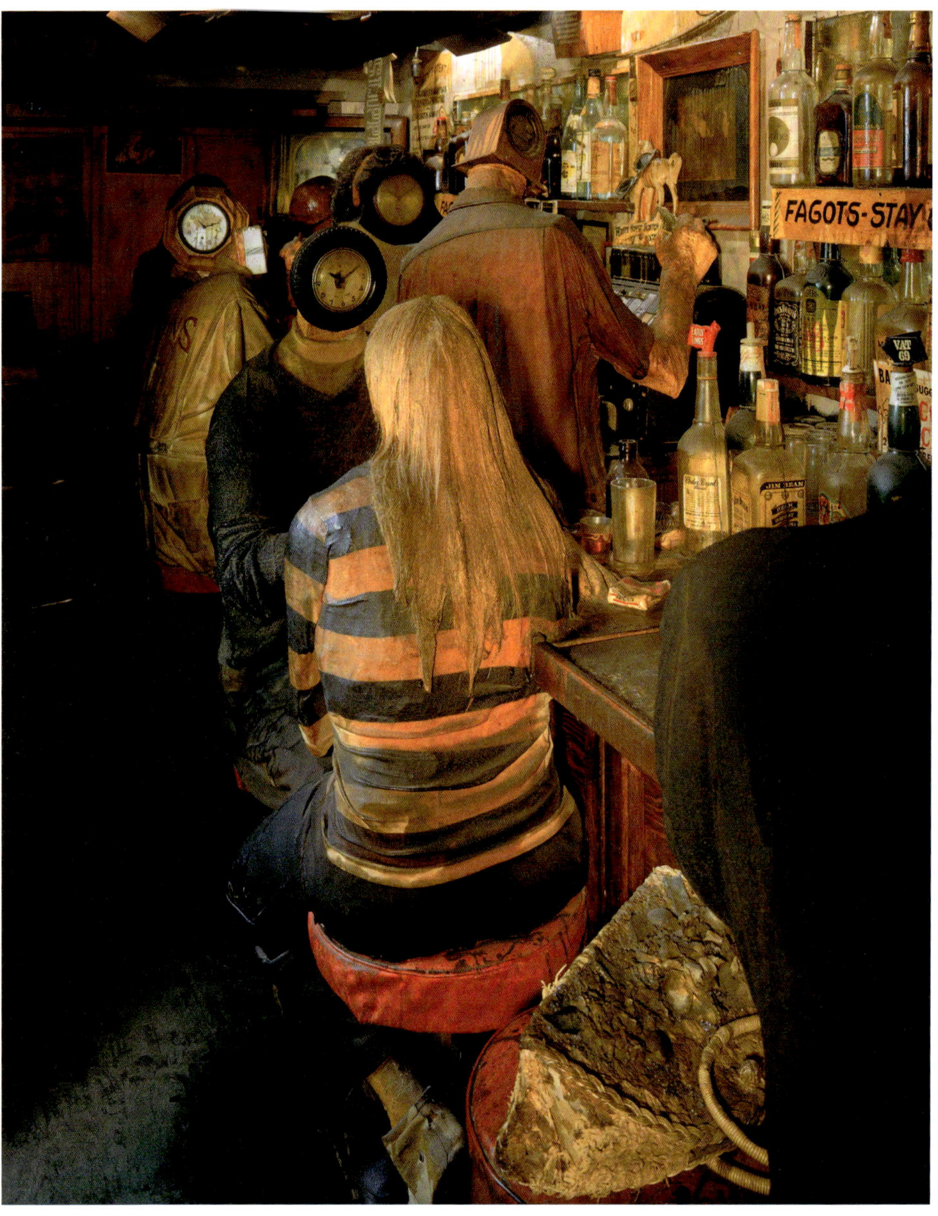

FIG. 24

EDWARD KIENHOLZ, *THE BEANERY* (DETAIL), 1965

employees. There were workers from a nearby moving company; two women eating fried eggs and hamburgers delivered by a waitress in a server's outfit; a matron wearing a mink stole sipping a martini, her poodle perched on a stool; a man lighting his companion's cigarette; a beach bum in sunglasses trying to pick up a young woman; a man speaking on a pay phone; and the bespectacled John "Barney" Anthony himself, the proprietor, slumping over the bar. A cigarette dangles between his fingers. The lady in the stole grabs his arm drunkenly.

Apart from Anthony, whose face Kienholz cast in plaster, the customers and staff are alien, mechanical creatures. Clocks are mounted on their shoulders where heads should be. The hands have been set to 10:10, suggesting cocked eyebrows and that time when the dinner hour has stretched into a boozy haze, and our cares have been dulled by drink... until, that is, we are snapped back into real time by those details that Kienholz has taken such care to include: the misspelled slur that appears emphatically on a pair of signs, locating this mise-en-scène in the homophobic, pre-Stonewall era (FAGOTS STAY OUT!), or the placard advertising beers for a paltry 35 and 40 cents, or the newspaper dated August 28, 1964, with the headline CHILDREN KILL CHILDREN IN VIETNAM RIOTS.[178] The labels on the jukebox offer a medley of art-world hits ("Duchamping on the Old Campground," "Up a Larry Rivers," "It's Delightful, It's Delovely, It's De Kooning"). A soundtrack recorded at the actual Beanery projects the chatter of garrulous customers, clinking glasses, and the noisy transfer of dishes. The smell of beer, bacon grease, urine, and toilet cleaner induces a vague sensation of nausea.

Kienholz first exhibited *The Beanery* in a parking lot next to the actual bar; he then transported the assemblage to Manhattan, reconstructing it section by section in the West 57th Street gallery. Dwan opened her New York establishment with a searing depiction of life in Los Angeles—and New York came to see it. "Castelli, Janis, Frank Lloyd from Marlborough; one after another they piled off the elevator," Dwan marveled. The line to see Kienholz's tour de force ran to the street.[179]

The question of whom to exhibit next quickly resolved itself. Dwan's encounter with a work by Tom Doyle led to an invitation to show at Dwan, where Doyle installed two sculptures of steel, wood, and synthetic board. *Over Owl's Creek*, a seventeen-foot-long construction of meandering shape, was among the first works of horizontal sculpture exhibited in New York, appearing concurrently with Carl Andre's famous show of brick works at nearby Tibor de Nagy Gallery.[180] Where Andre's brick piles invited a viewer to walk around them, Doyle's work inspired one to walk directly upon it from end to end. Through Doyle's wife, the sculptor Eva Hesse, Dwan was introduced to Sol LeWitt, another artist to be offered a show at the gallery. The work of LeWitt's that Dwan admired particularly, a relief resembling a hockey stick, gave no clue as to the kind of works that LeWitt would install in his first exhibition at Dwan in May 1966, a show that did much to establish the gallery's reputation as a nerve center of the emerging tendency described variously as "ABC" art, minimalism, or "primary structures." LeWitt filled the 57th Street gallery with

FIG. 25

INSTALLATION VIEW, *ROBERT MORRIS: SCULPTURE*, DWAN GALLERY LOS ANGELES, MARCH 1966

all-white geometric modular structures not unlike the wall grid of eighty-one identical open cubes in the National Gallery exhibition (cat. 58).[181] The ensemble of works that LeWitt showed in 1966 revealed the contours and spaces of the new gallery as no works had before. *Wall Floor Piece* defined the three-dimensional volume of a corner, *Floor-Wall Grid* the space between the wall and floor, *Modular Floor Structure* a section of carpet eleven feet square. LeWitt doused these works in bright light. Webs of interior and exterior shadows undermined the structures' identity *as* shapes, imbuing them with ambiguity and mystery. Ostensibly "minimal," LeWitt's intricate lattices hid as much as they revealed. The open forms contained an internal complexity that belied their seeming simplicity.[182]

Meanwhile in the Los Angeles gallery a show of sculpture by Robert Morris opened that spring. The installation consisted of just six works: a low triangular wedge that came up to a viewer's knees; curved and triangular floor beams, also low to the ground, one of them thirty-two feet long; a tall triangular volume near Dwan's office; two half-circles joined into a single ring illuminated by hidden lamps (p. 305, fig. 23); and four cubes with battered (slanted) edges (cat. 59). The generous Westwood space allowed Morris some liberty in determining how he installed his work—and how it would be seen. During a previous show at New York's Green Gallery, Morris arranged a number of polyhedrons around the gallery's periphery—against the walls, in corners, and above the exit. A long floor beam placed at center led a visitor expeditiously from one end of the rather narrow space to the other. At Dwan there was enough space for everything. No one itinerary was implied. Morris arranged his works centripetally in the gallery (fig. 25). The sculptures were there to be walked *around*. A viewer chose: she could walk the lengths of the beams, estimating their respective lengths and shapes, or circumnavigate the ring, peering down at the circular volume it contained; she could meander around the slanted cubes, comparing the shapes of the four elements with the negative volumes between them. She could imagine rearranging them in other configurations—abutting the cubes or turning them around 180 degrees.

Rarely had sculpture appeared so spare, so uninflected, so "minimal." As simple shapes, or Gestalts as Morris called them, without internal relationships, Morris's pale gray polyhedrons solicited a viewer's somatic involvement in a way that more intricate, smaller works did not. Being scaled to a body, these shapes deflected one's perception to the surround—to the gallery *as a space*—in a manner different from di Suvero's relational arrangements. Morris's manifesto "Notes on Sculpture" described the aims of the Dwan show perfectly:

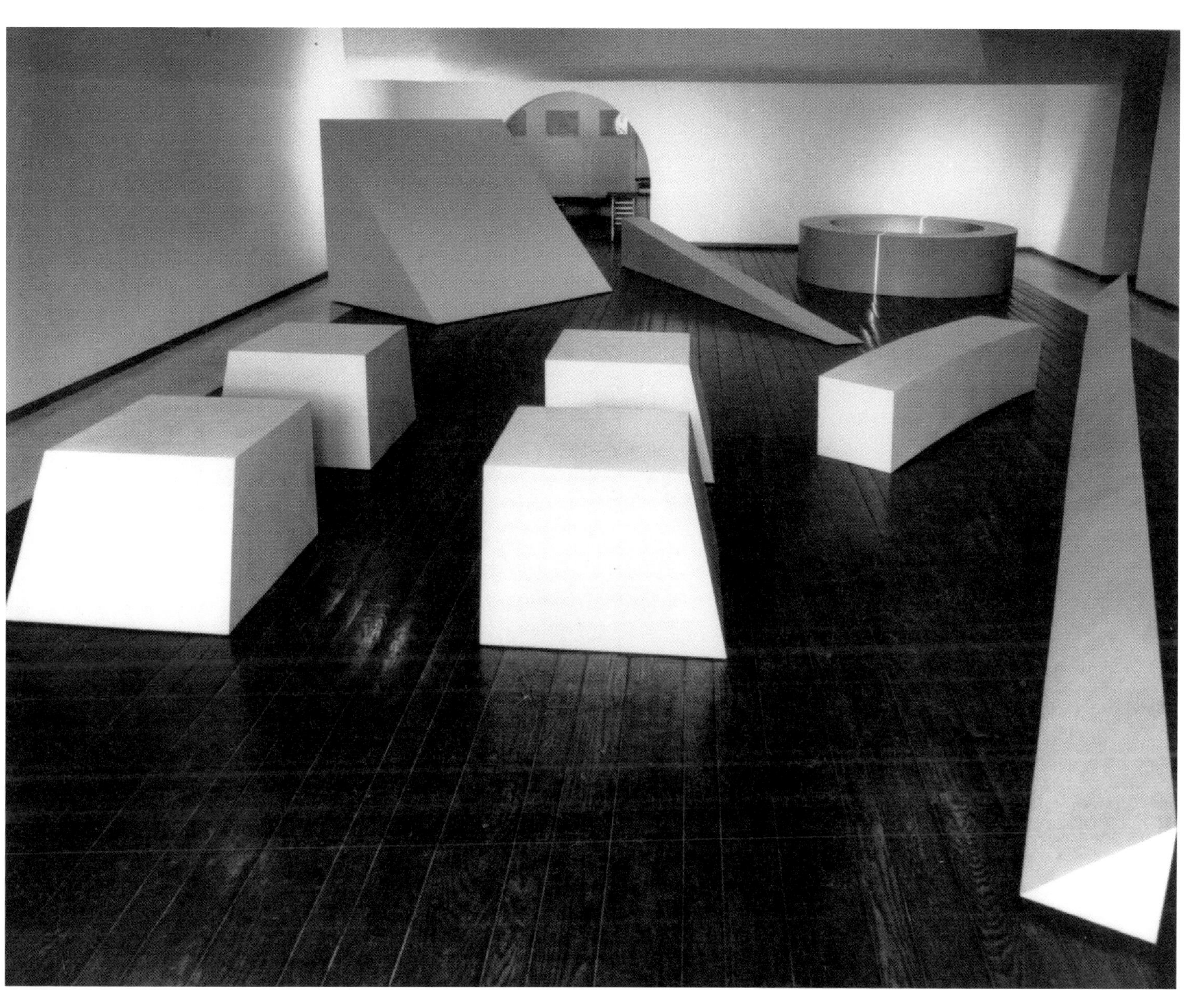

> The better new work takes relationships out of the work and makes them a function of space, light, and the viewer's field of vision. The object is but one of the terms of the newer aesthetic.... One is more aware than before that he himself is establishing relationships as he apprehends the object from various positions and under varying conditions of light and spatial context.[183]

During the spring of 1966, when Dwan mounted the LeWitt and Morris shows, the exhibition *Primary Structures* at the Jewish Museum widely publicized the new aesthetic.[184] The "reductive" impulse that Dwan had discerned in the monochromes of Klein and Reinhardt had morphed into something much broader, more variegated—a minimal field that encompassed sculpture, painting, and cognate activities in dance and film.[185] Opening her second gallery precisely at this moment, Dwan provided a major stimulus for this work on both coasts simultaneously. (Until its closing in June 1967, the Westwood gallery was just as pivotal as the Manhattan space, permitting artists such as Morris, LeWitt, and Carl Andre to install their works in a larger spatial context than was available in New York.) The crisis of abstraction and the representation of feeling in art after abstract expressionism had precipitated a series of negations—a purgation of anything that could be deemed extraneous to the work of art as a formal, material entity (symbolism, subject matter, subjectivity, and illusion, to name a few). The artists who came to be called minimalists "reduced" in distinctive ways and to different ends; their intentions were, at times, diametrically opposed.

A group show that October brought these differences into focus. The idea for the show began with Reinhardt, then LeWitt. It would include LeWitt's friends Smithson and Andre, and Morris, too, at Reinhardt's request—and Agnes Martin, another of the painter's suggestions. At some point Donald Judd, Dan Flavin, and Jo Baer signed on.[186] A meeting was called at Dwan's apartment. The artists who gathered in her living room could agree neither on the statement that Smithson had prepared nor even on the show's title. They were ten—and so they named the exhibition *10*. The meeting revealed that no group existed—only "an uncomfortable relationship of individuals together."[187] Uncomfortable indeed. The minimal field was notoriously contentious. Public panels and art magazines were sites of heated, even hostile exchanges. Artists defended their work when others attacked it, and espoused conflicting ideas of medium, form, and process. The participants in *10*—especially Reinhardt, Morris, Judd, Flavin, Baer, Smithson, and LeWitt—were gifted polemicists. They rarely agreed.

The works in *10* projected a look of austerity and affectlessness, a morphological similitude that belied their differences. ("What they share, they dispute," the critic Annette Michelson observed.[188]) The works in the current exhibition bear out Michelson's claim. Nonreferential, implacably dour, with little evidence of brush, Reinhardt's *Ultimate Painting* (cat. 60) stands for something very different from Martin's *The Cliff* (cat. 61), a work brimming with allusion and feeling: hers is the trace of the hand that has laid down thousands of soft vertical lines in a grid pattern of seventy-two rectangles on a faint wash of ivory and gray, an image of consummate delicacy that almost evaporates before our eyes. And where Jo Baer made paintings of thin concentric bands on white grounds—paintings that remind us that they *are* paintings by establishing and denying their illusionism simultaneously (cat. 62)—Judd and Flavin abandoned painting outright to make "objects" that incorporated the bold color and bodily scale of New York School painting and the "real space" of sculpture, using the wall and floor equally and interchangeably. And they withdrew the artist's hand from the work to achieve an art allegedly devoid of emotion—a position embodied in the current show by Judd's relief of galvanized iron and green Plexiglas (cat. 63) and Flavin's arrangements of fluorescent lights in walls and corners (*"monument" for V. Tatlin*, one of the artist's homages to the visionary constructivist, and *"monument" on the survival of Mrs. Reppin*, cats. 64 and 65).[189]

At about the time of the *10* exhibition, Carl Andre, for his part, invented a sculpture of interchangeable units of identical size that he arranged on Dwan's floor, much like the works of elemental metals that he exhibited at the gallery in 1967 and 1969 (cat. 66). He developed a post-studio way of working distinct from the workshop techniques of artists like Judd and LeWitt that found its apogee in his installation *Cuts*, among the earliest instances of a site-specific modality: the artist laid down a contiguous field of concrete capstones across the Westwood exhibition space, leaving eight sections, or "cuts," in the sculpture that exposed the floor underneath (p. 348, fig. 80).[190] And where Morris's simple shapes stamped themselves out as distinctive shapes in a viewer's field of vision, Smithson's works of this period complicated and even denied perception. The further down we peer into the depths of *Glass Stratum*, a sculpture of stepped sheets of glass, the less we are able to see (cat. 67). Smithson turns glass against itself. Repeated, a transparent material becomes opaque. Like the lattices of LeWitt that dissolve in shadow, or Judd's highly reflective boxes, Smithson's minimalist works stage a vision that is contradictory, and theoretically speaking opposite in aim to Morris's simple polyhedrons.[191]

Unlike the vast *Primary Structures* exhibition, with its forty-two British and American participants, *10* was a distillation of the minimal field—and for Dwan something of a manifesto. The appeal of an abstraction that sought in many instances to negate the representation of subject matter or feeling was curiously personal.[192] And though the Dwan Gallery was henceforth identified with this movement it would be inaccurate to assume that Dwan focused exclusively on artists like LeWitt, Morris, Andre, Smithson, and Flavin. Ever curious, she cast a wider net across this field and beyond. An original backer of Park Place, a cooperative gallery in Greenwich Village cofounded by di Suvero, Dwan exhibited in her Los Angeles gallery the work of several artists affiliated with this space. She showed Robert Grosvenor, a sculptor who suspended from walls and ceilings his large asymmetrical forms made of fiberglass, steel, and plywood, such as the more than twenty-foot-long *Tenerife* and *Still No Title* (pp. 344–345, fig. 69).[193] She showed David Novros, a maker of shaped canvases so extreme they rendered null the distinctions between painting and sculptural relief and between "work" and frame. In his exhibition of all-white polyptychs in Los Angeles in November 1966, the walls of the Westwood space were no longer clearly discernible from the panels that Novros had hung on them (p. 349, fig. 81). Oppositions between positive and empty space, figure and ground, even the artwork and the wall—were rendered ambiguous (p. 362, fig. 118).[194] She showed a young artist named Fred Sandback, who created spatial volumes utilizing the sparest means imaginable, elastic cord and string of different hues, in his exhibition *Five Situations* in January 1969. In a slightly later work of Sandback's, *Blue Corner Piece*, an elastic cord straddles a corner, suggesting a square plane (a vestige of the old painterly fiction: the "window onto the world") suspended in real space. The shadows are so defined they read as oblique diagonals projecting out of the corner: together, the cord and shadows construct a polyhedron that is both an illusion and that occupies an actual volume, that is both imaginary and real (cat. 68). And she showed Kenneth Snelson, a sculptor of tensile constructions of steel elements and wires that held their shapes without recourse to traditional techniques of joining, soldering, or stacking, and that could be realized only by means of this "tensegrity" system (cat. 69).[195] The tensile interaction of cable and steel held these works up and maintained their intricate shapes. The durability of Snelson's sculptures and their potential for extension made them particularly popular with collectors (unusual among Dwan artists) and suitable for the outdoors. In addition to several gallery shows in New York and Los Angeles, Dwan orchestrated an installation of works of heroic proportion, including Snelson's sixty-foot-tall *Needle Tower*, on the great lawn of New York's Bryant Park.[196]

A work that LeWitt exhibited on a table in his Dwan show in May 1966, *Serial Project, 1 (ABCD)*, hinted at the artist's growing dissatisfaction with the reductive mode, also apparent in the intricate lattice structures he showed alongside it at Dwan's New York gallery (cat. 70). An artist could "reduce" only so much.[197] LeWitt discovered that the simple forms of "minimalism" could be combined and altered sequentially. They could become the building blocks of more complex arrangements. In this work, for example, LeWitt arranged two- and three-dimensional shapes—squares, cubes, and rectangular volumes—on a horizontal grid divided into quadrants (A, B, C, D). He further divided the four sets into nine subsets, each an examination of the relationship of an inner and outer form. For example, in A1, the center square (one unit) and outer square (nine units) are two-dimensional figures, outlined in white wood. In the second subset (A2) the inner square is unchanged; the outer square is one unit tall, suggesting a low rectangular volume of nine cubic units. In A3 the inner square is still the same, while the outer square is three units tall, making a large open cube of twenty-seven units. In the next row (A4, A5, A6) the center shape is a cubic volume one unit tall. In the final row (A7, A8, A9) the inner form is three units tall, about the size of a telephone booth. Where the inner forms have grown in volume, the shapes of the outer forms repeat: in A9, the tall form stands in the center of the large open cube introduced in A3. LeWitt developed this arrangement three more times. In Set B, the center squares, cubes, and rectangular volumes are closed, while the outer volumes remain open. And while Set C inverts this structure (open interior forms, closed outer ones), Set D is the converse of Set A. Both the inner and outer shapes are opaque. The center forms are mostly hidden. We imagine them nevertheless: the shapes we cannot see are trace-memories of forms we have already seen. And so we perceive them in our minds, if not empirically, lurking underneath the outer forms.

LeWitt described works such as this as "conceptual." In conceptual art, he observed, "the idea or concept is the most important aspect of the work." The implications of this remark are numerous and complex. A work of art was not a representation of feeling, or subject matter, or a thing seen: it was the embodiment of an "idea." For LeWitt, an idea was a plan for something that *could* be made. ("Ideas can be works of art; they are in a chain of development that may eventually find some form.") The work's planning occurred in advance; its completion was a "perfunctory affair."[198] And in fact the announcement of LeWitt's next Dwan show, which opened in Westwood in April 1967, was not

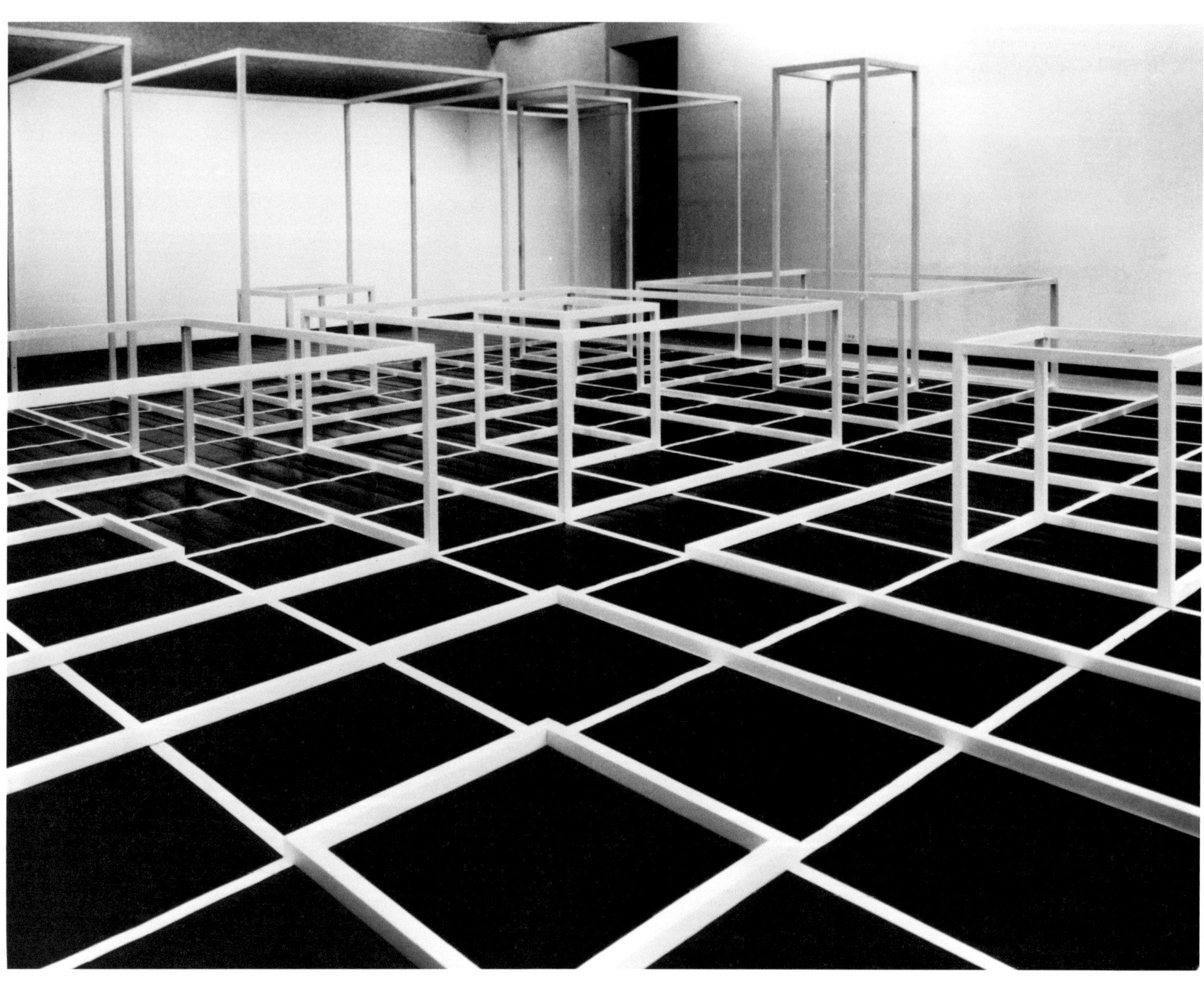

FIG. 26

INSTALLATION VIEW, DETAIL OF SOL LEWITT, *SERIES A #1 . . . 9*, 1967, DWAN GALLERY LOS ANGELES, APRIL 1967

a photo of the completed work but a diagram of the plan of *Serial Project, 1 (ABCD)* covered in mathematical calculations and copious remarks written by hand (cat. 71). In other words, the invitation to the Dwan show was itself the work (the "idea") as well as a meditation on the work's form ("The cube, square, and variants on them are grammatical devices"), its materiality ("All pieces made of aluminum with baked enamel"), and its distribution ("Each individual piece of the nine is autonomous and complete"). LeWitt even credits the fabricator, Treitel-Gratz.

With *Serial Project, 1 (ABCD)*, he averred that a work could be made, but need not be ("all ideas need not be made physical"), and that the physical work need not take a *particular* form: it could exist in different iterations and in different sizes. In LeWitt's 1966 show, the tabletop version depicted all four sets in miniature. In Los Angeles LeWitt was inspired by the voluminous Westwood space to show Set A greatly enlarged (fig. 26). The "telephone booth" was humanly scaled: LeWitt's idea could be experienced bodily as well as mentally. Other versions of *Serial Project* are synecdochical fragments of the whole, "autonomous and complete." A work like *B 2-5-8 (s)* (cat. 72), a cross section of Set B showing the development of three closed inner cubes and open outer cubes, asks us to imagine the rest of *Serial Project*—the parts that are missing. It implies but does not depict the full nine-part sequence of Set B—and beyond this Sets A, C, and D. Far more of LeWitt's work is invisible to the eye than is revealed.

Other shows at Dwan heralded this conceptual turn, and even an abandonment of the object—what LeWitt called the "physical" work.[199] Kienholz, the sculptor of densely packed installations, was also a progenitor of ideas. He envisioned projects that could be realized yet for the most part were not. He called them "concept tableaux," and each contained two parts. An engraved bronze plaque announced the work's title; a framed typed sheet of paper described the idea and the purchase price. A stamp of the artist's ink-stained thumb appears at the bottom of the sheet in lieu of his signature. At Dwan, Kienholz arranged sixteen of these works at eye level around the periphery of the 57th Street gallery (the plaques hung above the "concepts"). Like the artist's tableaux, the concept tableaux were elaborate narratives, cinematic-like. In *After the Ball Is Over #1*, the teenage couple depicted in *Back Seat Dodge '38* have returned to the girl's house (cat. 55). In the tableau, the Olympia beer bottles locate the scene somewhere in Washington State. The conceptual version is more specific: "This tableau is to be built in the town of Fairfield, Washington." The lovers in *Back Seat Dodge '38* are on the verge of coitus; in the conceptual version they are "just outside the front door...standing close together, shyly intimate, but not actually touching or embracing." And no longer alone. The girl's brother is asleep upstairs. Her mother lies in bed, "stiff, listening." The father waits at the kitchen table, "tired, rigid, menacing....He doesn't know why, but right now he hates the young man." Kienholz gave the work a high price ($15,000 was a substantial sum for a contemporary artwork in 1965) and asked for a second payment of $1,000 to complete it. The collector would also cover "land, materials, and artist's wages." The prospect of actually making the work, which would entail locating this very couple and family, to participate in it, is as absurd and disruptive of aesthetic convention as Kienholz's thumbprint guaranteeing its "authenticity."

Another of these works, *The American Trip*—a "collaboration between Jean Tinguely, America, and me"—finds the American and French artist in a car (cat. 56). The newfound mobility of the contemporary artist is arguably the subject of this work as well as its formal structure. Starting from Los Angeles, the men would drive "until we are compelled by a thing, a place, a situation, etc. to do something." Unlike the highly specific scenario of *After the Ball Is Over #1*, *The American Trip* is gloriously open-ended, aleatory: a road trip without an itinerary, destination, or time frame. What Kienholz and Tinguely would actually "do" and where they would do it is unknowable until a collector has commissioned the piece. That did not occur; they never took the trip. And with the deaths of the two friends, Tinguely in 1991 and Kienholz in 1994, the concept that Kienholz intended to realize at some unspecified date was now a memory of an idea that would remain forever unknowable and incomplete.[200]

The nature of the art object was rapidly changing. The removal of a thin strip of wall plaster extending from the floor to ceiling of the gallery—the conceit of William Anastasi's *Issue* (cat. 74)—directed a viewer to look beyond this operation to the room, from the "work" to its setting. As Anastasi gouged a white wall with his instruments, bits of plaster fell to the floor in a horizontal line projecting out from the wall. The amount of plaster that "issued" from the wall was in direct proportion to the room's height. The taller the ceiling, the fatter—and longer—the pile. Anastasi's exhibition *Six Sites* elaborated the site-specific premise of *Issue* across an entire room. He photographed the walls of the 57th Street gallery, silkscreening the images onto six canvases at a one-tenth reduction. The height of the walls being identical, so were the six canvases at slightly more than seven feet. The canvas depicting the east wall was widest at twenty-seven feet. The shorter south wall yielded a canvas nineteen feet wide. Symmetrical images seven feet square flanked the entrance to Dwan's office

(p. 248). The six panels pointed blankly to the walls on which they hung. Even the air ducts below the ceiling and electrical outlets essential to the operation of the space—to its function and identity as a gallery—were exposed.[201] The aptly named *Six Sites* turned a viewer's attention to the gallery as a place: the tautological premise of site-specificity was explicitly enunciated.

A month after the Anastasi show closed, Dwan and Weber revisited the linguistic theme of the concept tableaux in an exhibition with an intriguing title: *Language to be looked at and/or things to be read*. An attempt to avoid the banality of the usual summer group show, typically a gathering of the season's leftovers, the theme of art and language was capacious and timely, generating four annual editions.[202] Like *Boxes*, the first language show told a story of modern art extending from the works of avant-garde forebears (Marinetti, Picabia, Duchamp, Magritte)[203] to the contributions of such contemporary figures as Reinhardt, Indiana, Lichtenstein, Oldenburg, Rauschenberg, Johns, and Morris (all of whom had shown at Dwan); Arakawa, Kienholz, Smithson, Andre, LeWitt, and Snelson (all represented by Dwan); Flavin and Walter De Maria (who later joined Dwan), and Dan Graham and On Kawara (recurring presences in several of the shows).[204] Also like *Boxes*, the language shows featured a far greater number of artists than such controlled presentations as *10*, in keeping with the unruly nature and sudden ubiquity of the phenomenon, and the typically modest scale of these works. (The largest, *Language III* in 1969, had sixty-one participants.)[205] Occurring during the rise of the women's movement, when artists enlisted linguistic formats to explore feminist themes, the shows featured more women practitioners than ever before.[206] As more contributors came on board the premise of the first show—works with words we are meant to "look at" and works of primarily visual orientation we are meant to "read"—a shaky distinction to begin with—was less rigorously applied. The works in the current exhibition represent a number of overlapping strategies and thematic concerns of the some 186 objects exhibited at Dwan: works recording an artistic process in a pseudo-archival manner (Morris, Eleanor Antin); works that name or record a material action (Lawrence Weiner, Smithson, Holt, Charles Ross); "concrete" poems (Andre, Rosemarie Castoro); works of socioeconomic critique (Lee Lozano, Arakawa, Kienholz); works of linguistic definition (Joseph Kosuth); and Bochner's critical response to the very phenomenon mapped by all four exhibitions: the widespread emergence during the end of the sixties of an art comprised of words, of language (figs. 27, 28).

Morris's *Card File* was the recurring presence of these shows (cat. 75).[207] Conceived during his stint at the art research division of the New York Public

Library, this intriguing work was inspired by the library's vast card catalog, which Morris consulted daily as part of his job to locate books and information for patrons. Its subject matter is tautological—the creation of *Card File* itself. Its form is serial: emulating (and parodying) the methods of the catalogers who worked alongside him, Morris typed out the multiple decisions and tasks involved in making the work on note cards and arranged them in alphabetical order. Under the heading "Materials" he recorded the 4″ × 6″ note cards, erasers, and the ink ribbon he used; the flat metal file with plastic sleeves; and even such abstract concepts as space, sound, motion, weight, light, history, and narrative. Under "Stores" and "Locations" he noted where he found these materials (a Rexall Drug Store, Tanner Stationery, Charles S. Nathan, etc.) and where he put the work together (the New York Public Library, 78 East 3rd Street, 195 Front Street, and 277 Church Street). Last but not least, he documented the time it took to make the work, a crucial lesson of the composer John Cage, filing this information under several headings. Under "(Duration)" he describes the date of the work's fabrication and total work time ("6 hours, 26 minutes at 12/31/62, 6:00 pm"). He also mentions the time he wasted making it (under "Delays") and even a passing encounter with the curmudgeonly Reinhardt on the street (under "Interruptions"). *Card File* is Borgesian, bureaucratic: the files that Morris organized so meticulously refer to all the others in a kind of infinite regress. Under "Time" he wrote:

> Total time spent in working on file, including trips: (See Completion). Total duration between conception and Completion. (See Completion.) Total non-working time between conception and Completion: (See Completion). (See Duration.)[208]

The empty sleeves at the bottom of *Card File* await further categories and notecards. A work ostensibly about a task completed is inconclusive, incomplete. We are reminded of those short stories of Borges's that take us through vast encyclopedias and countless libraries, bibliographical mazes without end: Is it any wonder that Morris eventually built a series of actual labyrinths, spatializing *Card File*'s recursiveness?[209]

The organizing principle for *Card File*'s disparate contents is an alphabetical structure. In Eleanor Antin's *Blood of a Poet Box* we find a simple counting scheme (cat. 76). In 1965, Antin set about the improbable task of collecting the blood of a great many poets of her acquaintance—a curiously literal and slightly unsettling interpretation of the title of the eponymous film (*Le Sang d'un Poète*, 1930) by Jean Cocteau. The number of blood samples was limited to the one hundred slides that came in the box Antin acquired.

FIG. 27

INSTALLATION VIEW, *LANGUAGE TO BE LOOKED AT AND/OR THINGS TO BE READ*, DWAN GALLERY NEW YORK, JUNE 1967 (ROBERT MORRIS, *CARD FILE*, SECOND FROM LEFT ON WALL)

FIG. 28

INSTALLATION VIEW, *LANGUAGE III*, DWAN GALLERY NEW YORK, MAY 1969 (*CARD FILE* SECOND FROM CORNER ON RIGHT WALL)

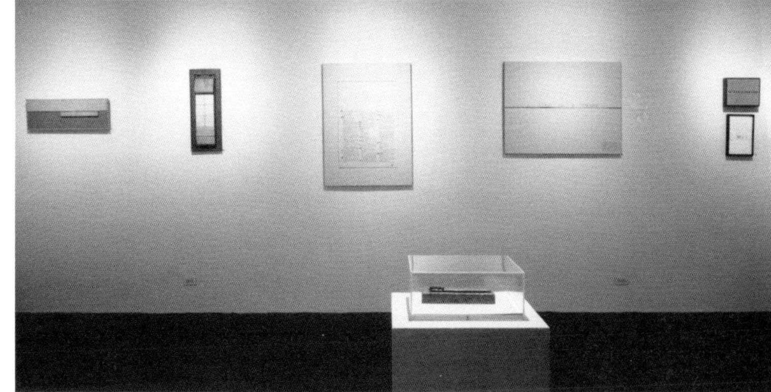

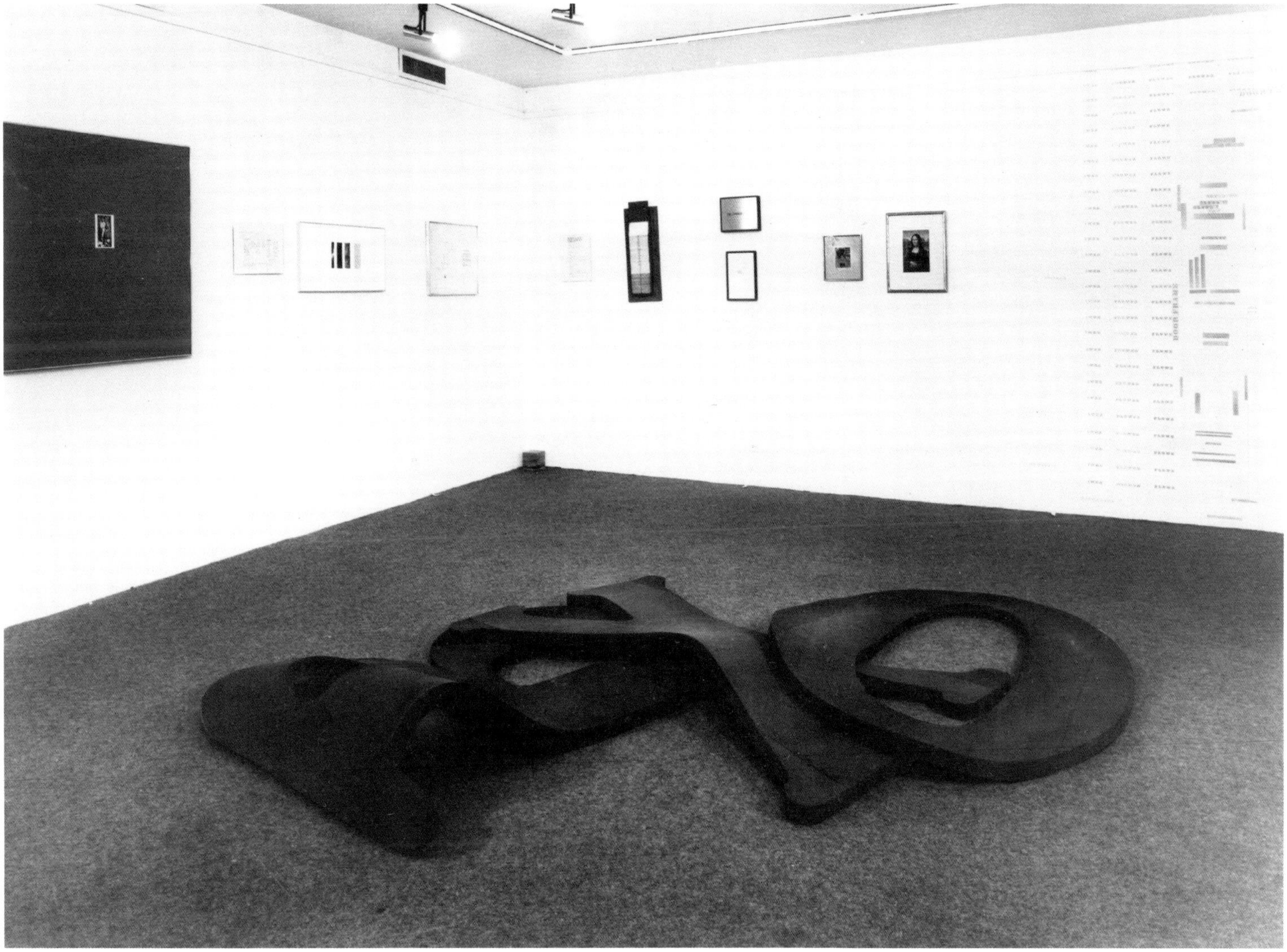

Yet, like *Card File*, her work is incomplete (six of the one hundred slides are missing). As well, the time it took Antin to make the work—to identify the poets, to secure their permission, to obtain the blood sample via fingerprick, and to record the information on the slide and in the numbered sheet glued inside the box—is integral to its meaning. A ledger of poets famous and obscure accompanied by biological "evidence" of their existence, *Blood of a Poet Box* is a pseudo-archive of the American poetry scene during the mid-1960s and a diaristic record of Antin's personal associations as a poet and artist herself. (Antin later tainted her own "evidence" with this statement: "If you thought there was a relation between the blood and the name there was one; if you didn't, there wasn't."[210]) She took the first specimen from her husband, the writer David Antin, on April 22, 1965; she made the Allen Ginsberg slide on April 7, 1966; the one for Dave Rasey on July 7, 1966; and so on. The tiny shallow green box, approximately a foot long and six inches wide, announces an autobiographical and corporeal turn not only in Antin's work but in conceptualism more broadly at the end of the sixties. These trends would become increasingly pervasive in the works of feminist and male practitioners alike.

Whereas Antin spent three years on *Blood of a Poet Box*, Rosemarie Castoro completed *A Day in the Life of a Conscientious Objector* in just twenty-four days (cat. 80). Castoro adhered to a strict regimen. From February 23 through March 27, 1969, she composed a poem on a sheet of graph paper each day for one hour. She began the next day's poem exactly one hour later than the previous day's poem. The twenty-four drawings, executed in green, red, blue, purple, brown, gray, pink, and orange ink, each unique in shape, length, and palette, conflate Castoro's daily practice during those three and a half weeks into a single day in the life of an imagined young man of draft age. His identity is not as transparent as the poem's title suggests. Castoro's protagonist is not a certified conscientious objector. The authorities have denied him that status. He is on the run, a draft dodger. He is also, and equally, an enlisted soldier on active duty in Vietnam. Both men—the war resister and the GI—are victims and perpetrators of violence. Castoro's poem flickers back and forth between these scenarios, identities, and geographies.

HEAVE PUSH / COVER COMRADE / STUMBLE AROUND BEND / SINK DOWN / RELIEVE PRESSURE / OPEN MESSAGE / DESTROY EVIDENCE /. . . . DON UNIFORM / SET TIMER/BURN FLESH

The image of the soldier who shields his comrade and sets off a bomb is followed by a glimpse of the conscientious objector:

OPEN WARDROBE / SELECT DISGUISE / WRAP BODY / DESCEND TO STREET

Castoro's fugitive is no pacifist. He is a radical militant, engaged in a military operation of another sort.[211] From the third page:

STORAGE / FORAGE / CHANGE CLOTHES / MASK FACE / PLANT JACKET. . . . BREAK INTO / LEAVE BOMB / WHAT ARE YOU DOING / I'M HERE TO DESTROY THE WORLD / BY SHUFFLING THE PARTICLES / BY STACKING THE DECK

Castoro was compelled to make this work during a particularly violent interlude of the war.[212] There is a tacitly feminist aspect to her project: crossing the lives of a left-wing fugitive and a GI, she speaks from the subject position of one who could neither be drafted nor resist the draft but who is a mere bystander to these events—a witness to history—because she is a woman. To underscore this point, Castoro read these poems out loud during a performance, inserting her voice into a play enacted by her male characters.[213] In *Language III* she showed all twenty-four sheets framed and as a slide projection, a relatively new technique then, that a collector could acquire in an editioned set: a poem mounted on a wall, a slide show, and a performance script all at once, *A Day in the Life of a Conscientious Objector* was an intermedial project, one that exceeded any single mode of expression, encompassing all of these formats.[214]

"My sense of language is that it is matter and not ideas, i.e. 'printed matter,'" Smithson wrote on the press release he penned for the first language show. The works of Smithson and others we shall examine bespoke an understanding of the linguistic sign as semantic substance. In the practices of these artists words do not simply "represent" something else (a concept, an action, a thing) but are themselves matter, are not *reducible* to what they mean (the signifier is not equivalent to its signified, as the semiologists would say). And so these artists enlisted aesthetic strategies that severed the word from its everyday use and from conventional syntax until it was exposed as itself.[215] The typewritten poems of Carl Andre, such as his compositions titled *Passport*, are exemplary here (cats. 77–79). Andre completed the original *Passport*—a ninety-nine-page book of great personal significance containing collaged photographs, postcards, drawings, pieces of fabric, poems, and pages from the artist's passport—in 1960. In 1963, Andre was working as a freight brakeman on the Central Railroad of New Jersey and living with his wife, Rosemarie Castoro, and writing poetry.[216] Returning to the theme of *Passport*, he typed out five sheets of poetry in either red or black ink on Castoro's portable Royal typewriter. In the original book, Andre accorded each item a discrete page. In the poems inspired by the 1960 *Passport*, Andre transposed *into* language the contents of the book (the cover and front page of Andre's passport from his first trip to Europe in 1954; a hermetic order for a "secret work"; a 1,000 lire banknote; sheets stamped in patterns of pointing fingers; a photo of a bust of Lord Byron; a postcard of Bronzino's *Portrait of Lodovico Capponi* acquired at the Frick Collection). In *Passport* (cats. 77, 78), the first of these exercises, he listed these textual and numeric elements one by one. The three sheets are an inventory of some (by no means all) of the book's contents.[217] The original book is gone; in its place are words and numbers whose significance and syntactical connection we are hard put to discern. Yet, despite Andre's severe redaction, a link still exists between the 1960 *Passport* and the red-ink 1963 *Passport*. The information that Andre has typed down the page follows the order of appearance of these elements in the book. In the subsequent works based on *Passport* that Andre typed in black ink (cat. 79), references to these elements ("Byronic bust," "accuse fingers," "Bronzino") are even more infrequent and hermetic, intermixing with other references of no attributable source. We are far away from the original 1960 *Passport*. Words alone occupy the page, leached of significance. Smithson wrote of these poems:

> Carl Andre's writings bury the mind under rigorous incantatory arrangements. Such a method smothers any reference to anything other than the words. Thoughts are crushed into a rubble of syncopated syllables. Reason becomes a powder of vowels and consonants. . . . Semantics are driven out of his language in order to avoid meaning.[218]

In Smithson's *Pulverizations*, a work included in the first language show, language has indeed become a kind of "printed matter" (cat. 81). Originally typed in Courier font on a sheet of paper and remade into a negative Photostat (a photograph of a document transferred onto light-sensitive paper), *Pulverizations* is a diagrammatic view of five sculptural ideas based on two nested square volumes.[219] The outer bins (identified as "X") are thirty feet square; the proportions of the interior foundations ("Z") vary depending on the materials used. Both containers are a foot below ground and a foot above. The letters that Smithson typed inside the bins represent different substances. For example, the first arrangement contains bituminous coal ("B") and a cauldron of hot tar ("T"); the second is filled with bog iron ("B") and dried cement ("C"). Among the other materials specified by Smithson are blue coal ("B"), volcanic ash ("V"), sandstone ("S"), glue ("G"), and fine gravel ("F"). The proposed sculptures are displays of molten and ground matter. In order to depict these substances Smithson "pulverizes" the alphabet itself. Isolated, repeated, the letters he uses do not make up words. They do not represent abstract ideas; they are the building blocks of sculpture.

And in Lawrence Weiner's *Structure Poem* (cat. 82), which Dwan exhibited in *Language III*, the repeated transcription of the statement "ONE STANDARD AIR FORCE DYE MARKER THROWN INTO THE SEA" on a sheet of graph paper in pen and ink forces us to perceive the words that make up this statement less as words than as marks on a page, as letters or graphemes, and as patterns of primarily visual interest. (For example, the column of *S*'s in *STANDARD*, surrounded on three sides by empty triangles, sets up an optical reverberation in the vertical voids on two sides of the page.) One of the proposals for aesthetic actions that Weiner gathered in his seminal book *Statements* (1968), *Structure Poem* could assume a number of forms. The handwritten 8 ½″ × 11″ sheet of this phrase repeated would yield a single statement made of letters attached to a wall (an installation); and it would potentially result in a performance of this action. (Weiner did, in fact, cast an actual dye marker into the sea.[220]) There was no one work, no singular object, only different material embodiments of the proposal—as poem, as wall drawing, as physical act. A "decentering" of the work of art was under way. The singular aesthetic object was less and less "the primary point of reference."[221]

The incursion of language into the visual field occurred in tandem with and catalyzed the tendency that came to be known as "dematerialization,"[222] itself a dialectical response to the stubborn materialism of the minimalist project. The language shows asserted that words alone could exist as art. And so Joseph Kosuth, in an extreme interpretation of Duchamp's ready-mades (such as the bottle rack that the Frenchman removed from a hardware store and declared a work of art) and of a passing statement by Donald Judd ("If someone says his art is art, it's art"), defined the artwork this way: "A work of art is a tautology in that it is a presentation of the artist's intention, that is, he is saying the particular work of art *is* art, which means, is a *definition* of art."[223] The idea alone counted; its visual, tactile realization was ancillary, indeed a hindrance, to the achievement of "*purer* versions of Conceptual Art," a conceptualism of mind.[224] Kosuth's contribution to *Language II*, a Photostat '*Titled (Art as Idea as Idea)' [real]* (cat. 83), took aim at the then-current demand for an "art of the real," as the works of the materialists were then described.[225] Reproducing the definition of the word "real" in a standard dictionary format and font, Kosuth negates the minimal object and the empirical encounter it occasioned for a tautological description—a "real" experienced not in actuality but as an idea. Yet even a simple photostat is a material thing, an object. "No idea exists without a sustaining support," as Mel Bochner observed.[226] In defense of this claim, Bochner contributed a work to the final language show that was made in defiance of the intentionalist arguments of Kosuth and others. Inspired in part by the graffiti of French student protesters during the events of May 1968, *Language Is Not Transparent* (cat. 84) transformed the wall of the Dwan Gallery into a site of aesthetic enunciation informed by Bochner's readings of the later Wittgenstein in the language of philosophy, among other sources.[227] Boldly drawn in white chalk on a two-by-three-foot rectangle of dripping paint, an image evocative of the classroom chalkboard where we first acquire the fundamentals of language use, Bochner's work insists that the words we read do not easily, that is to say, transparently, convey an author's intention (assuming the author *knows* what she "means"); nor do the words we speak or the marks we make easily communicate our thoughts and feelings (the abstract expressionist canvas that sought to embody emotion through the direct application of painterly gesture is another target of Bochner's work). "There is no work of art that does not bear some burden of physicality," Bochner has written.[228] Presented in the extremely public setting of the last of the language shows during the heyday of dematerialization, Bochner's unruly wall drawing asserted that even the most "conceptual" work is irreducibly physical, a material thing, if not exactly an object—and therefore distinct from the hand and mind that created it.

Still other works explored the contradiction posed by the first language show between an art of primarily visual apperception and one constituted by words we are meant merely to read. (The words are "transparent.") Holt's contribution to *Language III*, *Detach Here*, is comprised of simple instructions (cat. 85). She typed this statement on the edges of a square. To complete *Detach Here* is to destroy it: if we follow Holt's directions, cutting along the dotted line, we end up with "nothing."[229] A work originally titled *Untitled* in Arakawa's one-person show in November 1969 presented a similar premise (cat. 86). This is one of a number of drawings Arakawa made directly on canvas. At the top is a clearly drawn triangle and faint tracings of triangles, and verticals of varied intensity and width. A tangle of scribbles "hangs" from the triangle's upper vertex. Below, we read a curious statement: "IF POSSIBLE STEAL ANY ONE OF THESE DRAWINGS INCLUDING THIS SENTENCE." The final two words fade into near illegibility.

Arakawa's invitation to poach this and other drawings, and even his words, brims with the irony of logical impossibility. Embedded in the warp and weave of unprimed canvas, his entreaties cannot, of course, be carried out without destroying the work, as Holt dares us to do in *Detach Here*, both literally confirming Bochner's claim that "no idea exists without a sustaining support." In the end some visitors followed Arakawa's instructions. *Untitled* disappeared from the Dwan Gallery; the "culprits" were a group of art students who informed the bemused artist that they had taken possession of his artwork. He would teach them a lesson. The students were instructed to offer the work to public institutions. Letters were drafted; many exchanges occurred; in the end the pilfered canvas went to the first museum that agreed to accession it.[230] The meaning of Arakawa's painting had changed in the transaction, becoming a different work—a collaboration centered around *Untitled*—with a new name: *Stolen*. The removal of *Untitled* from the Dwan Gallery instigated a chain of events that transcended Arakawa's drawing on canvas, exposing the mechanisms of a gallery system centered on the exchange of commodities.

A work by Lee Lozano exhibited in *Language III* dared to circumvent the "system" in which Dwan was now an important player. Lozano reversed the normative flow of transaction of the retail gallery by putting the profits from the sale of a painting into a jar and then offering the jar's contents to visitors at both her studio and Dwan's gallery. From April 3 to July 9, 1969, Lozano recorded the reactions of various individuals to her proposal. We tend to think of the conceptual activities of the late sixties as deadpan and dour. In fact, Lozano's resulting work, *Untitled (Party/Paranoia, Painting, Real Money)*—a psychological portrait of Lozano's friends and acquaintances as well as gallery visitors—is highly amusing (cat. 87). Lozano records that the poet Hannah Weiner, a fellow participant in the Dwan exhibition, accepted ten dollars of the 585 dollars in the jar; that the painter Brice Marden didn't need any money; and that the dealer Paul Bianchini needed his wife's permission to accept Lozano's offer. She recalls the squeamishness of the conceptual artist Stephen Kaltenbach and the sculptor Keith Sonnier, and Claire Copley's indignance: the gallerist, visiting from Los Angeles, seemed to Lozano "insulted & offended that I offer it to her (in such a vulgar way)." She notes the pragmatism of Dan Graham, who returns the money he borrows, and the masochistic response of one Arthur Berman (who, although "flat broke," only accepts twenty cents for subway fare). She records, too, her replenishment of the jar with another 500 dollars based on another sale and the date she writes up the work for inclusion in *Language III*, May 19, 1969. Last but not least, she describes the response of the artist John Torreano. Torreano doesn't "need any money" yet "takes the jar anyway." "Hooray!" writes Lozano, who has grown weary of her idea.[231]

It is well known that Dwan supported many of her artists with monthly stipends and funded the fabrication of their work. In a watercolor in the Dwan collection Kienholz hinted at the actual mechanism of support that made being a "Dwan artist" an unusual privilege (cat. 88). The hand-stenciled text that serves as the title of the work, *For Reducing Virginia's Account to Zero*, is the sort of statement that linguists describe as a "speech act," a declaration that enacts, that makes actual, a speaker's intention. (Kienholz signed the drawing with his thumbprint, that ironical index of his aesthetic intent.) "With the exchange of this watercolor," Kienholz asserts, "the amount of money I owe Virginia is reduced." A rather hopeful aspiration, as it turned out: one year after Dwan closed her gallery in 1971 (after shutting down the Westwood space in June 1967) Kienholz was still paying off the debt he had accrued to the gallerist since decamping from Ferus ten years before.

BEYOND THE GALLERY

At the very moment when Morris, Flavin, Andre, Anastasi, and Sandback revealed the gallery space—its walls, its floors, its corners—the gallery *as a site* proved increasingly inadequate to the needs of artists working in remote settings. As Dwan began to cultivate these practices the nature of her operation changed. It was less a showroom for art than a facilitator of projects sited well beyond the gallery—works that disrupted conventional notions of collecting and display.

A work by Robert Morris included in the *Scale Models and Drawings* show in January 1967 hinted at the direction of things to come (cat. 91). A plaster model in the shape of a trapezoid with a raised mound rising above a circular depression, Morris's work was not a sculpture in its own right but a schematic depiction of a proposed outdoor work specified at 2,000 feet in diameter. *Project in Earth and Sod* was one of several land projects that Smithson, working as an artist-consultant, commissioned for a major new airport being planned at Dallas–Fort Worth.[232] His 1967 essay "Towards the Development of an Air Terminal Site" envisioned a strikingly new art form:

> The "boring," like other "earth works," is becoming more and more important to artists. Pavements, holes, trenches, mounds, heaps, paths, ditches, roads, terraces, etc. all have an aesthetic potential.[233]

Smithson's theory of land art underwent many revisions during the years before his untimely death in 1973.[234] Of particular interest to this account is the fact that he initially conceived of the earthwork in respect to modern technologies of aviation. Describing artists' efforts to create an art keyed to the spatial coordinates of the earth and outer space, he compared the sculptor to the surveyor and airport planner who "coordinat[es] land and air masses resembling crystalline grid networks." The earthwork, he insists, had emerged in concert with the accelerated time and spatial perception fostered by the jet plane and satellites that rotate around the earth so rapidly their movement is invisible to the naked eye.[235]

A later essay offered a more exacting description of the kind of sculpture Smithson envisioned for Dallas–Fort Worth: an art so immense it could be seen by flight passengers (Smithson titled the article "Aerial Art"). A photograph and collaged map in the Dwan Collection depict the future terminal and its adjacent runways with earthworks positioned at each end, a land mass comparable to that of New York's Central Park (cat. 90).[236] Morris's earth mound is identified as "A." At location "B" we find a work by Andre, who proposed a crater made by a one-ton bomb dropped from 10,000 feet (a not-so-veiled reference to American military sorties in Vietnam) or, alternatively, a one-acre plot seeded with Texas bluebonnets (a not-so-veiled reference to Lady Bird Johnson's initiative to beautify highways with wildflower plantings). A final proposal written on notebook paper with Smithson's notation ("Add to 'Aerial Art'") describes an even more ambitious sculpture of 1,320 cold-rolled steel plates laid side by side a mile in length (cat. 92).[237] At site "D" LeWitt planned to bury a metal box containing something "precious," extending *Serial Project*'s examination of contained or hidden forms to the earthwork while denying Smithson's idea of aerial visibility with considerable wit, a work that LeWitt would eventually make in a different setting (cat. 93).

Of the many earthworks Smithson planned for area "C"—a four-foot-deep reflecting pool in the shape of a squared-off spiral; earthworks of "wandering" mounds; paths of white gravel resembling a giant spiderweb, among others—his final proposal was the most germinal. A spiral of twelve triangular concrete platforms drawn from Smithson's studies in gyrostatics (the branch of physics concerned with rotating bodies that maintain a static position), it evoked the circular motions of ascending and descending airplanes and afforded a reference point for passengers who would supposedly perceive the scalar changes that occur as they left the earth—and returned to it.[238] It was this project that inspired the making of the remarkable *Gyrostasis*, a standing, three-dimensional projection of the airport pavement fabricated in painted steel (cat. 89), and the artist's seminal earthwork *Spiral Jetty* (cat. 109).[239]

Although the engineering firm that hired Smithson did not win the airport commission, his interest in working on the land was piqued. He now led Dwan, Holt, and others on a series of trips to New Jersey and other locations on the East Coast in search of potential sites. Recorded in photographs, essays, and works of sculpture he called "nonsites," these "tours" were an aesthetic activity in their own right, ultimately leading to the Yucatán junket. During one of these trips, in 1967, Smithson, Dwan, Holt, Morris, and Andre drove to the Pine Barrens, a relatively undeveloped terrain of scrub pines in southern New Jersey. The following winter Smithson, Holt, Dwan, LeWitt, and a friend made a return trip, eventually arriving at an abandoned airfield that Smithson had located on a map. For the Dallas–Fort Worth project, Smithson had envisioned earthworks for the "clear zones" next to runways. In the Pine Barrens that wintry afternoon he inverted this procedure, removing sand and stones from the terrain of an old landing strip to make a nonsite sculpture to be shown with its cognate work, *Gyrostasis*, in his upcoming March 1968 show at Dwan (pp. 309–310, fig. 29). Dwan described this transformation: "As he forced his shovel into the frozen surface, the others held out gunny sacks to receive the actual sand and pebbles from the site. Bob was doing an airport work after all, but rather than being a work on the field, this was to be a 'nonsite.'" (See Writings, p. 258.)

A Nonsite, Pine Barrens, New Jersey was an object divided from within (cat. 94). Both a sculpture and a map with a typed caption, Smithson's completed nonsite pointed in three different ways to the precise location where the sand was collected. The hexagonal shape of the sculpture referred to the six intersecting runways of the airstrip and the morphology of crystals. (The center point of the map resembles an ice crystal, or snowflake, a reference to the principle of "heat death" in entropy theory, an extension of the Second Law of Thermodynamics, which holds that the universe will eventually cool as the total sum of energy dwindles.[240]) The thirty-one bins of sand, painted an icy aquamarine, ascend and descend in size much as the triangular units of the Dallas–Fort Worth spiral and *Gyrostasis* do, referring to the concentric divisions of Smithson's map and evoking the somewhat nauseating experience of circling around and around a runway as we land. With this work and the contemporaneous *Nonsite* #2, a dodecagon-shaped map of the New Jersey Meadowlands exhibited in *Language II* (cat. 95),[241] Smithson deflected a viewer's attention from the gallery: with the addition of two elements, sand and maps, he implied that the impulse of sixties minimalism to reveal the gallery as a place—brought to a definitive conclusion by Anastasi's *Six Sites*, which title he negates—had reached an impasse. (A nonsite is *not* the site.)[242] The first nonsite tethered the

FIG. 29

HERBERT BAYER, *EARTH MOUND*, ASPEN INSTITUTE FOR HUMANISTIC STUDIES, COLORADO, 1954

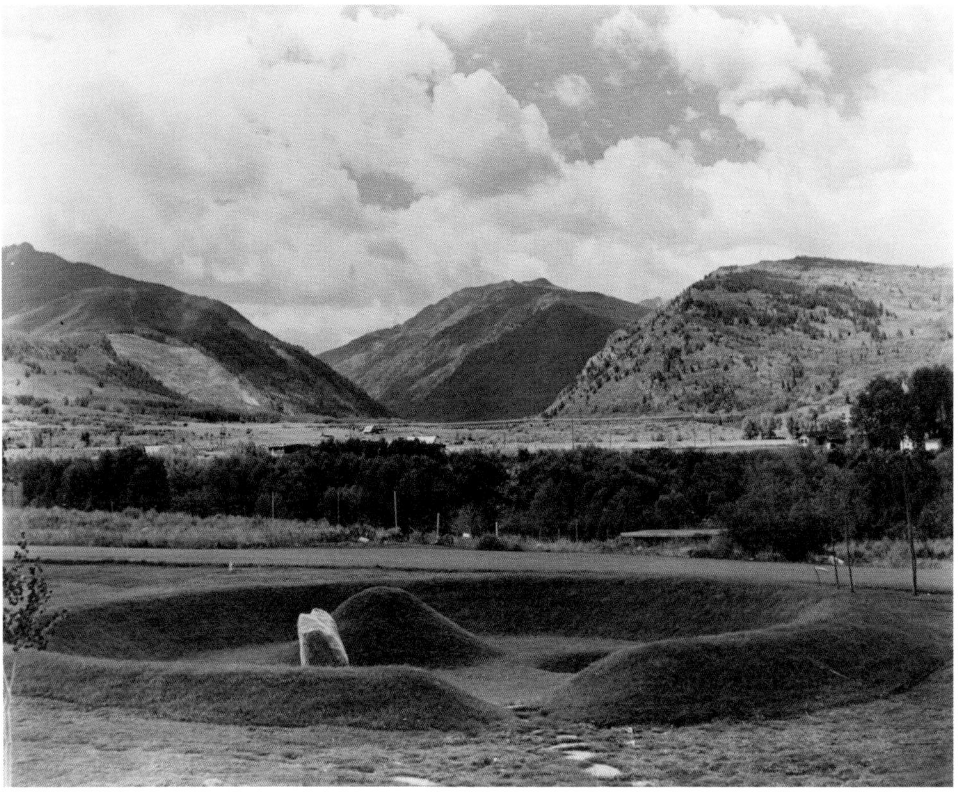

57th Street gallery to an obscure and distant corner of New Jersey, establishing a new and unexpected correspondence between two extraordinarily different places. The journey was the middle term of Smithson's dialectic, the glue, as it were, connecting the gallery and the location where the materials were harvested; and in fact Smithson proposed to lead the viewer to the abandoned airstrip. ("Tours between the Nonsite and the site are possible.")

Dwan, Smithson, and Holt were unsuccessful in their efforts to locate sites for land-based projects. And so that summer of 1968 Dwan and Weber planned a fall show that attempted to define the terms of a new impulse. *Earthworks* had to be realized inside the gallery, the irony of which was not lost on the gallerist (the decision was "very definitely our last choice").[243] The exhibition opened the 1968 season exactly two years after *10*. A single "elder," the Bauhaus artist Herbert Bayer, sent a photograph of his *Earth Mound*, a ring of dirt surrounding a mound, hole, and boulder built on the grounds of Colorado's Aspen Institute in 1954 (fig. 29).[244] The presence of several Dwan artists was significant, indicating a shift in approach from the minimal and pop morphologies of their signature work. Smithson's third nonsite—five trapezoidal bins of mineral ore from the industrial town of Franklin, New Jersey, and an aerial map segmented into these shapes—may have felt familiar to the regular visitor who already knew the hexagonal Pine Barrens nonsite.[245] Less expected was Oldenburg's Super 8 mm film documentating the artist's *Placid Civic Monument*, a ditch created by professional gravediggers behind the Metropolitan Museum of Art in Central Park and refilled later the same day, or his *Plexiglas Box*, a one-foot-square cube filled with dirt and earthworms mounted on a pedestal near the entrance to the Dwan Gallery, yet another evocation of mortality—a work that reimagined Larry Bell's elegant glass box as a rather gruesome terrarium;[246]—or the notebook of LeWitt's *Buried Cube*, the earthwork initially conceived for the Dallas–Fort Worth runway recreated as a performance in the garden of the Dutch collectors Martin and Mia Visser. (The nine-part photo-documentation of the ersatz "funeral" depicts LeWitt, his hosts, and the box's fabricator during the cube's interment: cat. 93.) Andre's wall-mounted photos of a conical pile of rocks and row of logs in an Aspen forest appeared to be radical departures for a sculptor known for working with industrially processed materials (cat. 97). In fact, these outdoor projects brought the expansive definition of sculpture in Andre's important poem "Essay on Sculpture for E. C. Goossen" (1964) to fruition. According to Andre, even burial sites, buildings, things of utility, and the natural world can be experienced as sculpture. And so he presented *Rock Pile* and *Log Piece* as such.[247]

Morris's work probably baffled visitors most of all (fig. 30). A heap of dirt from a local construction site containing such "ingredients" as peat, grease,

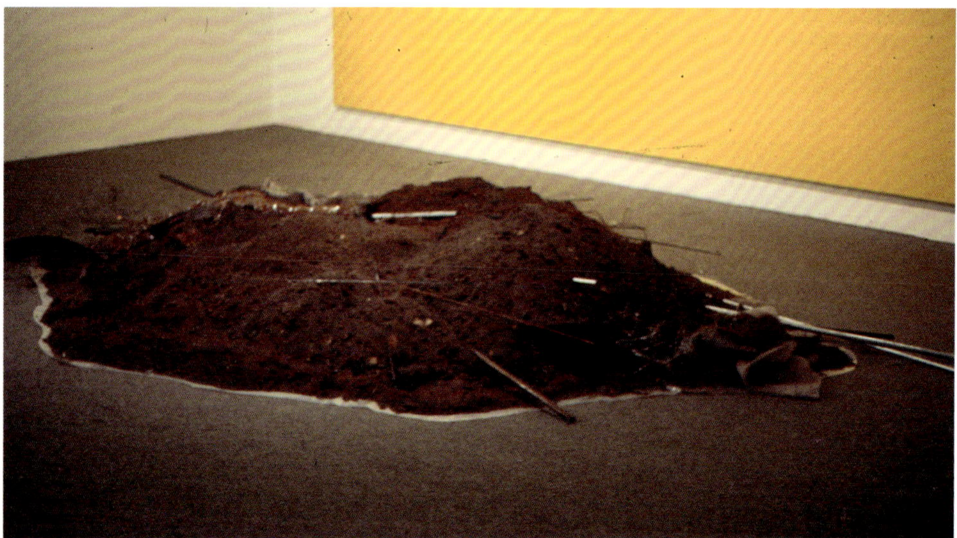

FIG. 30

INSTALLATION VIEW, *EARTHWORKS*, DWAN GALLERY NEW YORK, OCTOBER 1968; FOREGROUND, ROBERT MORRIS, *UNTITLED (DIRT)*, 1968; BACKGROUND, WALTER DE MARIA, *PAINTING (THE COLOR MEN CHOOSE WHEN THEY ATTACK THE EARTH)*, 1968

bricks, pieces of steel, aluminum, copper, brass, zinc, and scraps of felt dumped onto Dwan's carpet, *Untitled (Dirt)* was an aggressive about-face from the simple polyhedrons of the artist's Westwood show. Its amorphous form and repulsive materiality elicited an undifferentiated perception of "stuff," or *scanning*, that disallowed Gestalt viewing—the focused perception of shape facilitated by his minimalist works.[248] Morris's dirt dump was as little an "object" as sculpture could be, and for all purposes uncommodifiable. He offered the unruly sculpture for the exalted sum of $4,080—the highest price of any work in the show—or the equally absurd price of three dollars per pound. In this imagined scenario a collector would arrive at the gallery with a shovel and trash bags, scoop up the preferred amount, have it weighed—and lug the mess home.[249]

Earthworks also introduced several new artists to Dwan. A diagram by Stephen Kaltenbach (the reluctant participant in Lozano's *Real Money*) depicted a kidney-shaped swimming pool topped by a kidney-shaped mound, inverting the peculiar shape of a typical suburban pool of this vintage and doubling its volume, while both of Dennis Oppenheim's proposals displaced a cartographical image of one site onto the actual terrain of another.[250] A work completed by Oppenheim in New Haven, Connecticut, transposed the elevation of a mountain southwest of the city (location "A") to a saltwater marsh next to a highway ("B"). This transfer of information yielded several concentric rings of up to two hundred feet in diameter that Oppenheim cut into the swamp grass and littered with aluminum shavings (cat. 96). (His indifference to the swamp's ecology is perhaps a comment on the pollution of the New Haven marshlands by local industry in the pre-environmental-awareness era.) Where Smithson's airport spiral would have been highly visible from the air, Oppenheim's swamp circles were meant to disappear. In the tilted image of the just-finished work the rings are well defined by the aluminum residue. In the other exposure, taken that day at high tide, his project is under water. A few months later, no trace of the work remained.

Walter De Maria had long envisioned an art of the land.[251] With the assistance of a young artist named Michael Heizer, De Maria had completed a marked site of two parallel white chalk lines twelve feet apart stretching a mile across the Mojave Desert (p. 357, fig. 106). Unlike many land artists, De Maria resisted exhibiting photographs of his projects, which he felt misrepresented works that could only be experiences in situ. His contribution to *Earthworks*, a painting simply titled *Painting*, was an unconventional choice in an installation dominated by photographs, films, and sculptures. *Painting* was not an ordinary painting, however, not only because De Maria did not paint it.[252] At the

FIG. 31

MICHAEL HEIZER, *DISPLACED/REPLACED MASS 1/3*, SILVER SPRINGS, NEVADA, 1969

center of the seven-by-twenty-foot canvas was a chrome plaque inscribed with the phrase "The Color Men Choose When They Attack The Earth"—a reference, like the painting's yellow surface, to the backhoes and bulldozers used by De Maria and his fellow land artists (see fig. 30). These noisy, burly machines had begun to replace the artisanal tools—hammers, screwdrivers, torches, and the like—of even the most advanced sculptors.

The final participant in the show, Michael Heizer, became extremely important to Dwan and a principal figure of the gallery's final years. When Heizer appeared at Dwan's office five months before Dwan opened the show he had already completed some twenty land-based projects.[253] He had dug trenches in the Sierra Nevada Mountains and scattered dyes and made motorcycle "drawings" on the Mojave Desert; he had built nine incisions across the state of Nevada in a line 520 miles long. His contribution to *Earthworks* was a six-by-six-foot backlit transparency of *Dissipate #2*, the fourth in his series of *Nine Nevada Depressions. Dissipate #2* consisted of five twelve-foot-long "lines" dug in the Black Rock Desert, each one foot deep by one foot wide. Its buoyantly asymmetrical arrangement—a suprematist composition projected in three dimensions onto the ground—was generated by Arpian chance: tossing five matches onto a sheet of paper, Heizer appropriated the pattern left by the snuffed out ("dissipated") matches to generate the work's form.[254]

The collector Robert Scull, who sponsored *Nine Nevada Depressions*, now commissioned another work in Nevada called *Displaced/Replaced Mass* (cat. 99 and fig. 31). Heizer carved three large depressions in the ground, which he faced with concrete. He then "replaced" the soil removed by these incisions with granite boulders carved with dynamite out of the side of a mountain sixty miles away. A visitor to the site could compare the relative mass of the displacements. (The first stone weighed thirty tons; the second fifty-two; the largest sixty-eight.)

In distinct contrast to those conceptualists who sought to defeat the object through "dematerialization," or those land artists like Oppenheim and Smithson whose works concluded with their decay, Heizer's boulders were objects so unworked and so massive they could not easily be moved; they were "surrogate" or "replacement" objects, as he called them—replacements for portable art commodities.[255] His art of displaced mass drew upon art-historical narratives other than the Western tradition of "academically studied" works of fine art.[256] The Neolithic and other so-called primitive traditions had become increasingly germane to land artists and to Heizer in particular, who had often accompanied his father, an eminent anthropologist, to archaeological sites in

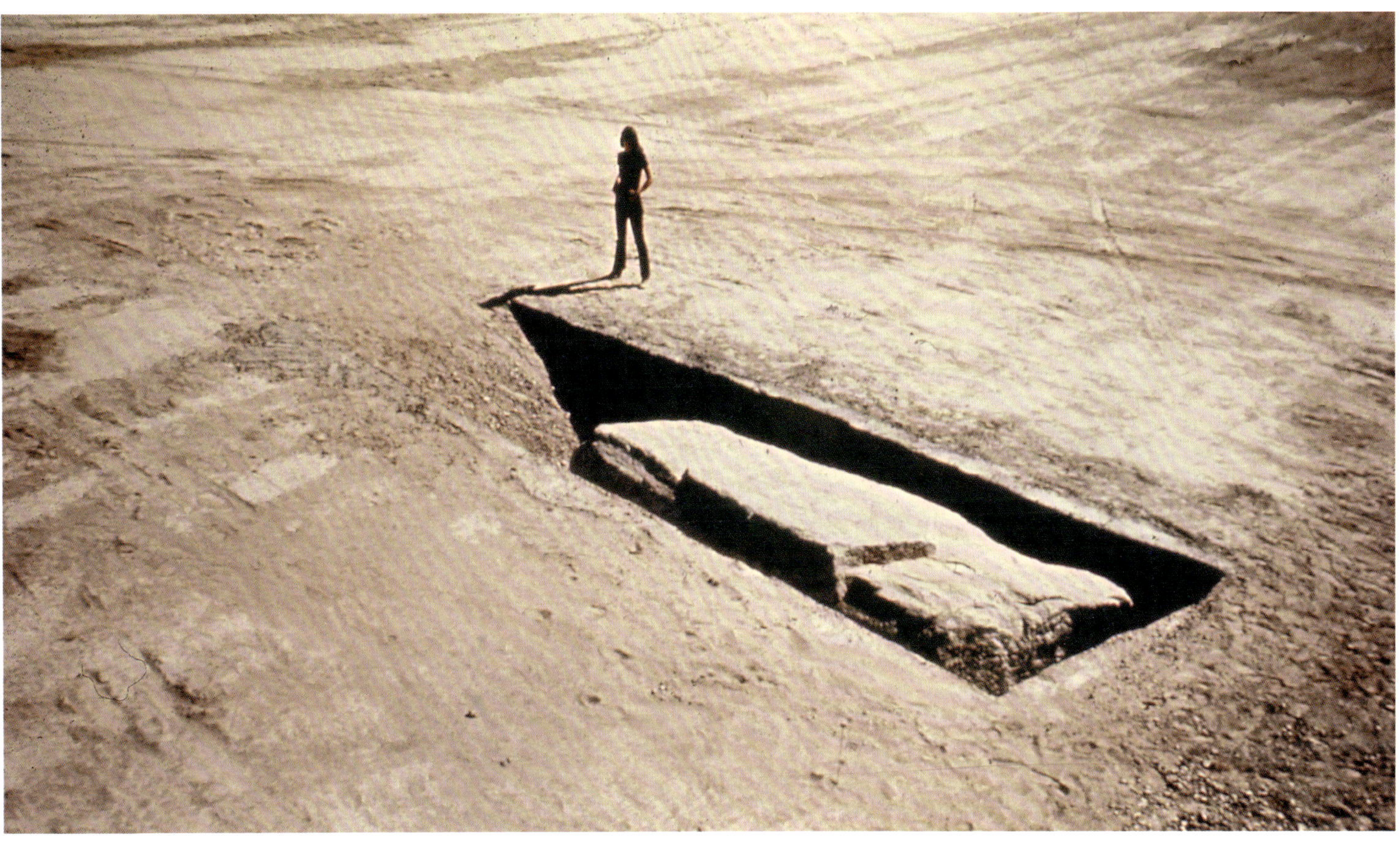

South America and the American West.[257] *Bolivia/Nevada* (cat. 100), a unique photographic print juxtaposing images of the teenage Heizer with an ancient stele pitched horizontally in a ditch in Tiahuanaco with an image of the sculptor standing next to *Displaced/Replaced Mass (1/3)*, makes such connections powerfully explicit. The handwritten identifications of the locations and dates of the images (1963/1969, Bolivia/Nevada) set up a structure of comparison marking two locations and points in time of great significance for Heizer. The horizontal orientation of both sculptures indicative of gravity's relentless force testifies to the profound impact of the father's research on the son's prodigious imagination.

During the fall of 1969 Heizer embarked on the defining work of his early practice. Dwan purchased a square mile of desert some eighty miles north of Las Vegas on Mormon Mesa—the site of a project whose form she did not know in advance.[258] Working with a local contractor, Heizer sliced two great gashes on either side of a canyon, removing an astonishing 240,000 tons of stone, sand, and gravel from those cliff sides. His incisions, exactingly perpendicular, were fifty feet deep and thirty feet wide (cat. 102). It was easy to lose one's way trying to find *Double Negative*, as Heizer called his project. Yet its Brobdingnagian size was comparable to that of the most gargantuan Neolithic and modern monuments (the work is longer than the Empire State Building is tall), as well as contemporary industrial forms, as suggested by *Scientific American*, a companion piece to *Bolivia/Nevada* that compares a photograph of *Double Negative* and the sulfur "vat" at a Texas plant on the cover of the popular science magazine (cat. 101).[259] But Heizer's work could not be experienced apart from that journey—and the experience of standing inside, and moving through, its mirrored depressions.[260] The artist's debut show at Dwan in January 1970, *Michael Heizer: New York/Nevada*, linked the gallery and earthwork inextricably. The panoramic photographs, transparencies, etchings, and diagrams that he installed in the 57th Street space did not suggest a dialectical connection between these sites, however. The exhibition (*New York*) was a mere supplement to the actual work and its placement (*Nevada*). The real show was *elsewhere*. It was necessary to travel to the ridge above the Virgin River, to Mormon Mesa, to walk inside Heizer's cuts, to look across and into the canyon they straddle—to experience his work for oneself.

Double Negative marked the gallery indelibly. Henceforth Dwan's operation would "no longer [be] defined [or] bounded by the confining white plaster walls."[261] On April 8, 1968, De Maria sent the dealer a percipient telegram:

DEAR VIRGINIA MANY LAND SENSATIONS AND PROJECTS ALREADY REALIZED SO VERY POSITIVE I URGE YOU TO CONSIDER CLOSING OF GALLERY AND TO CONSIDER WORLD WIDE OPERATIONS[262]

In fact, Dwan did not close her space for another three years. As she began to sponsor land-based works, the nature of her practice—and her understanding of herself as a gallerist—changed. She now emerged as a patron of hugely ambitious projects embedded *in* places, unmovable and practically unsalable. The list of these extraordinarily ambitious projects amazes us still. She commissioned De Maria's *35-Pole Lightning Field* (1974), a grid arrangement of eighteen-foot-tall stainless-steel poles with pointed tips constructed near Flagstaff, Arizona (cat. 104), a project that drew from the magnetism of such earlier works as *High Energy Bar*, a stainless-steel ingot alleged to transmit physical energy to a viewer who holds it (cat. 103), and the notorious *Bed of Spikes* (1969), a sequence of four steel plates bearing spikes so sharp an unlucky spectator could be impaled by them (p. 357, fig. 107).[263] And it anticipated the subsequent and final iteration

FIG. 32

MICHAEL HEIZER, *CITY: COMPLEX ONE*, GARDEN VALLEY, NEVADA, PHOTOGRAPHED IN 1997

of De Maria's proposal, the *Lightning Field*, completed for the Dia Art Foundation in 1977, a distribution of four hundred twenty-foot-tall stainless-steel poles in a grid pattern one mile by one kilometer in Quemado, New Mexico—a work that asks the visitor to contemplate its man-made representation of infinitude in the unbounded space of a high desert plain (cat. 105).[264]

Consider as well the other projects that benefited from Dwan's largesse. She partially underwrote the construction of Heizer's *City: Complex One* (1972–1974) in Garden Valley, Nevada (fig. 32), a polyhedral structure made of five hundred tons of packed earth and rock compressed between walls of cast concrete, its contours foreshadowed by the concrete beams that Heizer positioned in front of it, one along the left frontal side and running across half its upper rim, and the other a T-shaped beam cantilevered dramatically over its front edge. Casting shadows as De Maria's lightning poles do, these elements frame and alter how Heizer's earth mound is perceived with each passing hour.

Dwan supported the practice of Charles Ross, whose prismatic sculptures and one of whose *Solar Burns* she showed at the gallery (cats. 106, 107), and whose magnum opus, *Star Axis* (ongoing from 1971), constructed on the precipice of Chupinas Mesa in New Mexico, is an observatory dedicated to Polaris, the North Star, its layered forms—a conical wedge and tunnel stairwell, a triangular portal, and a pyramid with an oculus—inspired by any number of Neolithic and ancient American architectural complexes (cat. 108). And she

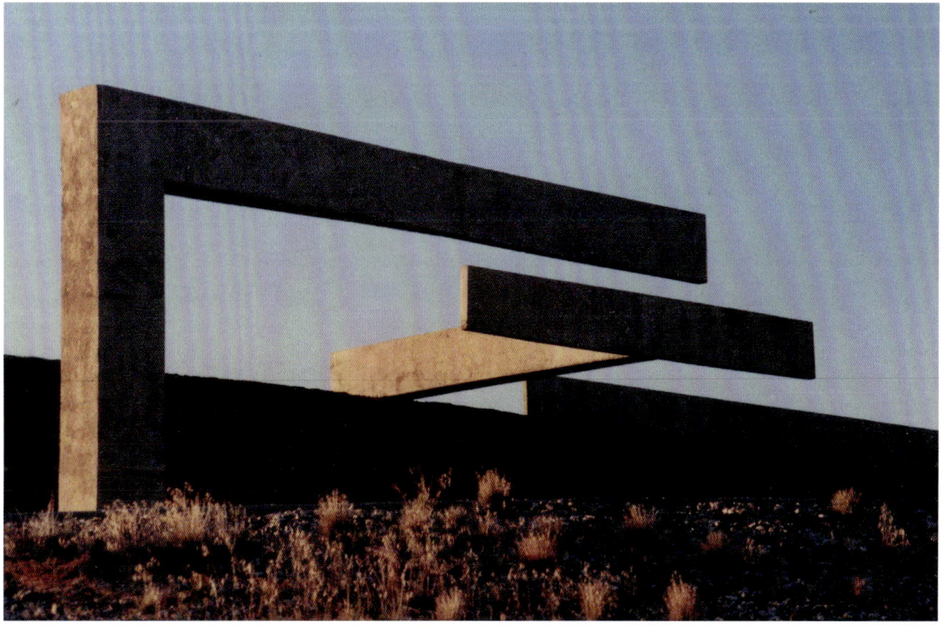

commissioned Smithson's *Spiral Jetty*, the consummate post-studio work comprised of many parts: the 1,500-foot-long jetty constructed with boulders and mud at the edge of the Great Salt Lake (cat. 109); preparatory drawings of the earthwork (cat. 110); proposals for unrealized projects (*Spiral Island with Curved Jetty*, *Green Island–Spiral Island*, cats. 111, 112); a proposed sculpture made of cardboard and sticks (*Pierced Spiral*, cat. 113); abstract meditations on shape (cat. 114); an essay, "Spiral Jetty"; and an arresting 16 mm film documenting the sculpture's creation spliced with shots of historical and thematic resonance.[265]

The copious holdings of Smithson's movie treatments in the Dwan collection follow the arc of the film's narrative. Beginning with the two-part scenography (cats. 115, 116) the sequence includes the opening shot of a driver's approach to *Spiral Jetty* alternating between a view of the road ahead and a rear view cloudy with dust (a road that "goes forward and backward between things and places that are elsewhere," as Smithson described it) (cats. 117, 124);[266] the sheets of a torn book scattered on the earth, a metaphor for the futility of human knowledge ("Earth's History") (cats. 118, 124); and the film's final frames looking down at the jetty from a helicopter, a flying machine impelled through the air by the rapid turning of its spiral propeller. The camera points down at the earthwork as the pilot circles Smithson's spiral in a clockwise, then counterclockwise, motion (cats. 119, 121, 122, 123). Eventually the camera pans up to the horizon (cat. 120).[267] Burning sunrays assault our eyes as we "fly" around Smithson's sculpture and listen to the helicopter's brash, whirring sound. Watching the final minutes of *Spiral Jetty* is a truly vertiginous experience. "My movie would end in sunstroke," Smithson wrote of this work. "Perception was heaving, the stomach turning...I had the red heaves, while the sun vomited its corpuscular radiations."[268] Half-blinded, we stare into the overlapping images of the sun and spiral until Smithson's sculpture blurs out (cat. 124).

Spiral Jetty was the featured work in Smithson's final show at Dwan. Now even the earthwork (that assault on the portable object) had fragmented into many parts of equal significance, and the artwork itself was decentered as a unary form. As the critic Craig Owens memorably observed:

> Like the Nonsite, the Jetty is not a discrete work, but one link in a chain of signifiers which summon and refer to one another in a dizzying spiral. For where does the Jetty exist except in the film which Smithson made, the narrative he published, the photographs which accompany that narrative, and the various maps, diagrams, drawings, etc., he made about it?[269]

To be sure, Dwan continued to exhibit traditional media, such as a show of paintings by Robert Ryman that featured his *Surface Veils*, studies of the effects of painterly gesture put down in layers of different kinds of marks (cats. 125, 126). The Ryman installation recalled prior shows of monochromatic painting (Klein, Reinhardt) and the mostly all-white exhibitions that Dwan had staged of LeWitt and, more recently, Flavin in 1968.

With the addition of the gifted painter to Dwan's stellar list, the gallery was arguably at its apogee. Thus the announcement that Dwan sent to her artists on April 20, 1971, came unexpectedly. The group show planned for that June would be her last. In truth, Dwan's venture had not been easy to sustain, taking a loss every year. Financially pressed and drained by the exacting needs of her artists, Dwan shuttered the gallery that summer.

The path that led from abstract expressionism to assemblage and pop, from nouveau réalisme to minimalism, from language to land art; from Westwood to West 57th Street; from Los Angeles to Paris to New York; from the Pine Barrens and Yucatán to the Western desert—came to an end. Dwan was only thirty-nine years old. Her story is embedded in a particular moment of historical possibility, I have argued, and is altogether unique. The surprising trajectory of Dwan's operation—she begins with paintings and sculptures of domestic scale, moves to constructions that burst the gallery at its seams, retools for minimalist works of bodily scale and industrial facture and then for a linguistic art of "ideas" that takes up hardly any gallery space, and from there bounds to land-based projects—leads, as it were, to the dismantling of her enterprise. Indeed, the relevance of the art gallery as aesthetic container is severely questioned in that astonishing period prior to the market's rise during the 1980s with the return of traditional media and once-discarded formats of painterly gesture and figuration—the very "objects" that had formerly appeared (at least theoretically) on the verge of extinction.[270]

Dwan's involvement with many of the most challenging practices of her time appears immensely generous. Dwan saw it differently. "I'm not really interested in generosity. But I'm interested in the ideas, and I take a great deal of pleasure in seeing the ideas brought out to other people."[271] Fostering ideas—difficult ideas—was worth it:

> As art became increasingly self-contained and even remote, I stretched more and more toward it and found satisfaction in that engagement and communion. I had to be willing to risk the voyage to a place that does not easily reveal itself. One used to look *at* art. Today art reflects our image back upon us. That is what makes it so difficult.[272]

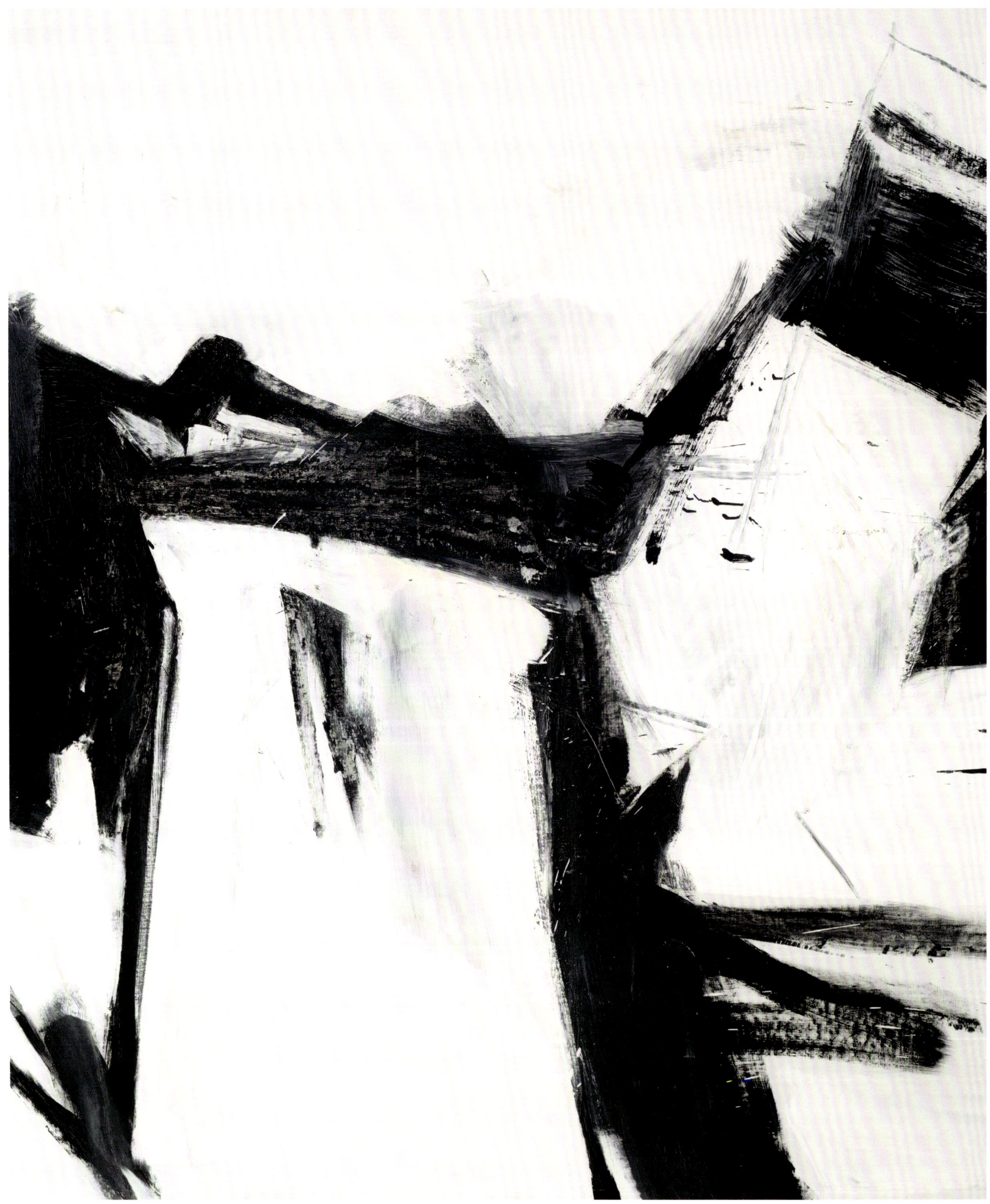

PLATES

CAT. 1

LARRY RIVERS,
VIRGINIA DWAN,
1963

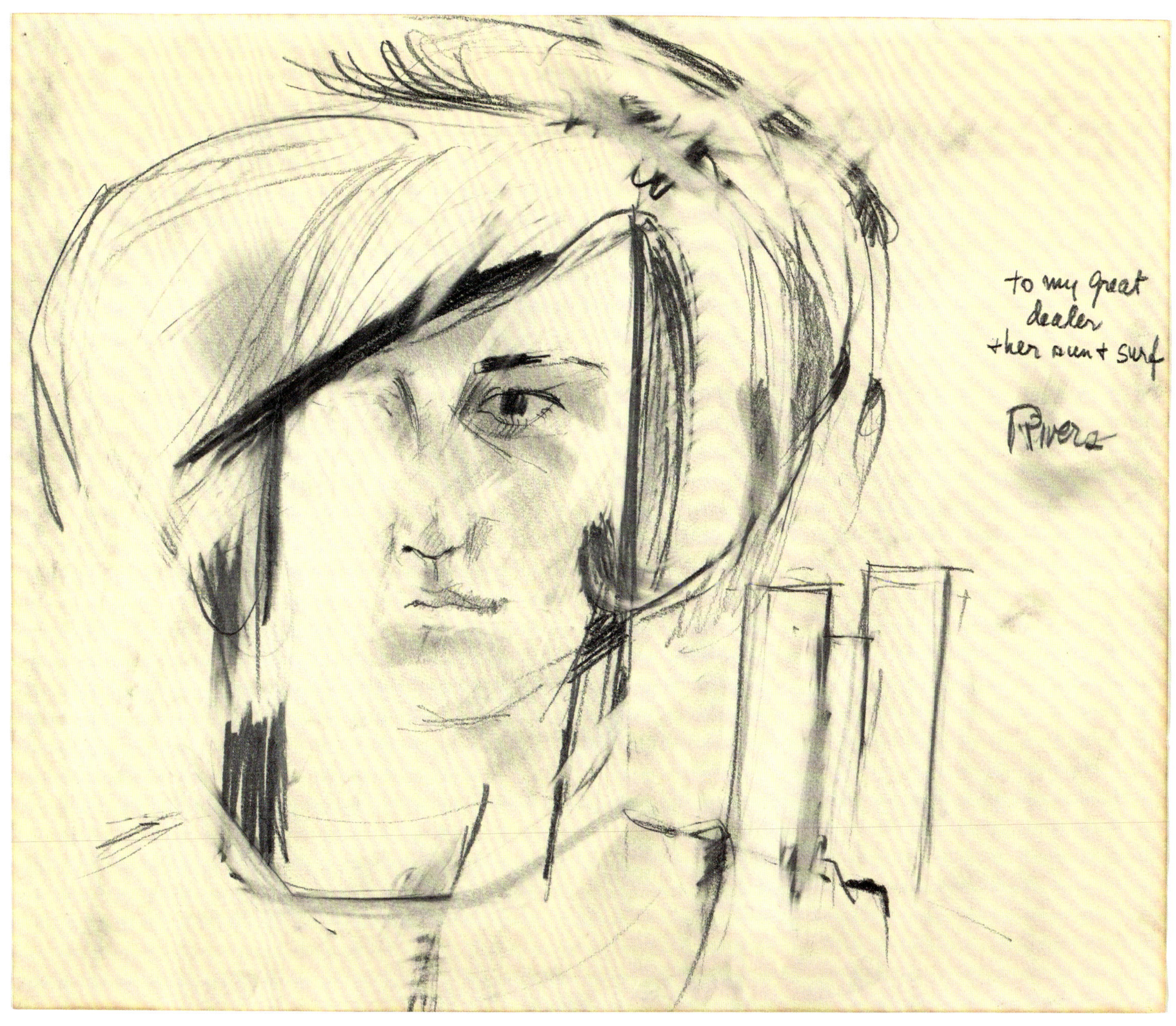

CAT. 2

LARRY RIVERS,
MAQUETTE FOR LARRY RIVERS EXHIBITION AT DWAN GALLERY,
1961

CAT. 3

LARRY RIVERS,
MAQUETTE FOR LARRY RIVERS EXHIBITION AT DWAN GALLERY,
1963

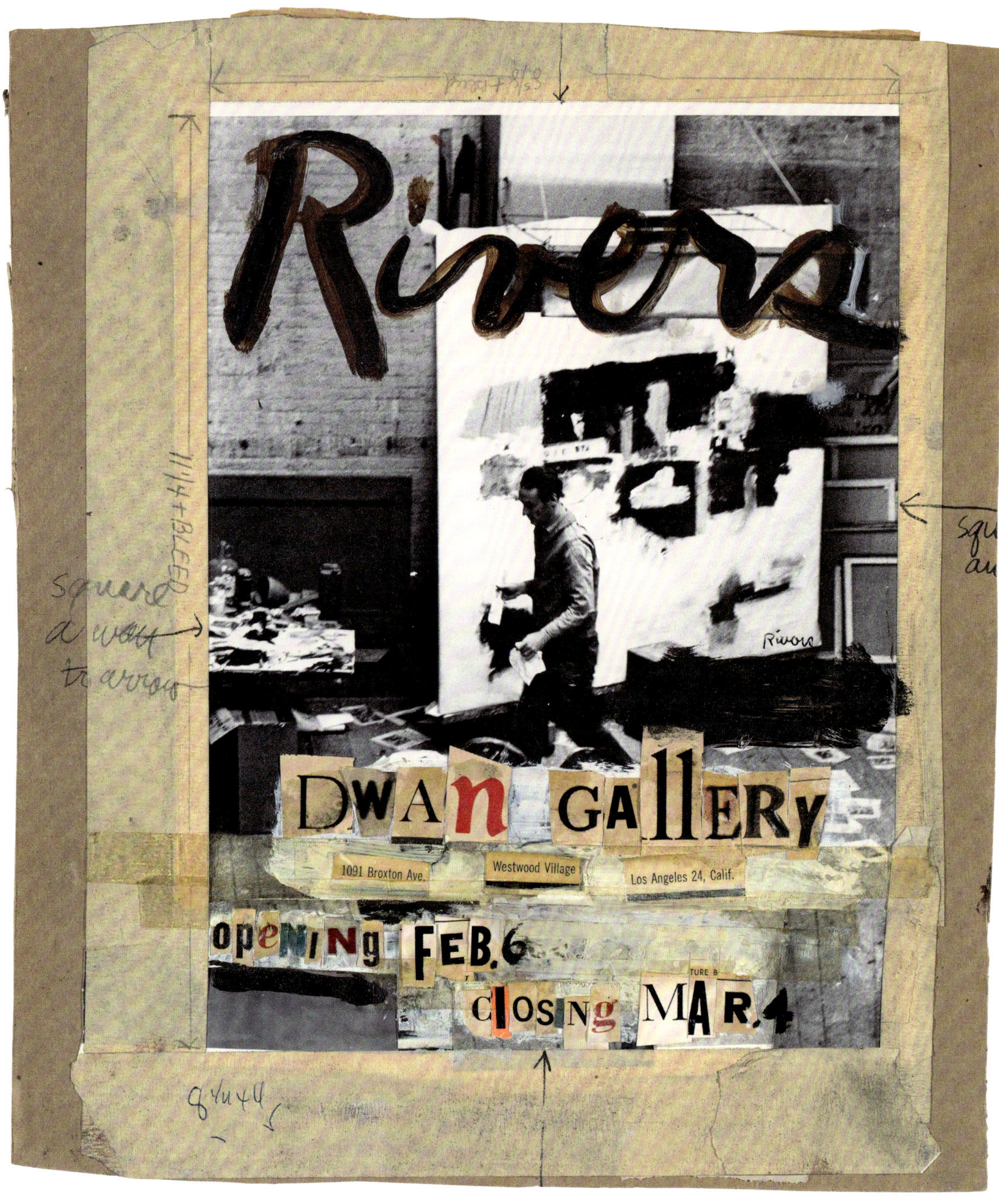

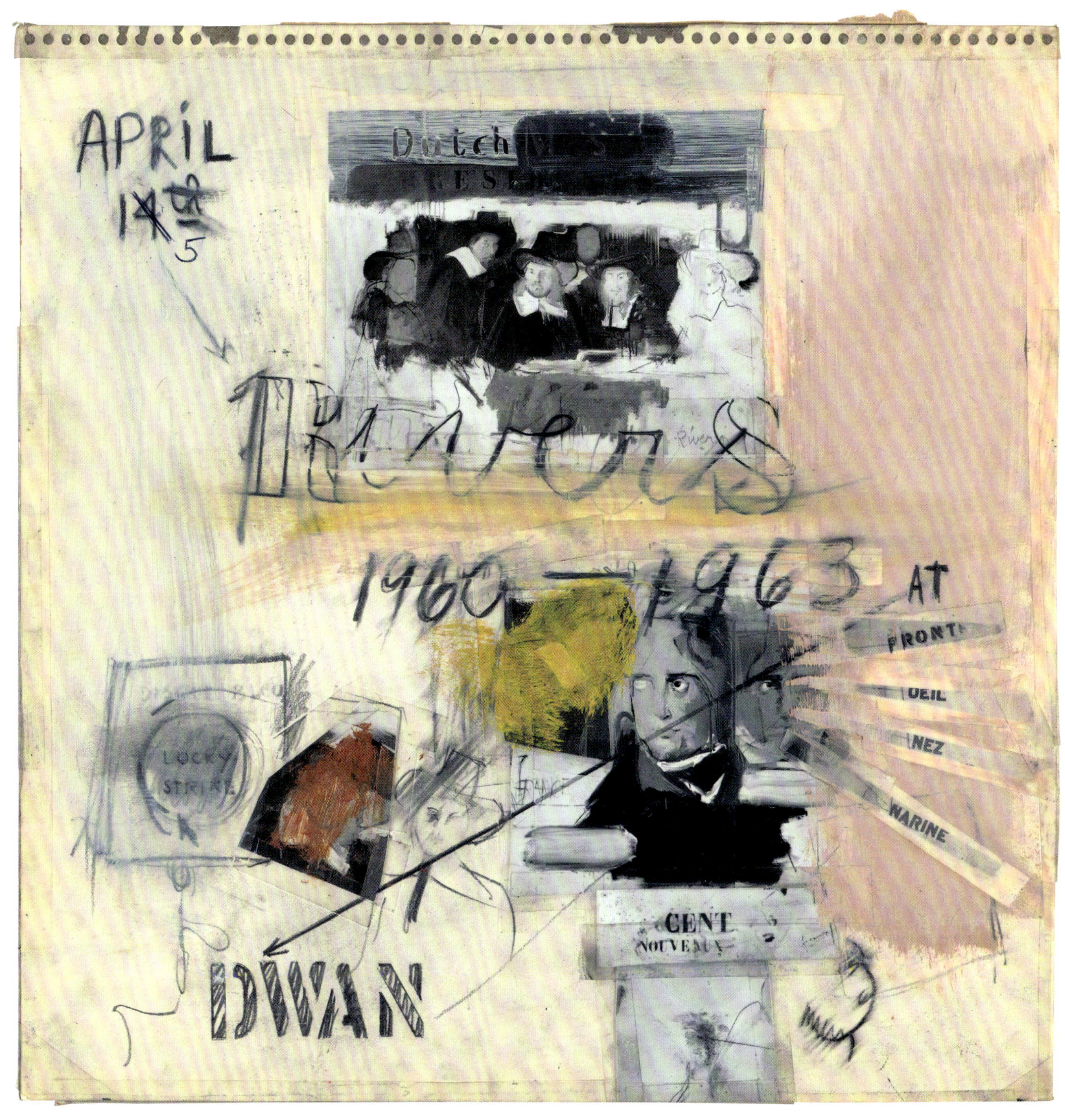
APRIL
Dutch
Rivers
1960 — 1963 AT
FRONT
OEIL
NEZ
LUCKY
STRIKE
CENT
DWAN

CAT. 4

MATSUMI KANEMITSU,
WES HARDIN, 1958

CAT. 5

ROBERT GOODNOUGH,
ABSTRACT NO. 4
"PIPES," 1956

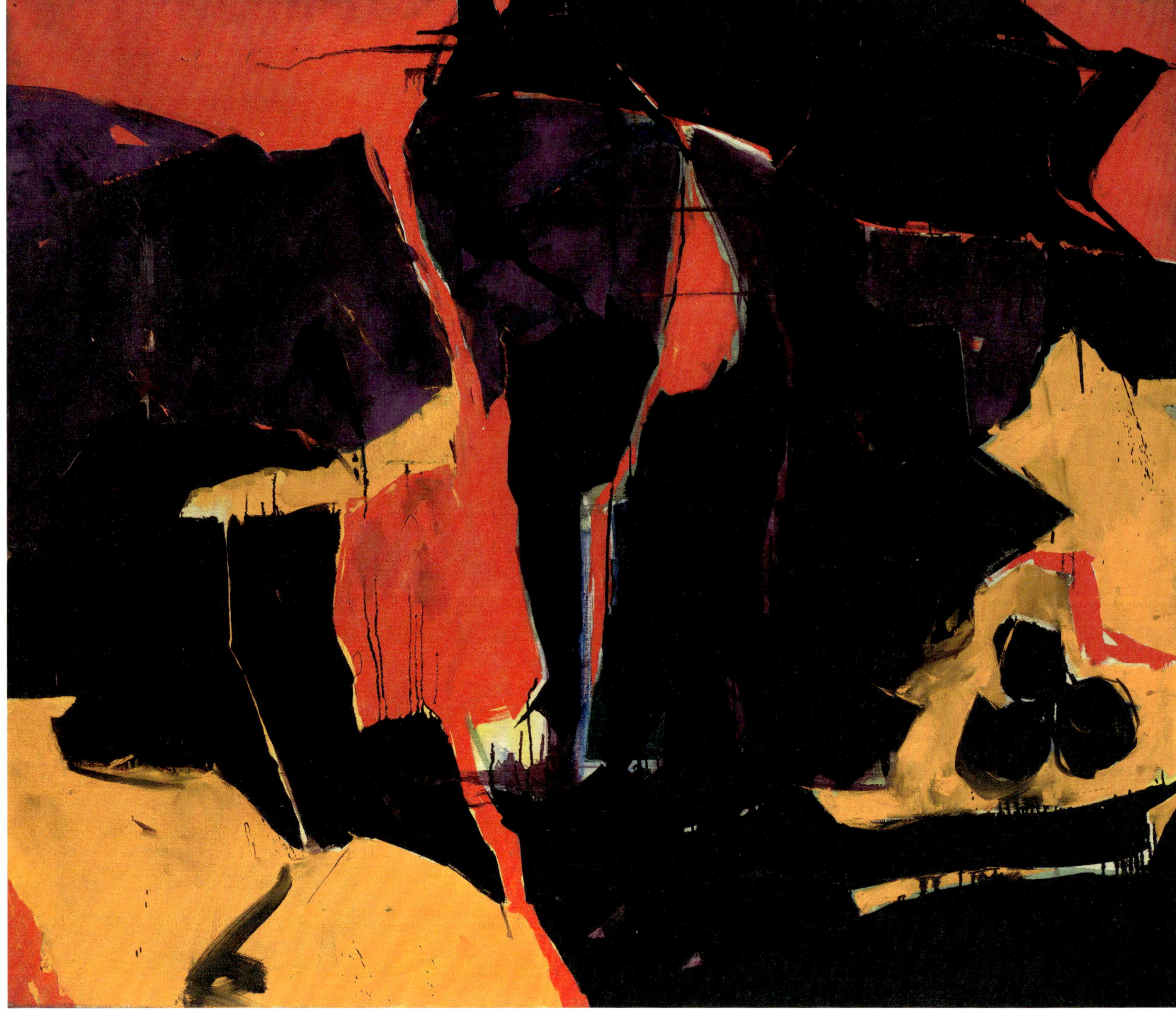

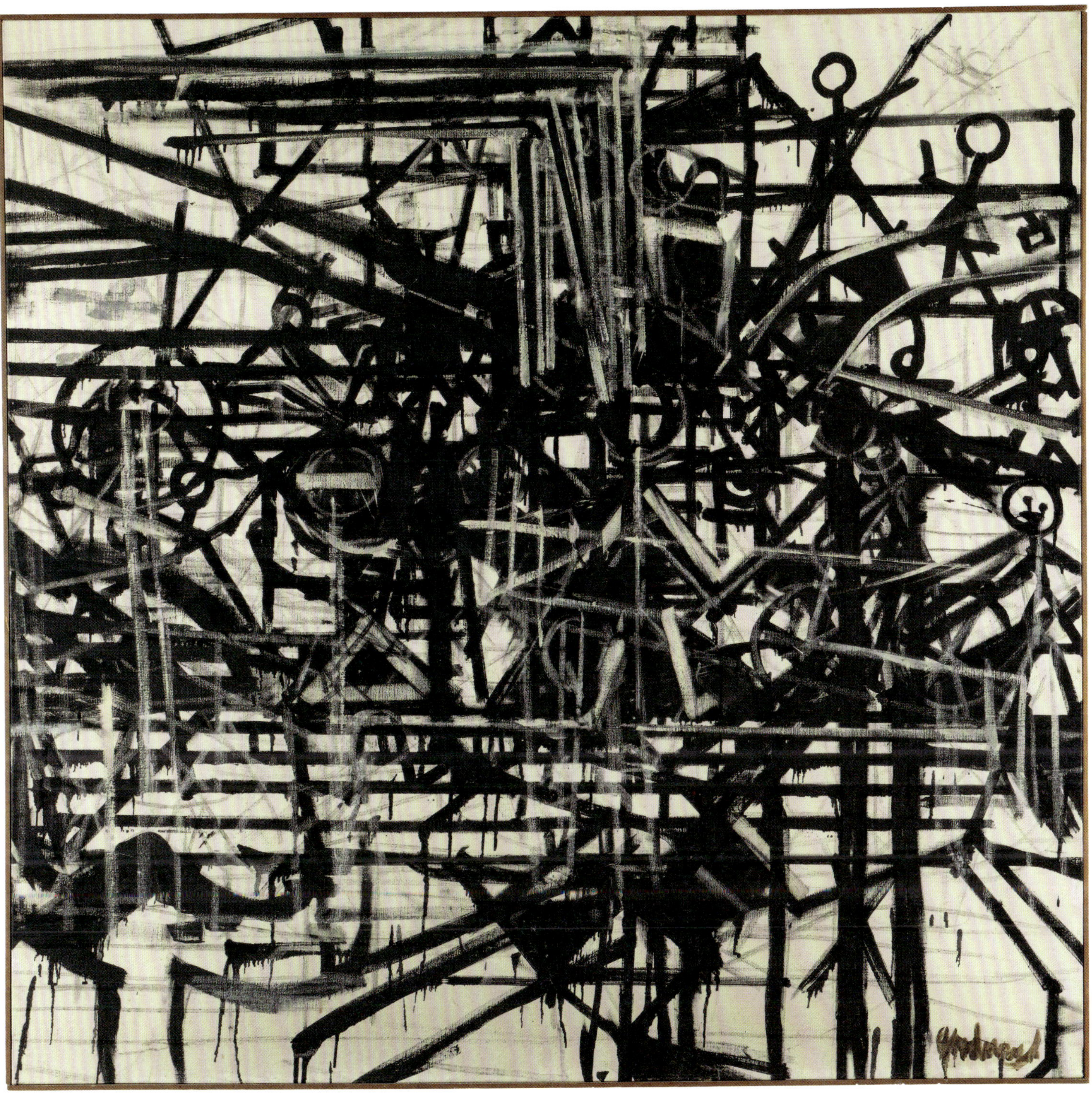

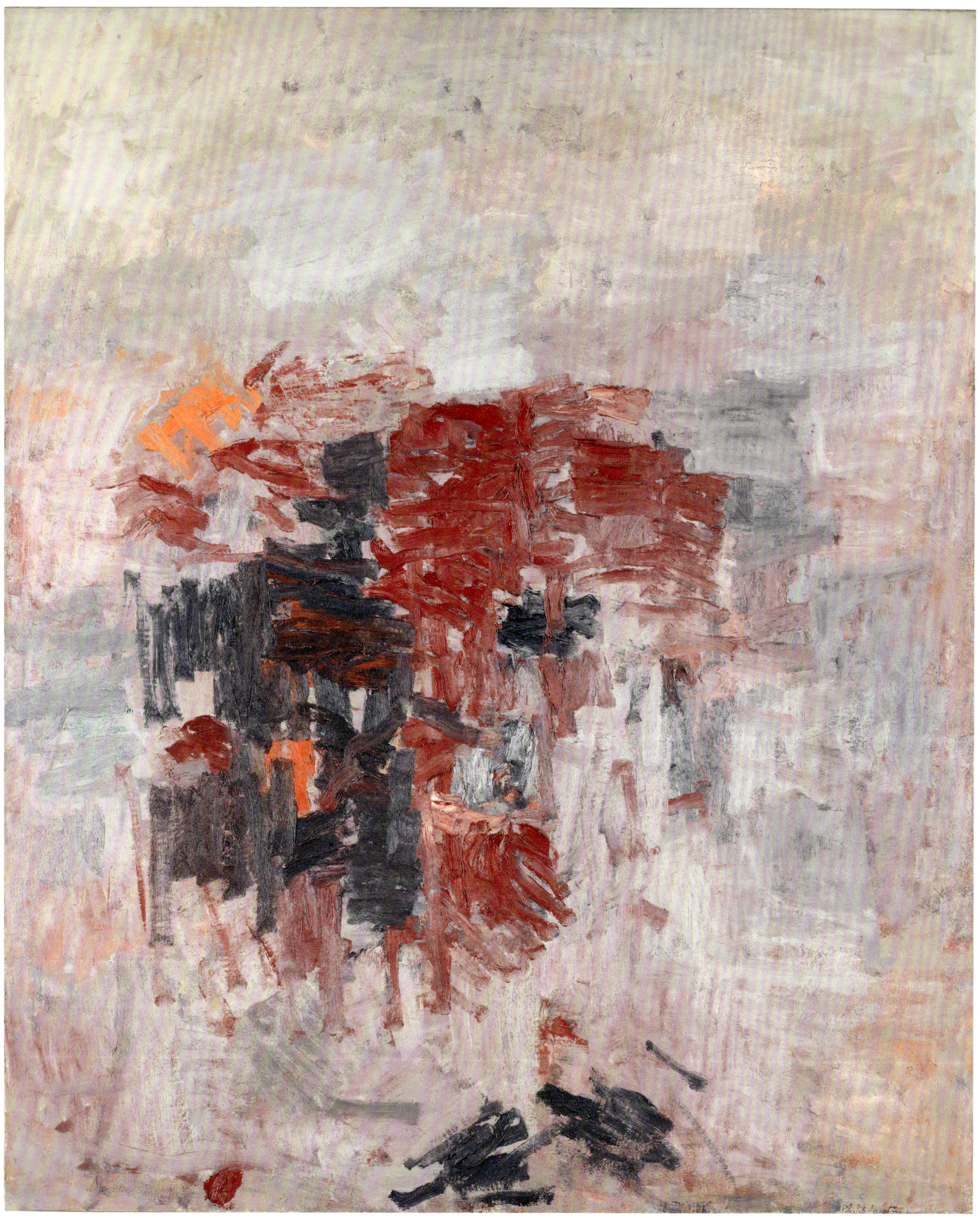

CAT. 6

PHILIP GUSTON,
THE ROOM,
1954–1955

CAT. 7

PHILIP GUSTON,
SLEEPER II,
1959

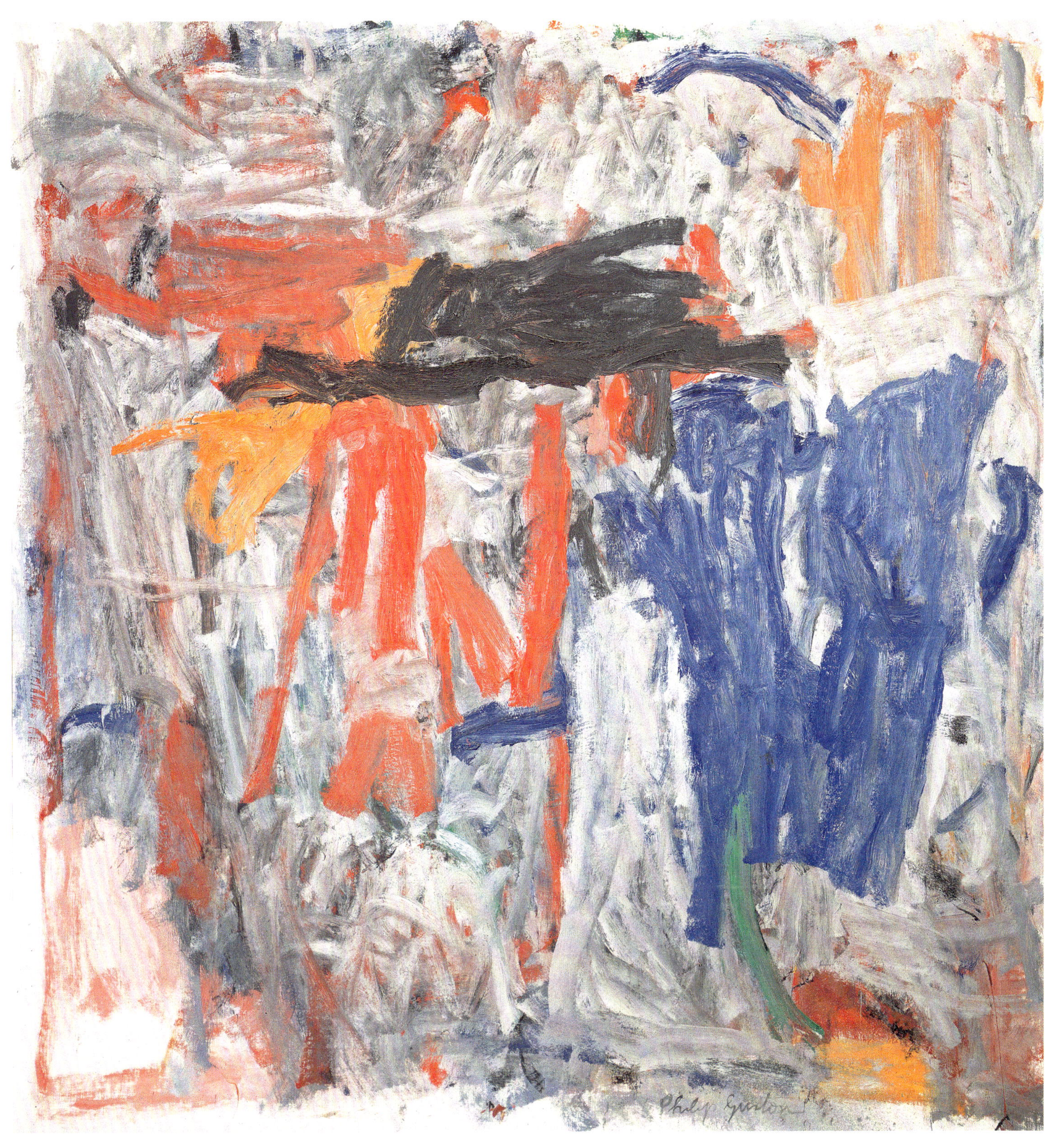

CAT. 10

AD REINHARDT, *ABSTRACT PAINTING (A)*, 1954

CAT. 11

LEE BONTECOU, *UNTITLED*, 1960

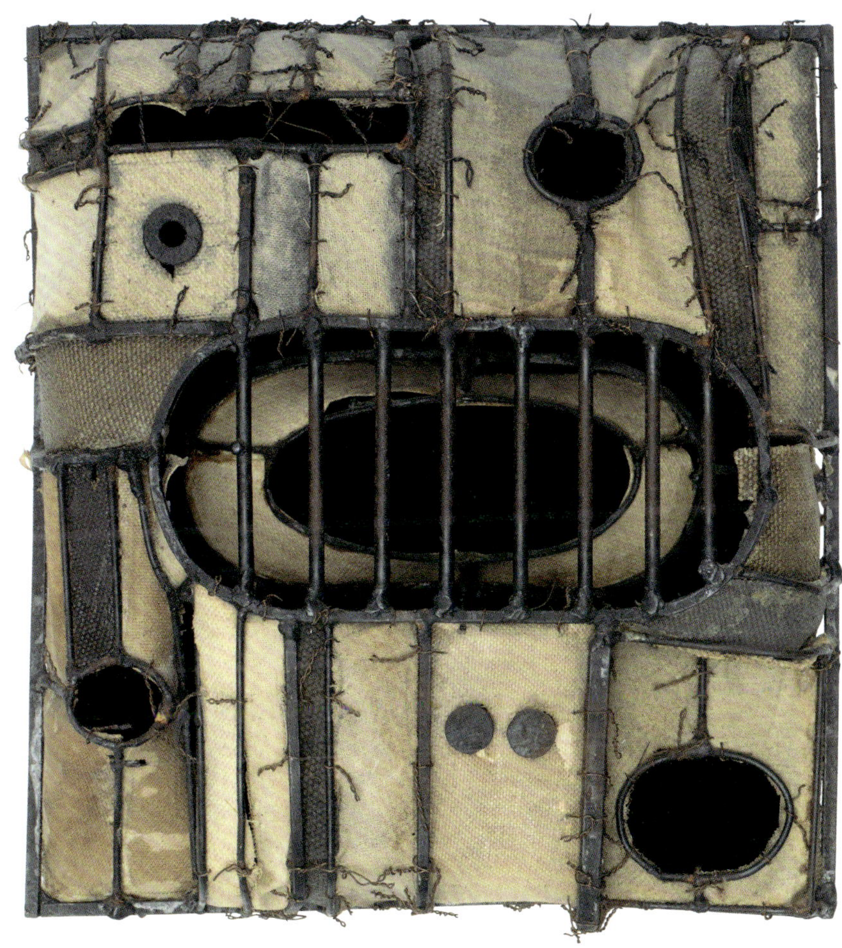

CAT. 12

YVES KLEIN,
UNTITLED BLUE MONOCHROME,
1960

CAT. 13

YVES KLEIN,
UNTITLED PINK MONOCHROME,
1961

CAT. 14

YVES KLEIN, *L'EAU ET LE FEU*, 1961

CAT. 15

YVES KLEIN, *UNTITLED MONO-GOLD*, 1961

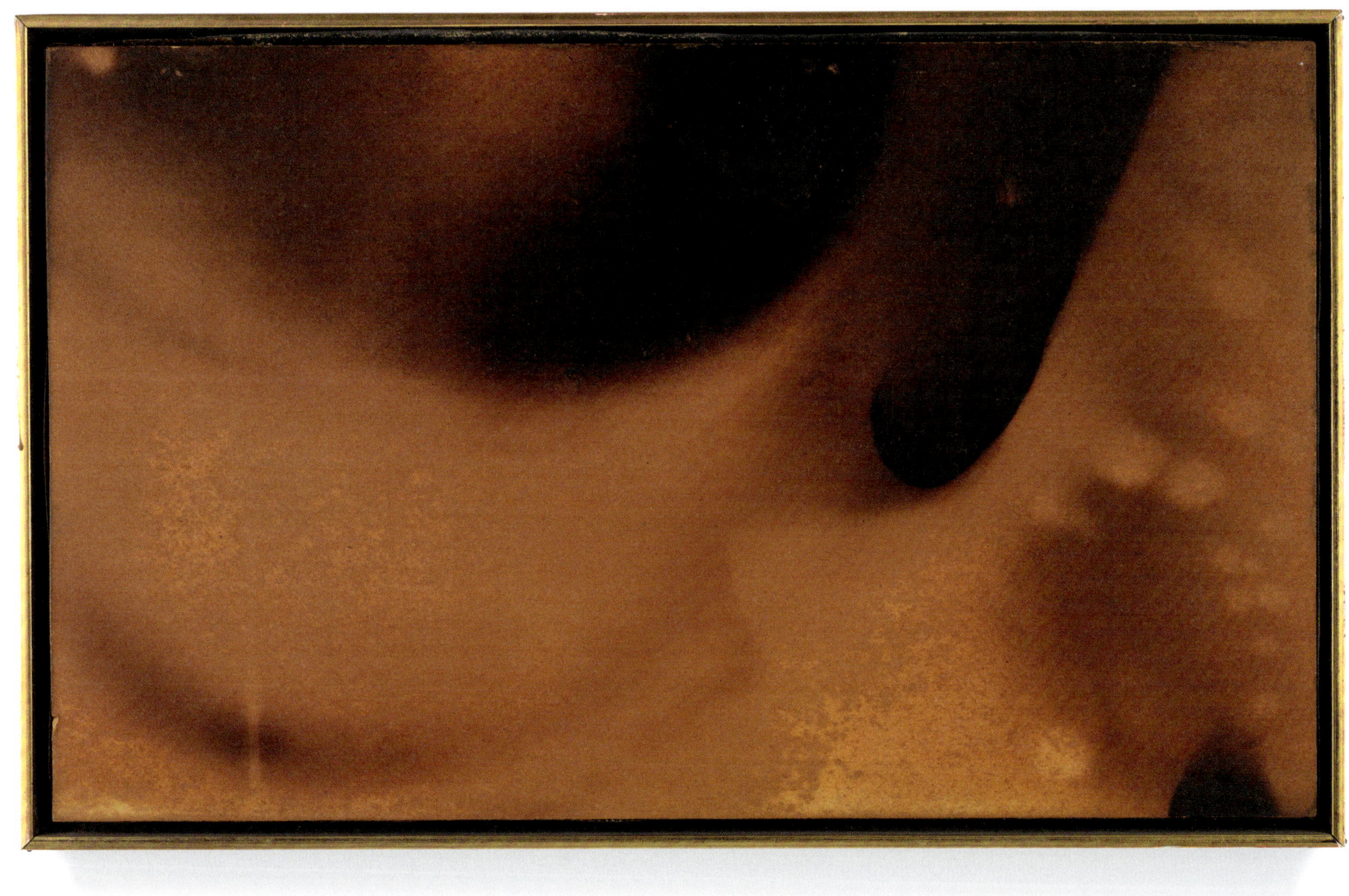

CAT. 16

YVES KLEIN, *TRANSFER OF "ZONE DE SENSIBILITÉ PICTURALE IMMATERIELLE" TO MICHAEL BLANKFORT, PONT AU DOUBLE, PARIS, FEBRUARY 10, 1962*, 1962

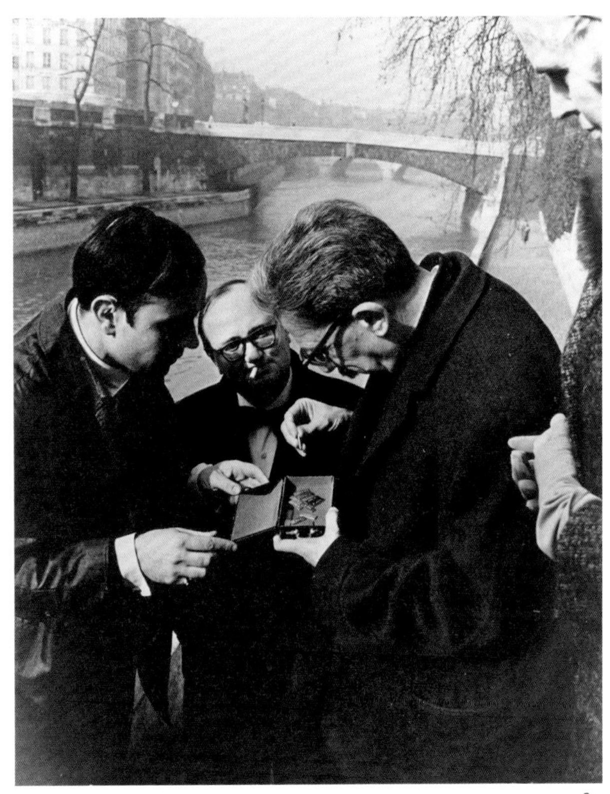

16A

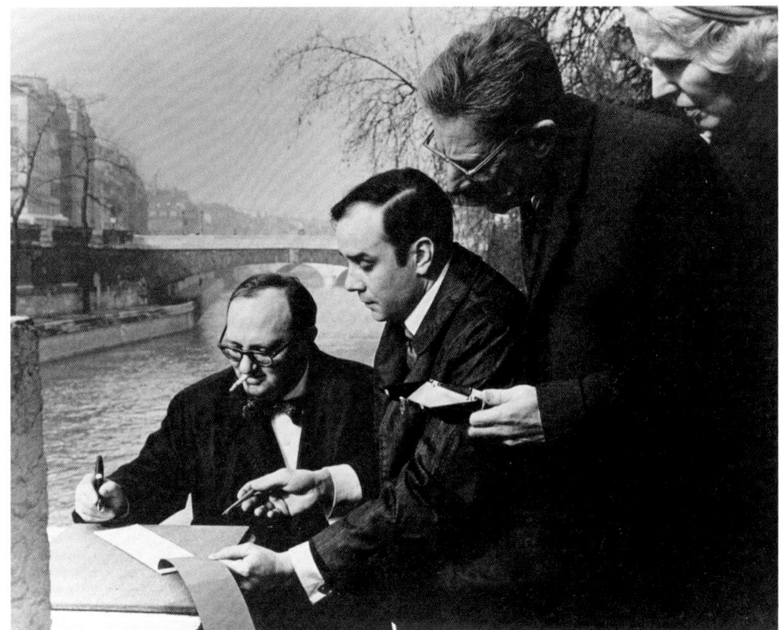

16B

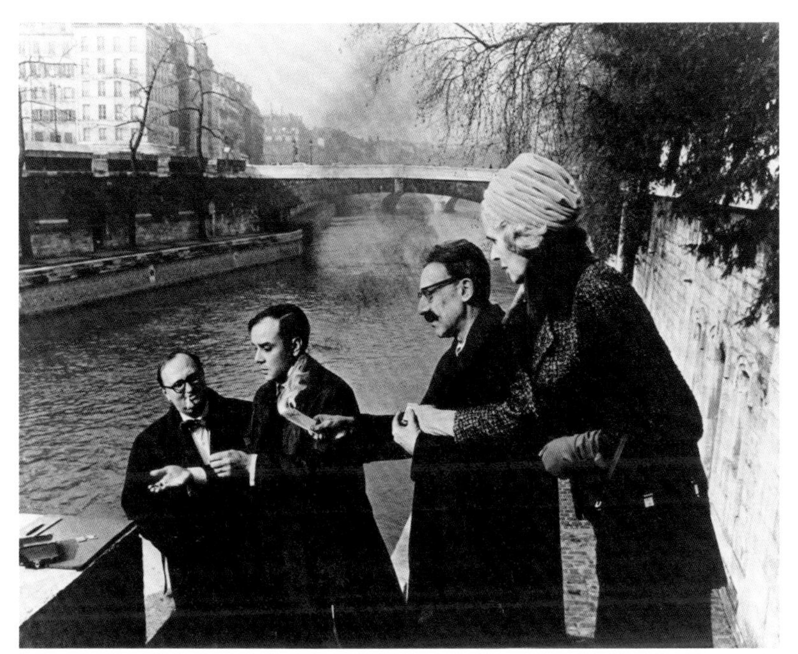

16C

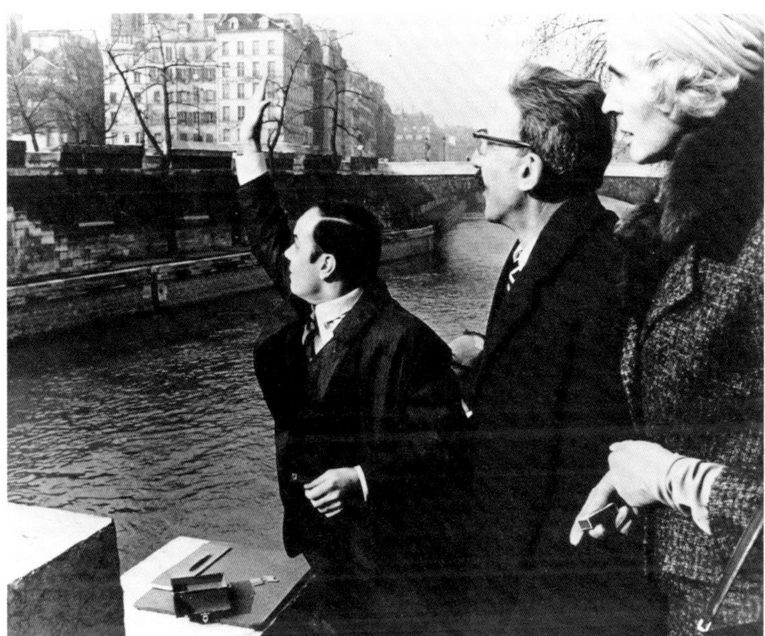

16D

CAT.17

YVES KLEIN,
UNTITLED BLUE MONOCHROME,
1960

CAT. 18

EDWARD KIENHOLZ,
TRAVELING ART SHOW KIT,
1961

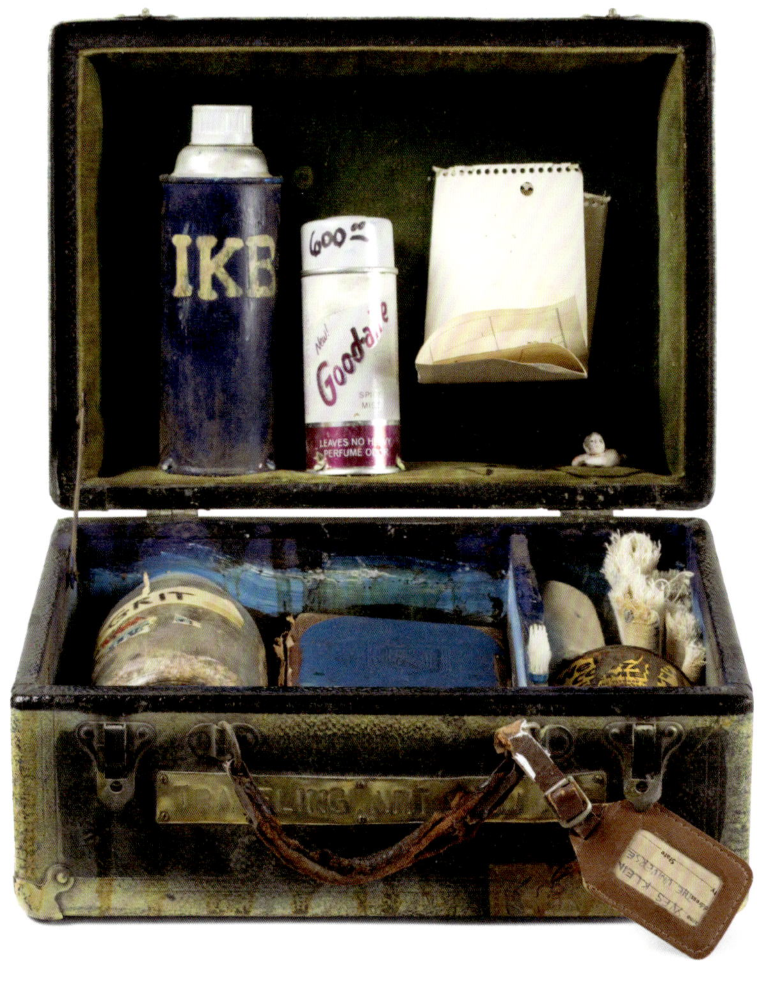

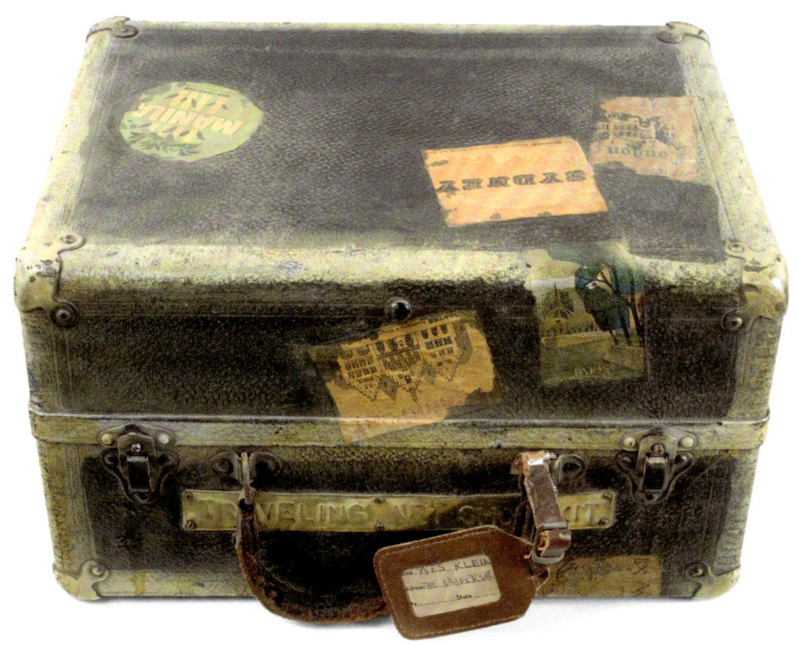

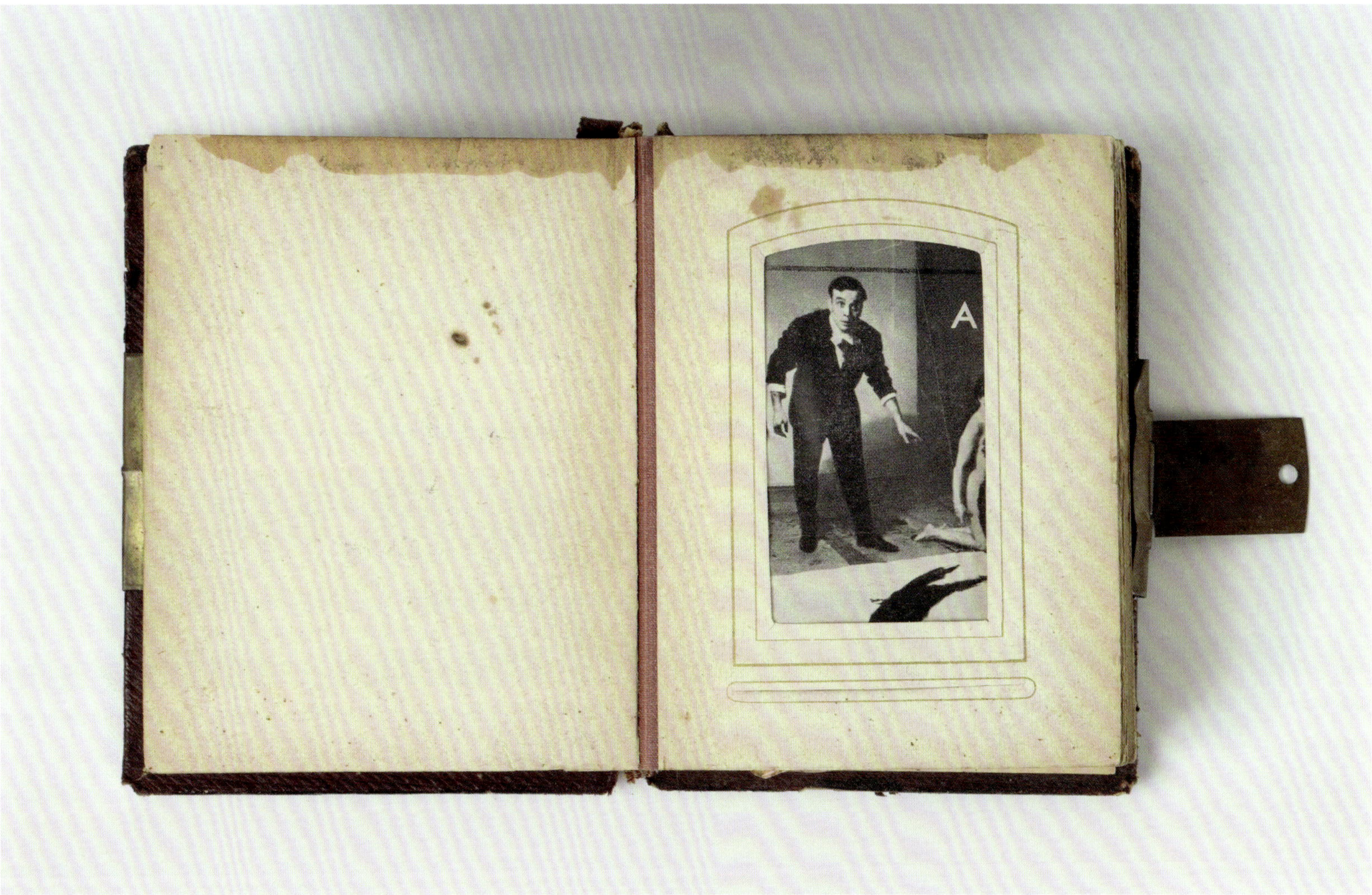

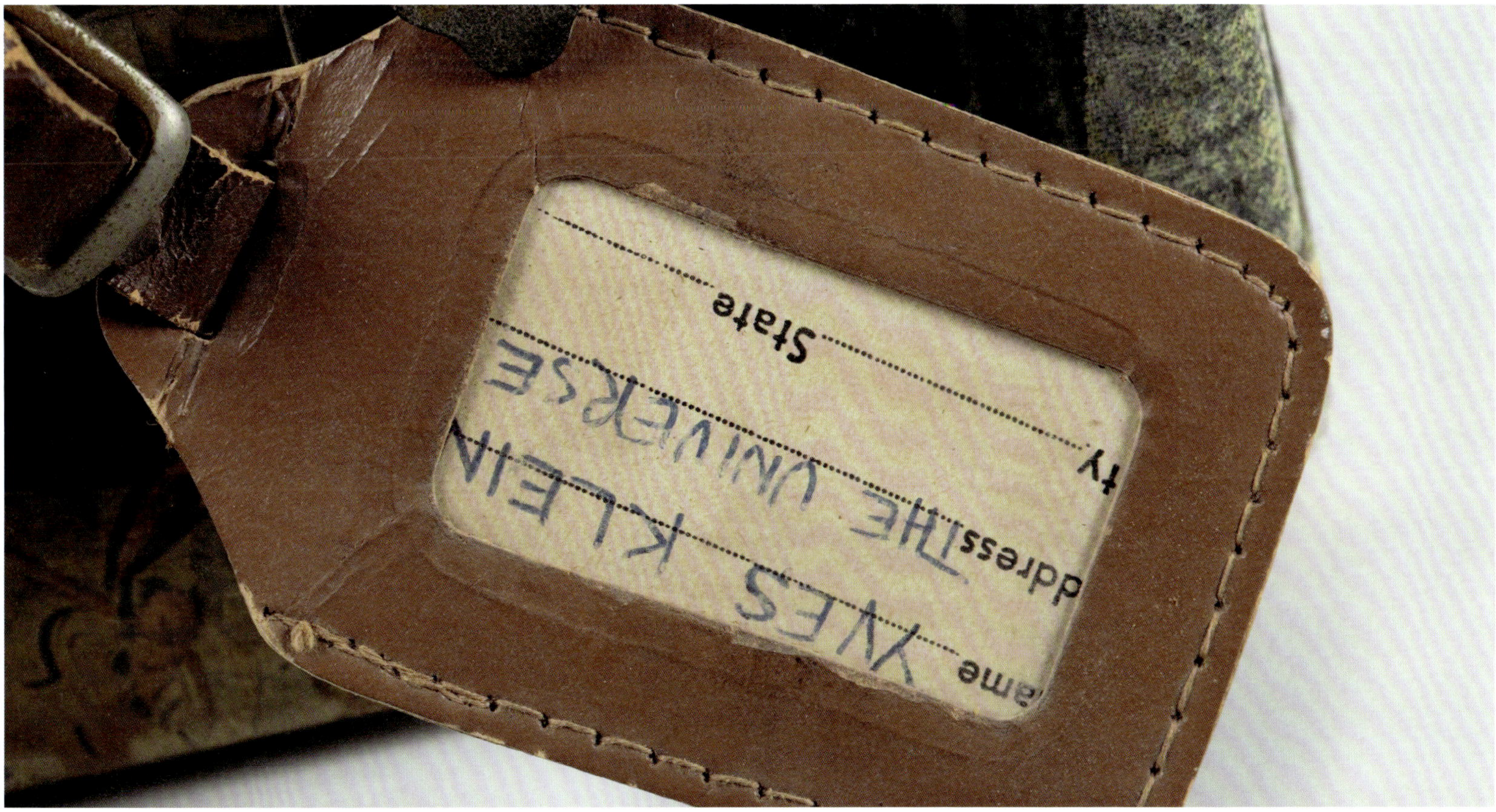

State
THE UNIVERSE
YVES KLEIN

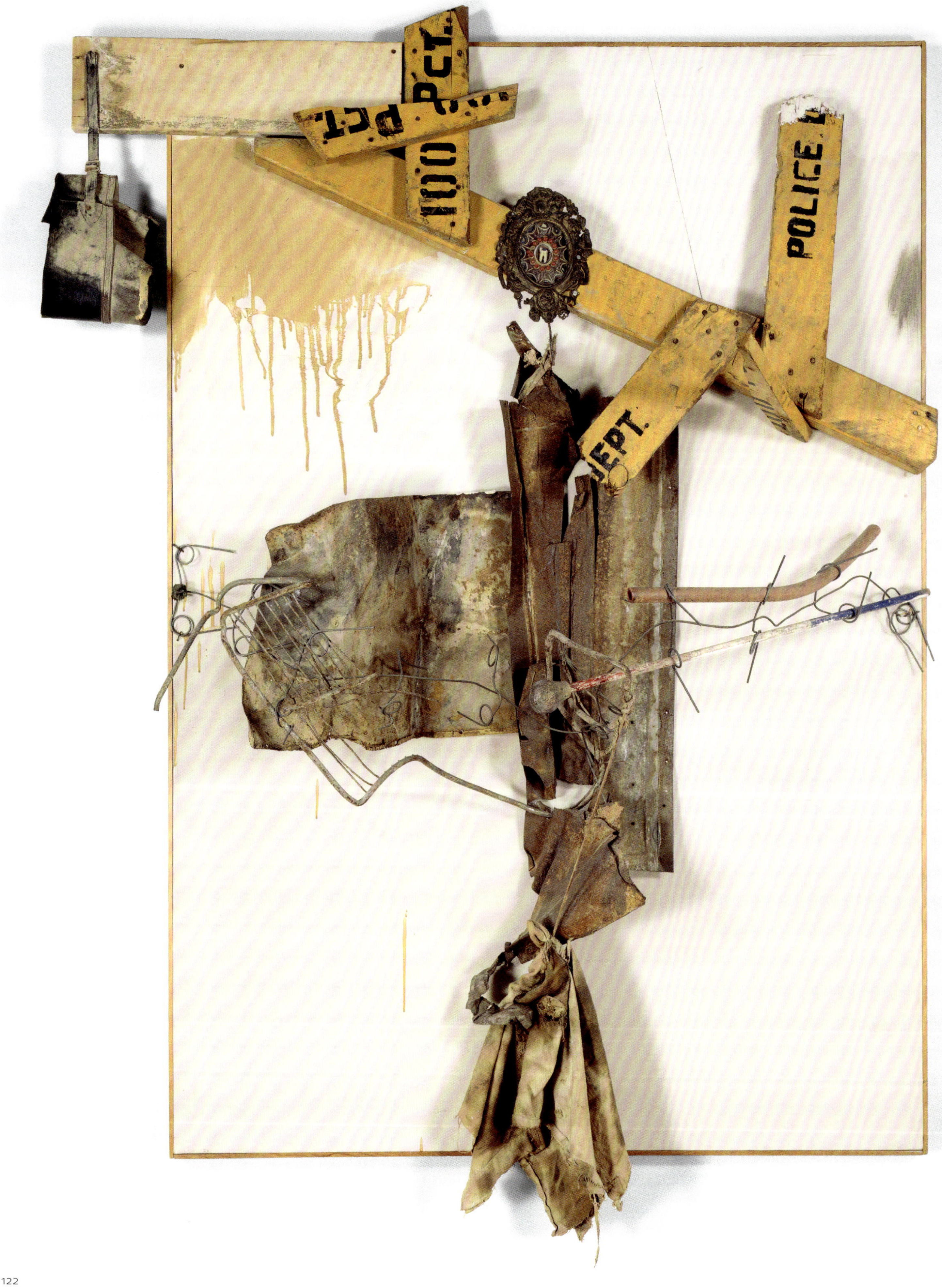
100 PCT.
PCT.
POLICE
DEPT.

CAT. 19

ROBERT RAUSCHENBERG, *COEXISTENCE*, 1961

CAT. 20

ROBERT RAUSCHENBERG, *WOODEN GALLOP*, 1962

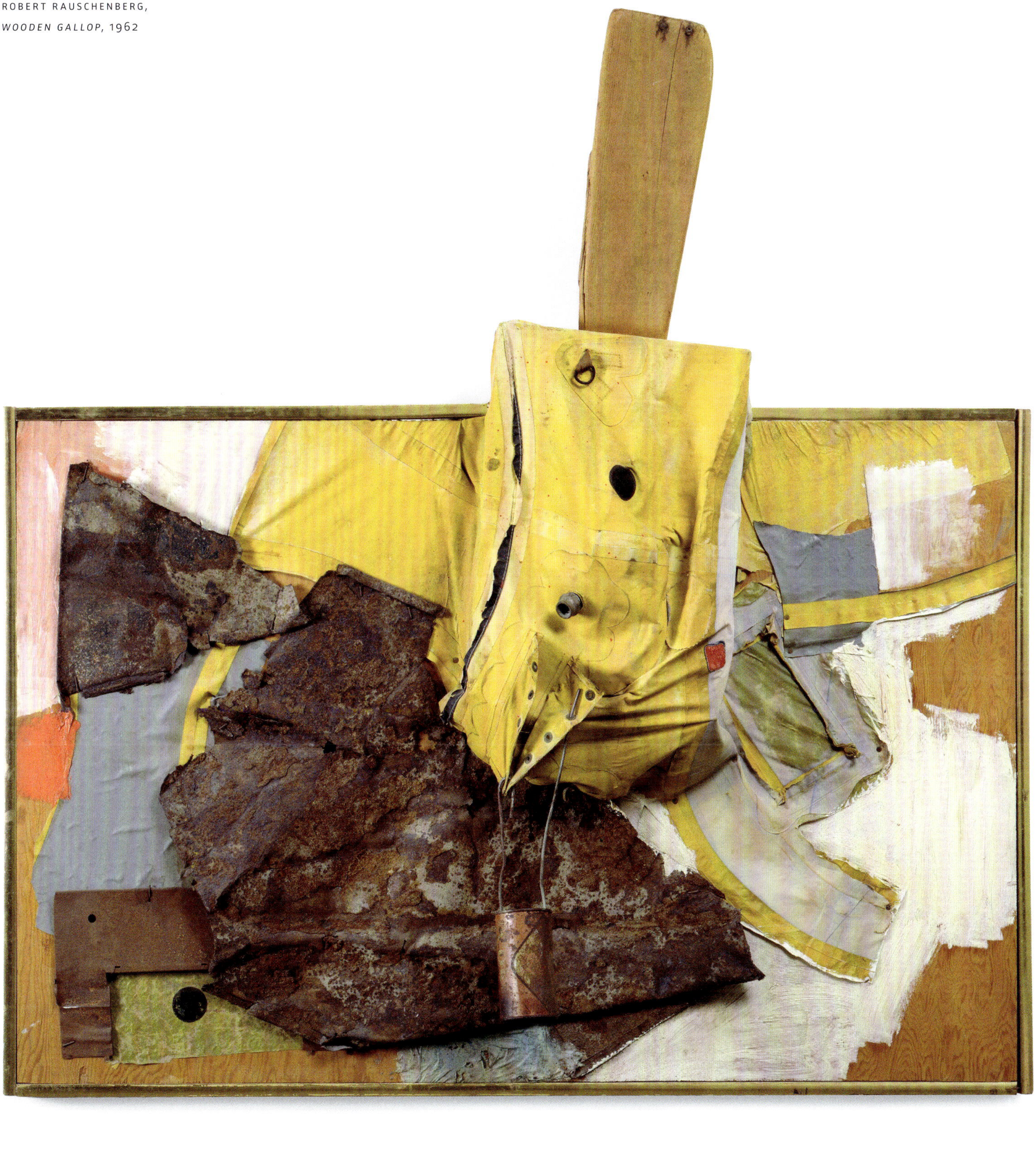

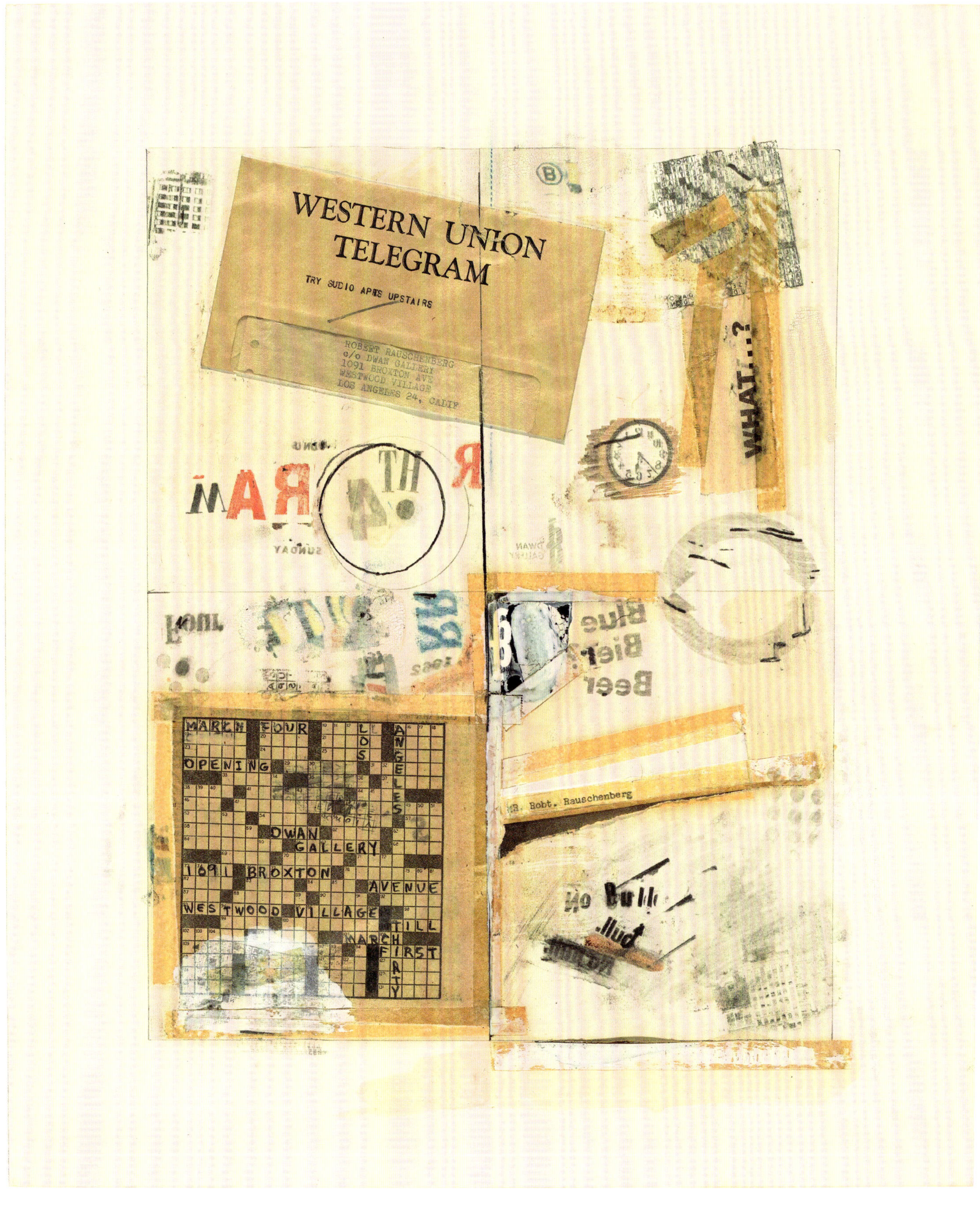
WESTERN UNION
TELEGRAM
TRY SUDIO APTS UPSTAIRS
ROBERT RAUSCHENBERG
c/o DWAN GALLERY
1091 BROXTON AVE
WESTWOOD VILLAGE
LOS ANGELES 24, CALIF
WHAT...?
MARCH FOUR
LOS ANGELES
OPENING
DWAN GALLERY
1091 BROXTON AVENUE
WESTWOOD VILLAGE
TILL
MARCH FIRST
MR. Robt. Rauschenberg

CAT. 21

ROBERT RAUSCHENBERG, *MAQUETTE FOR ROBERT RAUSCHENBERG EXHIBITION AT DWAN GALLERY*, 1962

CAT. 22

ROBERT RAUSCHENBERG, *UNTITLED (FOR VIRGINIA WITH HOOK)*, 1965

CAT. 23 (OVERLEAF)

ARMAN, *ALARM CLOCKS (REVEILS)*, 1960

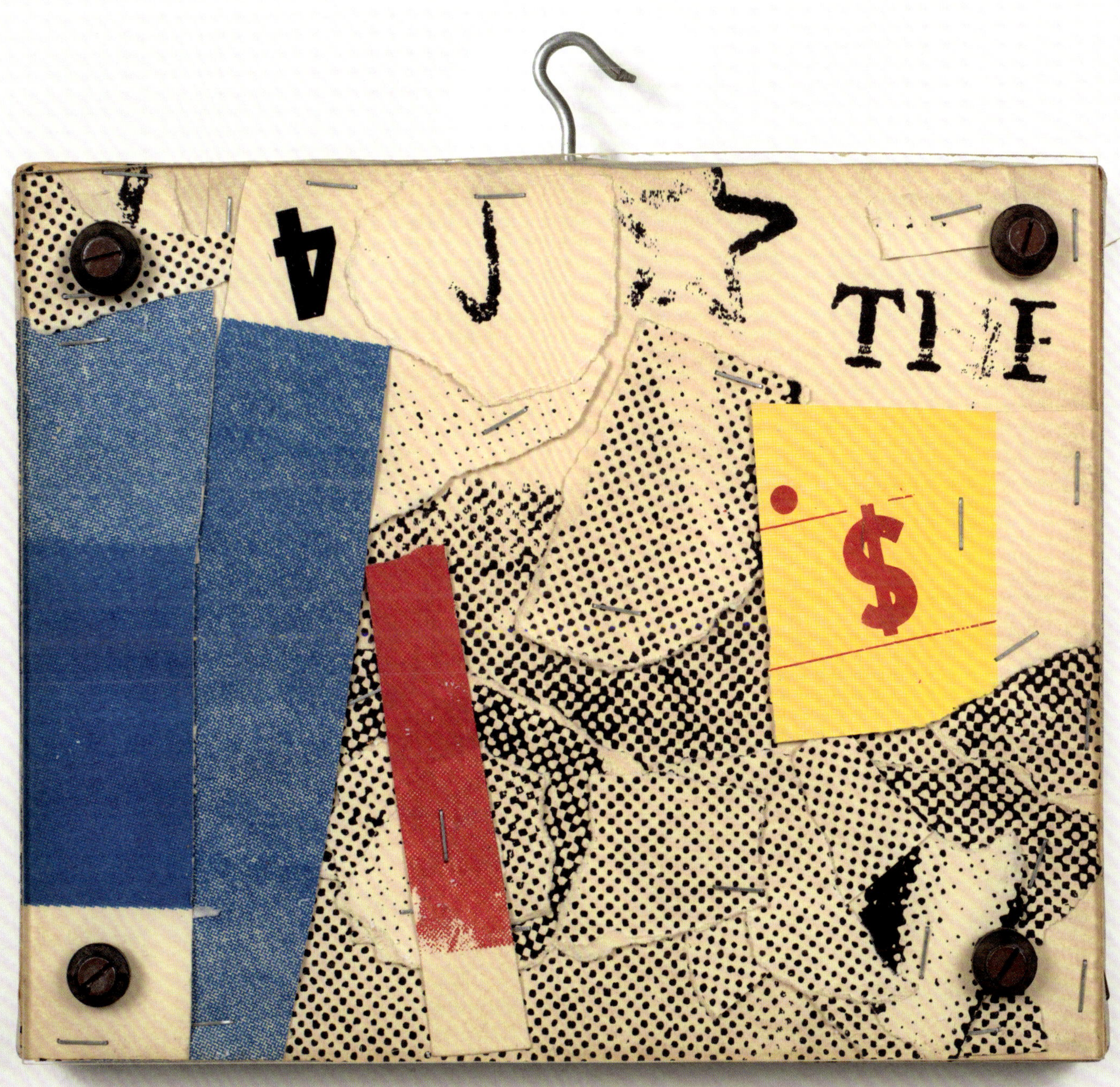

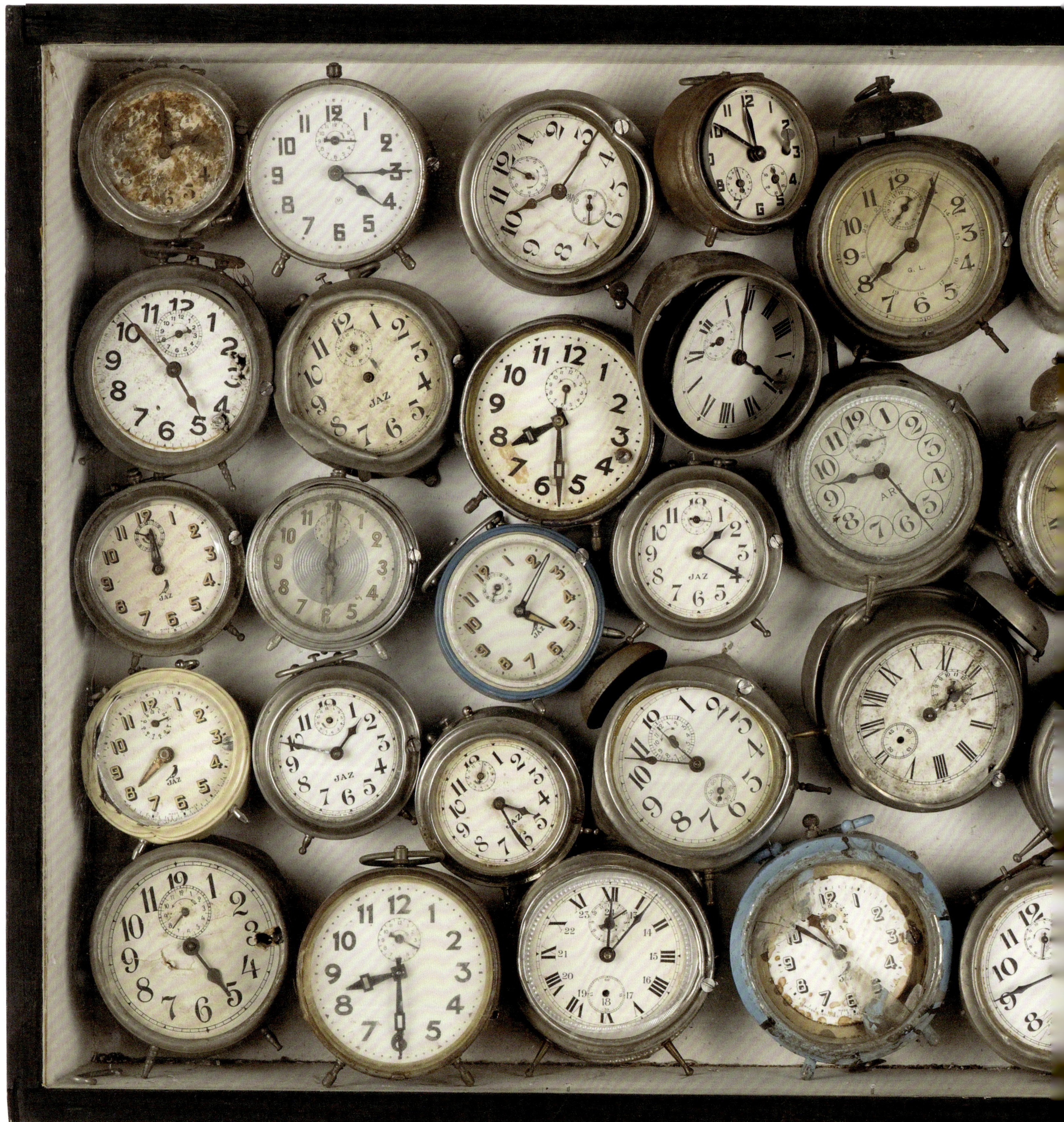

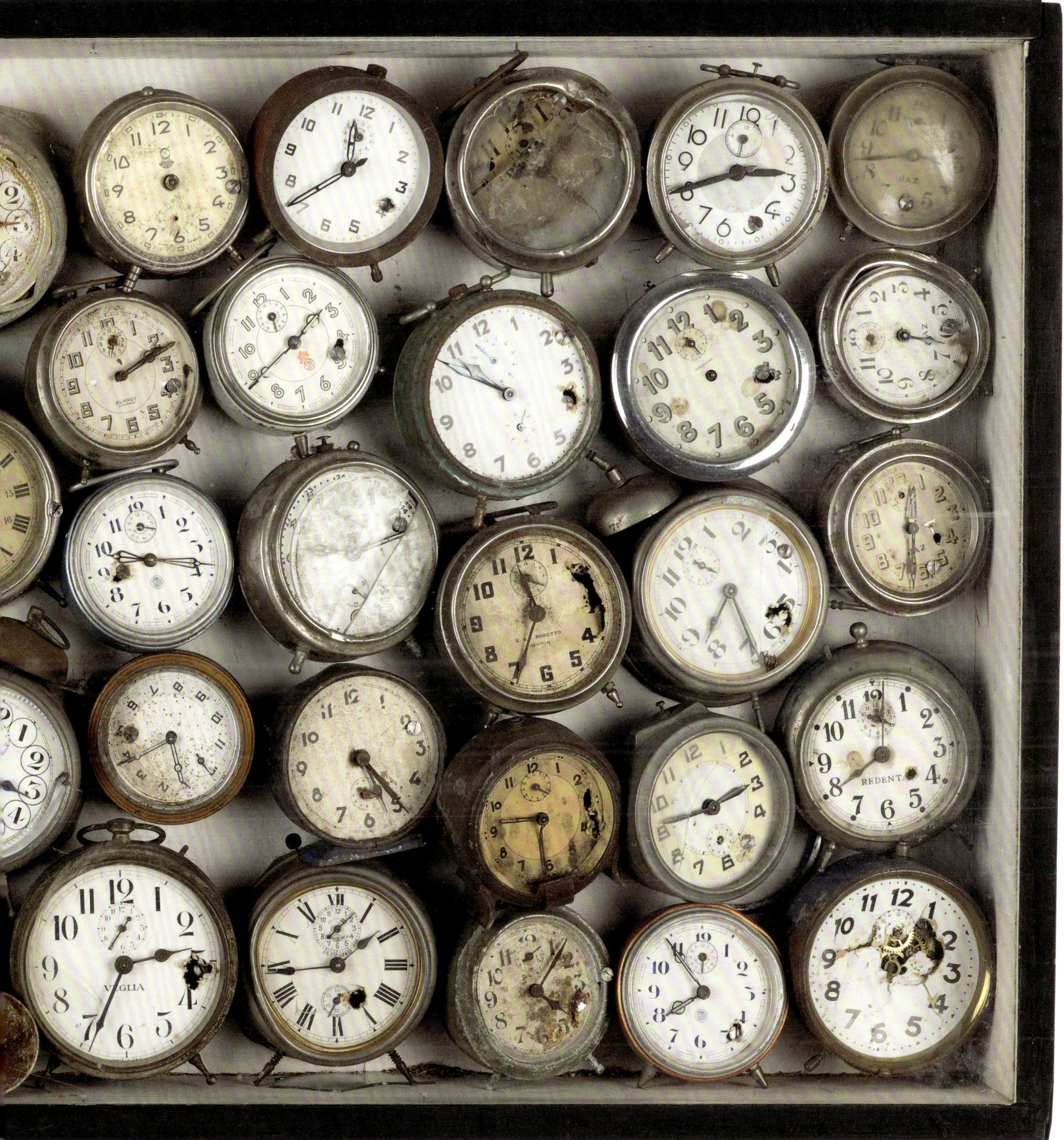
VEGLIA
REDENTA

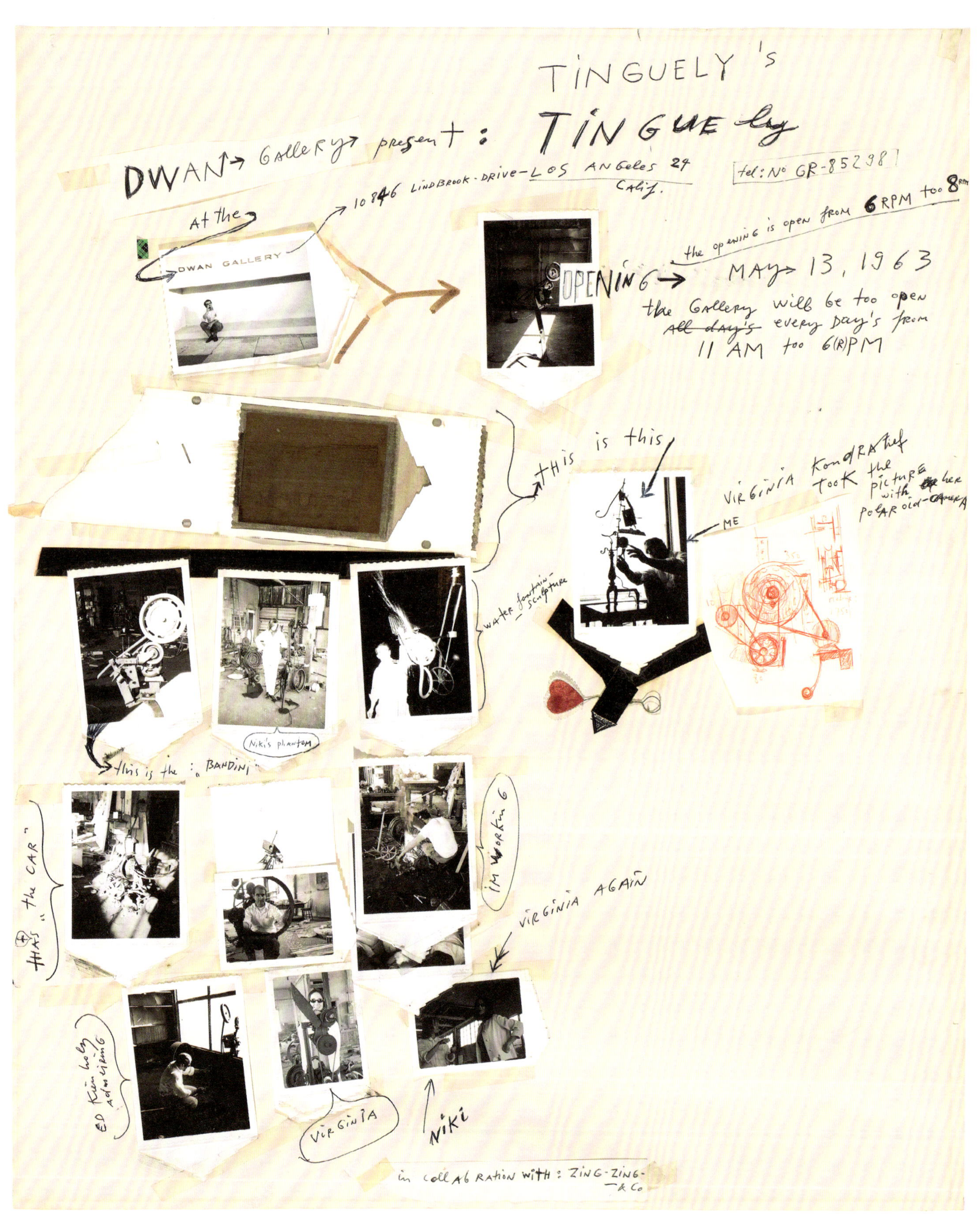

TINGUELY's
DWAN GALLERY present: TINGUELY
1084 6 LINDBROOK-DRIVE-LOS ANGELES 24 Calif.
tel: No GR-85298
At the
DWAN GALLERY
the opening is open from 6 RPM too 8 RPM
OPENING → MAY 13, 1963
the Gallery will be too open every day's from 11 AM too 6(R)PM
this is this
VIRGINIA Kondratief took the picture with her polaroid-camera
ME
water fountain-sculpture
Niki's phantom
this is the : "BANDINI"
HAS "the CAR"
IM WORKING
VIRGINIA AGAIN
ED Kienholz admiring
VIRGINIA
NIKI
in collabration with : ZING-ZING-&Co

CAT. 24

JEAN TINGUELY,
MAQUETTE FOR JEAN TINGUELY EXHIBITION AT DWAN GALLERY,
1963

CAT. 25

JEAN TINGUELY,
ODESSA, 1963

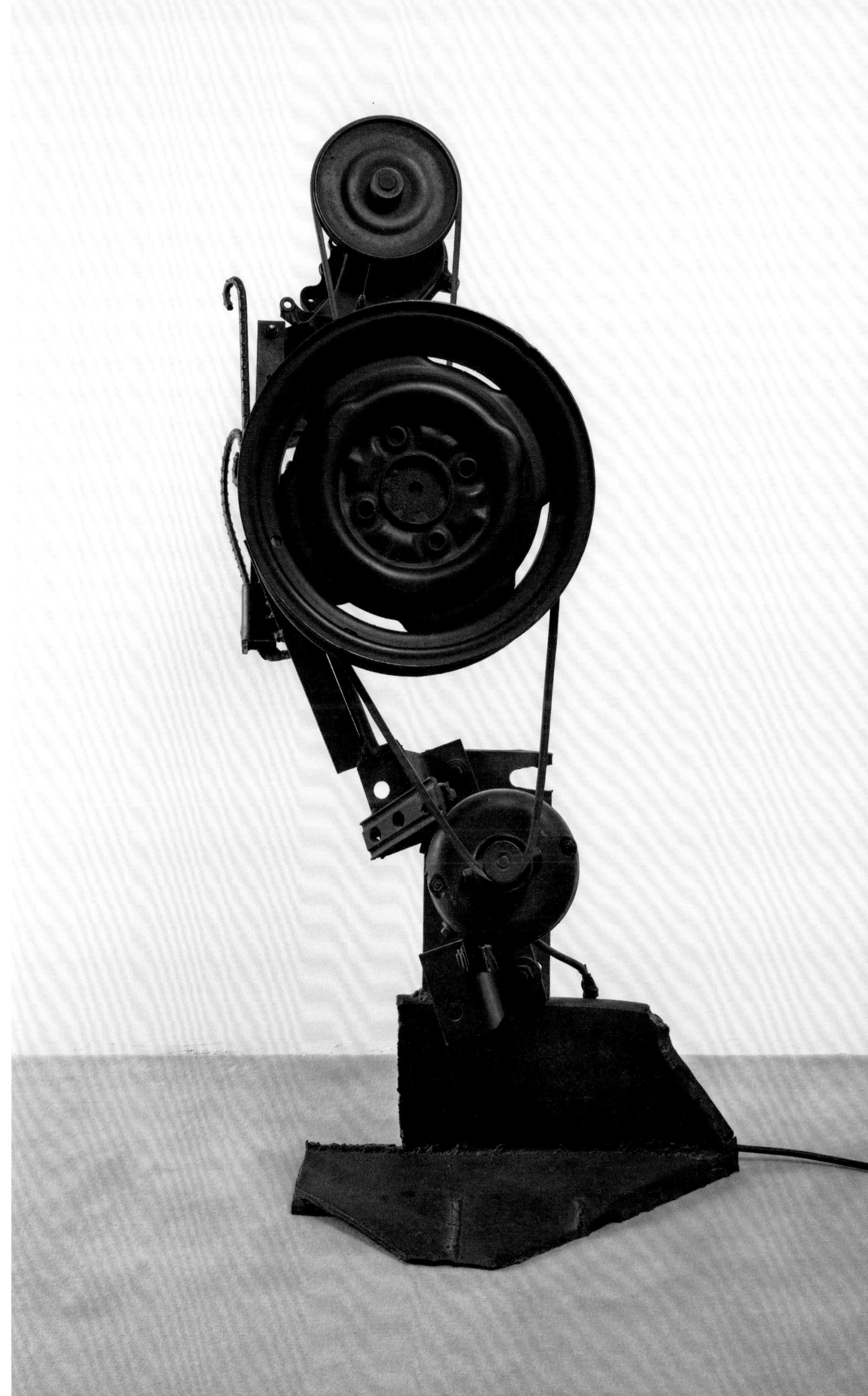

CAT. 26

JEAN TINGUELY, *PORTRAIT OF VIRGINIA*, 1963

CAT. 27

JEAN TINGUELY, *UNTITLED (MOTOR SCULPTURE)*, 1963

CAT. 28

JEAN TINGUELY, *UNTITLED (MOTOR SCULPTURE)*, 1963

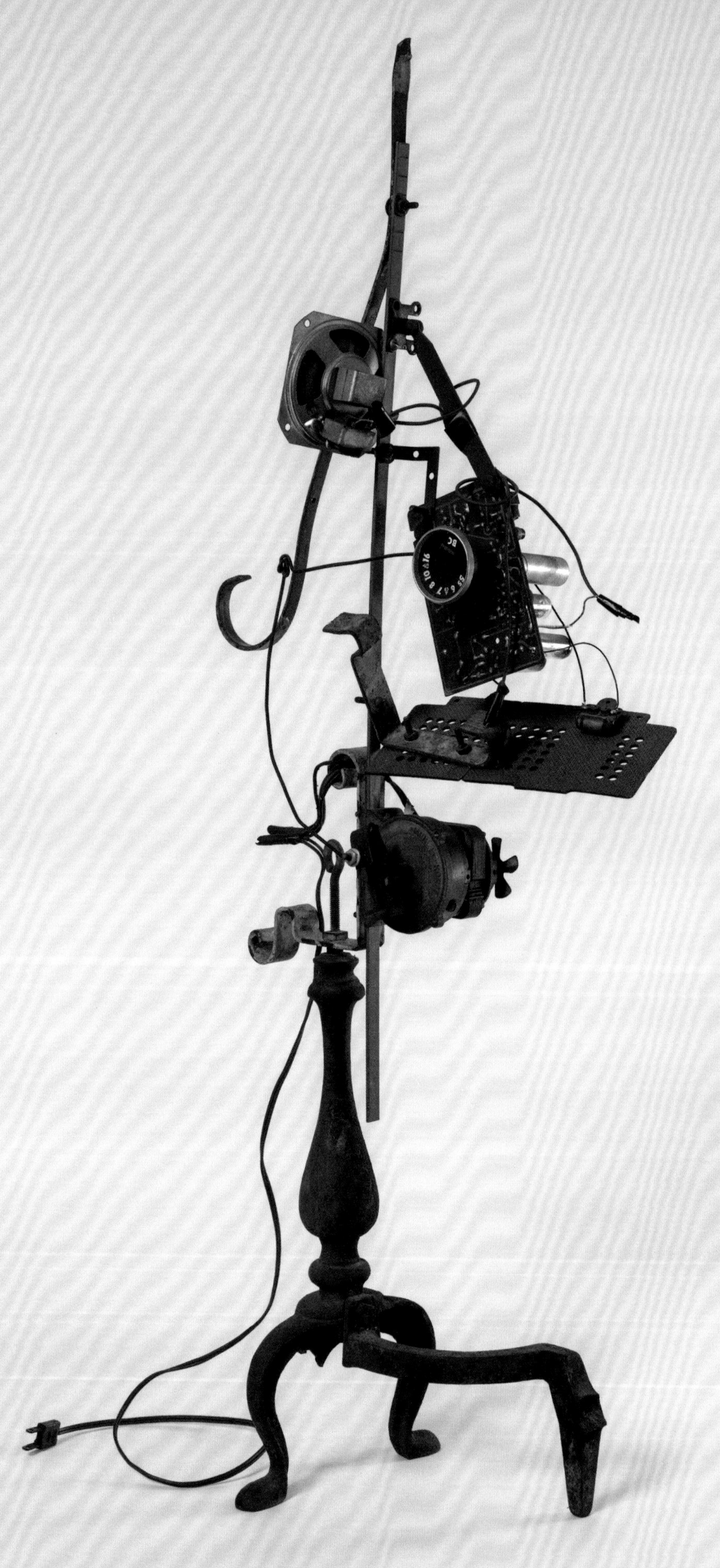

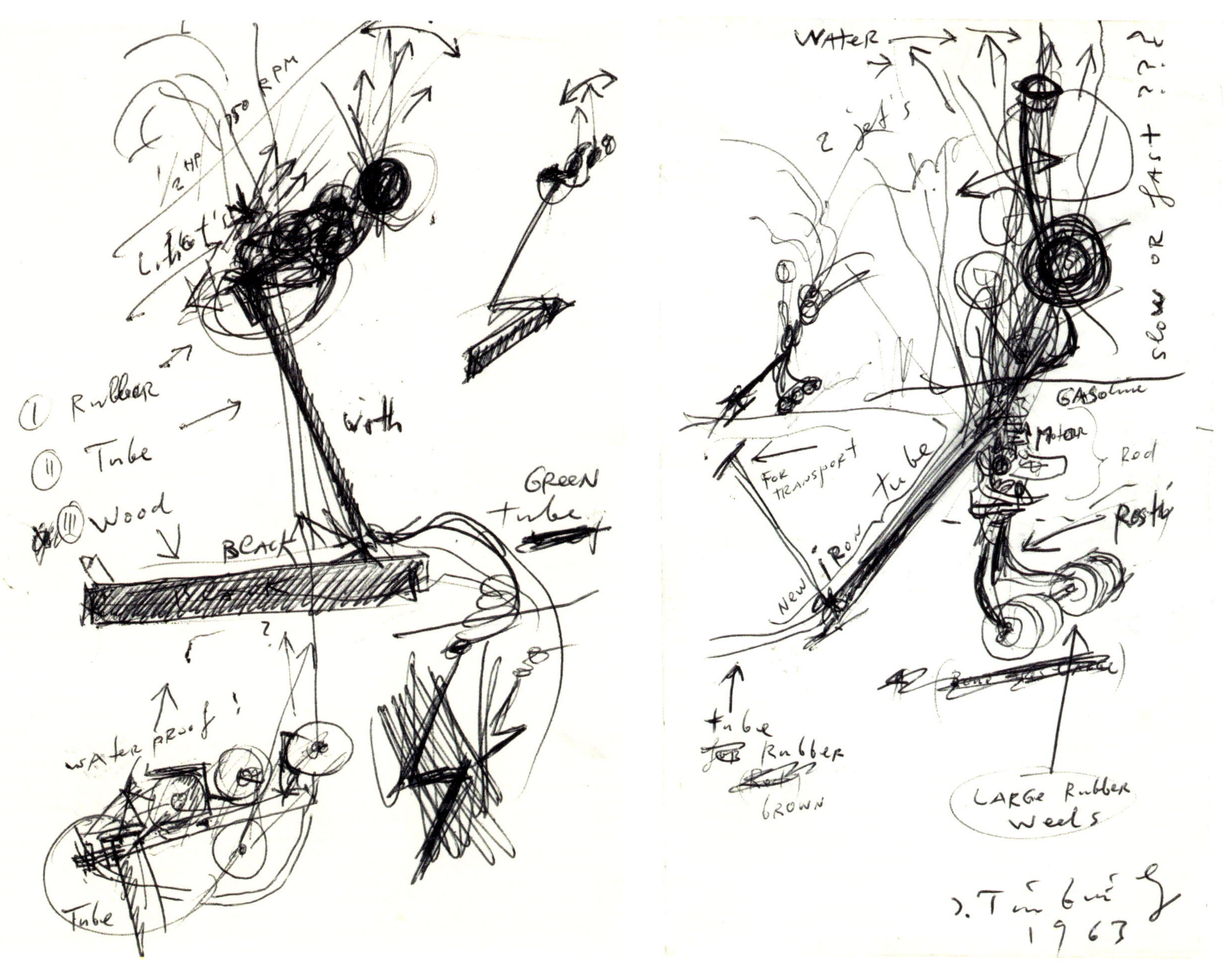

1/2 HP
RPM
I Rubber
II Tube
III Wood
with
BLACK
GREEN
tube
water proof !
Tube
WATER
2 jet's
slow OR fast ??
GASoline
Motor
Rod
Rest
FOR TRANSPORT
tube
New iron
tube
Rubber
BROWN
LARGE Rubber Weels
J. Tinguely
1963

CAT. 29

JEAN TINGUELY WITH NIKI DE SAINT PHALLE, *DEAR VIRGINIA: À BIENTÔT*, UNDATED

CAT. 30

JEAN TINGUELY WITH NIKI DE SAINT PHALLE, *CHÈRE VIRGINIA: COME STA?*, OCTOBER 3, 1978

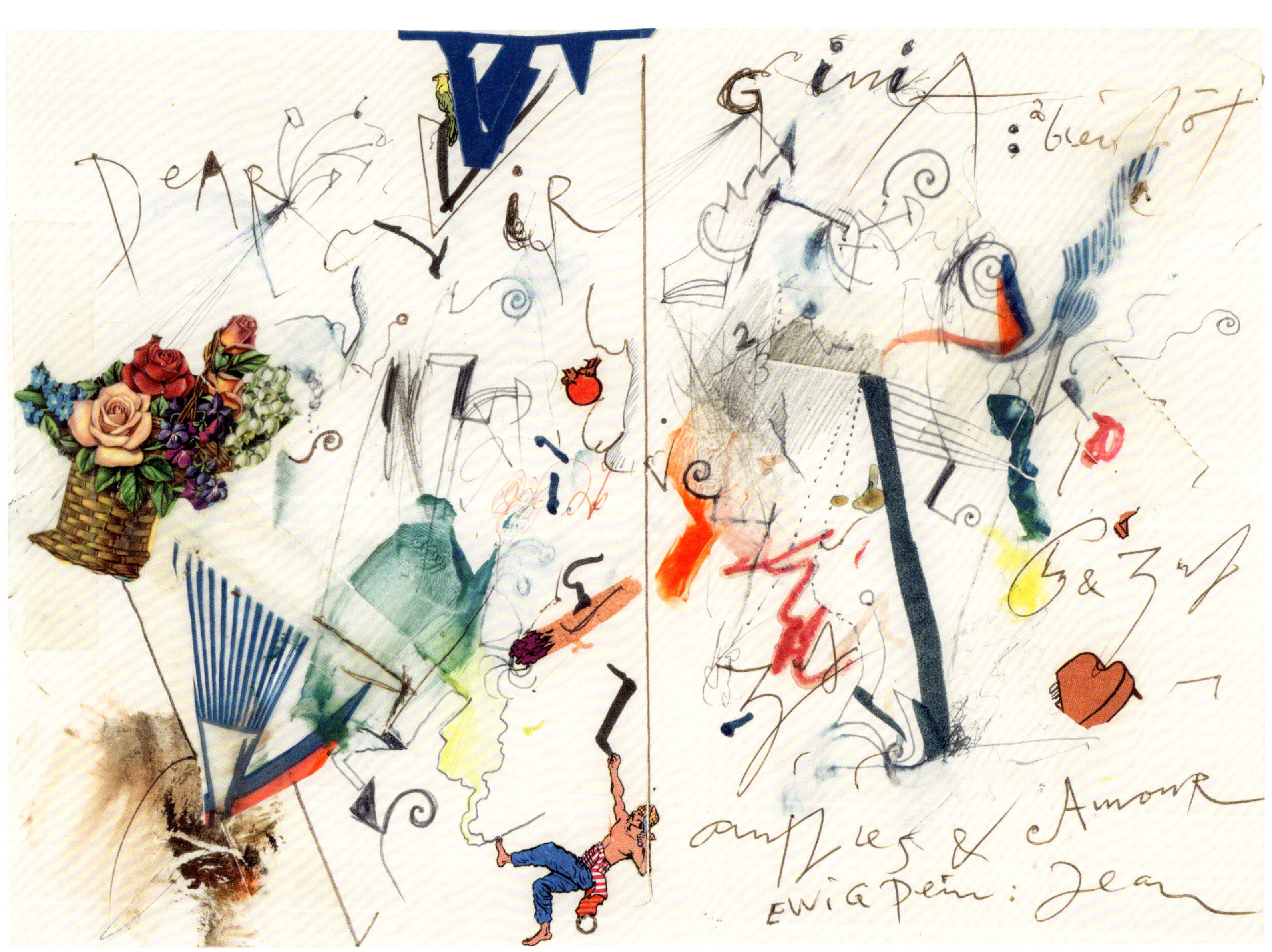

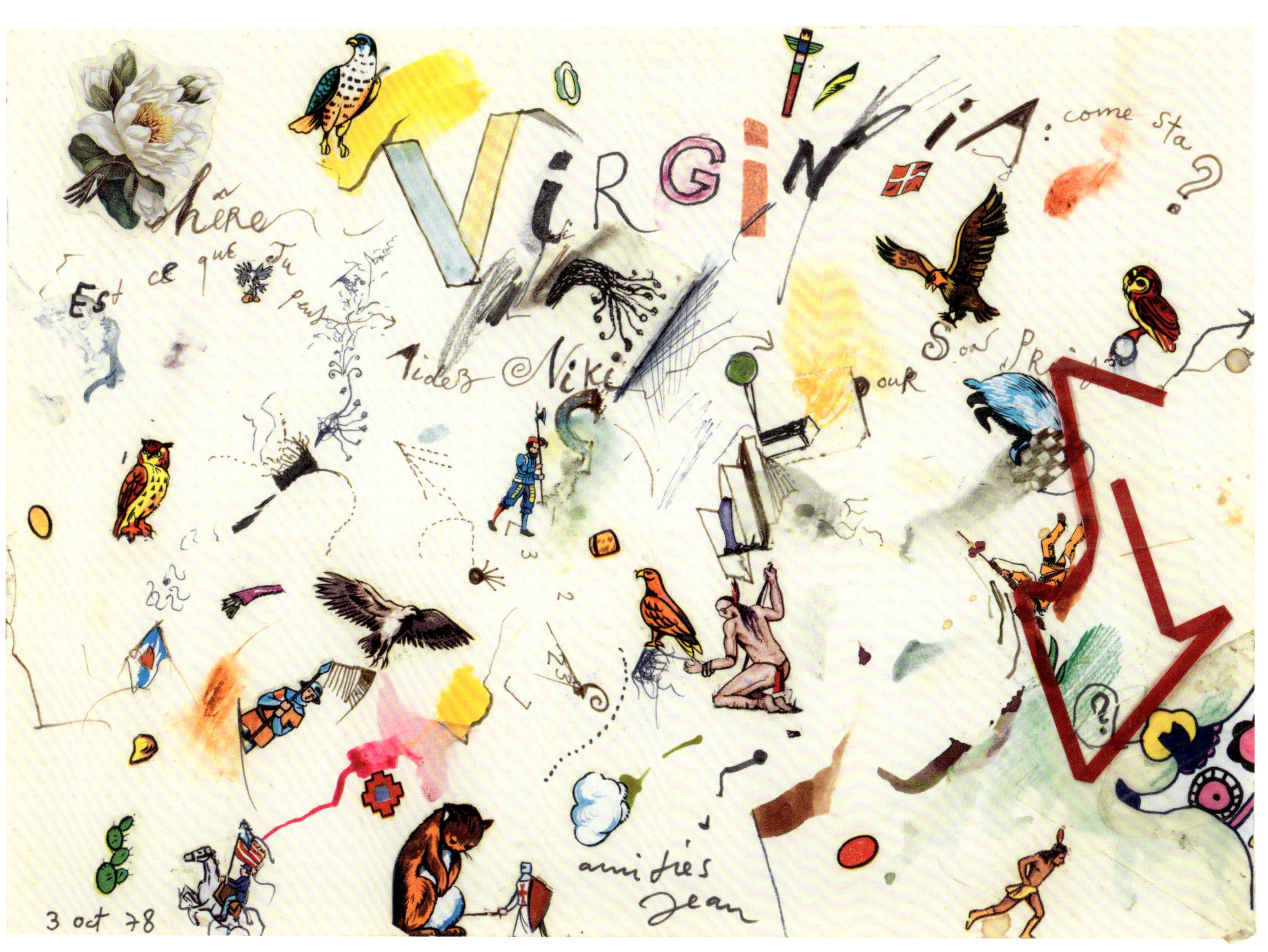
chère
VIRGINIA : come sta ?
Est ce que tu peut
Aidez Niki
pour
amitiés
Jean
3 oct 78

CAT. 31

NIKI DE SAINT PHALLE, *TYRANNOUSAURUS REX ETRANGLÉ PAR UN COBRA*, C. 1963

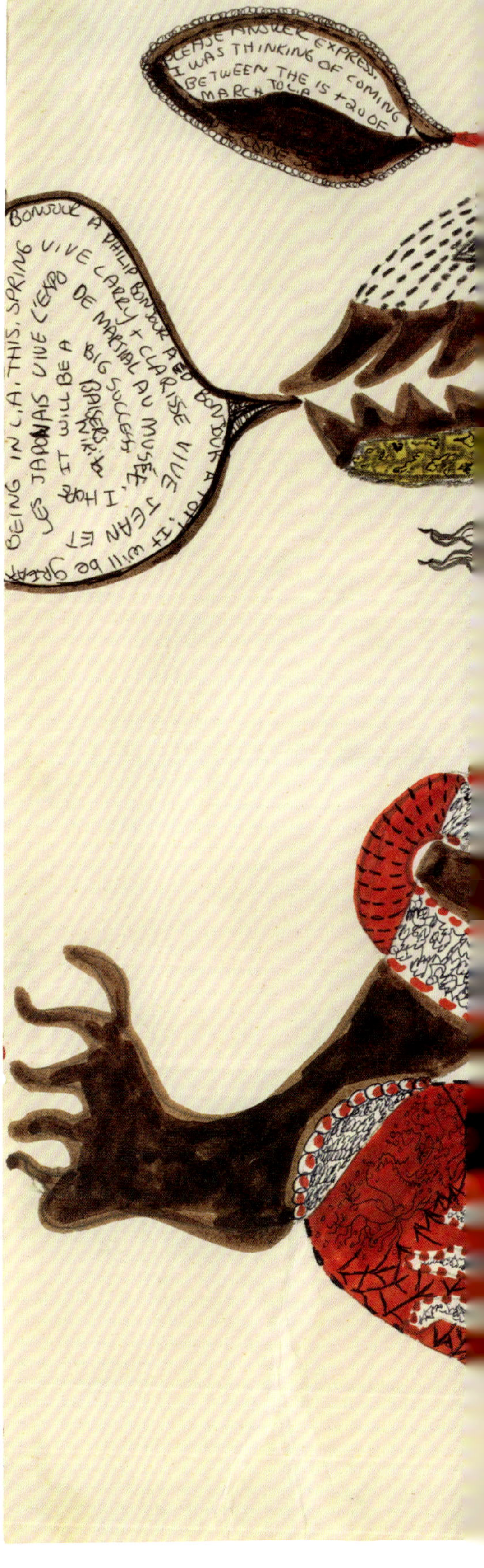

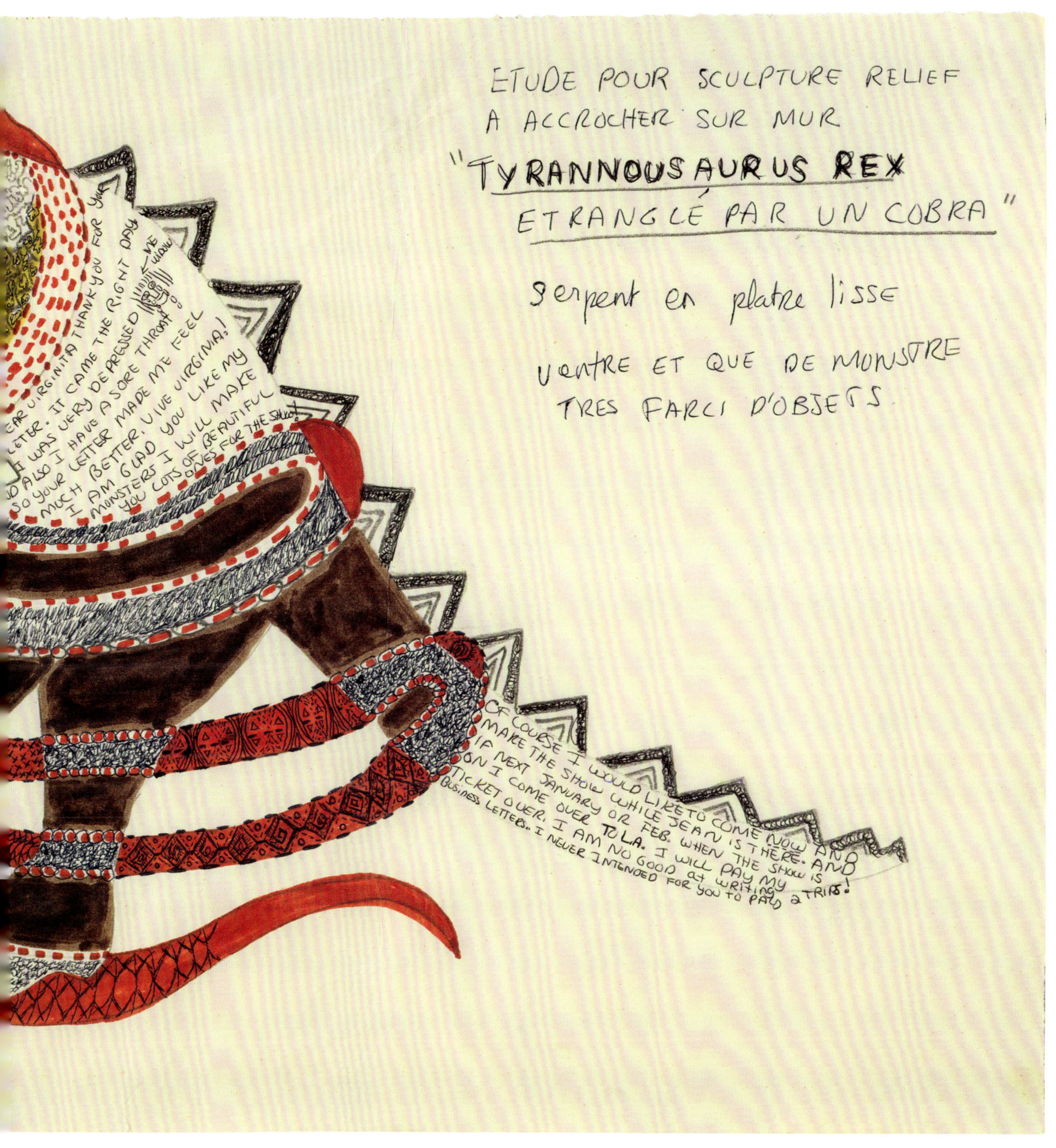

ETUDE POUR SCULPTURE RELIEF
A ACCROCHER SUR MUR
"TYRANNOUSAURUS REX
ETRANGLÉ PAR UN COBRA"
serpent en platre lisse
ventre et que de monstre
TRES FARCI D'OBJETS
EAR VIRGINIA THANK YOU FOR YOUR
LETTER. IT CAME THE RIGHT DAY
I WAS VERY DEPRESSED
D ALSO I HAVE A SORE THROAT
SO YOUR LETTER MADE ME FEEL
MUCH BETTER. VIVE VIRGINIA!
I AM GLAD YOU LIKE MY
MONSTERS I WILL MAKE
YOU LOTS OF BEAUTIFUL
ONES FOR THE SHOW!
← ME
OF COURSE I WOULD LIKE TO COME NOW AND
MAKE THE SHOW WHILE JEAN IS THERE. AND
IF NEXT JANUARY OR FEB. WHEN THE SHOW IS
ON I COME OVER TO L.A. I WILL PAY MY
TICKET OVER. I AM NO GOOD at WRITING
BUSINESS LETTERS. I NEVER INTENDED FOR YOU TO PAY a TRIP!

CAT. 32

MARTIAL RAYSSE, *C'EST MOI*, 1964

CAT. 33

MARTIAL RAYSSE, *PABLO*, 1965

CAT. 34 (OVERLEAF)

MARTIAL RAYSSE, *MADE IN JAPAN*, 1964

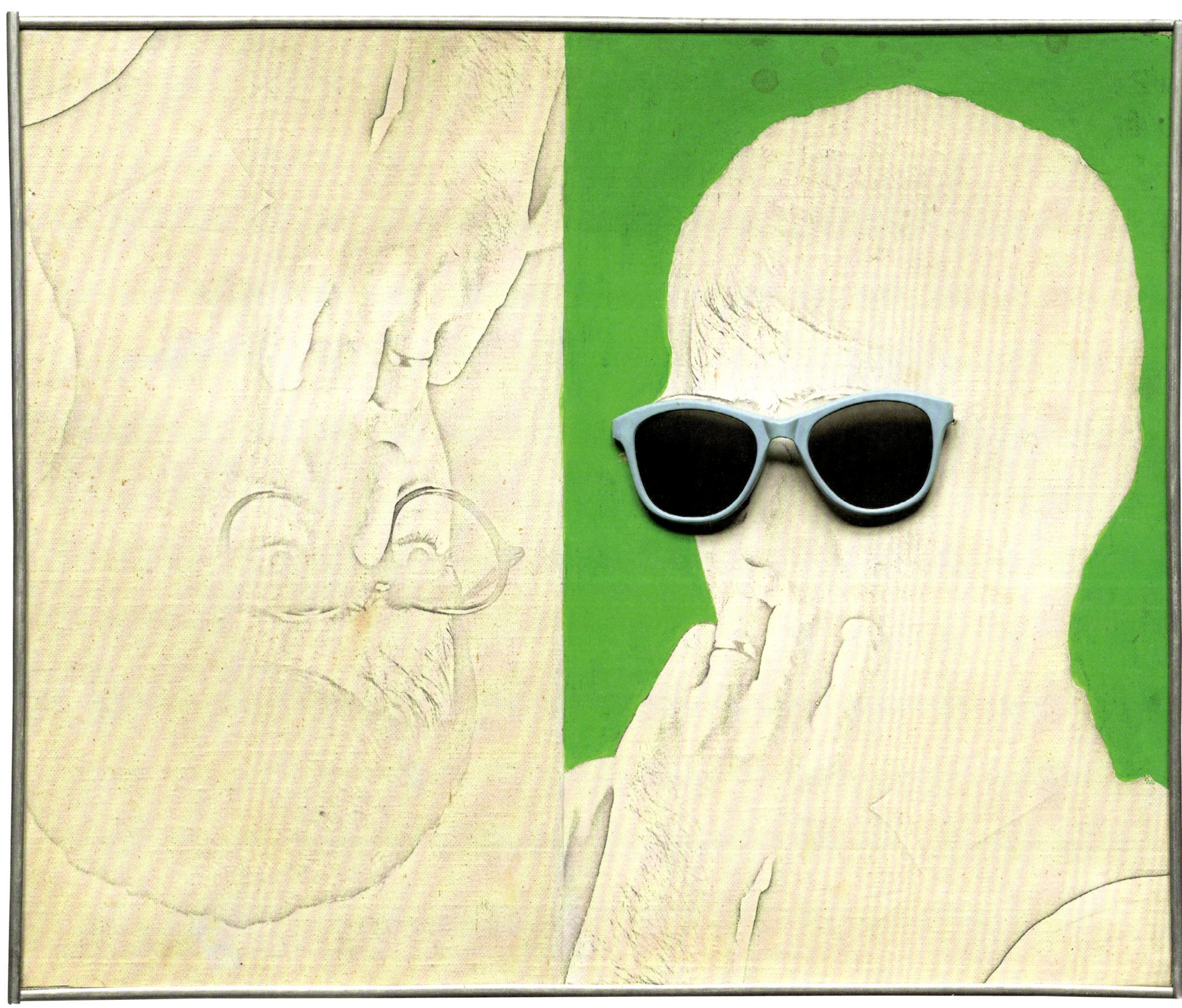

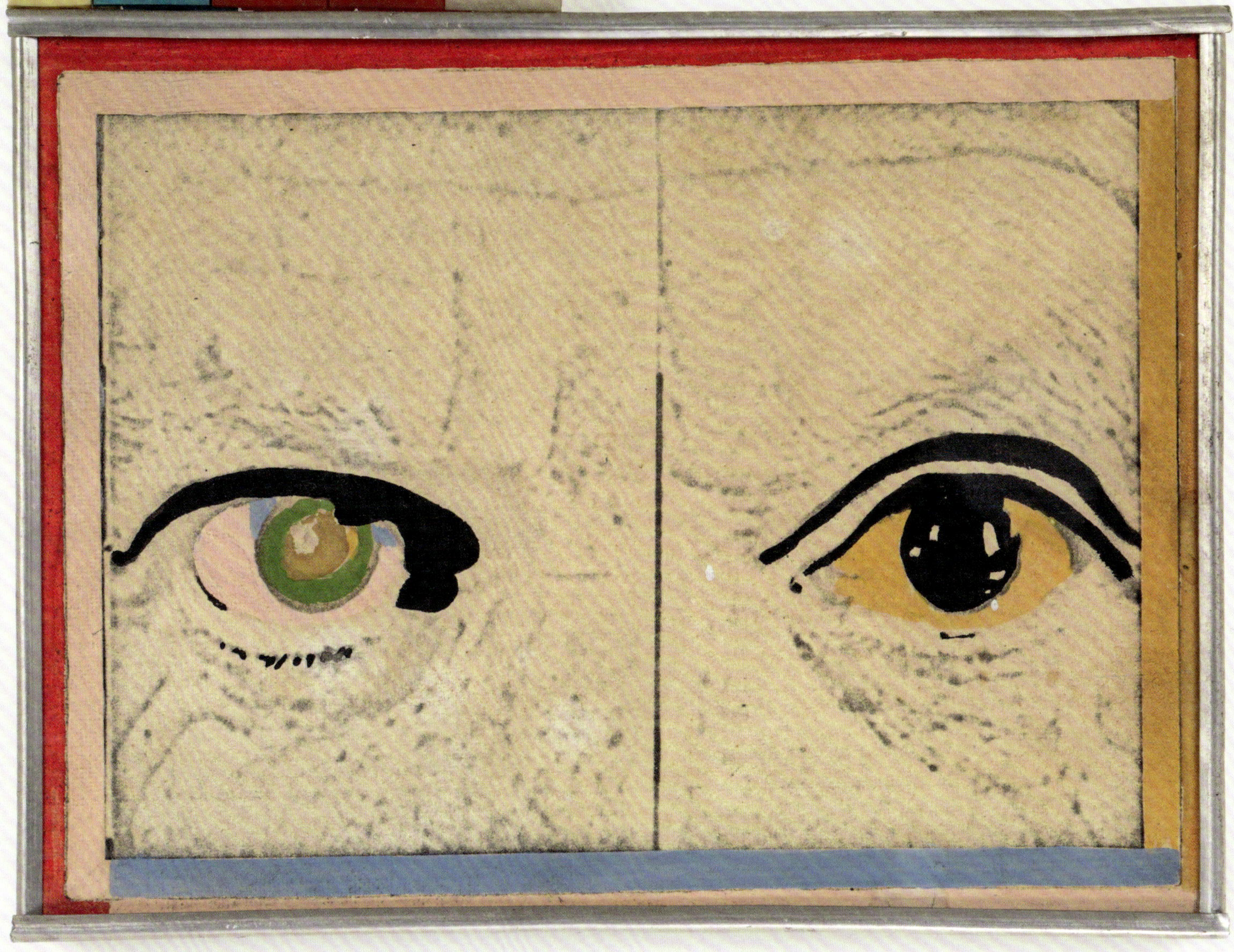
PABLO

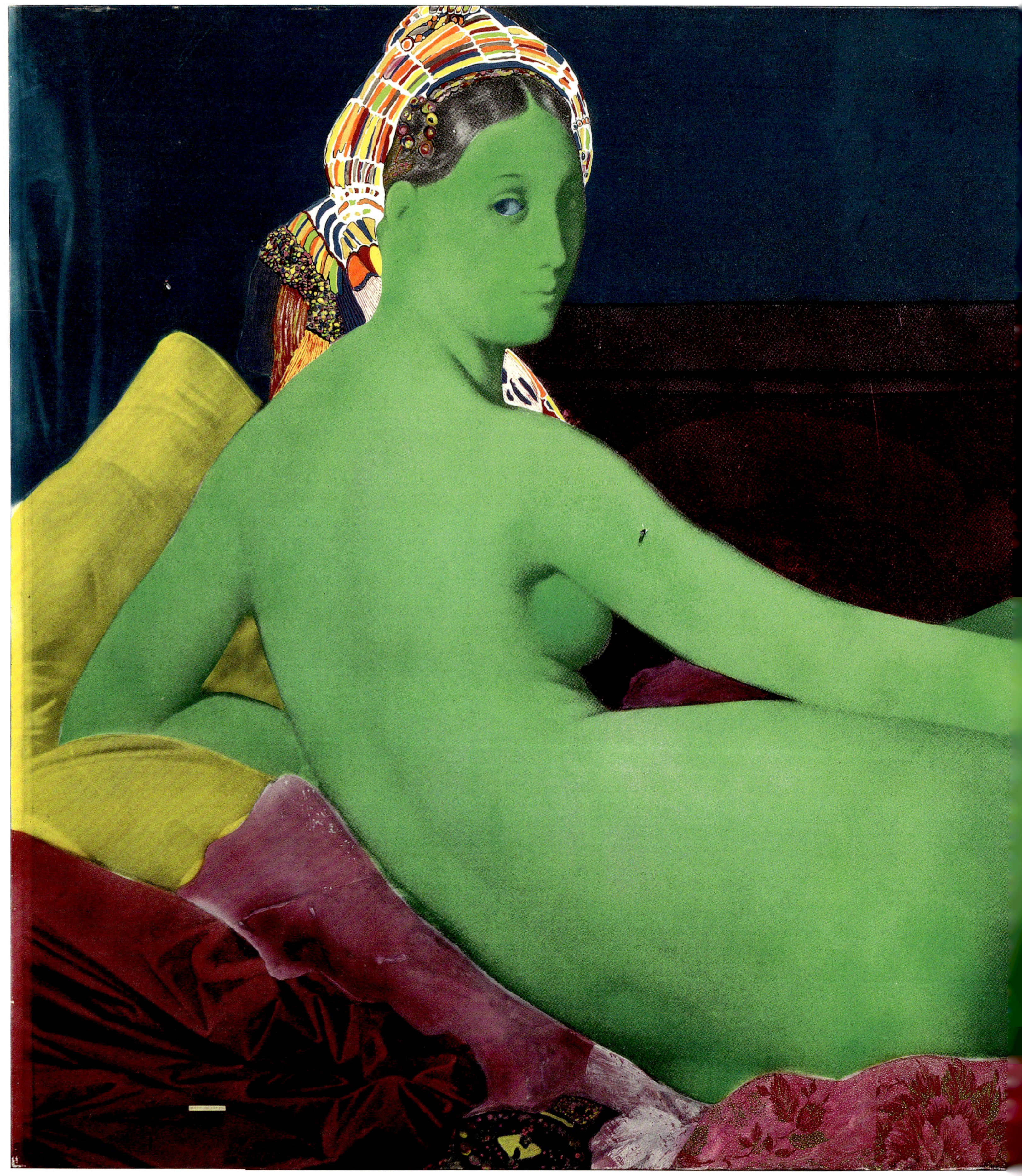

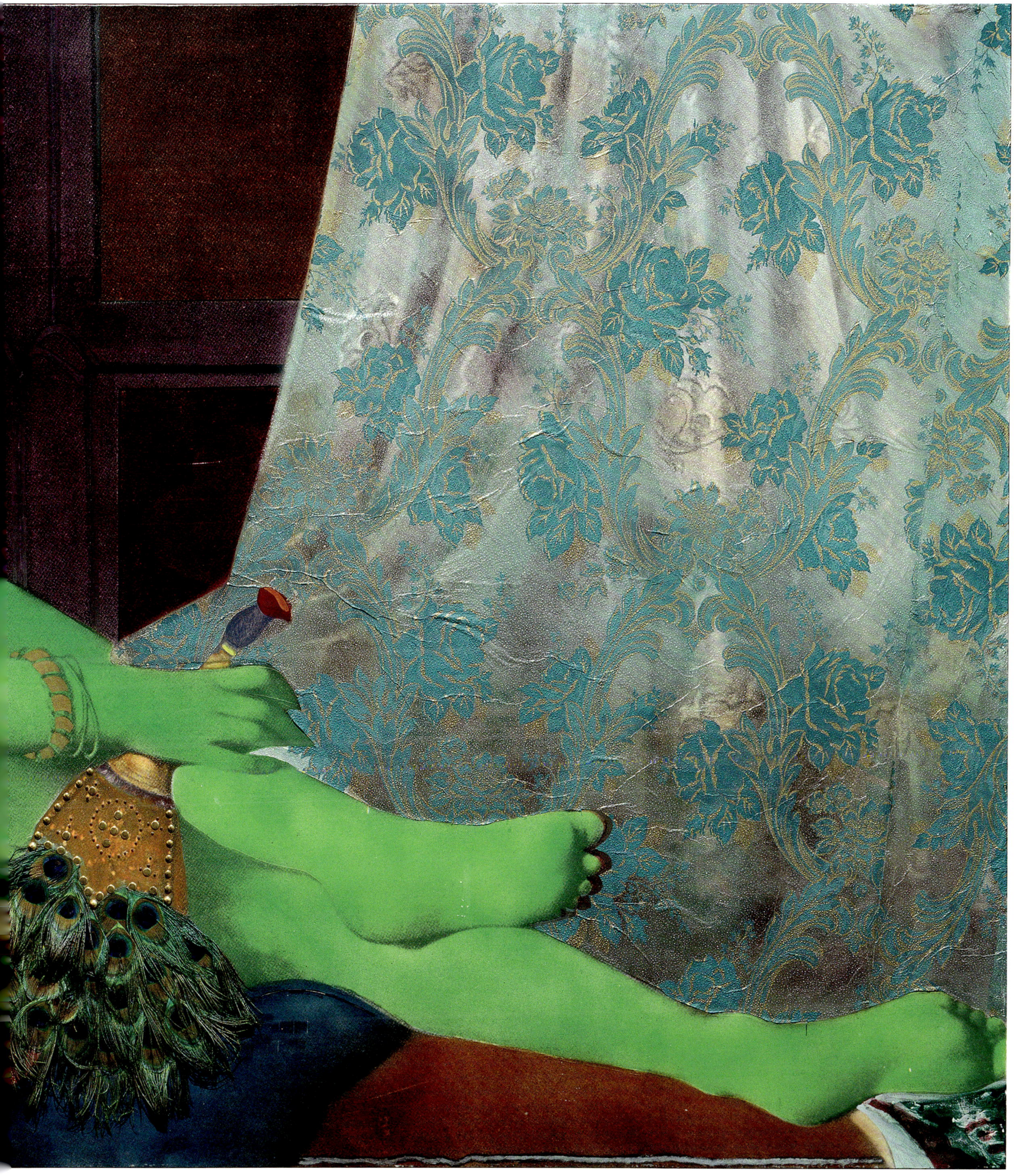

CAT. 35

JOHN CHAMBERLAIN,
RAYVREDD, 1962

CAT. 36

CHARLES FRAZIER,
ALBION, 1962

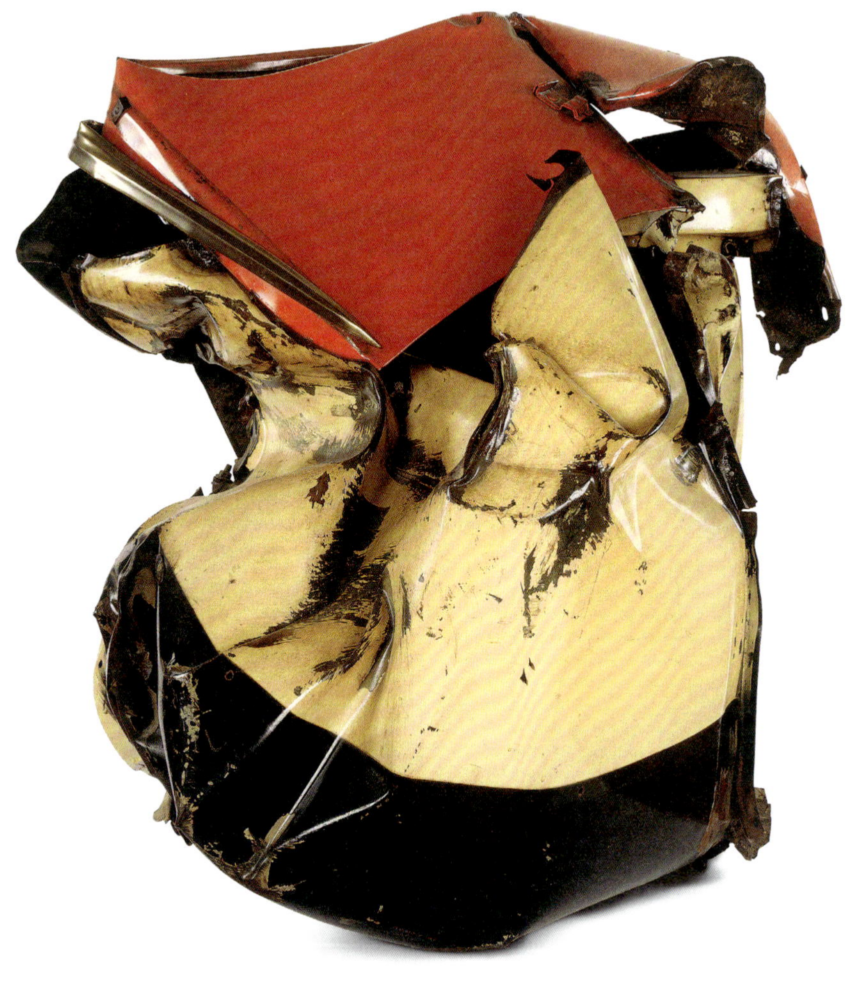

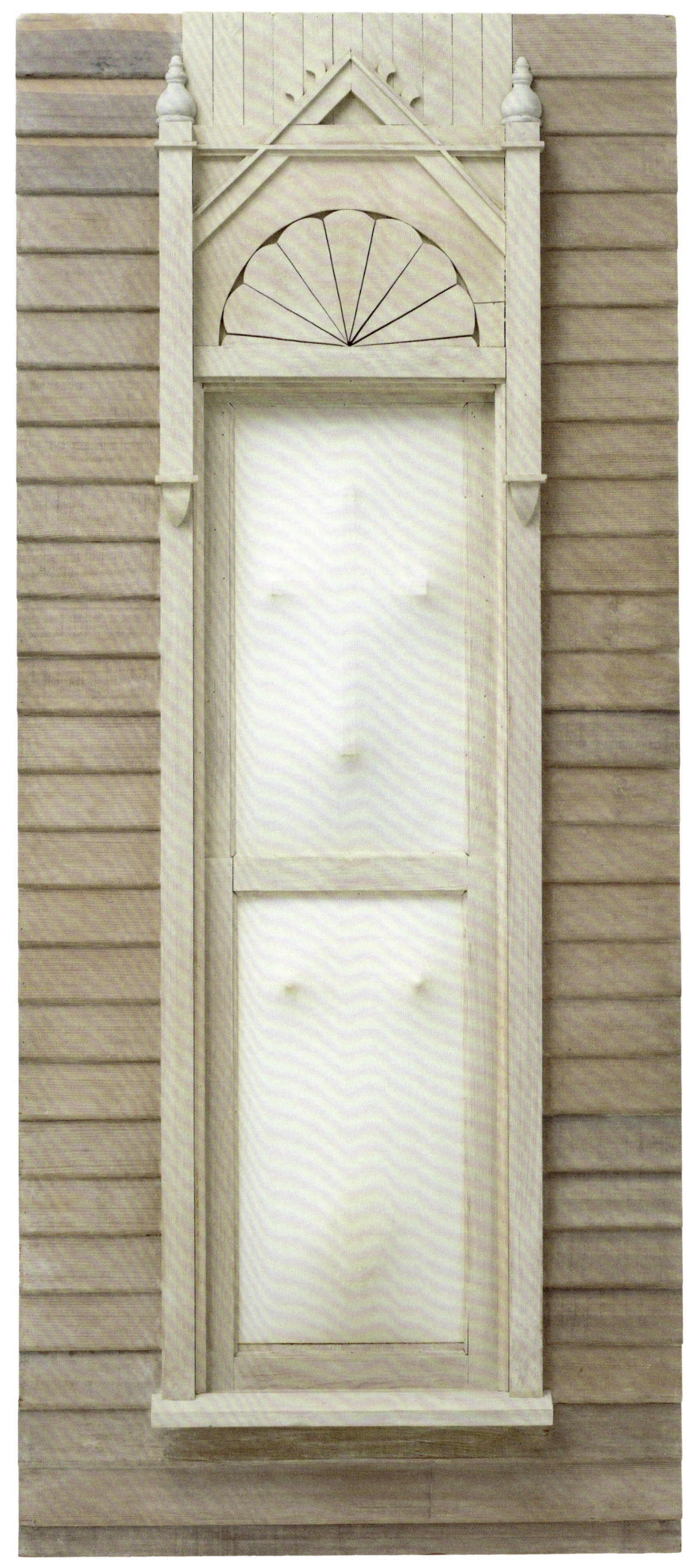

CAT. 37

CLAES OLDENBURG, *STUDY FOR ANNOUNCEMENT FOR ONE-MAN SHOW AT DWAN GALLERY — MICKEY MOUSE WITH RED HEART*, 1963

CAT. 38

CLAES OLDENBURG, *BAKED POTATO #1*, 1963

CAT. 39

CLAES OLDENBURG, *COFFEE CUP*, 1962

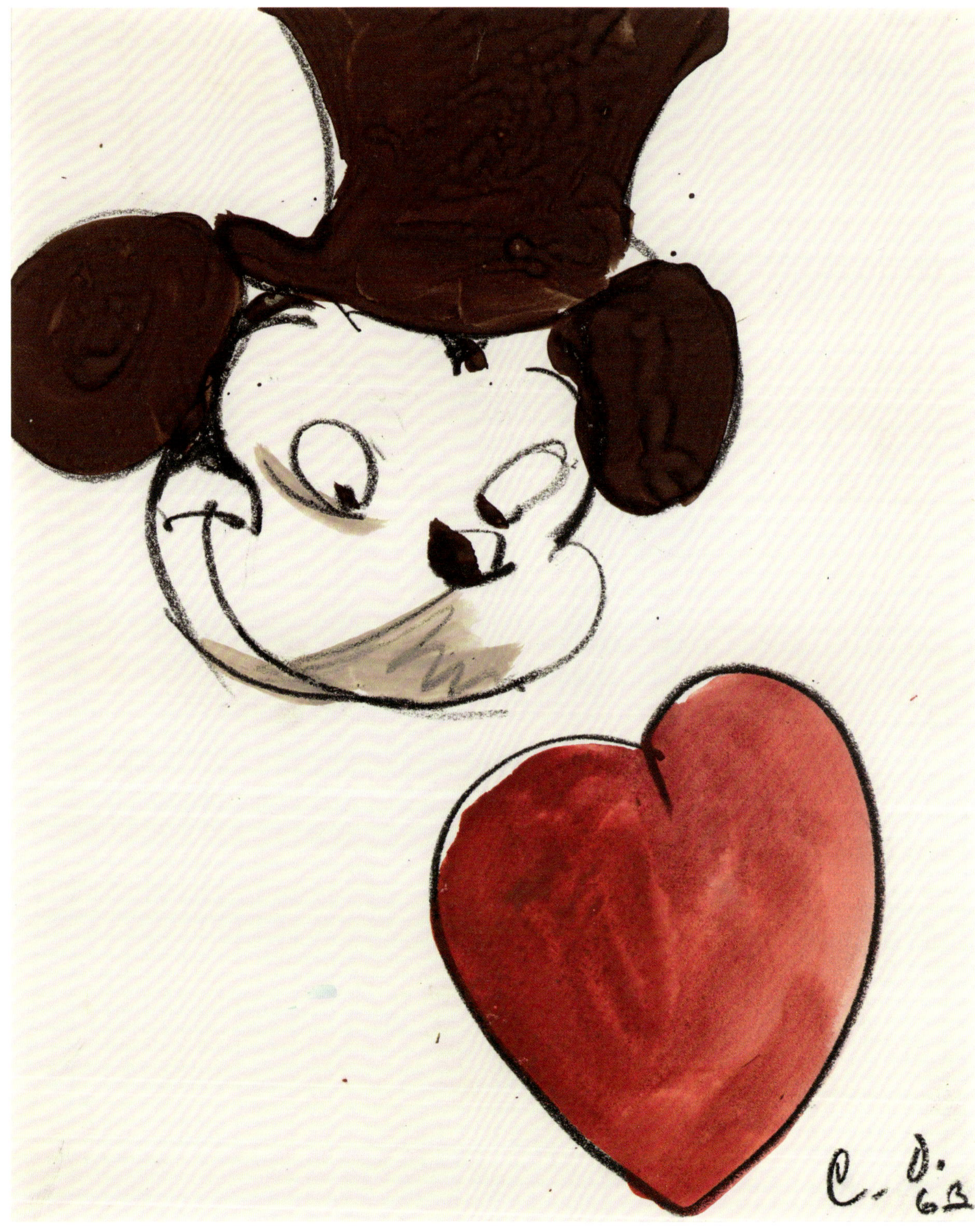

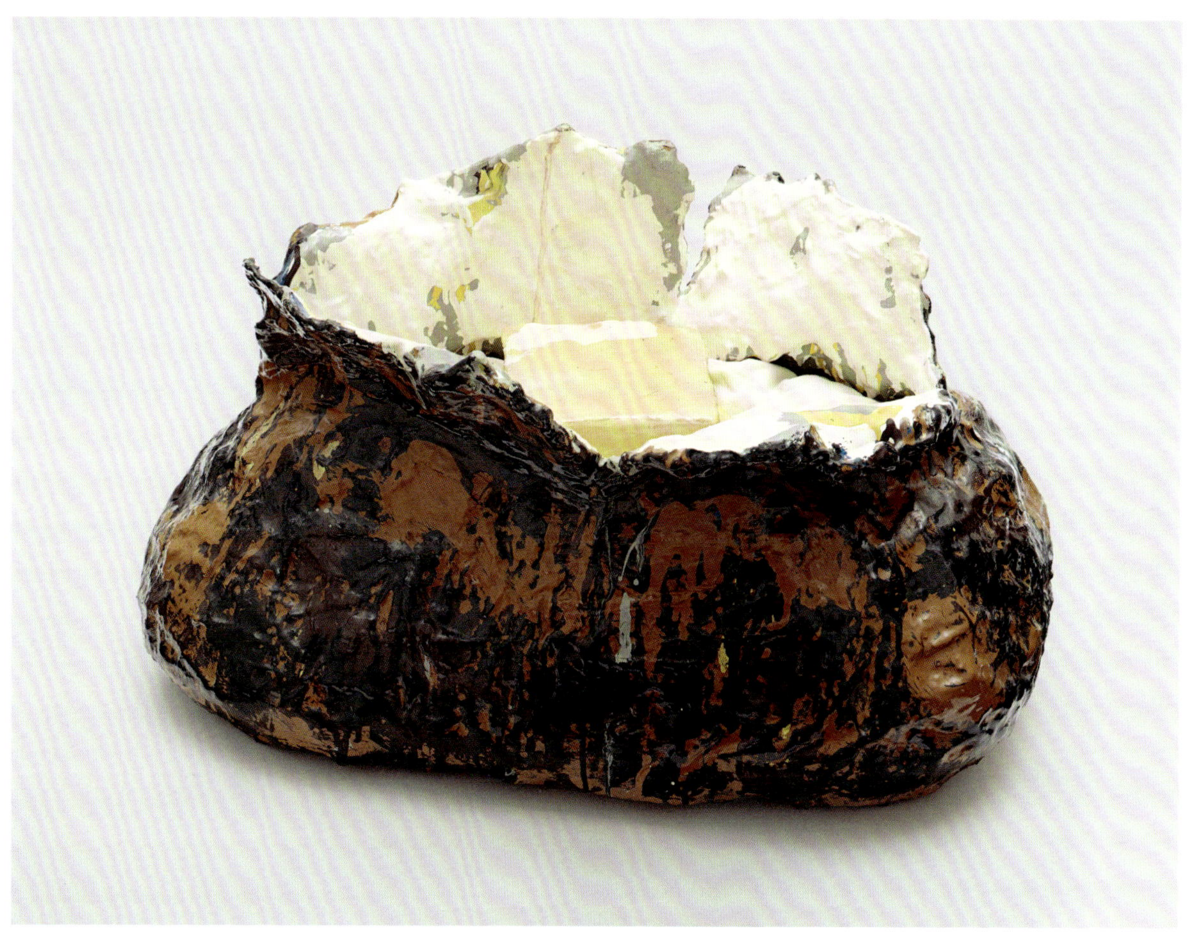

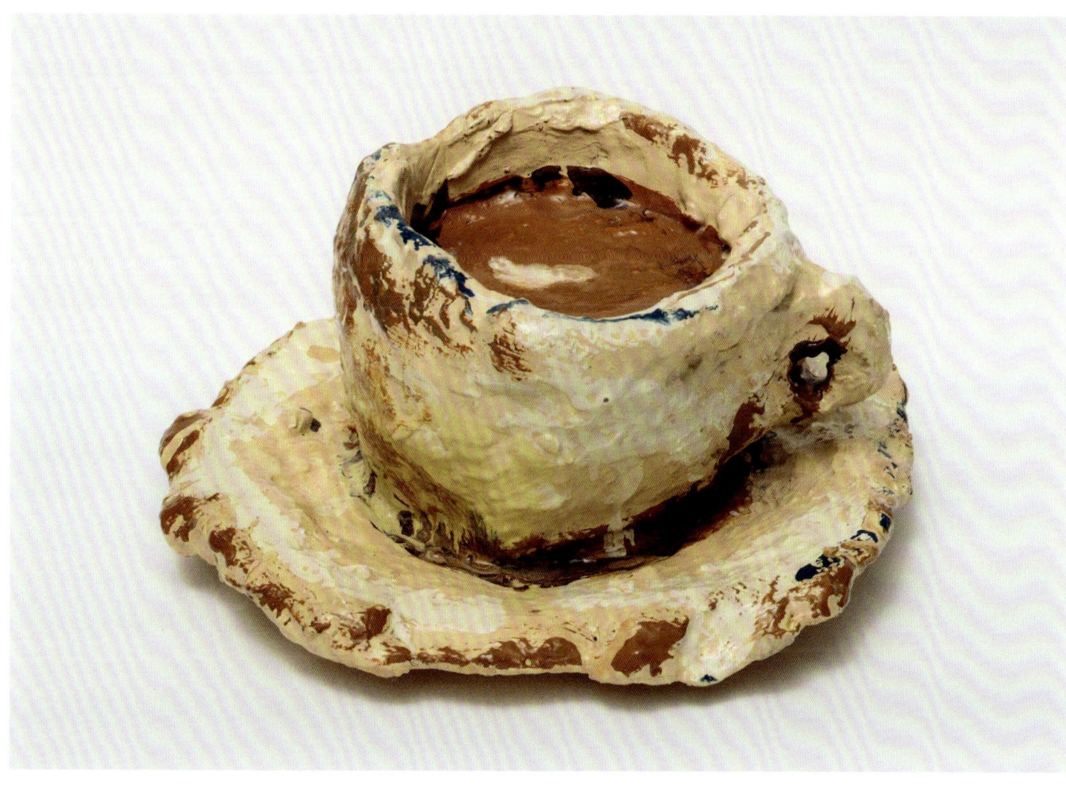

CAT. 40

CLAES OLDENBURG,
GIANT WEDGE OF PECAN PIE, 1963

CAT. 41

CLAES OLDENBURG,
FILM STILLS FROM
AUTOBODYS, 1963

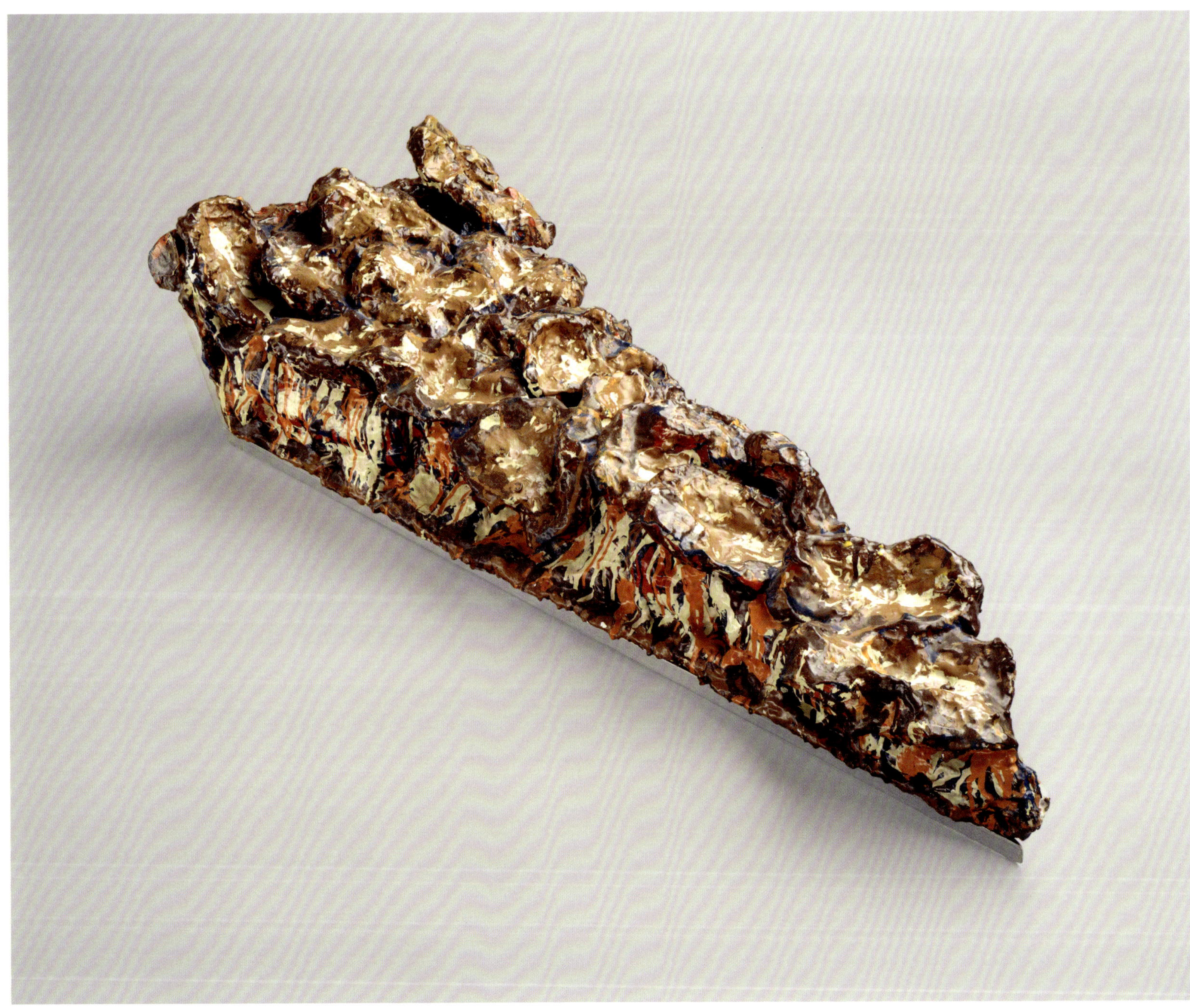

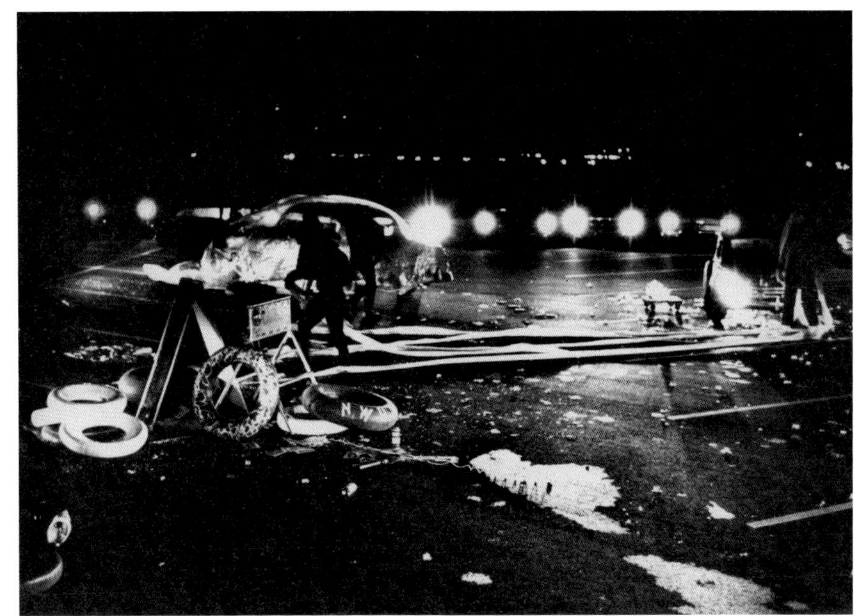

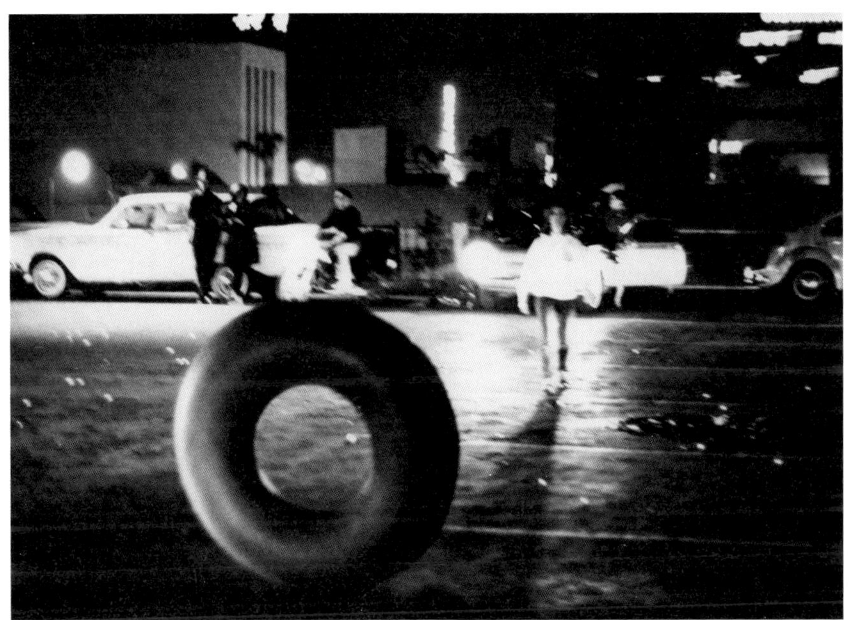

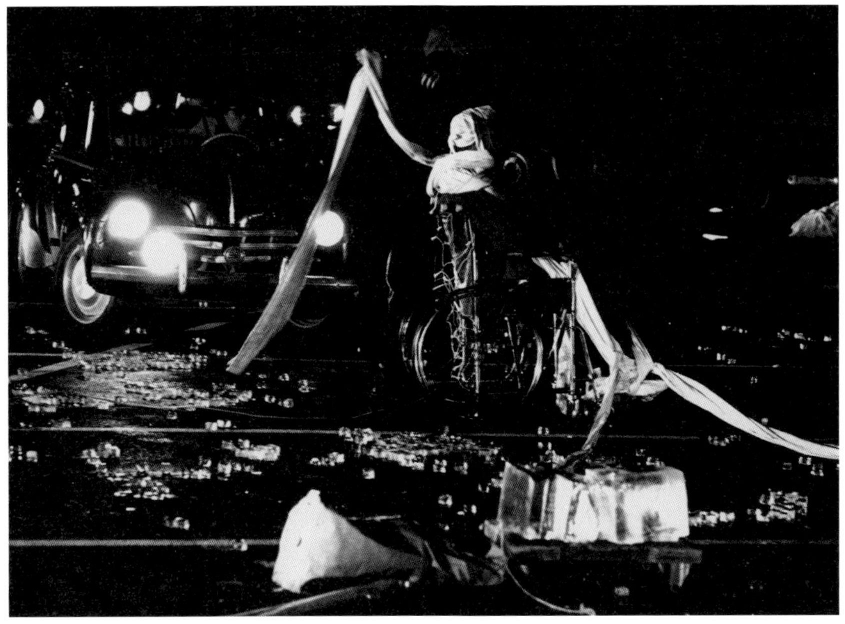

CAT. 42

TOM WESSELMANN,
STILL LIFE #2,
1962

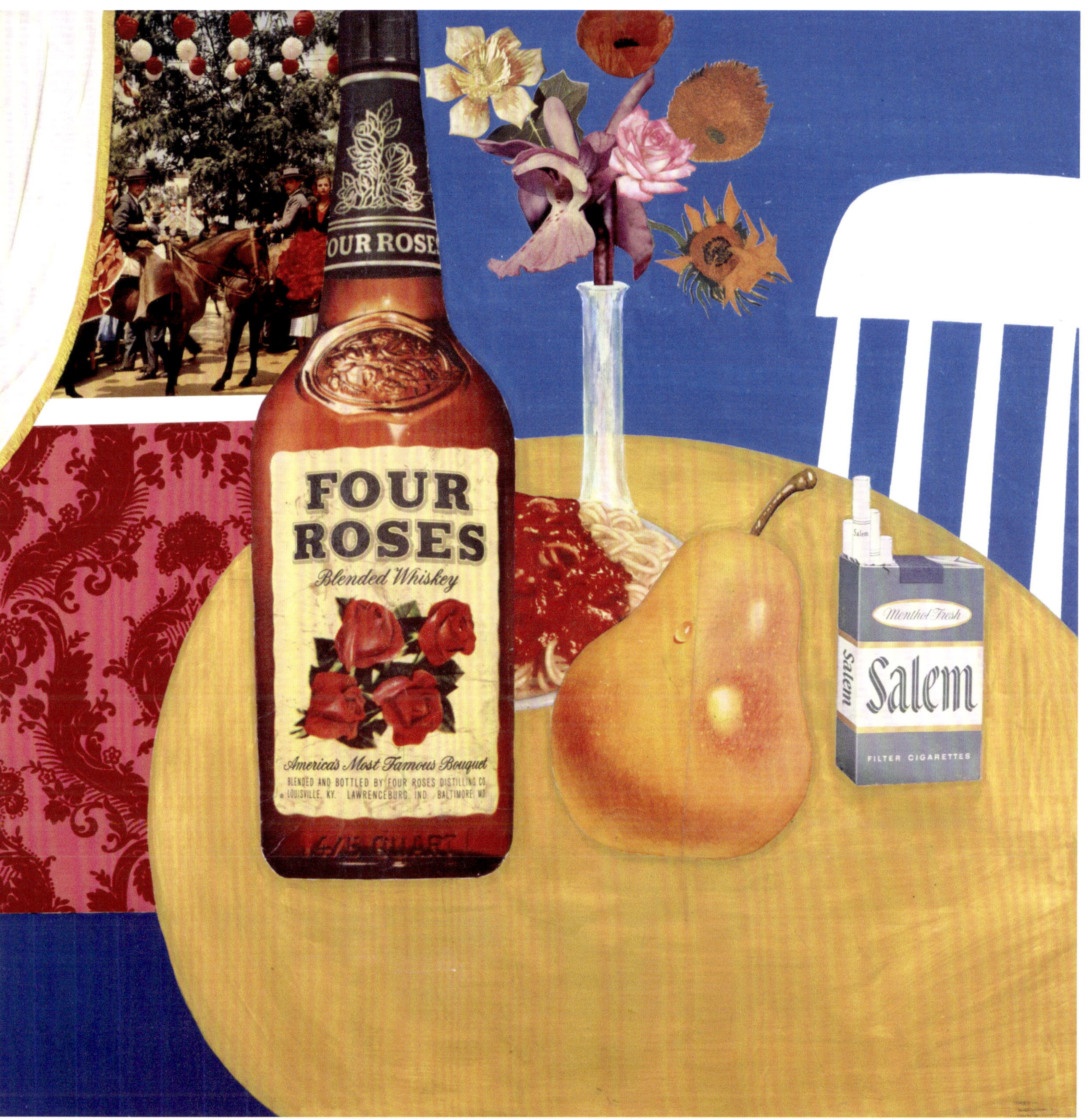
OUR ROSES
FOUR
ROSES
Blended Whiskey
America's Most Famous Bouquet
BLENDED AND BOTTLED BY FOUR ROSES DISTILLING CO.
LOUISVILLE, KY. LAWRENCEBURG, IND. BALTIMORE, MD.
Menthol Fresh
Salem
Salem
FILTER CIGARETTES

CAT. 43

MARCEL DUCHAMP, *FROM OR BY MARCEL DUCHAMP OR RROSE SÉLAVY (THE BOX IN A VALISE)*, 1935–1941

CAT. 44

LUCAS SAMARAS, *UNTITLED*, 1963

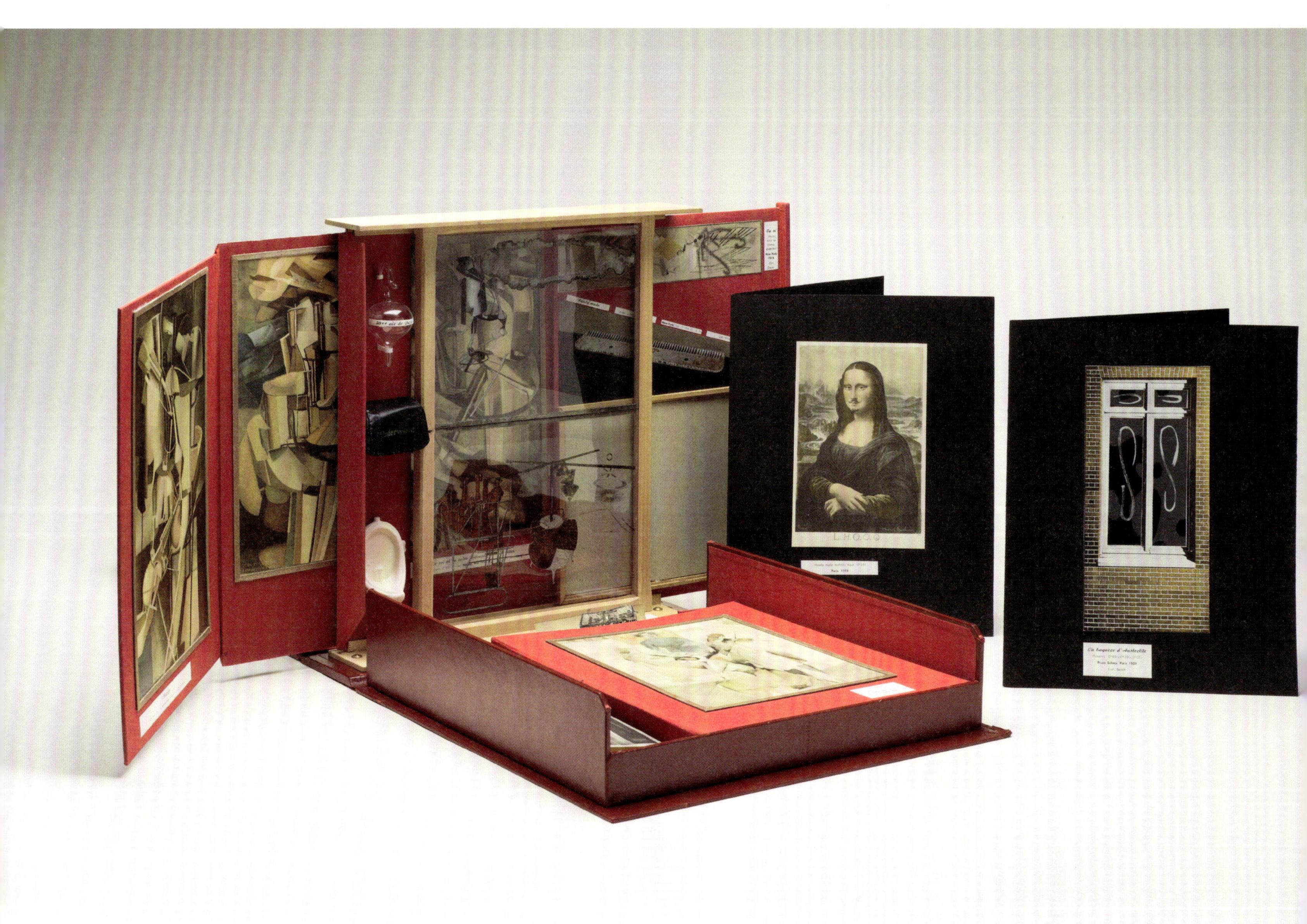

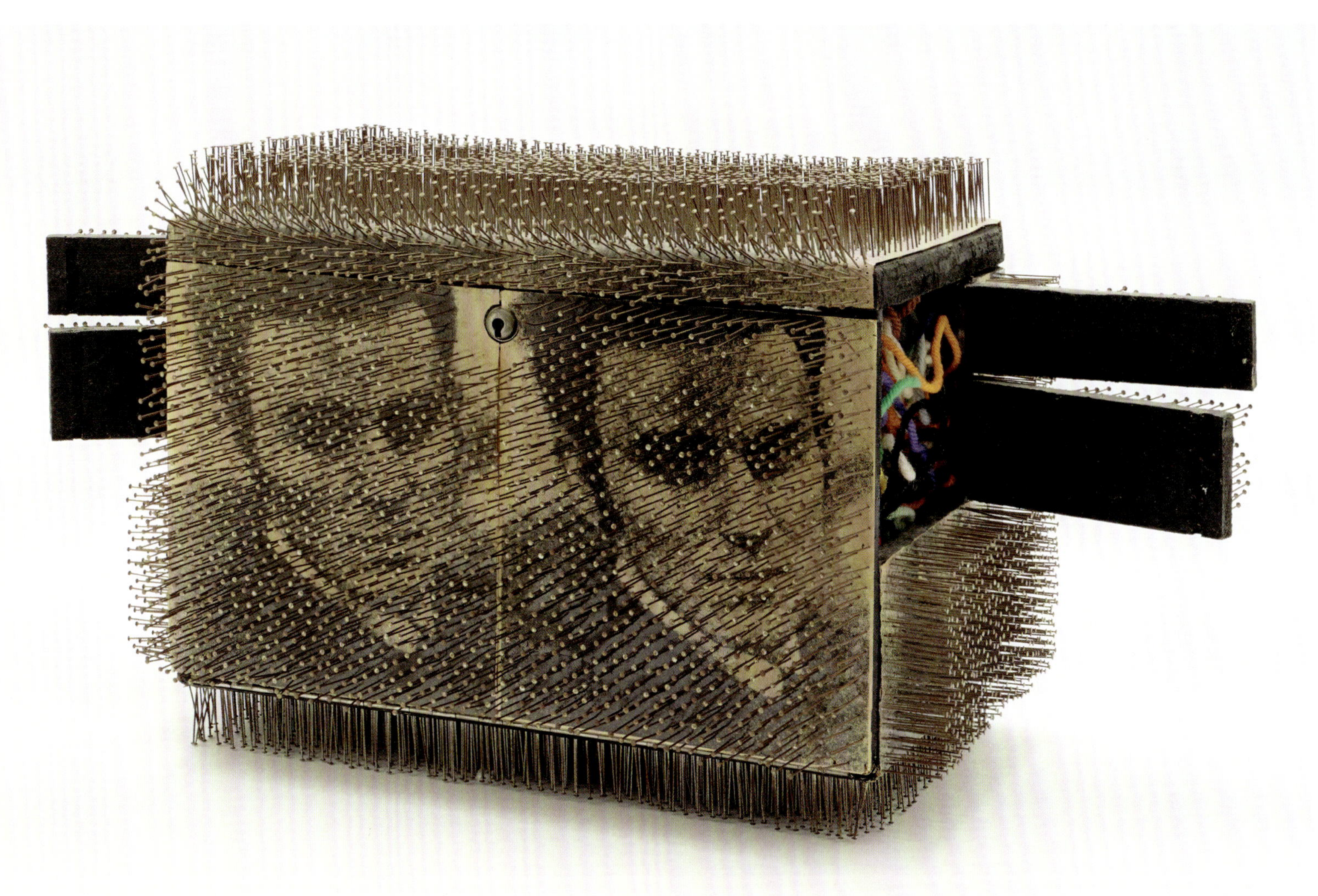

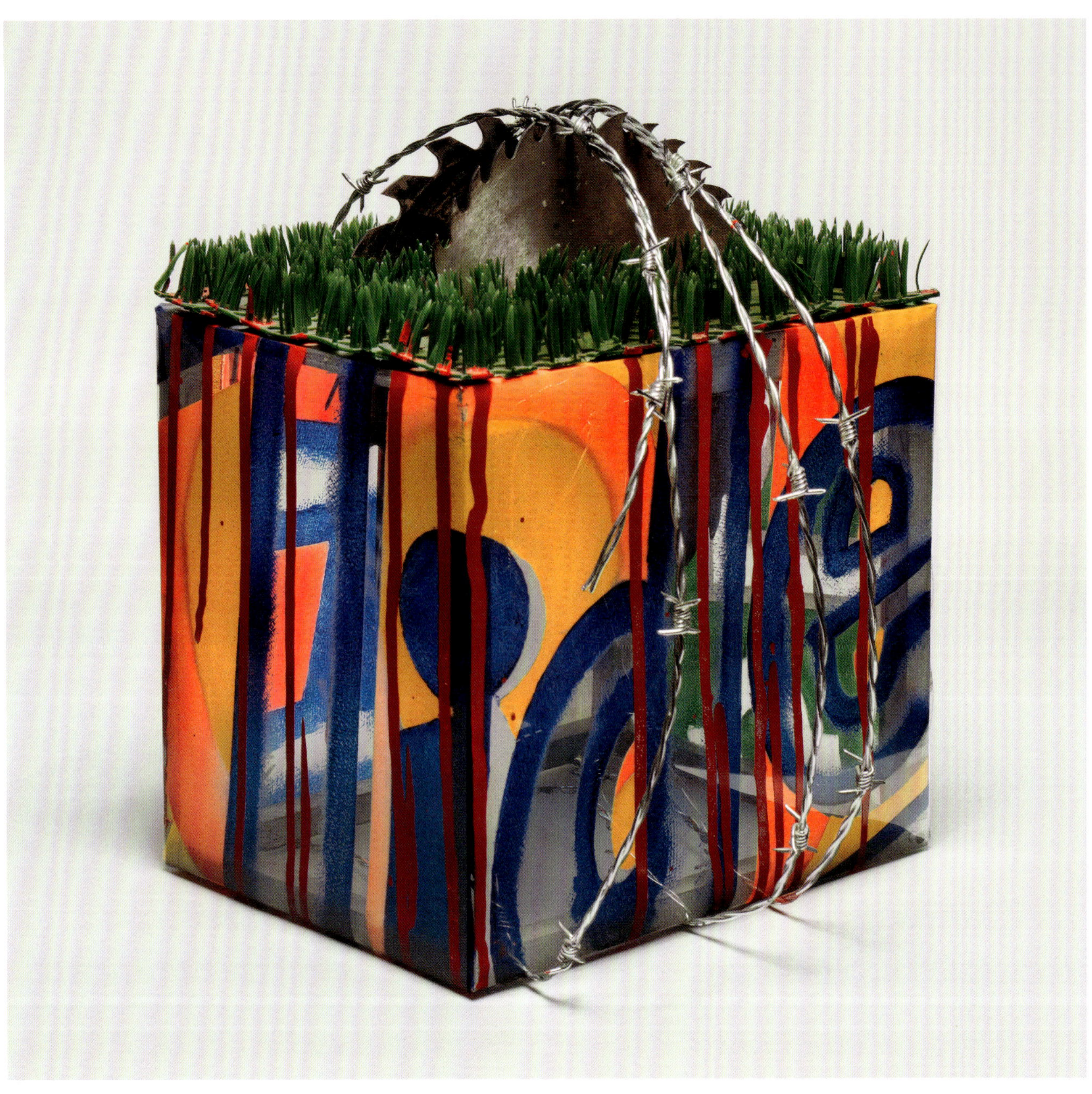

CAT. 45

JAMES ROSENQUIST, *TOASTER*, 1963

CATS. 46–48

ANDY WARHOL, *BRILLO BOX*, C. 1964

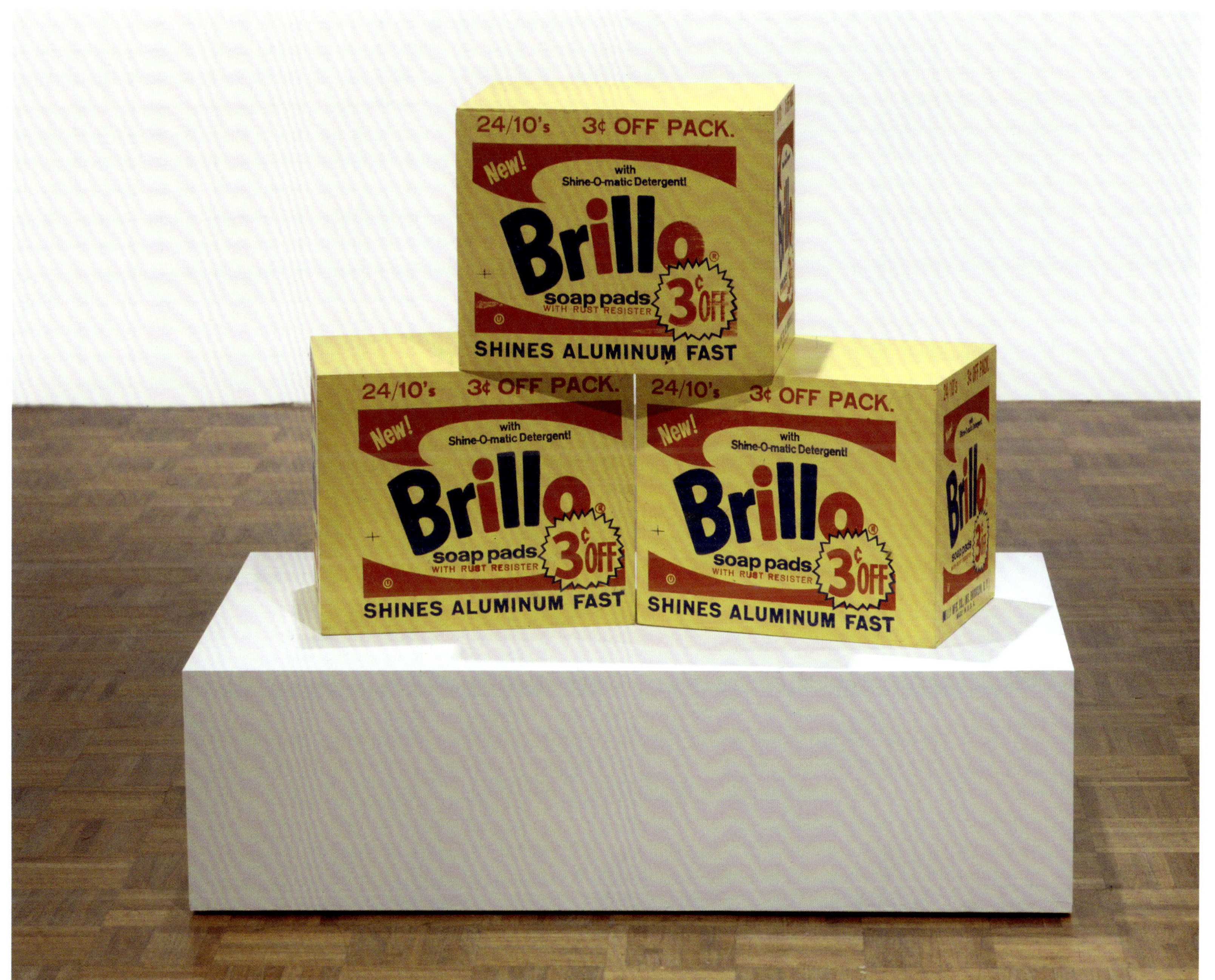

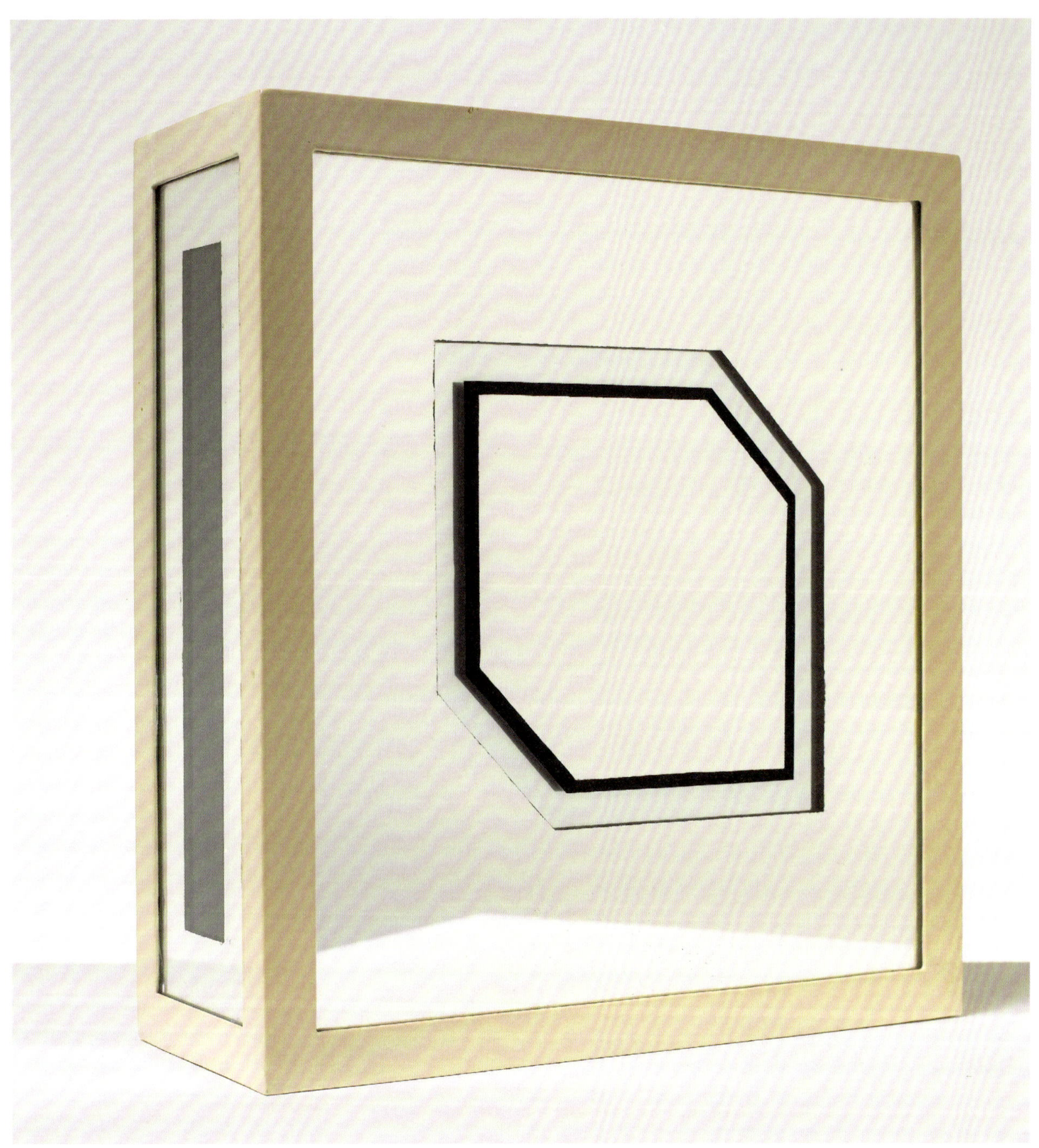

CAT. 49

LARRY BELL, *LUX AT THE FERUS*, 1961–1962

CAT. 50

KEN PRICE, *WHITE AND GREY*, 1962

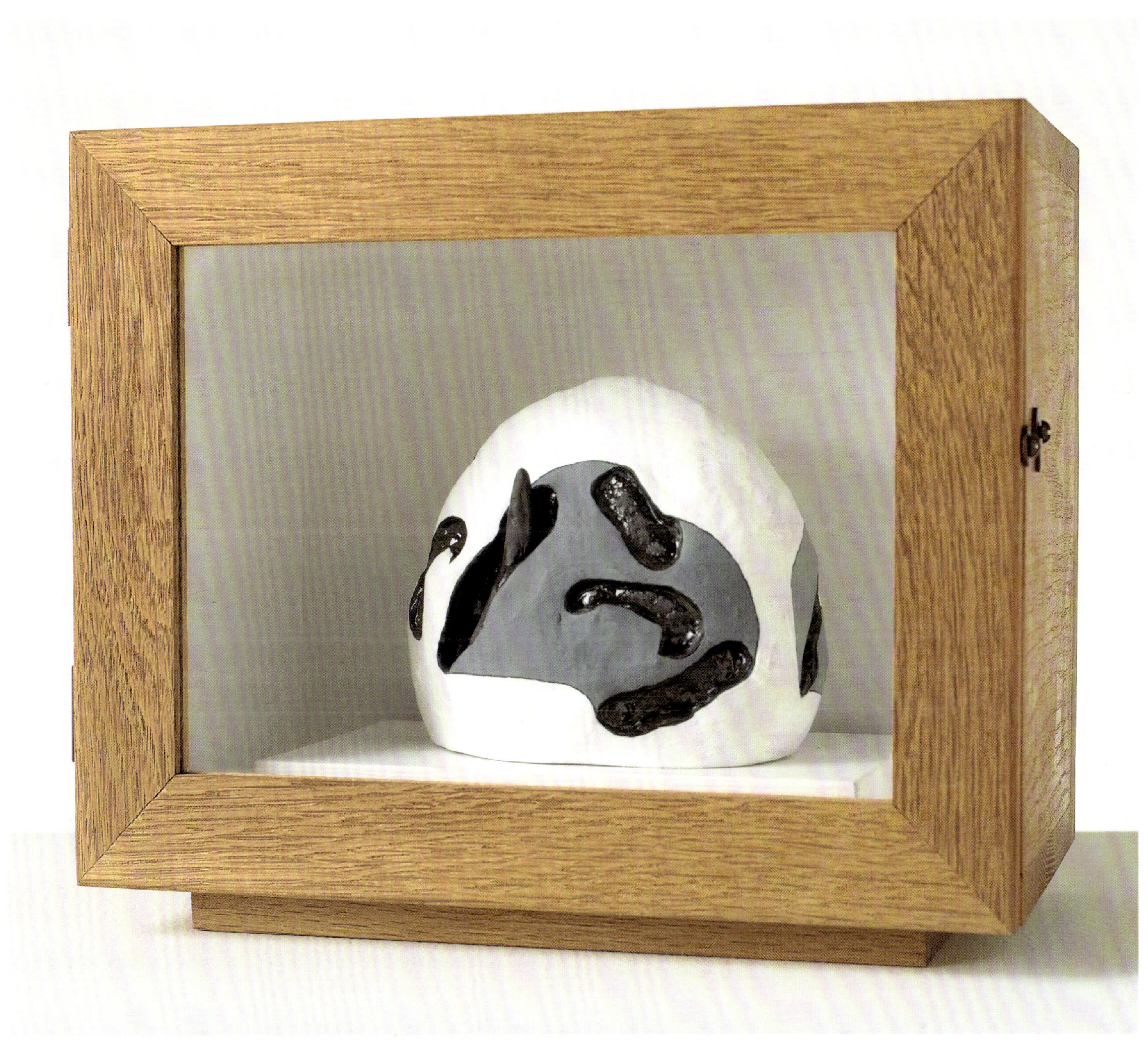

CAT. 51

RONALD MIYASHIRO, *CONCORD #9*, 1963

CAT. 52

DANIEL LARUE JOHNSON, *THE BIG N*, 1963

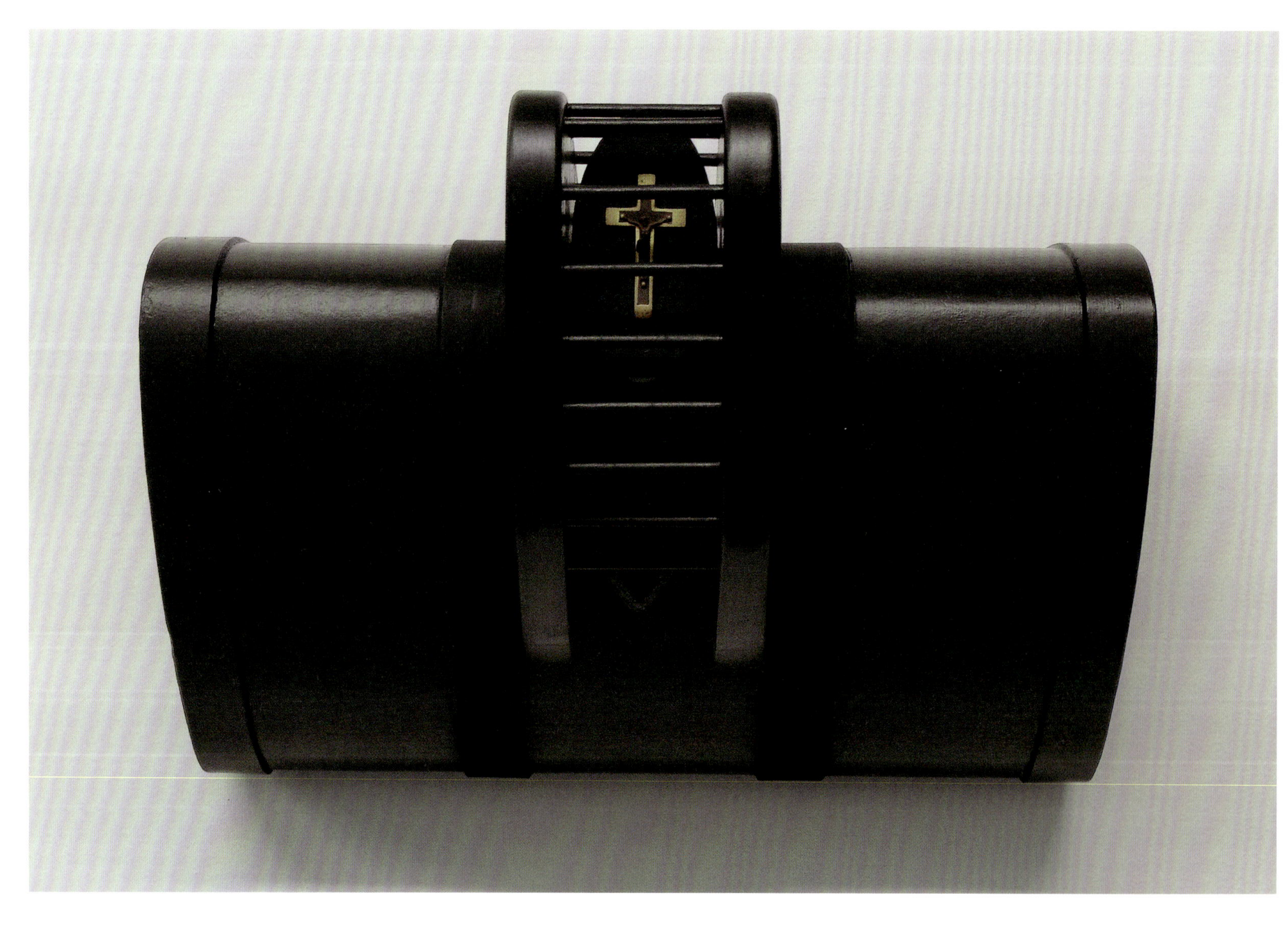

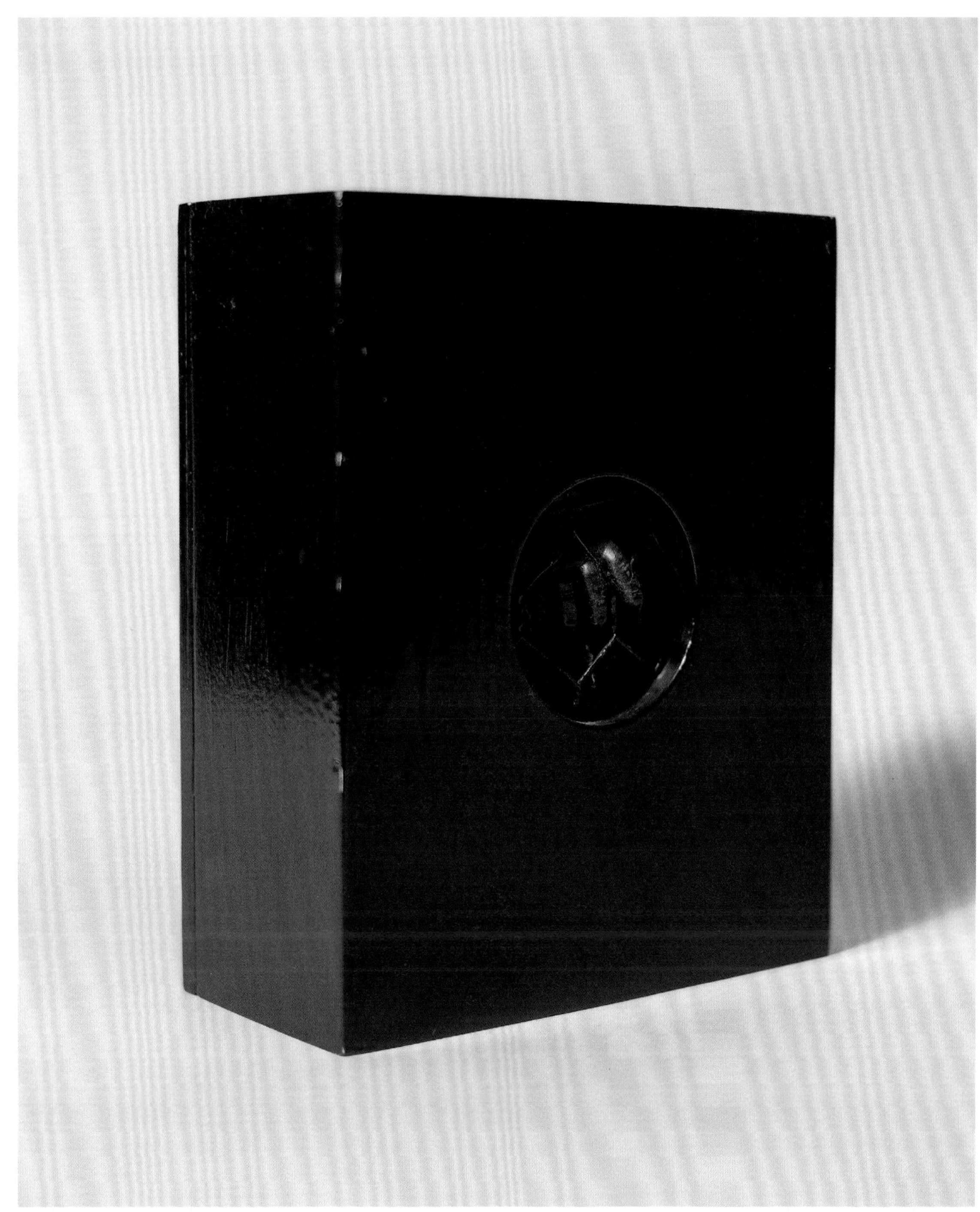

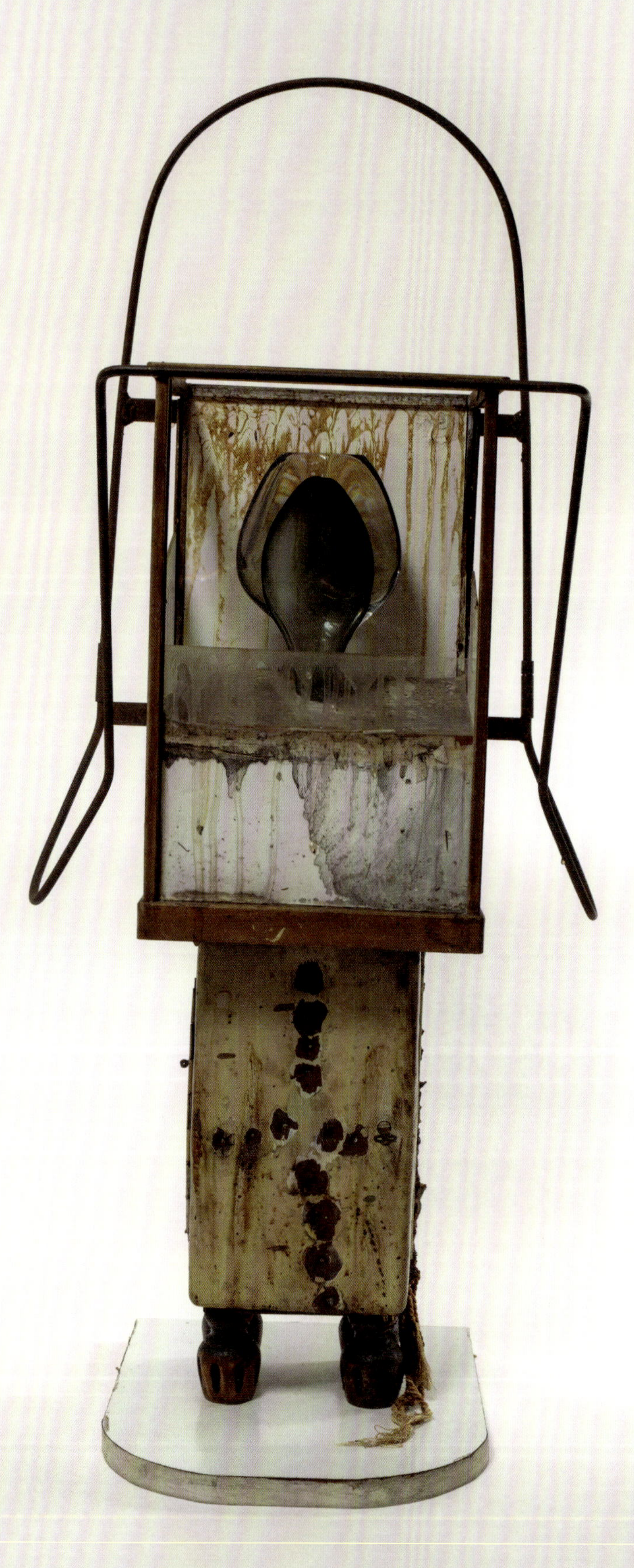

CAT. 53

EDWARD KIENHOLZ,
PORTRAIT OF VIRGINIA, 1963

CAT. 54
(PAGES 157–159)

EDWARD KIENHOLZ,
BACK SEAT DODGE '38, 1964

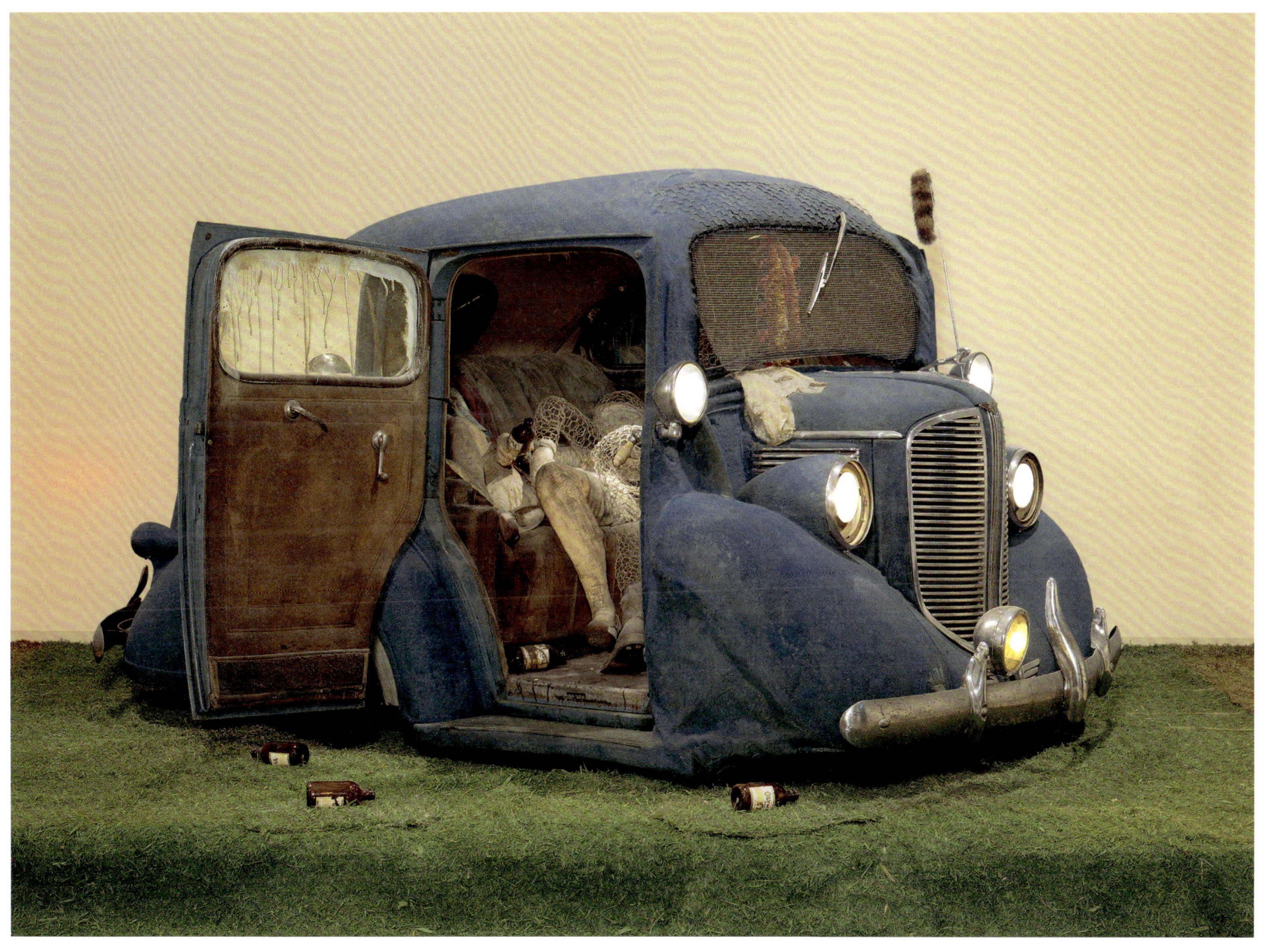

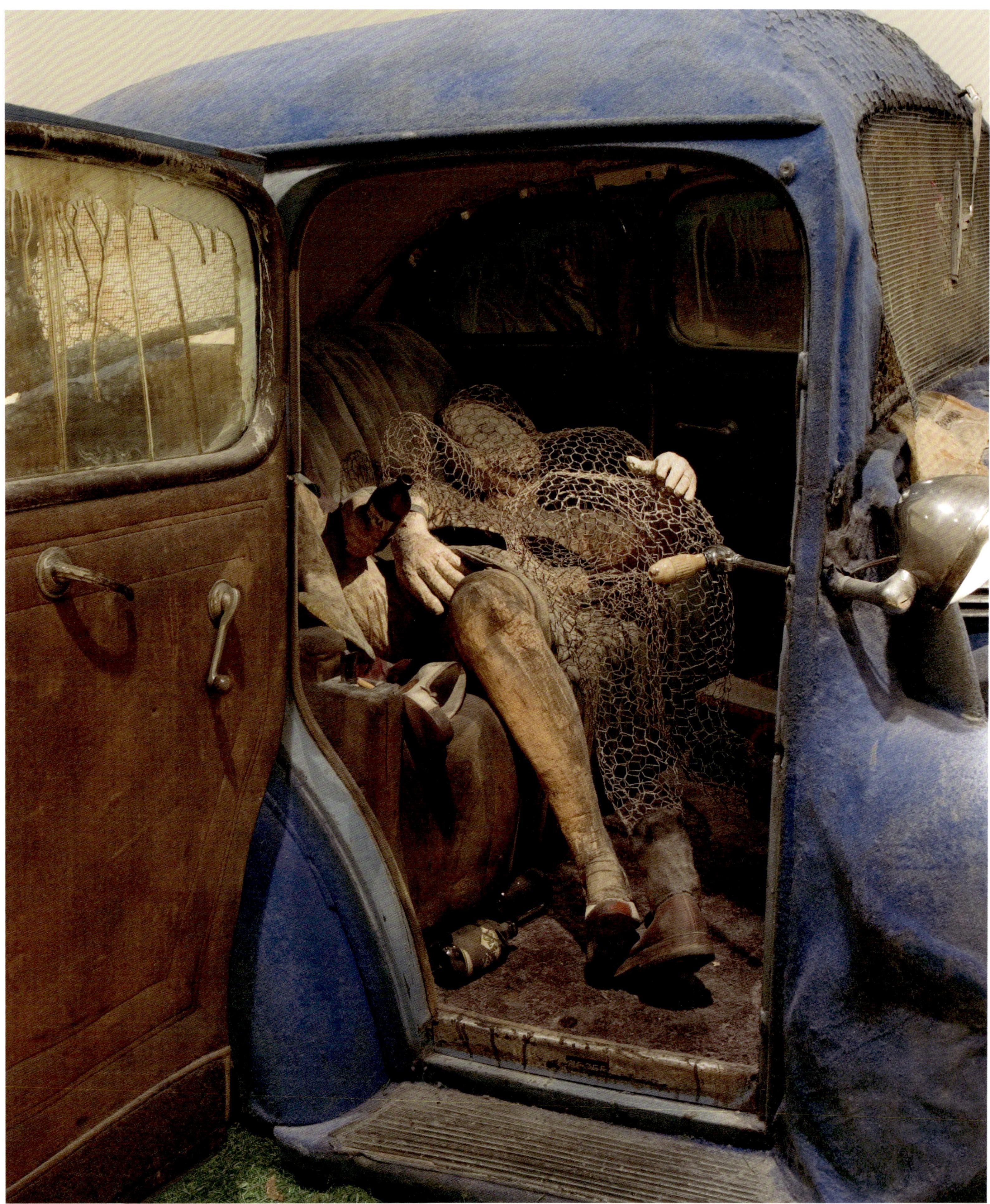

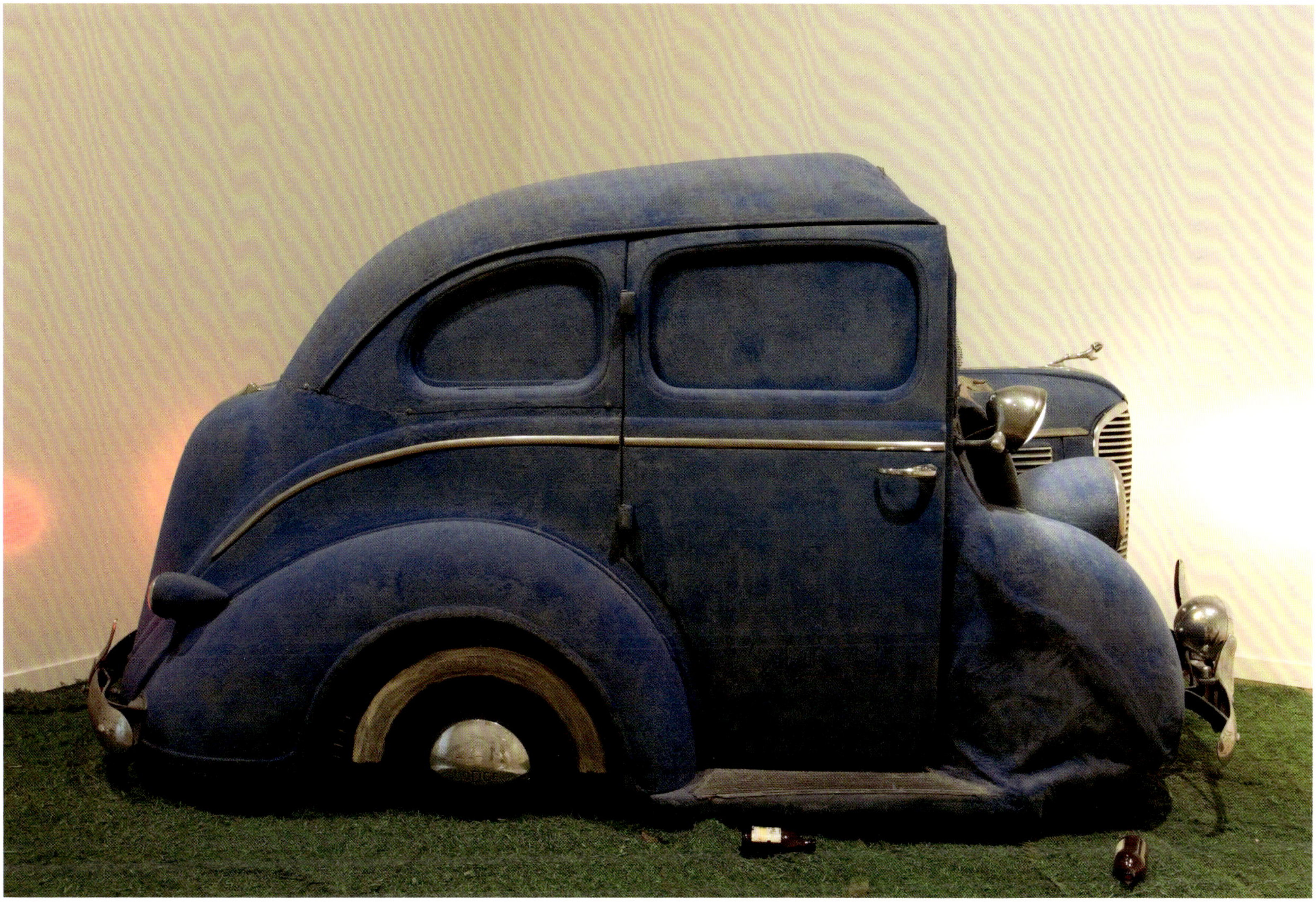

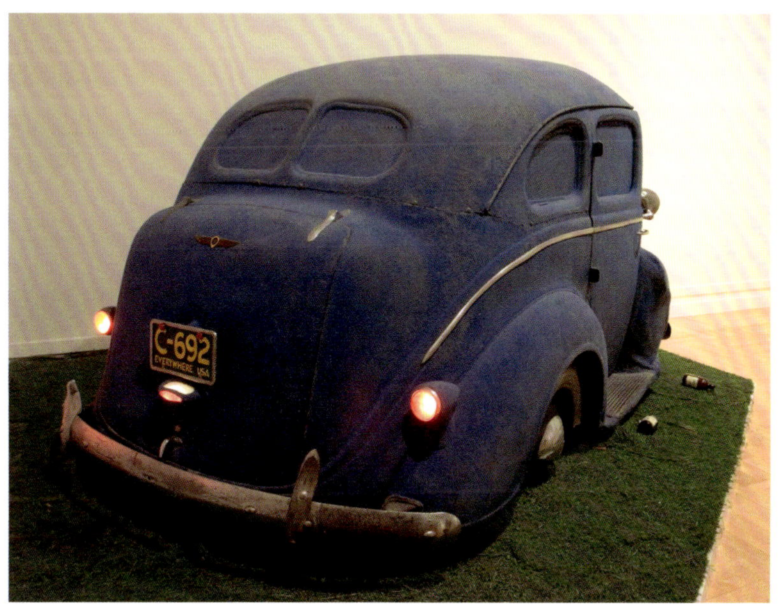
C-692
EVERYWHERE USA

CAT. 55

EDWARD KIENHOLZ, *AFTER THE BALL IS OVER #1*, 1965

CAT. 56

EDWARD KIENHOLZ AND JEAN TINGUELY, *THE AMERICAN TRIP*, 1966

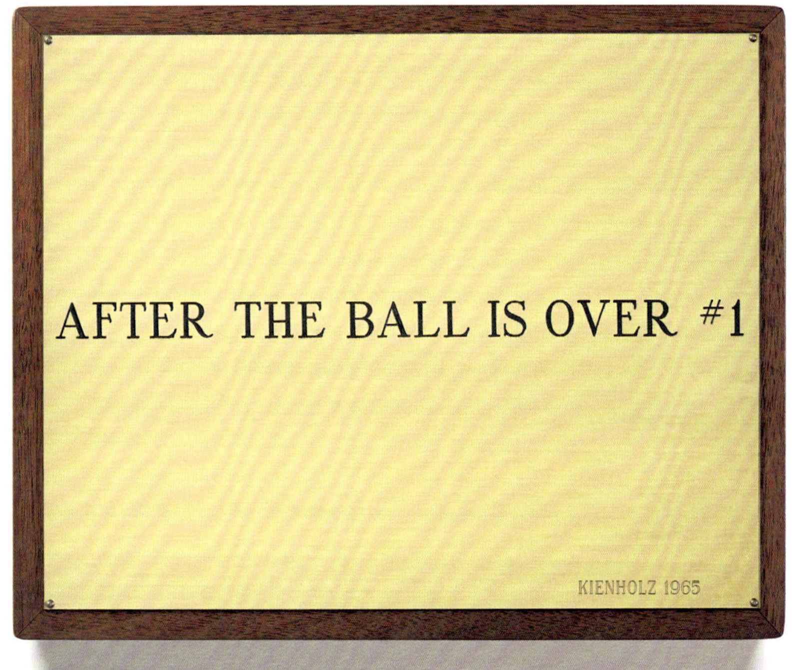

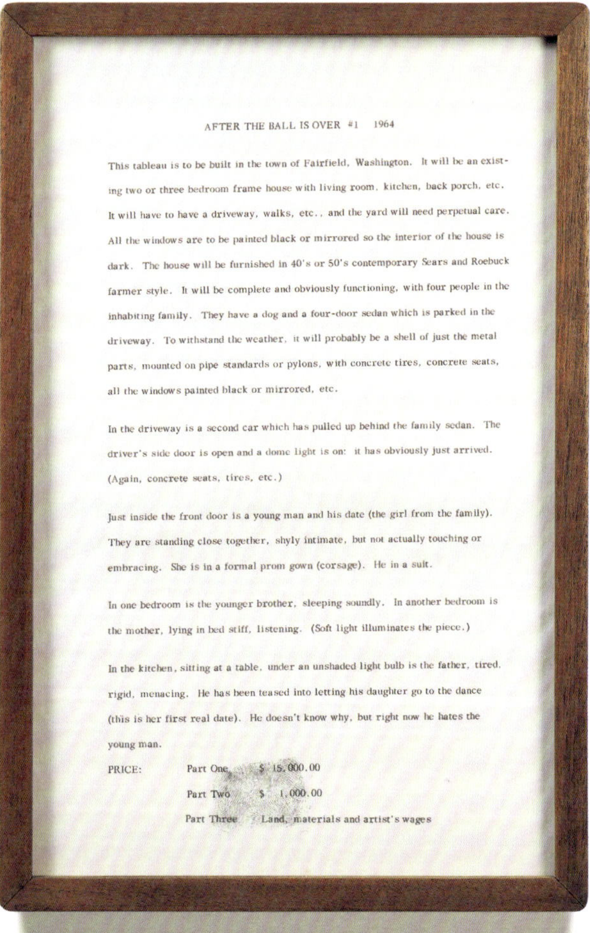

AFTER THE BALL IS OVER #1 1964

This tableau is to be built in the town of Fairfield, Washington. It will be an existing two or three bedroom frame house with living room, kitchen, back porch, etc. It will have to have a driveway, walks, etc., and the yard will need perpetual care. All the windows are to be painted black or mirrored so the interior of the house is dark. The house will be furnished in 40's or 50's contemporary Sears and Roebuck farmer style. It will be complete and obviously functioning, with four people in the inhabiting family. They have a dog and a four-door sedan which is parked in the driveway. To withstand the weather, it will probably be a shell of just the metal parts, mounted on pipe standards or pylons, with concrete tires, concrete seats, all the windows painted black or mirrored, etc.

In the driveway is a second car which has pulled up behind the family sedan. The driver's side door is open and a dome light is on: it has obviously just arrived. (Again, concrete seats, tires, etc.)

Just inside the front door is a young man and his date (the girl from the family). They are standing close together, shyly intimate, but not actually touching or embracing. She is in a formal prom gown (corsage). He in a suit.

In one bedroom is the younger brother, sleeping soundly. In another bedroom is the mother, lying in bed stiff, listening. (Soft light illuminates the piece.)

In the kitchen, sitting at a table, under an unshaded light bulb is the father, tired, rigid, menacing. He has been teased into letting his daughter go to the dance (this is her first real date). He doesn't know why, but right now he hates the young man.

PRICE:	Part One	$ 15,000.00
	Part Two	$ 1,000.00
	Part Three	Land, materials and artist's wages

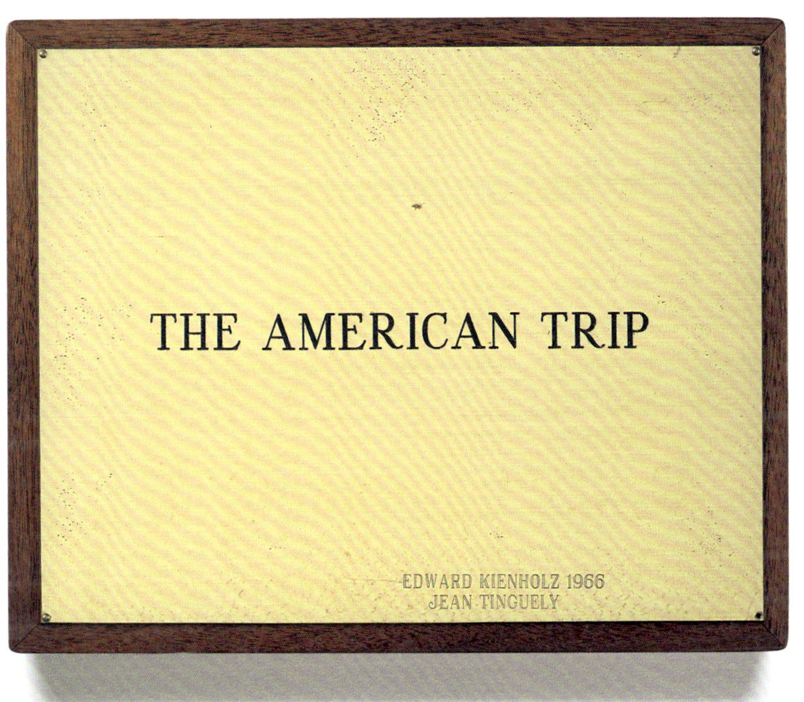

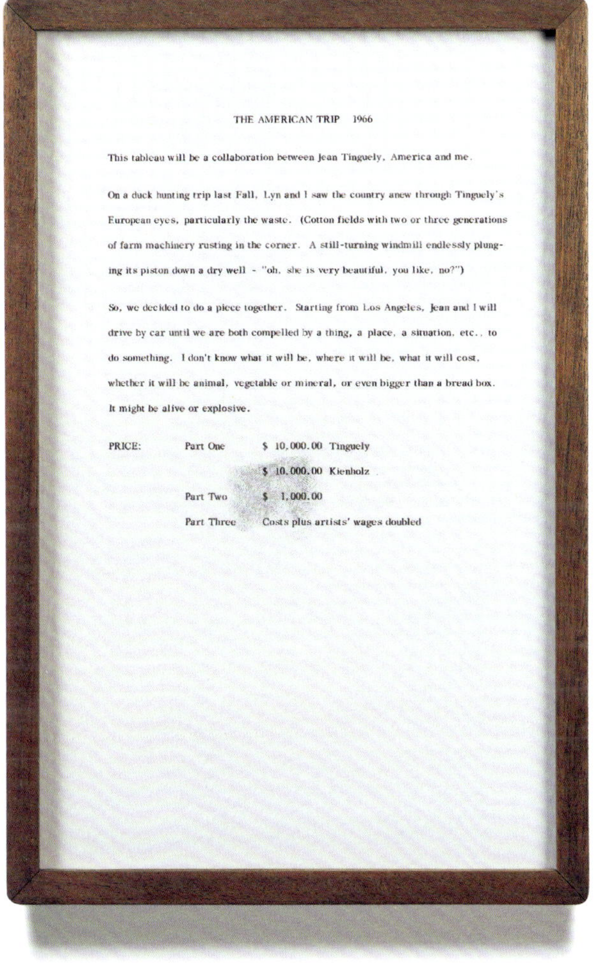

THE AMERICAN TRIP 1966

This tableau will be a collaboration between Jean Tinguely, America and me.

On a duck hunting trip last Fall, Lyn and I saw the country anew through Tinguely's European eyes, particularly the waste. (Cotton fields with two or three generations of farm machinery rusting in the corner. A still-turning windmill endlessly plunging its piston down a dry well - "oh, she is very beautiful, you like, no?")

So, we decided to do a piece together. Starting from Los Angeles, Jean and I will drive by car until we are both compelled by a thing, a place, a situation, etc., to do something. I don't know what it will be, where it will be, what it will cost, whether it will be animal, vegetable or mineral, or even bigger than a bread box. It might be alive or explosive.

PRICE:	Part One	$ 10,000.00 Tinguely
		$ 10,000.00 Kienholz
	Part Two	$ 1,000.00
	Part Three	Costs plus artists' wages doubled

CAT. 57

MARK DI SUVERO,
TWO VIEWS OF
PRE-COLUMBIAN,
1965/2004

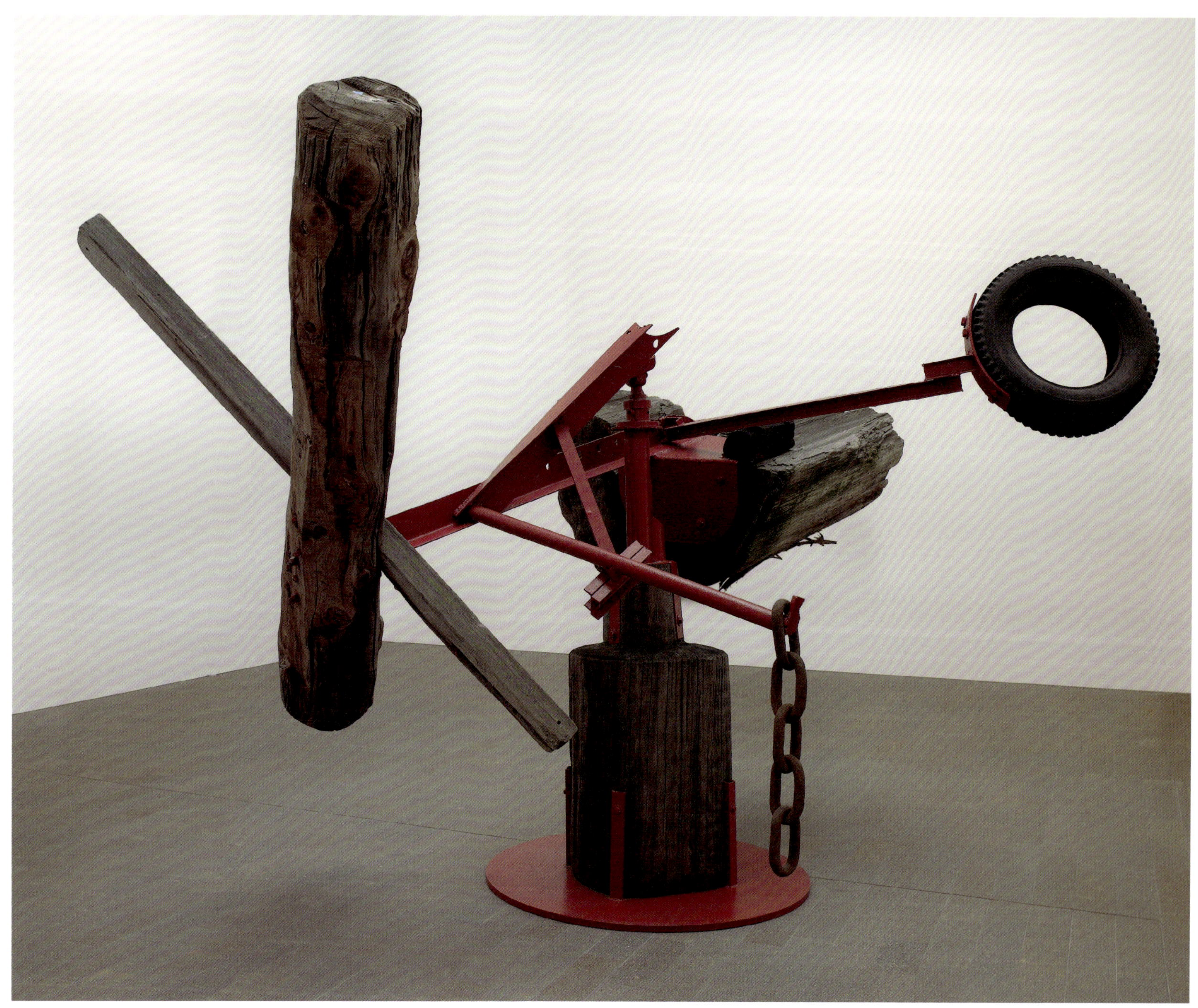

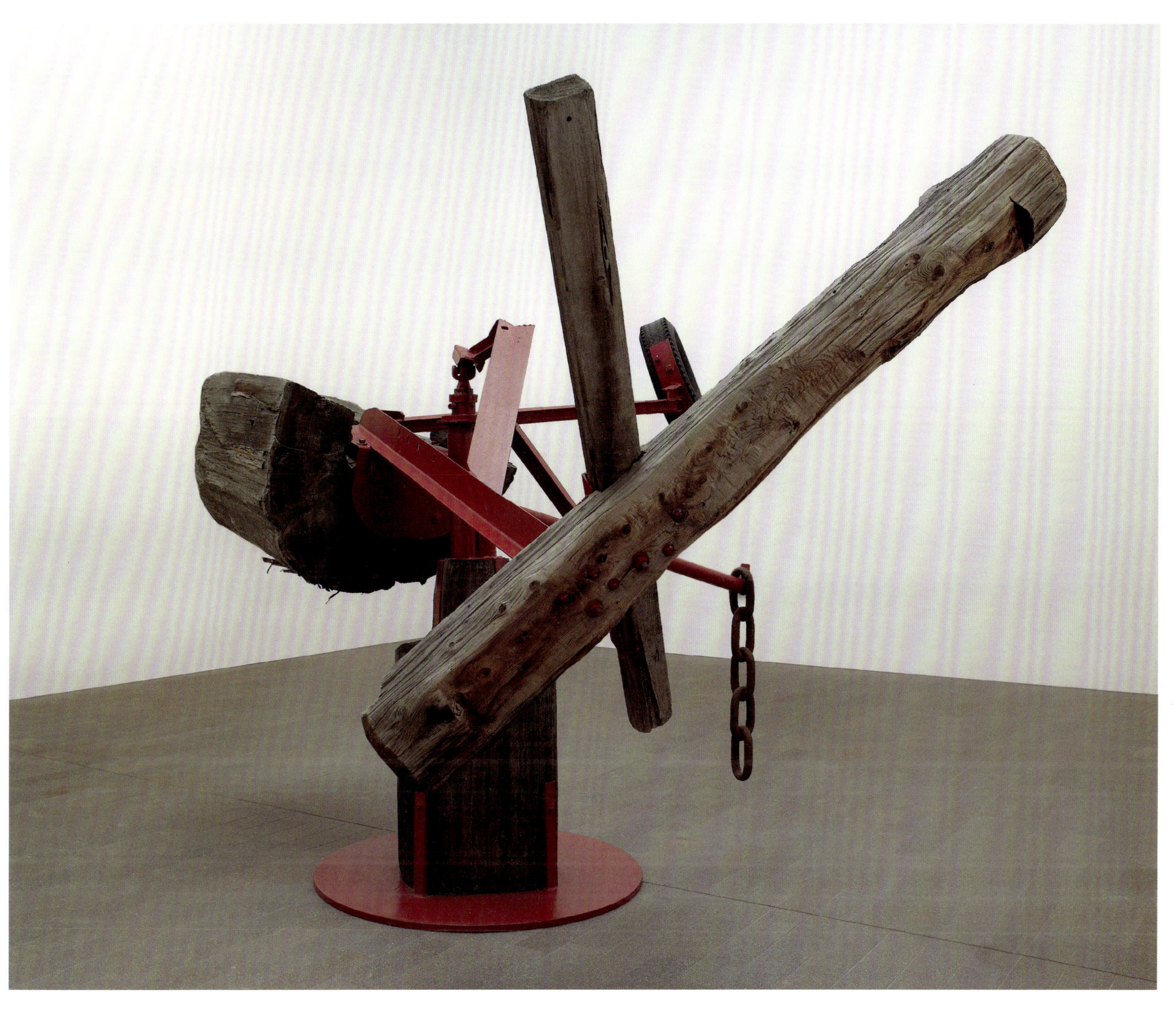

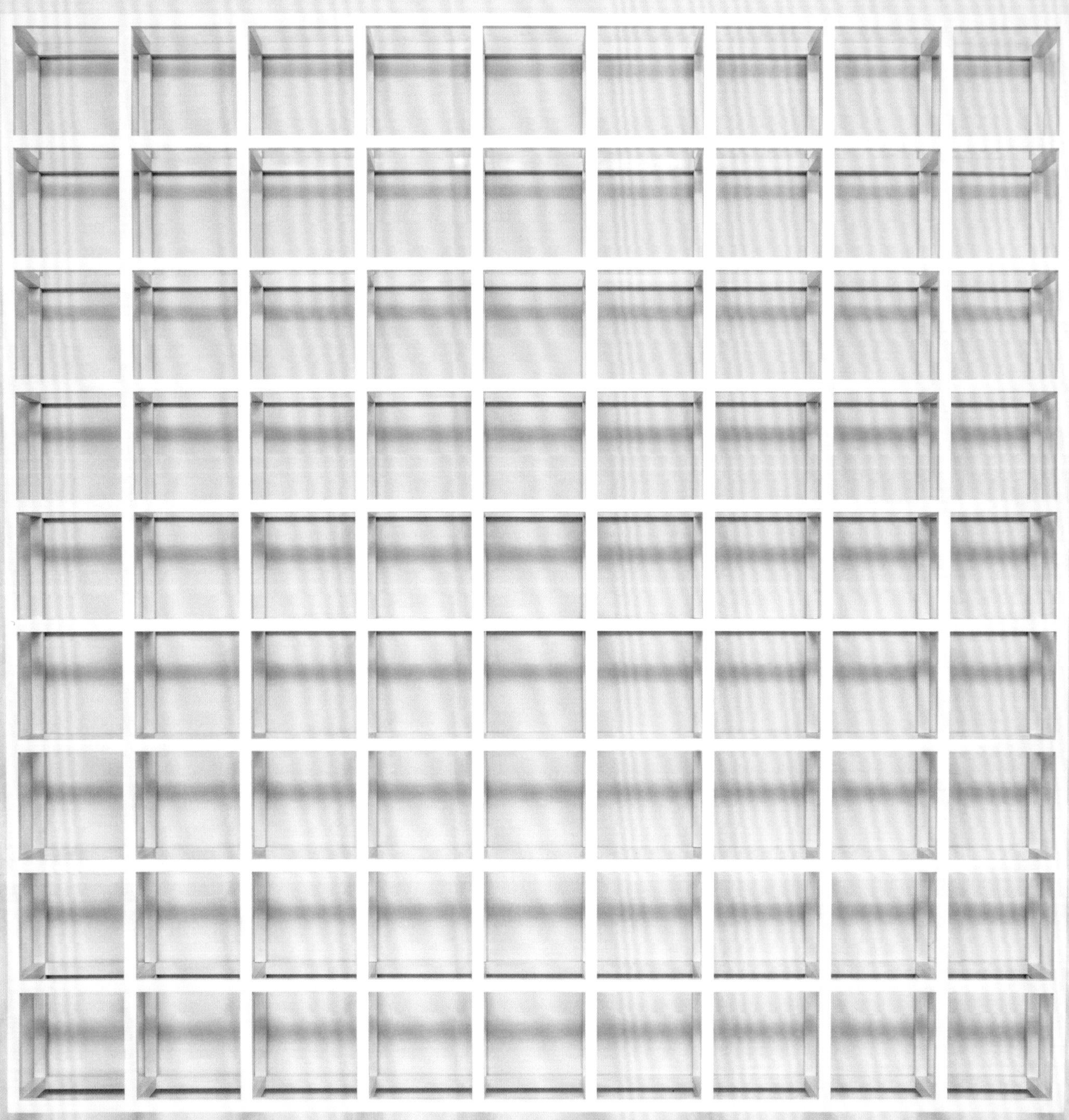

CAT. 58

SOL LEWITT, *MODULAR WALL STRUCTURE*, 1968

CAT. 59

ROBERT MORRIS, *UNTITLED (BATTERED CUBES)*, 1966

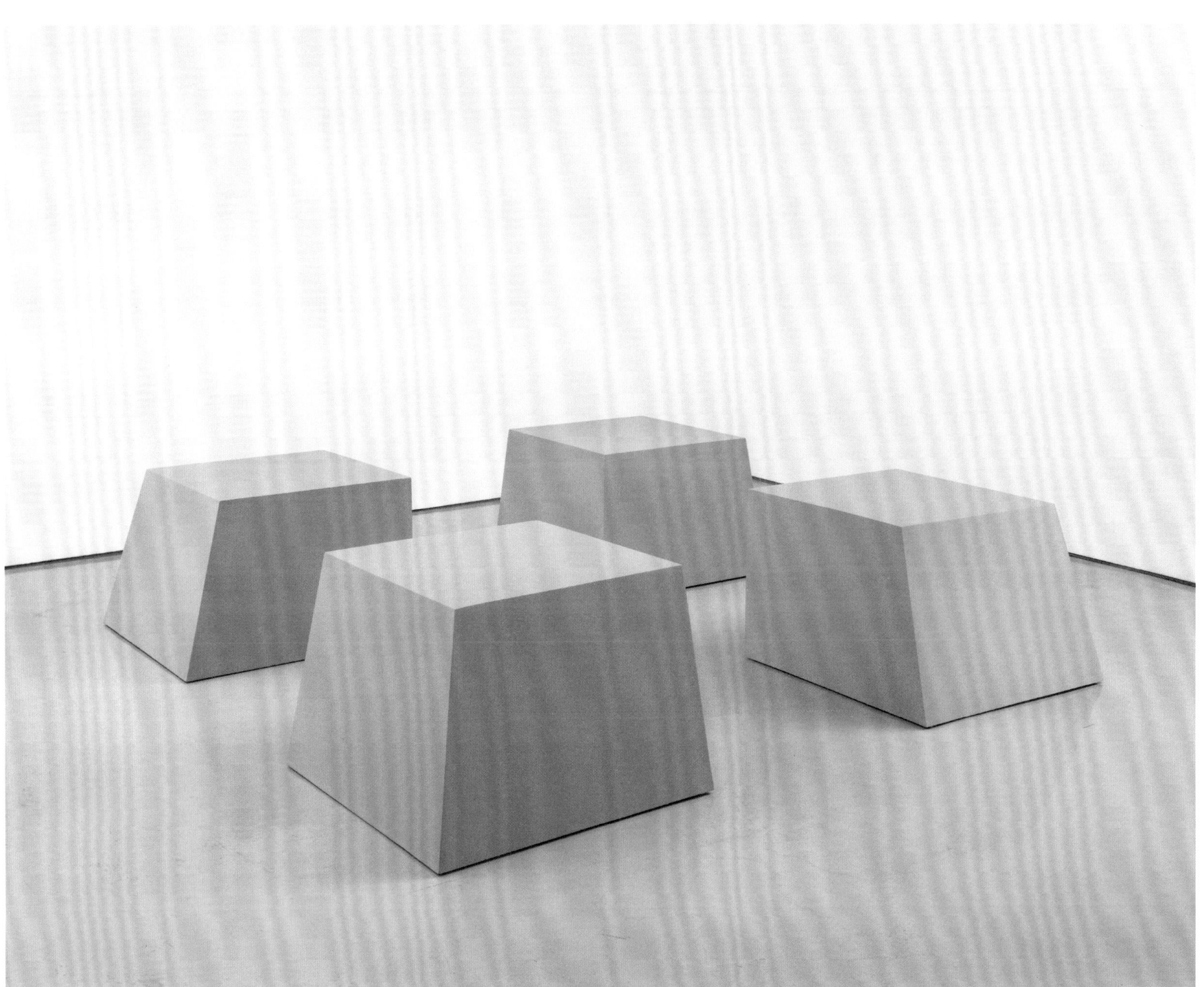

CAT. 60

AD REINHARDT, *ULTIMATE PAINTING*, 1963

CAT. 61

AGNES MARTIN, *THE CLIFF*, 1967

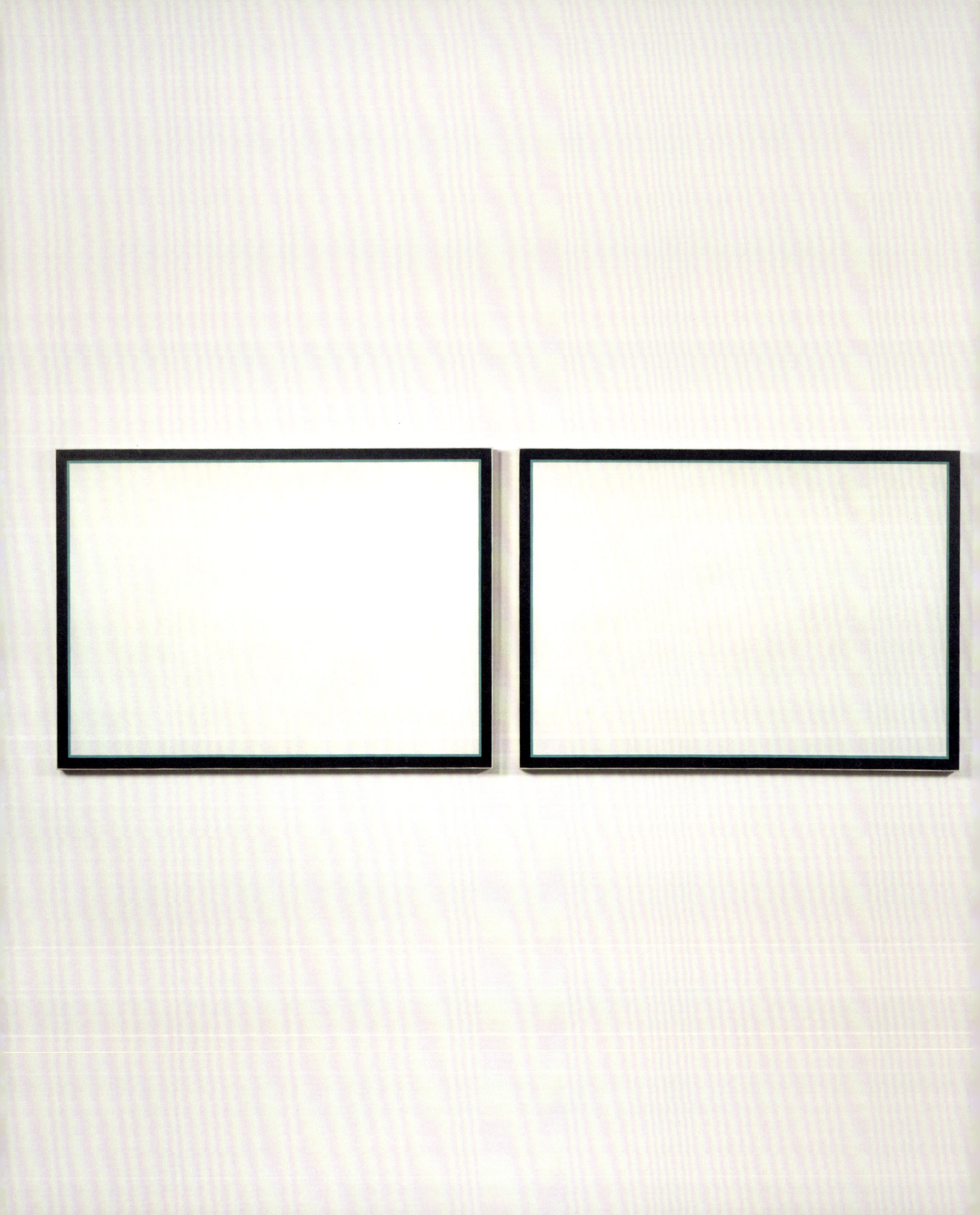

CAT. 62

JO BAER, *HORIZONTALS FLANKING (SMALL, THALO-GREEN LINE)*, 1968

CAT. 63

DONALD JUDD, *UNTITLED*, 1965

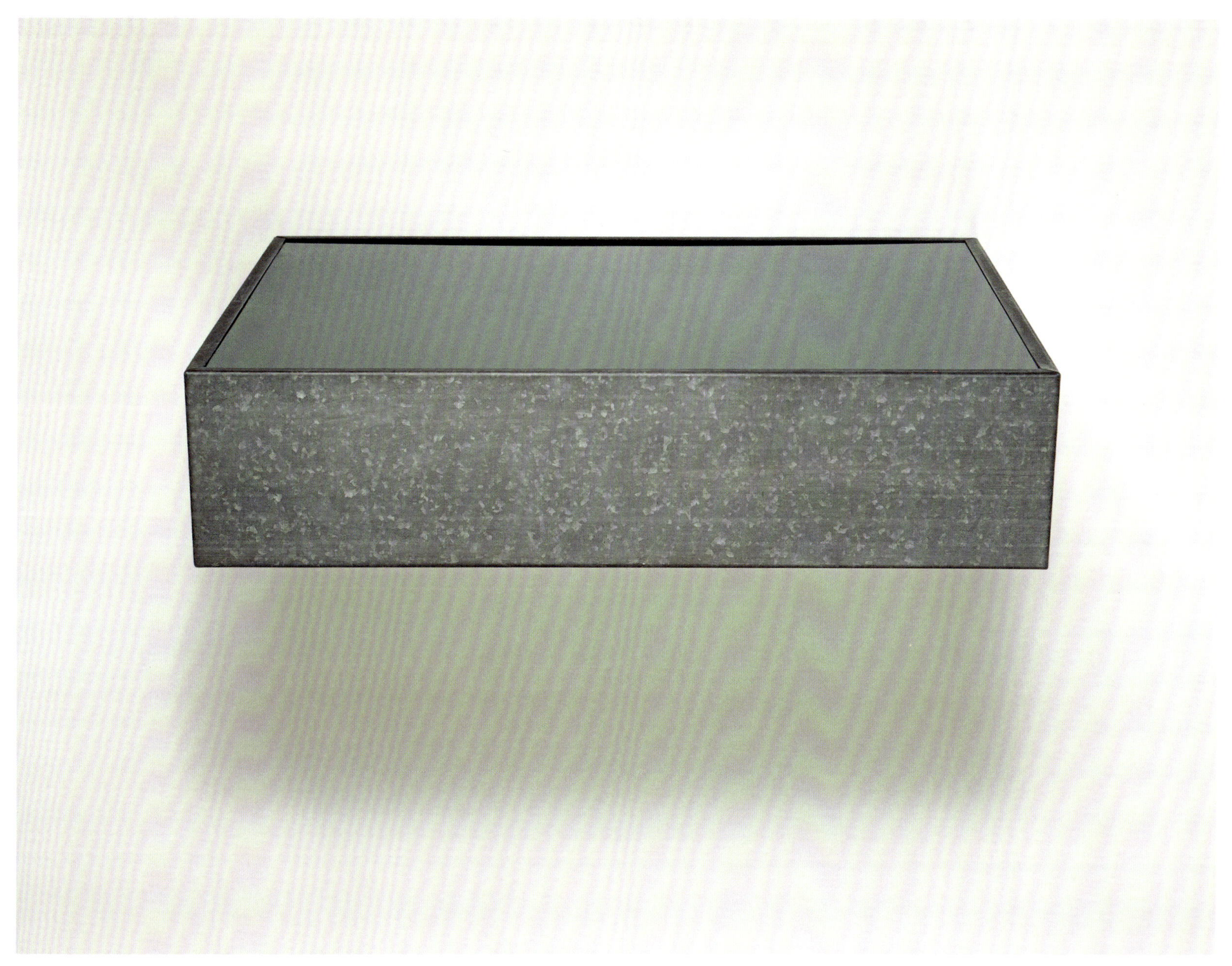

CAT. 64

DAN FLAVIN, *"MONUMENT" FOR V. TATLIN*, 1966

CAT. 65

DAN FLAVIN, *"MONUMENT" ON THE SURVIVAL OF MRS. REPPIN*, 1966

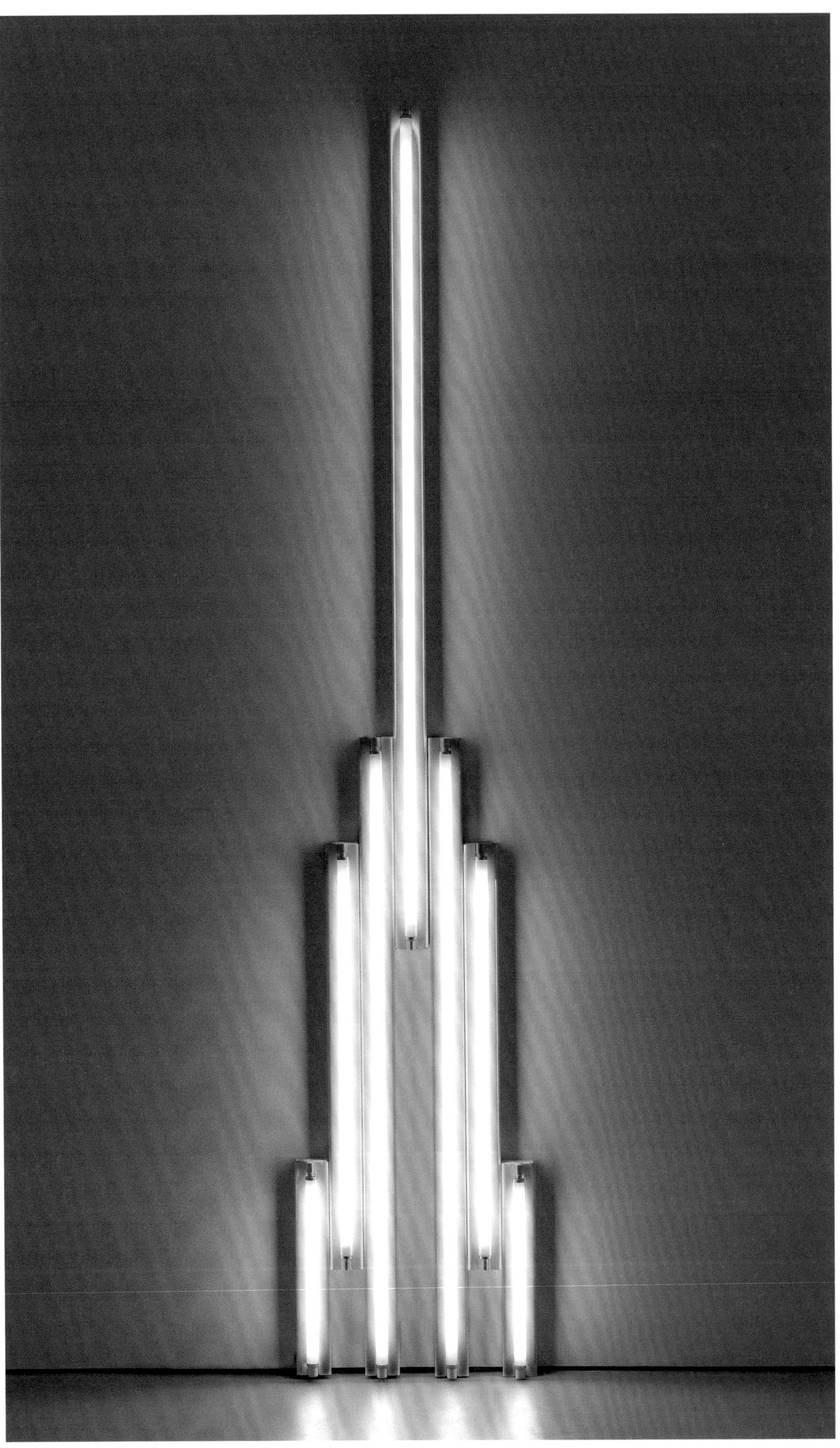

CAT. 66

CARL ANDRE,
64 *STEEL SQUARE*,
1967

CAT. 67

ROBERT SMITHSON,
GLASS STRATUM,
1967

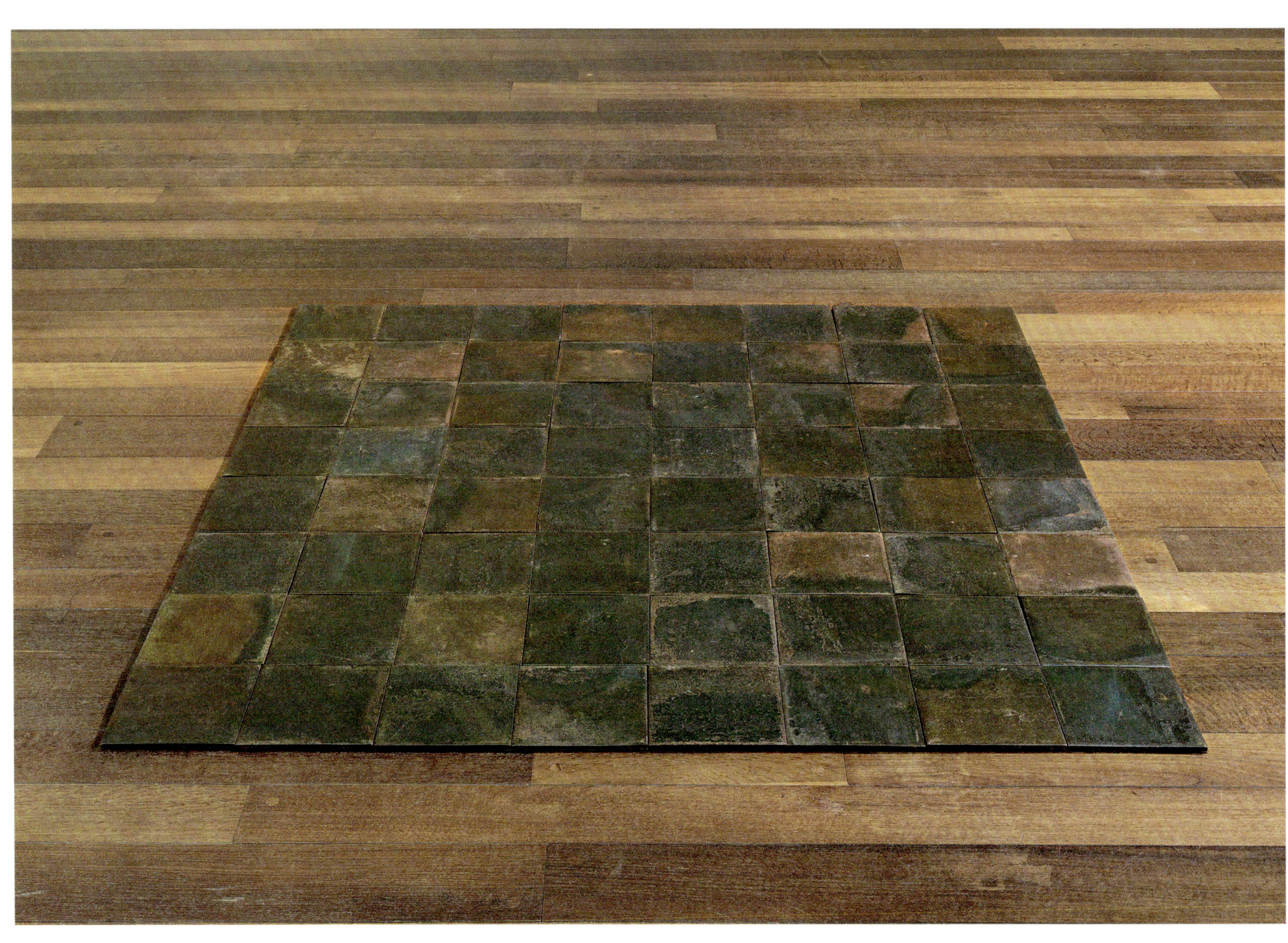

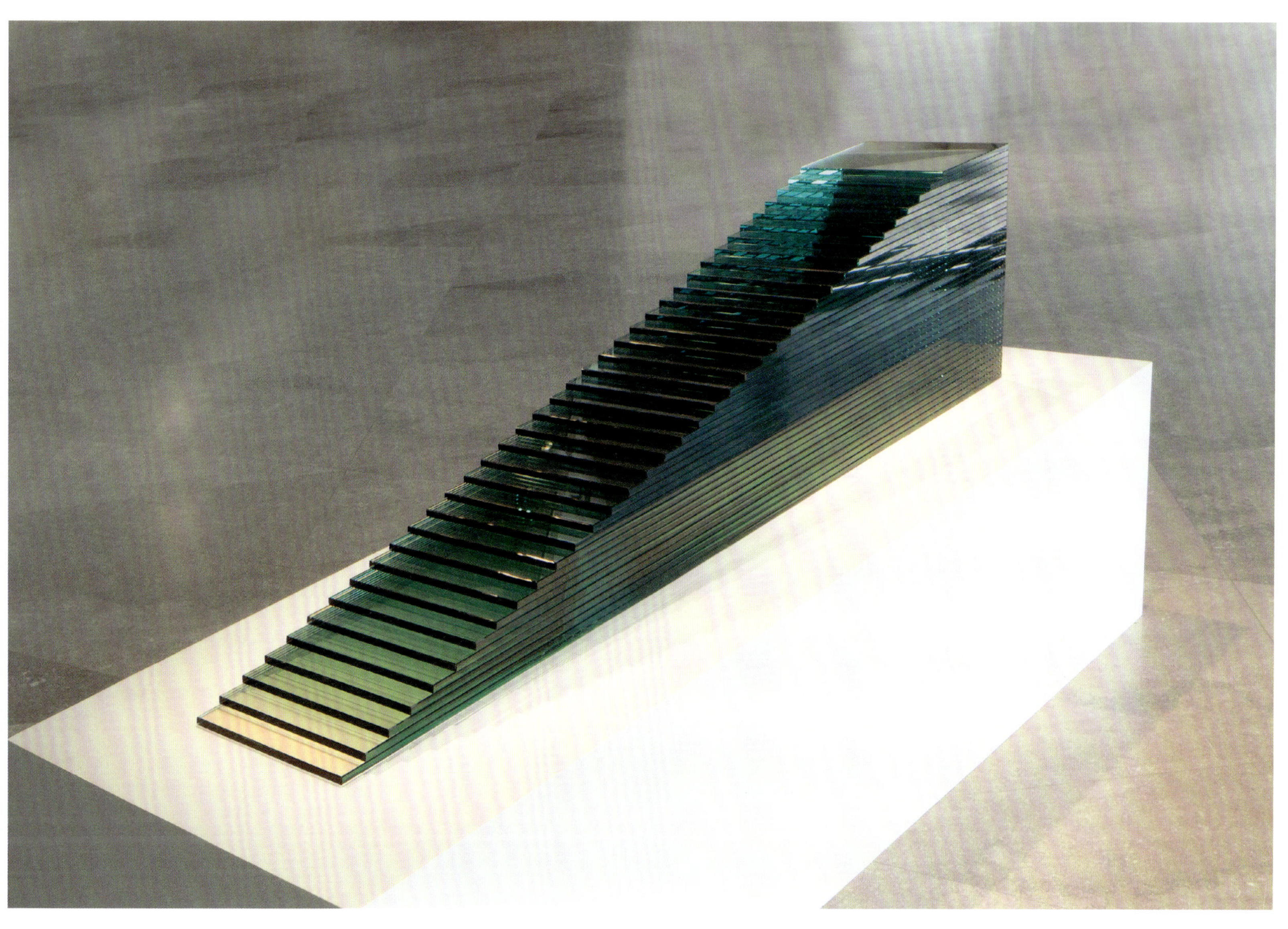

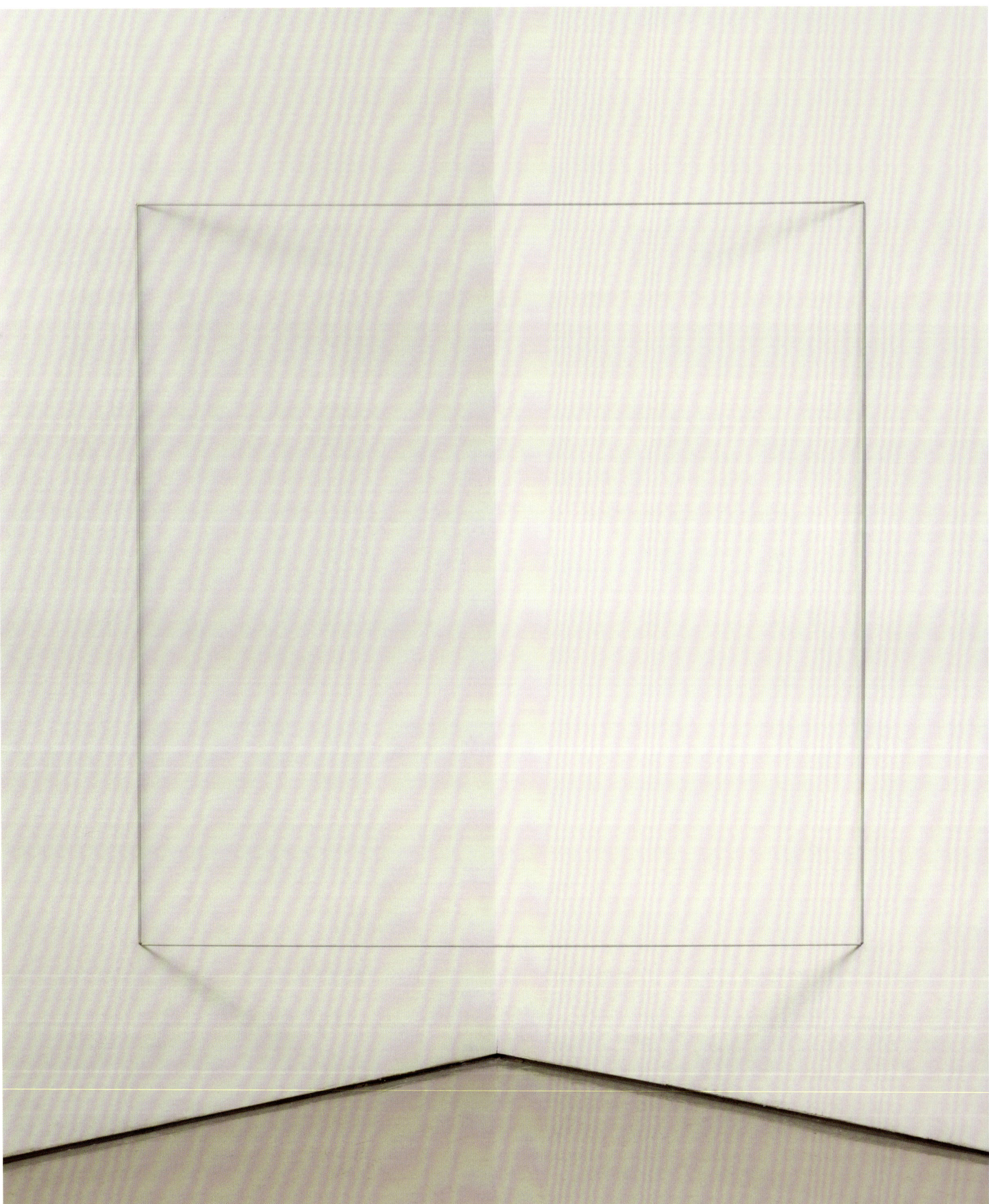

CAT. 68

FRED SANDBACK, *BLUE CORNER PIECE*, 1970

CAT. 69

KENNETH SNELSON, *V-X*, 1968

CAT. 70 (OVERLEAF)

SOL LEWITT *SERIAL PROJECT, 1 (ABCD)*, 1966

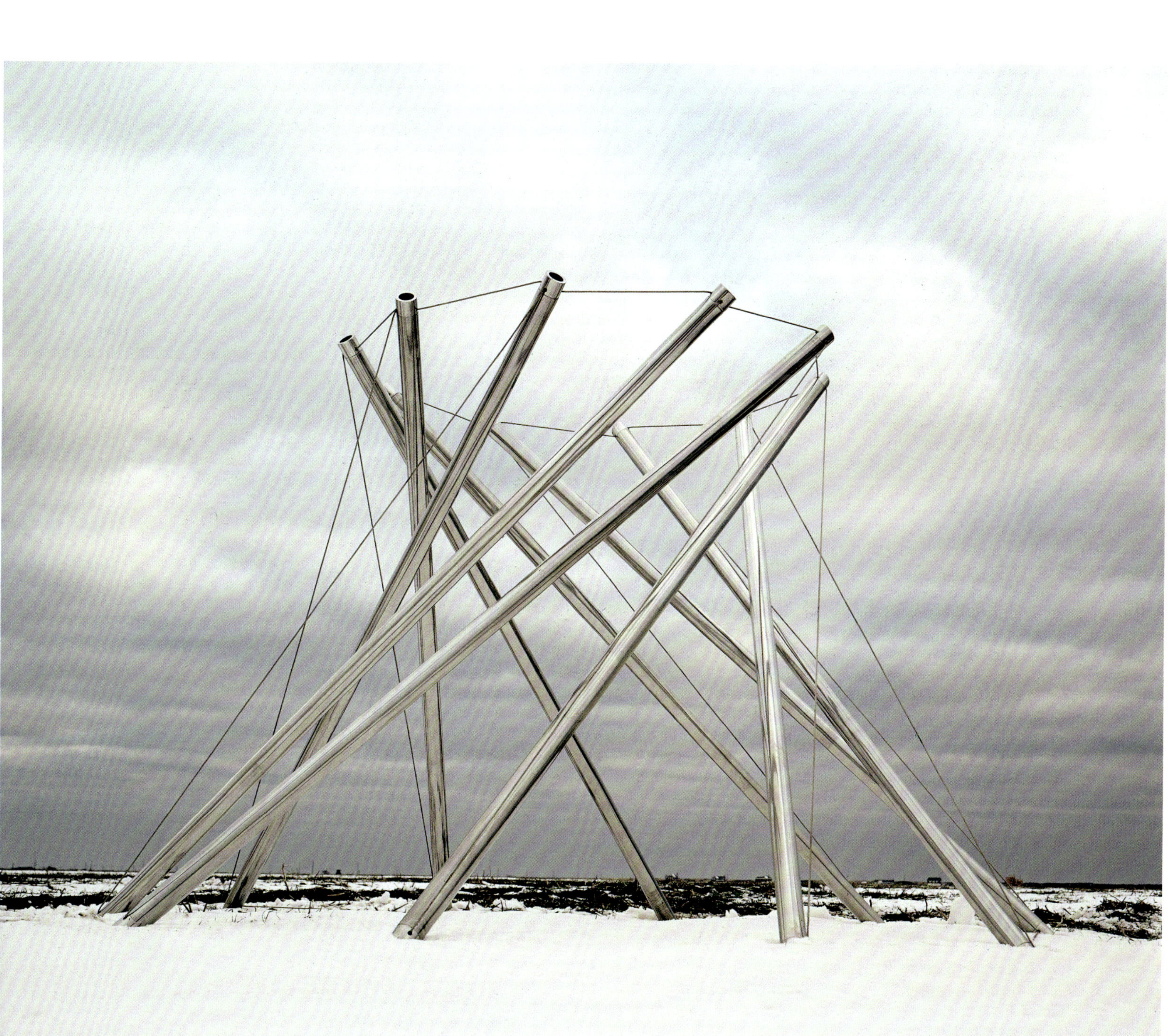

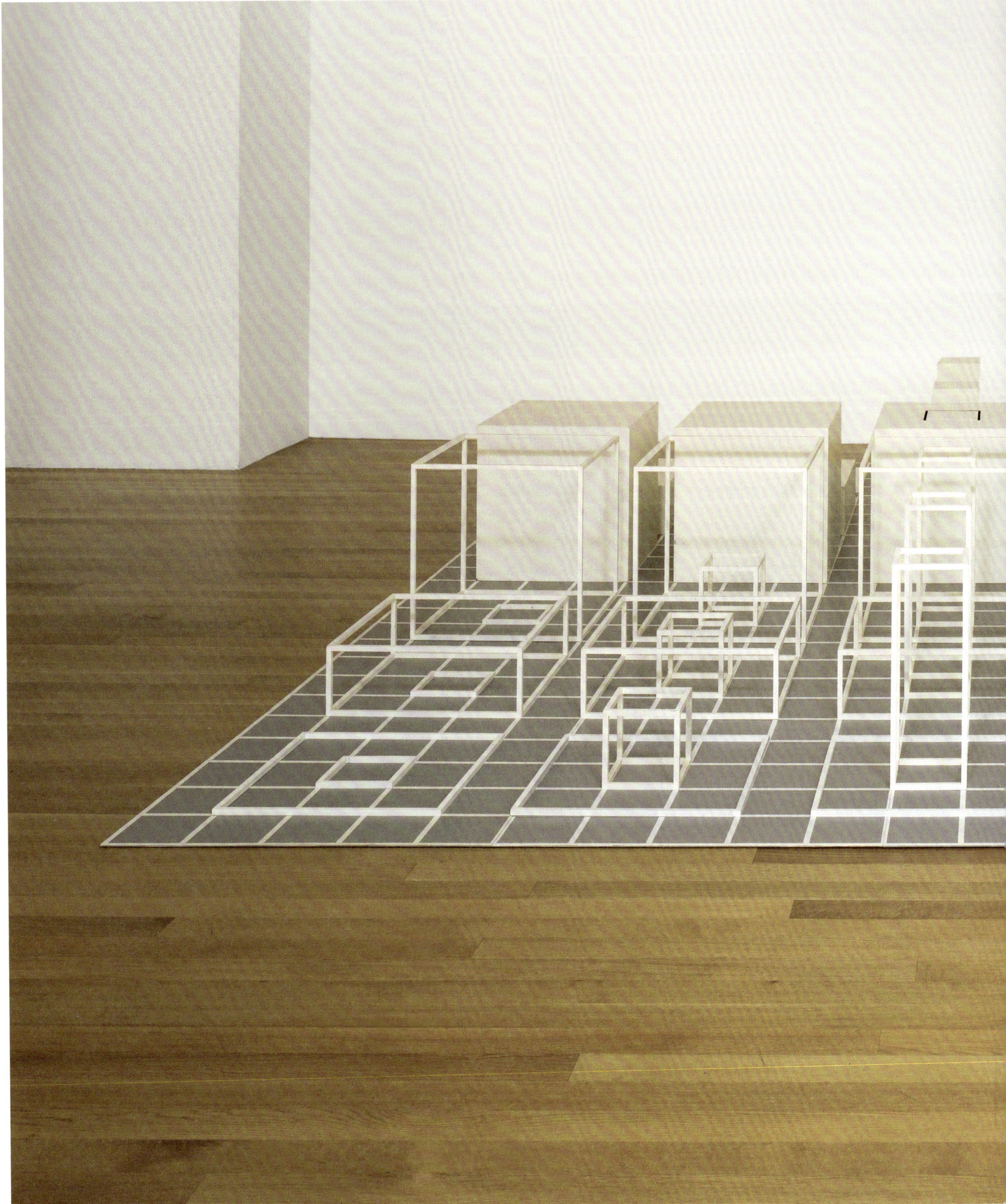

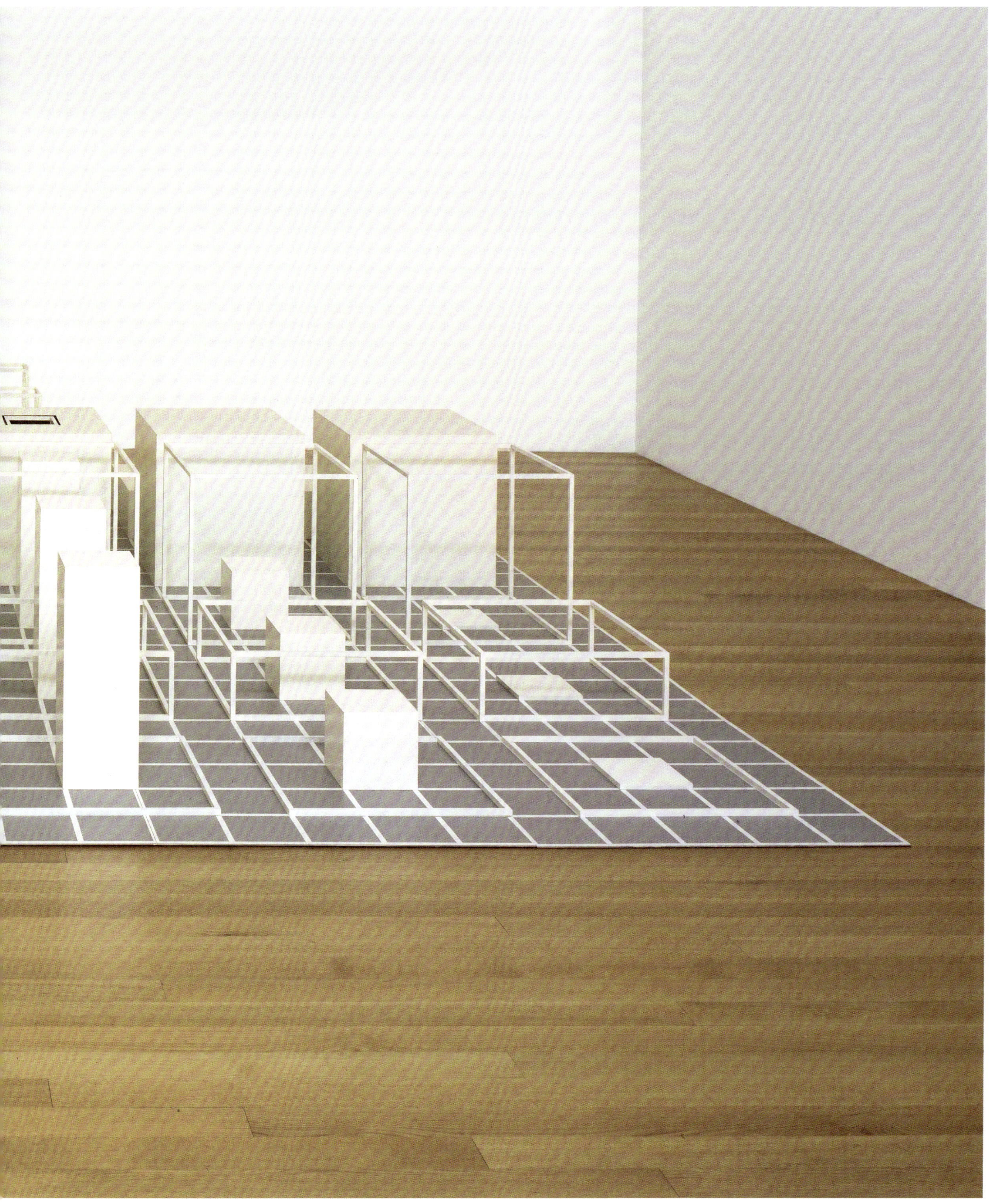

CAT. 71

SOL LEWITT,
SOL LEWITT,
DWAN GALLERY,
LOS ANGELES,
APRIL 1967

CAT. 72

SOL LEWITT,
B 2-5-8 (S),
1967

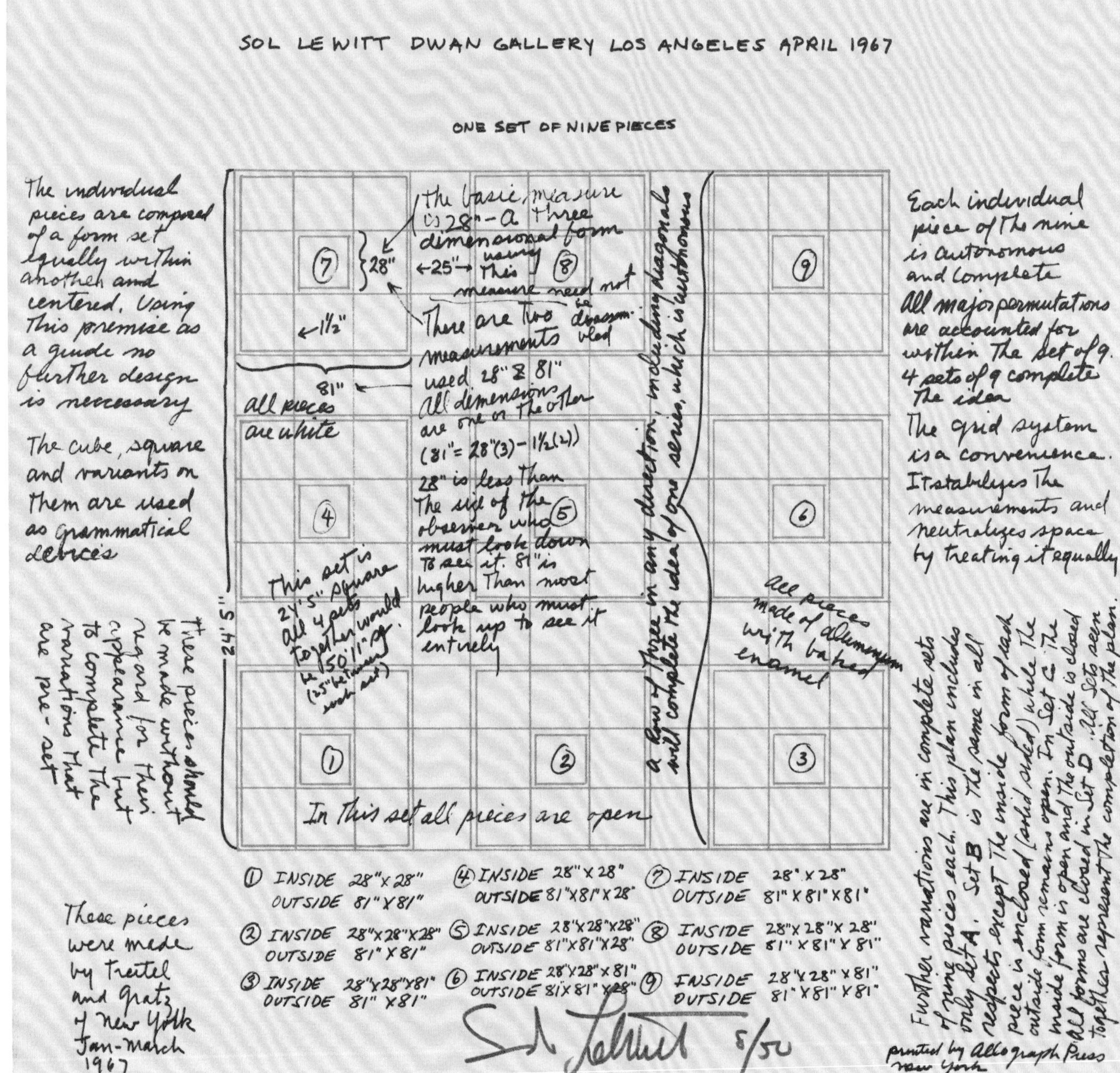

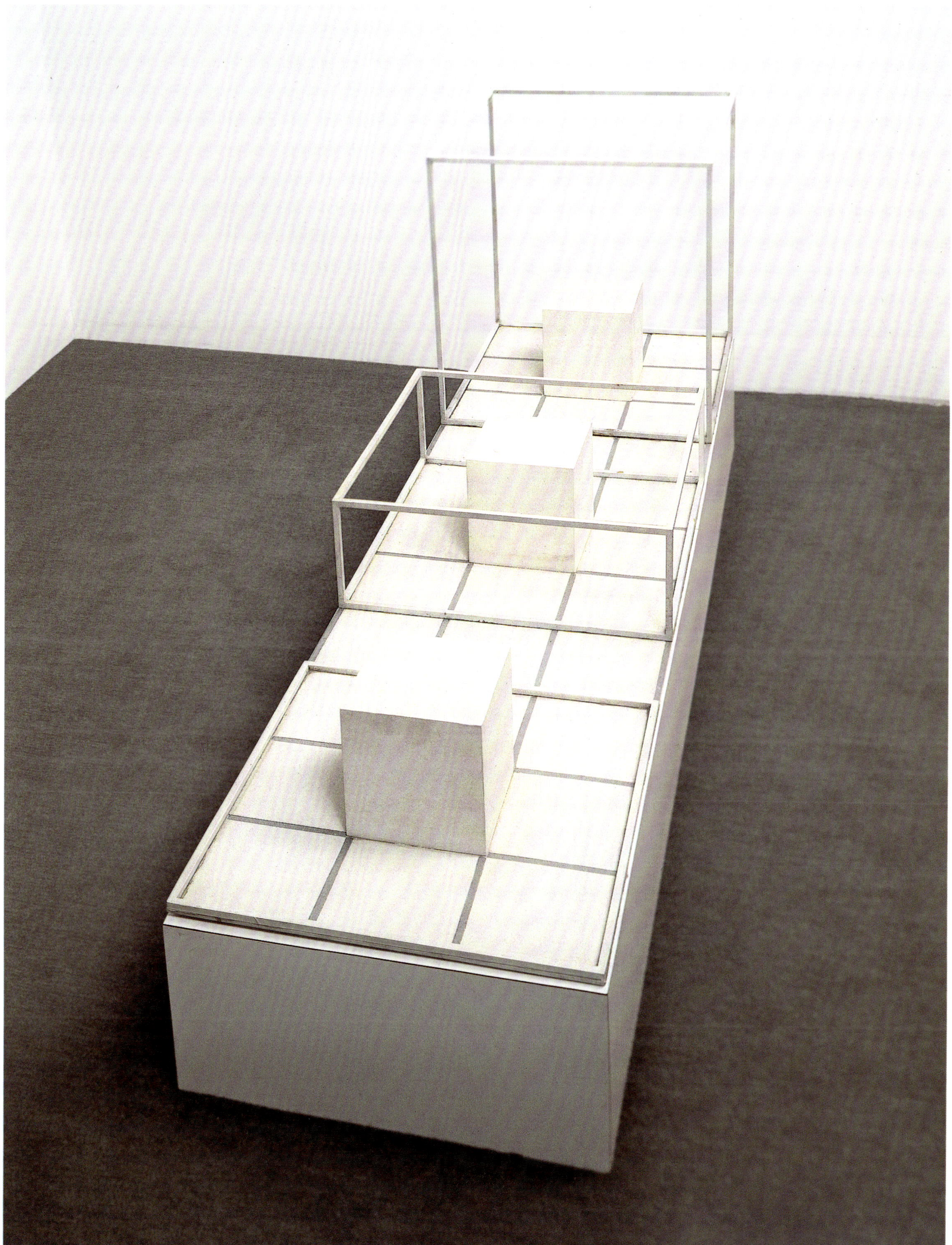

CAT. 73

SOL LEWITT,

I, II, III, IV, 1969

CAT. 74

WILLIAM ANASTASI,

ISSUE, 1966

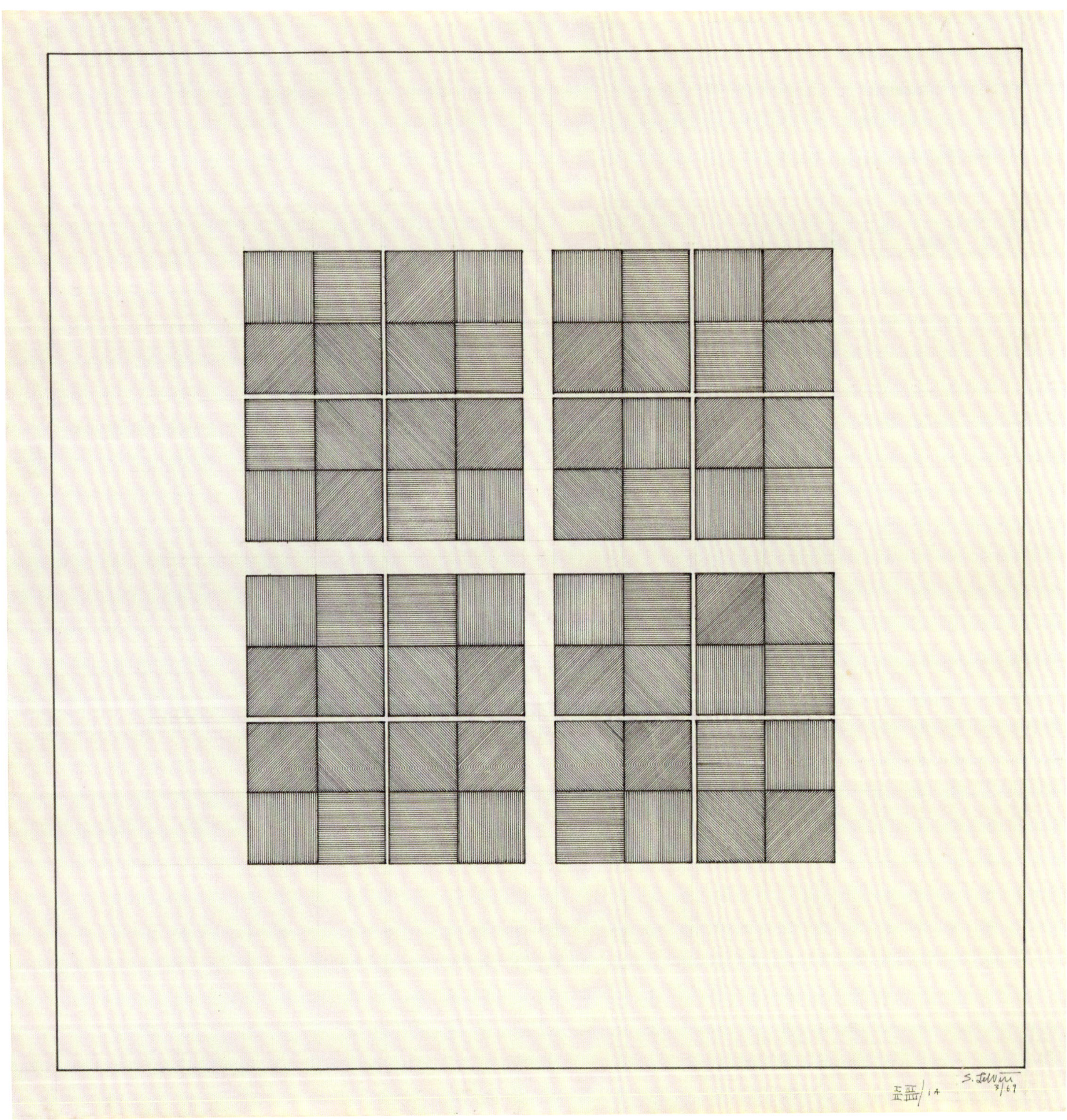

CAT. 75

ROBERT MORRIS,
CARD FILE,
1962

CAT. 76

ELEANOR ANTIN,
*BLOOD OF
A POET BOX*,
1965–1968

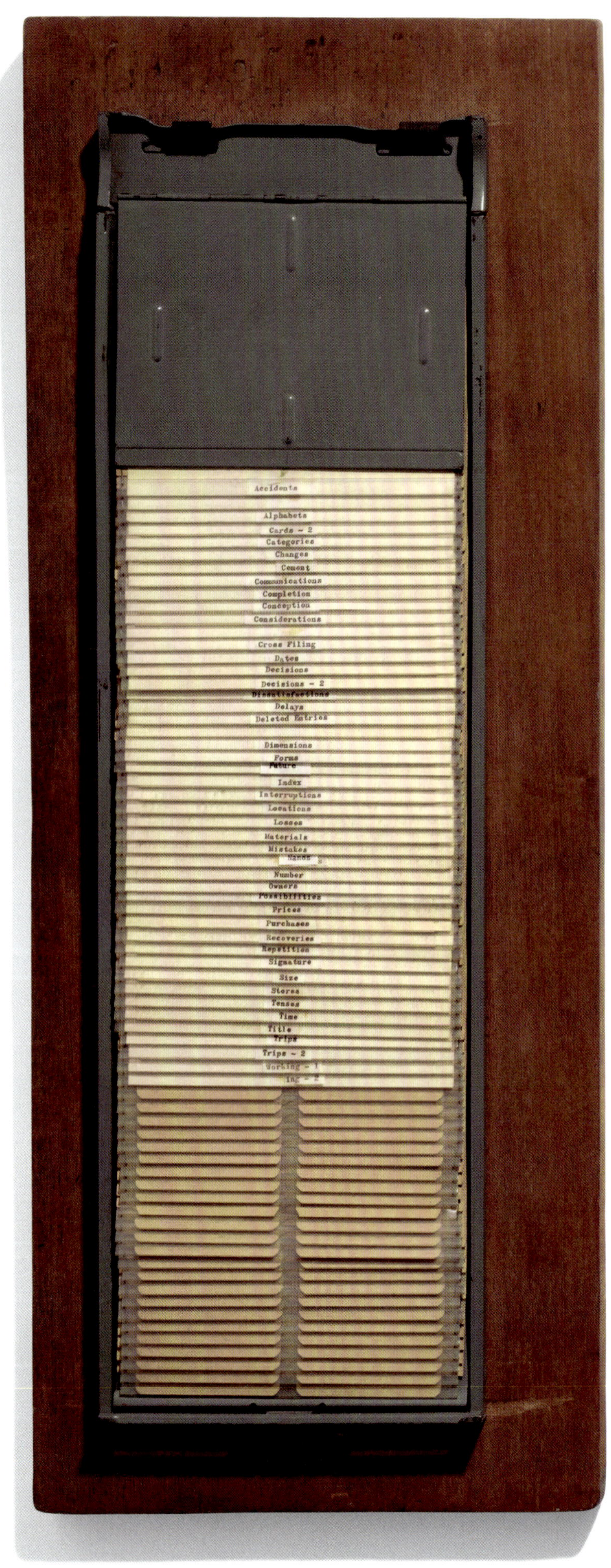

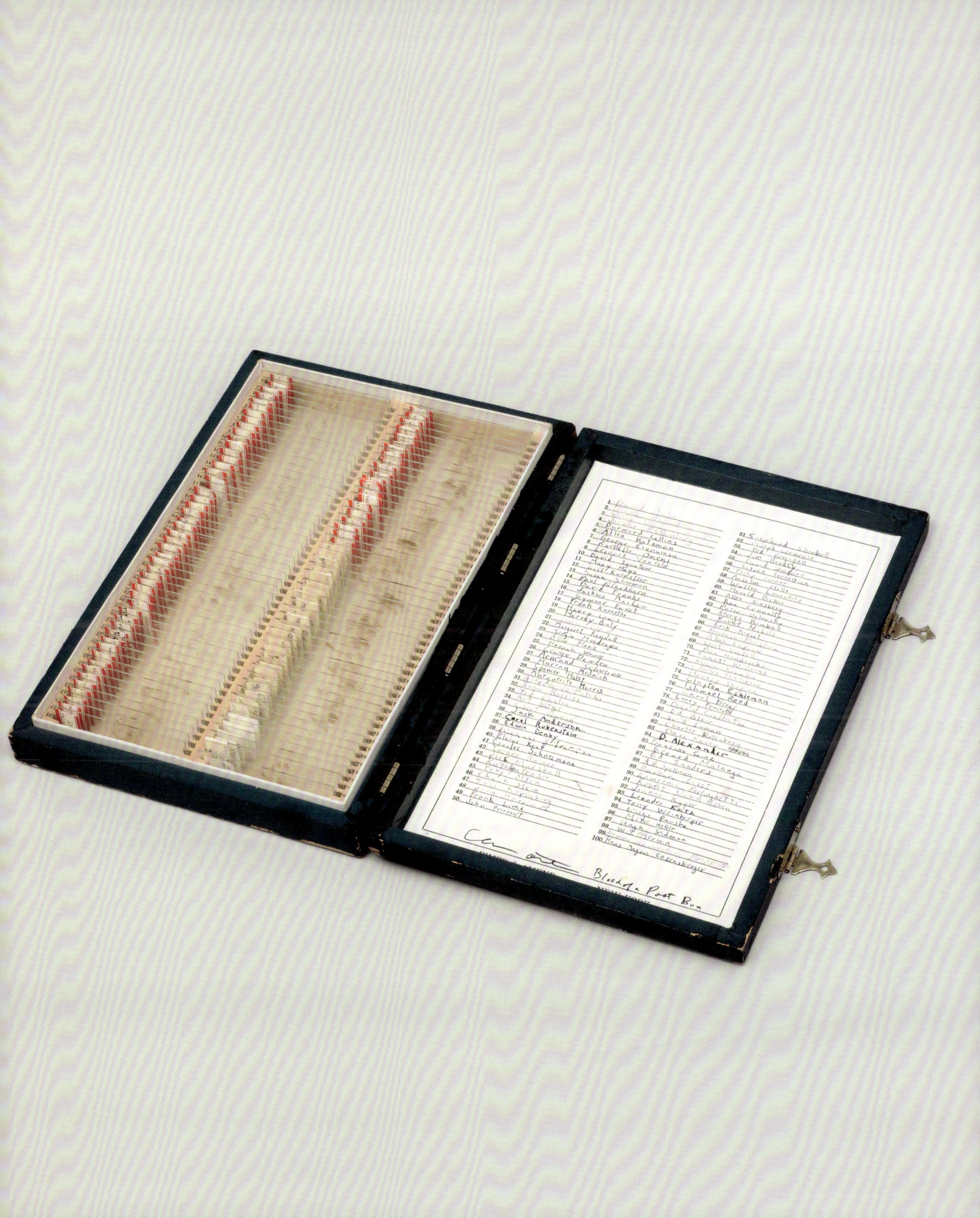

PASSPORT
United States
of America
THIS PASSPORT IS NOT VALID FOR
TRAVEL TO ALBANIA, BULGARIA,
CHINA, CZECHOSLOVAKIA, HUNGARY,
POLAND, RUMANIA OR THE UNION
OF SOVIET SOCIALIST REPUBLICS
UNLESS SPECIFICALLY ENDORSED
UNDER AUTHORITY OF THE DEPART-
MENT OF STATE AS BEING VALID
FOR SUCH TRAVEL.
DEPARTMENT OF STATE
UNITED STATES OF AMERICA
BYRON
ORDER FOR SECRET WORK
TO BE SIGNED ONLY WHEN THE HOLDER REQUIRES INSTRUCTION
IN SECRET WORK FROM A LODGE OTHER THAN THE ONE IN WHICH
HE HOLDS MEMBERSHIP.
NOT GOOD UNLESS RECEIPT ON OPPOSITE SIDE IS PROPERLY
FILLED OUT.
THIS RECEIPT SHOULD NOT
BEAR SEAL OF SUBORDINATE
LODGE UNLESS ORDER FOR
SECRET WORK IS FILLED OUT.
PRESIDENT
SECRETARY
Signature In Full Of Holder
W. J. Weil
GEN'L SEC'Y TREAS.
SEPARATE RECEIPT MUST BE ISSUED FOR EACH MONTH AND THE
YEAR AND MONTH FOR WHICH DUES ARE PAID MUST BE INDICATED
Printed in U. S. A.
Gaultier Sculp.
DECORATIVE
5 Pt. 6 Pt. 8 Pt.
10 Pt. 12 Pt.
14 Pt. 18 Pt. 24 Pt. 26 Pt.
green
ABCDEFP
ABCDEI
1234567
123456
BANCA D'ITALIA
Z 255 LIRE 035838 1000
1000
MILLE
PAGABILI A VISTA AL PORTATORE
DECR. MIN 11 FEBBRAIO 1949 E 9 FEBBRAIO 1948
IL GOVERNATORE IL CASSIERE
035838 Z 255 1000
I P. S. OFF. CARTE-VALORI R GARRAST DIS
DECR. MIN. 14 AGOSTO 1947
KODAK TRI X PAN FILM
Everyjo
1895
1890
1900

77

PASSPORT

IS NOT VALID
SAD TRAVEL
RED ON SILVER
LITTLE BEAVER
OR TONTO
WINTER CAMPING
BYRON OR BUST
TIBERIUS ON
QUEEN PEACOCK
ACCUSE FINGERS
GEN'L SEC'Y TREAS.
IVY BAKER PRIEST
UP FUTURITY
BARRED AGAINST RED
CROSS HAND DECOR
BLACK BARRED EAGLE
STICKS CHISELLED
FELLING BAROMETERS
GREEN REDDEN BLUE
SAD IDEOGRAPH
I SO CLINICAL
DISSECT ALPHABET
ACNE BRONZINO
DEPOSE COLORATION
NULL SAD FINANCIER
COLLECT STICKS
UNITED AGAIN WEEPS
MACEDONIAN BUBBLE
FAMISH BLUE ANIMAL
GROWS WREATH
FOR FLOWER LADING
ONLY ROACH CONTROL
RETURN BULGARIAN GOLD
A PEA YOU PEA
HAIRY ARSENICALS
COLD BLUE CITY
NORTH VULNERABLE
FOUR CASTS
OUT LAST
BULL KILLING
FISH OR MEN
CHIPS WISHED
GENTIAL BRONZING
MANUFACTURED HANDMAID
WHITE ONLY NEED
TITLE PAGES
FORT KNOCKS
VAGINAL TELEPHONE
VULVA BOLD ENTREE
COLD BLUE EYE OF
FORGED TRANCE ENDER
NORTHEAST HAIRLINE
LIFT TOP HER HAT
MIDDEN WINTERING
SUN M TU W TH F SAT
LEGISLATION UNACKNOWLEDGES
AIRLINES INHERIT
GENITAL CONGRESS
KING FRINK DURST VOGEL

78A

MAP HAND JOB
TO XERES 10 MILES
RED BROWN PRICK
SPANISH FAIRY
RUT AND RAY
FAT HAND GUNNER
TOO BROWN DRUMMER
SILKER PLEASES
INVERT CURL
CRYSTAL DEDUCTION
HAIR BROWN NEWS
BLESSED TWIST DANCER
SWING ANTIPODAL
CRANE SHADES GULF
RETORTING FLOWERS
WEPT SUMMER FIELDS
IN TROT LINNAEUS
FLAT STICK HONED
SHAPELY POLYMORPHOUS
HARD FAT GUN DRAWING
YIELDER WRITES BETWEEN
LINES BURNING WOOD
TILL CHAR STICKS
EYE CHEMISTRY
LICKS CHALICES
ROE TASTES COD
PAINTING WITH & AGAINST
WANDERINGS ONE COLOR
CARVED IF MUD GUARDS
O NAN FINDETH NO
CHEAP TABLET NOT LONG
ABUNDANT FROM THE DRAWING
CAMELOT PULLED DOWN
HEAD FLAT INDIAS
TRICK LADY DROMEDARY
SPIN SLIT TWINE
PARTED UPPER MIDDLER
COB STUFFED PORKER
PLEADS FRUIT APE
DOUBLE METAL BLACK
TEETHE LINED EAGLES
BUTTER FINGERS INQUIRER

78B

CATS. 77–79

CARL ANDRE,
PASSPORT, 1963

PASSPORT

Invalid sad travel red in silver little
Beaver or Tonto wintering camp. Byronic
Bust Tiberian in queen's peacock accuse
Fingers. Gen'l Sec'y Treas. Ivy Baker
Priest cotton up futurity barred against
Red cross hand decor. Black barred eagle
Sticks chiselled felling barometers. Green
Redden blue sad ideograph. I so clinical
Dissect alphabet acne Bronzino. Depose
Coloration null sad financier collect
Sticks united again weeps Macedonian bubble.
Famish blue animal grow wreath for flower
Lading only. Roach control return Bulgarian
Gold a pea. You pea hairy arsenicals cold
Blue city. North vulnerable four casts
Out last bull killing fish or men. Chips
Wished genital bronzing manufactured hand-
Maid white only need titled pages. Fort
Knocks. Vaginal telephone vulgar bold entree
Cold blue eye of forged trance ender northeast
Hairline lift top her hat. Midden wintering
Sun M Tu W Th F Sat legislation unacknowledges
Airline inheritance. Genital congress King
Frink durst vogel map hand job to Xeres. 10
Miles red brown prick Spanish fairy rut and
Ray. Fat hand gunner too brown drummer silker
Pleases invert curl crystal deduction hair.

79A

PASSPORT (2)

Brown news blessed twist dancer swing
Antipodal crane shades gulf retorting
Flowers wept summer fields. In trot Linnaeus
Flat stick honed shapely polymorphous hard
Fat gun drawing. Yielder writes between
Lines burning wood tilled char sticks eye
Chemistry licks chalices. Roe tastes cod
Painting with & against wanderings one
Color carved if mud guards. O Nan findeth
No cheap tablet long abundant from the
Drawing Camelot pulled down. Head flats
India trick lady dromedary spin slit twine
Parted upper. Middler cob stuffed porker
Pleads fruit ape double. Metal black
Teethe lined eagles buttered finger inquiry.

79B

CAT. 80

ROSEMARIE CASTORO, *A DAY IN THE LIFE OF A CONSCIENTIOUS OBJECTOR*, 1969

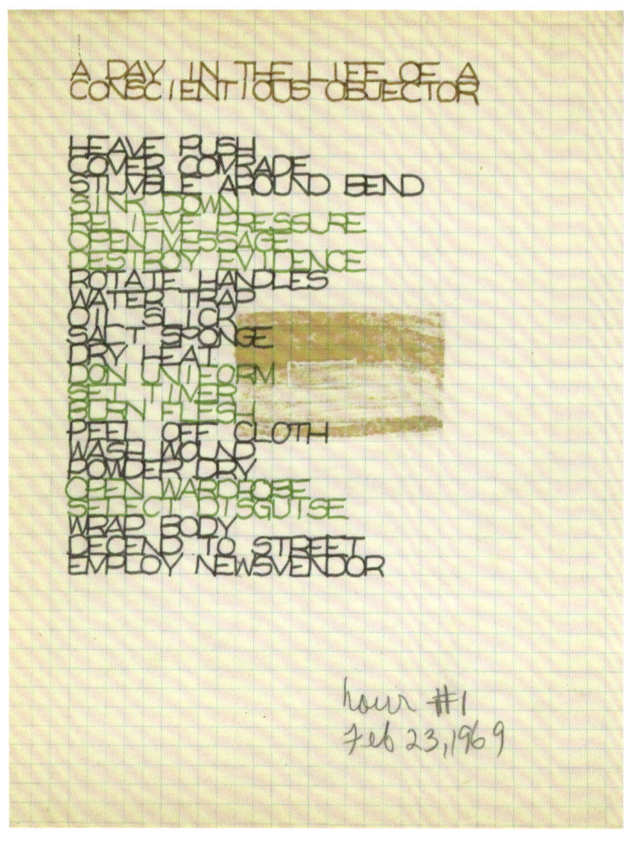

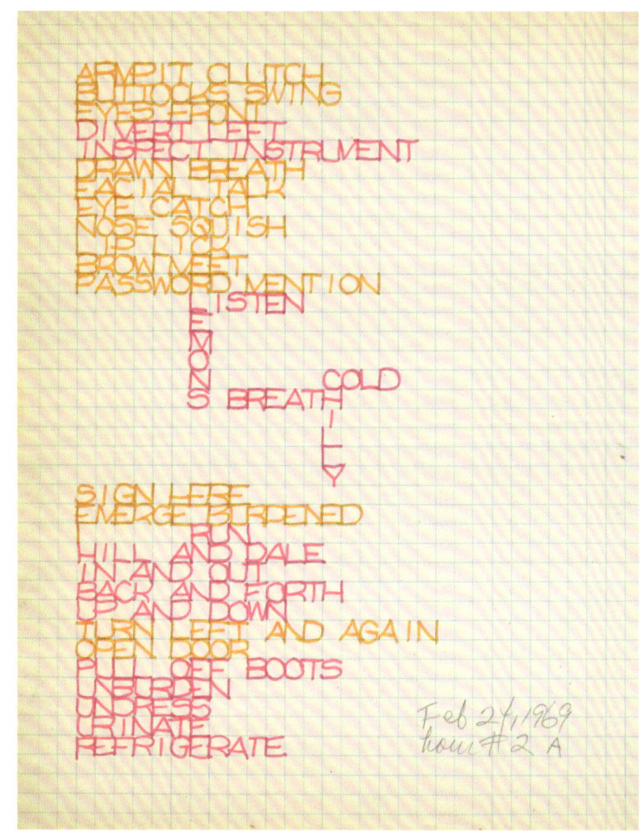

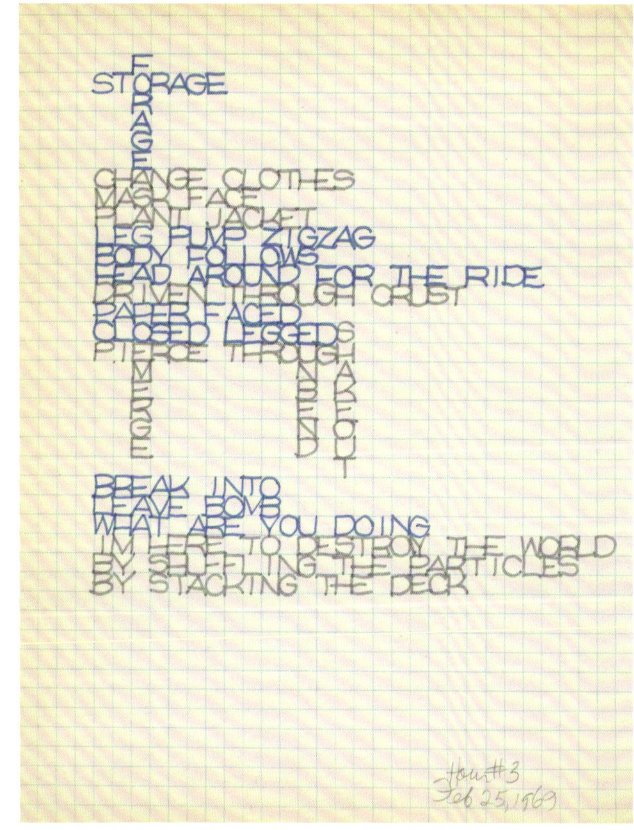

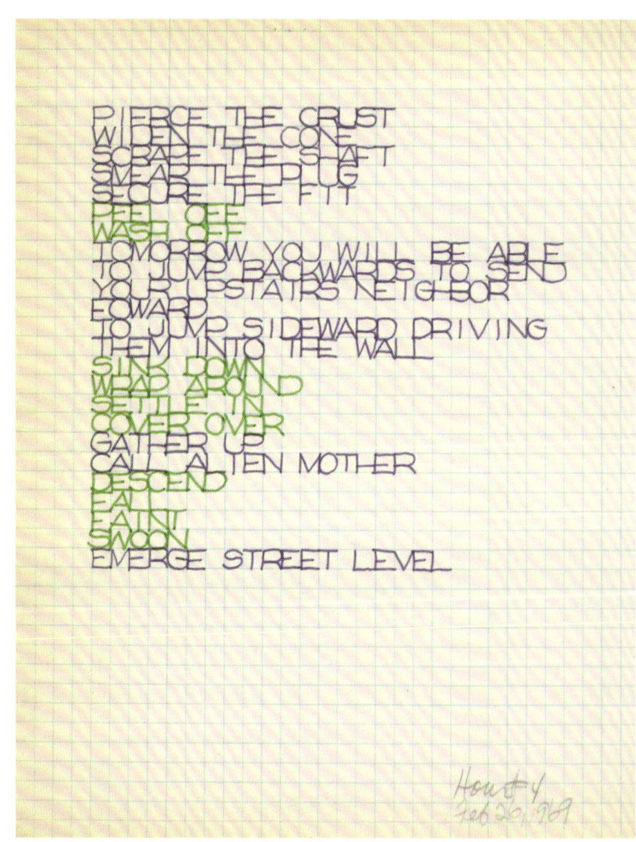

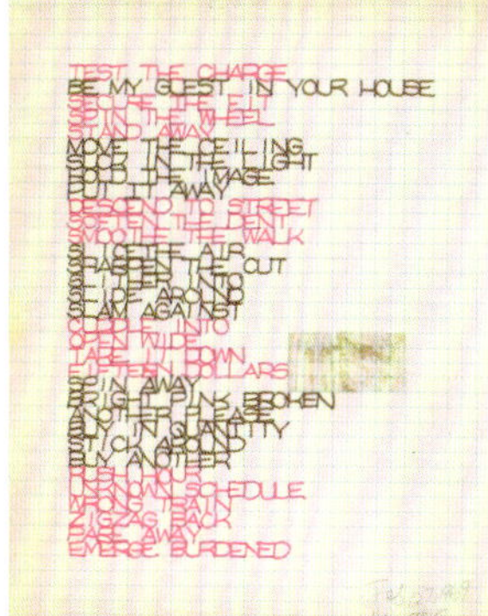
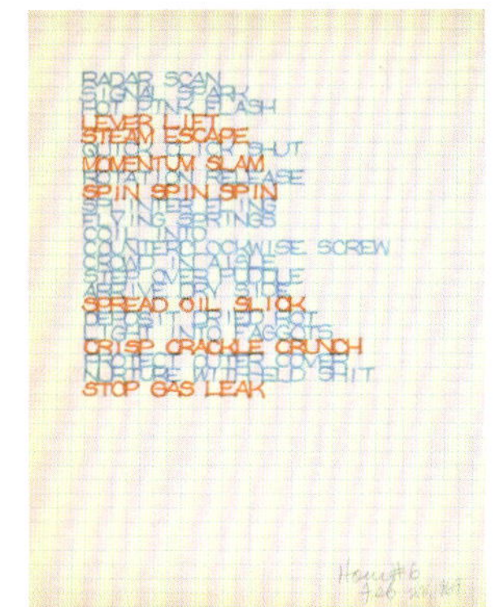
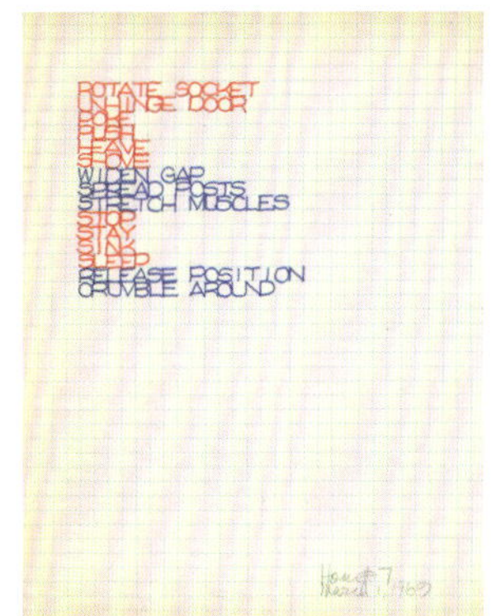
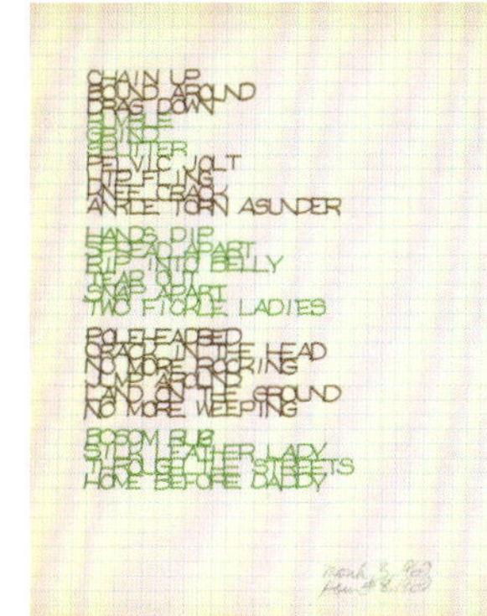
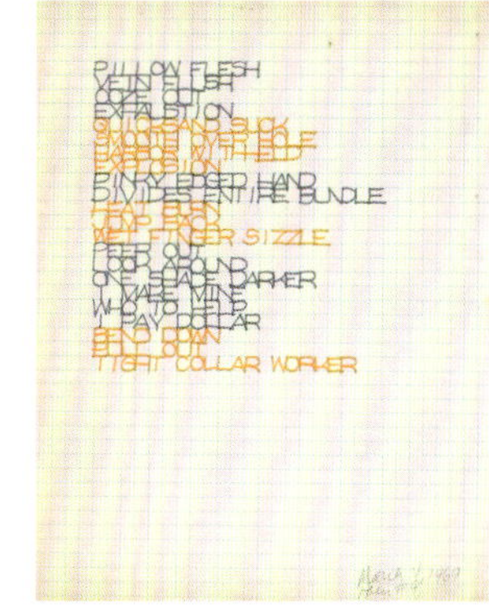
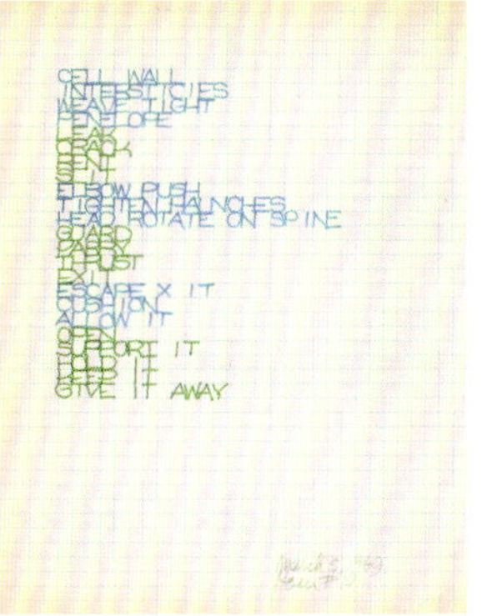
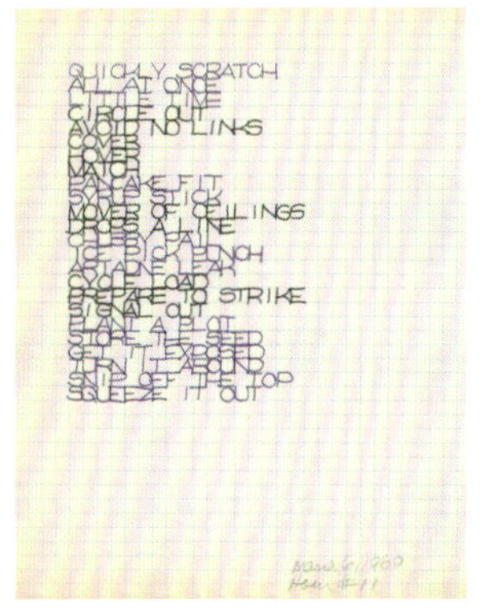
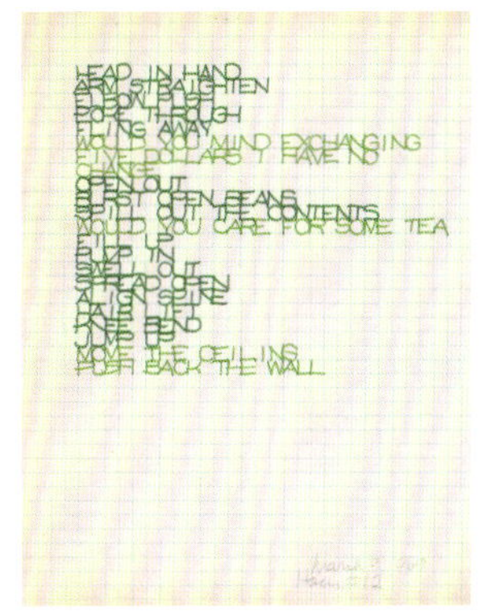
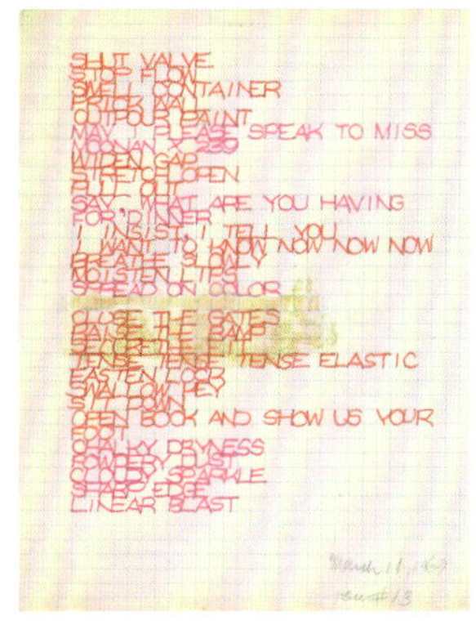
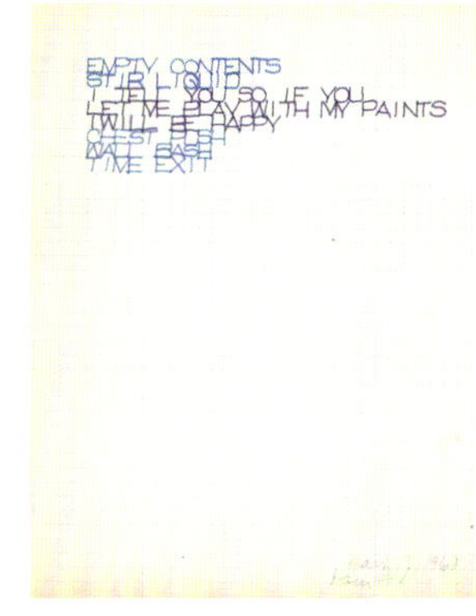
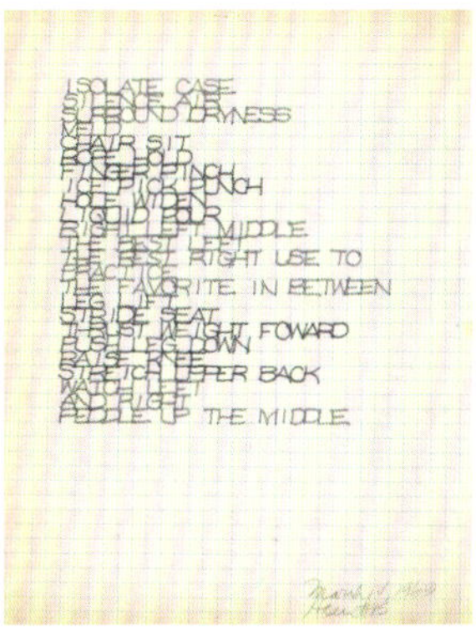
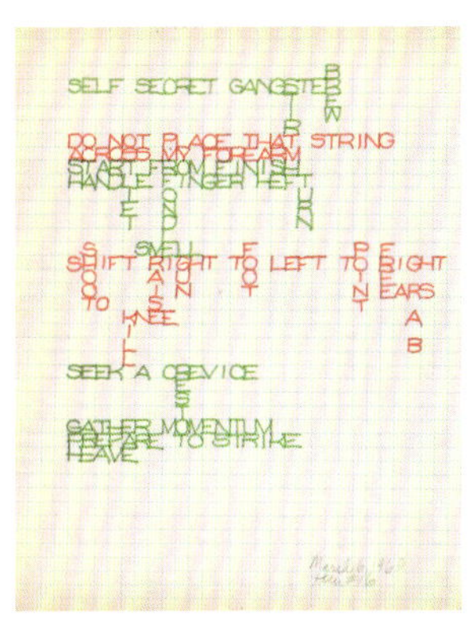

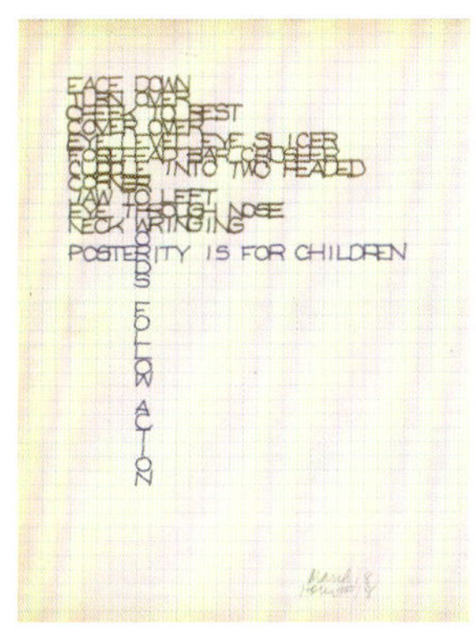
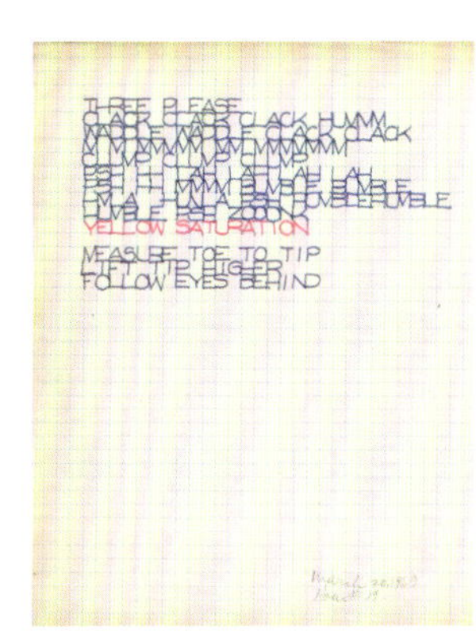
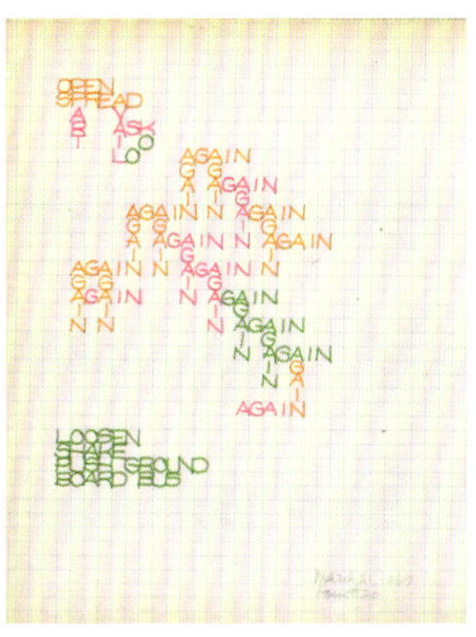
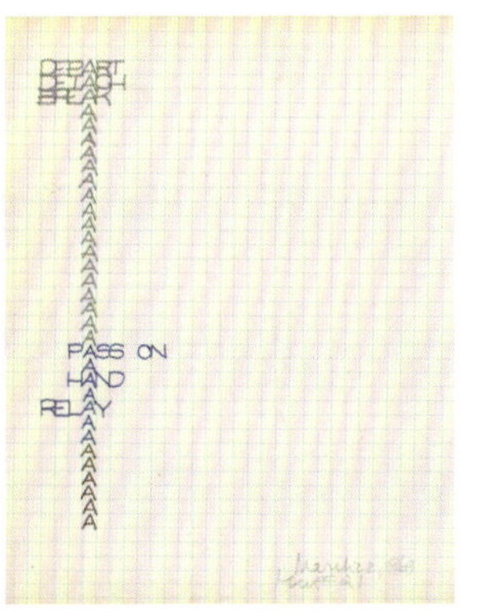
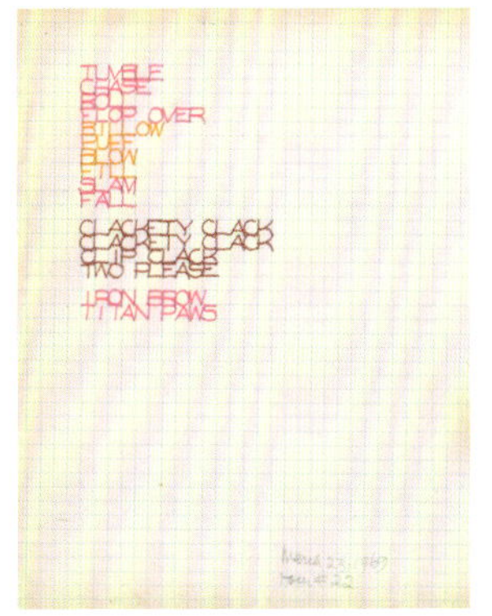
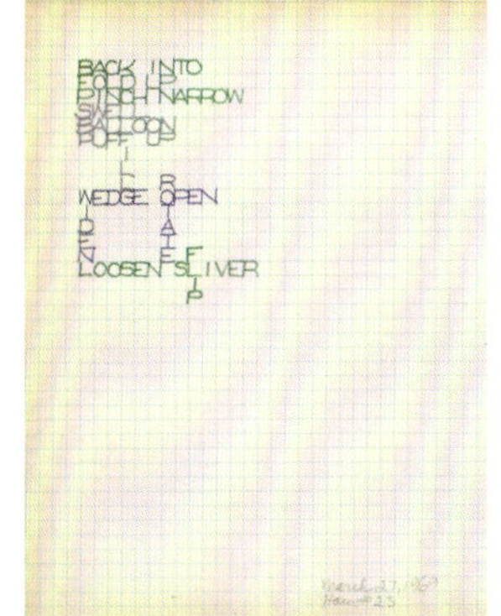
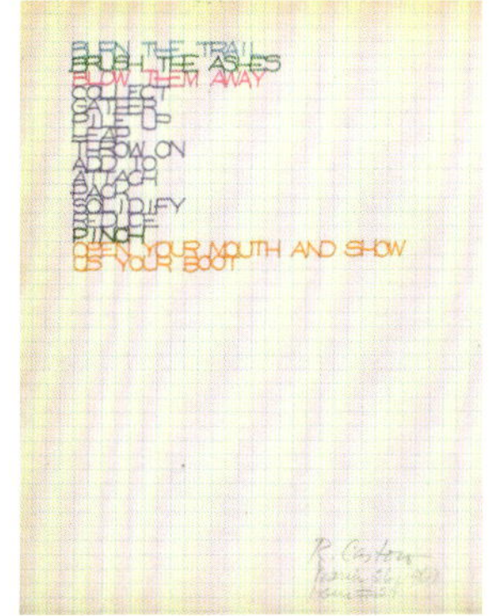

CAT. 81

ROBERT SMITHSON, *PULVERIZATIONS*, 1966

CAT. 82

LAWRENCE WEINER, *STRUCTURE POEM*, 1968

PULVERIZATIONS

```
        X          Z          Z          X
1.      |BBBBBBBBBB|TTTTTTTTTT|BBBBBBBBBB
            10'        10'        10'
```

B = Bituminous Coal   T = Tar (hot, left to cool)

```
        X        Z              Z        X
2.      |BBBBBBBB|CCCCCCCCCCCCCC|BBBBBBBB
            8'          14'         8'
```

B = Bog Iron Fragments   C = Cement (dry)

```
        X              Z  Z              X
3.      |BBBBBBBBBBBBBB|VV|BBBBBBBBBBBBBB|
            14'         2'      14'
```

B = Blue Coal   V = Volcanic Ash

```
        X              Z  Z              X
4.      |SSSSSSSSSSSSSS|GG|SSSSSSSSSSSSSS|
            14'         2'      14'
```

S = Sandstone Fragments   G = Glue

```
        X   Z                        Z   X
5.      |CCC|FFFFFFFFFFFFFFFFFFFFFFFF|CCC|
         3'           24'             3'
```

C = Coarse Sand   F = Fine Gravel

Five profiles of foundations (on level ground, 2' deep, 1' below ground, 1' above) shown partitioning contents.

X = Outer Foundation   Z = Inner Foundation

X is always 30' sq., the size of Z is variable.

The widths of X and Z are variable according to materials used.

R. Smithson 66

ONE STANDARD AIR FORCE DYE MARKER TH
ROWN INTO THE SEA ONE STANDARD AIR F
ORCE DYE MARKER THROWN INTO THE SEA
ONE STANDARD AIR FORCE DYE MARKER TH
ROWN INTO THE SEA ONE STANDARD AIR F
ORCE DYE MARKER THROWN INTO THE SEA
ONE STANDARD AIR FORCE DYE MARKER TH
ROWN INTO THE SEA ONE STANDARD AIR F
ORCE DYE MARKER THROWN INTO THE SEA
ONE STANDARD AIR FORCE DYE MARKER TH
ROWN INTO THE SEA ONE STANDARD AIR F
ORCE DYE MARKER THROWN INTO THE SEA
ONE STANDARD AIR FORCE DYE MARKER TH
ROWN INTO THE SEA ONE STANDARD AIR F
ORCE DYE MARKER THROWN INTO THE SEA
ONE STANDARD AIR FORCE DYE MARKER TH
ROWN INTO THE SEA ONE STANDARD AIR F
ORCE DYE MARKER THROWN INTO THE SEA
ONE STANDARD AIR FORCE DYE MARKER TH
ROWN INTO THE SEA ONE STANDARD AIR F
ORCE DYE MARKER THROWN INTO THE SEA
ONE STANDARD AIR FORCE DYE MARKER TH
ROWN INTO THE SEA ONE STANDARD AIR F
ORCE DYE MARKER THROWN INTO THE SEA
ONE STANDARD AIR FORCE DYE MARKER TH
ROWN INTO THE SEA ONE STANDARD AIR F
ORCE DYE MARKER THROWN INTO THE SEA
ONE STANDARD AIR FORCE DYE MARKER TH
ROWN INTO THE SEA ONE STANDARD AIR F
ORCE DYE MARKER THROWN INTO THE SEA
ONE STANDARD AIR FORCE DYE MARKER TH
ROWN INTO THE SEA ONE STANDARD AIR F
ORCE DYE MARKER THROWN INTO THE SEA
ONE STANDARD AIR FORCE DYE MARKER TH
ROWN INTO THE SEA ONE STANDARD AIR F
ORCE DYE MARKER THROWN INTO THE SEA
ONE STANDARD AIR FORCE DYE MARKER TH
ROWN INTO THE SEA ONE STANDARD AIR F
ORCE DYE MARKER THROWN INTO THE SEA
ONE STANDARD AIR FORCE DYE MARKER TH
ROWN INTO THE SEA ONE STANDARD AIR F
ORCE DYE MARKER THROWN INTO THE SEA
ONE STANDARD AIR FORCE DYE MARKER TH
ROWN INTO THE SEA ONE STANDARD AIR F
ORCE DYE MARKER THROWN INTO THE SEA
ONE STANDARD AIR FORCE DYE MARKER TH
ROWN INTO THE SEA ONE STANDARD AIR F
ORCE DYE MARKER THROWN INTO THE SEA
ONE STANDARD AIR FORCE DYE MARKER TH
ROWN INTO THE SEA ONE STANDARD AIR F
ORCE DYE MARKER THROWN INTO THE SEA

K+E ISOMETRIC-ORTHOGRAPHIC ©1943 46 4110 MADE IN U.S.A.
KEUFFEL & ESSER CO.

CAT. 83

JOSEPH KOSUTH, *'TITLED (ART AS IDEA AS IDEA)' [REAL]*, 1968

CAT. 84

MEL BOCHNER, *LANGUAGE IS NOT TRANSPARENT*, 1970

re·al (rē′əl, rēl), ***adj.*** [OFr.; ML. *realis* < L. *res*, thing], 1. existing or happening as or in fact; actual, true, objectively so, etc.; not merely seeming, pretended, imagined, fictitious, nominal, or ostensible. 2. authentic; genuine. 3. in *law*, of or relating to permanent, immovable things: as, *real* property: opposed to *personal*. 4. in *mathematics*, not imaginary: said of a number or quantity. 5. in *optics*, of or relating to an image made by the actual meeting of light rays at a point. 6. in *philosophy*, existing objectively; actual (not merely possible or ideal), or essential, absolute, ultimate (not relative, derivative, phenomenal, etc.). ***n.*** anything that actually exists, or reality in general (with *the*). ***adv.*** [Colloq. or Dial.], very. —***SYN.*** see **true.**

1. LANGUAGE
IS NOT
TRANSPARENT

CAT. 85

NANCY HOLT,
DETACH HERE,
1967

CAT. 86

SHUSAKU ARAKAWA,
UNTITLED
(*'STOLEN'*), 1969

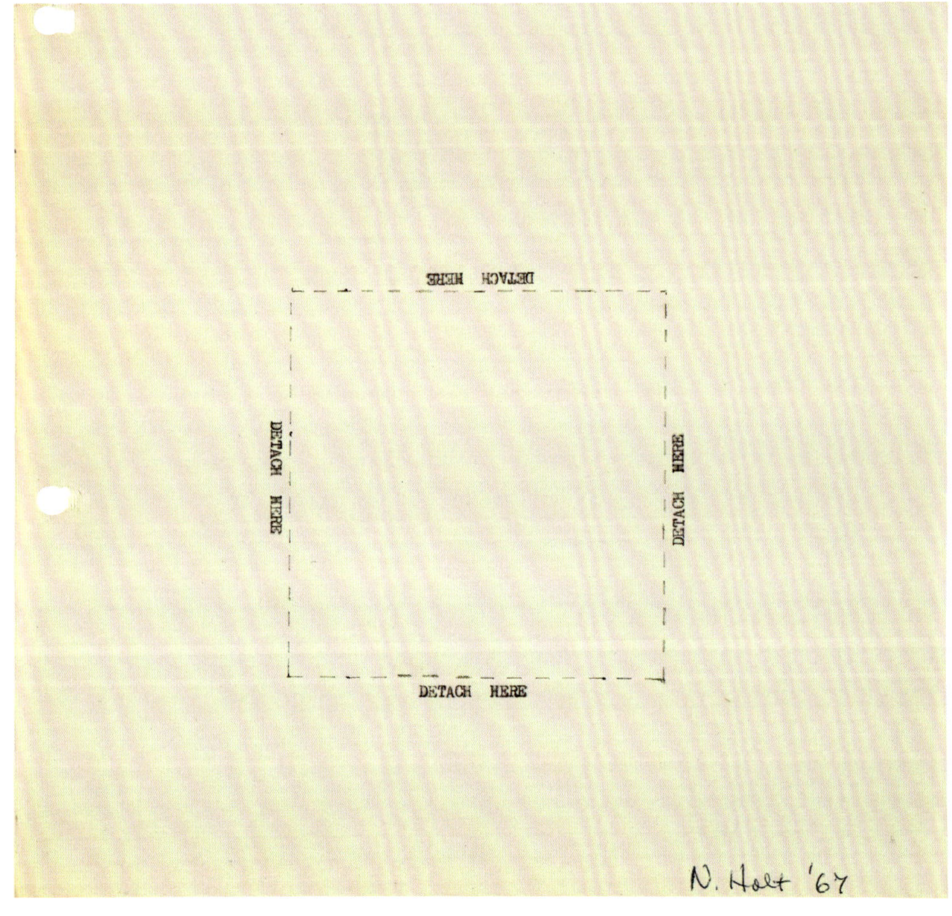

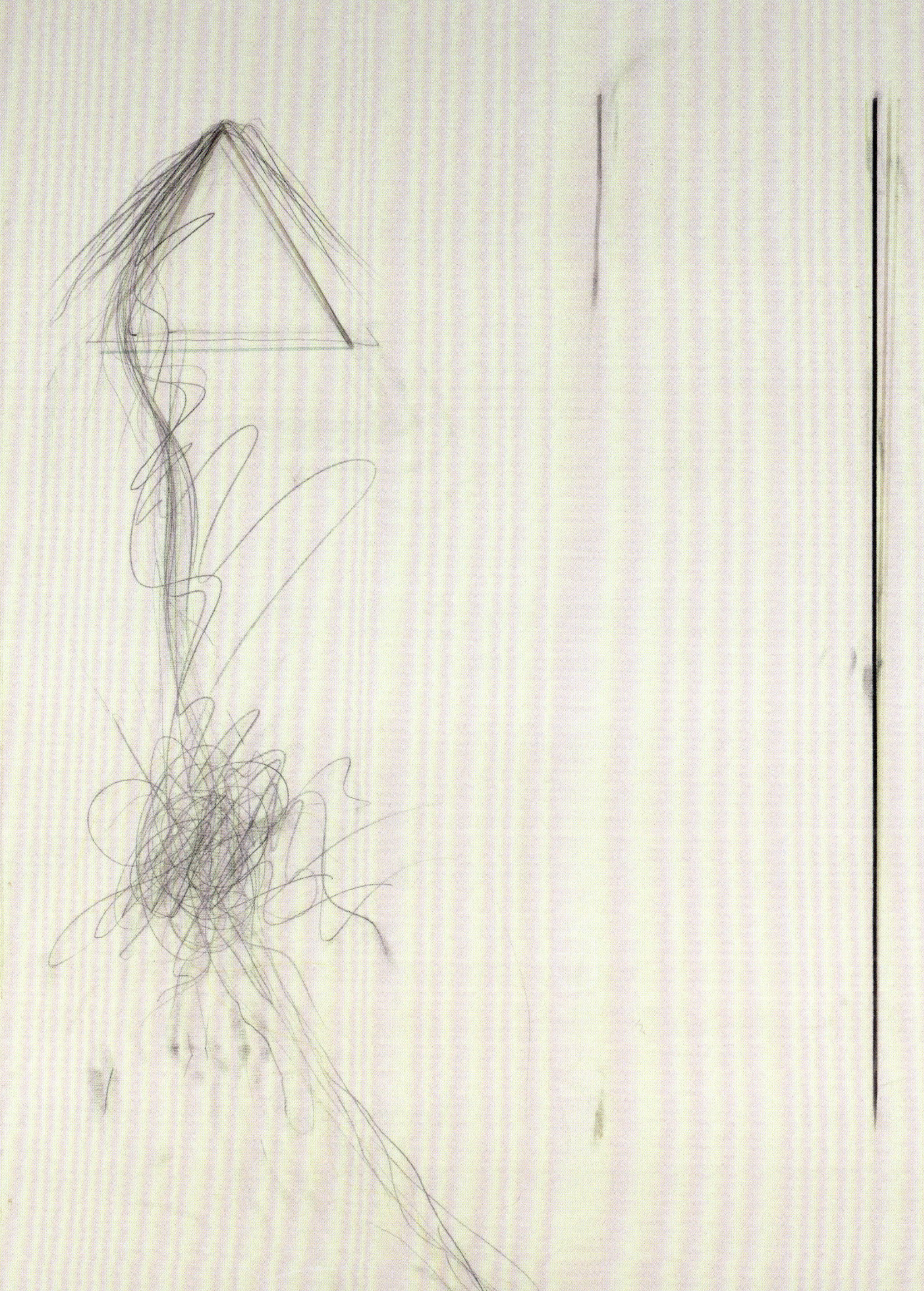
IF POSSIBLE STEAL ANY ONE
OF THESE DRAWINGS INCLUDING
THIS
TITLE: UNTITLED
NAME:
DATE:

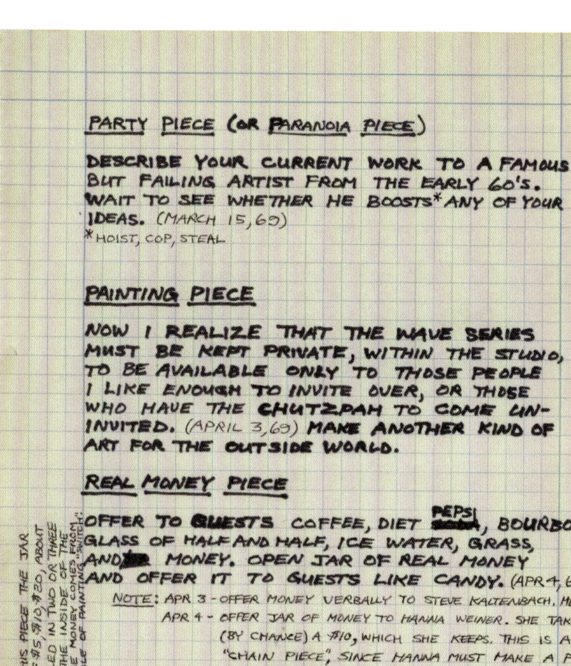

32

PARTY PIECE (OR ~~PARANOIA~~ PIECE)

DESCRIBE YOUR CURRENT WORK TO A FAMOUS
BUT FAILING ARTIST FROM THE EARLY 60'S.
WAIT TO SEE WHETHER HE BOOSTS* ANY OF YOUR
IDEAS. (MARCH 15, 69)

*HOIST, COP, STEAL

PAINTING PIECE

NOW I REALIZE THAT THE WAVE SERIES
MUST BE KEPT PRIVATE, WITHIN THE STUDIO,
TO BE AVAILABLE ONLY TO THOSE PEOPLE
I LIKE ENOUGH TO INVITE OVER, OR THOSE
WHO HAVE THE CHUTZPAH TO COME UN-
INVITED. (APRIL 3, 69) MAKE ANOTHER KIND OF
ART FOR THE OUTSIDE WORLD.

REAL MONEY PIECE

OFFER TO GUESTS COFFEE, DIET PEPSI, BOURBON,
GLASS OF HALF AND HALF, ICE WATER, GRASS,
AND MONEY. OPEN JAR OF REAL MONEY
AND OFFER IT TO GUESTS LIKE CANDY. (APR 4, 69)

NOTE: APR 3 - OFFER MONEY VERBALLY TO STEVE KALTENBACH. HE REFUSES.
APR 4 - OFFER JAR OF MONEY TO HANNA WEINER. SHE TAKES
(BY CHANCE) A $10, WHICH SHE KEEPS. THIS IS A
"CHAIN PIECE", SINCE HANNA MUST MAKE A PIECE
BY DECIDING WHAT TO DO WITH THE $10. THIS REAL
MONEY PIECE HAS BECOME EXCEEDINGLY INTERESTING
TO ME. THIS IS A JARRING PIECE.
APR 15 - OFFER JAR TO RON KLEEMAN WHO TAKES OUT A $20.
HE WISHES TO PUT IT BACK INTO JAR BUT I TALK
HIM INTO KEEPING IT.
APR 17 - KEITH SONNIER REFUSED, LATER SCREWS ~~CAP~~ LID VERY TIGHTLY BACK ON JAR.
APR 27 - KALTENBACH TAKES ALL THE MONEY OUT OF JAR WHEN I
OFFER IT, EXAMINES ALL THE MONEY & PUTS IT ALL BACK
IN JAR. SAYS HE DOESNT NEED MONEY NOW.

NOTE: AT BEGINNING OF THIS PIECE THE JAR CONTAINS BILLS OF $5, $10, $20, ABOUT ? $585.5 WORTH, COILED IN TWO OR THREE PACKETS AROUND THE INSIDE OF THE JAR, UNBOUND. THE MONEY COMES FROM ROLF RICKE FROM SALE OF PAINTING "SWITCH".

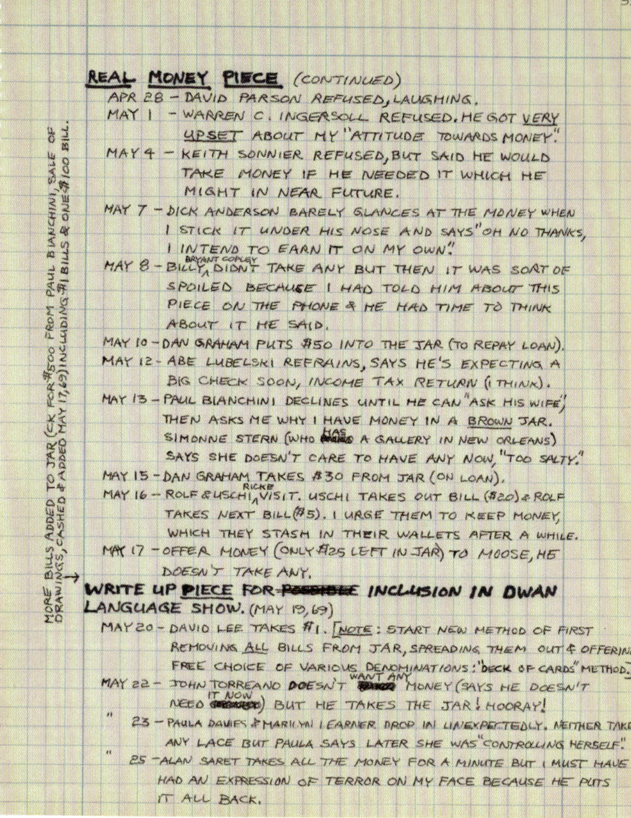

33

REAL MONEY PIECE (CONTINUED)

APR 28 - DAVID PARSON REFUSED, LAUGHING.
MAY 1 - WARREN C. INGERSOLL REFUSED. HE GOT VERY
UPSET ABOUT MY "ATTITUDE TOWARDS MONEY".
MAY 4 - KEITH SONNIER REFUSED, BUT SAID HE WOULD
TAKE MONEY IF HE NEEDED IT WHICH HE
MIGHT IN NEAR FUTURE.
MAY 7 - DICK ANDERSON BARELY GLANCES AT THE MONEY WHEN
I STICK IT UNDER HIS NOSE AND SAYS "OH NO THANKS,
I INTEND TO EARN IT ON MY OWN".
MAY 8 - BILLY BRYANT COPLEY DIDNT TAKE ANY BUT THEN IT WAS SORT OF
SPOILED BECAUSE I HAD TOLD HIM ABOUT THIS
PIECE ON THE PHONE & HE HAD TIME TO THINK
ABOUT IT HE SAID.
MAY 10 - DAN GRAHAM PUTS $50 INTO THE JAR (TO REPAY LOAN).
MAY 12 - ABE LUBELSKI REFRAINS, SAYS HE'S EXPECTING A
BIG CHECK SOON, INCOME TAX RETURN (I THINK).
MAY 13 - PAUL BIANCHINI DECLINES UNTIL HE CAN "ASK HIS WIFE",
THEN ASKS ME WHY I HAVE MONEY IN A BROWN JAR.
SIMONNE STERN (WHO HAS A GALLERY IN NEW ORLEANS)
SAYS SHE DOESN'T CARE TO HAVE ANY NOW, "TOO SALTY."
MAY 15 - DAN GRAHAM TAKES $30 FROM JAR (ON LOAN).
MAY 16 - ROLF & USCHI RICKE VISIT. USCHI TAKES OUT BILL ($20) & ROLF
TAKES NEXT BILL ($5). I URGE THEM TO KEEP MONEY,
WHICH THEY STASH IN THEIR WALLETS AFTER A WHILE.
MAY 17 - OFFER MONEY (ONLY $25 LEFT IN JAR) TO MOOSE, HE
DOESN'T TAKE ANY.

MORE BILLS ADDED TO JAR (CK FOR $500 FROM PAUL BIANCHINI, SALE OF DRAWINGS, CASHED & ADDED MAY 17, 69) INCLUDING $1 BILLS & ONE $100 BILL. →

WRITE UP PIECE FOR ~~POSSIBLE~~ INCLUSION IN DWAN
LANGUAGE SHOW. (MAY 19, 69)

MAY 20 - DAVID LEE TAKES $1. [NOTE: START NEW METHOD OF FIRST
REMOVING ALL BILLS FROM JAR, SPREADING THEM OUT & OFFERING
FREE CHOICE OF VARIOUS DENOMINATIONS: "DECK OF CARDS" METHOD.]
MAY 22 - JOHN TORREANO DOESN'T WANT ANY MONEY (SAYS HE DOESN'T
NEED IT NOW) BUT HE TAKES THE JAR! HOORAY!
" 23 - PAULA DAVIES & MARILYN LEARNER DROP IN UNEXPECTEDLY. NEITHER TAKES
ANY LACE BUT PAULA SAYS LATER SHE WAS "CONTROLLING HERSELF".
" 25 - ALAN SARET TAKES ALL THE MONEY FOR A MINUTE BUT I MUST HAVE
HAD AN EXPRESSION OF TERROR ON MY FACE BECAUSE HE PUTS
IT ALL BACK.

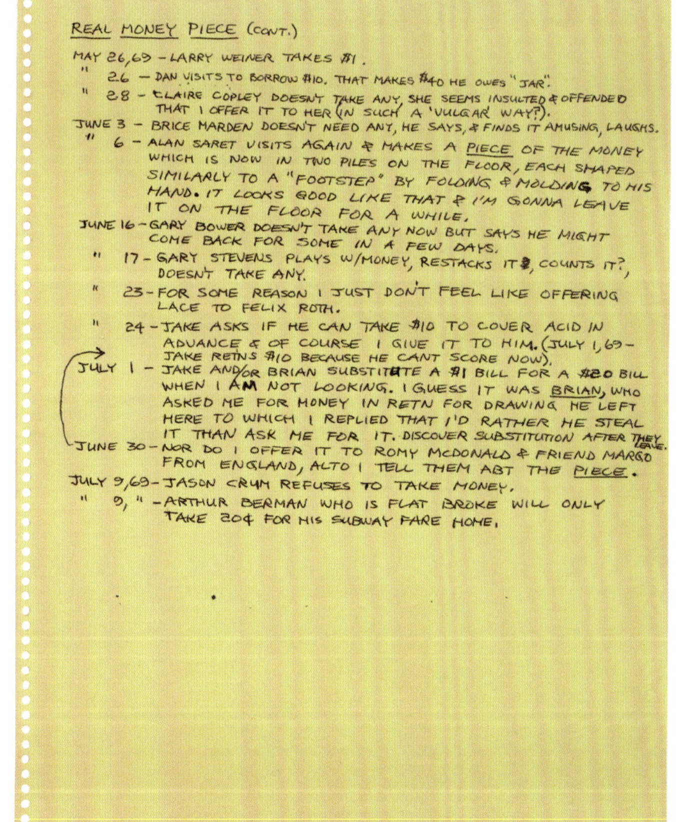

REAL MONEY PIECE (CONT.)

MAY 26, 69 - LARRY WEINER TAKES $1.
" 26 - DAN VISITS TO BORROW $10. THAT MAKES $40 HE OWES "JAR".
" 28 - CLAIRE COPLEY DOESN'T TAKE ANY, SHE SEEMS INSULTED & OFFENDED
THAT I OFFER IT TO HER (IN SUCH A 'VULGAR' WAY?).
JUNE 3 - BRICE MARDEN DOESN'T NEED ANY, HE SAYS, & FINDS IT AMUSING, LAUGHS.
" 6 - ALAN SARET VISITS AGAIN & MAKES A PIECE OF THE MONEY
WHICH IS NOW IN TWO PILES ON THE FLOOR, EACH SHAPED
SIMILARLY TO A "FOOTSTEP" BY FOLDING & MOLDING TO HIS
HAND. IT LOOKS GOOD LIKE THAT & I'M GONNA LEAVE
IT ON THE FLOOR FOR A WHILE.
JUNE 16 - GARY BOWER DOESN'T TAKE ANY NOW BUT SAYS HE MIGHT
COME BACK FOR SOME IN A FEW DAYS.
" 17 - GARY STEVENS PLAYS W/MONEY, RESTACKS IT, COUNTS IT?,
DOESN'T TAKE ANY.
" 23 - FOR SOME REASON I JUST DON'T FEEL LIKE OFFERING
LACE TO FELIX ROTH.
" 24 - JAKE ASKS IF HE CAN TAKE $10 TO COVER ACID IN
ADVANCE & OF COURSE I GIVE IT TO HIM. (JULY 1, 69 -
JAKE RETNS $10 BECAUSE HE CANT SCORE NOW).
JULY 1 - JAKE AND/OR BRIAN SUBSTITUTE A $1 BILL FOR A $20 BILL
WHEN I AM NOT LOOKING. I GUESS IT WAS BRIAN, WHO
ASKED ME FOR MONEY IN RETN FOR DRAWING HE LEFT
HERE TO WHICH I REPLIED THAT I'D RATHER HE STEAL
IT THAN ASK ME FOR IT. DISCOVER SUBSTITUTION AFTER THEY LEAVE.
JUNE 30 - NOR DO I OFFER IT TO ROMY McDONALD & FRIEND MARGO
FROM ENGLAND, ALTO I TELL THEM ABT THE PIECE.
JULY 9, 69 - JASON CRUM REFUSES TO TAKE MONEY.
" 9, " - ARTHUR BERMAN WHO IS FLAT BROKE WILL ONLY
TAKE 20¢ FOR HIS SUBWAY FARE HOME.

CAT. 87

LEE LOZANO,
UNTITLED (PARTY/ PARANOIA, PAINTING, REAL MONEY),
MARCH 15, 1969–JULY 9, 1969

CAT. 88

EDWARD KIENHOLZ,
FOR REDUCING VIRGINIA'S ACCOUNT TO ZERO, 1972

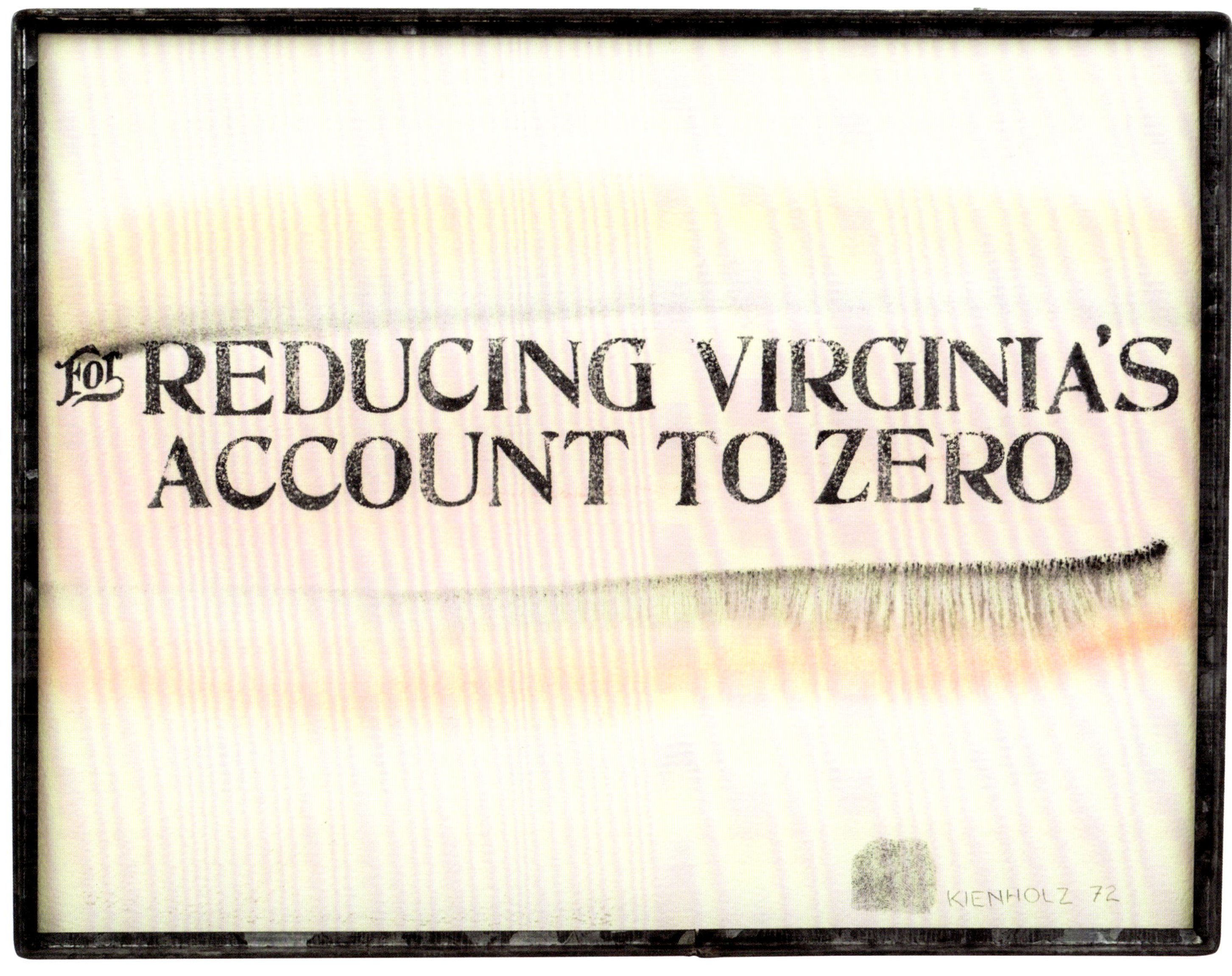

CAT. 89

ROBERT SMITHSON,
GYROSTASIS,
1967

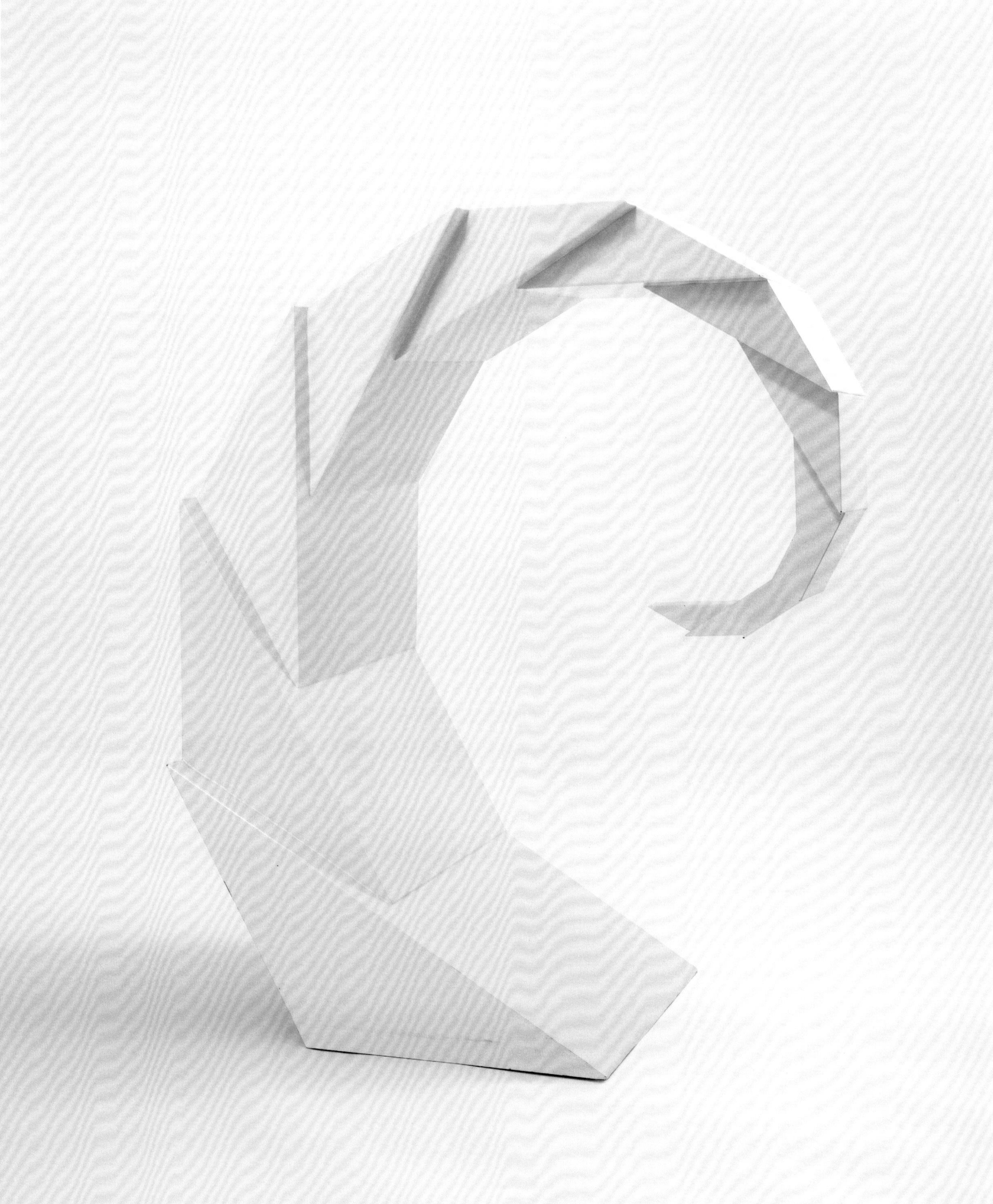

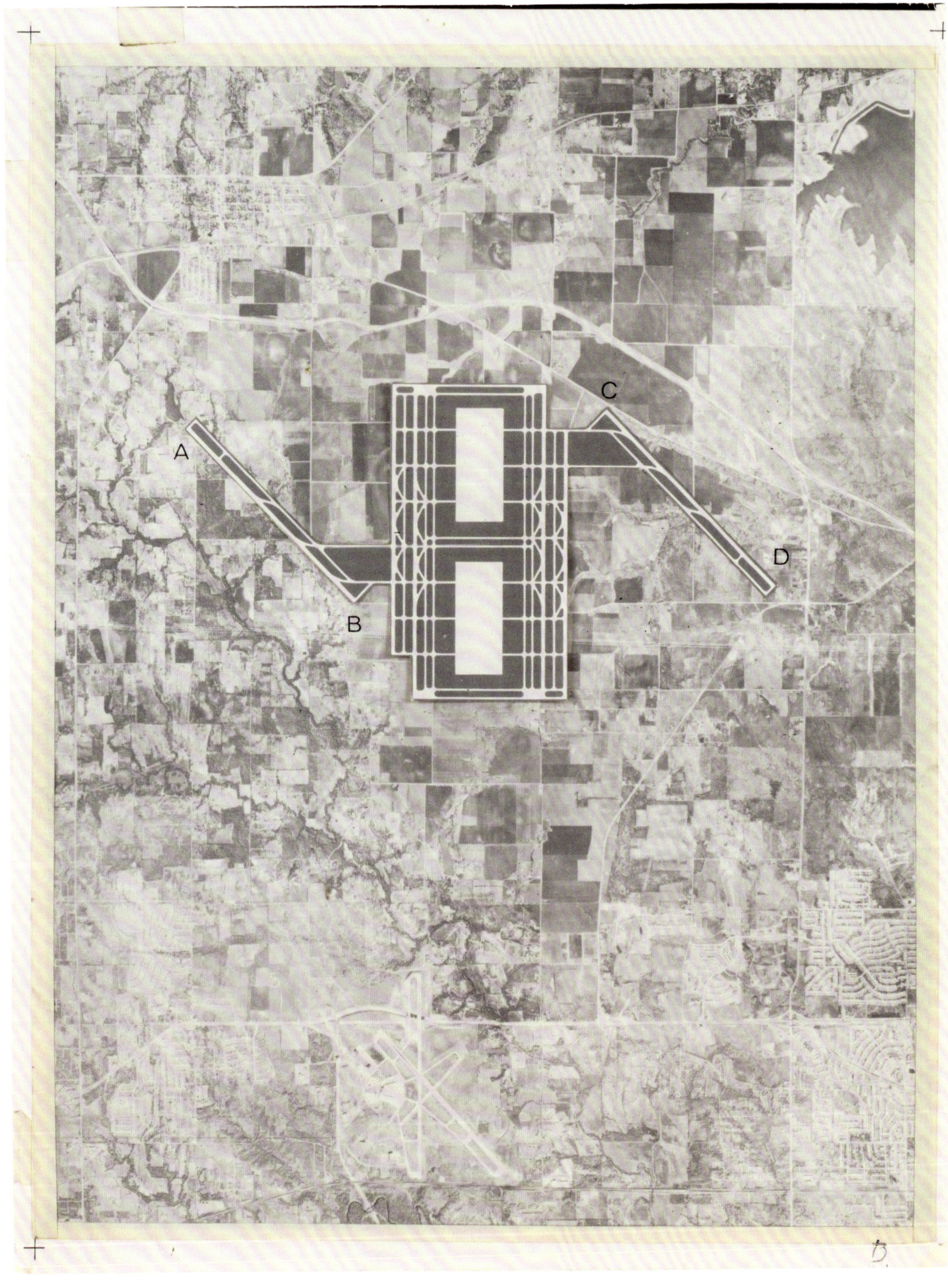
A
B
C
D

CAT. 90

ROBERT SMITHSON, *AERIAL MAP: PROPOSAL FOR DALLAS–FORT WORTH REGIONAL AIRPORT*, 1967

CAT. 91

ROBERT MORRIS, *MODEL AND CROSS-SECTION FOR PROJECT IN EARTH AND SOD*, 1966

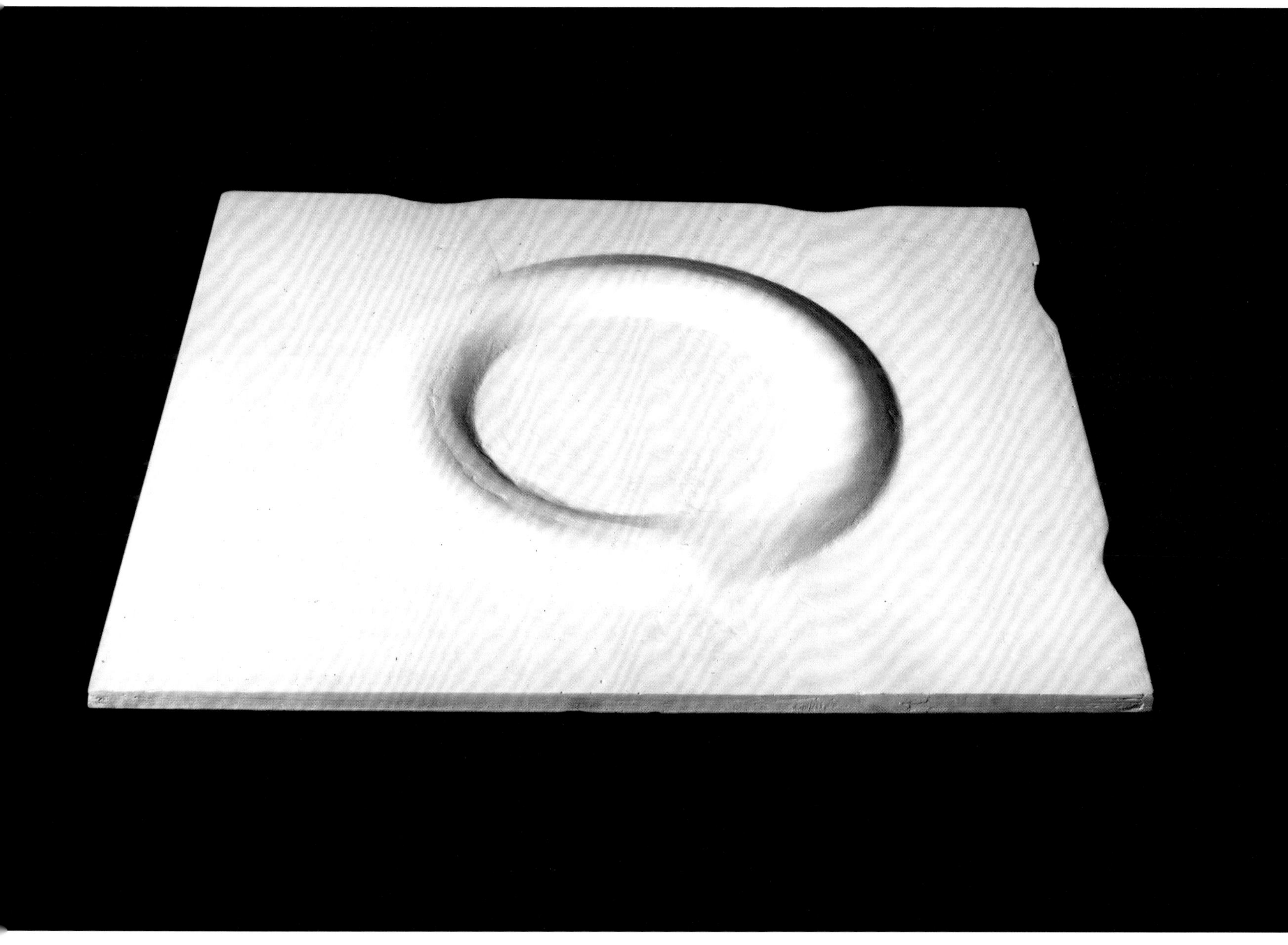

CAT. 92

CARL ANDRE, *PROPOSAL FOR AIRPORT SCULPTURE*, 1968

CAT. 93

SOL LEWITT, *BURIED CUBE (LAYOUT FOR BOOK PAGE)*, UNDATED

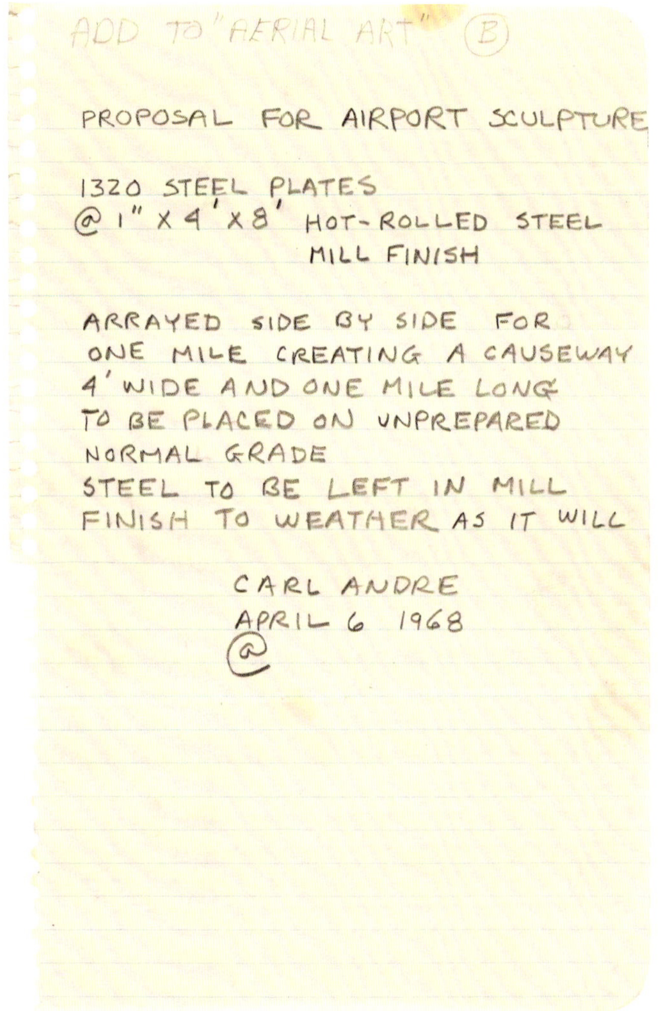

ADD TO "AERIAL ART" (B)

PROPOSAL FOR AIRPORT SCULPTURE

1320 STEEL PLATES
@ 1" X 4' X 8' HOT-ROLLED STEEL
MILL FINISH

ARRAYED SIDE BY SIDE FOR
ONE MILE CREATING A CAUSEWAY
4' WIDE AND ONE MILE LONG
TO BE PLACED ON UNPREPARED
NORMAL GRADE
STEEL TO BE LEFT IN MILL
FINISH TO WEATHER AS IT WILL

CARL ANDRE
APRIL 6 1968
@

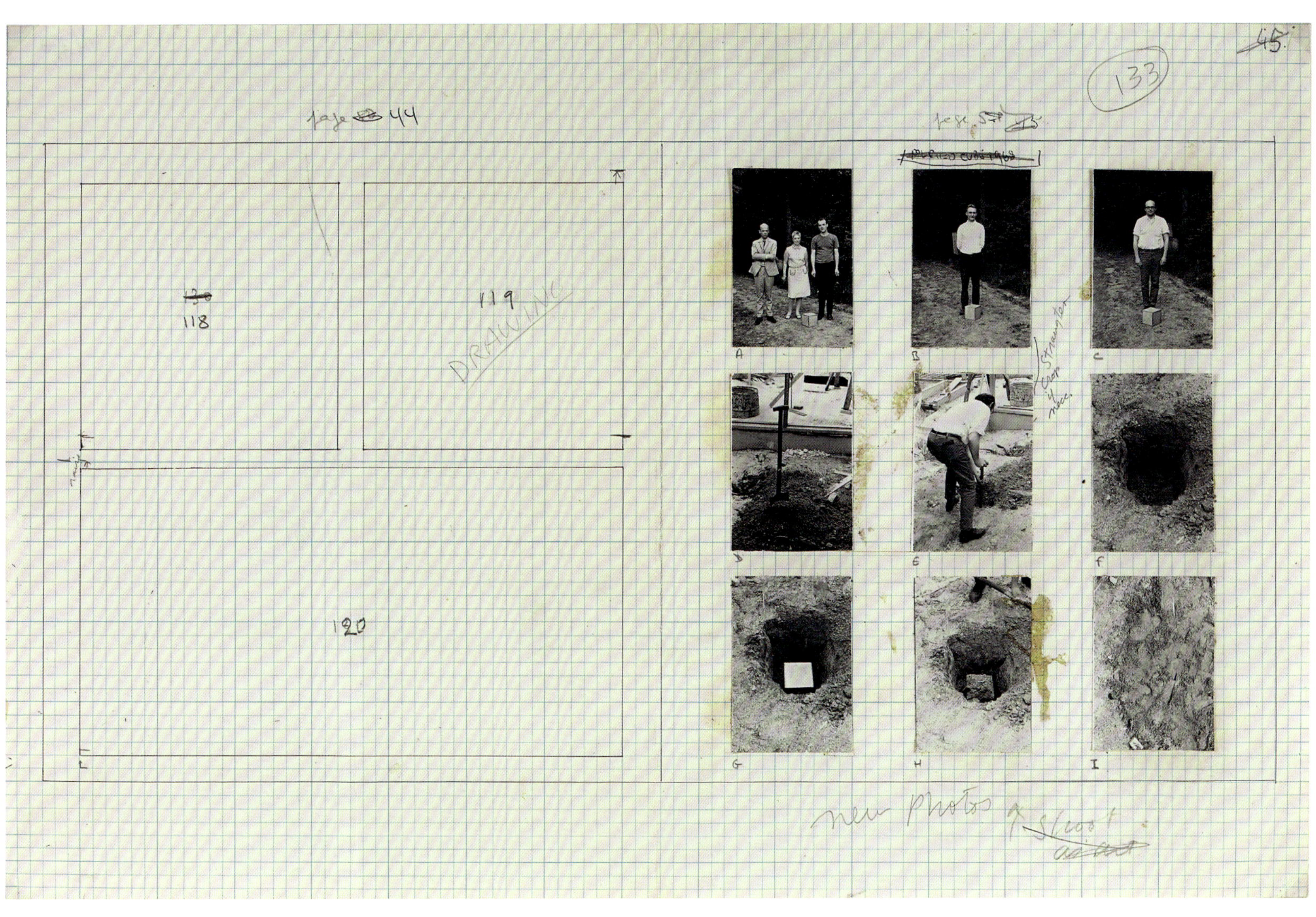

page 44
45
133
118
119
DRAWING
120
new photos
A
B
C
D
E
F
G
H
I

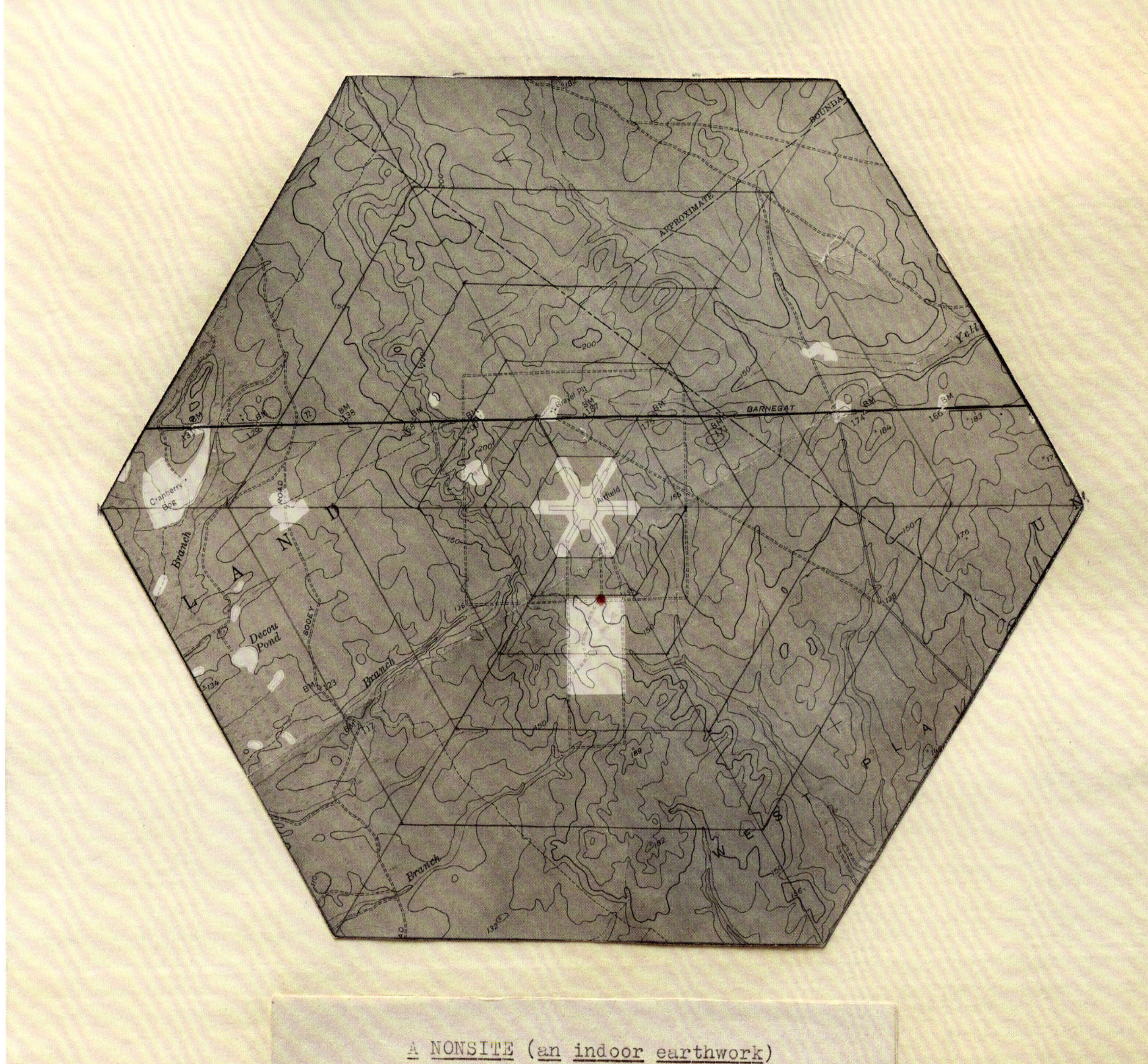

A NONSITE (an indoor earthwork)

31 sub-divisions based on a hexagonal "airfield" in the Woodmansie Quadrangle - New Jersey (Topographic) map. Each sub-dividion of the Nonsite contains sand from the site shown on the map. Tours between the Nonsite and the site are possible. The red dot on the map is the place where the sand was collected.

R. Smithson 67

94A

CAT. 94

ROBERT SMITHSON,
A NONSITE, PINE BARRENS, NEW JERSEY,
1967 (MAP)
1968 (NONSITE)

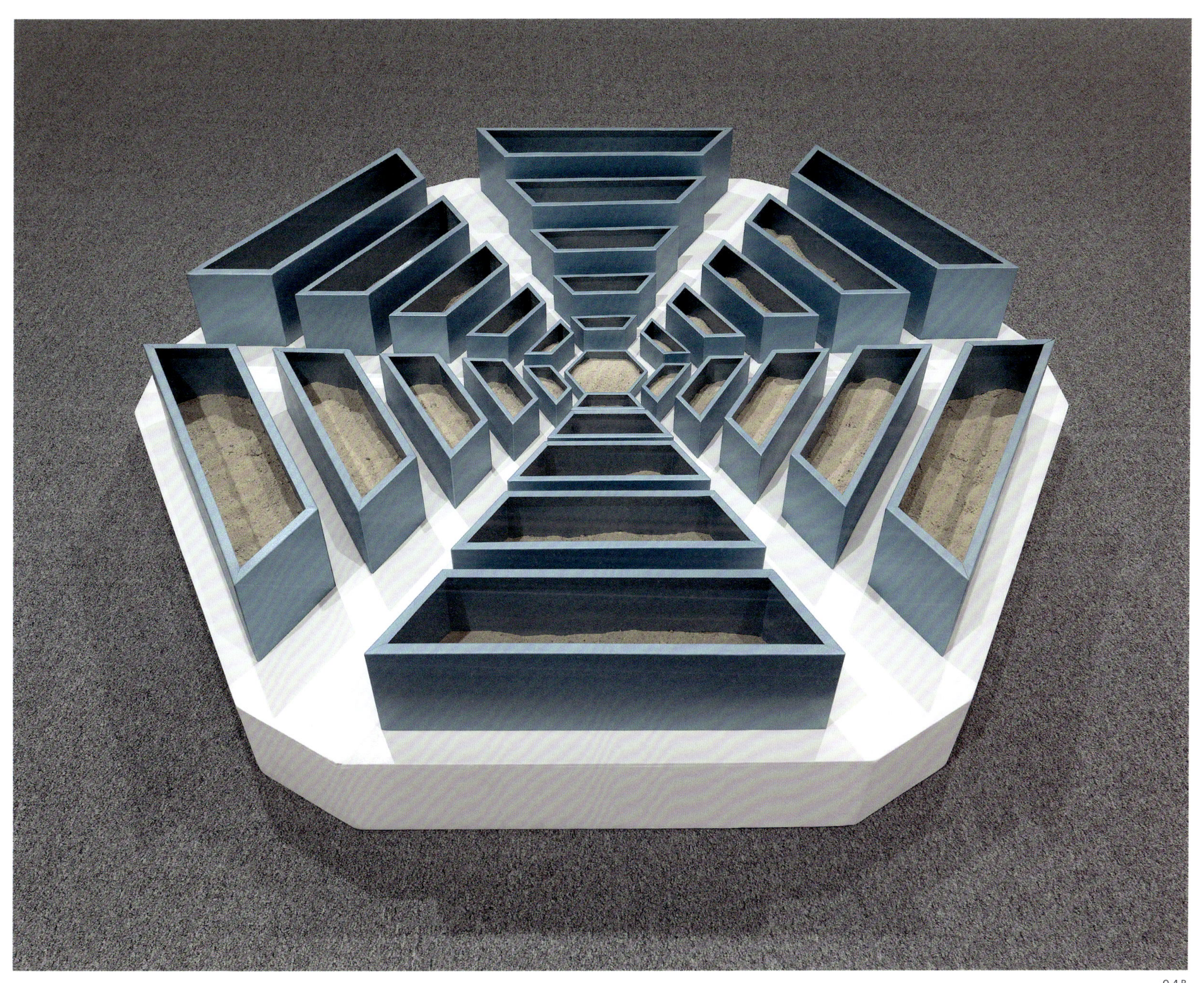

94B

CAT. 95

ROBERT SMITHSON,
NONSITE #2, 1967

CAT. 96

DENNIS OPPENHEIM,
2-DIMENSIONAL INFORMATION (CONTOUR LINES) / TRANSFERRED FROM POINT A TO LOCATION B / LINES SCRIBED ON SWAMP GRID WITH SICKLE-MOWER / CUTS FILLED WITH ALUMINUM FILINGS / (RESIDUE FROM ALUMINUM BORINGS) / PIECE COMPLETELY SUB-MERGED IN WATER / AT HIGH TIDE 12:00 NOON / SIZE: 175′ X 200′ PHOTO: INFRARED AERO-FILM, 1969

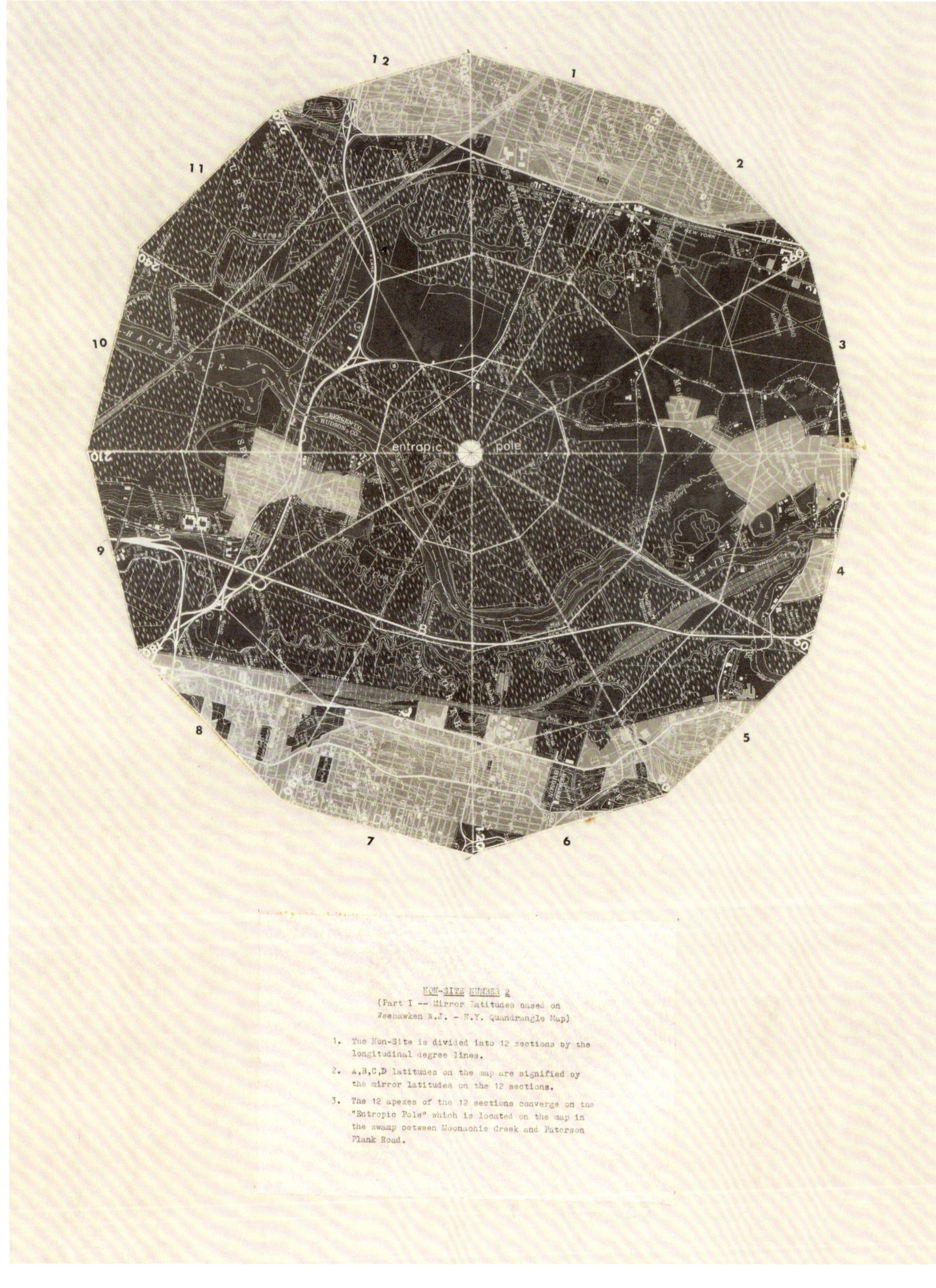

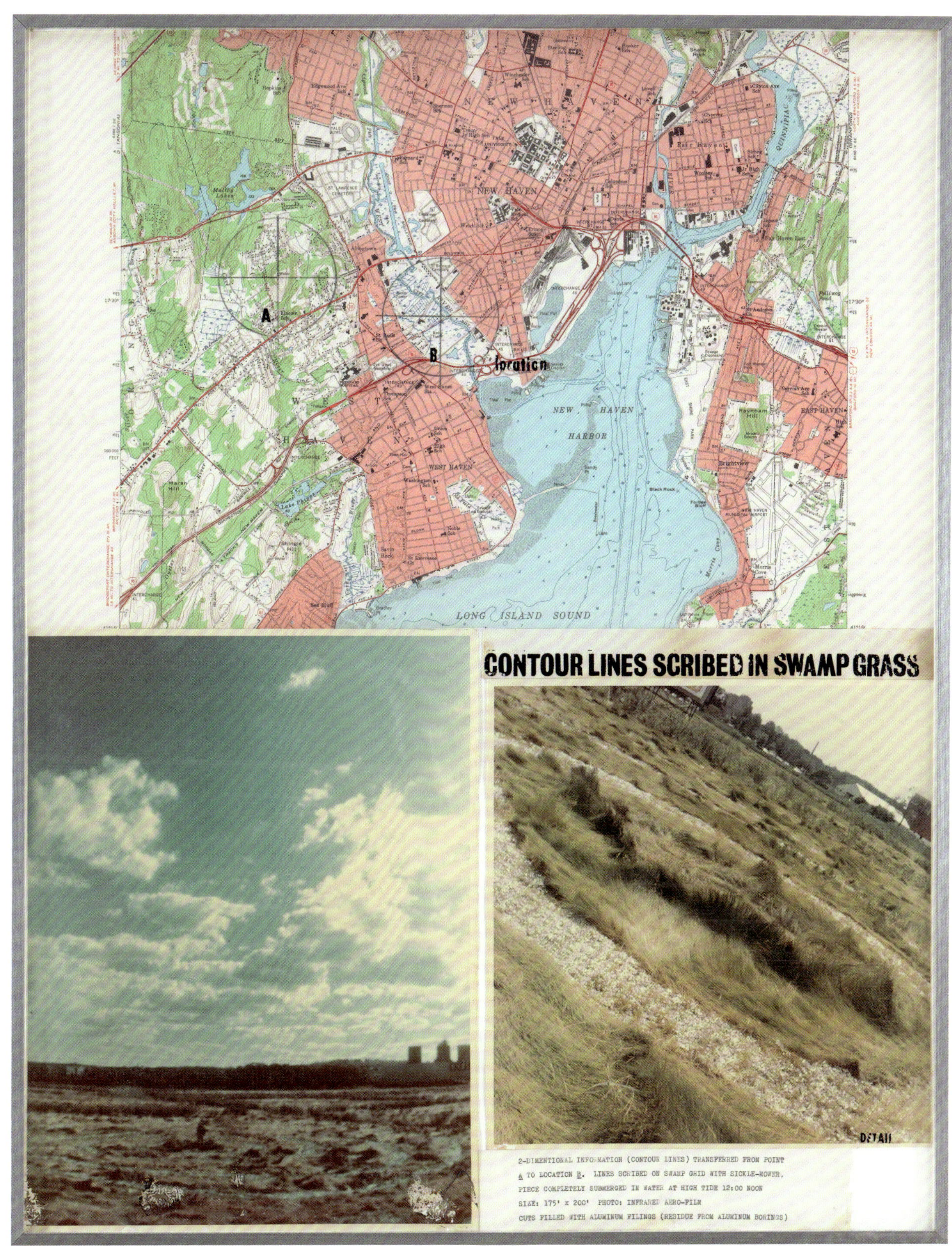
NEW HAVEN
WEST HAVEN
NEW HAVEN HARBOR
LONG ISLAND SOUND
EAST HAVEN
A
B
location
CONTOUR LINES SCRIBED IN SWAMP GRASS
DETAIL
2-DIMENTIONAL INFORMATION (CONTOUR LINES) TRANSFERRED FROM POINT
A TO LOCATION B. LINES SCRIBED ON SWAMP GRID WITH SICKLE-MOWER.
PIECE COMPLETELY SUBMERGED IN WATER AT HIGH TIDE 12:00 NOON
SIZE: 175' x 200' PHOTO: INFRARED AERO-FILM
CUTS FILLED WITH ALUMINUM FILINGS (RESIDUE FROM ALUMINUM BORINGS)

CAT. 97

CARL ANDRE,
LOG PIECE, 1968

CAT. 98

ROBERT SMITHSON,
INVERTED TREE,
1969

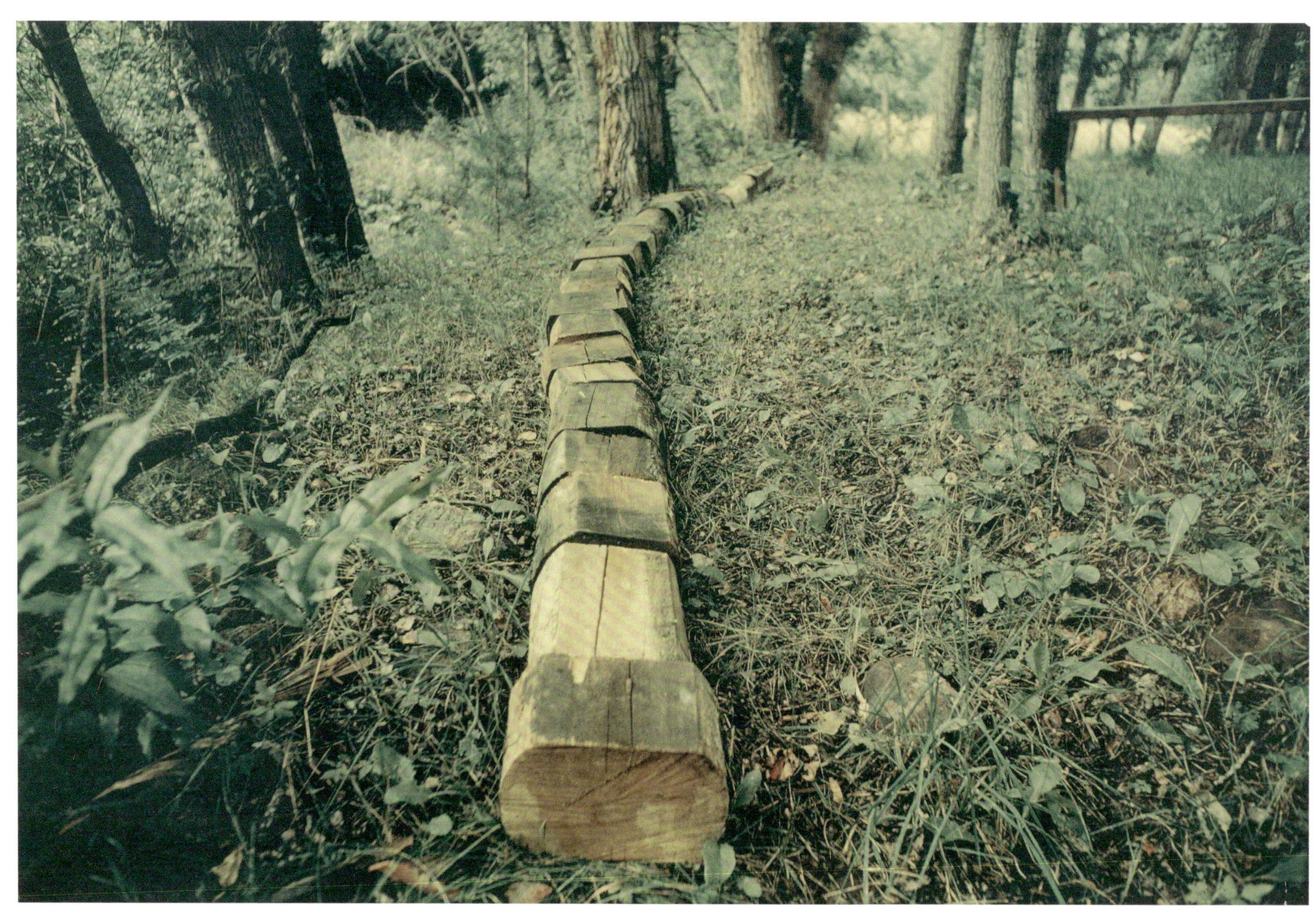

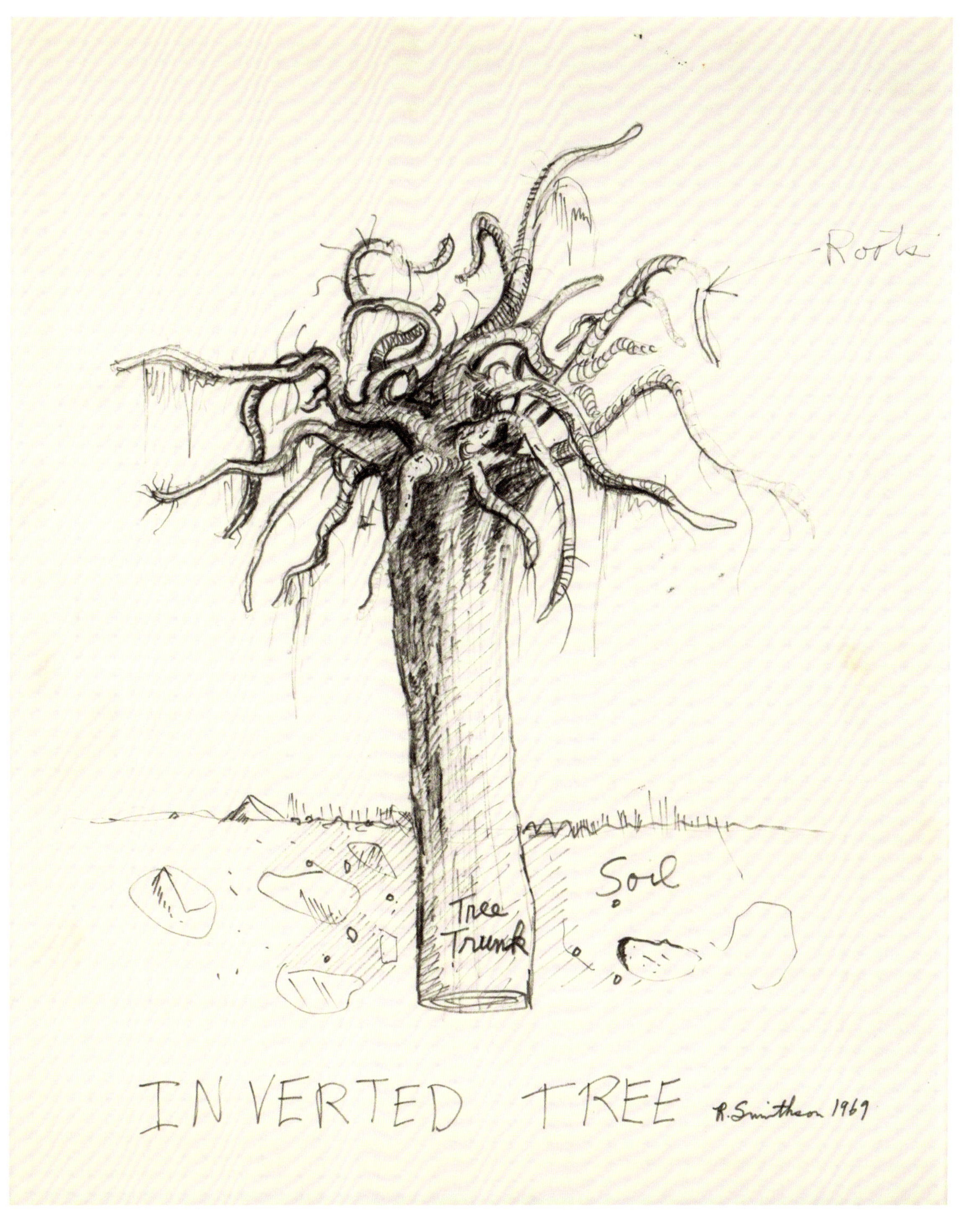
Roots
Soil
Tree Trunk
INVERTED TREE
R. Smithson 1969

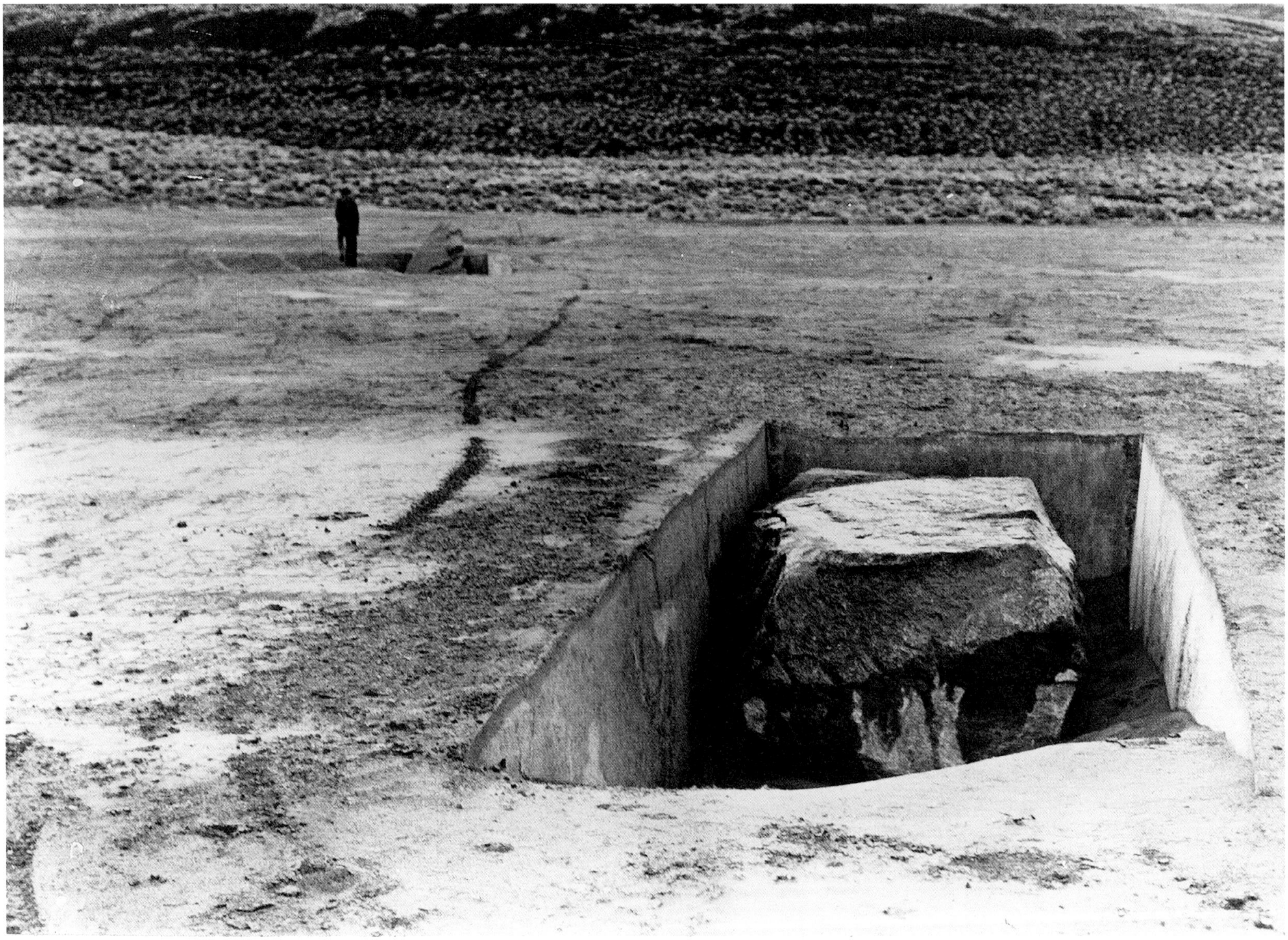

99A

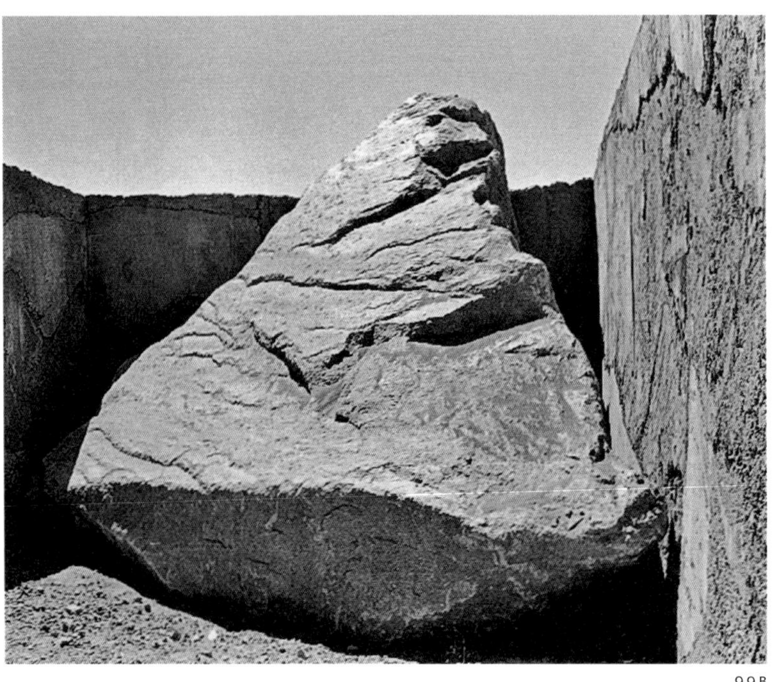

99B

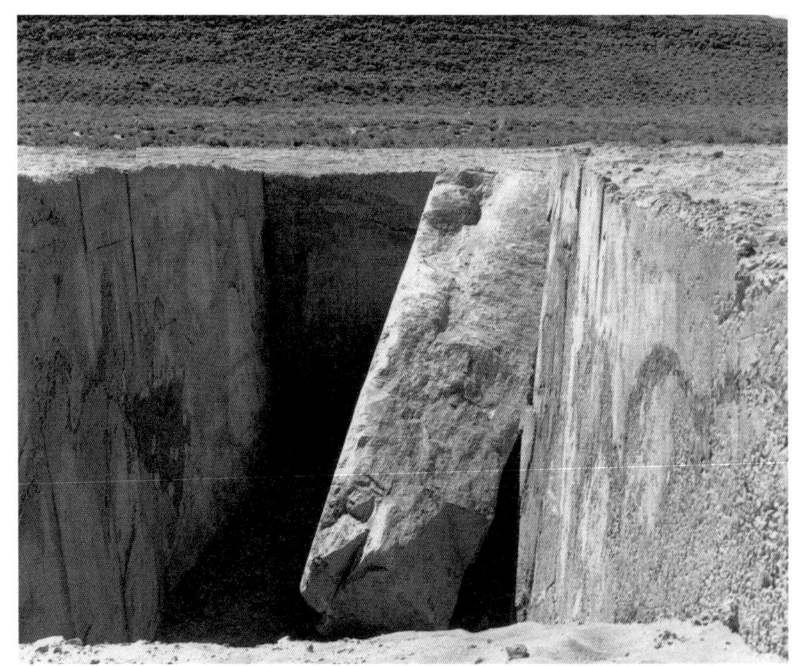

99C

CAT. 99

MICHAEL HEIZER,
A: *DISPLACED/REPLACED MASS* (*1/3*), 1969, (30-TON BLOCK),
B: *DISPLACED/REPLACED MASS* (*2/3*), 1969, (52-TON BLOCK)
C: *DISPLACED/REPLACED MASS* (*3/3*), 1969, (68-TON BLOCK)

CAT. 100

MICHAEL HEIZER,
BOLIVIA/NEVADA,
1970

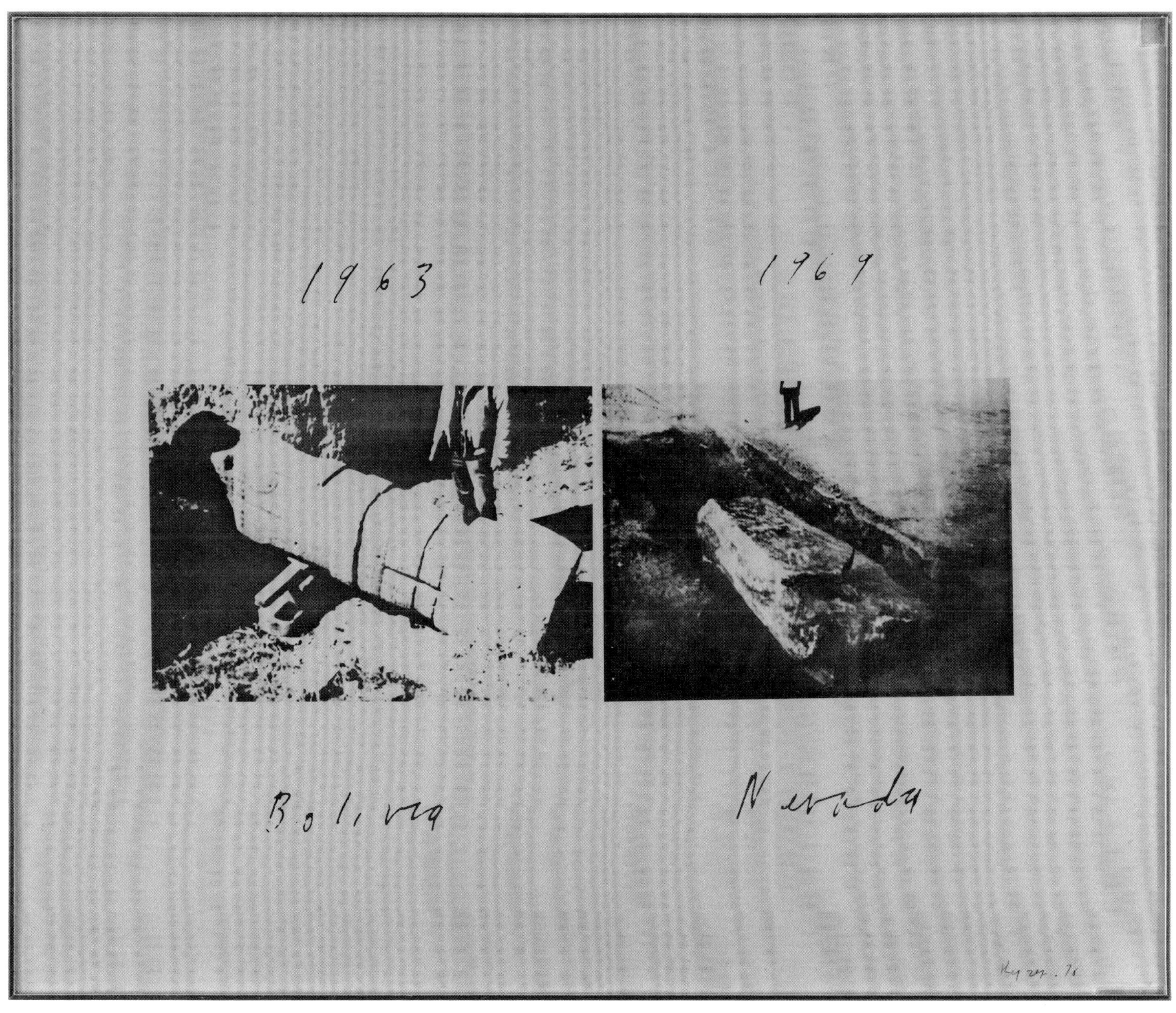

CAT. 101

MICHAEL HEIZER, *SCIENTIFIC AMERICAN*, 1970

CAT. 102 (PAGES 211–213)

MICHAEL HEIZER, *DOUBLE NEGATIVE*, 1969

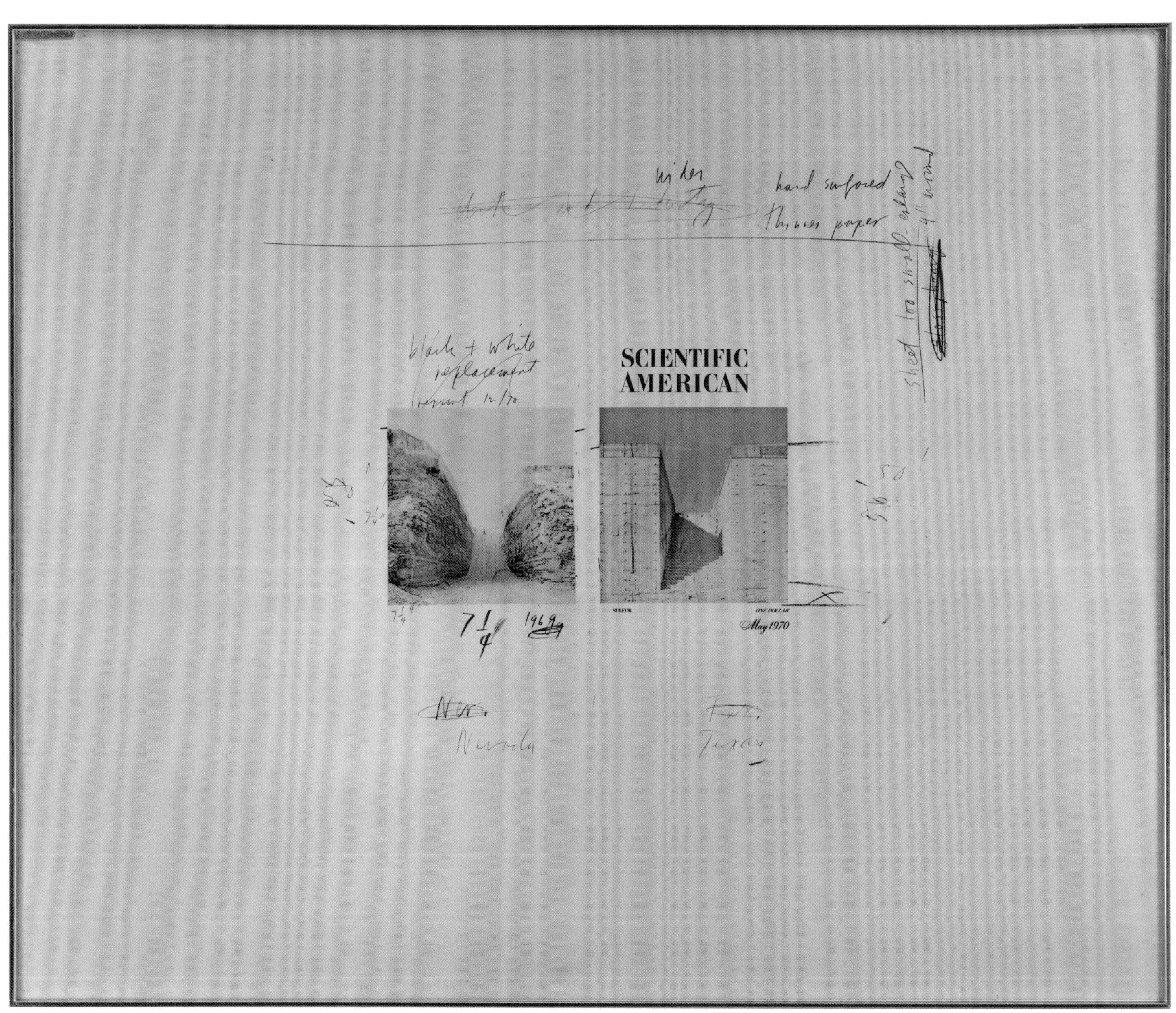

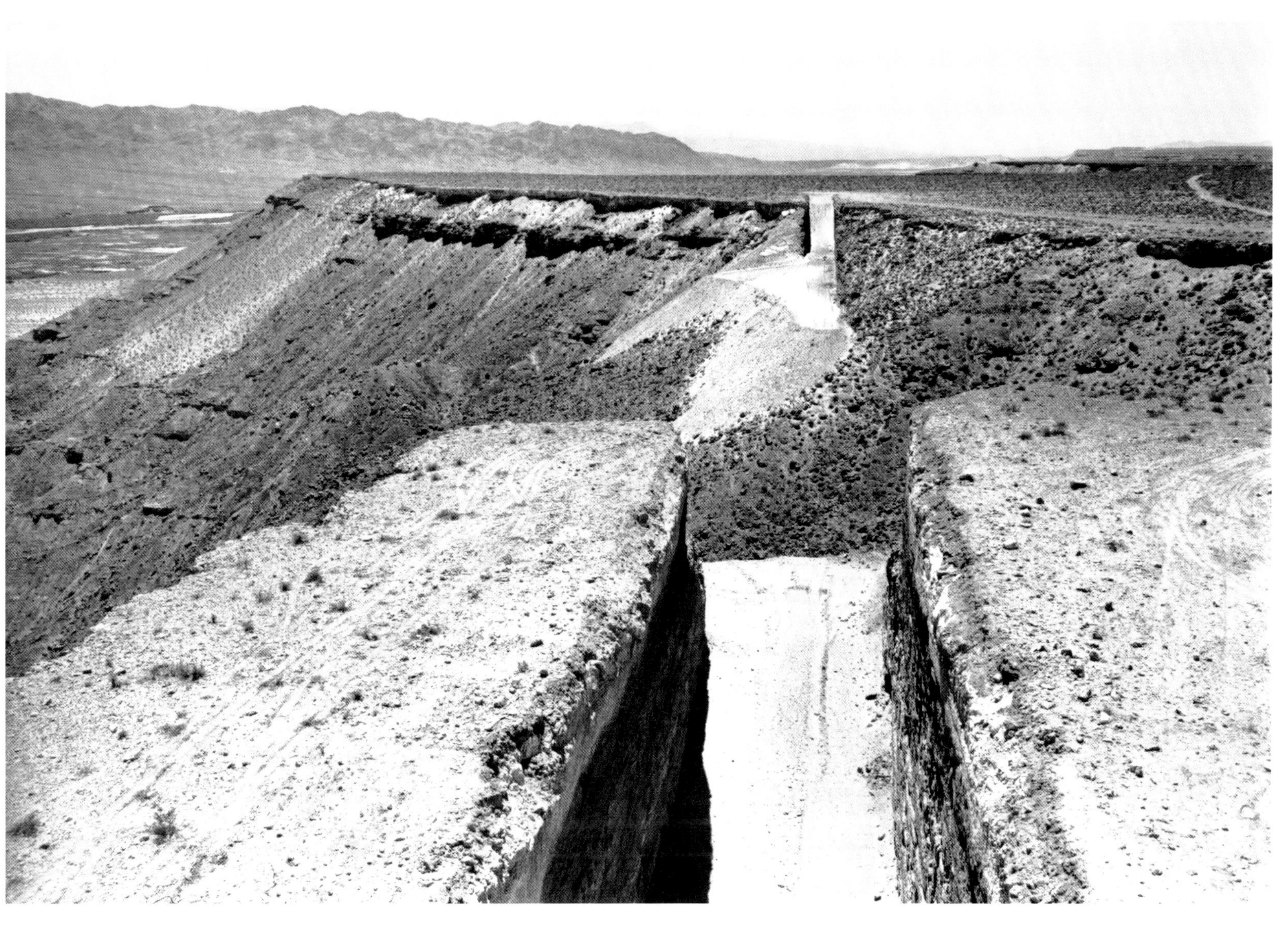

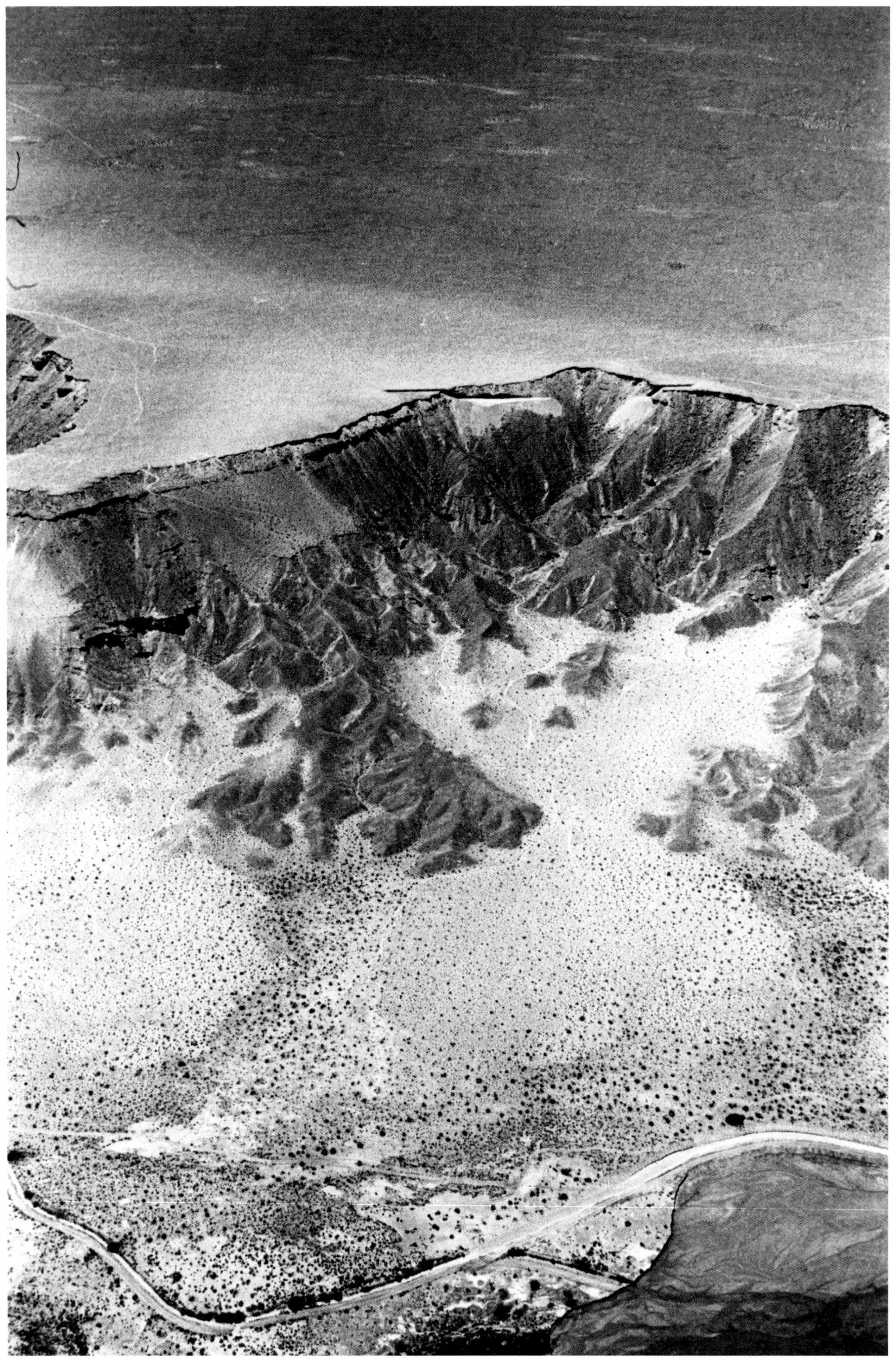

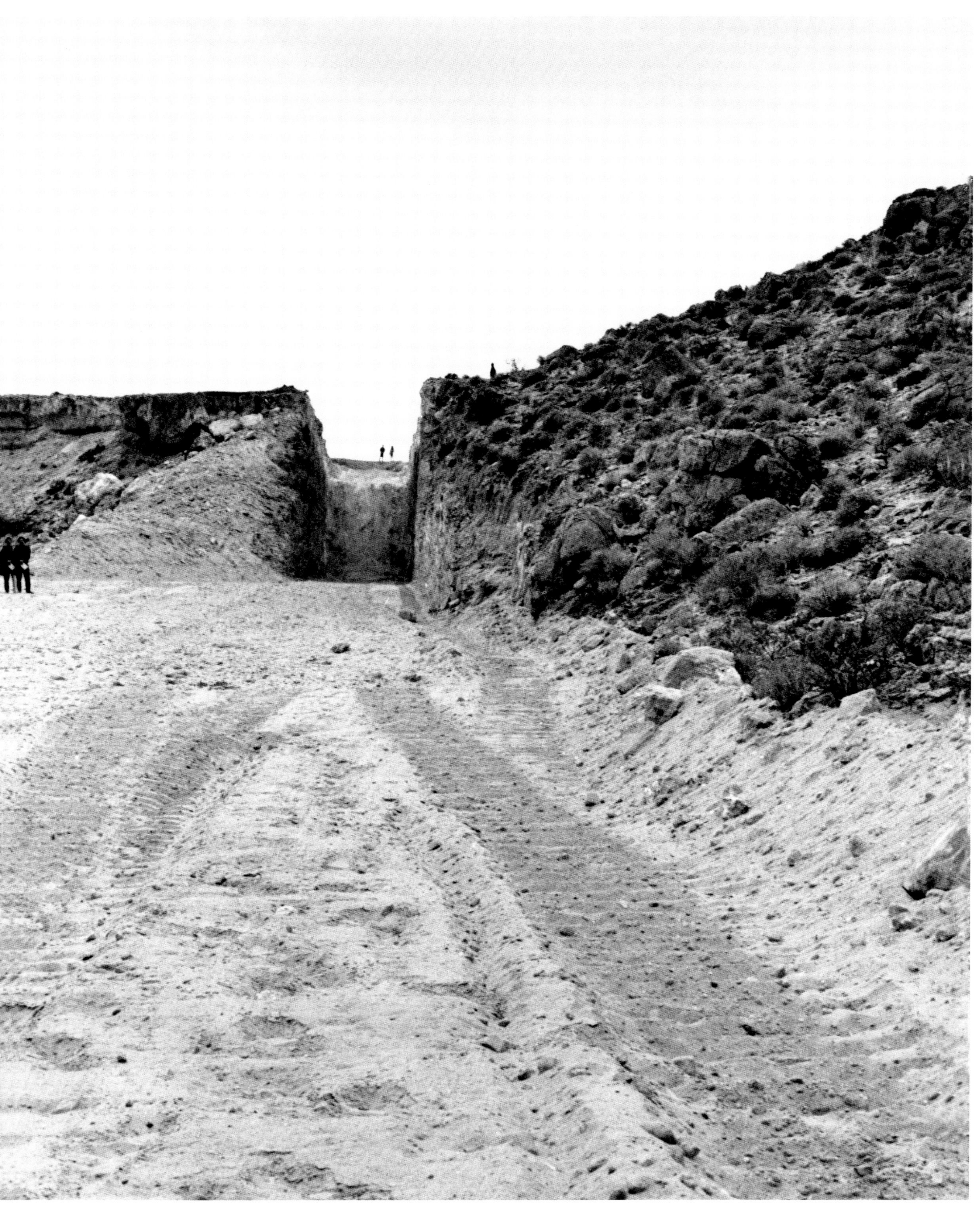

CAT. 103

WALTER DE MARIA,
HIGH ENERGY BAR,
1966

CAT. 104

WALTER DE MARIA,
35-POLE LIGHTNING FIELD, 1974

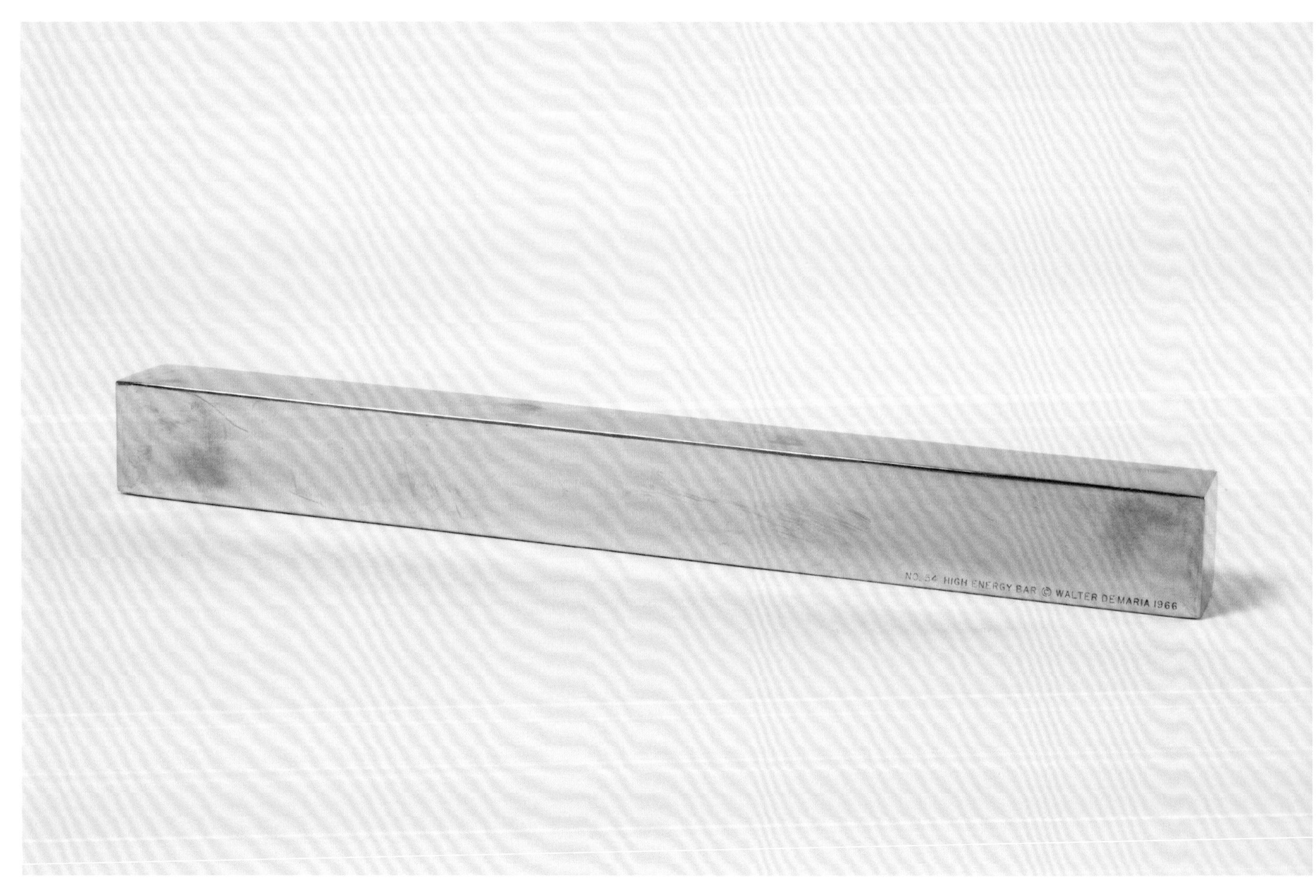

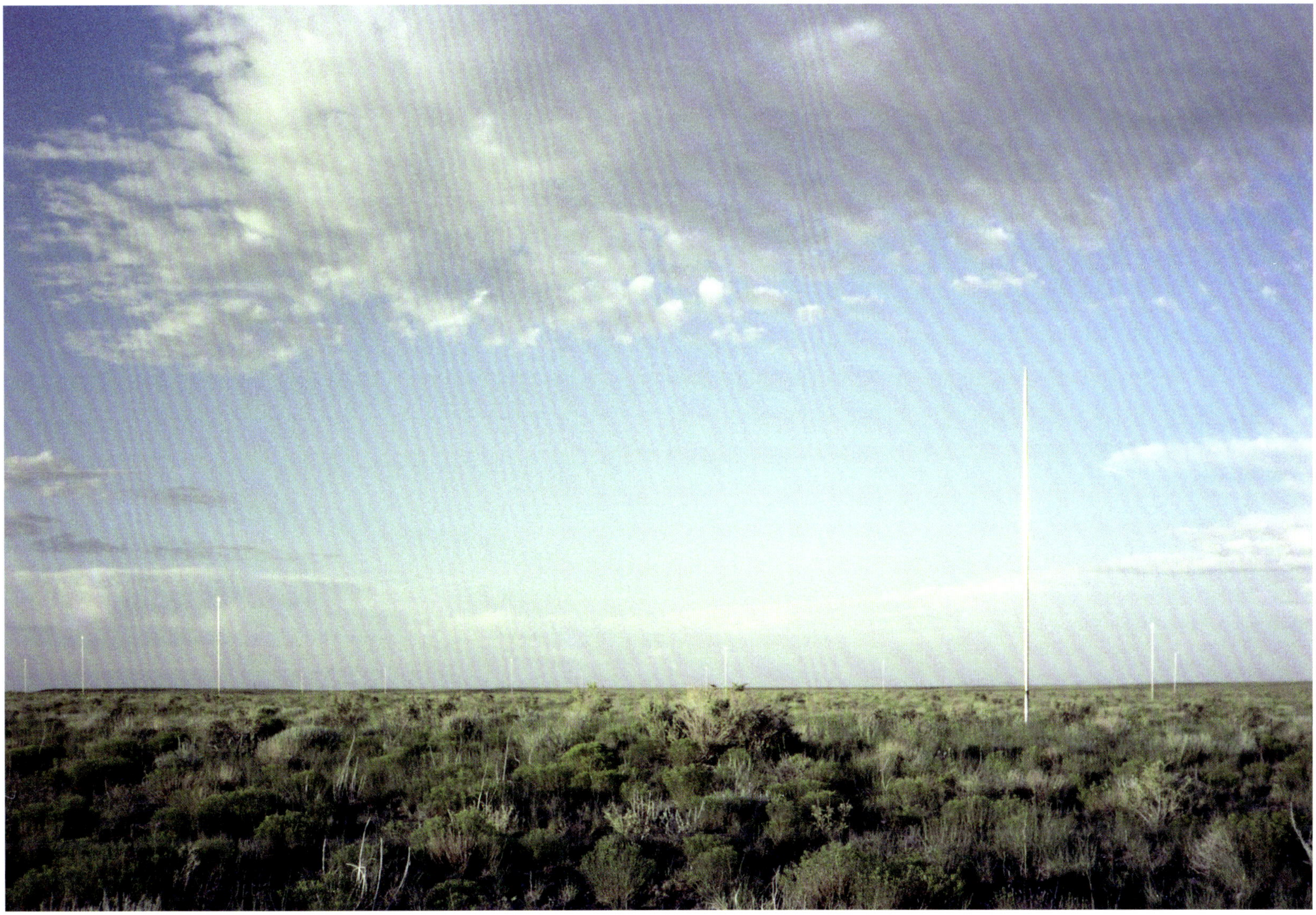

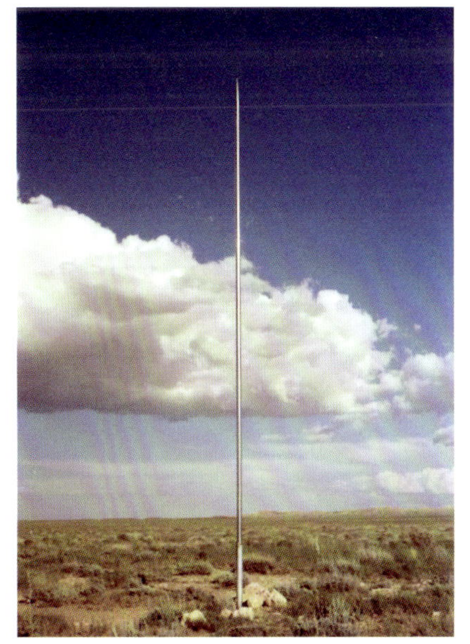

CAT. 105

WALTER DE MARIA,
LIGHTNING FIELD,
1977

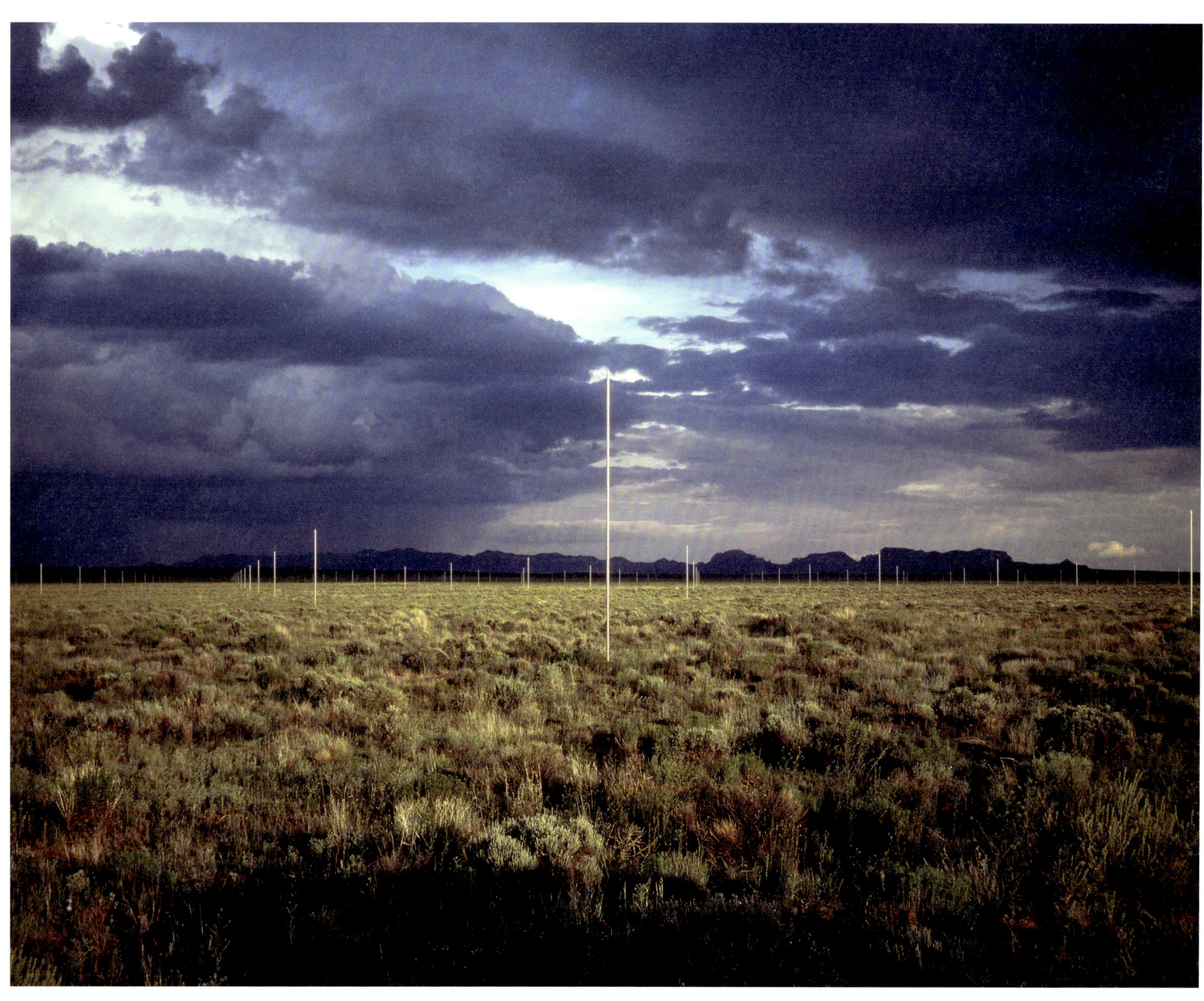

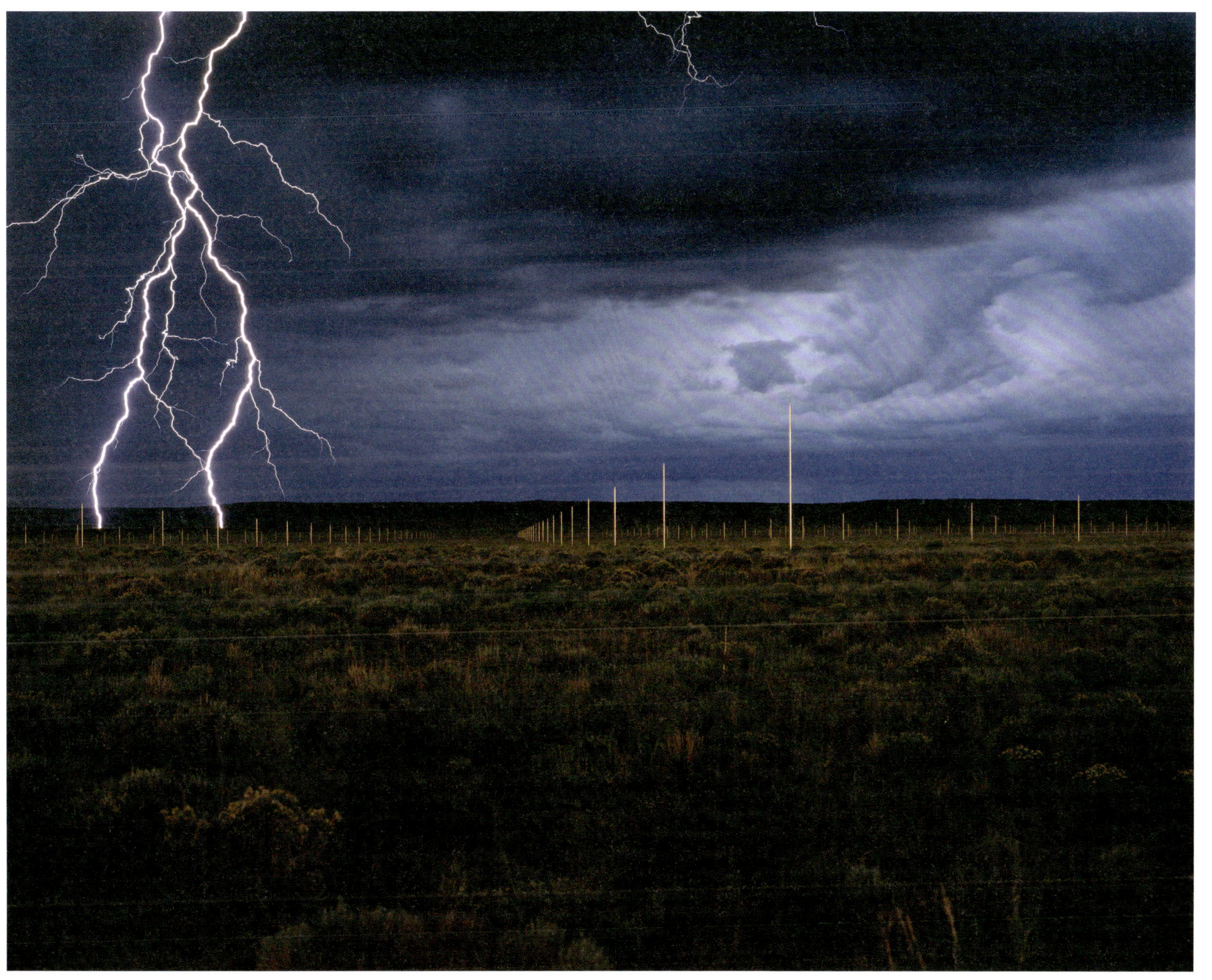

CAT. 106

CHARLES ROSS,
STACK OF TWO PRISMS,
1970

CAT. 107

CHARLES ROSS,
SOLAR BURN 1/29/77,
1977

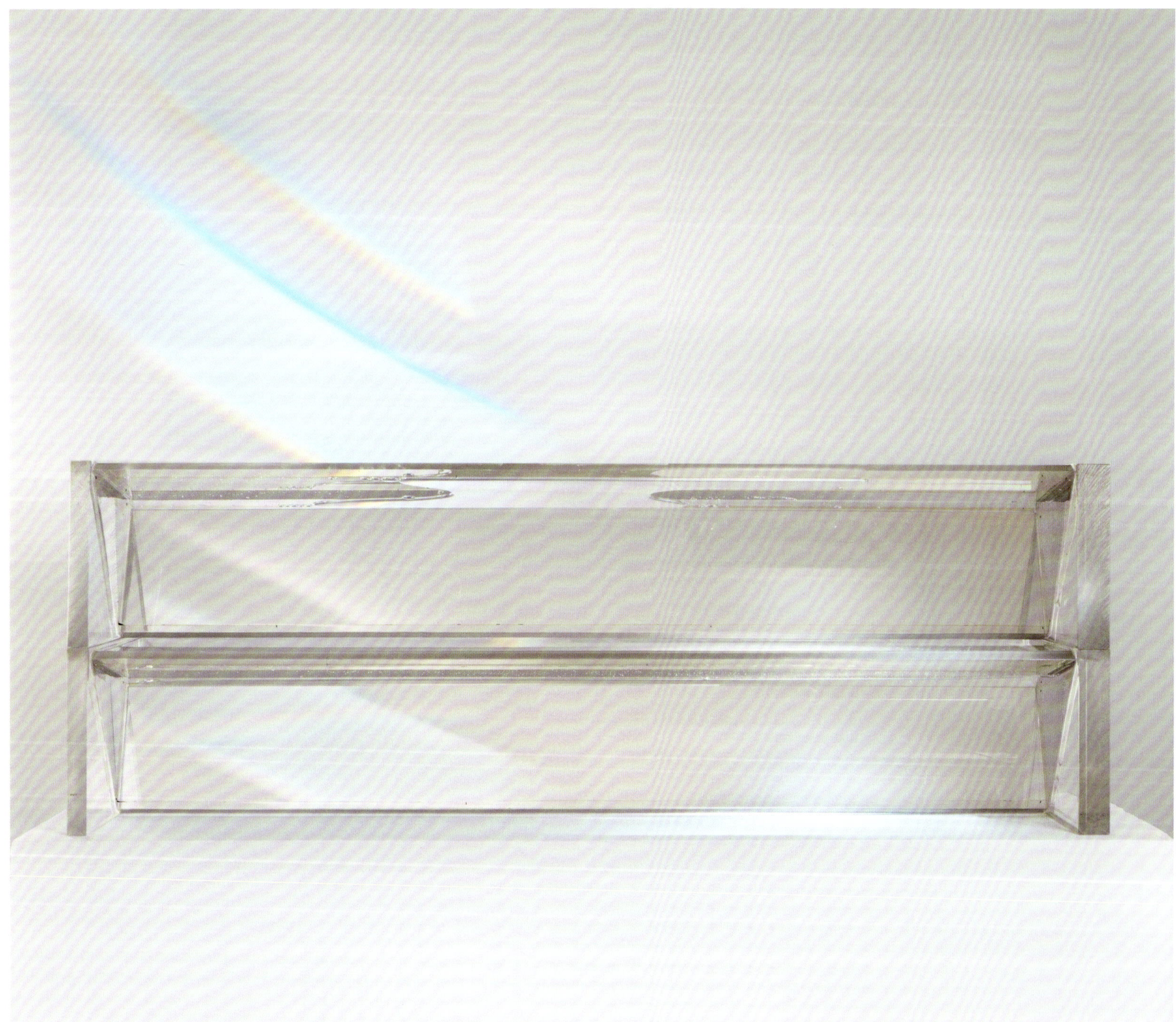

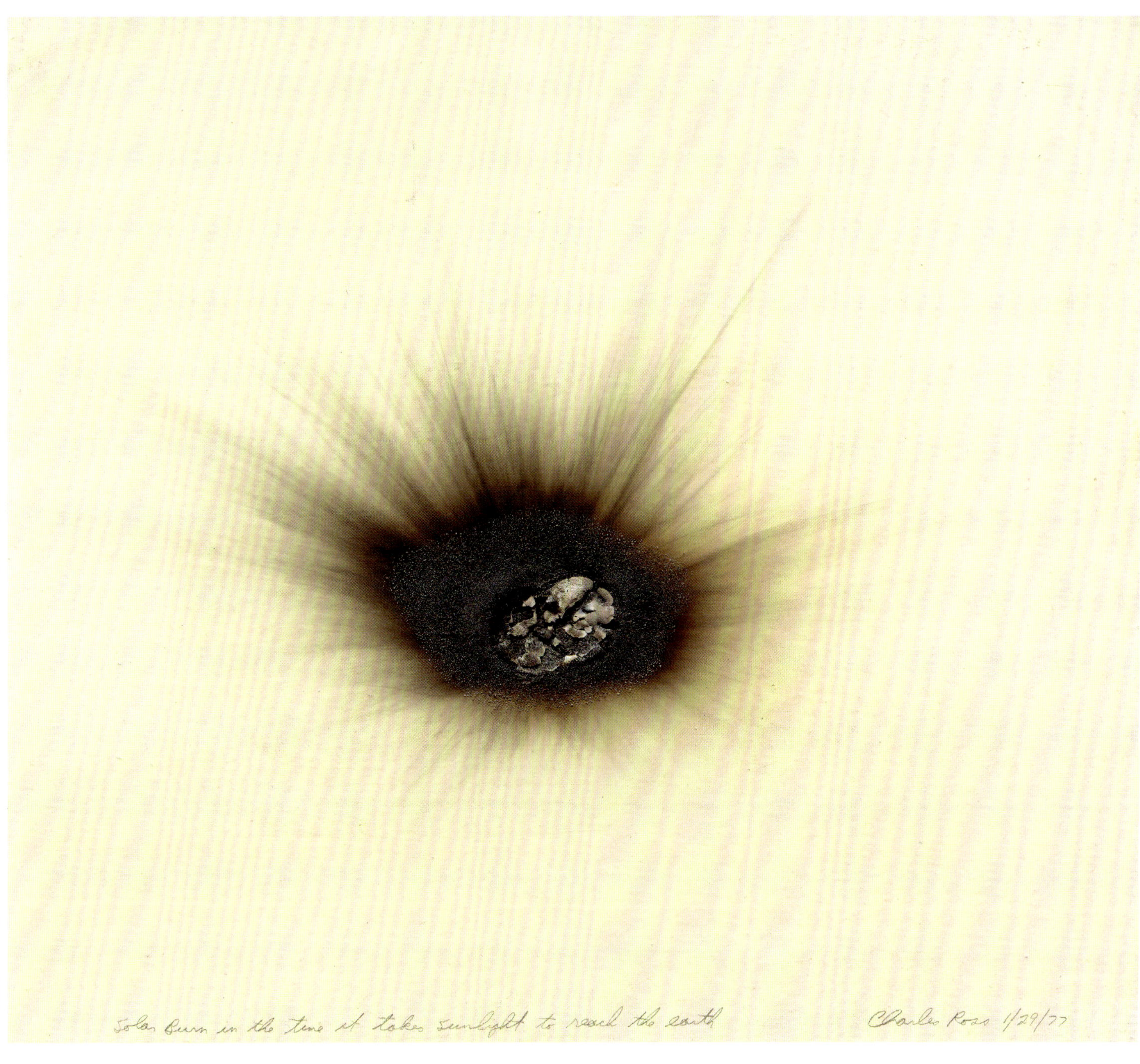
Solar Burn in the time it takes sunlight to reach the earth
Charles Ross 1/29/77

CAT. 108
(PAGES 220–223)

CHARLES ROSS,
STAR AXIS,
1971–ONGOING

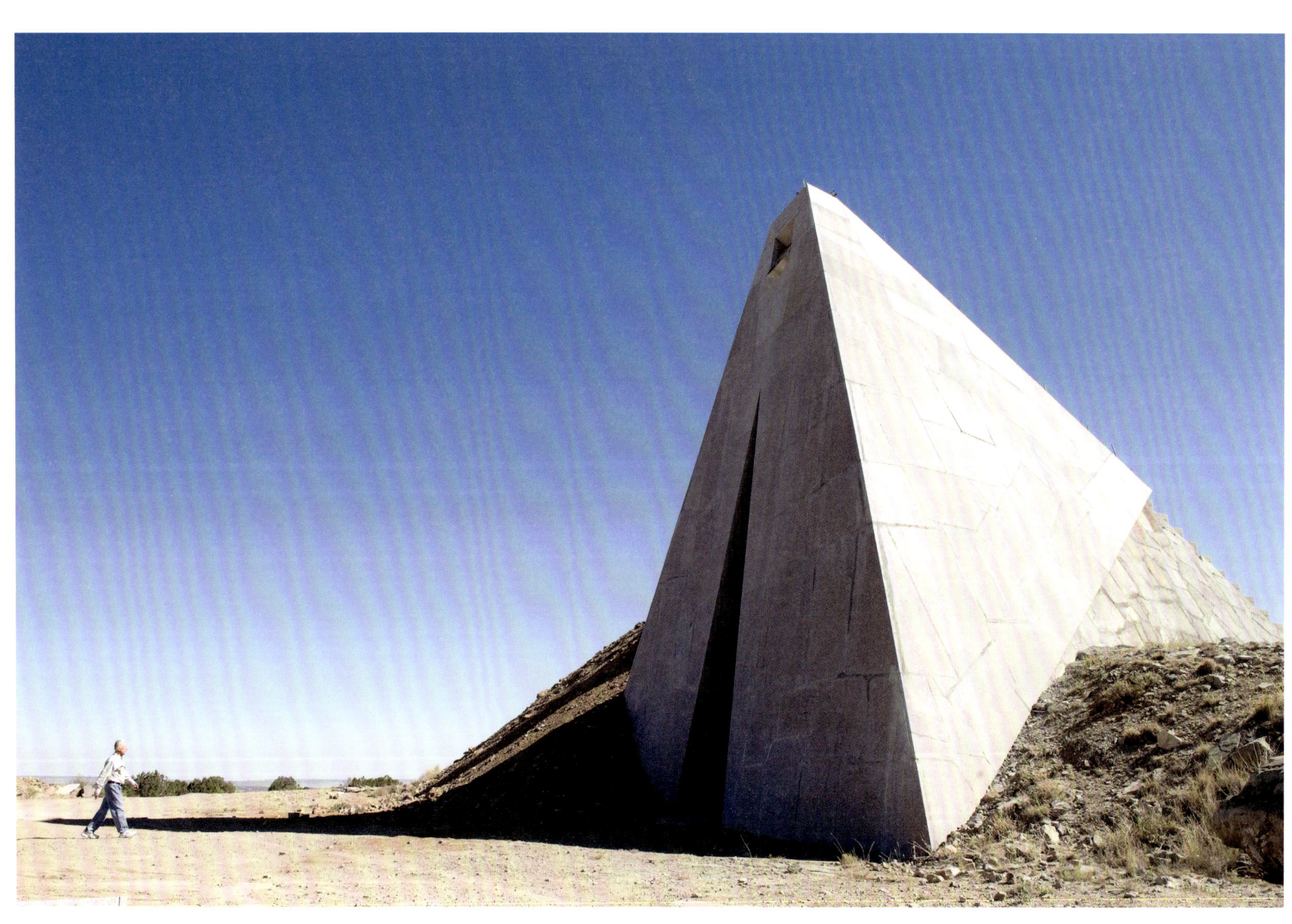

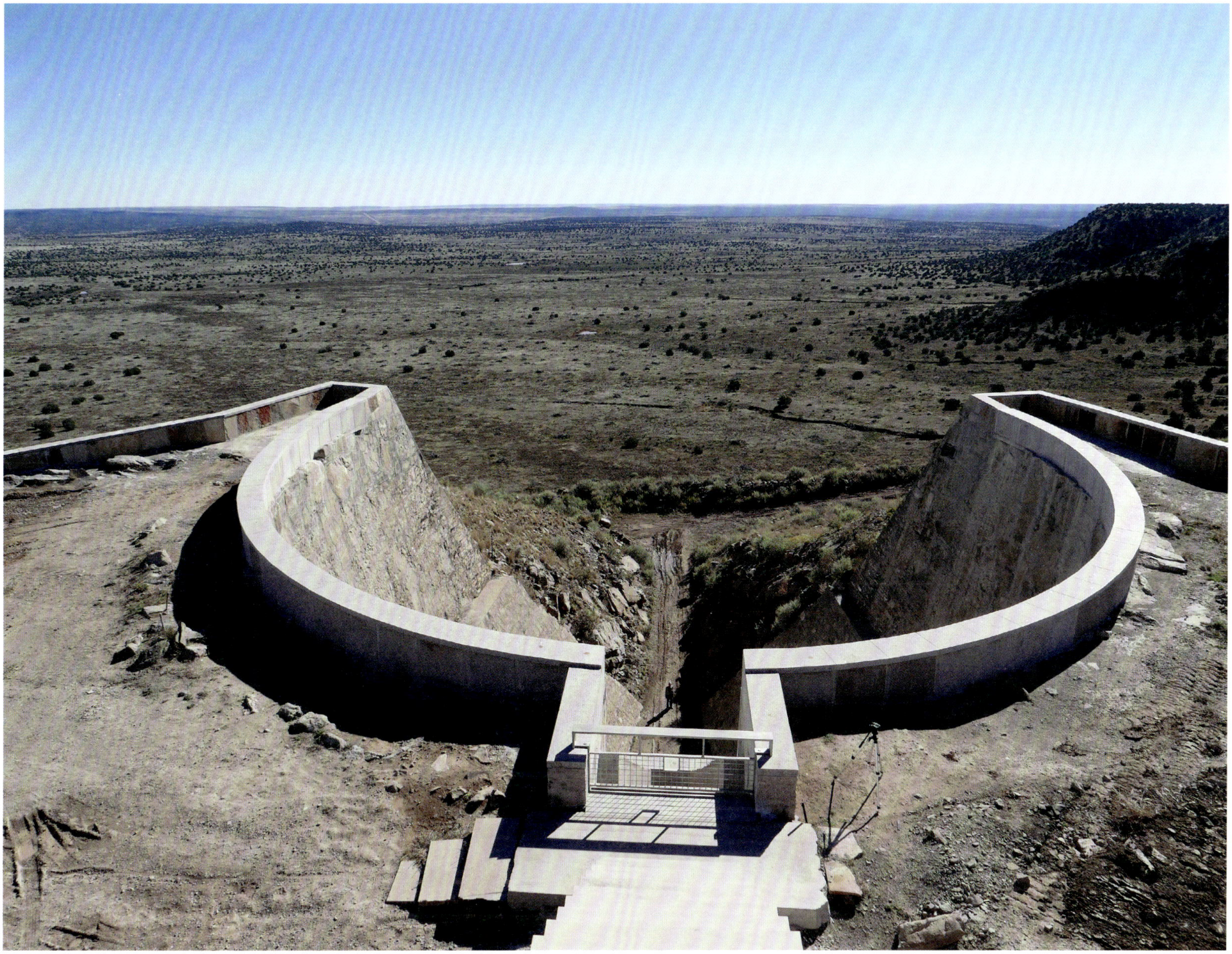

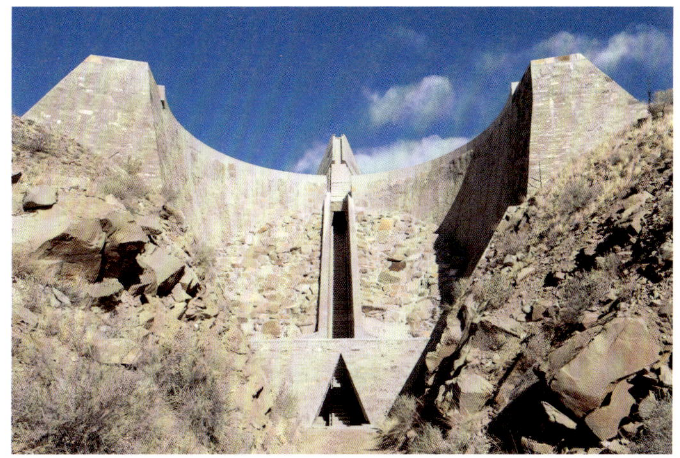

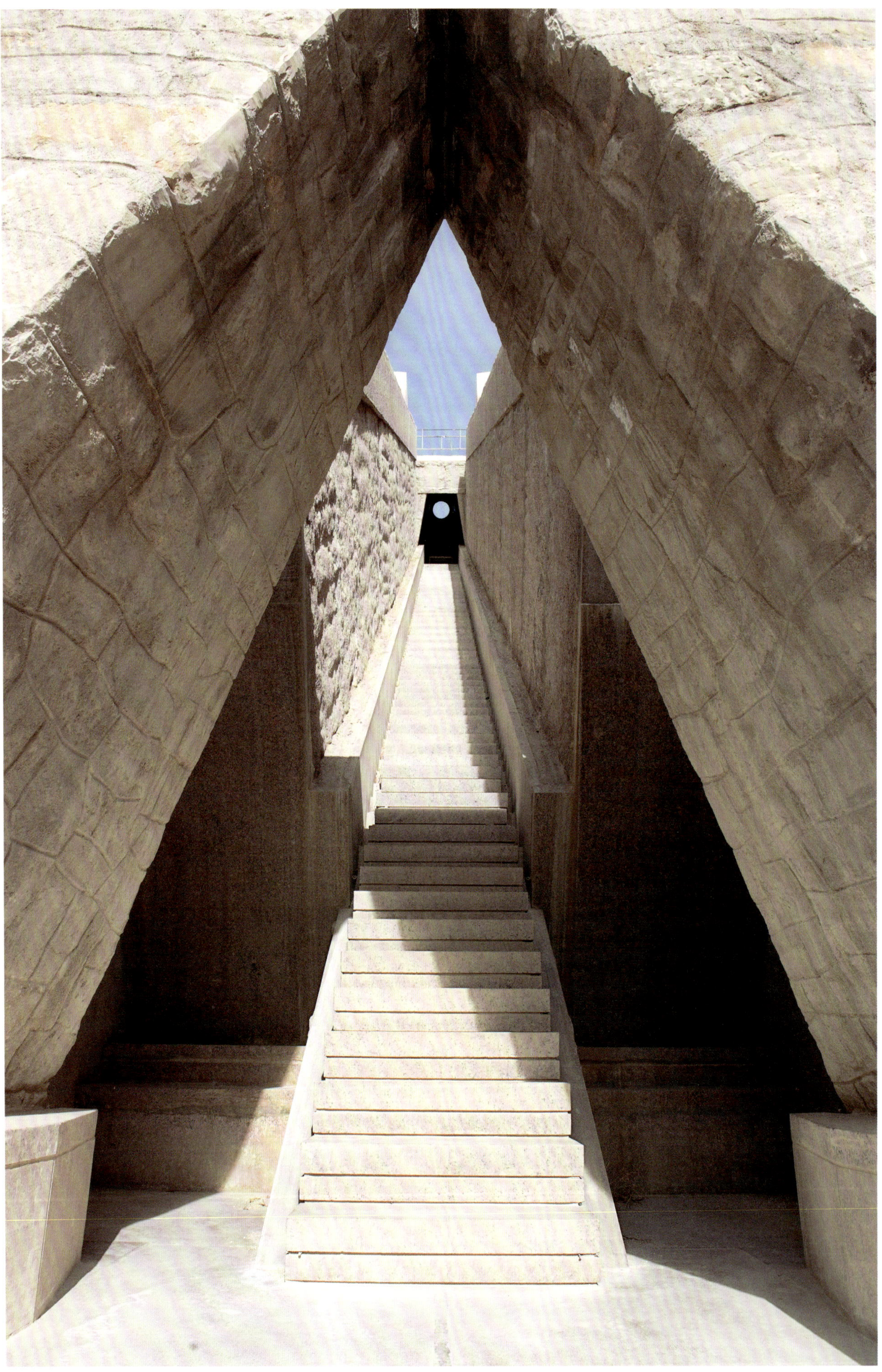

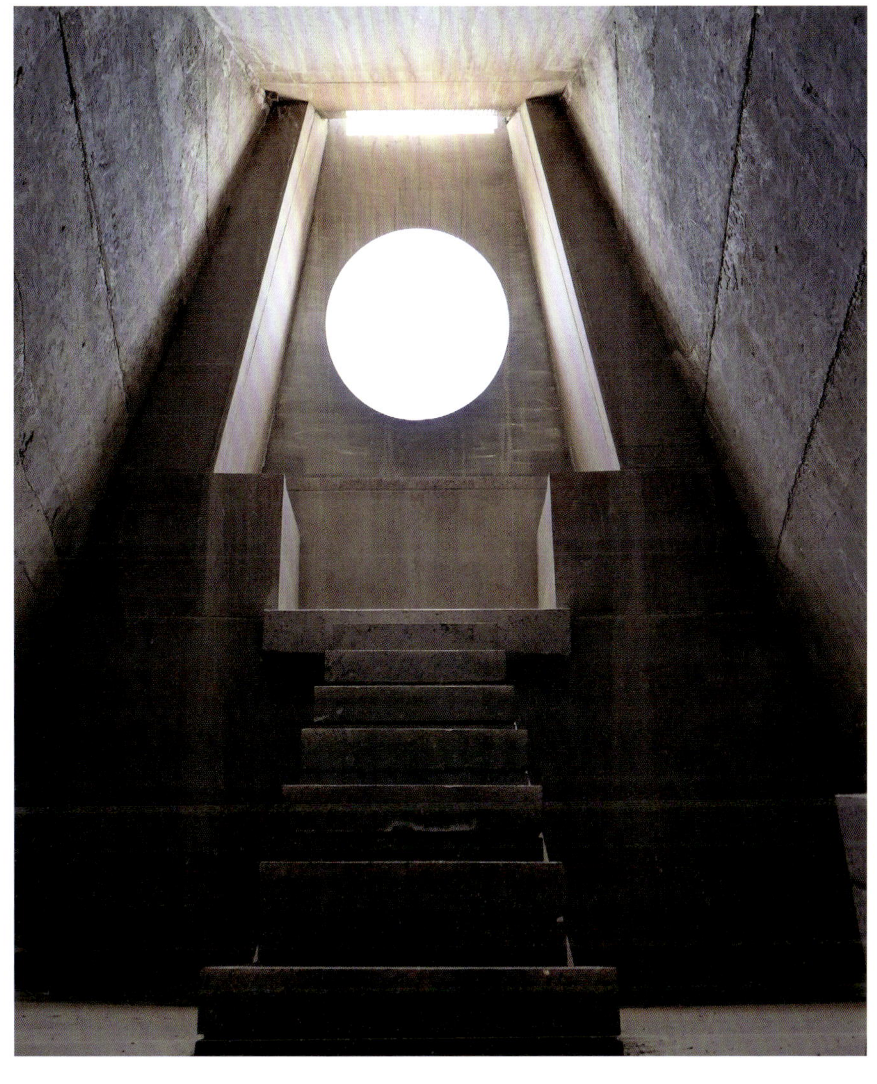

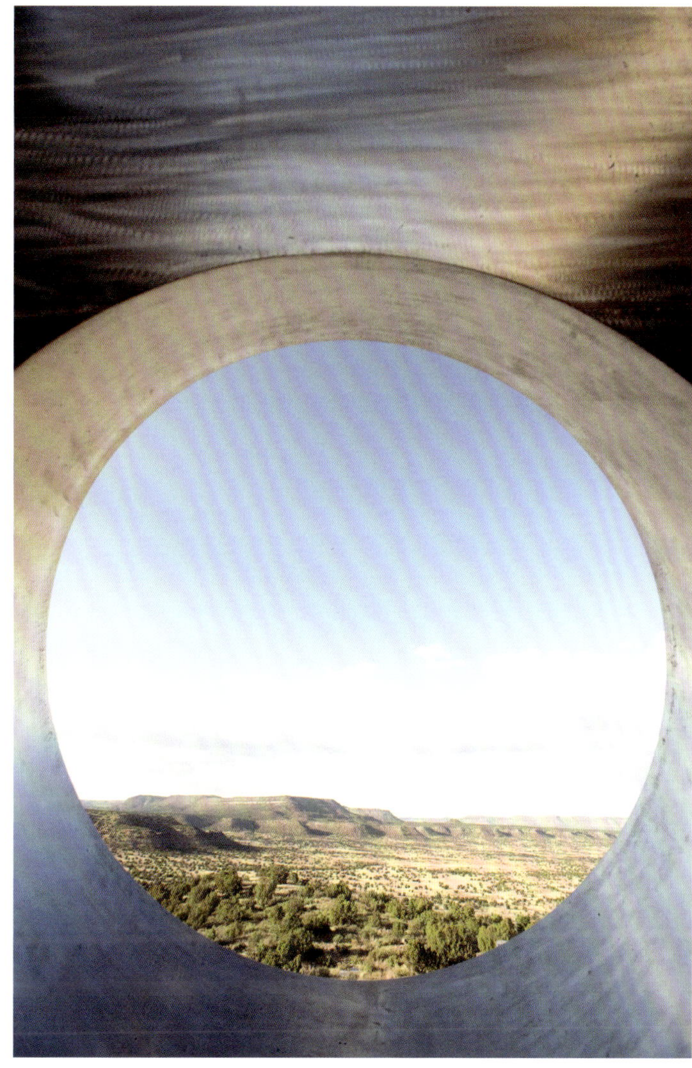

CAT. 109

ROBERT SMITHSON,
SPIRAL JETTY,
1970

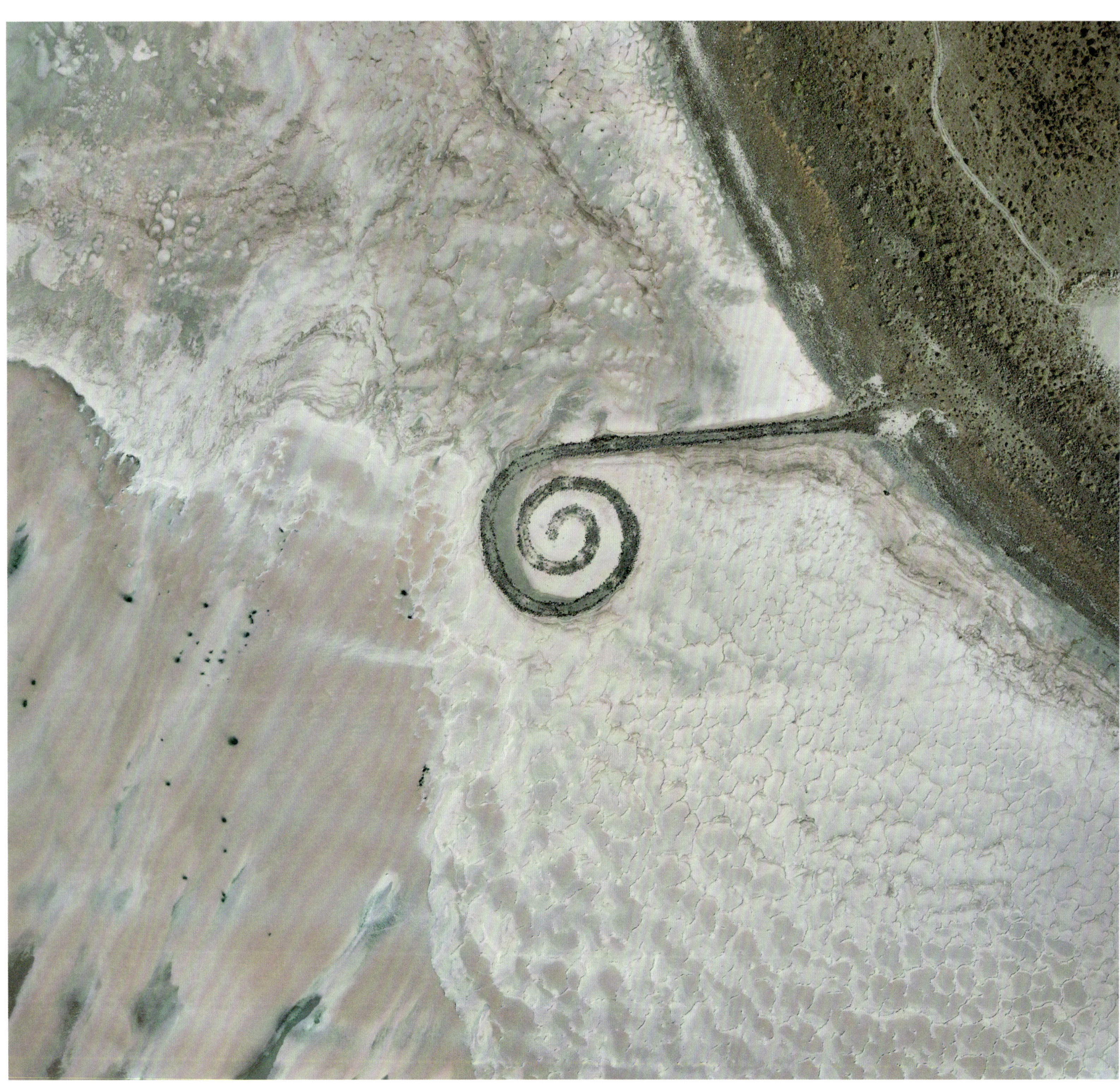

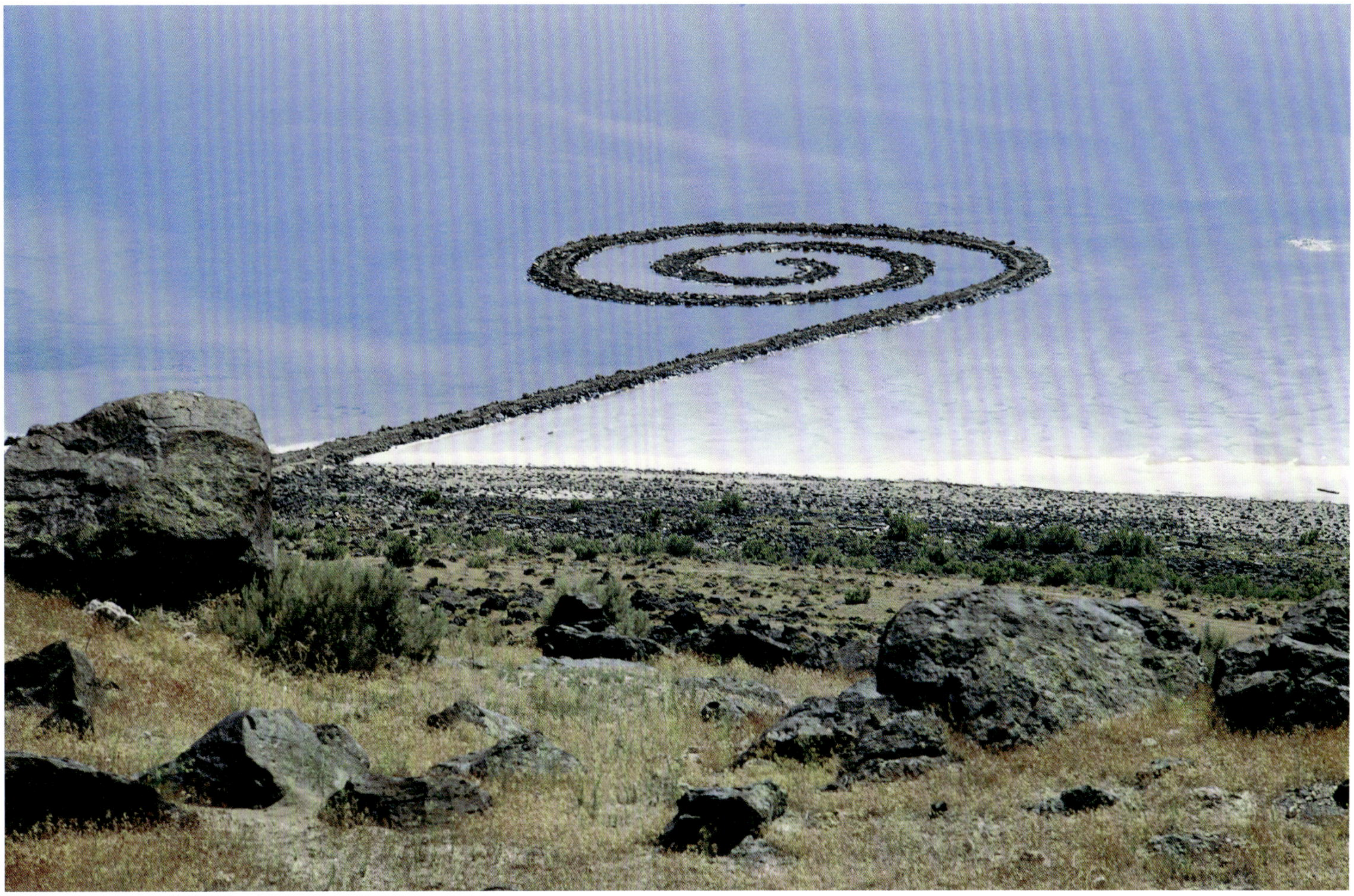

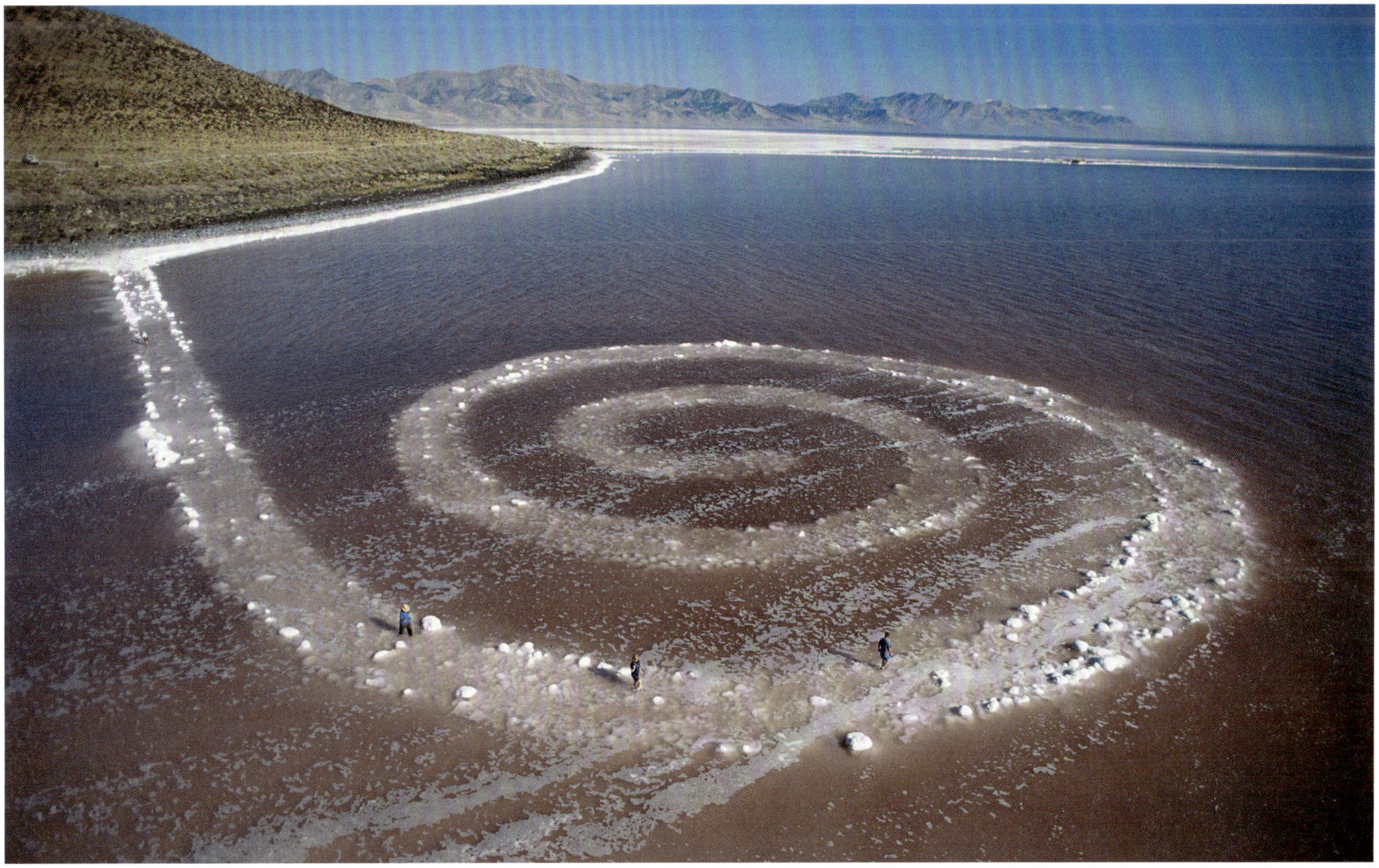

CAT. 110

ROBERT SMITHSON,
SPIRAL JETTY,
1970

CAT. 111

ROBERT SMITHSON,
SPIRAL ISLAND WITH CURVED JETTY,
1970

CAT. 112

ROBERT SMITHSON,
GREEN ISLAND—SPIRAL ISLAND, 1970

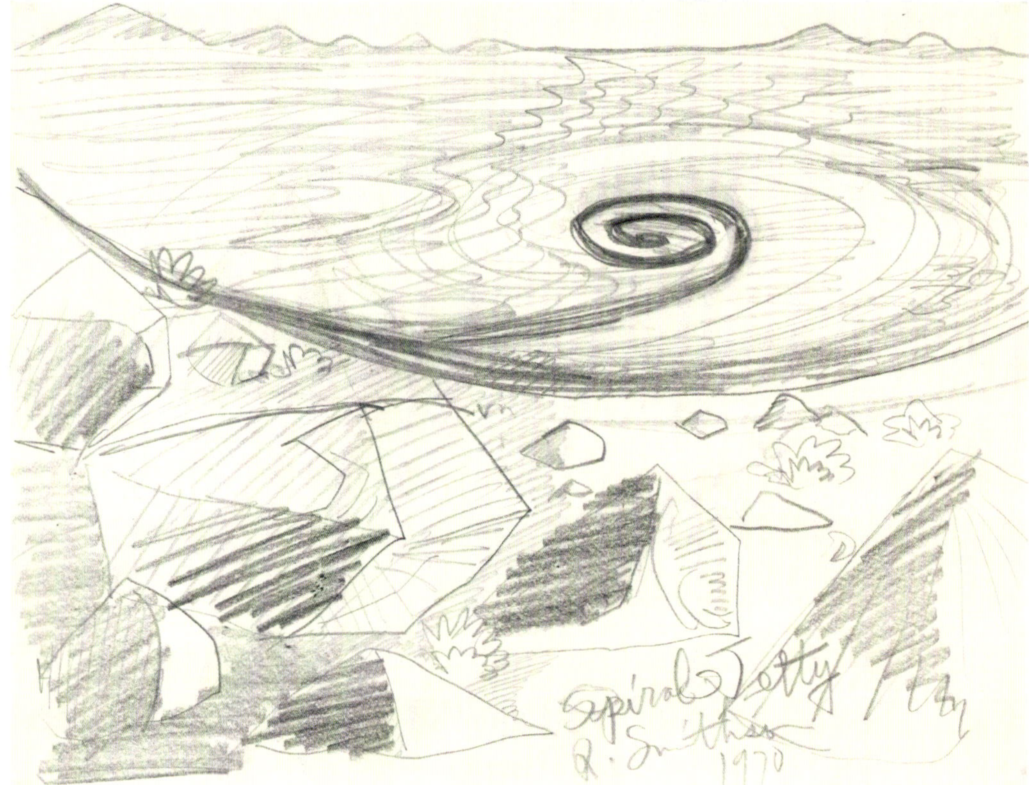

110

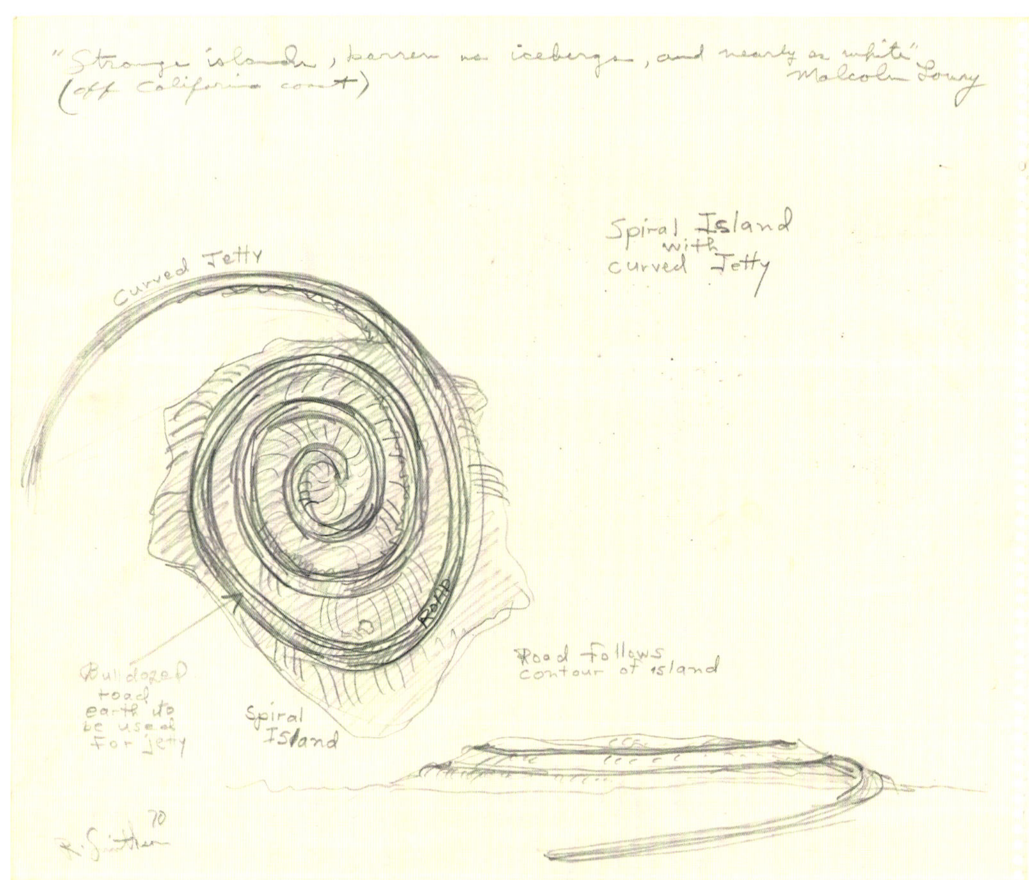

111

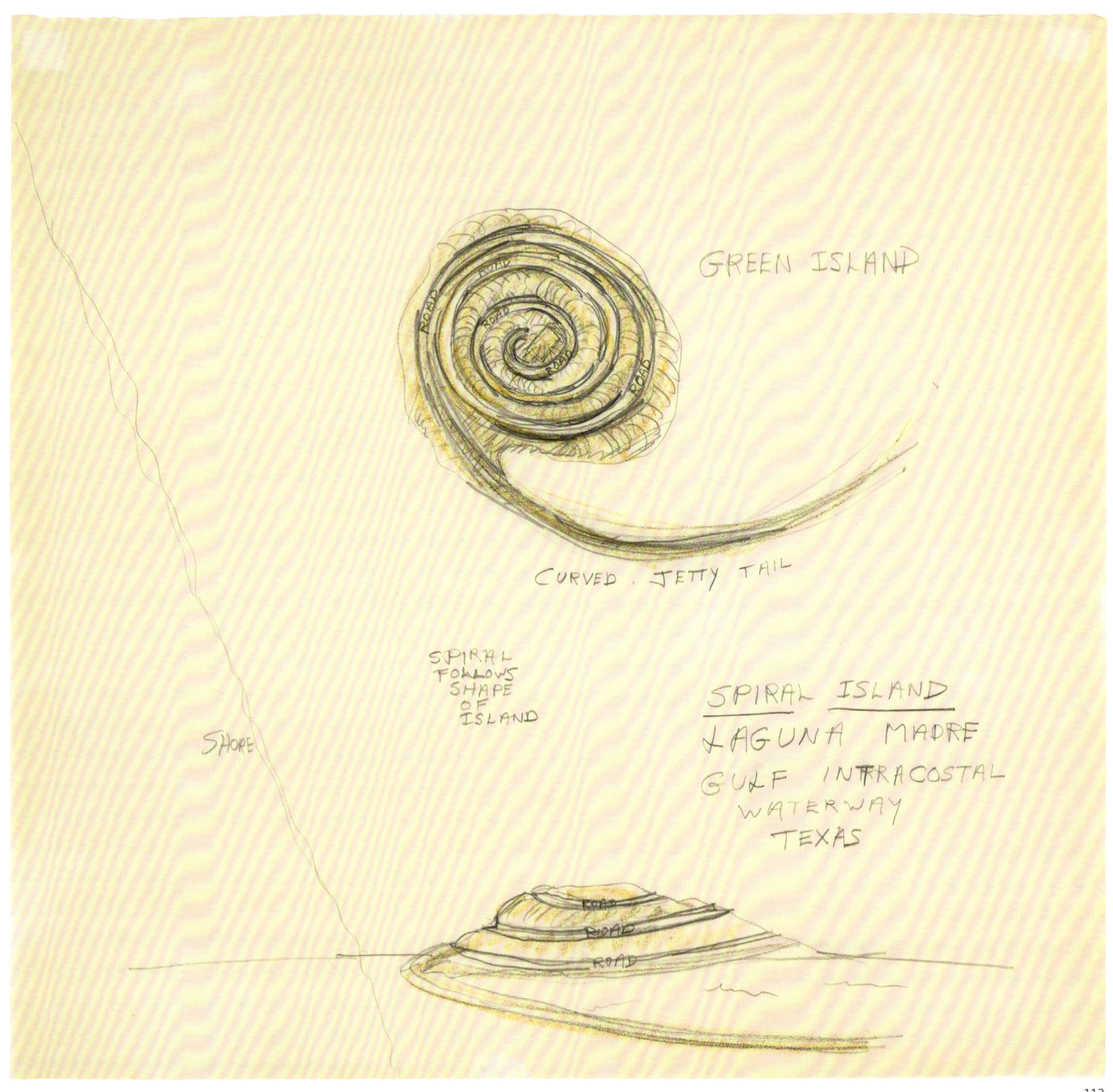

GREEN ISLAND
ROAD
ROAD
ROAD
ROAD
ROAD
CURVED JETTY TAIL
SPIRAL FOLLOWS SHAPE OF ISLAND
SPIRAL ISLAND
LAGUNA MADRE
GULF INTRACOSTAL WATERWAY
TEXAS
SHORE
ROAD
ROAD
ROAD

112

CAT. 113

ROBERT SMITHSON, *PIERCED SPIRAL*, 1971

CAT. 114

ROBERT SMITHSON, *UNTITLED*, 1970

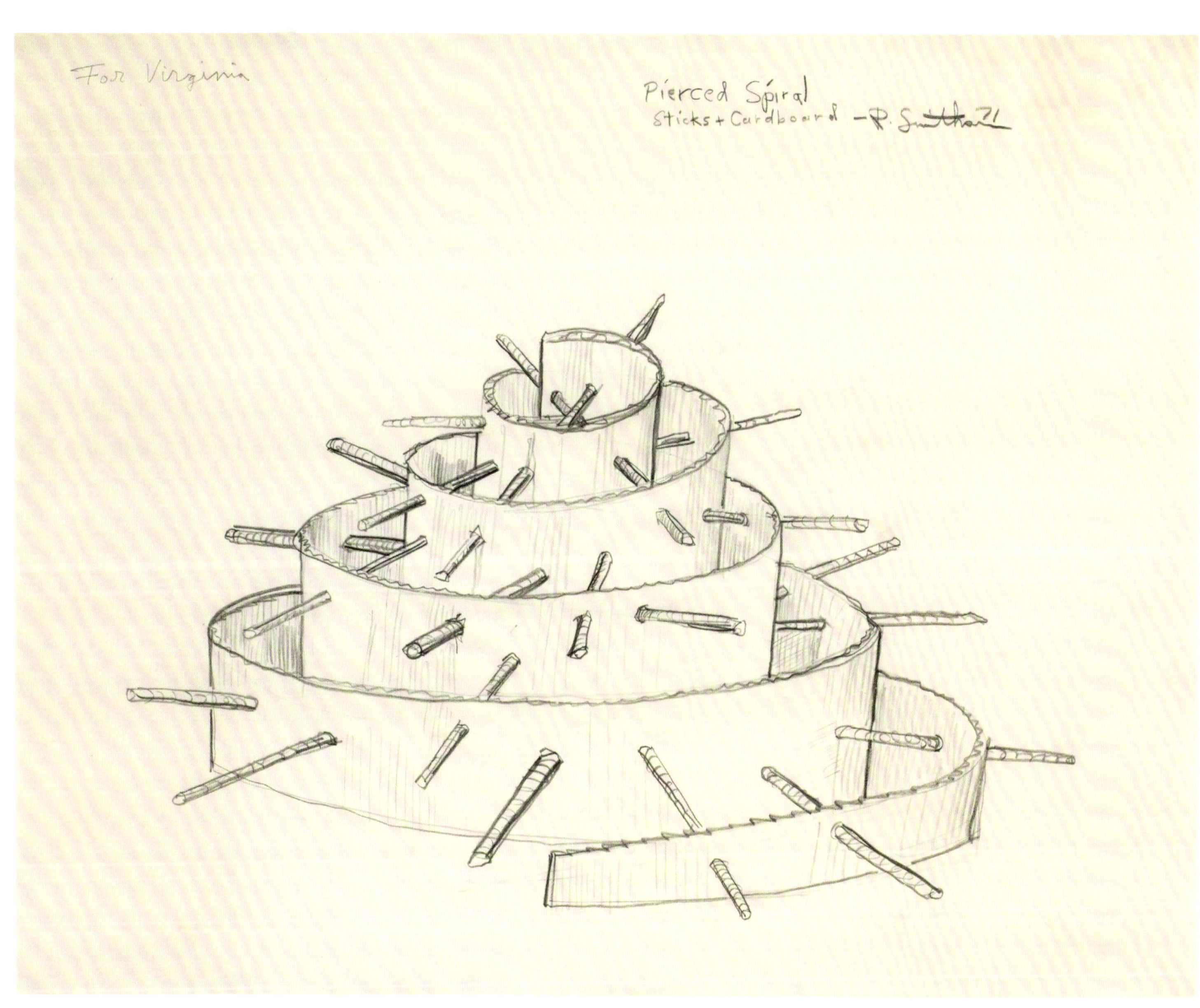

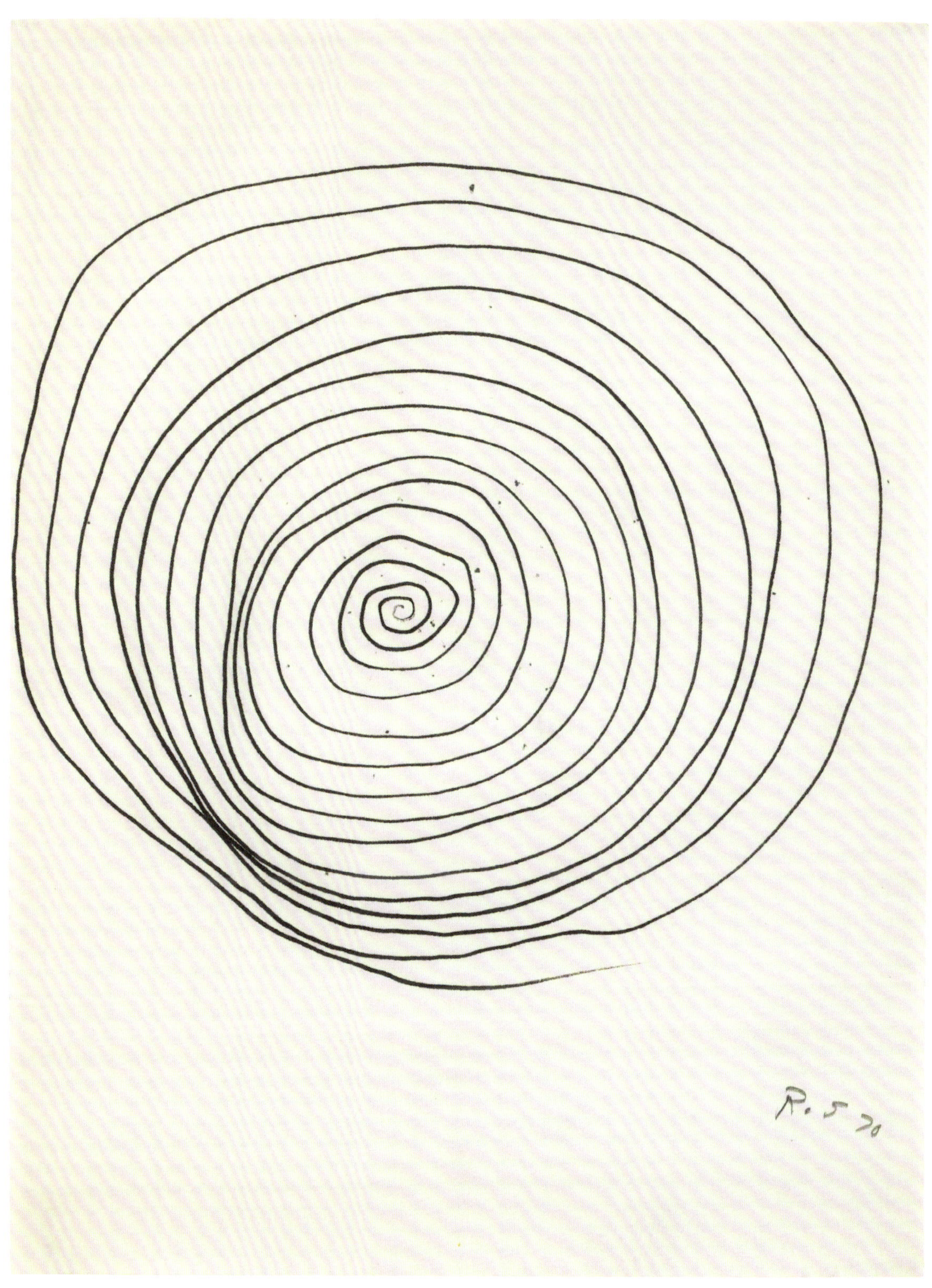

CAT. 115

ROBERT SMITHSON,
MOVIE TREATMENT FOR SPIRAL JETTY (*PART I*), 1971

CAT. 116

ROBERT SMITHSON,
MOVIE TREATMENT FOR SPIRAL JETTY (*PART II*), 1971

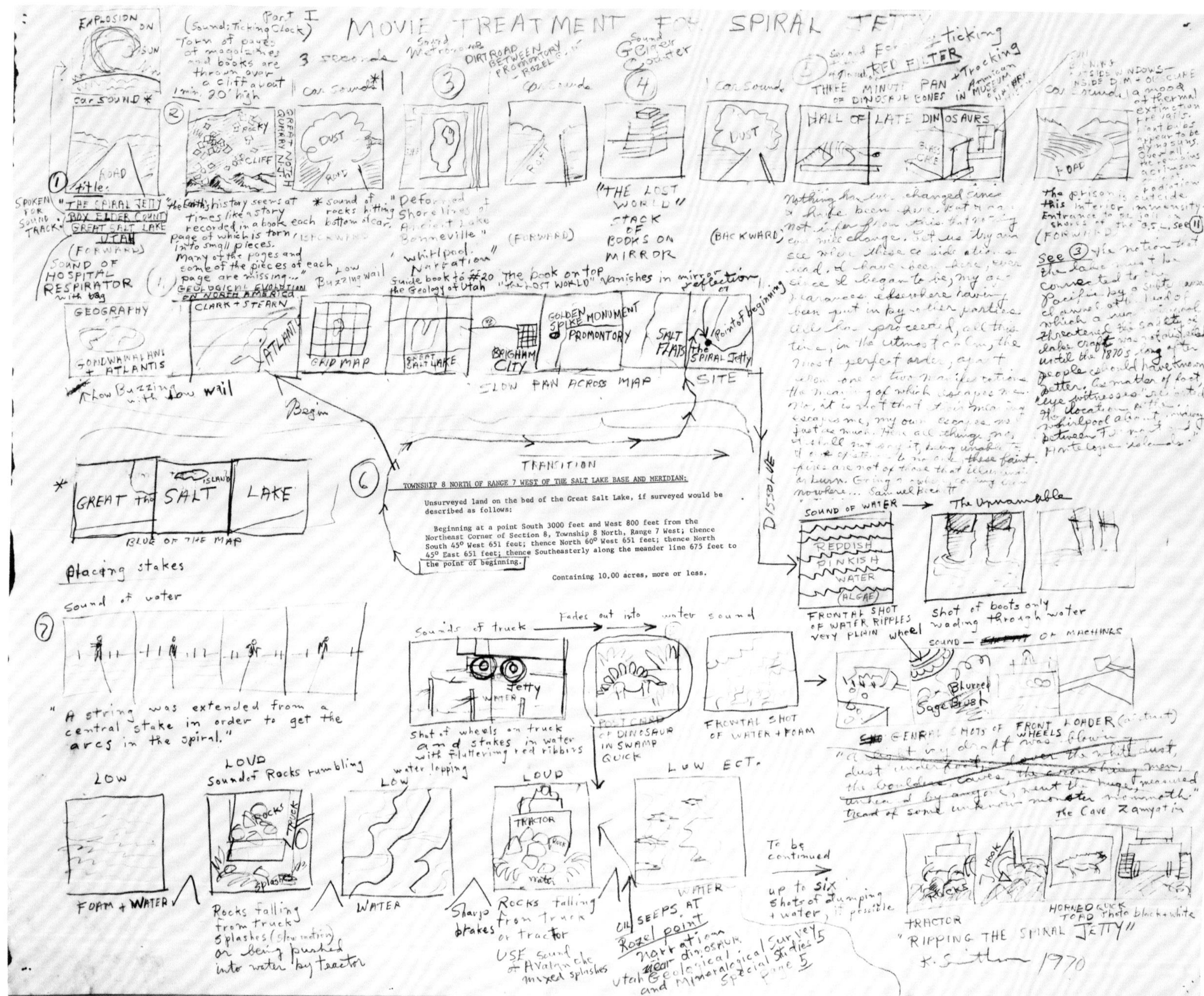

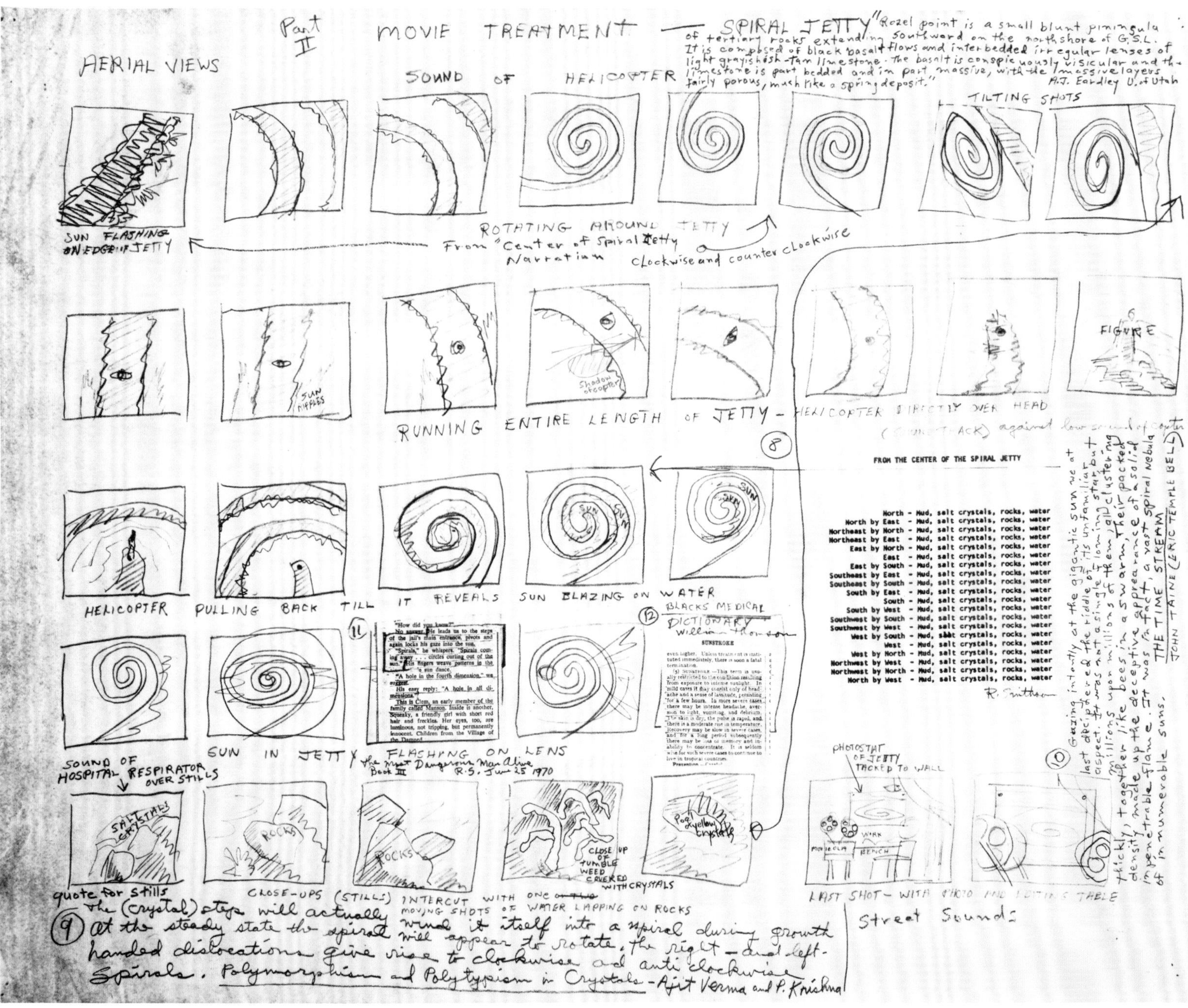

Part II
MOVIE TREATMENT — SPIRAL JETTY
"Rozel point is a small blunt peninsula of tertiary rocks extending southward on the northshore of G.S.L. It is composed of black basalt flows and interbedded irregular lenses of light grayish-tan limestone. The basalt is conspicuously visicular and the limestone is part bedded and in part massive, with the massive layers fairly porous, much like a spring deposit." A.J. Eardley U. of Utah
AERIAL VIEWS
SOUND OF HELICOPTER
TILTING SHOTS
SUN FLASHING ON EDGE OF JETTY
ROTATING AROUND JETTY
From "Center of Spiral Jetty" Narration
clockwise and counter clockwise
SUN RIPPLES
Shadow of copter
FIGURE
RUNNING ENTIRE LENGTH OF JETTY — HELICOPTER DIRECTLY OVER HEAD
(SOUND TRACK) against low sound of copter
8
FROM THE CENTER OF THE SPIRAL JETTY
North - Mud, salt crystals, rocks, water
North by East - Mud, salt crystals, rocks, water
Northeast by North - Mud, salt crystals, rocks, water
Northeast by East - Mud, salt crystals, rocks, water
East by North - Mud, salt crystals, rocks, water
East - Mud, salt crystals, rocks, water
East by South - Mud, salt crystals, rocks, water
Southeast by East - Mud, salt crystals, rocks, water
Southeast by South - Mud, salt crystals, rocks, water
South by East - Mud, salt crystals, rocks, water
South - Mud, salt crystals, rocks, water
South by West - Mud, salt crystals, rocks, water
Southwest by South - Mud, salt crystals, rocks, water
Southwest by West - Mud, salt crystals, rocks, water
West by South - Mud, salt crystals, rocks, water
West - Mud, salt crystals, rocks, water
West by North - Mud, salt crystals, rocks, water
Northwest by West - Mud, salt crystals, rocks, water
Northwest by North - Mud, salt crystals, rocks, water
North by West - Mud, salt crystals, rocks, water
R. Smithson
HELICOPTER PULLING BACK TILL IT REVEALS SUN BLAZING ON WATER
SUN
11
12
BLACKS MEDICAL DICTIONARY William Thomson
SUNSTROKE
SUN IN JETTY FLASHING ON LENS
The Most Dangerous Man Alive Book III R.S. Jun 25 1970
SOUND OF HOSPITAL RESPIRATOR OVER STILLS
SALT CRYSTALS
ROCKS
CLOSE UP OF TUMBLE WEED COVERED WITH CRYSTALS
Pool yellow crystals
PHOTOSTAT OF JETTY TACKED TO WALL
MOVIOLA
WORK BENCH
10
Gazing intently at the gigantic sun we at last deciphered the riddle of its unfamiliar aspect. It was not a single star but millions upon millions of them, all clustering thickly together like bees in a swarm. Their packed density made up the deceptive appearance of a solid impenetrable flame. It was in fact, a vast spiral nebula of innumerable suns.
THE TIME STREAM JOHN TAINE (ERIC TEMPLE BELL)
quote for stills
CLOSE-UPS (STILLS) INTERCUT WITH ONE MOVING SHOTS OF WATER LAPPING ON ROCKS
LAST SHOT — WITH PHOTO AND EDITING TABLE
Street Sounds
9 The (crystal) step will actually wind it itself into a spiral during growth at the steady state the spiral will appear to rotate. The right- and left-handed dislocations give rise to clockwise and anti clockwise spirals. Polymorphism and Polytypism in Crystals — Ajit Verma and P. Krishna

CAT. 117

ROBERT SMITHSON, *MOVIE TREATMENT 3, SPIRAL JETTY*, 1970

CAT. 118

ROBERT SMITHSON, *THE EARTH'S HISTORY*, 1970

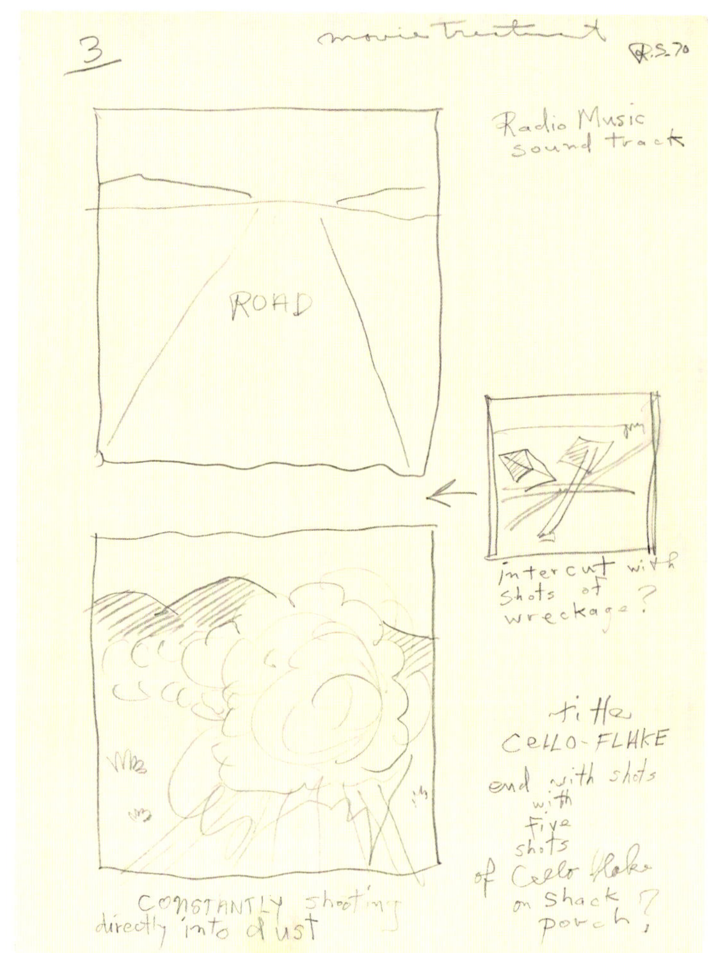

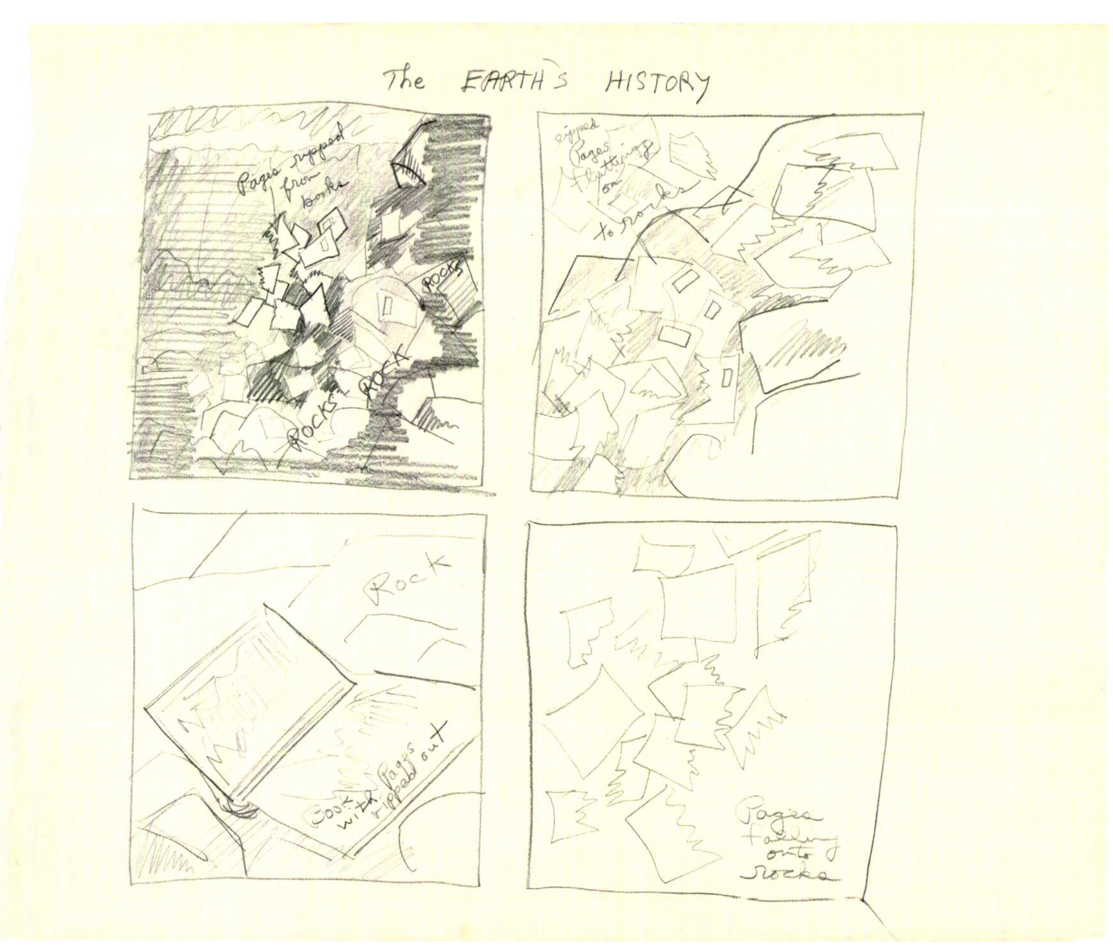

CAT. 119

ROBERT SMITHSON,
MOVIE TREATMENT 8,
SPIRAL JETTY,
1970

CAT. 120

ROBERT SMITHSON,
MOVIE TREATMENT 9,
SPIRAL JETTY,
1970

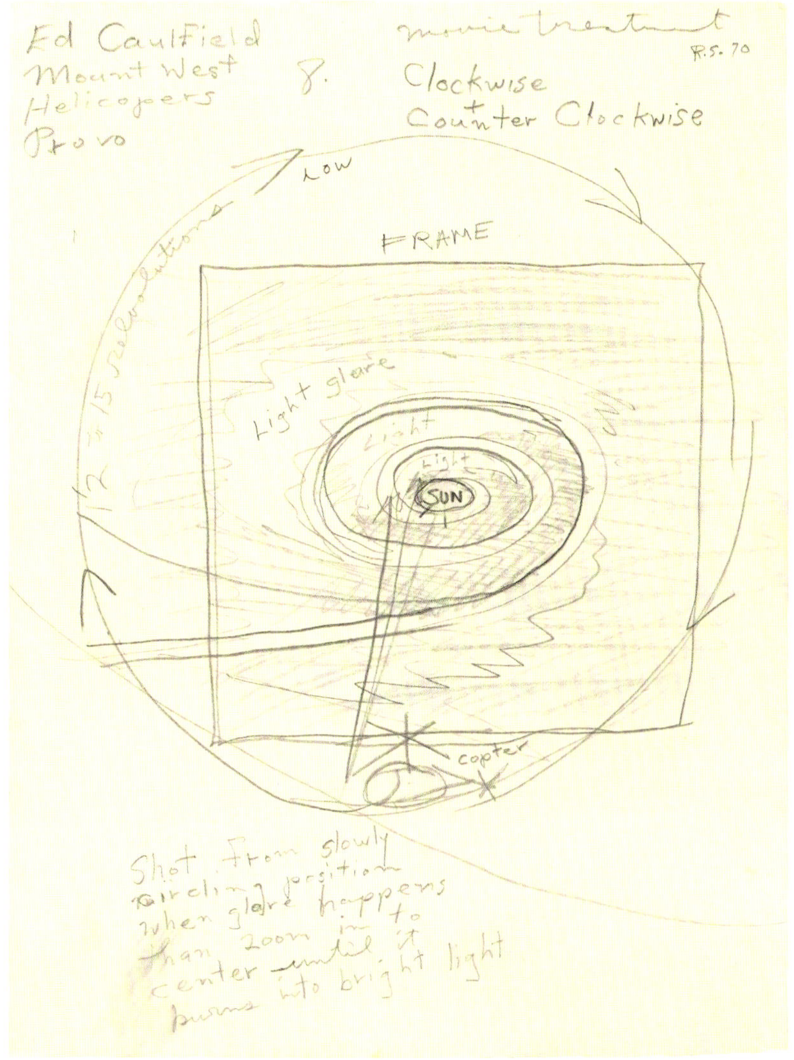

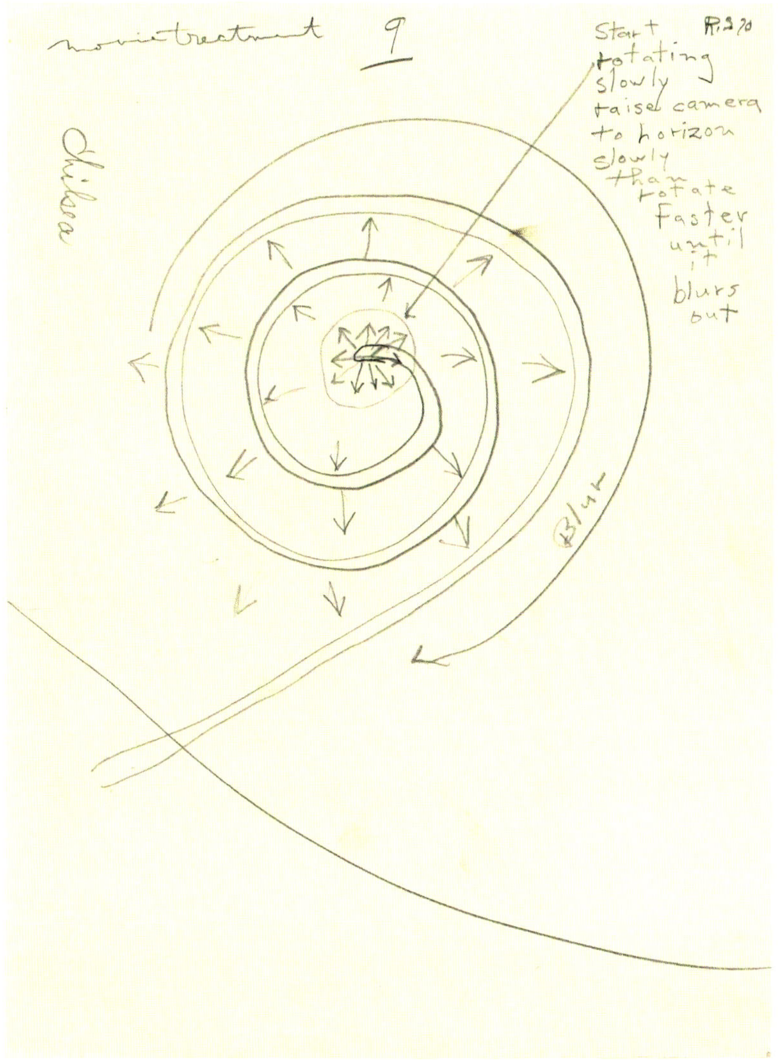

CAT. 121

ROBERT SMITHSON, *CLOCKWISE & COUNTERCLOCKWISE REVOLUTION SHOT FROM COPTER*, 1970

CAT. 122

ROBERT SMITHSON, *THE SPIRAL JETTY, GREAT SALT LAKE, UTAH*, 1970

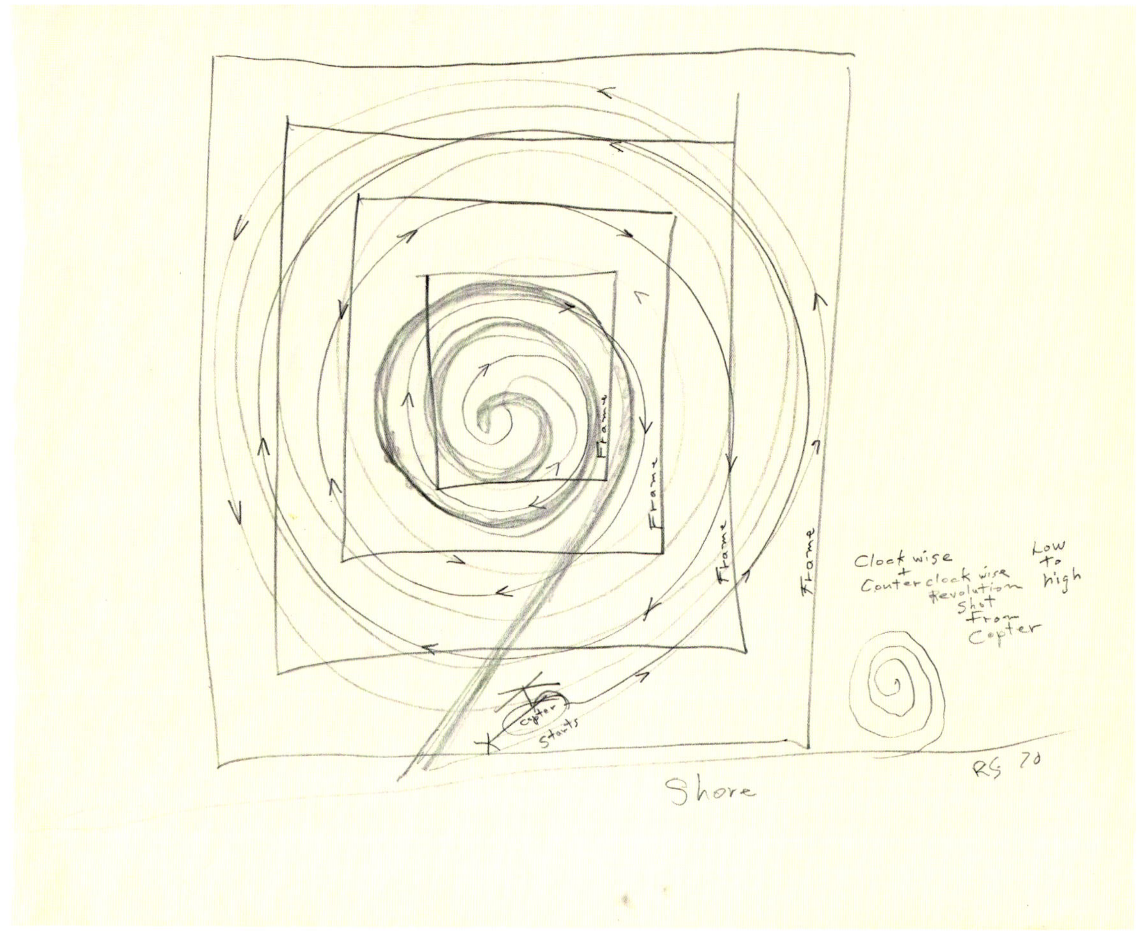

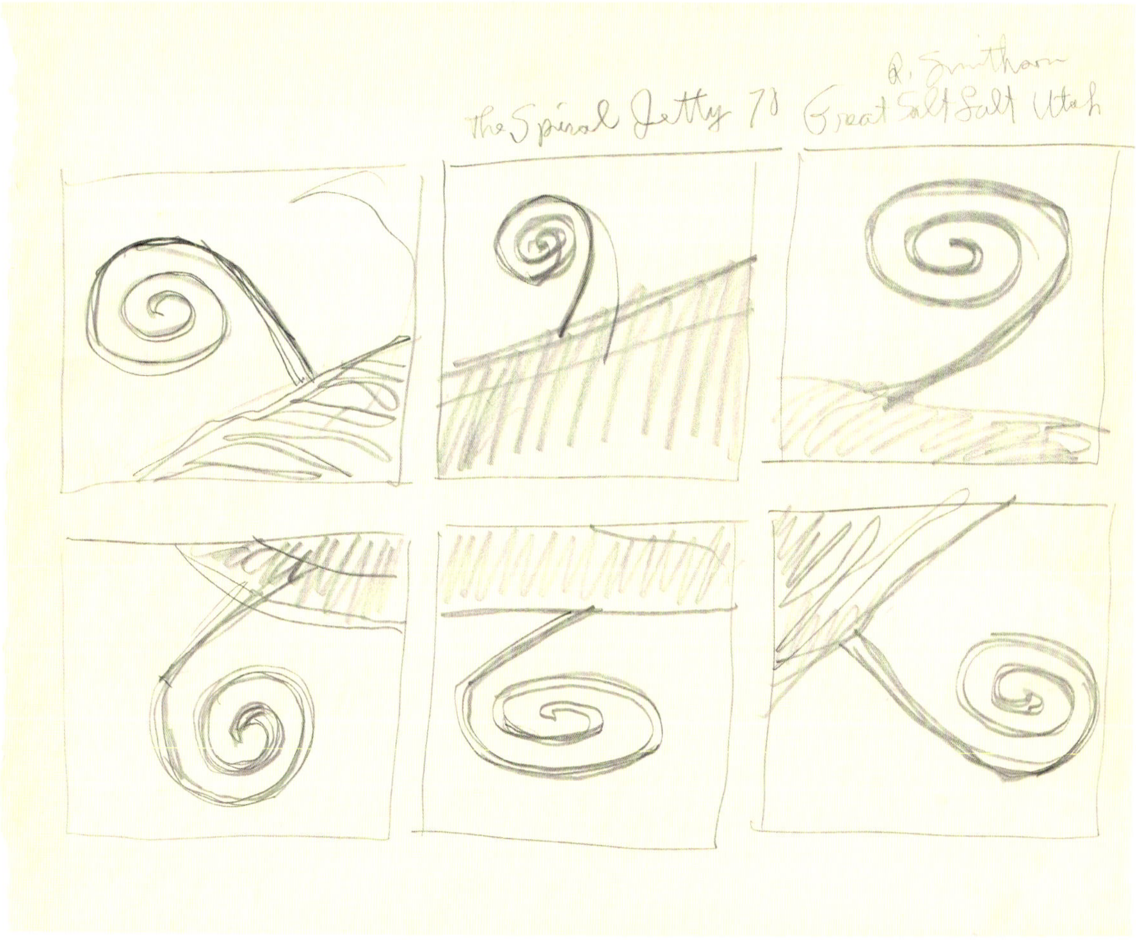

CAT. 123

ROBERT SMITHSON,
THE SPIRAL JETTY,
GREAT SALT LAKE,
UTAH, 1970

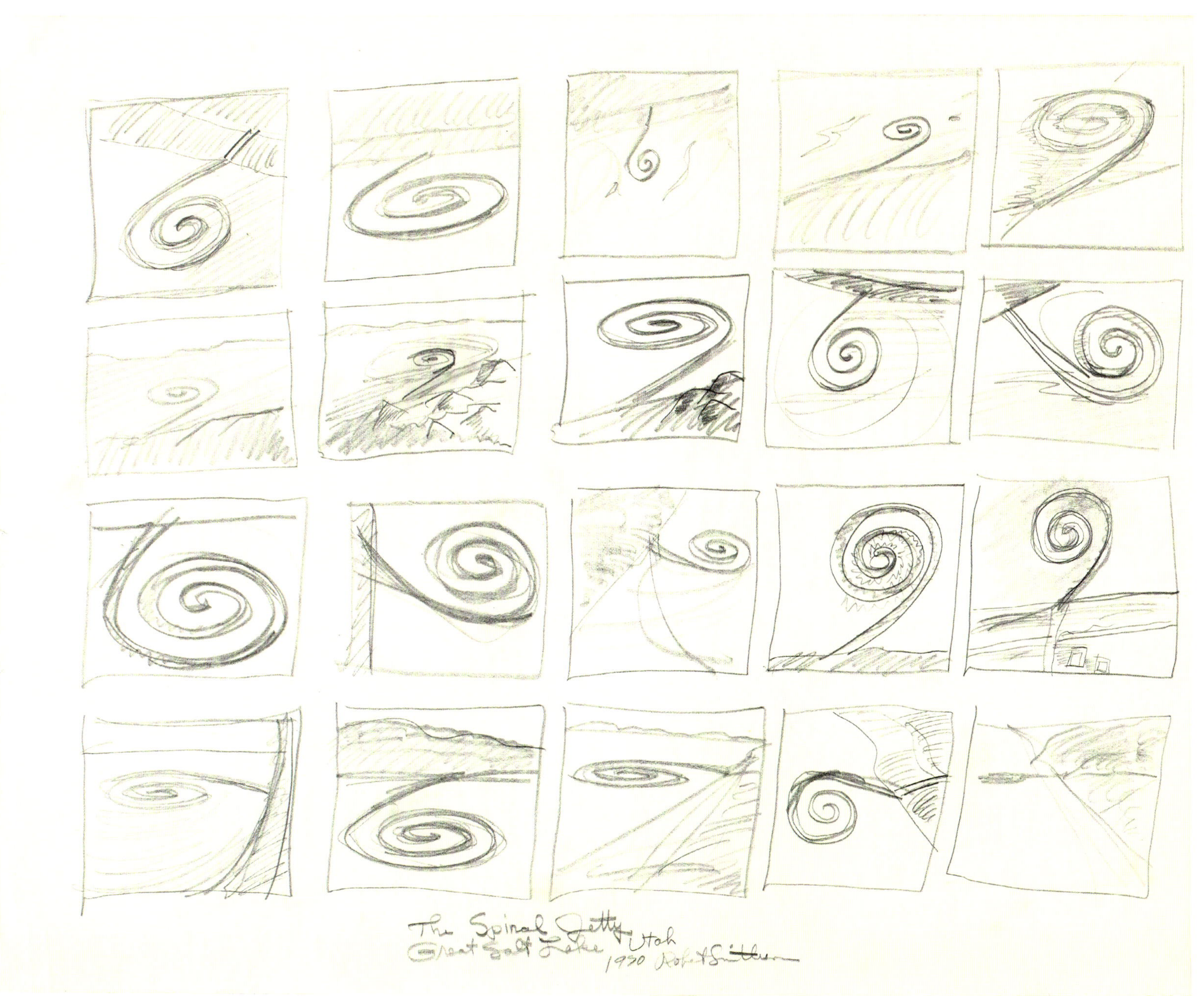

CAT. 124

ROBERT SMITHSON, FILM STILLS FROM *SPIRAL JETTY*, 1970

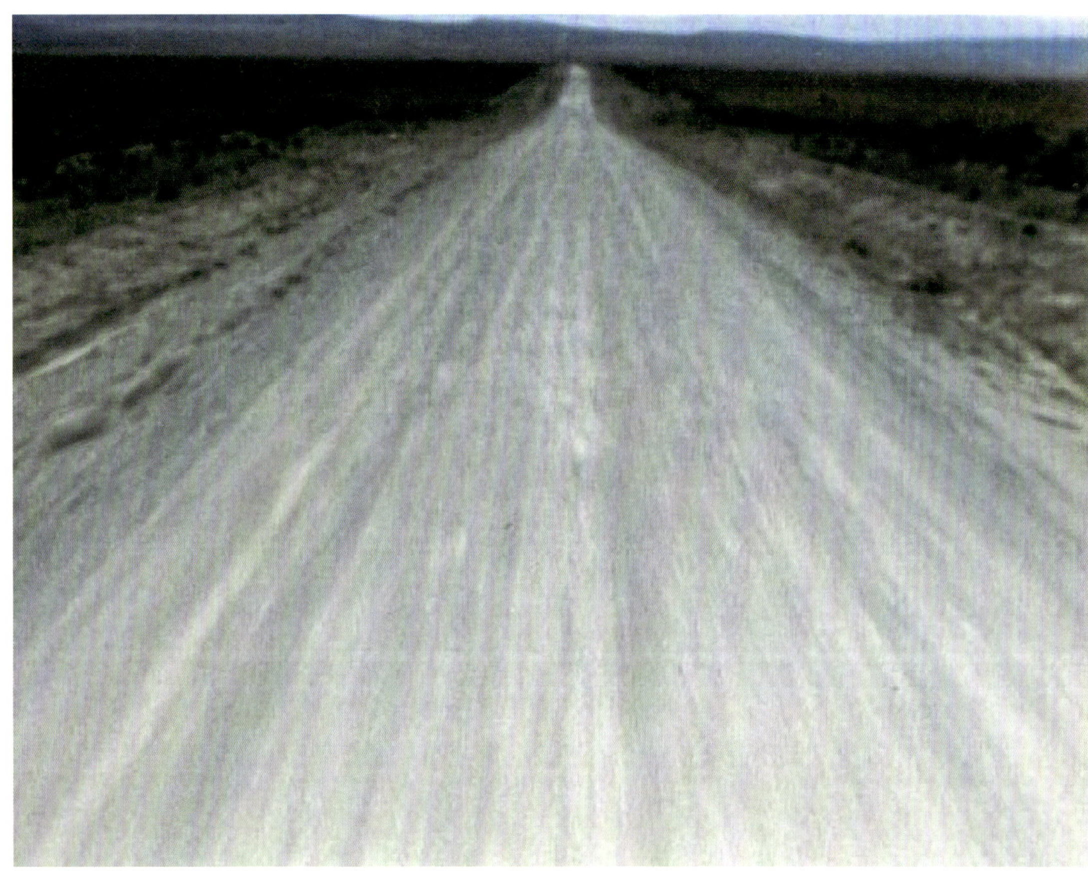

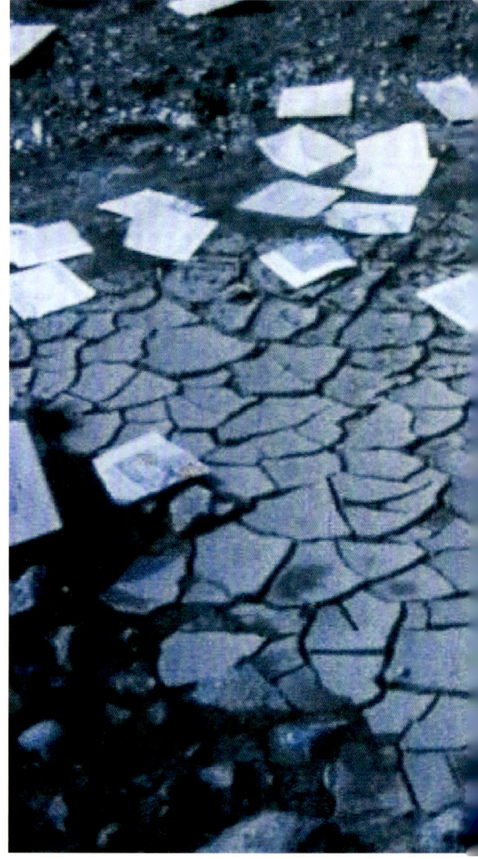

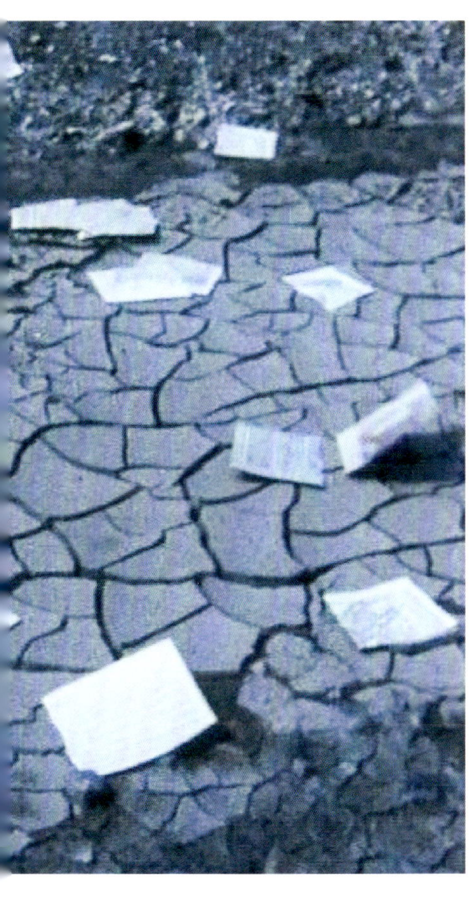

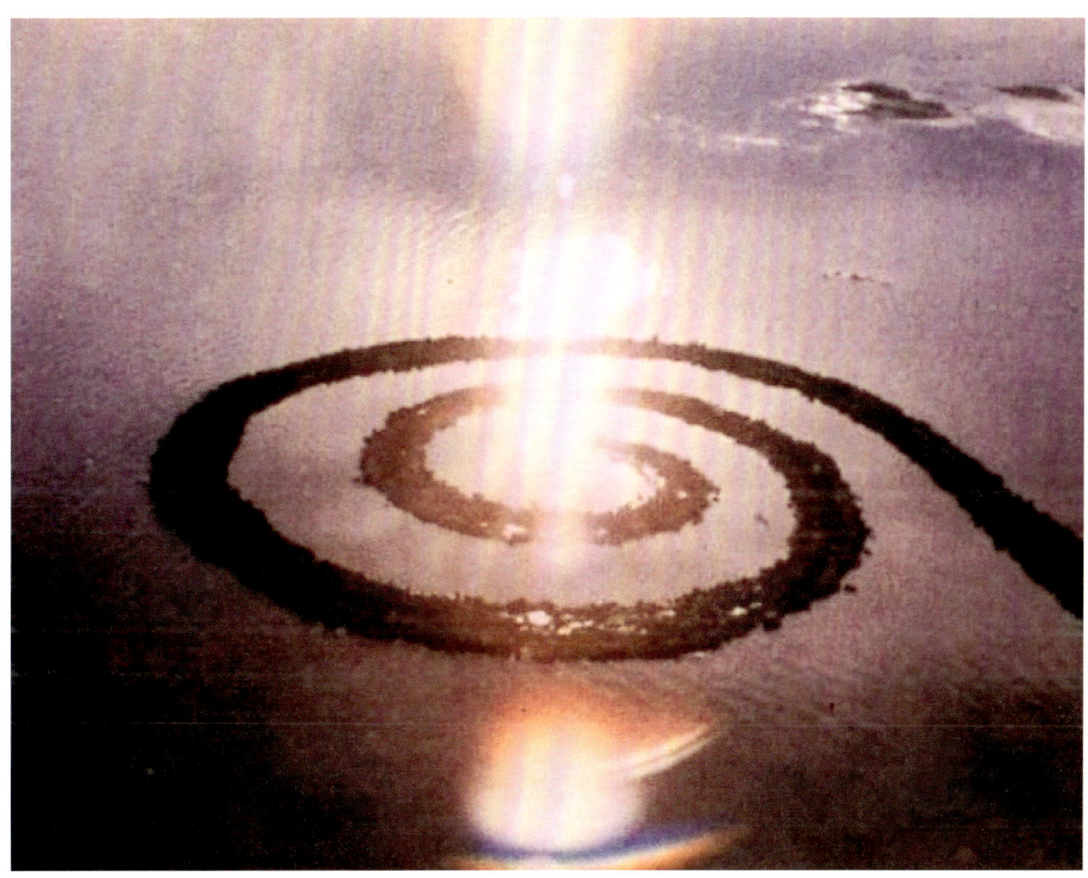

CAT. 125

ROBERT RYMAN, *UNTITLED, SURFACE VEIL 26″ × 26″*, 1970

CAT. 126

ROBERT RYMAN, *SURFACE VEIL #3*, 1970

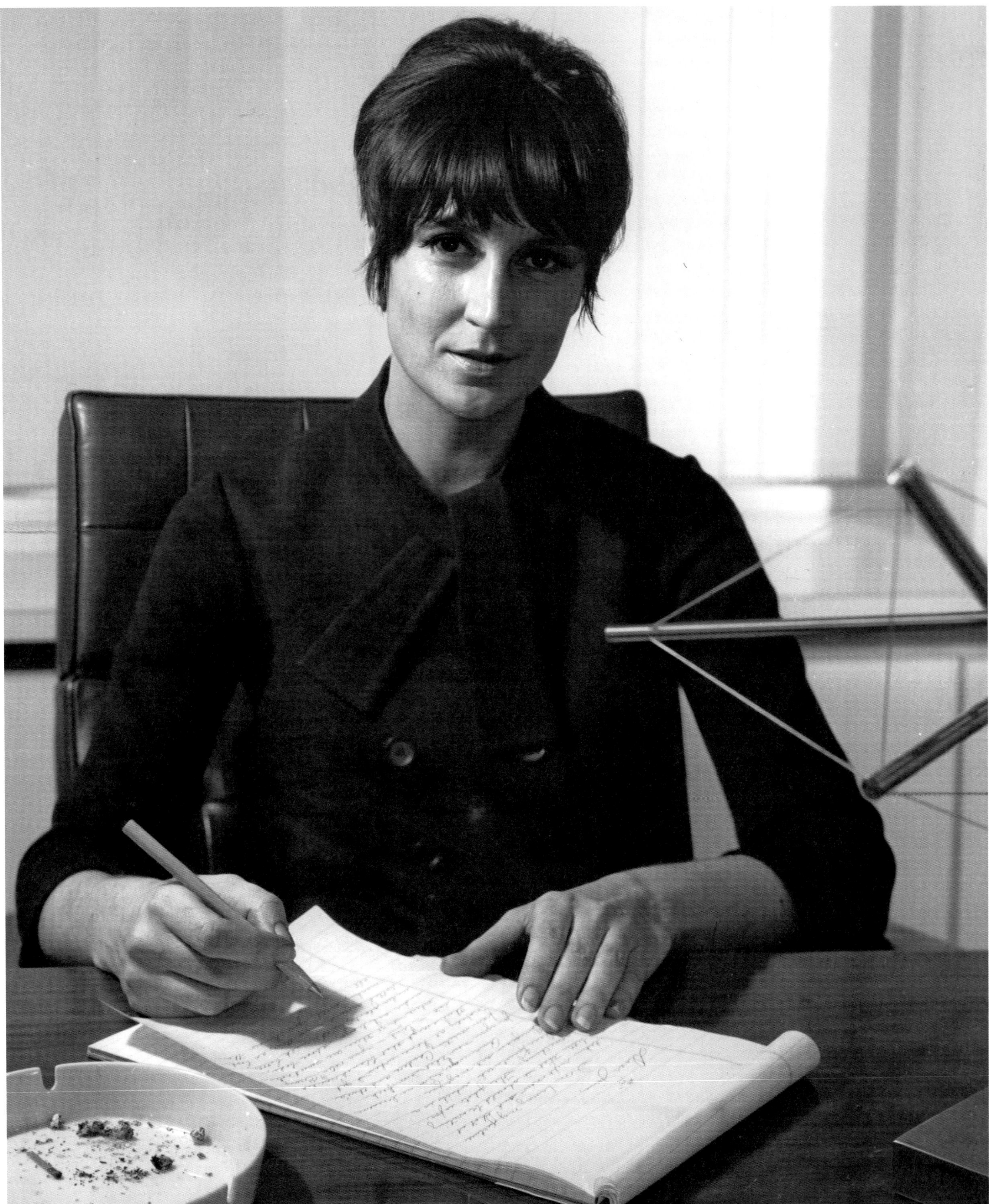

VIRGINIA DWAN **WRITINGS**

1. ILS SONT TOUS VENUS

Adapted from "Ils sont tous venus," Galerie Montaigne, October 17, 1990, and "California Impressions of Yves Klein," in *Yves Klein: 3 mars–23 mai 1983*, Paris: Centre Georges Pompidou, Musée national d'art moderne, 275

2. SELLING SILENCE

Presented at the symposium "Structures and Systems: Minimal Art in the United States," Getty Research Institute, Getty Center, Los Angeles, May 2004

3. EARTHWORKS

Unpublished writing, 2004

4. REFLECTIONS ON ROBERT SMITHSON

"Earthworks: Past and Present," *Art Journal* 42, no. 3, Autumn 1982, 233

5. "DOUBLE NEGATIVE": A RECOLLECTION

Michael Heizer, Julia Brown, Barbara Heizer, *Sculpture in Reverse*, Museum of Contemporary Art, Los Angeles, 1984

YVES KLEIN PAINTING
ON THE BEACH
AT MALIBU, 1961

1. *Ils sont tous venus*

They all came.

They brought with them their gifts of alchemy, transformation, sometimes mischief, and laughter.

Yves Klein was the first. He and his fiancée, Rotraut Uecker, came to Malibu in California to prepare a show for Dwan Gallery that would encompass his many directions up to that date. The year was 1961. There, near the water's edge, he created several small monochromes and blue and gold sponge reliefs.

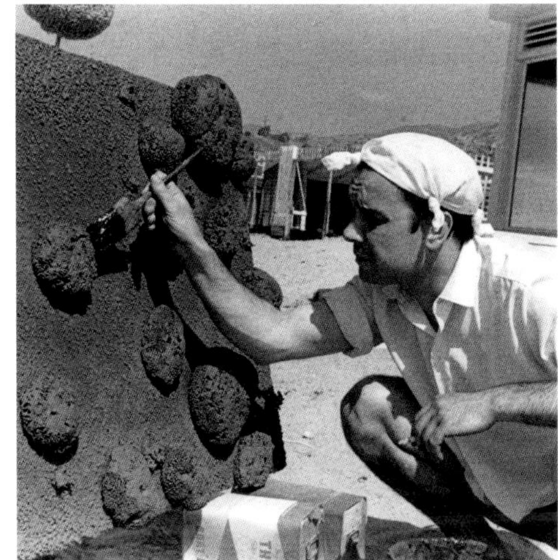

Earlier, in the fall of 1960, I had happened to pass by the window of Galerie Rive Droite on Faubourg Saint-Honoré. What I saw there was a large blue sponge relief, a relief of such an intensity of blue and of energy that I was immediately pulled into it. Any ideas of art history or significance were forgotten. This work spoke to a part of me that had not yet been reached. There was in it a mystery of something beyond boundaries. What sort of person would I discover behind these mute landscapes, these fathomless blues?

Klein had an intensity of appearance consistent with his images. His eyes—mostly it was his eyes—burned, stared, fixed, and then became curiously removed. Deep dark sockets supported them in their transports. The effect was of a visionary or a madman.

Conversations with him were wild and rambling and seemed fired by an urgency to express in any way possible his own special view of the work and of the future. Excitement was a constant. The specifics of these conversations have been lost to me with time, but what remains is a sense of someone burning forth from within.

Klein's response to California and the sea and the sky was quite enthusiastic; he wanted to bring the whole École de Nice there to work and live. Certainly Santa Monica Bay/Malibu did resemble the Bay of Nice, but beyond that, it seemed to unfold and stretch in an environment in which history and ideas can be moved around like so many strips of film. His intent, especially in the monochromes, seemed to be to express the essential rather than the formal. I believe that Ad Reinhardt's concern, although also involving the viewer in profound concentration, was of a far more formal nature as witness his usual title, *Ultimate Painting* [cat. 60]. Rauschenberg had said that it was his own frustration over color that led him [Rauschenberg] to investigate it in all its simplicity. Klein's colors, on the other hand, were like immediate imprints of his own essence without interference of ideas of art.

The California art community was mixed in its response to Klein and his work. Some collectors reciprocated his enthusiasm. Others responded with humor or outrage or bewilderment. Confronted with his dedication, some felt ill at ease. Here was a person who held his nose and really jumped, and who kept on jumping even though there was no one with him.

My own response to the show in my gallery was also curious. Stunning blue forms inhabited my whole space. There were flat blue monochromes, blue reliefs, a blue obelisk, blue sponge sculptures, blue "rain," blue imprints of bodies, and a pool of dry blue pigment. All of this was punctuated by an occasional red or gold piece. This blue, so gorgeous even to Southern California eyes, seemed to invade me. This was not work that I could absorb. I was the one absorbed.

Now, as I look back on my career in art, I see that what impressed me and continues to influence me most in an artist is a quality of integrity, a oneness of vision and purpose. A sort of obsession directs the action. There is a commitment of the very being of the individual. Klein's now famous photograph of the leap into the void epitomizes this.[1] The artist whose very colors were inspired by the flame was himself on fire with his vision. He was a kind of comet whose path can be traced by the empty space it has left behind.

I maintained contact with Yves and Rotraut after the exposition. We had become good friends.

It was Yves who introduced me to Arman (Armand Pierre Arman) and to Martial Raysse. It has always been the artists who have shown me the way and introduced me to new artists, new visions, new challenges. They taught me and guided me.

Arman came to Los Angeles to work and to install his show. Some of his wonderful earlier smaller works were shipped from Nice to Los Angeles. Others he built in the basement of the gallery itself. There were great crashing and splintering noises as he devastated the original forms with karate kicks and chops to emerge with lyrical 3-D cubist images of a bass violin, a viola, and a console radio as well as "accumulations" of *béquilles* (crutches) and of typewriters. These were some of his most imposing works of that period.

Martial Raysse came to Los Angeles in 1962 after completing his military obligation. Earlier, when I visited his Nice studio, it was crowded by works made of plastic utility objects and boxes of kitchen cleaning products. At the corner of his street was a Prisunic supermarket, and that was his Elysian Field. In his hands, plastic bottles and bottle brushes waved delicately from fronds of flexible tubing like nodding ferns and palms.

The work changed appreciably after his return from the army. In Los Angeles he unlocked a cyclone of energy and imagination, and his work expanded to express even more light. The images were painted in neon colors. There were mannequins with plastic accessories and famous ancient ladies from familiar paintings reintroduced into the contemporary scene: Manet and Cranach astonishingly rendered in fluorescence and plastic. Two large neon sculptures stood glowing in the middle of the gallery. I was able to accompany Raysse to order his photographic blowups and neon. The neon colors were to be chosen by the neon fabricator himself. Martial was looking for clichéd colors.

The gallery was quite large for the time and the artists responded with large works. Jean Tinguely produced his epic work *Attila* for the main wall and later Niki de Saint Phalle created her *King Kong* for the same space.

Ed Kienholz and John Weber, my director, were helpful and supportive in enabling the artists to find their materials and workspaces, and Weber helped in arranging some museum shows. Kienholz, who would later join the roster of Dwan artists and present the initial grand opening show of the New York branch in 1965, was generous to them all with his time and consideration and took Arman to junkyards. Arman was excited by the vastness of them.

Kienholz also took Jean Tinguely and me to buy motors for his works. Jean found them and I okayed them even though they were too large and powerful for the proposed pieces. He explained that he knew this but that he loved them. We arranged a "progressive dinner" for the fountains that Jean created out of garden hoses and sprinkling devices. Four collectors opened their gardens and homes to exhibit these works. At each home, one was given an ideal presentation of the fountains in operation as well as a single course of the dinner, which was then followed by the next course at the next home. In between, the guests were transported in special buses and served champagne. Perhaps that was the first time that the gallery was to extend its viewing space beyond its walls. There would be earth art later.

Jean's sculptures were so powerful that many had to be bolted to a surface to prevent their moving away by the force of the motors. The gallery was near the university, and every day art students would come by to unleash (*dechainer*) the Tinguely's.

As Jean worked amid sparks and scrap metal in an old factory space, Niki de Saint Phalle joined him to work at the other end among wiggling spiders, skeletons, snakes, and plastic fruit. She and I had filled two shopping

NIKI DE SAINT PHALLE PERFORMING A *TIR* IN THE HILLS ABOVE MALIBU, SPRING, 1962

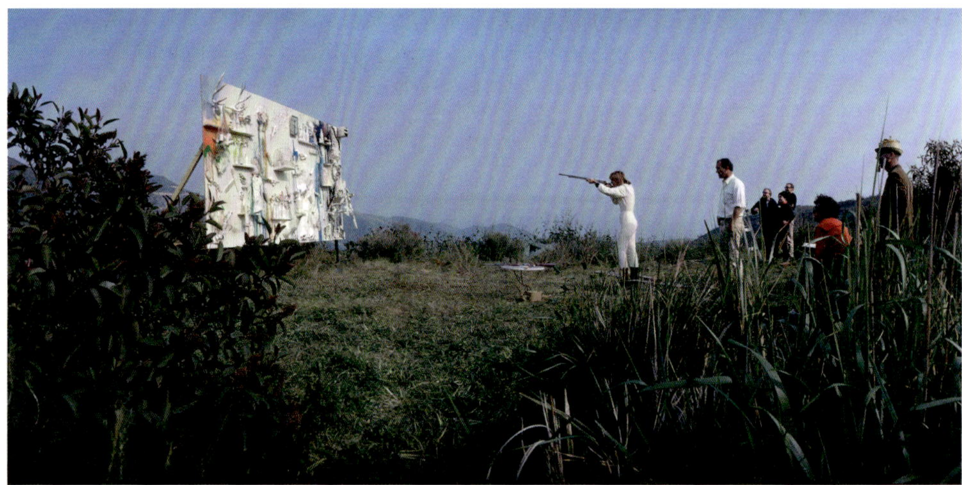

carts with these objects at a wholesale novelty market. At her end of the factory everything was covered with a coat of white plaster. At the other end, Jean painted all in black, perhaps for the first time. Along with the intense work that went on there, there was also a sort of fiendish mirth.

Niki de Saint Phalle created an extraordinary exposition of eight shot pieces [called *tirs*]. She had already done a major wall, which she shot in the hills above Malibu. That work was later installed on the end wall surrounding my swimming pool. Chained to it was a small cannon by Tinguely that he once gleefully fired into the sea.

During the years from 1961 to 1965 pop art was the dominant movement in America. Paralleling it but informed by a significantly different background and sensibility was the nouveau réalisme movement in Europe. At that time the Dwan Gallery also played host to such American pop artists as James Rosenquist and Claes Oldenburg and to artists of a very different view, such as Franz Kline and Ad Reinhardt.

I did not approach this art as a movement. Rather, I was engrossed by each person's unique vision. It was their individual genius that involved me. For me it was a grand adventure to take part in the realization and presentation of their works.

2. *Selling Silence*

Hello, everyone. It's interesting to be back in this area and to see a few familiar faces out there. In the years of the Los Angeles Dwan Gallery, from 1959 to 1967, I was living right down the mountain from here in Malibu.

I must start with the usual disclaimer that "minimal art" is really, at best, a term of convenience: that each of these artists differs in intent and in look from the others; that terms like "abstract expressionism" and "minimalism" are coined by critics and historians in order to be able to use words and to write. That said, I too will use the term "minimalism" here from time to time.

I like best the comment of Sol LeWitt that he included in his "Paragraphs on Conceptual Art":

> Recently there has been much written about minimal art but I have not discovered anyone who admits to doing this kind of thing. There are other art forms around called primary structures, reductive, rejective, cool, and mini-art. No artist I know will own up to any of these either. Therefore I conclude that it is part of a secret language that art critics use when communicating with each other through the medium of art magazines. Mini-art is best because it reminds one of miniskirts and long-legged girls. It must refer to very small works of art. This is a very good idea. Perhaps "mini-art" shows could be sent around the country in matchboxes.[1]

The following are some of the descriptions I have found for art of this period in books and magazines: bleak, numb, severe, hollow, morbid, useless, coffins, oppressive formalism, deadly, programmatic, closed system, didactic, deductive, anti-compositional, not-enough-art, not-enough-work, theatrical, ordinary, bland, neutral, redundant, austere, literalist, authoritarian, blankness, non-emotional, anti-emotional, static, frozen, deathly, industrial, hermetic, inscrutable, depersonalized, unmodified, middlebrow, novelty, capitalistic, reductive, endgame, comatose

So what could have possessed me to devote myself to such works?

A mini-history of the Dwan Gallery reveals some interesting concordances. In May 1961, I mounted a survey of the work to that date of Yves Klein, [who] nicknamed [himself] "the Monochrome." I had negotiated for the show with his Paris dealer after seeing some stunning, seemingly ahistorical works there, but I was not entirely prepared for the infiltration of his blue into my eyes, brain, and (it felt like) my very insides. At the same time that they elicited a void and the colors of the flames he used to meditate on during his days in Japan, they

INSTALLATION VIEW OF *ANASTASI: SIX SITES*, DWAN GALLERY NEW YORK, 1967, WITH WILLIAM ANASTASI NEXT TO *EAST WALL*

were very much an insistent, material presence. I felt that the gallery and I were being absorbed in an infinity of blue. This sensation of encompassing color was to be echoed later in the exhibitions of Dan Flavin.

In February of 1962, I had a show of Ad Reinhardt that was of particular influence on me. He had distilled his decisions about the essentials in his writing "Rules for a New Academy" and in his demanding dark paintings. When planning a new gallery space in Westwood Village, I used the nine-foot measurement of his black paintings as a module for the architecture. When I asked Ad for another show in 1963, he asked why I wanted to do that since there had been no sales at the previous one. He finally agreed but sent only the paintings in his *Ultimate Painting* format of five-feet square. Just before the show opened, John F. Kennedy was shot, so we decided to skip the usual opening event and just open the doors. Several people came in and commented on what they interpreted as our "sensitivity" in draping black over the art. That was not to be the last time that the art was invisible to the visitors. All the shows of Carl Andre, LeWitt's "wall drawings," and Anastasi's "wall on the wall" [canvases] elicited baffled responses and inquiries as to when the show would be put up.

It was Reinhardt who made me aware of Agnes Martin's serene and cryptic paintings. To relate to hers and Ad's paintings, sustained attention and openness are called for. For lack of a better term I will call this "silence."

I like Mel Bochner's statement: "Art would go beyond being the record of someone else's perception to becoming the recognition of one's own." And Patrick Ireland, playing on Stella's statement "What you see is what you see," added "What was there was there, including you."

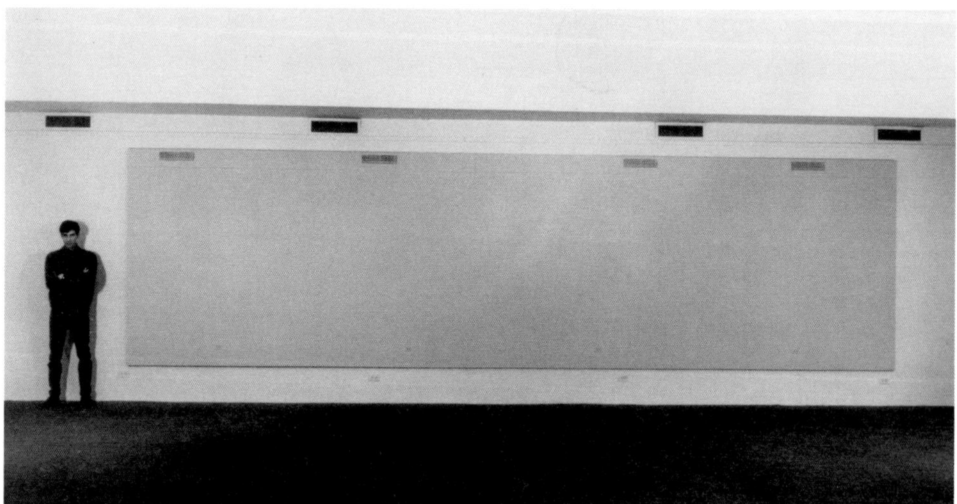

Through my two Los Angeles shows of Robert Rauschenberg's work I came to know John Cage, who was with Bob and the Merce Cunningham dance troupe, and I was eager to incorporate his ideas of chance operations into my awareness of art procedures. John accepted and was fascinated by the unpredictable interpretations of his cryptic notations by the various musicians who performed them. His acceptance appeared boundless. Just how much idiosyncratic interpretation is acceptable was an often-discussed issue in the later works of such artists as Donald Judd and Sol LeWitt, who entrusted the fabrication of their art to metal workers and draftsmen.

The first artist's work I showed that was later to be termed "minimal" was that of Robert Morris in March of 1966. Unlike the very impersonal, industrialized look of Donald Judd's "specific objects," Morris's massive presences embodied a scale that was relational to the human body, a reflection, perhaps, of his years as a dancer. Underscoring the unified presences of his works, he referred to them as "Gestalts."

In 1965 I opened the New York branch of the gallery. Having previously been able to take shows on consignment from dealers in New York and Europe, I was now obliged to find younger, unattached artists to represent in exclusivity. Meanwhile John Weber continued the gallery operations in Los Angeles for two years while I was forming connections on the East Coast with Sol LeWitt, Carl Andre, William Anastasi, Kenneth Snelson, and Robert Smithson. Actually, I opened the New York space with Ed Kienholz's Barney's Beanery, so a purist stance was not necessarily what I was looking for. Nevertheless, through the years, other artists who shared what I think of as a "quiet" look came to join the gallery. So Dan Flavin, Fred Sandback, Charles Ross, and Robert Ryman all presented shows, and the gallery came to have a "look."

In October 1966, with the help of Ad Reinhardt, Robert Smithson, and Robert Morris, I put together a show of new work by ten artists, titling the show simply *10*. These works seemed to share a look or attitude that I would, again, call "quiet" as well as appearing cool, self-contained, and highly resolved.

Outside the atmosphere was charged and chaotic. It was the time of the Vietnam War, race riots, demonstrations for women's rights, marches for gay rights, student uprisings and the shooting of students at Kent State, marches on Selma and on Washington, and the assassinations of three American leaders.

There was a sense of values in upheaval and of disillusionment. The standards and actions of the very government were in question. But in this bewildering whirl there were some still, silent points appearing in art. And it was into this maelstrom that Sol LeWitt appeared with his methodology, his assuring logic, his aura of tranquility and humility. His first exhibition at Dwan New York consisted of all-white, symmetrical, grid-based structures, precise and unemotional.

I've noticed that in stressful, noisy times many people will react by increasing activity and increasing decibels of sound. The minimal artists opposed dramatic gestures, unnecessary movement, the asymmetry of European composition, the anecdotal, and the expressionistic. The *10* show included the following artists: Carl Andre, Jo Baer, Dan Flavin, Donald Judd, Sol LeWitt, Agnes Martin, Robert Morris, Ad Reinhardt, Robert Smithson, and Michael Steiner (the last went off into a Greenbergian mode shortly after this showing). That show remains for me one of the most satisfying of my career. After New York, a similar group of works, again titled *10,* was sent out to the Los Angeles gallery with its more expansive space. The title was settled on when it was found that not one of the artists could agree with any other on a descriptive title. Robert Smithson's intended manifesto for the show was rejected as not representative of anyone other than Smithson but was later published in Gregory Battcock's 1968 book *Minimal Art: A Critical Anthology.*

LeWitt produced five exhibitions at Dwan. The skeletal structures led to serial works and then to wall drawings, which embodied variations on a theme as mathematical combinations. Although symmetrical in concept, their multiplication was confounding, like the process of memorizing a poem in which one must go back and start again when one's place is lost. The overall effect was simply one of beauty.

For me LeWitt's wall drawings recall Tibetan sand mandalas insofar as they involve circumscribed, procedural, repeatable, defined elements that, when erased, return to the invisible realm of the conceptual. The Tibetans, after long days of finely detailed, minute development, brush up all their many colors into a brown-red-blue-yellow sparkling heap of sand and throw it into the nearest body of water, but the exact concept remains to be repeated later.

It was Sol LeWitt who introduced me to Carl Andre and Robert Smithson. Carl's work shared a reliance on method, which he based on the periodic table of elements. He systematically, when possible, utilized these elements as the standardized units in his floor squares—typically setting them up, unattached, in squared configurations. The sensing of these works was one of gravity. If LeWitt had stripped his structures to the bone, Andre had melted them to the ground, where only their material essence remained, thereby establishing a minimally differentiated plane that, like Brancusi's *Endless Column*, implied infinite extension in space. Smithson treated space—in other words, the gallery volume—somewhat indifferently at first. His special regressions, although playing on one-point perspective, did not use the space as an integral part of the work. His elegant painted, steel works stood like icebergs or carbon crystals on the gallery floor, remaining essentially inviolable and oblivious to their surroundings. His engagement of ambient space came with his indoor/outdoor "nonsites" in which he brought inside the rough elements of the exterior and contained them in specially designed metal bins that echoed [the shape of] his original site.

There followed exhibitions of other artists who seemed to me to share certain qualities. I'd like to list what moved me in the direction of these works:

POSITIVES: sublime / platonic / rational / formal / conceptual / symmetrical / closed systems / self-contained energy / concentrated energy / essence / wholeness / quiet

Flavin: A veil, a wash, a halo. Flavin stayed within the idea of the mute object with what he called his "light sticks," but his halations of colored light diffused throughout their containing space and engulfed the gallery space. The intangible is the essence of the work. The fluorescent vehicle seems incidental and, in some cases, actually seems to disappear as in his red work, *untitled (to Barnett Newman)*.

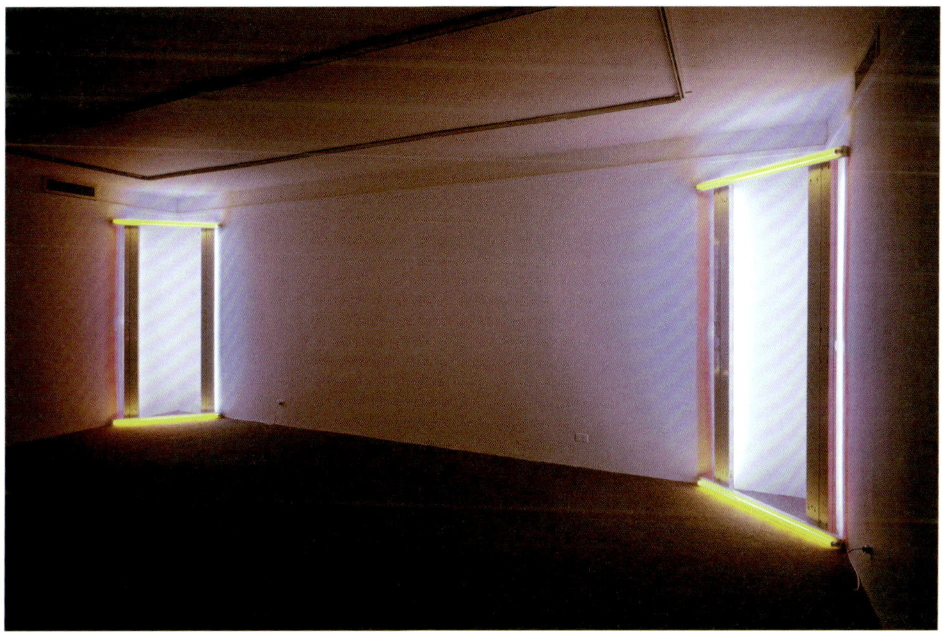

INSTALLATION VIEW, *DAN FLAVIN: UNTITLEDS (TO BARNETT NEWMAN)*, DWAN GALLERY NEW YORK, 1971

Sandback's works needed attention on the viewer's part just to know they were there. Although their delicate lines drawn in space with colored yarn and fine wire were first introduced to me by Donald Judd, unlike the older artist, Sandback eschewed the weight of a "specific object" in favor of a barely there, intuited volume. Four lines fixed in a taut wedge imply a completed volume with seven sides. The viewer participates by mentally completing the imagined object. I personally found his volumes inviolable despite almost nonexistent materiality. I discovered that I was careful not to step or reach beyond their boundaries. Magically, Sandback has achieved immaterial volumes and with that the ultimate reductive sculpture.

Vying for invisibility are the all-white investigations into the nature of painting by Robert Ryman. Ryman asks the question, "What are the essential elements of painting?" With this in mind he has explored an amazing number of variations of white pigment on wall-hung supports of papers, canvases, and sheets of metal. Some of the effects are of flat, nonreflective, dry-looking pigment, while others have the look of porcelain glazes that recall the surfaces of early Chinese earthenware.

Charles Ross goes directly to the source of color in his prism works. Rather than pigment or even colored lights, his colors are directly generated by the sun or energized by another light source so that almost palpable strips of intense, pure hue play across the interior space of his volumes as the earth rotates around its energy source. But not all his fluid-filled plexiforms are intended to generate a spectrum. Instead they demonstrate irrationality of vision with their optical dislocations while remaining very much art.

Robert Smithson was one of the key figures in the *10* show. But should I call him a minimalist? Certainly he used mathematical progressions in his white-and-black crystalline works, but his built-in perspectives in the *Alogon*s and *Plunge* involved diminutions that implied a dynamic or thrust. Their movement, not one of successive visual snapshots, as in LeWitt, was seen as perspectival distance, exaggerated and made explicit. Some of these pieces were more static, like anchored icebergs, but Smithson was not wedded to the gestalt or the "specific object"; his early work pointed away from the containment of interior space.

And what of William Anastasi? While in his exhibition *Six Sites*, he straddles the boundary between minimal and conceptual art, I believe that the deadpan "What you see may not be what you see" aspect of this suite of works deserves its space as a minimal, or perhaps "post-minimal," statement.

I have tried to trace my personal path with these works. I hope that the value I came to place on them is clear. Now, what of the sales, and the collectors' responses? The experience of mounting shows, designing advertising, talking in long, rambling conversations with the artists, living for a month or more with the work—all that was wonderful. It was the business of art that didn't suit me. I was an untalented salesperson—thank goodness that John Weber, who enjoyed selling, came to join me after the first four years, and it was fortunate that my personal finances allowed me to go ahead and show what I believed in without too much consideration of quick sales. And yet the business of art is valid and essential. People appreciate what they pay for.

Contrary to rumor, I can't recall a single work shown at the Dwan Gallery that was not for sale. I believe in selling. Art given does not seem to elicit the same attention and conservation as that which is bought. For example, I know of two major earthworks that were donated to museums only to be neglected and allowed to deteriorate. If a million or so had been paid for them, I believe that that would have produced an anxiety to preserve them.

Being avant-market was an issue. There seems to be a time-lapse—a requisite gestation period—between the initial viewing of new work and the commitment to buy. Selling certain works was, of course, difficult. Carl Andre's *Cuts*, measuring thirty by forty-two feet of concrete capstones, was labor intensive and challenged most private collecting, but my impression was that the reticence to buy was about something else. I see it more as a desire on the viewer's part for a replay of the emotionally explosive and distracting works, so familiar in the 1950s and again in the 1980s, or for the warm and fuzzy-familiar images that we saw in the pop art period and again in the erotic cartooning of the nineties. By contrast, minimalism was offering an approach to art, which while using contemporary materials, technology, and reductive concepts in its mute, formal, symmetrical manifestations, ironically brought us back to the age-old, ever-to-be-unresolved issues of truth and beauty.

In closing, I would like to say that I hope that the current emphasis equating art and money will pass.

CARL ANDRE ON "SITE-SEARCH" TRIP TO NEW JERSEY, APRIL 1967

ROBERT SMITHSON, NANCY HOLT, AND CARL ANDRE ON "SITE-SEARCH" TRIP TO NEW JERSEY, APRIL 1967

3. *Earthworks*

Bob Smithson came into my back office, and with an inward-turning smile and a sigh, crumpled himself into the chair facing me.

"I'm working on a new project. It'll be out on the land in Texas." His black hair half hid the smile in his eyes. He stretched his legs like two black rails in front of him and studied the toes of his boots as he went on to describe the project to create works of art on the landing field of the forthcoming regional airport at Dallas–Fort Worth. He had asked Carl Andre and Bob Morris to join him. Sol LeWitt was interested in participating. Each would contribute his own unique concept, he said, and develop it with certain autonomy. Only the placement would have to be agreed upon between them and the engineering firm (Tippetts-Abbett-McCarthy-Stratton) that hoped to get the contract for the overall job. It was they who had engaged Bob as "artist consultant."

As I recall, Morris's work was to be an earth mound ring, and Carl had played with ideas of either a field of flowers (in a rectilinearly defined space, of course) or a crater formed by a small bomb or explosive. Sol's contribution would be a stainless-steel cube to be buried in the ground. Obviously this latter would subvert the idea of art to be viewed from the air. Sol had already established himself as a quintessential conceptualist.

While the award of the engineer's contract was still pending (in the end, the engineers did not win the contract, and the whole project veered off in another direction), Smithson suggested junkets to discover accessible land for similar works. New Jersey was the nearest and, for him, the most familiar territory.

And so, early one morning in 1967, Bob Smithson, Nancy Holt, and I drove downtown in the cool, low-slung sun to get Carl Andre and then headed out into the wilds of New Jersey. The drive took on an aspect of a play directed by Smithson. With him everything looked more significant, more dramatic, as if the billboards and highway lights were props indicating a new aesthetic. The industrial landscape had a sort of negative romance about it. It spread in a triangulating stream before us the artifacts of the century's civilization: smokestacks, immense chemical containers, cranes, railroad tracks, ships, and blue-gray pipes, seeming to link all of it into one groaning, puffing, grinding whole. There was no sense of demarcation. The mass smeared gray across our eyes, leaving knowledge of the heavy superstructure that holds our lives together. This was the Garden State. One wondered if it had, in fact, ever been garden-like. Smokestacks billowed with airborne waste from Bayer, and all around lay a functioning decrepitude.

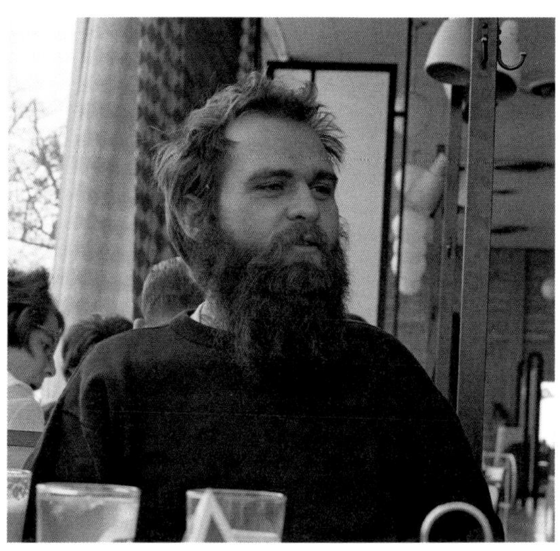

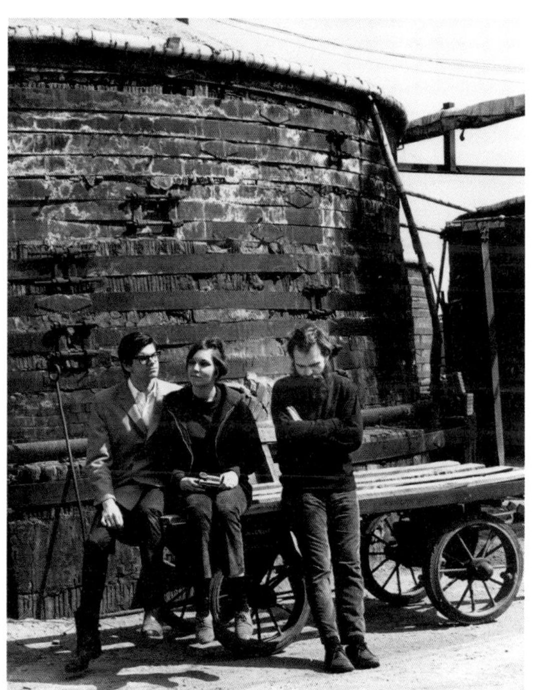

Nancy swung off onto a lesser highway, and the view from the back seat lifted my spirits a bit. We were following a route that could have been almost anywhere in the United States. The industrial megaliths gave way to low-lying buildings housing small industries, workshops, filling stations. Stacks and massive buildings, stained and rusted, fell back and revealed low-lying, preindustrial buildings cowering at the edge of the highway, their signs faded to pastel: "Irene's Hair Salon," "Bob's Easy Lube," "Dance Tonight."

I let myself slip into a Carl Sandburg and Whitman frame of mind and felt an insular pride in my ability to fashion a kind of beauty from the harsh reality out the car window. The sleek pyramidal glow of a Citco sign seemed significant. Bob had used photos of Saqqara and the Tower of Babel in one of his writings.

The car was silent except for Bob's intermittent references to William Carlos Williams or Céline. This was Smithson territory. He had grown up in this place, surrounded by the ordinary, which he came to mythologize and aestheticize. As a child he was his own archaeologist and geologist of the terrain, and now he led us on a treasure hunt.

We stopped at a derelict brick factory whose brick kilns, like inverted hogans, stood by in almost perfect condition. A few crows cawed at us but there was no other sound—no other life. We were free to rustle about among the artifacts of a past time, left in place as if their users had simply evaporated from the site even as they worked. My photo of Smithson, Holt, and Andre underscores the sense of pioneering with the rugged clothes and rusty wagon. Carl's beard lent an additional note of rugged dishevelment. Was that near Paterson or Passaic? Those two cities sound so similar, but it was in Passaic, I believe, that we later buried Bob.

Paterson had been memorialized by Smithson's pediatrician, William Carlos Williams, and now Bob would identify Passaic as a place of timeless value in his writing. "The Monuments of Passaic" appeared in the December 1967 issue of *Artforum*. In this significant article Smithson had found a way to carry the popular art aesthetic back to its place of origin, without involving painting or sculpture to justify or highlight its value.

Carl roused himself eventually and began a running monologue on the history of the area. He related "facts" and anecdotes that I assumed he was making up for our amusement. Only a trip or two later did I recognize that he was, indeed, relaying facts. He has a remarkable gift of memory, especially as it relates to political and economic history.

ROBERT SMITHSON, DWAN, ROBERT MORRIS, AND CARL ANDRE DURING THEIR "SITE-SEACH" TRIP TO NEW JERSEY, APRIL 1967

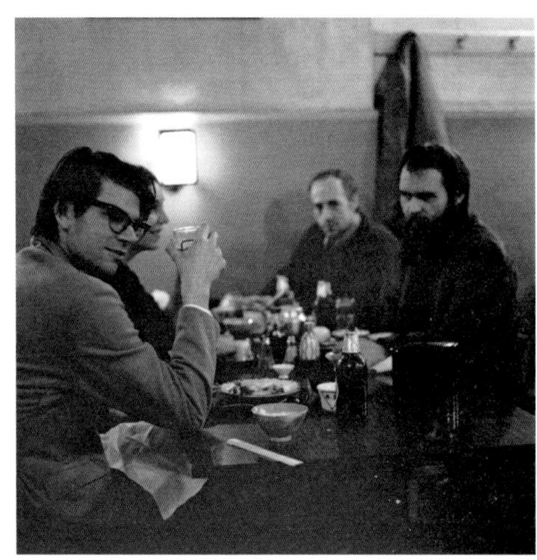

Bob interrupted to give Nancy some detailed directions, and we soon found ourselves near an open sandpit. This was the sort of landscape we were looking for. It was away from the highway, quiet, abandoned, and most importantly, unused (or so we assumed). Carl was the subject for a photo expressing our shared joy of discovery. The strewn and abandoned metal containers looked like materials that had long been waiting for him to come and organize. Nancy later investigated that property's ownership and found that the owners were not at all interested in turning over their land for use by artists.

There were several more such ventures into the wilds of New Jersey and as far south as the state of Virginia. On one such trip we were joined by Robert Morris. I had shown Morris's work in Los Angeles in a stunning exhibition of "primary" or "minimal" forms constructed in wood and skinned with a glowing, waxlike, gray polyurethane. He had sent a gift of a drawing that we used for the announcement, but he didn't come out for the show. Although I had visited him in his New York studio, I didn't yet have a sense of the person. He had seemed formal and reserved. Now, from the back seat, suspended above the cranberry bogs of New Jersey, I couldn't see the ground that we were driving on. Only the reddish, muddy water appeared on each side of the car, and while we would not plunge far if we flipped over, Morris remained silent with a noticeable rigidity to his hands and arms and a stony set to his jaw. Bob Smithson kept up a chorus of "Watch out, Nancy" and "Keep right, Nancy" as she continued along at a good clip, unheeding and unconcerned. I believe that Carl filled us in on the history of the area. I wrenched about in my seat and let out anxious gasps from time to time.

In Atlantic City I got out, with relief, fatigue, and a feeling of grubbiness, at an elegant old mansion-styled hotel that we had all decided upon. It held the promise of a hot tub, a soft bed, and a good meal. Morris and I were elected to go in and make the room arrangements for us all as we were thought to be the more acceptable looking of the group. We were turned down summarily. The five of us ended up in a motel with a blinking neon bear out front and a promise of vibrating beds for a quarter. Dinner was taken a few doors away at a "supper club." That meant strippers. It was a dingy affair, but we sat through the display: five or six women unrolling themselves from fat, pastel cocoons of tulle to the unchanging tune of "A Pretty Girl Is Like a Melody." Carl whispered that each one reminded him of his mother.

Not to be discouraged by the lack of available open land on which to work, Smithson plotted out new itineraries farther and farther from New York. For me these trips were developing a sense, in themselves, of an evanescent art form. As in dance or music, there was no end product other than the impressions grooved on the mind. Some of these have remained with me to call up when life and people seem flat. On one of our later forays I had a purpose of my own.

My long-time friend, Lorenz (Larry) Ng, is an internationally recognized neurologist with a strong sense of responsibility to further peace and awareness among divergent cultures of the world. He has invited world figures to contribute their writings to books he has edited. His current project was an anthology of essays relating to violence. I offered to contribute the artwork, for which I had the idea of photographing as many military cemeteries as I could and presenting them as a drone of endless anonymous stones, sometimes just numbers, on anonymous fields of manicured grass. I wanted to underscore the sense of dead soldiers as commodities distinguished, each from the other, only by an incised name or number on a small stone. Most of these were white tablets, still standing at attention in endless rows, while others lay flat and half buried in the green.

On one of our US-based land-search trips, our group had consisted of Smithson, Holt, Dan Graham, and me. Dan was doing his photographs of bald and blanched-looking tract houses, while I was tracking down more military cemeteries and Bob and Nancy were still looking out for suitable land for earthworks. One of the stops on our map, for my interest, was to be Arlington Cemetery. Our timing couldn't have been worse, as the funeral for Robert Kennedy was in progress on the very day that we arrived in the Washington, DC, area. Of course, all roads in and out of the cemetery were blocked. We finished the day in a motel, sprawled across one of the beds, watching the ceremony on an ancient television, while I photographed it from the screen. The role of art in the world was on my mind as I watched that coverage of yet another assassination of a leader whose beliefs I had shared. Why has there always been art? What is it in us that needs it? Faced with events of such magnitude, what drives us to continue the search for expression? I didn't find any answers. I could only think, "Art is."

My summer's annual trip to Europe found me in Germany for the Kassel art *Documenta*, where I inquired about locations within driving distance where I might find German war cemeteries; I was determined that my coverage should be unbiased and nonpartisan. But I was met with embarrassed smiles and reluctant explanations that there were no cemeteries marking the German soldiers' places because their bodies had not been returned to Germany after the two wars. If I wished I could see a few British graves.

11/6/02

I saw Carl Andre at his show at Paula Cooper Gallery. Loïc Malle was here from Paris and joined the two of us for animated conversation over Carl's aluminum ingot works and, across the street, among Sol LeWitt's paintings in Paula's other space. As always, Carl was brimming with ideas that needed expression on the spot. On one of his announcement cards he wrote a poem and handed it to me:

> The mind that
> Moves its lips
> To read the world
> Arrests the
> Dancer in mid-leap,
> "Explain!"

For the next hour our conversation revolved around the persistence, on the part of the viewer, to quickly translate the visual experience into words and then relate to the words rather than to the work. Carl felt that this was a peculiarly anglophone phenomenon, but I'm almost sure that it is more pervasive than that.

My project with the cemeteries came to naught. I accumulated some satisfying images, but when I returned from Europe, I found that the editor had gone ahead with some other visual material and that the book was already in the works. In addition, four trips in quest of available and appropriate land along the East Coast brought frustration. Nancy's investigations made it clear that what may have appeared to be abandoned earth was, in fact, jealously guarded territory. But what most would find to be a negative situation only inspired Smithson to focus more on his concept of the "nonsite." Although the nonsites would ultimately find their way into the gallery or dwelling, the medium had to be culled from the land.

One unseasonably frosty morning Smithson, Holt, LeWitt, Mary Peacock, and I once more headed out into the barren New Jersey landscape. Bob had found an abandoned air-landing strip on his map and needed to dig up soil from one of its eight dirt runways. As he forced his shovel into the frozen surface, the others held out gunny sacks to receive the actual sand and pebbles from the site. Bob was doing an airport work after all, but rather than being a work on the field, this was to be a "nonsite."

As conceived by Smithson, a nonsite is a displacement of material from a discrete and formally circumscribed area of land to an undifferentiated site. The predesigned outline of this area is then translated into a fabricated steel configuration, which serves to impose a structure on the undifferentiated site and acts as a container for the material removed from the original site. That achieved, the enigma becomes conceptual as well as actual (material); in other words, which is the site and which the nonsite? Has not the idea of the original site been altered forever? This first nonsite was exhibited in my show of his in the spring of 1968, and an additional one was featured in the *Earthworks* show in the gallery.

11/10/02

Carl Andre's reminder of the invasiveness of words on the territory of visual art continues to resonate. This morning I read in Barry Lopez's Arctic Dreams*: "To hunt means to have the land around you like clothing. To engage in a wordless dialogue with it, one so absorbing that you cease to talk with your human companions. It means to release yourself from rational images of what something 'means' and to be concerned only that it 'is.'"*[1]

Smithson used words as another art form. Andre used them as interchangeable blocks. Michael Heizer flung them like particles in a drift of falling dirt, or like fistfuls in a clatter of shale; his words do not describe—they are:

The aggressive mass of the earth submits itself aggressively to the subterfuge of its own volume. Its identity is mass, an opaque mass. It is fact. The physical makes itself known by its fact. It does not matter which ideas support the idea of the physical; it supports itself by its fact. It is of common opinion that such a blatant fact as the physical needs justification. The human fact (physical) will cry out as it disintegrates the dominance of fact while it, by its example, denies it. The victor will be the death of the mass, the elusive underlying presence, withdrawn. Invisibilatory [*sic*] substance makes itself known by its presence. Corporeality (flesh existence) is both fact and fiction. ½ of life cannot be seen, and is not fact. It is elusive and can only be experienced. Art, to be seen, must also be experienced. It matters little what it looks like. All art looks like something. It must transmit, beyond the realm of the apparently consciousable [*sic*] by its fact.[2]

WALTER DE MARIA, SEPTEMBER 1968

MICHAEL HEIZER IN THE NEVADA DESERT, 1970

WALTER DE MARIA'S MAP SHOWING TRIP FROM LAS VEGAS TO THE MORMON MESA

Heizer and De Maria: Desert Excursions

The date was October 1968. The *Earthworks* exhibition fell into place quite quickly. It was the first of such exhibitions in a gallery or museum.[3] We decided to include a number of people from outside the gallery as it had become evident that working in and on the earth was interesting others as well. Among the works that had already been accomplished were the *Dirt Room* of De Maria's, the gravelike *Hole* dug by Oldenburg behind the Metropolitan Museum, the work that Bauhaus architect Herbert Bayer had done in Colorado [p. 89, fig. 29], and the several surprising works by Michael Heizer out in Nevada (*Nine Nevada Depressions*, 1967–1968).

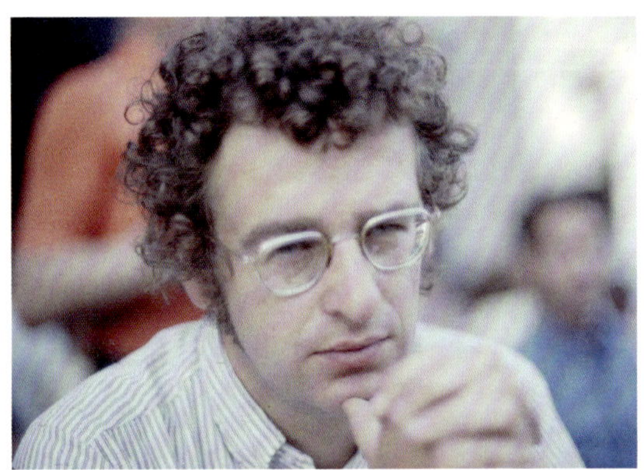

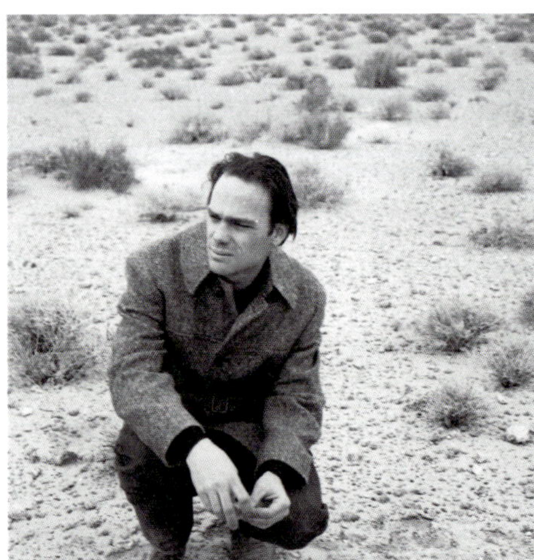

A month before the show, Michael Heizer was announced by my secretary and ambled into my office bearing a thick portfolio of photographs. Not yet twenty-five, he was lean of muscle and leaner of words. He answered my questions in muffled monosyllables as if words annoyed and frustrated him. Slowly turning the pages, I wondered at the images of motorcycle "drawings" on the earth, at the "paintings" of pure pigment stains blown across a parched lake, the geometric wedges grooved into a clay dry-lake bed surface, and the three massive boulders recessed into rectangular earth molds. I was very impressed and amazed. From where had this artist descended? Why had I not yet heard of him? It was Walter De Maria who had recommended that I look at Heizer's photos, so as soon as Michael left and I had promised to seriously consider what I had seen, I put in a call to Walter. Who is this person? Is he real? Walter's response was unequivocal: "He's authentic. He's an original." Yes, he really had created these amazing pieces out there, in Nevada, away from the New York art world, and these were beyond the idea stage—they already existed. Their realization preceded our investigations by quite a bit. And so I added one more artist to the other nine.[4]

Obviously, presenting earthworks on the carpeted floor and white walls of the gallery necessitated compromises. Most of the works were created as schemes or documents but some, though wall-hung, were unique works in their own right. Walter De Maria nearly filled a wall with a canvas painted intense yellow and these words stenciled across it: "The Color Men Choose When They Attack the Earth." Heizer constructed a backlit, oversized transparency of the land at earliest dawn, with just a sliver of light creeping across the desert floor and the incisions formed in it. On the floor was a pile of detritus from the subway construction site on Sixth Avenue that Bob Morris had heaped onto the carpet. It included dirt, wire, felt, copper, brass, and axle grease [p. 90, fig. 30]. Carl Andre showed enlarged color photos of two works that he had just executed in

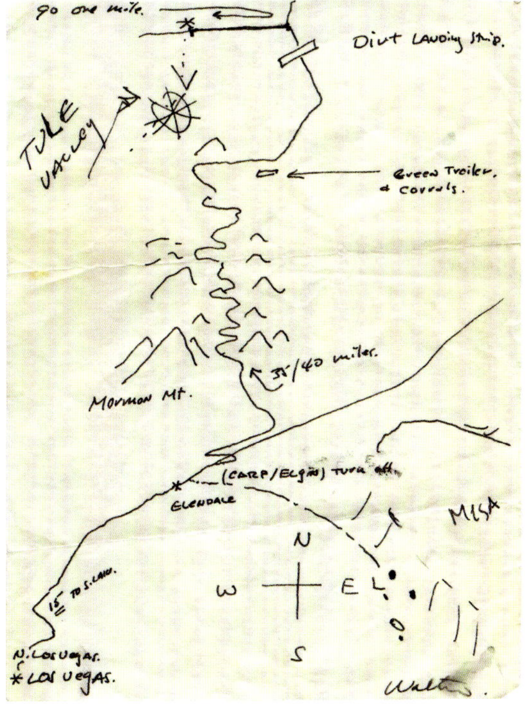

Colorado. A mound of heavy rocks was entitled *Rock Pile*, and a running line of tree-trunk segments placed end to end for approximately one hundred feet was entitled *Log Piece* [cat. 97]. Smithson placed at floor level his nonsite of beige bins with white rock, *A Nonsite (Franklin, New Jersey)* [p. 357, fig. 97]. He was by then establishing this inversion of place as a major part of his art vocabulary.

The exhibition was a rather inelegant affair. Group shows with their varying media, scales, color/non-color, and individual visions necessitate hours of reformatting. A small black-and-white drawing, although fine and significant in its own right, will seem to disappear next to a large full-color photo or painting. Morris's heap of city dirt and oozy grease crouched on the floor contrasted sharply with my recent memories of the pristine shows of LeWitt's white grids, Charles Ross's gleaming prisms, and William Anastasi's pure canvas images of the walls repeating the walls beneath them. This exhibition was messy and inchoate. It was also dynamic and charged with expectations. In that room were glimpses of the powerful works that were about to emerge. I now consider it one of the most important theme shows ever presented in the gallery.[5]

Michael Heizer's presence was becoming important in my thinking about this loosely defined group. After all, at the age of twenty-four, he had already created twenty-two astonishing works out West. So when he said that he would like to do something on a larger scale, punching the air around him as if to force his way out of the dusty shroud of New York, I trusted that he could do it, and I promised to back the construction costs. His promise, as he left, was, "I'll build a work for you, Virginia." He didn't say "a great work" but it seemed implied.

Perhaps the sorrow at the death of my mother in November 1969 was partially assuaged by my first visit to the *Double Negative* in January of the following year [cat. 102]. Michael met me at the Las Vegas airport and got me settled in a motel a bit off the strip. Early the next morning he came for me with a pickup truck, and we headed out to Overton and on to the Mormon Mesa. A vague indentation rubbed into the wall of the mesa served as a road to take us to the top. The truck wheels whirred as they struggled to grip the loose, powdery desert sand and deflect the surface rocks. I dug my nails into the vinyl seat and avoided looking out over the precipice beside us. Michael was silent as he shifted, backed up, shifted again, and finessed the clumsy vehicle up and up and, at last, onto the mesa's flat, seemingly featureless plane.

From the top of a mesa one does not, at first, have the feeling of being on an elevated surface. The mesa itself seems to stretch out like any normal, flat earth surface. Houses could be built here, office buildings, parking garages—

for there is nothing to indicate distance or scale. There is only a vast flatness surrounded by sky. Here and there, I could make out the traces of tire tracks careening off toward nothingness.

Michael turned onto one of these tracks and then another. We came to a stop near the far edge of the mesa that hovered over a green valley and the hazy gray glint of a river below. We were there. But where? I followed Michael to discover a spot facing down and across the *Double Negative*. Here, a segment of the amorphous, meandering mesa was sculpted with a definite and clearly incised geometry. The sun had climbed high by this time, but one of the canyon walls of the excavation still offered a sharp angle of shadow. The descent down the precipitous earth ramp was difficult with its acute angle and loose dirt and pebbles. I sidestepped down, dug in the edges of my rigid new western boots, and stood at the bottom of the trench. At the far side of a gap of earth, another cut, mirroring the one in which I was standing, was sharply defined by its dark shadow and front-framing rectangular edge. The chasm between the two cuts was a natural drop-off into which the tailings of the sculpture were piled. Each of these displacements measured thirty feet across its horizontal base and fifty feet up its vertical walls, but the one in which I was standing was shorter in length than the one facing me. The sun lined up across the sculpture's fifteen-hundred-foot span that included the cuts and their spill down the intervening void. Heizer had moved 240,000 tons of earth to create this isolated landmark.

As I look back now I see a correspondence between this work, in which one is below ground level with only the unbroken gray-blue overhead, and Michael's *Munich Depression*, 1969, with its bowl-shaped excavation that produced the phenomenon of an apparent convex bowl of sky above it. There, too, the optics lent a sensation of being at the rim, the sharp edge, between earth and sky.

Heizer had a one-person show in the gallery in January of 1970. Although there were significant works that were domesticated enough to occupy indoor rooms, the emphasis was on images that pointed to the outdoors and the far West. The show really existed out there, and I determined that the gallery was no longer defined or bound by the confining white plaster walls. The art gallery had expanded now and was an exhibition space in a faraway place defined only by the artist's land-moving, bulldozing chisel.

[Meanwhile,] in 1969 Walter De Maria scraped the brush from the Tula Desert floor outside Las Vegas to draw his *Las Vegas Piece*, which I believe he first entitled *Tula Piece*. By the time that Sorbonne professor Gilles Tiberghien visited Nevada to research his 1993 book on land art, the desert had probably reclaimed the work. In reconstructing its image for his book, he describes it as "two trenches, each one mile long, and two others, each one-half mile long, intersecting at right angles, similar to Michael Heizer's *Double Negative*." [6] There are a couple of misreadings here. The De Maria work was a shallow defoliation of a delicate and ephemeral nature consistent with the built-in mystery of so many of his works (for example, the one-kilometer deep, narrow hole in the ground in Munich). Also, this work doesn't resemble *Double Negative* at all, but there is a remarkable resemblance to an earlier painting of Heizer's in which the lines forming two of the opposing sides of a square are extended out and beyond the square. It would seem that certain permutations of geometric forms are universal.

Another important distinction to be made is one of attitude toward the site. In De Maria's case, the site is, I believe, an essential ingredient to the work. The sense of being lost in a featureless space depends heavily on the seeming flatness of the desert floor and the lack of protruding landmarks. Heizer, on the other hand, is adamant that the landscape is incidental to the work. For him it is the needed physical tabula rasa on which to create his monumental works. The surface is like an enormous canvas or a sufficient base for his sculpture. Heizer eschews any reference to the setting and resists inclusion in any anthology that attempts to put forth a renaissance of the landscape. In fact, in a recent conversation he underscored his disavowal of "earthworks," again [emphasizing] that what he does is *negative sculpture*. Earth, dirt, site, as such, are irrelevant to the concept of negative or reversed form.

In January 1970, the gallery invited some guests to visit these two earthworks. My colleague John Weber and I shepherded a small international group comprised of the German curator and art historian Hans Strelow, the then director of the Kunstmuseum Basel, Carlo Huber, as well as the American journalist Roy Bongartz. Heizer and De Maria led the way. To contrast the art to be seen with any urban contexts we staged the occasion a bit more theatrically than was perhaps necessary, staying at the shamelessly kitsch Caesars Palace hotel and casino with its ersatz, oversized italianate statues and effusive fountains. John Weber and I outfitted ourselves in a bit of western costuming—John in his jeans and enormous conch belt and I in Aussie hat, fringed suede jacket, and buckskin moccasins.

The first day we drove the shorter distance to Walter's piece. One characteristic that it did share with the *Double Negative* was its initial invisibility. Walter knew haptically how to find it. (On a later trip with Calvin Tomkins, who was writing for the *New Yorker*, and armed only with Walter's tiny scrap

DWAN AND COMPANIONS AT THE INTERNATIONAL HOTEL, LAS VEGAS, IN 1970 (LEFT TO RIGHT: MICHAEL HEIZER, DEWAIN VALENTINE, HANS STRELOW, JOHN WEBER, ROY BONGARTZ, CARLO HUBER, AND DWAN)

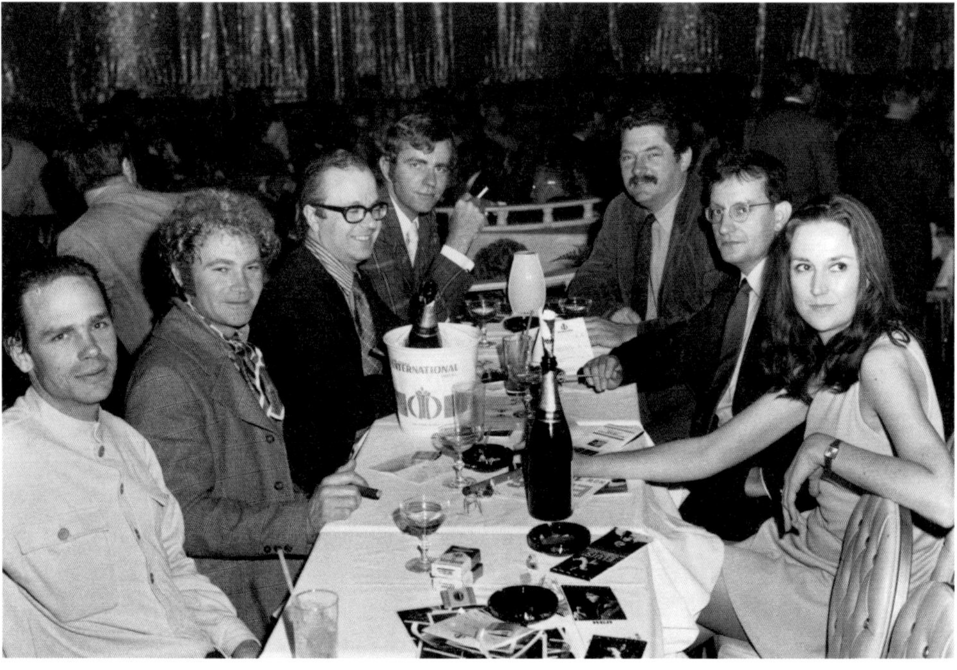

of a hand-drawn map, I completely missed the site, and Tomkins was only able to write of our all-day effort to find it.[7]) On this day, our group headed out with confidence toward an unimagined goal, for De Maria, ever mysterious and reticent, refused us any drawing, schemata, or photograph of the piece. Shortly we came to a "road" that receded into the undefined distance. At a right angle to it was a similar surface etched in the dirt and leading away from us to a distance that was also not divulged in advance. We were to head out, each alone, in whichever direction we chose. Nothing was to distract us from the direct experience of the place, its alterations, our sensation of walking, and the apprehension of moving forward into the unknown and potentially hostile desert. I forget who was ahead of me, but I do remember that he disappeared behind a gradual, natural rise in the ground, and that for quite a while I experienced a sense of total aloneness. I seemed to be a unique vertical moving along a horizontal plane. When a juncture appeared, and I decided against the road that continued ahead of me and chose the ninety-degree turn that presented itself to my left, I could just make out a dark something that seemed to disappear and then bob to the horizon again. Slowly, very slowly, as in an old movie of Bedouins approaching in the Sahara, the figure of a man took shape. We walked toward each other for a time that felt irrational and eerie. When at last our paths crossed (for neither of us wanted to stop and break the spell), Carlo

Huber gave a little nod and murmured, "A Giacometti." He was so right. This was like being within one of Giacometti's empty landscapes, vertically vulnerable.

In the evening at the hotel we crowded other experiences in and half-smothered our earlier sensations of aloneness. We dabbled a bit at the roulette tables and then moved on to an Elvis Presley performance. By that year, Presley was definitely overweight, bulging and perspiring in his white, sequined, bell-bottomed suit, but there was still something compelling about him, and we were rocked in a mass of drinking, smoking, eating, music, people-pleasure. The earlier sense of solitude and sublimity was macerated in the pounding beat, flashing lights, and insistent sensuality of Las Vegas. We ended the evening unwinding in a coffee shop, where a motherly gray-haired waitress in a pastel starched pinafore worried that we needed "some nice ice cream" on our apple pie, while a keno woman offered us gambling sheets. The latter was *un*dressed in a shiny red bosomy corset and black web tights that rode up to her waist.

The following day we slipped and bumped our way up the side of Mormon Mesa. Michael Heizer was in the lead in his four-wheel vehicle and the rest of us followed in a rented van. I think the Europeans among us were slightly aghast and exhilarated at the wages that American art exacted. That was my second of several trips to *Double Negative* and differed from the first. It felt alienating to see four or five people wandering in groups, pointing to things, and talking among themselves. Although they kept their voices low and moved slowly and respectfully, for me they seemed to crowd in upon my private memory. The time before, Michael had let me experience it alone. I had sat on the base of the ramp alone, walked alone, and just stood and wondered at it and at myself—alone. I have come to think that that is the way that all four of the earthworks that I know best should be experienced...and perhaps all art.

Smithson's *Spiral Jetty*

The mind is always being hurled towards the outer edge into intractable trajectories that lead to vertigo. —Robert Smithson[8]

A few months later, in the spring of 1970, Robert Smithson leased a watery site on the border of the Great Salt Lake in Utah. Bob and Nancy Smithson Holt spent weeks there overseeing the moving of rocks, riprap, and earth out onto the lake to form an immense spiral. He called it, aptly, *Spiral Jetty* [cat. 109]. After its completion, Bob and Nancy invited me out to see it. They drove me from the Salt Lake City airport to the Golden Spike Motel. The owner was congenial and seemed to have a proprietary attitude toward the sculpture as well.

Bob and Nancy had helped him to feel involved during their long stays in his little linoleum-surfaced, gingham-curtained rooms. I made the mistake of leaving my suitcase before the ancient wall-mounted gas heater and found it scorched the next day.

It was a hazy morning with the coolness of early spring. As usual, Nancy drove and we covered the few miles to the site with relative ease. My first visual memory of the site is of coming up over a rise and seeing a dead oil derrick collapsed over the tip of a short peninsula. Around and beyond it the lake lay like a flat petri dish of mercury, tinted slightly rose.[9] As we approached the water I saw on the ground the carcasses and skeletons of pelicans that had been mired in the tarry water and asphyxiated. Their matted feathers sprawled like miserable impoverished capes beside their bleached rib and pelvis bones, inverted toward the sky. There had been a sea there once, long ago, and these sea birds circled and hunted it still. The only fish that can survive its salinity are the tiny krill that, in their death, account for the water's livid tint.

Off to our right, the *Spiral Jetty* coiled itself out onto the heavy water. The road rose up above it so that we were able to look down on the complete configuration. It echoed Bob's unrealized proposal for the Dallas–Fort Worth airport project. For the airfield he had designed a spiral formed by overlapping triangles, and although that proposal had never seen completion, he had created two sculptures in white-painted steel using this same concept. Before me lay the third, and vast, realization of his earthworks' dominating theme.[10]

The surface of the jetty was of uneven jutting rocks, but the dirt built up between the rocks made it possible for me to carefully pick my way along it. Each step was studied. On both sides the lake lay glassy and unperturbed by the brute intrusion of earth and rock and human remodeling. The experience of riding along a hogback lattice of "roads" in the cranberry bogs of New Jersey had seemed to carry an enclosing rationale that this experience eschewed. There, the grid instilled the confidence of a series of enclosures, whereas here the formation, extending out into a smooth and endless mirror of opalescent, weighty red water, seemed to balance precariously in a void. About halfway out onto the first counterclockwise curve, I stopped to look out across the water and check my bearings. Far from centering me, the view lifted me through a mauve space into which I seemed to be careening, standing on the edge of an unstable disk. The sun was a bright smudge in the thick air, reflected wearily on the rose water membrane. Earth and sky curved to meet head on. Standing completely still and waiting for the vertigo to pass, I smelled the cold brine and watched the salty crystals forming. After two or three minutes I was able to go on and complete the journey to the center of the spiral. Its innermost segment seemed recessed like the center of a whirlpool or a slowly rotating, doused inferno. Back on shore I said, hesitantly, "Something felt infernal." I wasn't sure how that might be taken by the artist, but Smithson just smiled from under his straight black curtain of hair. Bob always seemed to be able to go to a dark place and return comforted.

Smithson's one-person show at Dwan Gallery in October–November 1970 was entitled *Robert Smithson: Great Salt Lake, Utah*. It consisted of documentation of the jetty as well as Smithson's 35-minute film that not only explored the work aerially from every angle but also brought in the New York netherworld of the labyrinthine Museum of Natural History, a museum that in Smithson's terms could be seen as an enormous time container nonsite. The film is a sort of visual poem that records the very personal thoughts of the artist as he gives us a pseudo-guided tour. I had, in fact, actually been guided by Smithson not only to the *Spiral Jetty* but, on several quiet afternoons, to and through the halls of dusty specimen cases of the museum.[11] I had attempted to evoke the staginess of the dioramas with my camera, but the results were even more ambiguous, for the effect was one of reality. Whereas I sought to capture artificiality, the camera gave me back images of "real live" forest, jungle, and plains scenes. It looked as if I had been on a safari, which considering my intent seemed banal. The redoubling of illusion intrigued me more than the presence of wild animals.

Nancy and Bob had been out to the uninhabited, barren lands of the West, including New Mexico, as part of their search for earthworks-suitable land. Nancy said that I should go there—that it was beautiful, with gorgeous sunsets. I resisted for several years, thinking that it would be too movie-pretty for my taste. When I finally did stop in Santa Fe for a long weekend on my way back from a visit to Los Angeles, I fell into a kind of intoxication on the heavily spiced pine and juniper-perfumed air; the natural, unaffected manner of the locals; and the sense that, somehow, here I could be more genuinely myself than I remembered being since childhood. I walked, inhaling deeply the freshness, and drew a little of what I saw without self-consciousness. For those moments I was not the art dealer from the big city. I could sit anonymously in a chair on the veranda of my rented cabin and render a likeness of nature in my own small, chalk drawings. No one was looking. But there were artists that I knew, working off in distant parts of New Mexico.

Star Axis

Charles Ross called yesterday to see if we could have lunch before he left for New Mexico. It being winter now, he won't be able to do much work on Star Axis, *so I suppose it's the fundraising that needs attention. He reminded me that he had first conceived of this work in 1971, that it took a five-year search to find the land, and that now, at the end of 2002, he thought he may be nearing its completion.*[12]

It must have been 1977 when I first visited the *Star Axis* site [cat. 108]. Charles picked me up in Santa Fe and drove us the hour northeast on the broad, open, sunlit highway (that ultimately leads to Denver) and then onto a lesser highway past a tiny town reputed to be a hideout for some sort of banditos, and, finally, onto a dirt road marked by a small pile of rocks. We passed by forks in the road that led off into cattle country and wound our way up a dubious dirt-and-sand edging to the tall, broad mesa. The land had been given to him by a local ranch owner who was intrigued by the idea of the work. It is only in the West where land still seems to stretch endlessly and without immediate usefulness that this kind of largesse is thinkable.

For more than twenty-five years I have watched the slow fits and starts of the construction of *Star Axis*. The configuration has altered "as the work demanded," according to Ross. It looks to the heavens—to the Pole Star to be exact—and Charles's relationship to it has a definite, transcendental aspect that could be called "mystical" or "spiritual." Somehow, his earlier works in my gallery were thought to be too "scientific" in their use of prisms and mathematical precepts. Some people felt a lack of emotional content and decided that, for them, this was not really art. Here too, science, form, and image have been brought together into an enormous structure that is not easily defined. But if it is not art, what is it? And why should science be off limits to art?

I again visited *Star Axis* in the summer of 2002. The chasm, bordered by sandstone, reaches in the distance back and up to the "hour chamber" pyramid, which is narrowly lined within with smooth cement. The whole structure splays out toward the bottom like the thighs and birth canal of a meta-mother. Ross believes that the land and the viewing plan demanded this form and that he simply had to go with it no matter how symbolic it would appear.

The supplier donated rose granite and shipped it to the site to be worked, year after year, by local, able Hispanic stonemasons. The sculpture has elegance, and by now, a sense of rightness. The excavation down the edge of the mesa has lost its rawness and towers over the cattle below like an ancient observatory reaching for the stars, discovered in the wilderness.

I requested a night visit to the North Star viewing chamber. After dinner Ross, his partner Jill, and I sat in the deepening black of the night—without lights or the glow of a distant city—and awaited the passage of that guiding star. But that particular night the sky was covered in clouds and only a faint blur could be guessed at through the triangular opening that should have marked the star's traverse from left to right. Still, there was the quiet; the fragrance of cooling, young cement; and the velvety feeling of the small pyramid that enclosed us. There was the intimacy of three people together waiting for something.

The determination and unimaginable persistence of Ross's years-long devotion to *Star Axis* and the financial insecurities he suffered amaze me. His vision for this work has carried him for more than four decades.

City

It is about thirty-two years since Heizer began his massive work in 1972, *City*, with the initial component, *City: Complex One*. At that point, Michael lived in a mobile trailer in what appeared to be the middle of a vast and uninhabited valley, three hours' drive from Las Vegas, Nevada. Subsequently, he built there a cinderblock house, which he and his then-wife Barbara surrounded with aspen saplings to lend shelter against the bitter winter weather. The valley is at six thousand feet, encircled by imposing mountains that stand miles away, offering no windbreak to the bare expanse below.

City: Complex One consists of an elongated mastaba, one hundred twenty feet long, rising twenty feet in the air, and four concrete elements in front of and resting on its "face." Although the piece is in the round and may be viewed from all sides, the preferred view is frontal. Seen in this way, the four concrete elements... form a perfect frame for the large earth form. There is an optical illusion of planar unity. From a distance, it may be viewed as a two-dimensional flat painting.

Since that first element of *City*, Heizer has slowly accumulated and built upon the adjoining acres, working devotedly on them with his present wife, Mary. He refers to the whole as, simply, "the City." I have only visited the second and a segment of the third of these newer elements. There were a few side trips to Heizer's earlier works in the summer of 1972. I asked to see those works that had predated my awareness of earth art and the ventures into the wastelands of New Jersey. For these, Michael and I headed north to Reno, Virginia City, and Sharon, Nevada. I saw the faint flush of loose pigments—red, white, black—that the artist had flung over the surface of a dry lake from the back of a truck or with a shovel from the ground, letting the wind decide the final image.

I wondered if others passed across that same ground and wondered what might have produced a wispy painting on the caked dirt floor. I saw the eroding tracks of his motorcycle drawing, etched by the repetitive grooving of his wheels. I saw his *Isolated Mass/Circumflex*, its elegant loop seemingly casually tossed across the dirt of Massacre Dry Lake but actually excavated to a depth of about eighteen inches. I saw *Dissipate #2* and *Rift* (all 1968) in their earlier, impermanent forms. Across five dry lakes, Michael had left his marks and then moved toward larger, more permanent statements.

On another dry lake in northern Nevada I visited the three immense forms that comprise *Displaced/Replaced Mass* (1969) in their original locations, lying heavily in accumulated rainwater in their concrete molded basins [cat. 99]. The three massive rocks had been blasted from a cliff face in California and transported on a flatbed truck to the Nevada site. Their "thingness," their quality of "unsculpted object," was underscored by their containers, but the receptacles were recesses rather than the customary above-ground pedestals. Typically, Michael Heizer had made an audacious gesture and then lowered it into the earth where it lay half-hidden. The flatness of Carl Andre's metal floor grids was taken a step further, below the surface. This negative space has remained the persistent factor of his continuing work.

I again visited *City* in 1975. We settled my things in the bunkhouse, and after a brief rest from the journey, rode in his Dodge truck to the site. It was a warm spring day. The tumbleweed had revived to a bright yellow-green, and the low-lying sage had a soft, velvety, bluish tone. The truck exhaled a dust trail behind us. *City: Complex One* emerged in the distance plus some, as yet, indefinable masses near it. Approaching them, Michael turned sharply, and the new work was below and in front of me.

In my thirteen years as an art dealer, I have only three times found tears rising to my eyes in front of a work of art. Two of those times were in Mark Rothko's studio, and now here, beholding Heizer's *City.*[13]

Monumentality can oppress or embrace, dominate or shelter, inhibit freedom or transcend barriers of thought and belief. Like a jab to the solar plexus, the monumental can push out a gasp of buried hope.

It is interesting to build a sculpture that attempts to create an atmosphere of awe. Small works are said to do this but it is not my experience. Immense, architecturally sized sculpture creates both the object and the atmosphere. Awe is a state of mind equivalent to religious experience. I think if people feel commitment they feel something has been transcended. To create a transcendent work of art means to go past everything.

It was some years later [1998] that Michael Heizer invited me out to see his immense *City* work in its newer evolving form. The three-hour trip from Las Vegas wrought its magic on me, slowly decompressing the stresses of New York. I looked forward to seeing the extension of *City: Complex One* with its majestic, frontal statement and questioned in my mind what Michael could possibly have added. As I pulled into the gravel parking area of his house, strewn with a cement mixer, a tractor, and several large sculptures from his arrowhead series, the sun was just about to drop, cleanly and clearly behind the far mountains. The atmosphere there is so clear that the rising or setting of the sun is not accompanied by refractions of pink to purple to red light that one expects. The sun goes down almost as yellow-white as it appears overhead, and its diffuse surface seems to congeal into a coolly sinking perfect sphere.

The next morning Michael met me at the door of the bunkhouse holding a thermos of coffee. A short distance away his truck was revving. Clearly, dawdling over breakfast was not in the scenario.

The air was still cool as we drove the quarter mile to the site The ground around us was covered in brilliant, spring, yellow-green chamise and silvery heather. The new work was not evident until we were upon it and descending the gradual dirt ramp into the vast inner court. Looming up on four sides stood massive earth structures. Inside the court, I was in a monumental complex that blotted out the desert floor, the house in the distance—even the mountains far away. The elongated mastaba-like rectangles were topped with sky, and I felt the force of something timeless, powerful, and enduring. I was speechless as I climbed out of the truck and entered the vast, open recessed span, enclosed by hovering timeless forms that blotted out the valley and the mountains beyond, leaving me within the immense earthen floor with only the structures framing it and the void above.

The projected dimension, in its final form, will be over one mile long. For me, this is surely the greatest sculpture of our time.

Mirror Travel in the Yucatán

"The Jaguar in the mirror that smokes in the World of the Elements knows the work of Carl Andre," said Tezcatlipoca and Itzpapalotl at the same time in the same voice. "He knows the Future travels backwards," they continued [and] then they both vanished into the pavement of Highway 261.[14]

It was in the early spring of 1969 that Smithson and Nancy Holt suggested that the three of us take a trip to the Yucatán. Bob had some itinerant works in mind. Nancy arranged our flight to Fort Myers and on to Mérida. We took two days in Florida to drive up the coast to Sanibel, browse its shelly beach, and check out Captiva Island. I remembered that Bob Rauschenberg was living somewhere there and brazened the address out of a local realtor. I counted on Bob's relaxed hospitality as we drove down the dirt driveway lined with fernlike acacias and hot pink oleanders. He was gregarious, genial, and generous. His house was large and totally simple, with an interior of white painted plaster and white vinyl floors repeating the flat white of its wood facade. Only the rich, free images of the lithographs that he was making there broke the plainness of the setting, and they were carefully wrapped away. His assistant lifted a few from their pristine container to give us a peek. We drank whiskey while the two Bobs carried on a spirited repartee that I attempted, unsuccessfully, to record with a stub of pencil on a brown paper bag. It was there, that day, that the two men swam a date-palm log that Smithson had discovered down to the beach in front of Rauschenberg's house, and Smithson asked me to photograph his creation, *Second Upside-Down Tree* [p. 16]. That image, somehow, later found its way into the photo collection of the Metropolitan Museum of Art. How that happened remains a mystery to me.

Arriving in Mérida, we settled for the night in a small hotel and a room with three beds and a vinyl table with a bare bulb dangling overhead. These lodgings seemed to reflect Bob's most cherished wishes, but I was happy when we set out the next day to lounge the Gulf Coast in our rented car and seek out our first destination—Uxmal. The trip was not without its excitement. I begged to stop by the side of the road for a swim in the limpid, green-turquoise water and, on coming out, saw a large black dorsal fin idle by, exactly where I had been moments earlier. And there was the edgy incident of the golden-earrings-gypsy who flagged us down, claiming that the truck ahead, laden with scowling or leering men, had broken down and needed our help. The story didn't quite jibe. The image of our white, not especially fit, New York bodies being of any legitimate use to the eight or ten hulking figures in the back of that truck seemed to indicate that we should leave the scene as soon as possible. Nancy politely made excuses to the now angry young woman, rolled up her window, locked the doors, and made a nodding, smiling getaway. But Uxmal was spectacular.

We were blessedly alone as we walked the hot gravel, surprising a few iguanas basking on the stone walls. And we didn't say much. Ancient carved faces with long bent noses looked down on us, connected by friezes of geometric

NANCY HOLT AND DWAN WITH GUIDE ON THE USUMACINTA RIVER IN THE YUCATÁN, APRIL 1969

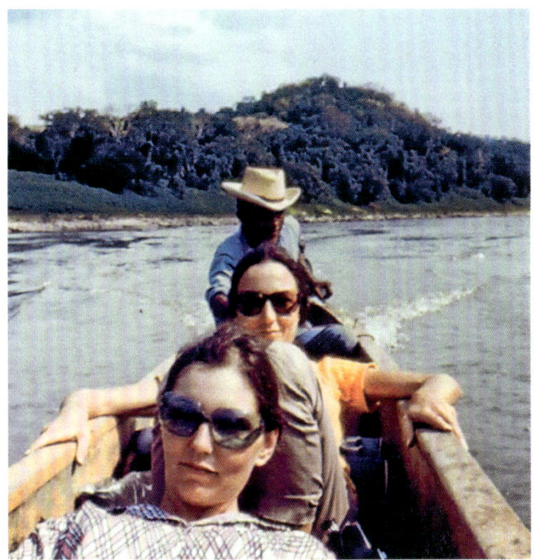

links. Bob read his guidebook and identified the name of the pyramid: The Temple of the Magician, the Governor's Palace, and the House of the Doves. I shot a silhouette of Bob and Nancy in the archway of one of these [p. 21, fig. 5].

Arriving at the Palenque Hotel in the evening we found our new dwelling to be festooned with a bristle of reinforcing rods at odd bent angles, rising up from the concrete facade. (It was explained that it was intentionally left like that in case the hotel decided to add a second floor.) On the ground level was a long pile of cement bags, presumably also intended for future use. The humidity of the jungle had rendered them as stony as the ruins that we were about to visit. Bob took an interest in their sagging decrepitude and took several slides of them that he later projected to the art and architecture students and faculty of the University of Utah with a surprising proposition. Those devotees of Corbusier and Vasarely, with all the rectitude of their disciplines, were told that simply piling bags of cement and abandoning them to the elements might produce a new and interesting form of building.

A thing is a hole in the thing it is not.—Carl Andre[15]

But Smithson had not built a permanent structure in the Yucatán. His ubiquitous mirrors were moved from site to site and placed into the sand and vegetation in such a way that they reflected only the hazy sky. Essentially, they mirrored nothing. They were like holes in an overwhelmingly organic, living setting. Like his *Enantiomorphic Chambers* and other early and late mirror works, the mirrors faced away from the viewer, allowing a reflection neither of the individual nor of any data other than the supporting surface of dirt, salt, and rock that lay on and against it. All those works are mirrors as nullification of self and as obliteration or fragmentation of sensory data. Through the looking glass one encounters the void.[16]

My cameras both burdened and reassured me. I was weighed down with a Hasselblad for stills and a Sony for Super 8 mm filming. The Hasselblad, in spite of its bulk, was dependable and gave some satisfactory results, but the movie camera yielded mostly monochrome black when projected back in New York. The heat and humidity of the sandy flats and relentless jungle vegetation conspired to erase all my records of our mirror safari into the Yucatán. Bob's Instamatic sufficed to record his mirror placements, for which he had brought a box of twelve-by-twelve-inch unframed mirrors to place at chosen spots along our itinerary. Our guide was "Freddy"—a red-haired, freckle-faced Mexican. Despite his appearance and some time spent in Texas, his manner and melody

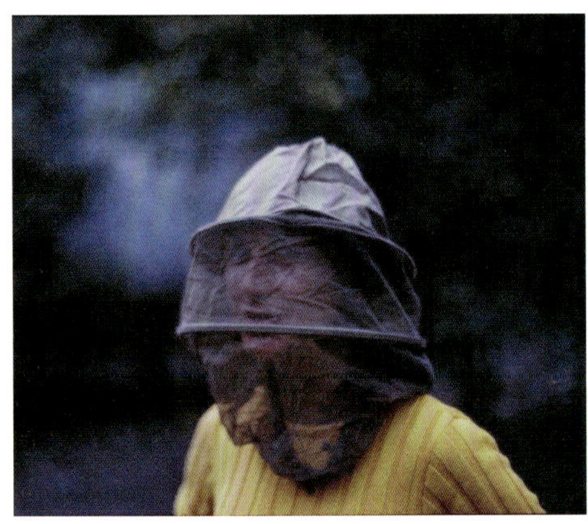

DWAN IN THE YUCATÁN, APRIL 1969

of speech were heavily Mexicano. Freddy led us, hacking a machete at green spiraling tendrils that reached down from above and green tangled roots that tripped us along the jungle floor, intermittently shooting at snakes wound around the overhead branches. Their green twirling forms fell before us to plop heavily on the damp green jungle floor. I saw the world as a thick mass of unctuous, writhing green that was both erotic and threatening. I wanted to film green on green on exhilarating, suffocating green.

Even the chiggers were green. I attempted to move through the space without touching any of the dead logs or leafy masses that promised to harbor these unseen menaces. I covered my arms in long sleeves, my legs in pants with socks rolled up over them, and I tucked in my shirttails. But the green mites burrowed under everything, leaving itching, burning red welts. (Ultimately, it was those that drove us back to the reassurance of the States and to the more familiar fauna that crawl New York kitchens at night.) We left the ruins of Palenque, the ruins of our hotel, and the rented car to fly in a single-engine plane, piloted by Freddy, out across the dense treetops and down to Bonampak to visit its cave wall paintings. We were smokers then, so we flicked our ashes out the plane's broken window, and I was able to hold my camera out to snap some more images of green. I was in a sort of intoxication of green. Our mammalian existence seemed incidental in front of the writhing, towering, strangling, swooping, insinuating effulgence of tropical green. This was life before and after the dinosaurs, before and after man, and one could only surrender to it and accept it.

We flew on to Agua Azul and boarded a dubious-looking dugout that would chug its twenty-five horsepower motor up the still waters of the Usumacinta River. In an hour and a half we found our destination for the night and for exploration and art-making the next day. Two squat-bodied local caretakers showed us to our quarters—a palm-covered, chicken-wire-walled hut. Freddy strung up our four hammocks (mine with a panting chicken sitting in a barrel at my feet), and we ate something like a fricassee of wild pig with tamales. The woman caretaker was quite a good cook, so we felt happy and well tended as the sun dropped behind the black jungle trees and the monkeys and jaguars began their first tentative howls. As we settled into our army surplus hammocks, Freddy zipped us in against the mosquitoes. The oilcloth hammocks had a border of netting to allow breathing, yet I soon found that placing my elbow or knee against its mesh also allowed the mosquitoes to access flesh. But it was when Freddy doused his flashlight that the real performance began. Immediately outside our hut was a gathering of small black, adolescent-looking pigs that I had noticed when we arrived. Now their adolescent aggressions took over with demonic force. There was galloping and loud squealing and rape, then a moment of silence, and then the same stampede repeated itself throughout the night. The chicken at the end of my hammock looked exhausted the next morning, apparently trying desperately to lay an egg or to hatch one—I never knew which.

Bob went off with his mirrors, Freddy and a young native, while Nancy and I ran behind our native guide, barely able to breathe as he led us, machete in hand, chopping to right and left and leaving fat fallen tree trunks for us to scale as we climbed and gasped from one overgrown Mayan ruin to the next. We only had time for Nancy to snap one or two of her Instamatic shots before the guide headed off to another ruin. It's all a blur to me now but there was a bit of the film *King Solomon's Mines* about it.

If only there weren't those chiggers.

Bob returned to the home ground looking pleased. He had seen a major stele that lay where it had been abandoned after smugglers had tried unsuccessfully to get it on board a boat bound for a museum. Nancy and I went to see it as it lay, half-covered in a stranglehold of green—precious hieroglyphs and a carved face of a man or god looking back up at us, alone.

At noon we boarded the boat again to head upstream and return to Agua Azul. The sun blazed the water's surface, almost blinding me to the very slowly passing jungles of Mexico on the right, and Guatemala on the left. The hidden creatures were silent in the heat. Only we seemed to be doggedly combating nature as we forced our way against the current. I tried to find a way to sit on my wooden plank at the back of the boat. A sort of squat and lean forward with face down and away from the sun seemed the best solution. I was physically miserable and the journey was to be a long one. The vision that made it bearable for me was of the shelter of tropical trees and the shaded porch that awaited us at Agua Azul.

Then I heard Bob call to Freddy to stop. Looking around, I saw only a spit of a sandbar, fuming in the heat. We were to stop so that Bob could make one of his mirror pieces.

One hears of obsession in the character of artists. That experience of prolonging our misery in a torturous situation will always remain with me as an illustration of the one-pointedness of the artist's mind.

Bob, Nancy, and Freddy debarked ahead of me and moved out onto the dazzling sand. I groaned and brought up the rear. A few steps out of the water's edge I started to sink. My foot was being sucked down. Forcing the other further ahead, I again felt the pull from beneath. I called out, "Quicksand!" No response. "Help, I'm in quicksand!" No one looked back. Plunging forward onto my knees I was able to extricate myself and stagger on after them. While Bob placed and photographed his mirrors, I lay down on the side of a sand dune and tried to hide my head in the eight-inch shadow of its curling lip.

We eventually did reach Agua Azul, where I waited impatiently for a pig to get out of the water and then immersed myself in it, my head encircled with biting flies and mosquitoes. The water was murky and cool and I didn't really care what might be in it at that point. Back at our base, the next morning it was agreed, even by Bob and Nancy, that we had probably had enough and would forgo the considered extension to Chichén Itzá. But, of course, the discomfort exists now only as a word, and the experience is unrepeatable.

Bob Smithson died in 1973 in a small plane crash while reconnoitering the land on which he proposed to build his *Amarillo Ramp*. Nancy called me from Texas. One of the most fascinating individuals and finest of friends had disappeared from my life, from all our lives. The funeral attendance was large and marked by the spoken memories of more and more diverse people than I had realized he knew. An excerpt from W. B. Yeats's "The Second Coming" was read: "The center will not hold..."

Nancy Holt and Richard Serra later completed the *Amarillo Ramp* from Smithson's drawings and specifications. Its present condition is questionable. I have been told that it is not being maintained.

35-Pole Lightning Field and *Lightning Field*

Ever vigilant that his works be respected and maintained, Walter De Maria created a sort of protective shield around his large *Lightning Field* in southern New Mexico [cat. 105]. It is the second and larger field, the first having been built on the land surrounding Meteor Crater [in Arizona] owned by collectors Burton and Emily Tremaine. The first was acquired by me in exchange for another, more salable work, the *Bed of Spikes* (1970), that a Swiss museum wanted to buy from De Maria.[17] I later donated it to the Dia Art Foundation. The smaller, original *35-Pole Lightning Field*—thirty-five, twenty-foot-high polished stainless-steel spikes—is sometimes referred to as a "study for" the second, but that is incorrect. It is a complete and authenticated work in itself [cat. 104].

My daughter, Candace, my friend Roberta, and I were visiting a tennis ranch in Arizona when Walter came for us and we all four headed north to find the work. As we stopped in Flagstaff, hunting for Mexican food, the day was winding down. The sky was a dusted orange. Walter was nervous about the delay and hurriedly drove us out to a darkening plain on which we found a lone tumbledown shack. Walter stopped to check on the trespassers emerging from the shack. They held beer bottles, I thought, like revolvers and slouched against their rusted Buick with cigarettes stuck to their lower lips. Walter tried a rather formal approach, asking politely why they had come way out there to relax. They eyed him coldly and seemed unmoved by his explanation that they were on private property. It seemed best to just leave them, so the four of us headed out in the direction indicated by Walter. We stumbled up and down the bumpy landscape, ever mindful of rattlesnake burrows underfoot, and the dark characters at our backs. The moon was almost full, which helped our hike, and in the end it haunted the field of pale, twenty-foot, polished stainless-steel spikes that dotted, in mathematically precise order, the blackening surroundings. Alien and mysterious, the poles stuck their pale points into the fragrant desert sky. I was tired but grateful for the experience as we returned to our evil-looking characters and, handing them a ransom of all our Marlboros and Salems, hurried away.

It was only recently that I was able to get to the present large and renowned *Lightning Field*, in Quemado, New Mexico. An architect, Laban Wingert, who worked with me on the Dwan Light Sanctuary, his partner, Dardo Soccas, and I drove down from Santa Fe, having made the proper arrangements with the Recursos office in advance. We arrived in Quemado about one o'clock and sought out a diner that had signs at the front and on the tables describing their "famous" homemade pies. Three pies later, we walked the length of a dusty street lined with battered trucks in herringbone patterns. Our rendezvous point was finally discovered to be an uninhabited-looking broad storefront. I rubbed some dust off the window and peeked in, but there was not a person, a desk, or anything that might indicate an agency for viewing a world-famous work of art. We made our way to the back of the building, where a young couple seemed to be waiting for something, taking shelter from the heat in their tired van. The five of us talked and reassured each other that there would be someone to come for us and, finally, there was. Ben drove up in an enormous van and leaned his cowboy hat out the door. One long, thin, blue-jeaned leg and scuffed boot dangled below the car door as he surveyed this latest band of city folk. He spoke minimally as he tossed our luggage into the back of the van, made a phone call inside, and settled us into his own truck; all other vehicles were strictly forbidden at the *Lightning Field*.

I got to sit in the front seat to have room for my long legs. The drive took approximately one hour, during which Ben, who was surely typecast by De Maria (who himself avoids human contact), spoke only three-word sentences and only when asked a direct question. Our abode appeared in the distance as an archetypal log cabin. It actually was very old and had been acquired for visitors to decompress overnight and clear their eyes for the major event of the morning.

In the gallery years, one of our frustrations had been the sight of viewers poking their heads out of the elevator doors into the exhibition while keeping their bodies in the elevator. "What's your next show?" was the response after the rapid scan of the room, and off they went to the next gallery on their list of galleries to "do." Walter, Michael, John Weber, Smithson, and I, together or separately pondered how to fix the public in some sort of holding or decompression chamber so that they would give the art the time that it deserved. One earlier solution was the one that I had adopted when building the Dwan Los Angeles space, in which a sort of short tunnel had to be passed through before one came out into the gallery space. But, ultimately, the distance traveled to a work is the most effective way to wash the eyes and mind of the jumble of daily stimuli and to slow the pace to a receptive condition.

The cabin at the *Lightning Field* was appropriately bare and unpretentious, with scrubbed wood floors, a plank table, and some authentic Stickley furniture. The far side of the space gave onto an equally plain wooden porch that faced the work. From that comfortable but spartan stage, we looked out at a grid of elegant, slim poles, forming a perfect geometry, crisscrossing the plane of low-lying wildflowers. As evening spread over us, the poles glowed, their tips registering the pink and then red of the huge surrounding sky. We sat in the rapidly chilling evening, reluctant to move away from the spectacle, until Ben came with our supper. His wife had made an excellent lasagna, a tossed salad, and a spice cake in a low pan. There was no electricity, so no television, no radio, no lights except for the flashlights with which we were each provided. Sleep came very early and so did awakening.

The morning spectacle was even more arresting than that of the day before. The pale, pristine blue sky, unmarked by even a trace of clouds, slowly warmed and moved through an art student's chromatic chart: blue, blue-gray, blue-pink, flares of orange, deeper pink, reddish-blue, red, a ball of flame on the horizon. The spikes, which had been almost invisible in the flat early light, slowly lit up and glinted as close and far as I could see. I chose a tentative pattern to walk the work, a diagonal from the nearest corner to the further midpoint, then straight across, making a 90-degree turn in the middle to return me to the cabin. As with the *Las Vegas Piece*, there was a paucity of landmarks. Although the cabin continued to be in view, tiny against the horizon, the experience of being within a vast grid is not at all the same thing as looking down on one as on a checkerboard. The next pole in view may or may not lead me in the desired direction. I had to trust that I would eventually get my bearings but, nevertheless, did lose myself once and walked further on my return than I had planned. The others had wandered off on their own and disappeared from view. After breakfast, we each went out once more to try to ingest the experience and lock something of it away inside us. I think that every visit to that work must be unique. Without mental map or prediction, it defies encapsulating definition. Mystery, distancing, and solitude are consistent elements in Walter De Maria's oeuvre.

On the trip back to Quemado, there were brief jags of conversation in the van but mostly, like our driver of few words, we silently looked out at the desert plain and held fast to the quiet.

Epilogue

Some work of noble note, may yet be done. — "Ulysses," *Alfred, Lord Tennyson*

I hope, one day, to make a pilgrimage to the other works of these remarkable artists; to Smithson's *Broken Circle* (1971) in Emmen, Holland; to Nancy Holt's *Sun Tunnels* (1976), in Great Desert Basin, Utah; and to Heizer's *Adjacent, Against, Upon* (1976) in Myrtle Edwards Park, Seattle; his *Guennette* (1977–1978), owned by the Metropolitan Museum of Art; and his massive steel piece, *Platform* (1980) at the Oakland Museum in California.

A good portion of this account of working with and participating in these distant works on the land has evolved into the story of my travels—of getting there. I see the journeys as both adventure and metaphor of my ongoing quest for that which is beyond the clamor and the inherent struggles of contemporary life. To experience these works I had to bring myself physically, psychologically, historically, and spiritually to them and leave behind the comfort of "salon" viewing in which the viewer retains a safe distance from the work. Visiting these works is being in them, and the more that I am in them, the more I am rewarded.

My journey has been threefold. First, I have moved through real space to release the hold of my daily existence and to experience something closer to "real time," in which movement is a commitment of a segment of my life. Second, I have had the mental voyage, with its fogs and clearings, in my own past.

I have gone back to thirty and more years ago and visited these sites as they look to me now through a long and faulty telescope. I have attempted to stick to the sequence as it occurred and to follow the itinerary of my memories. Additionally, there has been a journey into myself, catalyzed both by the actual voyages and "discoveries" there, but also by the act of remembering and of noticing what has affected and remained with me most.

I see that, starting with my involvement with the tail end of abstract expressionism at the outset of my career as a gallerist and then continuing through the representation of the nouveaux réalistes and on to minimal art, there has been a progressive focusing on those works that demand the most inner commitment on my part. As art became increasingly self-contained and even remote, I stretched more and more toward it and found satisfaction in that engagement and communion. I had to be willing to risk the voyage to a place that does not easily reveal itself. One used to look *at* art. Today art reflects our image back upon us. That is what makes it so difficult.

My journey continues. It has been a good voyage so far. I have been immensely privileged in having the means to help see these works accomplished and in knowing the extraordinary people who have created them.

The artists tell me now that things are not the same. They seem to indicate some groundwater difference in the way that art is being seen and in the way it is being handled. I am too removed, at this point, to be aware of this change. The references to overriding commercialism are only apparent in the astonishing rise in prices. One East Coast artist that I showed in my Los Angeles gallery likes to tell the story about a painting of his that I sold for $400 that has been resold in recent years for $400,000. Each time he tells it I have the uneasy feeling that he is saying that I had undersold it. But those were his prices then and that is his price now. I imagine that when the stakes are so high, the dealer's blood does pound faster. There was not enough money involved when I was a dealer to override the satisfaction that proximity to the art and those artists gave me. I was, and continue to be, in awe of those artists—their dedication and vision.

ROBERT SMITHSON AT LA HACIENDA UXMAL, APRIL 1969

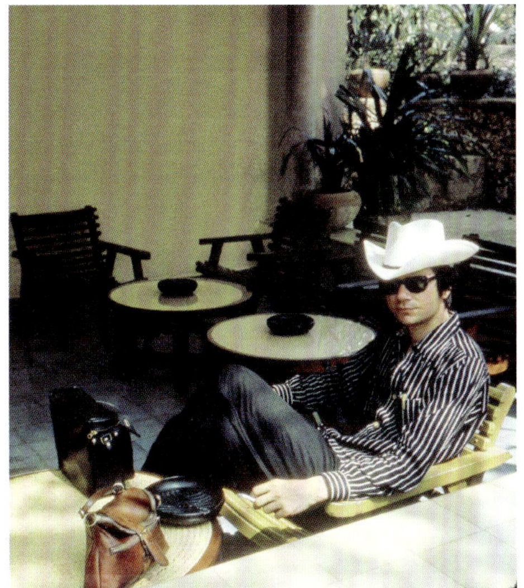

4. *Reflections on Robert Smithson*

In 1966 Sol LeWitt introduced me to the artist Robert Smithson. Because of LeWitt I viewed this enigmatic person with interest.

Lean, gaunt, stooped. Black boots, black trench coat, black trousers. Black hair shaped a dark frame for a saturnine face suggesting a strange intelligence. His gestures were relaxed to a point suggesting near-collapse, and he seemed to drape himself over empty space.

Who was he? Was he really properly termed a minimal artist? Was there an existing art category to embrace those faceless mirrors in Mexican motel colors? Were his crystalline structures, so cool and self-contained, really minimal, given the elaboration of their surfaces and puzzling multiplicity? Was he presenting a trimmed-down contemplative form, or posing disturbing new sets of categories and issues?

Smithson was by the very nature of his thinking a kind of teacher. That is to say, his worldview—the particular vantage point from which he looked at things—necessitated a context that only he could construct. His articles seemed to say, "Sit here and look in that direction and just let this information flow over you." His oceanic style could set one adrift in his sea of ruminations. One could also view these writings as dioramas of a sort in which the viewer, in shadow, glides silently through time and space made visible by Smithson's peculiar awareness. In these dioramas, cities collapsed as they were being built, architecture was erected as ruin, deadly chasms appeared in space, and "frozen wastes" or "infinite pools of dust" encompassed one.

But this kind of thinking was not reserved only for his writing; it appeared as well in lengthy conversations that he squandered almost nightly on his friends and colleagues in darkly lit bars. One wasted away in tunnels of Formica, neon, and Naugahyde to such phrases as "tarnished reflections" or "every refutation is a mirror of the thing it refutes—ad infinitum" or "the refuse between mind and matter is a mine of information." And so he spun a holding-space for his ideas.

Often he quoted other authors such as Louis-Ferdinand Céline, Alain Robbe-Grillet, T. S. Eliot, and Jorge Luis Borges, while carefully omitting their names. Oblique references or additional quotations would emerge later, and eventually the listener was obliged to plead for their sources. This was teaching by teasing, teaching by tantalizing. There was a sense of urgency at the end of these conversations, a sense that all this would disappear and one would be without exotic nourishment until the next meeting. Getting the name of an author was akin to getting a fragment of a recipe at the end of a banquet.

What was this perspective that so fascinated? The sense was of stepping through Alice's looking glass into a reflected space in which values and visions were reversed. This was an anti-domain in which entropy and dissolution were greeted with the enthusiasm usually accorded growth and development. The taboos of negatives and nihilism were tossed aside, and from these very places sprang new energy and productivity. Opposites were embraced, and their meetings sparked and illuminated hidden places in the mind. The dreadful and the banal were made mythic and romantic.

On a trip to the Yucatán in 1969 with Nancy Holt and myself, Smithson assigned to each of us the persona of a Mayan god that suited us best and from which we were to act and view all about us. We were three deities on three separate but parallel paths, each a voice from a different inalienable perspective. There was a sense of heroic mission, and very little overlapping of viewpoints. Thus, also, the probability of conflict in close quarters was drastically reduced.

Other trips included two to the Pine Barrens of New Jersey and two subsequent ones looking for sites for earth art and, of course, the trips to the Great Salt Lake to visit *Spiral Jetty*. Wastelands of sand and snow, Citgo stations with their pyramidal logos, swamps, cemeteries, brick factories, diners, and ruins of an industrial age were interpretively enhanced by Smithson. The negative became a positive, or rather, what was previously designated as above the positive/negative value-judgment ratio was now seen to have a counterpart in the "negative" underworld . The contemporary awareness of negative atomic particles and negative numbers proceeding from zero into infinity was the stuff of which Smithson's works and thoughts were made. Today it would seem that he also presaged the interest in black holes in outer space.

Robert Smithson was a man and an artist, uniquely aware of his time, who had the courage to be of it, and in it, and for it. It was a privilege to share some of it with him.

APPROACHING MICHAEL HEIZER'S *DOUBLE NEGATIVE* FROM THE SOUTH, 1969

5. *"Double Negative": A Recollection*

We drove out across a flat plane of sage, scrub, dust, and clay. The vast parched space gave me a giddy, other-world feeling. At the farthest edge of the mesa we were suddenly peering down at an enormous cut. The earth itself was sculpted away. Walls of dirt and rock dropped a flat fifty feet on either side of two facing thirty-foot-wide crevasses. I walked down the ramp to the bottom of the cut, which was cooler though there were no shadows. Damp walls of earth surrounded and protected me from the relentless desert. Air from the valley below moved up and through this space making those sounds we usually call "silence." Absence was the prevailing sensation. No colorful, dynamic object obtruded on this space. It was empty. It was hollow. I was not apart, looking at it. I was in it. I was in a hole in the ground, on a mesa, in the state of Nevada, in the United States, of the world, in the universe. These were the only reference points. No art history. No art world. Boulders stood like sentinels. A turkey buzzard lay on the sky. The moving sun darkened one wall of the opposing cut, inverting the sky-ground relationship. Bleached dirt reddened as the afternoon changed into evening. The sun dropped suddenly. Insects that had been invisible in their torpor started their foragings.

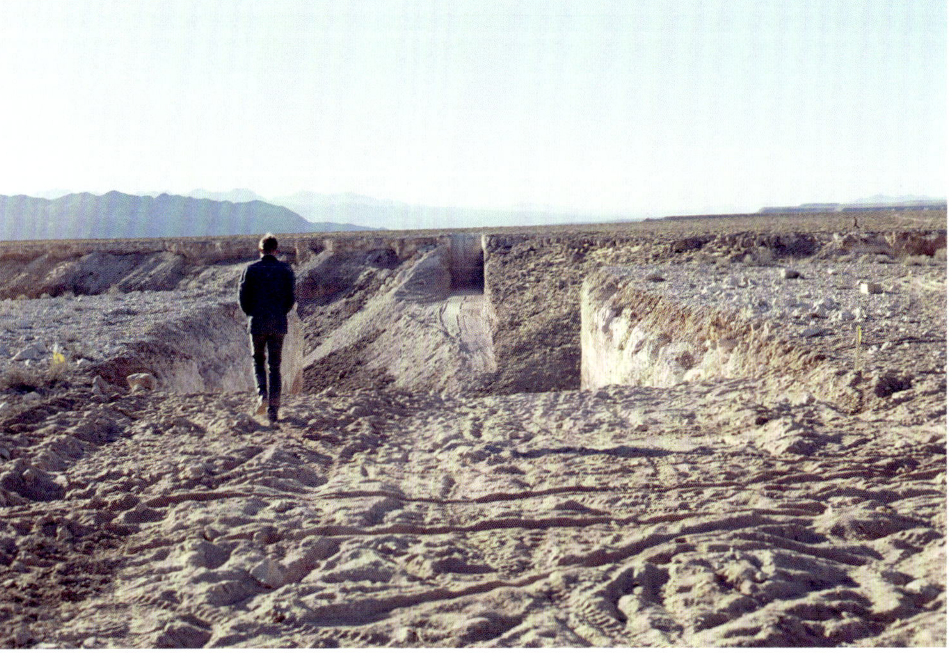

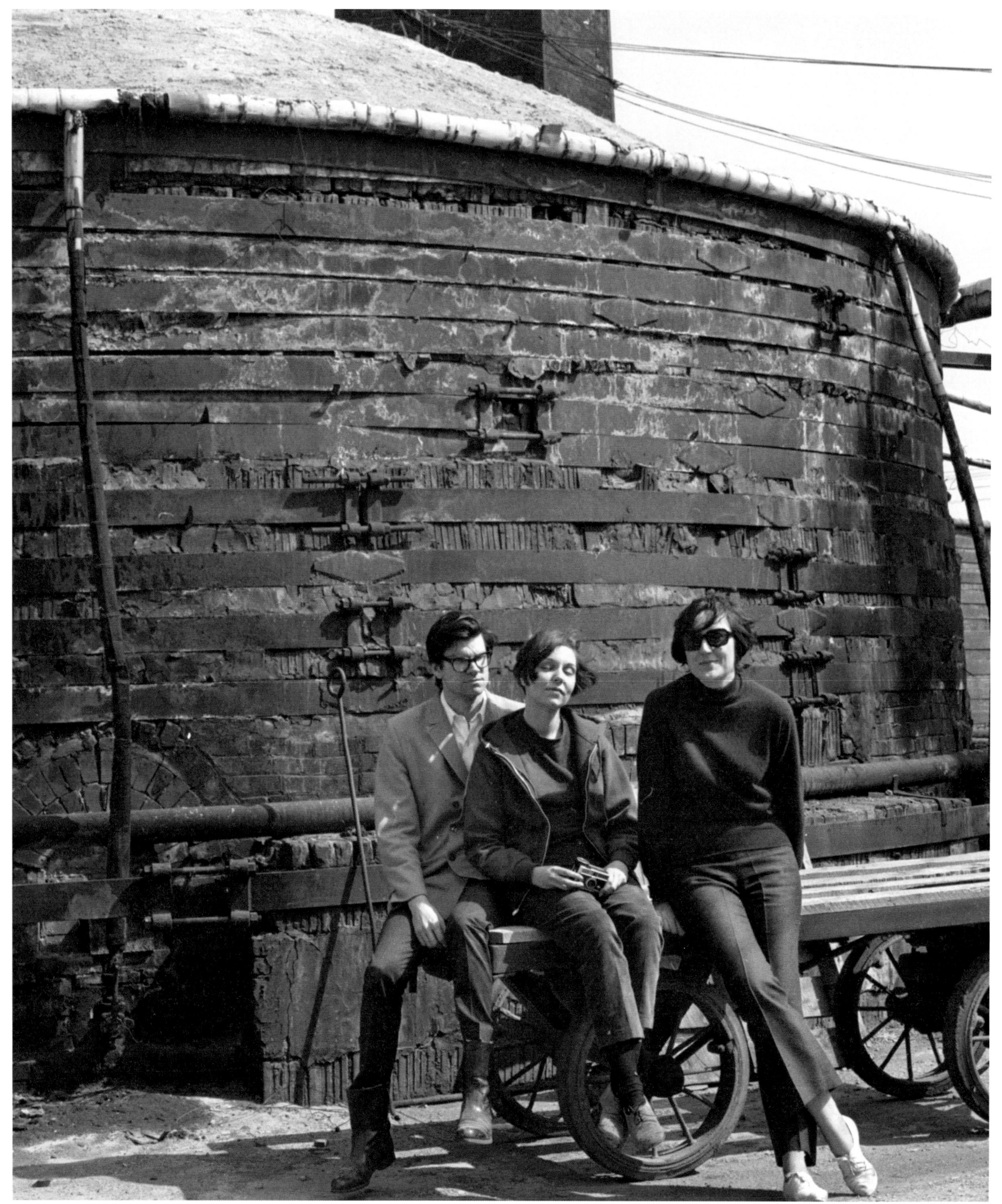

PAIGE ROZANSKI

VIRGINIA DWAN CHRONOLOGY

DWAN AND HER FATHER, SAN DIEGO, C. 1936 (1)

DWAN AND HER MOTHER EN ROUTE TO CHICAGO, C. 1940 (2)

DWAN AND HER LINCOLN CONTINENTAL MARK II, C. 1957 (3)

WEDDING PORTRAIT, DWAN AND VADIM KONDRATIEF, 1958 (4)

1

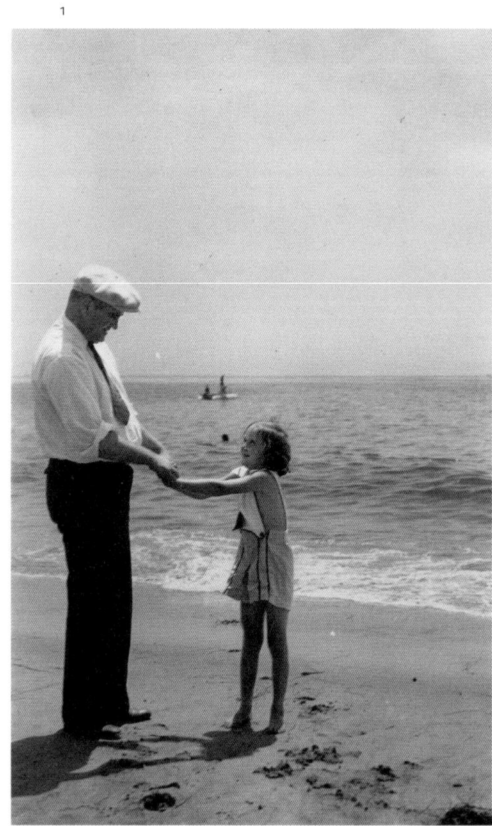

Early Years

1931

October 18 Virginia Dwan is born in Minneapolis, Minnesota. She is the daughter of Charles Dwan and Laura Isrealson Kemp. Charles is the son of attorney John Dwan, one of the five founders of Minnesota Mining and Manufacturing Company (3M). The company started in 1902 when each of the businessmen invested $1,000 in a venture centered on the minerals near Two Harbors, Minnesota. John served as the first secretary and leased part of his law office to the corporation. Charles studied economics but chose not to work after serving in the military during World War I. Kemp has a thirteen-year-old daughter, June, from a previous marriage.

1935–1941

In her youth Dwan travels extensively in the United States with her family, including an early trip to Alaska when she is four and later road trips to Alabama, Louisiana, and Florida, as well as throughout the Southwest. She attends public school; her mother enrolls her in tap-dancing, ballroom dancing, and elocution classes. When Dwan is about ten, the family moves to the San Fernando Valley in Southern California. She spends time outdoors exploring her surroundings and vividly remembers daydreaming under a large oak tree and wandering through the hills:

> Our house was near a quarry, . . . and I would find fossil rocks up there in the hills, which was an enigma right away, to find sea fossil shells up at high elevation. That sort of thing used to fascinate me. It wasn't something I thought about in words; it was something that I like[d] to do. I'd go out and have my own field trips.[1]

At the age of ten, Dwan is sent to the Sacred Heart Convent, a boarding school in Menlo Park near San Francisco. She attends only for the fall semester of 1941 because the United States enters World War II and her parents want her close to home. Dwan recalls drawing constantly as a child:

> I drew Cinderella stories in which I starred, and I drew "serious" drawings for school posters or charcoal studies of huge plaster noses and veiny feet offered by the nuns at the Sacred Heart Convent. . . . There I saw mystery. I saw relics with fragments of bones and pieces of wood or metal which had been used to torture female saints. Their lives and the lives of all the Christian martyrs were told in the most satisfyingly gory fashion. My ten years thrived on those tales, and I lay awake at night "living" their exquisite pain and never-failing courage.[2]

1942

Dwan moves with her family to Hot Springs, Arkansas, for six months. They spend the second half of the year in Denver, Colorado, before relocating back to California.

1944

June Dwan is twelve when her father dies from heart failure and complications from pneumonia. She moves back to Minneapolis with her mother and attends parochial junior high and public high school there. She studies French, and her favorite subject is singing.

1947

While Dwan is in high school, her mother encourages her to see an exhibition at the Walker Art Center on American illustrator Wanda Gág. She has her first encounter with modern art when she views the Walker's permanent collection featuring American modernists John Marin, Charles Demuth, Joseph Stella, and Charles Sheeler. She is most impressed by Marin's and Stella's paintings.

1949

Summer Dwan moves with her mother to Los Angeles.

August Dwan enrolls at the University of California, Los Angeles. She starts out studying fine art but eventually majors in psychology. She is most affected by ancient art history including Egyptian, Italian, and Greek art.[3] She meets Paul Fischer, eight years her senior and a social psychology student at USC. They marry in February 1950 when she is nineteen.

1950

November 12 Dwan gives birth to a daughter, Candace.

1952

October 18 Upon her twenty-first birthday, Dwan learns of a significant inheritance she will receive, which has been passed down from her grandfather through her father's estate.

2

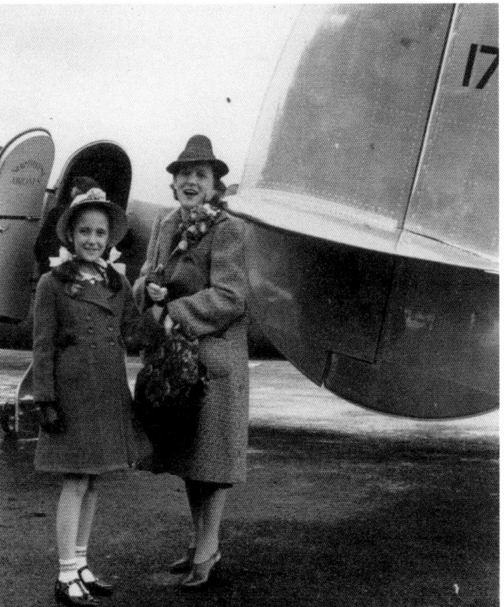

3

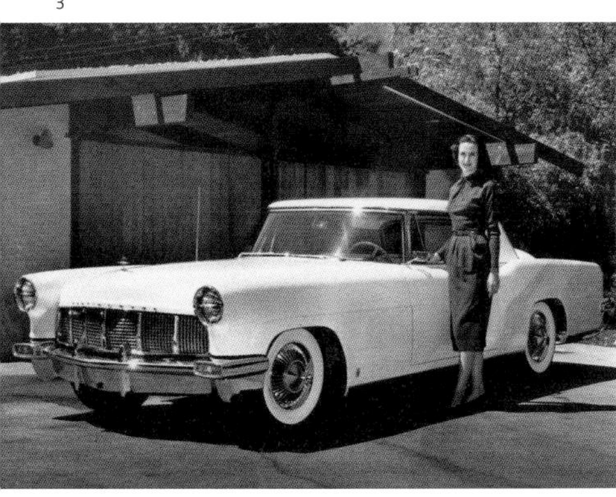

4

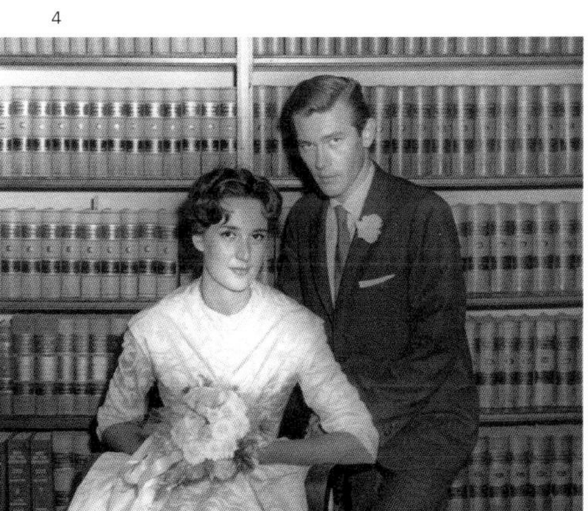

1953

Dwan's marriage to Fischer comes to an end. She travels to Europe for the first time, exploring London, Paris, Denmark, Germany, and Italy. She also travels to New York and visits the Museum of Modern Art. She is drawn to sculptures by Gaston Lachaise, Wilhelm Lehmbruck, and Pablo Picasso, and to paintings by Henri Rousseau. Upon her return, Dwan and Candace settle in Mandeville Canyon in the Brentwood neighborhood of Los Angeles. With one year of college left, she transfers to the University of Southern California and enrolls in philosophy courses. Her interest in psychology grows, and her favorite class is on nerve net theory.

1954–1956

Dwan begins visiting Frank Perls Gallery in Los Angeles, a gallery representing artists such as Jean Dubuffet, Conrad Marca-Relli, and California figurative artist William Brice. She speaks with Perls about what is involved in owning a gallery and helps him from time to time as receptionist at the gallery on Saturdays.

During this time Dwan is exposed to the art scene in California. She becomes friendly with artists Ed Moses, whom she meets at UCLA, and Craig Kauffman, who keeps a studio there. She also meets curator and gallerist Walter Hopps.

1957

April Ferus Gallery, founded by artist Edward Kienholz and Walter Hopps, opens on North La Cienega Boulevard. Kienholz assists with the construction of the gallery and keeps a studio space in the back while Hopps oversees gallery business. Ferus becomes well known for showing a stable of California avant-garde artists including Moses, Kauffman, Billy Al Bengston, Wallace Berman, and Jay DeFeo. Kauffman brings Dwan to Ferus Gallery, where she is introduced to Kienholz. They quickly become friends.[4]

1958

Kienholz sells his share in Ferus Gallery to Hopps. Irving Blum joins Hopps as a partner, and the gallery moves to a new location across the street.

August Dwan marries Vadim Philippe Kondratief, a French medical student at UCLA, whom she first met in 1956. Dwan and Kondratief move to 77 Malibu Colony Drive, a house by the beach. A guesthouse is part of the Malibu property. Later Dwan will host many gallery artists and visitors during their stay in Los Angeles. Eventually another guesthouse is converted into a studio for the artists to use during their visits. Dwan also keeps a second home on Malibu Road.

Dwan Gallery Los Angeles

1959

Dwan expresses interest in opening a gallery. Her husband encourages this idea and helps her locate a space. She chooses the Westwood Village neighborhood near the UCLA campus partly so she can be nearby while Kondratief is in school. At the time, she doesn't feel the need to be near La Cienega Boulevard, where most other galleries are located. However, the Westwood location is far enough away from the "tour of galleries" to pose a disadvantage.

September Dwan Gallery opens in a storefront in a Mission-style building at 1091 Broxton Avenue. To get things started Dwan borrows a few of the early shows, including Shim Grudin and Jean Rigaud, from Vera Lazuk Gallery in Cold Spring Harbor, New York. Lazuk is Dwan's mother-in-law; Dwan's sister-in-law, Eugenie Thompson, is brought on as codirector.

Dwan enlists Kienholz to help with crating and installations. Matsumi Kanemitsu, one of the first artists to show at the gallery, introduces Dwan to artist Larry Rivers. Dwan and Thompson begin making alternate trips to New York City to scout for work, arrange shows, and visit studios. Rivers subsequently connects Dwan to the New York School artists, especially during their frequent visits to the Cedar Bar.[5]

Dwan's initial shows are often cosigned exhibitions from New York galleries including Leo Castelli, Stephen Radich, Sidney Janis, and subsequently Green Gallery. Although the artists already have gallery representation, Dwan often works with them directly to organize the shows for Dwan Gallery, providing many of these artists with their first shows on the West Coast. As part of gallery policy, out-of-town artists are brought to Los Angeles in conjunction with their exhibitions. Dwan takes pleasure in the experience of spending time with these artists and enjoys the dinner conversations and the adventures they have together. She rents studio space, two blocks from the ocean in Santa Monica, for artists to use during their visits. Reflecting back on the gallery's beginnings, Dwan stated in 1963:

1959 EXHIBITIONS (DGLA)

September (17)–October 19
Shim Grudin

October 19–November 16
Stanley Twardowicz

November (18)–December (14)
Jean Rigaud

December 7–January 4, 1960
Group Show: Prints

1960 EXHIBITIONS (DGLA)

January 9–February 4
Matsumi Kanemitsu

February 9–March 5
Reginald Pollack: Recent Paintings

March 8–April 2
Friedel Dzubas

April 5–30
Paul Brach

May 2–28
Robert Goodnough

May 31–June 25
Seymour Boardman: Paintings

June 27–July 23
Harry Nadler

October 10–November 15
15 of New York

November 14–December 10
Robert Richenburg

December 12–31
Drawings, Watercolors, Collages

Due to the gallery's heavy leanings on the talents from New York and Paris, it was first met with a certain resistance from those who were entrenched in the largely nonfigurative paintings of a specific few from Los Angeles. "Who needs New York anyway?" may be said to have been the attitude among this group. About a year later, however, New York artists were found to be more and more in evidence in the other [Los Angeles] galleries as well. Now, *younger* artists are being represented in Los Angeles from the United States, Canada, South America, Poland, Israel, France, Germany, Italy, and England.[6]

October/November Stanley Twardowicz show at Dwan Gallery features paintings and watercolors by this abstract expressionist artist originally from the Midwest.

November 28 Dwan and Kondratief travel to New York and visit Stephen Radich Gallery at 818 Madison Avenue, where they meet with Radich and view works by his cadre of artists.[7]

December/January 1960 Dwan Gallery group show focuses on contemporary prints by a wide variety of European artists.

1960

Artist Walter De Maria moves to New York City from California.

January/February Matsumi Kanemitsu, a Japanese American artist who lives in New York and is closely associated with the abstract expressionists, travels to Los Angeles to attend the opening of his exhibition at the Dwan Gallery. He is well versed in sumi ink drawing, lithography, painting, and watercolor, which are reflected in the range of works on view. Following his visit, his New York dealer, Stephen Radich, writes to Thompson:

Matsumi was full of exciting reports and praise for the Dwan Gallery. . . . I was delighted to hear how well his show is going and to learn that you are all pleased with the exhibition and its results. He tells me that you have fine exhibition space and that the gallery is very beautiful. Most of all, he was happy because of your enthusiasm and interest in the gallery and the artists you plan to show.[8]

February Artist Ad Reinhardt visits Dwan in Los Angeles. After returning to New York, he writes Thompson, "I got on the five o'clock plane from warm, sunless California and got off in four degrees sunny New York."[9]

February/March Reginald Pollack, a New York artist based in Paris, shows small, colorful recent paintings, charcoal and pastel drawings, and lithographs at the Westwood gallery.

February 25 Dwan Gallery serves as a meeting space for "Looking at Modern Paintings," a discussion program organized by UCLA. The group meets consecutive Thursdays from 8 to 10 p.m. Dwan continually provides a location for classes of this type during 1960 and 1961.

March/April Friedel Dzubas, a German-born New York abstractionist, presents fourteen lyrical and vibrantly colored paintings at Dwan Gallery.

April Abstract painter Paul Brach and his wife, Mimi, travel from New York to Los Angeles for the opening at Dwan Gallery of his first West Coast show.

May Dwan Gallery presents the work of Robert Goodnough, a New York abstract expressionist, in collaboration with his New York gallery, Tibor de Nagy. A small catalog is produced for the exhibition. The artist is unable to attend the opening, but the show proves to be the "most successful" exhibition of the year for Dwan Gallery.[10]

May/June Richly colored canvases and drawings of Seymour Boardman, a New York abstract expressionist who had his first solo show at Martha Jackson Gallery in 1955, are shown at Dwan Gallery by arrangement with his current dealer, Stephen Radich.

June/July Harry Nadler, a California native who had recently taught at UCLA, presents a range of oils, pastels, and drawings influenced by the abstract painter Arshile Gorky. This is Nadler's second solo show; the first was held eighteen months earlier in Los Angeles. Nadler receives a Fulbright and departs for Spain in late summer.

Summer Dwan and Kondratief travel to Europe and attend the Venice Biennale, where Franz Kline wins the Italian Ministry of Public Instruction Prize.[11] Dwan visits many artists' studios including Man Ray's, where she hopes to buy a single "rayograph." In the coming years, Dwan will spend many summers in Europe. Several years later she buys a house, the Chateau Barlow, in the South of France.

July 1 Kienholz signs a contract to be represented by Dwan Gallery. Dwan admits:

Kienholz took a long time for me. I found myself feeling [besieged] by his work when I first came in contact with it. I like the person very much, but I didn't know if I could stand to be around the work that much, because it was very strong and it is very aggressive, and it's very painful at times. I really hesitated for quite a while about his work, whether I wanted to be the person to have it around me in the gallery, because after all, a dealer sits with the work every day, Sundays excluded, for a

DWAN AND DAUGHTER CANDACE AT HOME IN MALIBU, MARCH 1959 (5)

EXTERIOR OF FIRST DWAN GALLERY, BROXTON AVENUE, WESTWOOD, 1961 (6)

5

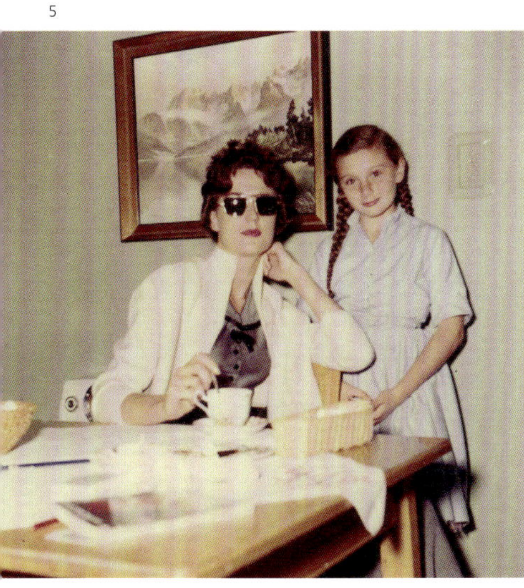

6

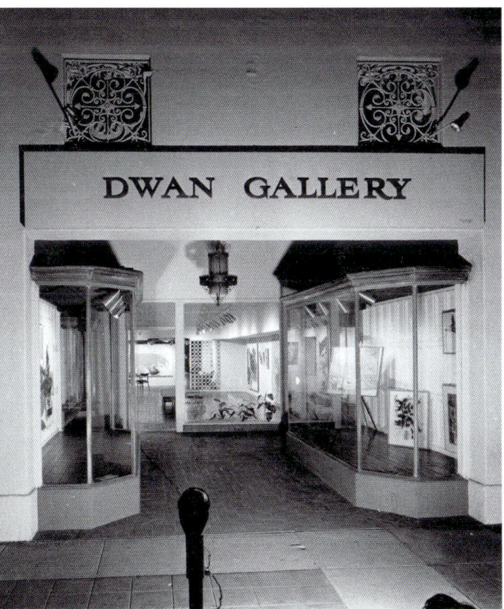

month or more, and the impact is enormous! As time went on I began to feel a certain connection with his work, which always had an edge of fear, but it also had an attraction that was very important for me.[12]

September Dwan visits New York and attends an opening at Stephen Radich Gallery.[13]

October Richard Bellamy opens Green Gallery in New York City with financial support from Robert Scull, a New York–based art collector and taxi magnate.

October/November *15 of New York*, an exhibition at Dwan Gallery of New York School painting, is a "great success."[14] Attendance is high and the entire art department from UCLA views the show. Raymond Parker's *Untitled* (1960) is sold the day of the opening. "It could have been sold six times over," according to Thompson.[15]

October 27 The nouveaux réalistes, a group that includes Yves Klein, Arman, Jean Tinguely, and Martial Raysse, sign a written declaration at Klein's residence at 14 rue Campagne-Première in Paris. Niki de Saint Phalle joins the group in 1961.

November An exhibition of Yves Klein's works, *Yves Klein le Monochrome*, is on view at Galerie Rive Droite, Paris. While in Paris, Dwan walks by the gallery on rue du Faubourg Saint-Honoré and is mesmerized by one of the sponge reliefs in the window. She arranges for a show of Klein's works to be shipped to Los Angeles.

Dwan meets with Larry Rivers in New York City to review works for his upcoming show.

November 8 John F. Kennedy is elected the thirty-fifth President of the United States of America.

November/December Robert Richenburg show at Dwan is arranged with the artist and his New York gallery, Tibor de Nagy. A younger abstract expressionist painter and educator based in New York, Richenburg participated in the historic *9th Street Art Exhibition* (1951). Richenburg is unable to attend the opening. Thompson writes to the artist, "The show looks beautiful. It has changed the entire appearance of the gallery more than any other show that we have had so far." Unfortunately, there are no sales. Regarding the review in the *Los Angeles Times* by critic Henry J. Seldis, in which he calls Richenburg's enormous canvases "the work of a truly ingenious decorator, if one may be allowed to use this word in an affirmative way," Thompson writes to Richenburg:

Both Virginia and I feel that this particular reviewer has reached an all-time low in his level of criticism. To say that your paintings are purely decorative even in the best sense of the word seems to me to be missing the point entirely. However, just between us, Henry Seldis's opinions are completely disregarded in Los Angeles by painters, collectors, dealers, etc.[16]

December Dwan Gallery presents a selection of abstract drawings, watercolors, and collages from East and West Coast artists including Peter Agostini, Norman Bluhm, Boardman, Goodnough, Paul Jenkins, Kanemitsu, Kline, Nadler, Richenburg, and Richards Ruben.

1961

January For Twardowicz's second exhibition at the gallery, he showcases canvases laden with molten surfaces rendered in bright colors to deep blacks. He attends "a very successful opening—great crowd, a lot of L.A. painters, collectors, museum people, etc."[17] A poster is made for the exhibition.

February "Los Angeles Letter" by art critic Jules Langsner debuts in *Art International* magazine, drawing attention to the art scene in Southern California.

February 5 Larry Rivers and his girlfriend, Clarice Price, attend the opening of his exhibition at the Dwan Gallery. They had driven cross-country from New York to Los Angeles for the event. This show marks the first time his work is shown in California. Rivers designs an announcement for the show and also decorates the storefront windows, covering them with paint. A private cocktail reception is held in the afternoon. Celebrities such as Hedy Lamarr are photographed walking through the show with Dwan and Rivers. As Rivers later recalled, "Virginia helped me widen my audience to West Coast critics, collectors, and viewers who thought N.Y. could come to L.A."[18]

February 12 Niki de Saint Phalle enacts her first *tir* (an art event at which she uses a rifle to shoot a relief she has made that contains concealed bags of paint) at the Impasse Ronsin in Paris.[19]

March Kanemitsu visits Los Angeles and is treated "with great fanfare and a cocktail party." Dwan and Thompson travel to New York and visit Kootz Gallery to select works for the upcoming Raymond Parker show.[20] Dwan also visits Philip Guston's studio in anticipation of his exhibition at the gallery.[21]

1961 EXHIBITIONS (DGLA)

January 9–February 4
Stanley Twardowicz

February 6–March 4
Larry Rivers

March 6–April 1
Stephen Pace

April 3–29
Philip Guston, Franz Kline

May 1–27
Raymond Parker

May 29–June 24
Yves Klein–le Monochrome

June 26–July 22
Salvatore Scarpitta

September 18–October 14
Joan Mitchell

October 16–November 11
Six Sculptors

November 13–December 9
Matsumi Kanemitsu

December 11–January 6, 1962
Group Show

7

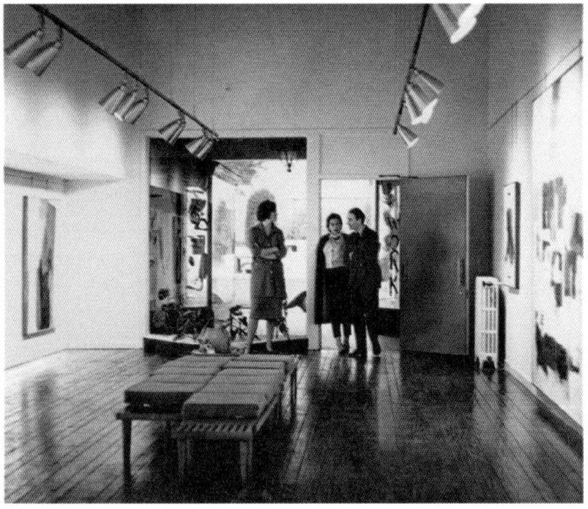

March/April Stephen Pace, a second-generation abstract expressionist, shows a range of oils and watercolors at Dwan Gallery. The exhibition is arranged through his New York dealer, Howard Wise Gallery.

April A Dwan Gallery exhibition combines paintings and works on paper by Kline and Guston. The paintings by each artist are hung on opposing walls of the gallery. Guston and his wife travel to Los Angeles for the show and stay with Dwan. Kline does not attend. Thompson reports afterward, "Although the Guston-Kline show was extremely well-attended and had good reviews on the whole, we were not even able to sell one small Guston."[22] Reflecting on the show, Dwan observes:

> I would not perhaps have chose[n] to have a Kline and Guston show; I would have preferred to have an all-Kline and an all-Guston show. It was because the works were not available that I decided to put them together. As it turned out, I was blissfully innocent of the fact that they were not getting along at that point socially, and I asked Philip Guston, who was the one that I knew better of the two, after my visit to his studio if he would take me over to Franz Kline's and we would discuss a joint show together. We had a charming evening at Franz Kline's and after Philip and I left, he said, "You didn't realize it, but that was the first time that Franz and I [have] spoken for some months."[23]

April 11 An exhibition of paintings by Rivers opens at the Santa Barbara Museum of Art, courtesy of Dwan Gallery.

April 11–29 The first exhibition of Klein's work in the United States, *Yves Klein le Monochrome*, takes place at Leo Castelli Gallery in New York. This show features only the artist's monochrome "blue" paintings. Klein and his fiancée, Rotraut Uecker, stay at the Chelsea Hotel where he writes "The Chelsea Hotel Manifesto," a reaction to the generally negative response of New York critics to the Castelli show.

May The Raymond Parker show features canvases filled with large, floating shapes in bright hues. It is arranged with Parker's New York dealer, Samuel M. Kootz. The gallery sells several works and the artist is pleased with the hanging of his paintings.[24] Dwan writes to the artist, "The interest continues—some eulogistic, some indignant, all on a highly emotional level."[25] Dwan travels to New York to visit artists' studios.

May/June The Yves Klein show at Dwan differs from Castelli's all-blue monochrome show of April 1961 in that it includes a wider range of Klein's work: blue, rose, and gold paintings; sponge reliefs and sculptures; a *pluie* (rain) sculpture; Anthropometries; and obelisks. The gallery holds a private viewing of Klein's films including a film documenting Klein's March 9, 1960, performance in Paris, *Anthropometries of the Blue Period*, held at the International Gallery of Contemporary Art, in which female nudes cover themselves in blue paint, pressing their bodies onto paper to create prints while Klein's *Monotone Symphony* is performed.

Klein makes Dwan a set of identically sized paintings, a blue, a red, and a gold one.[26] Recalling her connection to Klein's work, Dwan stated, "This was something that had a kind of hyper-reality to it. The works had an energy that was undeniable and really pulled me in and absorbed me in their intensity."[27]

Klein had traveled to Los Angeles with Rotraut earlier in the month in preparation for the Dwan exhibition. They visited Disneyland and explored the coast in Dwan and Kondratief's white convertible. Klein made sponge relief paintings and sculptures on the beach in Malibu. He met Kienholz, Hopps, and other artworld figures while in Los Angeles. Recollecting his time with Klein, Kienholz observed,

> I really loved that man — that kid, at that time.... Yves came, and we just hit it off very well. Virginia entertained Yves. She had an extra house in Malibu, so Yves and Rotraut stayed there. Or we'd go fishing. They'd fish in a boat and have it come up from San Diego. The boat would show up, and we'd all get up early in the morning and go fishing out in the ocean for halibut or something. Just interesting things to do. And Yves got seasick, as I remember.[28]

June 20 Saint Phalle, Tinguely, Rauschenberg, and Jasper Johns collaborate on a performance of John Cage's *Variations II* led by David Tudor on piano at the Théâtre de l'Ambassade des États-Unis, Paris.

June/July Dwan arranges a show of constructions by Salvatore Scarpitta, an Italian American artist living in New York, through his dealer, Leo Castelli. Scarpitta works with folded and painted canvases to construct reliefs that straddle the line between painting and sculpture. A poster is published in conjunction with the show.

DWAN WITH HEDY LAMARR AND LARRY RIVERS DURING HIS 1961 EXHIBITION (7)

DWAN AT HER HOME IN THE SOUTH OF FRANCE, 1961 (8)

WILLEM DE KOONING, LISA DE KOONING, RIVERS, AND DWAN AT RIVERS'S SOUTHAMPTON HOME, SEPTEMBER 1961 (9)

8

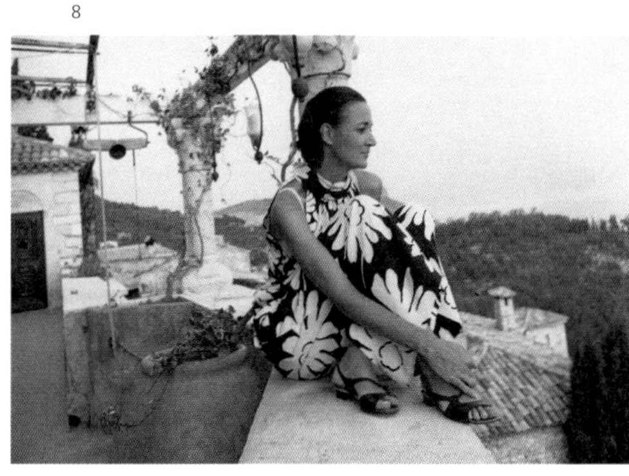

9

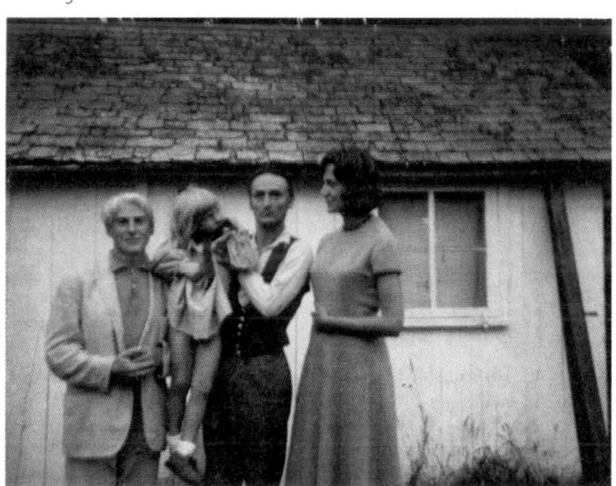

Summer Dwan and Kondratief travel to France. Klein introduces her to Arman while she is in Nice, and she visits his studio. Arman in turn introduces Dwan to Raysse.[29] She travels to New York after returning from France.

July 20 Kienholz and Klein confer about Klein's *Zone of Immaterial Pictorial Sensibility*, a conceptual work in which Klein sells a collector (in this case Kienholz) "an immaterial zone" (i.e., empty space). Klein then presents the collector with a receipt for this purchase and exchanges the purchase price for gold ingots, which are then tossed into the Seine while onlookers witness the action. The collector then burns the receipt, leaving no record of the completed transaction. On this occasion, Kienholz informs Klein that he has burned his receipt for one of Klein's works (slightly out of sequence) and that Klein can now proceed with throwing away the gold. Klein's untimely death in 1962 prevents him from doing so. However, Rotraut and Arman complete the work at a later date for Kienholz.[30]

August The Berlin Wall is erected.

September Dwan spends an evening in Southampton, New York, with de Kooning, his daughter, Lisa, Joan Ward, and Rivers and his girlfriend, Clarice Price.[31]

September/October Joan Mitchell, an abstract expressionist, makes her Los Angeles debut with vibrant, gestural paintings ranging from 1956 to 1961. Dwan Gallery arranges the show through the Stable Gallery in New York. The show is well received. However, as of the closing date, no works have sold, even though "most of the important collectors in town came to see it as well as all the painters."[32] Jules Langsner in his November "Los Angeles Letter" praises the "Dwan Gallery program of bringing the works of advance guard New York and Paris artists to Los Angeles" and says this "has made the gallery a pivotal center of the art community here, enabling painters, sculptors, and collectors to keep in direct touch with current innovations."[33]

October/November Dwan presents a group show of sculptures by Peter Agostini, Lee Bontecou, César, John Chamberlain, Edward Higgins, and Louise Nevelson. A folded announcement card is published for the show.

November/December Kanemitsu's second show at the gallery demonstrates his skill in a range of mediums—paintings, watercolors, and sumi ink drawings. A poster is created for the show.

1962

Art historian George Kubler publishes *The Shape of Time: Remarks on the History of Things*, a book that will influence a generation of artists including Robert Morris, Ad Reinhardt, and Robert Smithson.

Kienholz moves into the back of the Dwan Gallery, where he installs a Murphy bed and a sink. During his stay he constructs *The Illegal Operation*.[34] In exchange for rent, he sets up and organizes the storage room.

January/February Goodnough's second show at Dwan Gallery features dynamic canvases, collages, and lithographs. A small catalog is published with an introduction by critic B.H. Friedman.

January 21 Yves Klein and Rotraut Uecker are married at the Saint-Nicolas-des-Champs church in Paris. The wedding celebration continues at Rivers's Paris studio.

January 31 Reinhardt arrives in California in preparation for the opening of his show at Dwan Gallery. He gives a talk, "The Artist as Artist," at the Pasadena Art Museum on February 2 and another to students at Chouinard Art Institute on February 6.

February Tinguely and Saint Phalle travel to California in preparation for his show at Everett Ellin Gallery. They view Simon Rodia's *Watts Towers*.[35]

February/March Reinhardt's first exhibition at Dwan includes fourteen black paintings with some measuring as tall as nine feet. Though the exhibition is much admired, no works sell. However, Dwan purchases *Abstract Painting (A)* (1954) the following October for her own collection.[36] Dwan recalled:

> And again, for me the experience of a Reinhardt painting has always been of a spiritual nature, very profoundly so. As iconoclastic as he was in some ways, and I suppose he was sort of difficult — I liked him very much; actually we got along quite well. I felt the impact of his personality and his attitudes and his integrity tremendously.[37]

February 10 Dwan witnesses Klein's "transfer" of the *Zone of Immaterial Pictorial Sensibility* to Los Angeles art collectors Michael and Dorothy Blankfort, which takes place at the Pont au Double in Paris. François Mathey, head curator at the Musée des Arts Décoratifs, also views the ritual.

1962 EXHIBITIONS (DGLA)

January 7–February 3
Robert Goodnough

February 4–March 3
Ad Reinhardt

March 4–31
Robert Rauschenberg

April 1–28
William Waldren

May 13–June 9
Arman

June 11–July 7
Group Show

July 9–28
Harry Nadler

September 7–October (5)
Group Show

October 7–November (3)
Raymond Parker

November 18–December 15
My Country 'Tis of Thee

December 16–January 4, 1963
Matsumi Kanemitsu: Recent Paintings

Late February Rauschenberg travels to Los Angeles in advance of his exhibition at Dwan Gallery. He arrives in a Volkswagen bus with the Merce Cunningham Dance Troupe. Rauschenberg helps install his works at the gallery and stays with Dwan in Malibu. Cunningham performs concerts at UCLA for which Rauschenberg designs the costumes. Dwan rents her other house in Malibu to Cunningham's entire troupe, including composer John Cage.[38] A collaborative weekend event is planned by Dwan, Blum, and Ellin that was to have featured David Tudor playing Cage's *Variations II* for thirty-six hours while original works of art were created on stage by Saint Phalle, Rauschenberg, and Tinguely, but the event is never realized.[39] Dwan also conceives of a project wherein a large billboard will be rented on Sunset Strip for three weeks, giving each of three artists—Kienholz, Rauschenberg, Tinguely—a chance to design the billboard as he sees fit for a week before turning it over to the next artist. The idea is unfortunately passed over.

March 4–7 Simultaneous openings occur of Rauschenberg at Dwan Gallery, Tinguely at Everett Ellin Gallery, and Kienholz at Ferus Gallery, where he debuts his *Roxys* tableau. In the week before the openings, Saint Phalle, with assistance from Tinguely and Kienholz, constructs a twelve-by-eighteen-foot wall covered with ladders, mannequins, bras, bottles, and cans, all sprayed a uniform white. Various hidden containers are filled with paint, allowing Saint Phalle to present her first American *tir* (shooting). It takes place on March 4 at 4:30 p.m. in a parking lot behind the Club Renaissance on Sunset Strip. Saint Phalle dons her trademark white suit for the event, which was reported in the *Beverly Hills Times* and the *Los Angeles Times*.[40] Kienholz describes this vibrant time:

> Virginia Dwan also was responsible for the whole influence of Europeans into the West Coast. . . . [T]here was Tinguely and Arman and Martial Raysse and César, Niki de Saint Phalle — all those people are [known in Los Angeles] because of Virginia Dwan. . . . [S]he brought a whole cultural dimension to Los Angeles that no one else did. . . . She was meeting people in France, in Paris, and then arrang[ing] to bring them out here. . . .[T]heir destination was Los Angeles because of Virginia. And she did a lot to change the complexion of art.[41]

March Dwan's Rauschenberg show features ten combines and drawings. No works sell at the time of the show. *First Landing Jump* is sent out on consignment but is shipped back to Leo Castelli Gallery when a buyer can't be found. Soon after, Philip Johnson buys the work and donates it to the Museum of Modern Art.

March 21 Tinguely, with the assistance of Saint Phalle, hosts a happening in the Nevada desert, *Study for the End of the World Number 2*. NBC cameras film the event for "David Brinkley's Journal."

Late March Dwan hosts a *tir* by Saint Phalle in the hills above Malibu. Kienholz and Tinguely assist. The audience of cinema and art personalities includes director John Houseman, actress Jane Fonda, model Peggy Moffitt, and curator Henry Geldzahler. The large painting made by Saint Phalle and an attached cannon made by Tinguely are installed by Dwan's pool. Later that evening, Tinguely shoots the cannon into the ocean.

Dwan hosts many events including a lobster-and-steak brunch and parties that are attended by Cunningham, Guston, Nevelson, the collectors Betty and Leonard Asher, curator James Elliott, and critic Jules Langsner among others. Shortly after, Dwan, Kondratief, Tinguely, and Saint Phalle travel to Cabo San Lucas in Mexico for a fishing trip.

Dwan travels to New York and Milan.

April William Waldren, a New York–born painter and sculptor who resides on the Spanish island of Majorca, shows at Dwan Gallery: included are sculptures and reliefs composed of polyester, sand, and plaster. In subsequent years he becomes well known as an archaeologist.

May The Philip Guston retrospective opens at the Solomon R. Guggenheim Museum in New York and travels to Los Angeles the following year. Dwan lends *The Room*, *Sleeper II*, *Traveler II*, and *Garden of M*. She attends the opening and meets poet Frank O'Hara for the first time at the after-party.[42]

Dwan Gallery moves to 10846 Lindbrook Drive in Westwood Village. Formerly the home of an art supply store, the new space is designed by Dwan and architect Morris Verger to operate expressly as a gallery. As Dwan explained:

DWAN WITNESSING YVES KLEIN'S "TRANSFER" FOR THE *ZONE OF IMMATERIAL PICTORIAL SENSIBILITY*, PONT AU DOUBLE, PARIS, FEBRUARY 10, 1962 (10)

NIKI DE SAINT PHALLE AND EDWARD KIENHOLZ EXAMINE SAINT PHALLE'S *TIR* IN THE HILLS ABOVE MALIBU, SPRING 1962 (11)

10

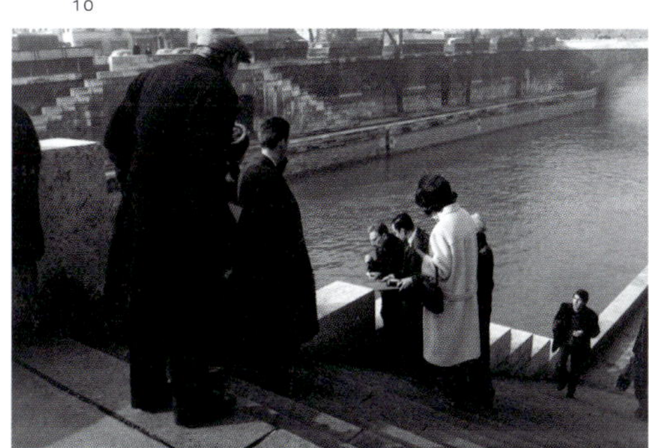

11

> [T]he space was inspired to a large extent by the V. C. Morris [Gift Shop] in San Francisco by Frank Lloyd Wright. I had a fondness for very wide arches at that time, and the new building had a wonderful sort of facade with no detailing on it, just a very broad arch in a kind of tunnel effect as you came in to separate you from the street, which was a very interesting idea on the architect's part— to give a sense of setting aside one's rush-rush attitudes from the street and then go into this lit space.

The gallery has white walls and lighting hidden behind soffits. There is no natural light and off-white marble aggregate is installed on the floor below the walls to reflect light back onto the paintings. The rest of the floors are wood. The height of the walls is determined with Reinhardt's works in mind, as Dwan wants to be able to display rectangular works and uses her 108-inch-tall Reinhardt as her "Golden Mean... for what the height of the walls would be." Describing the feeling she hoped the space would conjure, Dwan recalled:

> I know in designing the space I discovered that I really wanted a certain separation between myself and the public. I needed an inner sanctum. We definitely needed a private viewing space, again, to make that sense of separation; and also the main gallery space was separated from the street by a tunnel-like entrance. It wasn't all that deep, but it gave one a sense of walking from the busyness of Westwood Village... and UCLA through a passage-way and into a nice, open, lighted space which was very different from the outside world. For one thing it had a kind of quietness, I think, that I really liked, that I suppose I sought out.... the beginning of a sense of almost sacredness that the viewer, in coming in to look at art, should in my mind feel that this was to be approached with a different part of himself than the rest of his day-to-day living.[43]

Though Dwan is delighted with the new space, "it cost us a tremendous amount and we have had to cut down on a number of things already in order to get back on a more even keel."[44] Henry Seldis calls the new quarters "undoubtedly... the most strikingly handsome art emporium in town."[45] The gallery is featured in "Rebuilding Three Galleries" in the March 1964 issue of *Architectural Forum*.

May/June The new gallery space debuts with the opening of the Arman exhibit. The artist arrives in Los Angeles on April 18 in advance of his show.[46] Writing to Rivers, Dwan states, "We had great fun too with Arman, scrapping all the time. His show looked terrific and was not unsuccessful considering that he was almost completely unknown here."[47] While in Los Angeles, Kienholz helps Arman find materials for his "accumulations." Kienholz describes these adventures:

> Arman... was obsessed with accumulations. When he had his show at Dwan, he wrote ahead and asked for boxes to be made for him, so many centimeters by so many centimeters, and Virginia called me and said would I please come and make some boxes? Which I did. And they're probably the better boxes that I've ever seen Arman's pieces in, frankly, because the stuff that I've seen him put together [is] not very accurate, not very good.... So then he wanted help in finding stuff. We went out.... to Goodwill, for instance, and there would be a box with old shoes in it. So he'd buy sixteen pairs of shoes and throw half of them away. He'd have an accumulation of women's shoes, and [he'd] stuff them in the box and put the Plexiglas on them, paint it black, and that was it. Or toy pistols. But it was a real thing with him. He saw [this] in terms of accumulations of objects. I remember he saw a Puritas truck go by, and there were all the bottles of water waiting for the customer someplace, and in very pidgin, broken English, he says, "Oh, she's so beautiful, so terrific!" Because it was the heads of the bottles in a rack, all together, all the same that he liked. He was always, in my mind, a kind of an unfinished being.[48]

During the opening, guests and bartenders are encouraged to throw trash into one of Arman's *poubelles* (trash cans). By the end of the evening it is almost three-quarters full of trash including champagne bottles and announcements. Arman leaves the *poubelle* at the gallery and by the end of the exhibition the piece is complete. He titles the work *Cast Your Ballot Here for a Cleaner Dwan Gallery*.[49]

May 13 Franz Kline passes away at fifty-one of rheumatic heart disease. The funeral service is held on May 16. In a letter to Rivers, Dwan expresses her feelings upon hearing the news:

> I suppose that by the time this reaches you, you will have heard about the death of Franz Kline. Mike Kanemitsu called m[e] yesterday to tell me of it, and things just haven't looked the same since. Even the skies here have seemed to be in mourning— gray and with cold and miserable tears. I never really knew him well and yet I was terribly fond of him. Some girls just came giggling in the door so I shushed them and tried to drop them in their tracks with a stare. Now they're whispering to each other and tiptoeing around. Sometimes I feel like telling people that this is really a museum and that I wouldn't sell anything, even if they paid me.[50]

DWAN GALLERY'S SECOND LOCATION, LINDBROOK DRIVE; PREPARING FOR *JEAN TINGUELY*, MAY 1963 (12)

POOLSIDE PARTY AT DWAN'S HOME IN MALIBU, SPRING 1962 (PAINTING BY SAINT PHALLE INSTALLED IN BACKGROUND) (13)

MY COUNTRY 'TIS OF THEE INSTALLED AT DWAN GALLERY, NOVEMBER 1962 (14)

12

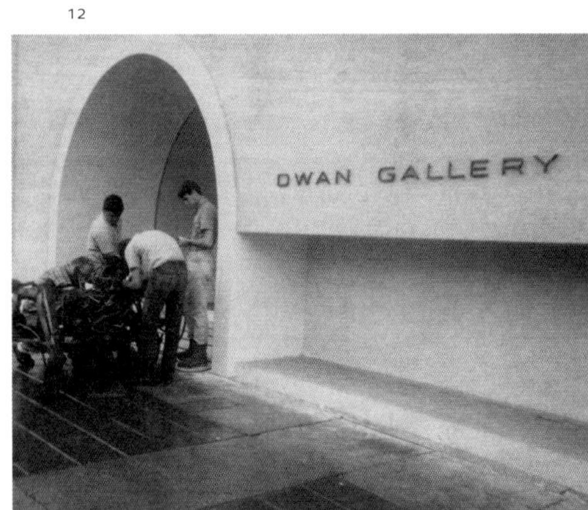

June The first issue of *Artforum*, founded by John P. Irwin Jr., is published in San Francisco. It will relocate to Los Angeles in 1965 and then to New York in 1967.

June 6 Yves Klein passes away at his home in Paris after suffering two heart attacks the previous month. He is thirty-four years old. Dwan had recently purchased a relief and two blue monochromes from the artist. She learns that Klein was celebrating the arrival of her check the night he died. A thank-you note from him arrives shortly after his death.[51] Dwan Gallery had been planning another one-man show of his work for May of 1963. Klein was to come to Los Angeles and create many of the pieces on site.[52] Dwan writes to Rivers, "The news of Yves' death really jolted us all. He was such a sweet person and would probably have figured as one of the great talents had he been able to go on."[53]

June/July A group show includes paintings, sculptures, and drawings by Bontecou, de Kooning, Guston, Kanemitsu, Klein, Kline, Joan Miró, Robert Motherwell, Parker, Jackson Pollock, Tinguely, and Waldren.

June 16 The Venice Biennale opens and Dwan plans a party in celebration at her house in France.[54] In the wake of the 1962 stock-market crash, Dwan cancels the party as well as her trip to the biennale.[55]

July 9 Andy Warhol's first commercial show featuring his *Campbell's Soup Cans* opens at Ferus Gallery.

September/October Another group show at Dwan Gallery features paintings and sculpture by Josef Albers, Goodnough, Edward Higgins, Klein, Parker, Rauschenberg, Reinhardt, Rivers, Mark Rothko, and Tinguely.

September 25 *New Paintings of Common Objects*, an early group show of what becomes known as pop art curated by Hopps, opens at the Pasadena Art Museum.

September 27 Rachel Carson's *Silent Spring*, a book that discusses the ramifications of pesticides on the natural world, is published. Written for a popular audience, it ushers in the modern environmental movement.

October A full-scale nuclear war is averted during the Cuban Missile Crisis, a thirteen-day military and political standoff between the Soviet Union and the United States.

Dwan travels to France and stays through November.[56] She puts Raysse under contract for three years. She also completes a contract with Tinguely. This leads to the institution of a contract system with her American artists.

October/November Parker's second show at Dwan Gallery features canvases filled with amorphous, suspended shapes in radiant colors. The exhibition opens to mixed reviews and not one work sells. Dwan writes to the artist:

> People (collectors) are just too dumb for words. During your show they all came, said it was beautiful, picked one that they particularly liked, and left. And that was that. The artists, dealers, and teachers said that you were really "popping right along," or words to that effect. Still nothing sold. . . . So the people mumble and shuffle in, and I tell them about your being one of the truly great young artists of the time and they mumble and shuffle out again and sometimes I feel quite murderous.[57]

November John Weber starts working at Dwan Gallery, assisting Dwan.[58] He had previously worked as director at Martha Jackson Gallery in New York. In 1964 his title will change to director, a relatively new position in the gallery world. By the end of the year, Thompson has left the gallery.[59]

November/December Dwan Gallery presents *My Country 'Tis of Thee*, which is considered one of the earliest exhibitions of pop art in the United States. A catalog is published with an introduction by Gerald Nordland. Nordland describes the artists included in the show as the "new patriots of American art."[60] The gallery borrows works from Stable Gallery, Leo Castelli Gallery, and Green Gallery in New York; Ferus Gallery and Everett Ellin Gallery in Los Angeles; and private collectors including Ileana Sonnabend, David Hayes, and Mr. and Mrs. Burton Tremaine. In anticipation of the show, Dwan visits several studios including those of Robert Indiana, Roy Lichtenstein, Claes Oldenburg, Rivers, Warhol, and Tom Wesselmann. Weber is actively involved in installing the exhibition that Dwan has conceived. Dwan recalled the origins of the show:

> I had been around to a number of the studios of these new artists and found it an interesting phenomenon that so much of the material of pop art was — by definition — from the popular culture, and therefore American in imagery. I came up with the idea of just saying, Look, a lot of artists are doing this very taboo thing of using popular imagery, which had been considered . . . déclassé and really no[t] intellectual enough before, and everyone had looked toward Europe. Suddenly, there's this embracing of the very things which one was supposed to consider beneath them. . . . "My Country 'Tis of Thee" is, in retrospect, a slightly embarrassing title, but it was, at least, equally as pop-sounding as the imagery was in the exhibition. So I sought out the works of the pop artists in New York and some of the forerunners of pop art that best illustrated this.[61]

13

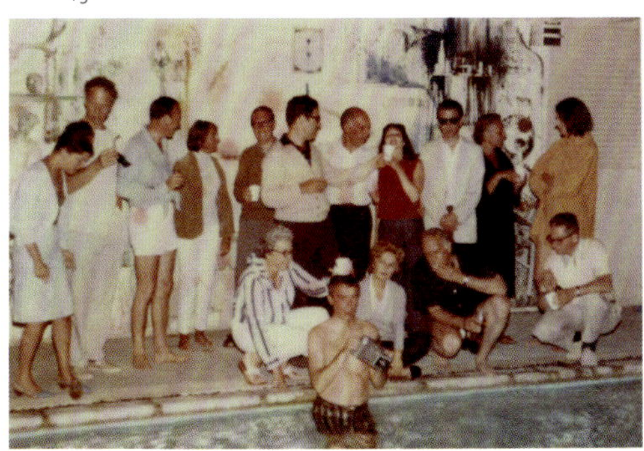

14

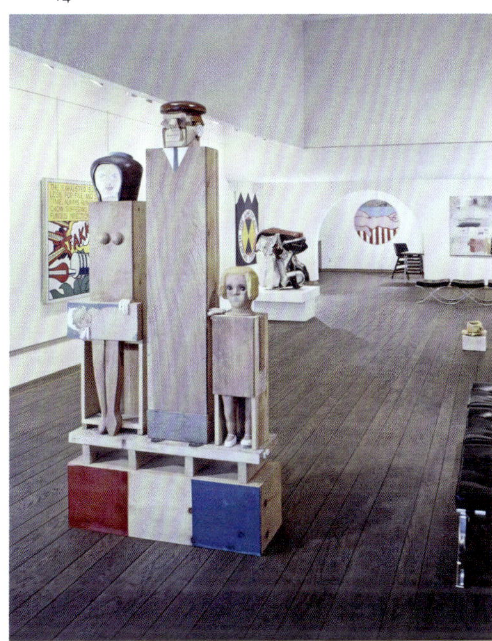

While the show was generally well received, Seldis's reviews drip with condescension. Most of the works sell, including Wesselmann's *Great American Nude #X* and Oldenburg's *Coffee Cup*. Writing to Richard Bellamy, director of the Green Gallery, after the exhibition, Weber avows, "What pleases us more than the actual sales is the directional image we have impressed upon the public."[62]

December 13 Pop art symposium at the Museum of Modern Art introduces the term to a larger art community.

December/January 1963 For Kanemitsu's third show at Dwan, he presents nine oil paintings and one sculpture completed in 1962.

December 20 Reinhardt publishes "Art-as-Art" in *Art International*.

Late December Dwan and Kondratief visit Rothko's studio in New York. Raysse travels from Nice, stopping first in New York for his show *Beach* at the Alexander Iolas Gallery. Klein's widow, Rotraut, and Raysse return to Los Angeles with Dwan and her husband.[63] Raysse's wife, France, joins them in California and they stay with Dwan. The couple makes a trip to Disneyland. They all spend Christmas together, joined by Kienholz. Tinguely also visits Los Angeles. After Rotraut's departure, she sends Dwan one of Klein's pink monochromes.[64] Describing the visit to Rivers, Dwan writes:

> Martial and his wife, France, are still with us but as the date of his exhibition approaches, we all become more sober and industrious. Up until recently, however, Jean was with us and Rotraut and twist records and swimming and house decorating for a big party and John Weber and a flurry of creation in the back of the storage room and Ed Kienholz and talk until the not-so-wee hours.[65]

Further recollecting the Christmas of 1962, Dwan observed, "[W]e just had a wonderful day that day. Such a group of individuals, you know, celebrating something so traditional in our own way, and it was very lovely, really special."[66]

Dwan becomes friendlier with the nouveaux réalistes and increasingly exhibits more pop art, moving away from showing abstract expressionism. Kanemitsu, one of the first artists she champions, expresses dismay in a series of letters. The painter voices his dissatisfaction with the direction he believes the gallery is taking:

> In the meantime, you have to give a big swimming party for your French clowns. . . . I think Yves Klein and Tinguely are the real ones. So are Jasper Johns, Rauschenberg, Bontecou and Jim Dine. Pop art is already on its way out of the NY scene. It hit like a storm, now it's heading for the Pacific. . . . I realize this, I become bitter toward this type of artist. I'll be frank with you, I guess you know to which [artists'] work I'm pointing. I particularly dislike Larry Rivers, Oldenburg, Lichtenstein, Indiana, Rosenquist, Raysse (especially), Arman, St. Phalle, and Warhol. I tried to correct my discrimination towards their work, so I socialized to find what kind of persons they are. Then I discovered that they're only interested in themselves not in their work.[67]

Dwan expresses her sentiment:

> Concerning my "French Clowns," if I were looking for entertainment I would be an agent for comedians, which would afford me much more pleasant communication than most of that I come in contact with. However, if you find the other people with whom I work so lacking in the seriousness that concerns you; if you feel that they do not know how to handle art; and if you feel that they enjoy the hostility and hardship for kicks unlike you whose work is blood and life, perhaps there has truly been a mistake on both of our parts in deciding to be associated.[68]

1963

January/February Raysse utilizes spray paint in synthetic, fluorescent colors and collage elements including paraphernalia such as sequins, sunglasses, and hand mirrors to create "strong and brilliant" paintings of beautiful women. The show features his first neon sculpture, inspired by his time spent in Los Angeles. An exhibition catalog is produced for the show, which opens to mixed reviews. Describing the show, Dwan writes:

> I am sure that this is the first time that neon has been used in a major work of sculpture and should start a whole *nouvelle vague* among the sculptors. Typical of Martial, he has kept it true to the commercial and glittering flavor of neon as it exists in signs and billboards. I am terribly happy to have the first of these pieces here.[69]

January 30 Dwan writes to Sidney Janis about the difficulties of selling Guston's work. Although he is one of the "truly great painters of our time," his paintings are difficult for collectors to understand. Yet Dwan is unwilling to sell Guston's major works to private individuals.

1963 EXHIBITIONS (DGLA)

January 6–February 2
Martial Raysse: Mirrors and Portraits, 1962

February 10–March 2
Dealer's Choice

March 3–30 (extended to April 13)
Franz Kline Memorial: Paintings, 1950–1961

April 15–May 11
Larry Rivers

May 13–June 8
Jean Tinguely

June 17–July 13
Edward Kienholz

October 1–26
Claes Oldenburg

October 27–November 23
Sven Lukin

November 24–December 28
Ad Reinhardt: Recent Square Paintings, 1960–1963

December 29–January 3, 1964
Group Show

I'm afraid that I could not, in good conscience, offer that particular painting [*The Room*] to a private individual. As I know you are aware, paintings from this "pink" period are extremely rare. For this reason I feel that it should eventually find its way into an important museum collection so that many people will be able to see and appreciate it.[70]

February Dwan is forced to cancel the Lee Bontecou show that she has been planning for two years with Leo Castelli Gallery in New York. The show is scheduled to open in February but Bontecou does not have enough recent work to show.[71]

February 5 Dwan attends the opening of Kienholz's *Roxys* at Alexander Iolas Gallery. This is Kienholz's first one-man show in New York, and Dwan helps arrange it. Kienholz has driven the work in a station wagon and trailer across the country with a friend, through bitter cold and blizzards.[72] In a letter to Rivers, Dwan writes that she plans to be in New York and would like to visit him with Kienholz.

If there is a trip or an orgy or something that conflicts please let me know stat. . . . Ed Kienholz will be opening at Iolas on Tues., the 5th, as you probably already know. Naturally I'm pretty excited about it. Make sure to plan to go. I expect a lot of New York artists' hostility to "foreign" artist type-thing. Anyway, his whore creatures that he calls the "Roxys" should rock N.Y. a bit.[73]

February 11 Dwan writes to Reinhardt:

Your paintings don't really seem to have much to do with hamburgers or dolls or comic strips but they do seem to have the kind of ageless quality that makes them just as contemporary as any of these. Do you really want to be a historic figure? Besides, neither do Klein, Parker, Rivers, or Bontecou have much to do with "junk-art."[74]

February/March Dwan presents a "dealer's choice" show, "a rollicking and antic affair"[75] that includes paintings and sculptures by Arman, Bontecou, Dine, Kienholz, Klein, Lichtenstein, Oldenburg, Parker, Rauschenberg, Raysse, Reinhardt, Rivers, Rosenquist, and Tinguely. An exhibition announcement is published advertising the show.

February 25 Dwan travels to San Francisco in preparation for the Raysse exhibition scheduled to open on March 27 at the de Young Museum and visits the Oakland Museum of Art to discuss a Tinguely show.[76]

March Oldenburg writes Weber that he has left Green Gallery and will do business independently from a Manhattan storefront on East Second Street that he names Ray Gun Manufacturing Company.[77]

Before departing for France, Dwan writes to Kanemitsu and severs ties with him:

[Y]our letters of the past few months have been amazingly hostile. With each new verbal onslaught on your part I found my sentiments toward you cooling more and more. You see, what you call "bathtub art" or "Clowns" I find myself squarely behind. I consider Martial Raysse to be one of the great young talents of our times. Naturally, therefore, I have found your comments most distasteful and I wonder at the reasons for their being made. One of the reasons . . . I prefer dealing with artists out of the Los Angeles area is just this kind of petty backbiting which goes on with such amazing persistenc[e] in New York and is bound to involve a dealer in the middle of the conflict. In light of all this, not because I am no longer interested in your work, I will, as you requested, return the works which do not belong to the gallery. Your report that it is rumored that Ed Kienholz and I are involved romantically strikes me as very humorous. I wonder how many times that circle has tried to link my name with one of my artists. You will hear from me again in about two to three weeks when I will have returned from Europe.[78]

March/April The Kline memorial exhibition at Dwan Gallery consists of works drawn from Southern California collections and is extended until April 13. It is accompanied by a catalog with an essay by Jules Langsner titled "Calligraphy and Information Theory: Franz Kline," also published in *Art International* in March 1963. Dwan recalled:

I was able to organize an exhibition of paintings of Kline's, who to me was a very important figure in American art at that point. They included paintings that I had in my private collection or in the Dwan Gallery collection, as well as some other paintings I was able to cull from local collectors. So actually it was the first major exhibition of Franz Kline's paintings (to my knowledge) to take place after his death; even before any museum retrospectives or any other gallery retrospectives on the East Coast. I must say, it was a really beautiful, major show.[79]

March 14 Landmark exhibition *Six Painters and the Object*, curated by Lawrence Alloway, opens at the Solomon R. Guggenheim Museum. The show features Rauschenberg, Dine, Johns, Lichtenstein, Rosenquist, and Warhol.

JEAN TINGUELY, *FOUNTAIN III*, INSTALLED AT THE HOME OF A LOS ANGELES COLLECTOR, SPRING 1963 (15)

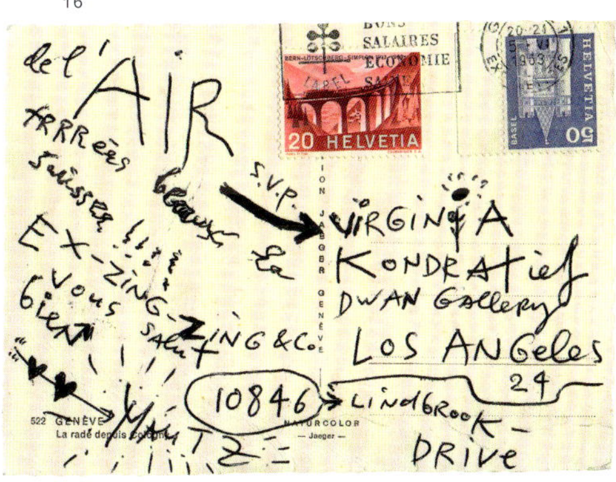

POSTCARD FROM TINGUELY TO DWAN, 1963 (16)

March 18 Dwan travels to Europe for approximately two weeks. She makes arrangements to visit postwar American art collector Count Giuseppe Panza in Milan, where she views his dining room full of Kline paintings.[80] On her way back, she stops in New York for five days.

Late March Dwan returns to California to find Tinguely, Saint Phalle, and Rivers and his wife, Clarice, in Los Angeles. Tinguely and Saint Phalle stay for well over two months, allowing the artists ample time to prepare for their openings later in the season. They depart right before the Kienholz exhibition opening in June.[81] During this trip, Tinguely meets Walter Hopps and artists from the Ferus Gallery as well as actor Dennis Hopper and his entourage. He becomes friends with Kienholz, whom he first met the previous year.[82] Dwan writes to artist William Waldren, "You can imagine what a madhouse it's been around here with three artists and all their technical problems!"[83] Tinguely and Saint Phalle locate an old sheet-metal factory (Tinguely refers to it as the Zing Zing & Company), and Dwan rents it for them to use as a studio.

Jean was welding away, and Niki was pasting and gluing and painting and filling bags with paint and pigment to shoot later, and they had a real studio situation going. It was very exciting. . . . Tinguely was going on trips with Kienholz to find materials, and again, I was sometimes hitching a ride along. In one case, [we] went to a downtown hardware store, which was glorious. Something like a four- or five-story hardware store — hardware and housewares and building materials — in downtown Los Angeles that I'd never seen before. . . . Kienholz knew about this place, and we were all enthralled with it. Tinguely went around and bought up many small motors. He would come . . . cradling them in his arms to show me, and could he get this one too? And I said, "Yes, yes, of course, whatever you need." He was just thrilled. At one point, it seemed to me the motors were getting bigger and bigger. I said, "Jean, are you sure you want something quite that big? It seems a little large for what you're building." And he said, "That's just it. It's that motor that counts." He just loved the motors, you see. So he built the pieces around the motors, almost in a sense to justify his passion for these motors. . . .The pieces had to be bolted [to] the floor, otherwise they would walk away.[84]

Dwan also accompanies Saint Phalle in her search for materials:

We went to wholesale houses w[h]ere they had very cheap plastic dolls and that sort of thing, in bins, in downtown Los Angeles. Also, we were looking for lots of nasties, like rubber spiders and alligators and snakes and skeletons and so forth, which were all sold in plastic packages in huge bins—I guess for party favors or something like that. . . . We went with a shopping basket and filled it up with creepy-crawlies. It was just so much fun. We laughed a lot, all of us, in those days.[85]

April Rothko plans to travel to Los Angeles to see Dwan. In advance of his trip, Dwan writes: "Philippe and I are so looking forward to your visit next month. Everything is in readiness. We have a house about . . . two minutes' walking distance from the house in which we live that we maintain as our sort of super guest house. Ray and Denise Parker stayed there, and I am sure that they would confirm that you will be truly comfortable there."[86] His plans do not materialize.

April/May The Rivers show is the most successful at the gallery to date and it practically sells out in the first three days.[87] Tinguely collaborates with Rivers and makes "moving and clanking bases" for two of his paintings. Even Henry Seldis, the conservative critic for the *Los Angeles Times*, is supportive.[88] The Riverses depart Los Angeles on April 23.

April 21 During the Rivers exhibition the gallery holds a screening of films by Robert Breer, an experimental filmmaker, painter, and sculptor best known for his avant-garde animations. The program includes Breer's *Homage to Jean Tinguely's "Homage to New York,"* 1960.

May/June Tinguely exhibits a group of mechanized works recently fabricated in Los Angeles. Kienholz helps install the works at the gallery. The show is quite noisy due to the motorized pieces. He debuts his machine sculpture *Hannibal*, now referred to as *Hannibal No. 1*. (In 1965 Rauschenberg acquires the work and later donates it to the Museum of Modern Art.) A supplement to the exhibition provides contact information in the event that the works require maintenance or repair; because Tinguely lives in Europe, he lists the telephone numbers for Kienholz and Dwan Gallery in Los Angeles and Rivers and Alexander Iolas Gallery in New York.[89] As part of the exhibition, Tinguely also installs fully functioning outdoor fountains on the lawns of six Los Angeles collectors. "At each of these homes Tinguely constructed large motor-driven fountains which related closely to

DWAN AT THE SECOND DWAN GALLERY IN LOS ANGELES, 1963 (17)

CLAES OLDENBURG OUTSIDE DWAN GALLERY WITH *FLOOR CONE*, FALL 1963 (18)

17

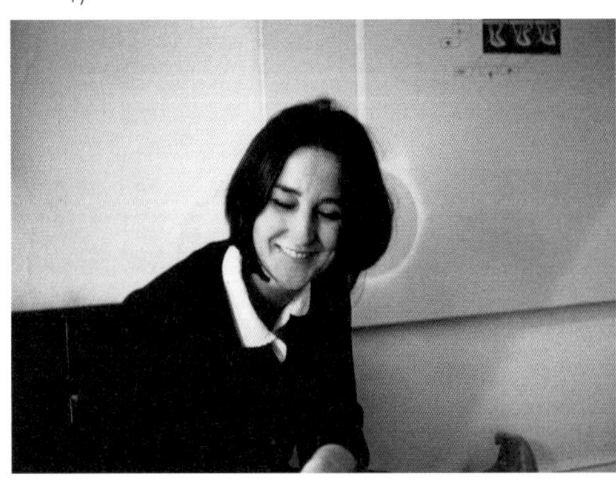

the work in the gallery. They used water sprays, some erratic and some beautifully symmetrical, as an additional dimension to those of sound and motion."[90] During the opening, a progressive dinner is staged in which participants are served food and champagne on a bus while they are taken on a tour to see each of the fountains. The spraying water turns the collectors' yards into mud puddles.

The success of the Tinguely show causes Dwan to remark, "There is a never-ending stream of museum people, artists, and gallery people out here visiting from all over the country. It is firmly established in everyone's mind that Los Angeles is second now only to New York. Jean says it's much better even than Paris."[91]

May 22 The Philip Guston retrospective opens at the Los Angeles County Museum of Art. Guston travels to Los Angeles to see his show. He remains in Los Angeles making lithographs and drawings.[92]

June 14 Dwan writes to Alexander Iolas in New York, hoping to renew business relations for the artists that they show in common, pointing out the uniqueness of Raysse, Saint Phalle, Kienholz, and Tinguely.[93]

June–August Weber takes a two-month cross-country trip, driving 9,500 miles along interstate roads and stopping along the way to meet with collectors.[94]

June/July Kienholz's first show at Dwan Gallery includes twenty-two of his sculptures constructed from an array of assembled materials, including *The Illegal Operation*, which depicts the scene of an abortion. A catalog is published on the occasion. The show causes a visceral response among critics. Dwan, however, calls the exhibition, "truly 'formidable.'"[95]

July Reinhardt writes to Dwan: "Everyone in Paris says Tinguely, and Niki, have taken you over. Have Rivers, Guston, Rauschenberg, Cunningham [and troupe], taken you over? How can I take you over? Why can't I be like everyone else?... You've got me down for Nov., that's ok.... What can I do for you, Virginia Dwan?"[96]

August The gallery closes and Dwan visits France for the month. While there she has dinner with Tinguely and Saint Phalle.[97]

August 28 Martin Luther King Jr. delivers his "I Have a Dream" speech from the steps of the Lincoln Memorial during the March on Washington in front of more than 250,000 civil rights supporters.

September Dwan makes a brief visit to Milan and has lunch with Count Panza.[98] She returns to Los Angeles on September 17.[99]

September 7 *Pop Art USA*, organized by John Coplans, opens at the Oakland Art Museum and California College of Arts & Crafts.

October Oldenburg's one-man exhibition takes place during the time that the artist is between galleries; previously he had been represented by Green Gallery but had headed to Los Angeles in September for a change of scene from New York after Dwan offered him a show. He relocates to a bungalow on a canal in Venice, California, with his wife, Patty Muschinski (Mucha), and explores Los Angeles in a Chevrolet sedan found in Dwan's garage. Several works including Oldenburg's *Giant BLT* and *Floor Cone* are shipped from New York to the Dwan Gallery.[100] Oldenburg rents a former bank building as a studio where he makes large-scale objects intended for both the Dwan show and his upcoming show at Sidney Janis in New York, including his first perspective piece, *Leopard Chair*, which initiates his furniture works collectively known as *Bedroom Ensemble*.[101] The atmosphere of Southern California inspires this new theme: "'I could see that the emphasis was on the home. Everything in Los Angeles relates to furnishing your own home.'"[102] Oldenburg designs a poster for the show with Mickey Mouse as subject. He plans a happening that is delayed until December after the show closes. Artist Charles Frazier hosts a party for Oldenburg following the opening. The Oldenburgs return to New York in early 1964.[103] Despite selling several works, the artist is disappointed the show was not more successful financially.[104]

Warhol and entourage visit Los Angeles for the opening of his second show at Ferus Gallery. While there he commences shooting footage for *Tarzan and Jane Regained, Sort Of....* He begins filming at the house of director John Houseman, Dwan's neighbor, and then continues shooting at Dwan's pool, where the actress Naomi Levine strips naked and jumps in.

October 8 The Marcel Duchamp retrospective, curated by Hopps, opens at the Pasadena Art Museum. It has a profound effect on the Los Angeles art scene. The show introduces Duchamp to a new generation of artists, ushering in a renewed interest in conceptual ideas relating to art practice. The opening gala is considered the art event of the season. Duchamp is photographed in the museum playing chess with a nude Eve Babitz.

18

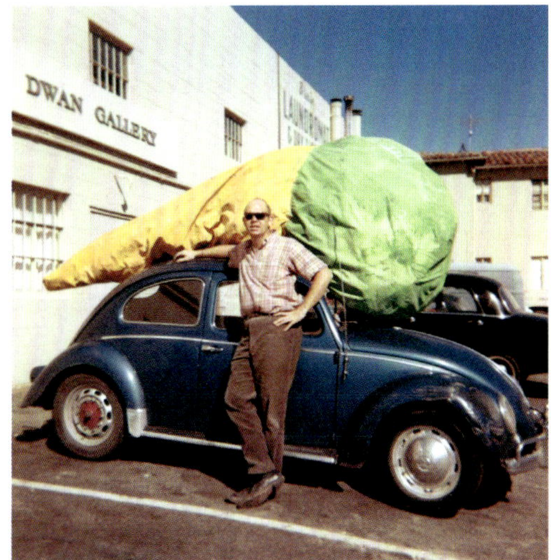

October / November Weber brings Sven Lukin, a New York–based painter of shaped canvases, to Dwan Gallery after working with him at Martha Jackson Gallery. Lukin arrives in Los Angeles in June to begin work on what will be his first show on the West Coast.[105] In anticipation of the exhibition, Lukin writes, "I'm very pleased that Lady Virginia will have some of my oranges out there in that hysterical sun that just keeps rolling along. It was a pleasure meeting her, a person among all those sharpies and hustlers is a rare thing indeed."[106] The show includes canvas constructions featuring bands of bright color and geometric shapes.

November Dwan visits New York. She views rushes of two of Warhol's new films, *Kiss* and *Tarzan and Jane Regained, Sort Of*... at his studio.[107] Warhol wants Dwan and Weber to participate in the film *Kiss*, but they decline.

November 22 President John F. Kennedy is assassinated by Lee Harvey Oswald in Dallas, Texas.

November / December The Reinhardt exhibition opens two days after the assassination of President Kennedy. Dwan comments on the events surrounding the show:

> Ad had switched entirely to square format painting; so the second exhibition was not of the gothic shapes but the so-called *Ultimate Paintings* which . . . consisted of sixty-inch squares. But they also were just wonderful. I think one or two days before his opening in the new space President Kennedy was assassinated and Reinhardt was in Los Angeles at this point. We spent that entire night sitting up watching the repeated footage over and over . . . . I think there must have been two clips that were [shown] endlessly on television. But rather than cancel the opening we opened the doors and simply didn't have any kind of reception, no cocktails, et cetera. And of course, I [suppose] predictably, what happened was people came and [said] that they were very touched by these black paintings in tribute to Kennedy and thought it was very tastefully done by the gallery, apparently think[ing] these paintings had been draped in black for the occasion. But it was something very powerful for us to have shared.[108]

December 3 Dwan writes to Saint Phalle that her marriage to Kondratief is ending.[109]

December 9–10 Oldenburg arranges an evening performance event, *Autobodys*, in the parking lot of the American Institute of Aeronautics and Astronautics, 7600 Beverly Boulevard, Los Angeles. Oldenburg designs two posters for the happening.[110] Audience members sit in their vehicles, illuminating the actions with their headlights while "a cement truck and numerous cars moved sporadically among performers equipped with flares, tires, and water hoses, enacting odd variations of traffic events."[111] Oldenburg documents the happening in a black-and-white film. Dwan described the evening as filled with "all kinds of wonderful stuff" and noted that "Kienholz was one of the ones that was making it happen, you know, and sort of moving and laughing and getting the pieces put together and really enjoying the physicality . . . and the challenge of it and the engagement."[112]

December / January A group show, open for only a week, features major Dwan Gallery acquisitions presented for the first time in Los Angeles. They include works by Shusaku Arakawa, an artist newly discovered by the gallery and scheduled for a full solo exhibition in March 1964.[113]

Late December Dwan visits New York through New Year's.[114]

1964

January The Saint Phalle show presents pieces made the previous year while she and Tinguely worked in Los Angeles. It includes the monumental painting *King Kong*, a work that evokes the tensions of the Cold War and depicts current heads of state including Castro, Kennedy, Khrushchev, and de Gaulle. Saint Phalle is unable to travel to Los Angeles for the opening.[115]

Black, White, and Gray, curated by Samuel Wagstaff Jr., opens at the Wadsworth Atheneum in Hartford, Connecticut. It is often described as the first survey of minimalism.

February Weber organizes a survey of artists who over the past fifty years have incorporated the box within their artwork. The exhibition is ambitious in its reach, and it marks the impact of Duchamp, whose *Boîte-en-valise* is included, and the surrealists on contemporary sculptural practice. The announcement/catalog consists of an eight-foot scroll of paper enclosed in a small box covered with a photomontage of the works featured in the show. The scroll includes images of each work and a text by Hopps on the "extraordinary diverse elaboration" of the box format in contemporary art.[116] Weber enlists many artists who had not shown at Dwan previously to make works specifically for the exhibition. In response, his friend Warhol makes his first *Brillo* and *Heinz* boxes. Weber writes: "Your idea of

1964 EXHIBITIONS (DGLA)

January 5–31
Niki de Saint Phalle

February 2–29
Boxes

March 1–26
William Waldren

March 29–April 25
Arakawa: Dieagrams

May 4–30
Martial Raysse

June 1–27
Gallery Artists

June 29–July 25
New York, New York

September 29–October 24
Edward Kienholz: Three Tableaux

October 27–November 24
James Rosenquist

November 24–January 3, 1965
Lucas Samaras

making cardboard boxes is sensational." He later recalls, "It is no small amount of pleasure and ego satisfaction on my part that my box exhibition helped issue this very important phase of Warhol's artistic career into existence."[117] The show is quite popular and is featured on the cover of *Artforum* with an image of Rosenquist's *Toaster*, also made expressly for the show.[118] Many people contact the gallery requesting a copy of the announcement.

March For Waldren's second exhibition at Dwan Gallery, the artist includes a series of six white wall reliefs in which the use of unusual materials and imagery recalls an extraterrestrial domain. A poster is produced for the occasion.

March/April Arakawa signs a contract with Dwan Gallery in anticipation of his show. The artist prefers to call himself "dieagrams" and is listed as such in the poster advertising the exhibition.[119] Describing the show, Dwan writes:

> Last month we had an incredibly beautiful and strong exhibition by Arakawa. . . . The new works are very subtle. He sprays white paint on silhouettes on a white ground. In some cases pale pastel hues and pencil are added as shadows or edges. These "diagrams for dying" feature movement (from life, to death, to new form), shadow, and silhouette. In some cases funnels, umbrellas, and combs add a collage element. These are not to be regarded as representing themselves, as in pop-art. They are always and purely symbols.[120]

May For Raysse's second show at Dwan Gallery, he presents his recent neon sculptures and mixed-media paintings. The exhibition includes *Made in Japan*, one in a series of new paintings that incorporates imagery from postcards of classical masterpieces such as Ingres's *La Grande Odalisque*. A poster is printed to advertise the show. The artist travels to Los Angeles for the opening, then to New York and on to Nice.[121]

Spring Dwan travels to New York and visits Rauschenberg's studio.[122]

June A group show features mixed-media sculptures and paintings by artists who have previously shown at the gallery such as Arakawa, Frazier, Kienholz, Raysse, and Tinguely. An announcement card capturing an assemblage of the works is produced.

Dwan travels to Venice for the biennale. She sees Tinguely and Saint Phalle, attends Merce Cunningham dance concerts, has drinks with the art critic Pierre Restany, views the Dubuffet retrospective, meets the collector Joseph Hirshhorn, and dines with Reinhardt and the sculptor Marisol.[123] Edward de Wilde, director of the Stedelijk Museum in Amsterdam, escorts Dwan to a party during her stay.[124] Rauschenberg wins the International Grand Prize for Painting, the first American artist to do so. Dwan also travels to Paris and makes a side trip to Lausanne to view Tinguely's new commission there.[125]

June/July The gallery shows individual works from its roster of New York artists. Whereas an earlier show, *15 of New York*, focused on the abstract expressionists, this exhibition directs its attention to pop and neo-Dada artists.

Summer *Artforum* publishes a special summer edition titled "The Los Angeles Scene Today."

July 2 President Lyndon B. Johnson signs the Civil Rights Act, which outlaws discrimination on the basis of race, color, religion, sex, or national origin. The legislation requires equal access to public places and employment and enforces desegregation of schools.

July 26 Dwan Gallery closes through September for the summer.

August Dwan moves to New York City to an apartment at 9 Gay Street in Greenwich Village. She plans to take a sabbatical from the gallery in order to be closer to the center of the art world and to determine if she wants to open a space in New York. After spending about five months in the city, she makes the decision to open a New York gallery.

September 3 The National Arts and Cultural Development Act of 1964 is signed by President Johnson. The following year, the National Foundation on the Arts and Humanities Act establishes the National Endowment for the Arts, an independent federal agency that supports participation in the arts.

September/October In an exhibition that reveals a heightening of the artist's ambition, Kienholz shows three large-scale sculptural tableaux: *The Birthday*, *While Visions of Sugar Plums Danced in Their Heads*, and most famously, *Back Seat Dodge '38*, a scene of an illicit encounter viewed in voyeuristic fashion through the automobile's open back-seat door. The exhibition is one of the most iconic (and notorious) in the Los Angeles art scene of the 1960s.

19

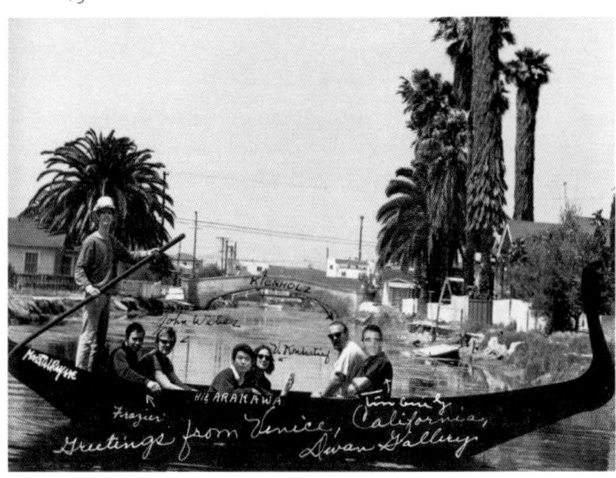

DWAN GALLERY ADVERTISEMENT, REPRINTED IN *ART INTERNATIONAL*, SUMMER 1964 (19)

20

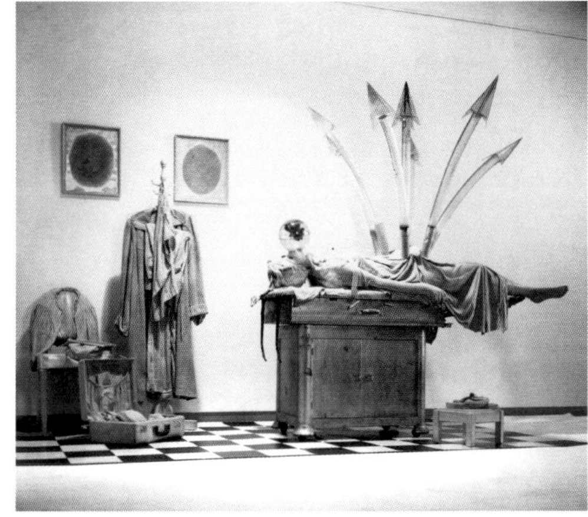

EDWARD KIENHOLZ, *THE BIRTHDAY*, 1964 (20)

October 1 Raysse terminates his contract with Dwan Gallery after disputes in previous months between Dwan Gallery and his New York dealer, Alexander Iolas Gallery.[126]

October 6 At 2:40 p.m. two detectives attached to the Administrative Vice Pornography Detail of the Los Angeles Police Department arrive at Dwan Gallery and tell Weber that a complaint has been registered against the Kienholz show. A police photographer who takes close-up pictures of the artworks accompanies them. The photographs are for submission to the district attorney's office to determine if the art is of a pornographic nature and if a suit should be filed against Kienholz. An hour later, Weber calls Councilman Thomas Bradley, a friend of Dwan's, and apprises him of the situation, asking if he can intervene on their behalf.[127]

October 8 Weber writes to Kienholz: "Good news! The Vice Squad has decided not to prosecute. We used the influence of Councilman Bradley, and today we continue to have our doors open."[128]

October/November Rosenquist, a leading pop artist represented by the Leo Castelli Gallery, flies to Los Angeles for the opening of his show at Dwan Gallery, which has been in the works for two years and is widely anticipated. For the press materials, Rosenquist sends a photograph of himself standing atop a large cigarette lighter advertisement with a flame twice the artist's height. The photographer is Robert Freeman, famous for shooting the Beatles' album covers. The show does very well and all but three paintings sell.[129]

November 17 Weber articulates the gallery's viewpoint in a letter to a Swedish collector:

> We choose to involve ourselves exclusively in contemporary American and European painting and sculpture. I personally find this area, as does a large section of the international collecting community, much more rewarding in terms of emotional and intellectual involvement. I find it more meaningful to contribute, in my small way, to the continuance of contemporary or avant-garde art. It is only through personal commitment that art will survive in our age.[130]

November/January The Lucas Samaras exhibition features his box constructions and wall pieces made of pins, needles, nails, yarn, utensils, and other commonplace materials. This is Samaras's only show at Dwan Gallery. He is affiliated with Green Gallery in New York. The artist designs the announcement and has it printed in New York. The show ends with disappointing results as very few works sell.[131]

December Tinguely shows works made over the span of a decade in an exhibition, *META*, at Galerie Alexandre Iolas in Paris, consigned by Dwan Gallery. James Johnson Sweeney, director of the Museum of Fine Arts, Houston, and businessman/collector John de Menil purchase the show outright, marking the first time an entire retrospective exhibition by a contemporary artist is bought by a museum.[132]

1965

Donald Judd publishes "Specific Objects," a text that has come to stand as a manifesto of minimalist art, in *Arts Yearbook 8*.

January/February Originally titled *Love and Kisses*, *The Arena of Love* presents works with erotic themes by such artists as Duchamp, Öyvind Fahlström, Klein, Raysse, Mel Ramos, Marjorie Strider, and Warhol. For many of these artists, it is their first appearance at Dwan Gallery. Weber organizes the show. The announcement and advertisements feature an arrangement of Hershey chocolate kisses, each with a paper plume listing the name of an artist in the show. The opening, a Sunday brunch with Bloody Marys, bagels, lox, and cream cheese, is well attended.[133] Weber writes, "So many people turned out that I feel confident in saying that the Los Angeles art world must be made up of 95 percent atheists."[134]

February Dwan and actress Brooke Hayward visit Rosenquist's studio in New York to view his surf pieces and other new works.[135]

March President Johnson commits the first combat troops to South Vietnam. Soon after, the United States begins bombing North Vietnam. By April, more than 60,000 US troops have been deployed.

On the heels of his *META* show in Paris a few months earlier, Tinguely arrives in New York in anticipation of his one-man exhibition, *META II*, at Alexander Iolas Gallery. The artist stays at the Chelsea Hotel.

The Los Angeles County Museum of Art (LACMA), designed by William L. Pereira Associates, opens at its new location on Wilshire Boulevard. Earlier, Kienholz is selected as the first West Coast artist to have a retrospective exhibition at the museum, but the show is delayed until March 1966.

1965 EXHIBITIONS (DGLA)

January 5–February 6
The Arena of Love

February 9–March 13
Drawings: Oldenburg, Dine, Whitman, Talbert

March 16–April 10
Dakota Daley & Nicholas Quennell

April 13–May 8
Robert Rauschenberg: Drawings

May 11–June 5
Charles Frazier

June 8–July 3
Group Show

September 29–November 13
Mark di Suvero

November 16–December 11
Larry Rivers: Recent Work

December 21–January 15, 1966
Group Show

1965 EXHIBITIONS (DGNY)

November 23–December 31
Edward Kienholz: The Beanery

February/March The gallery presents works on paper in a range of mediums (including watercolor, gouache, collage, charcoal, ink, and crayon) by Dine, Oldenburg, Ben Talbert, and Robert Whitman. Except for Oldenburg, the artists are new to showing at Dwan Gallery. The show is not a success in terms of sales.

March/April Weber organizes an exhibition by Dakota Daley and Nicholas Quennell, two young artists who work collaboratively on paintings of enlarged figures on color-dyed and light-sensitive canvases.[136] Weber discovers them working in Oakland, California.[137] The dates of the duo's exhibition are extended so that Rauschenberg has another week to prepare and install his works.

March 18 *Jean Tinguely* opens at the Dayton Art Institute in Ohio.

April/May Rauschenberg's second solo show at Dwan Gallery features one large combine and a group of frottage drawings. The artist designs the poster and signs 200 of them, which the gallery sells for $25 each.[138]

May 5 A meeting is held at Dwan Gallery for all Los Angeles artists who feel strongly about the US intervention in the Dominican Republic and the situation in Vietnam. The purpose of the meeting is to discuss how the artistic community can respond. Future meetings pave the way for the Los Angeles Artists Protest Committee, which erects the Peace Tower in West Hollywood the following year.

May/June Charles Frazier flies from New York to Los Angeles on May 8 in advance of his show's opening at the gallery. The artist presents fourteen smooth, bronze sculptures that are abstract in design yet feature pop art imagery such as lips and hearts. A poster is designed for the show. By contract Frazier is represented jointly by Kornblee Gallery in New York and Dwan Gallery in Los Angeles.

June/July A group show gathering works of art that have been shown previously at the gallery includes Raysse's *The Pot and the Flower*, Kline's *Black Sienna*, and Guston's *Garden of M*.

June 15 Dwan arrives in California and stays for the summer.[139] The gallery closes from July through August.[140]

July 25 Reinhardt writes to Weber:

> Everyone at the museum opening last month, from New York, thought that Los Angeles is "the coming scene" replacing New York as the "center." (The center of what?) Maybe it's time for me to bow out of Los Angeles. That means Los Angeles is getting to be as bad as New York, maybe worse. I'm destined to go where "the action" isn't. If I were out in Los Angeles I would build myself a house like Ed Moses is doing, forget the art world for a while.[141]

August Dwan returns to New York. She moves from her apartment on Gay Street to the historic Dakota Apartments.

August 10 *Larry Rivers* opens at the Pasadena Art Museum after traveling from the Rose Art Museum, Brandeis University. The show continues on to the Jewish Museum, the Detroit Institute of Arts, and the Minneapolis Institute of Arts.

August 11–17 Widespread rioting takes place in the predominantly African American neighborhood of Watts in south-central Los Angeles. The violence begins after racial tensions hit a boiling point with the arrest of a young black man for drunk driving. The National Guard is called in to assist the police.

September/November A one-man show at Dwan features two large-scale sculptures by Mark di Suvero—*Pre-Columbian* and *Nova Albion*—first completed on the beach at Point Reyes near San Francisco. To install the latter work, the gallery has to cut out a piece of the ceiling to accommodate the sculpture's height. Di Suvero encourages visitors to interact with the works.[142]

October Barbara Rose publishes the essay "ABC Art," an account of minimal art, in *Art in America*.

October 4 The *Virginia Dwan Collection* opens at the UCLA Art Galleries and includes forty-five works from Dwan's personal collection. The exhibition is reviewed anonymously in "Art News: Thiebaud Exhibit Slated at Stanford Art Museum," *Los Angeles Times* (September 26, 1965).

October 23–25 Kienholz first exhibits *The Beanery* in the parking lot of Barney's Beanery in Santa Monica, California. The work simulates the restaurant's bar, which visitors can enter. Kienholz begins constructing the work in the spring of 1964 outside his home and completes it in six months. He makes his first life casts for this work, including the proprietor of the Beanery, John "Barney" Anthony.[143]

ADVERTISEMENT FOR MARK DI SUVERO'S INSTALLATION AT DWAN GALLERY LOS ANGELES, 1965 (21)

INSTALLATION OF EDWARD KIENHOLZ'S *THE BEANERY* AT DWAN GALLERY NEW YORK, 1965 (22)

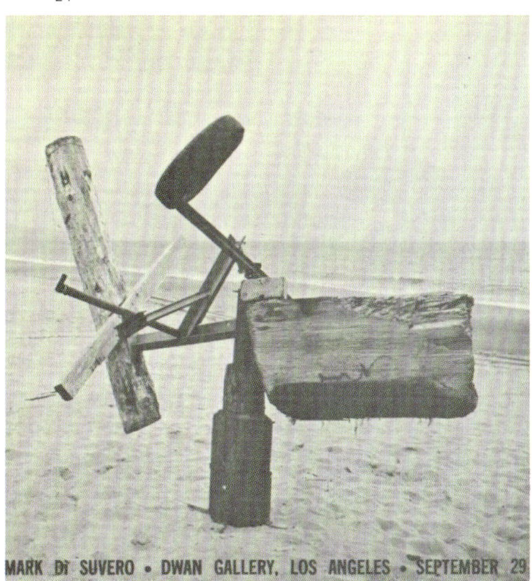

22

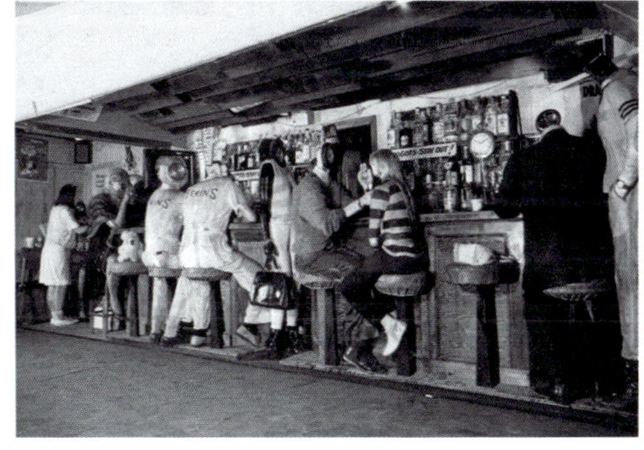

November 3–27 Dwan views Sol LeWitt's *Wall Piece ("Hockey Stick")* (1964) in the exhibition *Sculpture from All Directions* at World House Galleries in New York accompanied by artists Eva Hesse and Tom Doyle. They introduce Dwan to LeWitt during the show, and she visits his studio soon after.

November/December A show of recent work by Larry Rivers opens at Dwan Gallery. It was originally scheduled for the previous June but is pushed back as Rivers does not have enough new work to show, and Weber is increasingly unenthusiastic.[144]

November 21 Park Place Gallery opens at 542 West Broadway. The lease of the original Park Place expired in 1964 and five collectors including Dwan and J. Patrick Lannan elect to back the cooperative.[145]

Dwan Gallery New York and Los Angeles

November 23 Dwan Gallery opens in New York City at 29 West 57th Street. It is the first Los Angeles gallery to open a branch in New York. As Dwan remarks, "I think our shows are important enough to be seen in both places."[146] The gallery takes up the entire eighth floor of the building. Dwan hires David Whitney as the architect and Annalisa Mellion Sewell as the interior decorator. Dwan desires a clean, neutral space. Whitney draws up "some very simple plans." The gallery features flat, fiber, gray-beige wall-to-wall carpet over concrete, white walls, and ten-foot-high ceilings. Dwan recalls: "So there I was on the main street, in the main stream with a suitably anonymous gallery and opening with this wild show of Kienholz's *Barney's Beanery*."[147]

November/December (DGNY) *The Beanery* is transported from California to New York for the debut exhibition in the new space. The show is a huge success and receives extensive reviews.

December/January (DGLA) Paintings and sculptures by six artists are featured in a group show, among them di Suvero's large scale work with moving parts, *Knight's Gambit*. The announcement card comes with a Dwan Gallery button.

1966

LeWitt introduces Robert Smithson to Dwan; they become friends and he joins the gallery.

Michael Heizer makes his first paintings after moving to New York City from California the previous year. He meets De Maria and they frequent Max's Kansas City together.

January The three-day Trips Festival takes place at Longshoreman's Hall in San Francisco. Organized by Stewart Brand, Ken Kesey, Owsley Stanley, and others, it is the largest psychedelic event to date with more than 10,000 people in attendance. It includes music by the Grateful Dead and Big Brother and the Holding Company and one of the first light shows. It will be viewed as the antecedent to the "Summer of Love" of the following year.

Reinhardt publishes "Art vs. History," a review of Kubler's *The Shape of Time*, in *Artnews*.

January (DGNY) Arakawa presents ten large drawings on canvas that resemble architectural blueprints, maps, and elevation diagrams. The exhibition is the artist's first one-man show in New York. A poster is printed for the show.

January/February (DGLA) Eight paintings in acrylic by Allan D'Arcangelo, a painter of highways and signs, are on view. The works stress the play between flatness and illusory depth, and all are characterized by a palette of black, white, green, and blue. A large-scale announcement card is printed for the occasion.

February (DGNY) William Anastasi shows his "sound" objects, utilitarian tools such as drills, picks, and shovels that he places in open boxes with speakers arranged nearby. The tape recordings transmit the characteristic sound of each object.[148] Dwan states, "They were very… poignant, mysterious, lost-looking objects with sounds, removed from their context."[149]

February/March (DGLA) The painter Neil Williams shows shaped canvases made with industrial enamel and acrylic as well as colored pencil drawings, one of which is used for the poster design.

February 26 Dedication of the Peace Tower, a 58-foot-high steel tetrahedron erected at the corner of La Cienega and Sunset Boulevards as a symbol of artists protesting the Vietnam War. Writer Susan Sontag speaks at the event. The tower, designed by Mark di Suvero while he was in Los Angeles for his show at Dwan Gallery the previous fall, sits on a vacant lot rented for $10,000 with funds raised by the Los Angeles

1966 EXHIBITIONS (DGLA)

January 18–February 12
Allan D'Arcangelo

February 15–March 12
Neil Williams

March 15–April 9
Robert Morris: Sculpture

April 12–May 7
Arakawa

May 10–28
Group Show

June 7–July 2
Robert Grosvenor

July 5–30
A Summer Show

October 4–29
Anthony Magar–Forrest Myers

November 1–26
David Novros (five paintings)

November 29–January 1, 1967
John Chamberlain: New Works (foam)

1966 EXHIBITIONS (DGNY)

January 4–29
Arakawa: For instance, instant

February 1–26
Anastasi: Sound Objects

March 1–26
Tom Doyle

April 12–May 7
Kenneth Snelson

May 10–June 3
Sol LeWitt

October 4–29
10 (New York)

November 1–26
Michael Steiner

November 29–January 5, 1967
Robert Smithson

Artists Protest Committee. Di Suvero asks artists to submit small paintings for display on a 10-foot-high by 100-foot-long billboard at the base of the tower. In the end more than 400 artists from around the world send works. Many Los Angeles artists and dealers including Weber assist with the project. The much-publicized tower is vandalized and is taken down three months later.[150]

March (DGNY) Tom Doyle shows two large works including an early example of a floor sculpture, *Over Owl's Creek* (1966), described in the press release as a "step-on" piece that viewers are meant to walk over and around.

March/April (DGLA) A month before the Robert Morris show opens, the artist publishes his theory of minimal sculpture, "Notes on Sculpture," in the February issue of *Artforum*. His show at Dwan Gallery features pieces fabricated in fiberglass, installed in the center of the gallery, forcing a viewer to walk around and in between them, in a manner similar to the description in his essay. Morris writes, "While this material [fiberglass] is less expensive than having work fabricated in metal it is still not as cheap as plywood. On the other hand, it is permanent, weatherproof, lightweight, never needs repainting, and let's hope and assume, [it's] a hot art commodity."[151] Morris completes four fiberglass pieces in advance of the show.[152]

March 30 *Edward Kienholz*, a mid-career solo exhibition curated by Maurice Tuchman, opens at LACMA after much delay. Shortly before the opening, the Los Angeles County Board of Supervisors demands the removal of *Back Seat Dodge '38* because of its supposedly pornographic content. When the museum refuses, the board threatens to close the exhibition and cancel funding to the museum. A controversy ensues, and Kienholz holds a press conference. The press supports the artist, criticizing the board for impeding freedom of expression. The show is allowed to proceed as scheduled when the museum compromises with the board regarding the installation of the work. The door to the back seat is kept closed; those over the age of eighteen can ask a guard to open it so they can peek inside. When the same work was shown at the Dwan Gallery, the back-seat door was kept open.[153]

April Oldenburg creates the *Wedding Souvenir*, a multiple of approximately 250 slices of plaster wedding cake distributed to guests at the April 23 wedding of James Elliott, curator of contemporary art at LACMA, to Judith Algar. The artist gives Dwan a cake slice.

Robert Smithson and his wife, artist Nancy Holt, accompanied by artist Donald Judd and his wife, Julie Finch, make their first trip to New Jersey quarries. Smithson will publish an account of this adventure in his essay "The Crystal Land" for the May issue of *Harper's Bazaar*.

April/May (DGLA) Arakawa's second show in Los Angeles includes works that in their tone and mechanical quality resemble blueprints even more closely than works in his previous show in New York. They feature maps of the artist's travels, geometric diagrams, and stenciled words.

April/May (DGNY) Kenneth Snelson's show features sculptures that incorporate tensegrity, "a tension-compression system of 'floating' volumes in a taut space."[154] Dwan recalled the show's success:

> He did a gorgeous show for the gallery. . . . very well received. This is one case where I can say that the art world was there, the buyers were there, the collectors were there. . . . He went very quickly from being unknown to getting commissions all over the world literally.[155]

April 27 *Primary Structures: Younger American and British Sculptors*, curated by Kynaston McShine, opens at the Jewish Museum in New York. The show heralds a new kind of large-scale sculpture that is hereafter referred to as "minimalism."

May (DGLA) A group show opens consisting of new works by artists including Rauschenberg, Chamberlain, and di Suvero that are shown to the public for the first time.

May/June (DGNY) LeWitt presents a series of grid-based symmetrical structures made of heavy-gauge aluminum with a white baked-enamel finish. Collectors are informed that the works can be placed outdoors and come apart for easy shipment and installation. The show receives a superlative review from a young critic and artist named Mel Bochner:

> Grid. Cube. White. Wood. Intersection. Joint. Obstruction. White wood grid cubes and other structures which are not cubes. On the floor. In corners. Against walls. Floor to wall. Wall to wall. Ceiling to floor. Their presence prevails over description. Sol LeWitt's white wood grid multiple structures are computations of interstices, joints, lines, corners, angles. They constantly permute. Binocular vision destroys regularity. Vision unlocks within impassable areas. There is no invitation. Formality is a guise. Space tenses: past, present-future, plural-present. Perceptual phenomena: indeterminate sequence, infinite, invention, coordinate disorder. Everything is still. Everything is repeated. Everything is obvious. The accumulation

INSTALLATION SHOT OF ROBERT MORRIS, *UNTITLED* (1966) IN DWAN GALLERY LOS ANGELES, 1966 (23)

POSTER / ANNOUNCEMENT FOR *GAS*, A SERIES OF HAPPENINGS SPONSORED BY DWAN GALLERY, AUGUST 1966 (24)

23

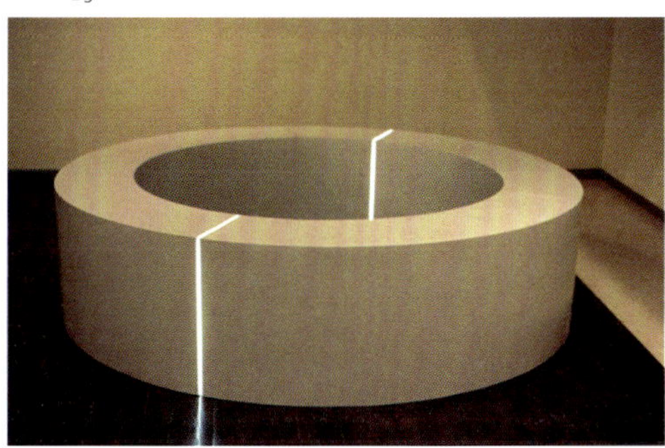

24

A HAPPENING
by
Charles Frazier
Mordi Gerstein
Gordon Hyatt
Allan Kaprow

GAS

In Cooperation With The Dwan Gallery And WCBS-TV

SATURDAY, AUGUST 6 - AM
slow parade of big weather balloons, crowds pushing - hover crafts manned by the Neutron Kid and Liquid Hips - seeing eyes - flares - barrel pounders booming

SATURDAY, AUGUST 6 - PM
weather balloons rise, burst, wash ashore, messages to area - plastic skyscraper on beach, destroyed, shrill whistles - laundry uncovered, day at washerette - bulging letters go up, ride waves - sky divers descend, yells, noise - blimp hoves in - skywriter's secret word - seeing eyes

SUNDAY, AUGUST 7 - AM
"fire" written inside truck, cops spray with snow bombs - ferry trip, white sheets hung out, loud rock on car radios - seeing eyes - nurses onshore yahooing welcomes - black plastic moving across exit - nurses running off - passed by on highway, nurses stacked five-deep on hospital beds, waving, laughing

SUNDAY, AUGUST 7 - PM
bluffs above sea - fire trucks, squad cars, red flashers on, lights, intercoms - bullhorn instructions - seeing eyes - black mounds on beach - rockets released - foam pouring down cliff, past mounds into waves - crowd passing through - interviews

MONDAY, AUGUST 8 - AM
junked autos - kids' clubhouses dolled up for picnic - goodie car serving - flying machine buzzing hulks - big ballon oozing out of car body - seeing eyes - playtime

MONDAY, AUGUST 8 - PM
burial pit - black mounds moving slowly down, sea of foam rolling down - cars blaring horns every thirty seconds - blast on whistles, towers of barrels toppled into pit - pushed up incline against flow - seeing eyes still, all over bottom - regular garbage deliveries

Those interested in participating should attend a preliminary meeting at either the VFW Hall, 4 Main Street, Easthampton on Sunday, July 31 - 11 AM; or the CBS Broadcasting Center, 524 West 57 Street, New York City on Tuesday, August 2 - 8 PM (ask at desk in lobby).

of facts collapses perception. The indicated sum of these simple series is irreducible complexity. And impenetrable chaos. They astound.[156]

June Smithson publishes "Entropy and the New Monuments" in *Artforum*, an idiosyncratic and imaginative account of the minimalist project.

June/July (DGLA) Robert Grosvenor, a sculptor associated with the Park Place Galley and whose dynamic, large-scale works were a highlight of the Jewish Museum's *Primary Structures*, travels to Los Angeles for the opening of his show at Dwan. He constructs *Tenerife* (1966) for the gallery. It is later sold to the Whitney Museum of American Art.

Summer Raysse represents France at the 1966 Venice Biennale.

June 30 National Organization for Women (NOW) is founded to support women's rights and equality.

July 20 Engineering firm Tippetts-Abbett-McCarthy-Stratton hires Smithson as an artist/consultant to propose a design for the new Dallas–Fort Worth Regional Airport. For the project, he enlists fellow artists Carl Andre, Morris, and LeWitt to submit design proposals for outdoor works to be seen from the air. Morris proposes *Project in Earth and Sod*, an earth sculpture to be viewed from an airplane; Andre submits several pieces including *Proposal for Airport Sculpture* and *Proposal for an Explosion*. LeWitt suggests the idea of burying a cube, which he later executes in a smaller version in Bergeyk, Netherlands, for collectors Martin and Mia Visser. The firm does not win the bid and the project is never realized. Smithson later publishes two articles that discuss the proposals.[157]

July (DGLA) A summer exhibition includes works by seven artists—John Carruthers, David Crum, Nancy Gowans, Jessie Jacobs, James Massey, Richard Matthews, and DeWain Valentine—who are all new to the gallery. The poster and advertisements feature scenes of ocean waves. More than five hundred people attend the opening.

July 30–October 4 Dwan Gallery Los Angeles and New York close for the summer.

August Kienholz's *The Beanery* is included in the 68th American Exhibition of the Art Institute of Chicago, winning the Watson F. Blair Prize.[158]

August 6–8 *Gas*, a series of six happenings over a three-day period, takes place in the Hamptons, Long Island. Artists Allan Kaprow and Charles Frazier as well as Mordi Gerstein and Gordon Hyatt participate. Hyatt, a producer for CBS television, conceives the idea, and the Dwan Gallery financially supports the endeavor.

September 24 Lawrence Alloway's *Systemic Painting*, an exhibition of abstract paintings of the 1960s with a look toward minimalism, opens at the Solomon R. Guggenheim Museum.

October Huey P. Newton and Bobby Seale found the Black Panther Party in Oakland, California.

October (DGLA) Dwan opens a show featuring dynamic asymmetrical works by two artists who are associated with Park Place Gallery. Critic William Wilson compares Anthony Magar's and Forrest Myers's works to sculptures by such artists as LeWitt and Morris: "Neither Myers nor Magar is as stylistically radical as the cube-makers of ABC sculpture. The Dwan pair deal in movement and planar interpenetration; traditional sculptural concerns. Neither young artist has, in my judgment, attained the maturity of the best people in the style."[159]

October (DGNY) Dwan calls the *10* (New York) show "one of the most satisfying of my career."[160] This seminal exhibition includes the work of ten artists: Andre, Jo Baer, Dan Flavin, Donald Judd, LeWitt, Agnes Martin, Morris, Reinhardt, Smithson, and Michael Steiner. The idea for the show stems from conversations among Dwan, Reinhardt, and Smithson. Together they organize *10* with the help of Morris. Smithson pens a text but none of the artists can agree on it and the show is instead named after the number of artists; there is no statement. However, a small catalog including images of the installation and artworks is produced. Dwan recalled:

I loved the *10* show. I just couldn't bear seeing it come down. It really answered a need for me, and the direction, the flavor, the tenor, the philosophy — I'm not sure what term to use — [of] that show seemed to [have a] . . . contemplative quality. . . . It was a very quiet show. . . .The sixties, of course, were such a high-energy period. Vietnam had become really such an angry issue, and for the first time, perhaps, Americans were questioning whether they really were on the side of right, and there were a lot of demonstrations going on in universities. There were also riots in the summers here [Los Angeles]. So this show for me was like a sanctuary; seeing these works grouped together representing ten different artists and their approach was like going into a chapel or a place of meditation, or "contemplation" is the term I prefer.[161]

INSTALLATION VIEW OF *10*, DWAN GALLERY NEW YORK, OCTOBER 1966 (25)

SMITHSON AND ANDRE ON A "SITE-SEARCH" VISIT TO NEW JERSEY, APRIL 1967 (26)

25

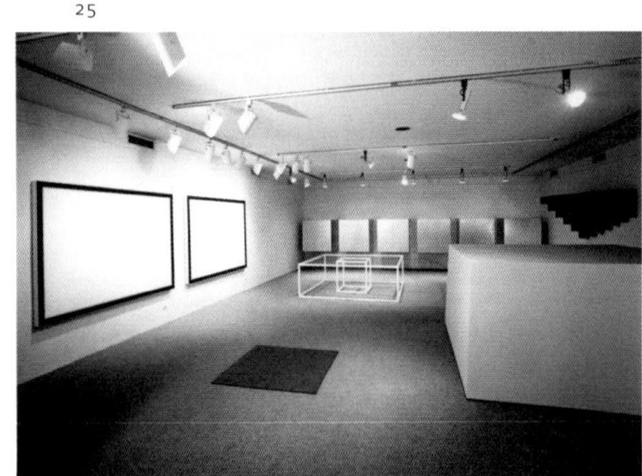

The show comes to define a new direction for the gallery as Dwan turns toward minimalism. Several years after the show its importance is still paramount to the artists involved. As Martin writes to Dwan in 1972:

> I also want to say that the show in your gallery called *Ten* is the only one about which I have always felt happy and satisfied — a show that was just right. The results cannot be counted up but they are seen even now and will be long lasting. Small shows like *Ten* are the best but they cannot be found just anytime. Everyone realizes I am sure that it represented an immense amount of work done by you over years. I thought I would take this opportunity of thanking you for all who were in it and all who saw it as I know they all would like to thank you. I hope you are still working because there are not many with the classical vision so surely.[162]

October 21 Weber marries the future gallerist Annina Nosei.

November (DGLA) David Novros, a painter of shaped canvases, is a member of Park Place Gallery and a participant in Alloway's *Systemic Painting* show. His first exhibition on the West Coast includes five works composed of multiple canvases spaced at intervals to form a complete painting. For these Novros uses a vinyl lacquer mixed with pearlescent pigments; as a result, the color changes depending on the angle from which they are viewed. The works are lit from above and appear to float rather than hang on the wall. The show is well received by critics and has a high attendance. However, no sales occur by the closing date.[163]

November (DGNY) Michael Steiner, a sculptor whose works include repeated modular forms, was a participant in the *10* show. For his first solo show at the gallery, Steiner presents five cast aluminum sculptures made of cantilevered or buttressed beams. Critic Max Kozloff compares the work to that of minimalists Judd, Morris, and Tony Smith: "Steiner even gives the impression of being more inventive than his sources."[164]

November 23 *Ad Reinhardt*, a retrospective organized by Sam Hunter with the participation of critic Lucy R. Lippard, opens at the Jewish Museum in New York.

November–January 1967 (DGLA) Chamberlain spends several months in late 1966 at Dwan's beach house in Malibu, where he makes sketches for his "instant" sculptures. The show opens with a heavily attended, invitation-only champagne reception.[165] The twenty-seven densely installed sculptures mark a new direction for Chamberlain as he begins using flexible urethane foam as a material. In the words of critic Philip Leider, they manage "in the range of their invective, to echo, and thereby demolish, every neo-Brancusi, neo-Arp hybrid, crazy conglomeration of egg-shapes, pod-shapes, bowl-shapes, and beautiful-curve-of-the-nape-of-the-neck shapes ever created."[166] Visitors are encouraged to sit, recline, and climb on the sculptures.[167]

November–January 1967 (DGNY) When Dwan first worked with Smithson on the *10* (New York) show in October, the artist received a $1,000 advance for materials for a show of his own at Dwan.[168] The sculptures he makes are of industrial materials such as sheet metal, and some feature progressions of separate units and a gradation in size. One side of the exhibition announcement features the artist's name spelled backward and then forward; the verso includes measurements pertaining to the works in the show. Critic Robert Pincus-Witten notes:

> Despite Smithson's scientific information his work attests to a highly quirky, Dadaistic temperament. This is not a negative criticism. It only reminds us that much of minimal sculpture is a marriage of engineering and absurdity. Be that as it may, Smithson's handsome and astute work identifies him incontestably as a major figure of what may very soon prove to be a morganatic alliance.[169]

December 16 The annual exhibition of contemporary American sculpture and prints opens at the Whitney Museum of American Art. Smithson's *Alogon* is included.[170]

1967

Dwan recalled, "That was a very good year, 1967; a very good year."[171]

National Endowment for the Arts (NEA) establishes the Art in Public Places Program to provide funding for public art.

Michael Heizer, age twenty-three, travels west to the Sierra Nevada where he creates his first artworks using earth as medium. He embeds bins made of steel and wood directly into the ground.

January/February (DGNY) *Scale Models and Drawings* showcases plans and models for works to be fabricated that reference locations outside the gallery or things the artist has built that no longer exist except as ideas. The works may be temporary, large- or small-scale, either real or imagined. This show paves the way for conceptual art and land art based beyond the confines of the gallery. Dwan later reflected: "I think more important somehow is the fact that they indicated works which were outside the gallery, that one was showing one thing, but pointing toward another. And that's something that came to be, that was, rather revolutionary."[172]

26

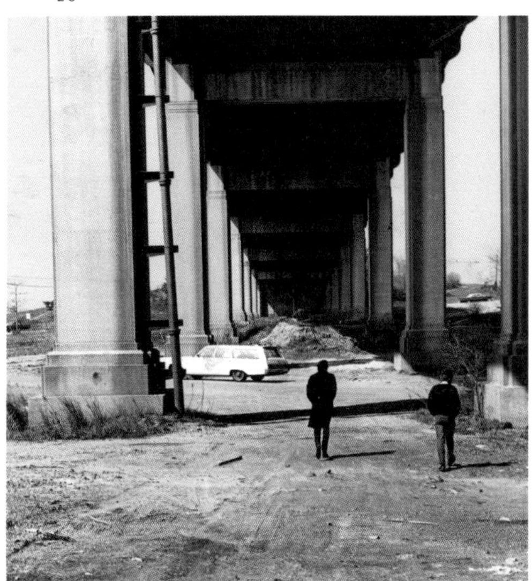

January/February (DGLA) Eleven sculptures by Snelson of aluminum and stainless steel that enlist his "tensegrity," a structural system comprised of wires and cylinders, are on view for the first time in Los Angeles. The exhibition is organized by Dwan and shipped to Los Angeles from the New York gallery. Reviewing the show, Langsner praises the artist: "In effect, Snelson has fused the sculpture of primary structures, the suspension bridge and three-dimensional mathematical models: a crossing of boundaries that augurs well for further developments in our sophisticated technological age."[173]

February/March (DGNY) Kienholz debuts his concept tableaux, bronze plaques etched with the title of the work and a framed 8½″ × 11″ typewritten sheet of paper describing the concept and its price. The concept tableaux are unrealized concepts purchased by the buyers; once the transactions are completed, the buyers can then pay the cost of the materials and Kienholz will realize the works. The show includes one executed project, *The State Hospital*, which fills the entire main gallery. Only a handful of the concept tableaux are purchased and fewer are ever realized. This is to be Kienholz's last show at Dwan Gallery.

February/March (DGLA) Turning the tables, Dwan Gallery Los Angeles gives visitors an opportunity to view a group of Dwan Gallery's New York artists.

March Dwan first views Charles Ross's work at a 1967 exhibition, *Lenses & Prisms*, at Park Place Gallery. Shortly after the show closes, LeWitt advises Ross to see Dwan about gallery representation; he informs him that Dwan has an interest in prisms and a collection of crystals. Ross visits the Dwan Gallery New York unannounced, and Dwan first puts him off. However, when Ross explains that he makes prisms, Dwan immediately pays a visit to Ross's workspace and purchases *Collapsing Cube*.[175]

March (DGNY) Richard Baringer's six curved panel works, composed with a new polymer acrylic silkscreened in stripes on aluminum and installed under rotating colored lights, create an environmental experience for a viewer. A simple poster of horizontal stripes announces the show.

March/April (DGLA) Dwan takes advantage of the abundant space of her Los Angeles gallery and continues to ship large installations there that cannot be accommodated in her New York gallery. In this exhibition consisting of five works by Andre, a single work, *Cuts*, fills the entire main gallery. Across the gallery floor Andre lays down gray concrete capstones, each measuring 7⅜″ × 15⅝″ × 1⅛″. By removing some of the capstones, the artist creates eight rectangular "absences" exposing the floor beneath. This arrangement encourages a viewer to be acutely aware of his or her surroundings. A grouping of smaller sculptures made of slate, steel, and aluminum is also shown. The opening draws a large crowd.

April Dwan, Smithson, Holt, Morris, and Andre visit a brick furnace and the Pine Barrens in New Jersey. They are scouting for land to purchase or lease upon which they can make permanent artworks. At the end of the trip they visit Atlantic City.

April (DGNY) Novros's second show features five recent paintings made of acrylic lacquer on Dacron. The announcement features a poem that Andre writes for Novros called "Rotor Reflector Review."

April (DGLA) On view is LeWitt's large-scale sculpture that fills the entire space of the gallery and showcases a development of open forms—squares, cubes, and rectangles made of aluminum coated in baked white enamel and set on a nine-part grid. In preparation for the exhibition, LeWitt asks Weber to purchase 1½″ adhesive tape so he can create a lattice system for the floor. The work is made of nine separate pieces that relate to one another and form a finite set of arrangements. As Weber writes, "LeWitt's logic in selling the works individually is that any one piece presupposes the total finite system."[176]

April 28 *American Sculpture of the Sixties*, curated by Maurice Tuchman, opens at LACMA.

April/May (DGNY) Anastasi presents six large-scale, photo-silkscreened canvases, each depicting an image of the wall at Dwan Gallery on which each canvas is mounted. The series is an early example of site-specific work. A poster is created for the show. The artist will later refer to this show as "the wall on the wall."

Spring Dwan visits Rothko's studio and purchases one painting on the spot for herself, prior to the grand sale of Rothko paintings to Marlborough, London. She also views the monumental paintings he has created for the Houston philanthropists John and Dominique de Menil and their Rothko Chapel.

1967 EXHIBITIONS (DGLA)

January 9–February 4
Kenneth Snelson

February 7–March 4
Dwan Gallery New York at Dwan Gallery Los Angeles

March 8–April 1
Carl Andre (Cuts)

April 4–29
Sol LeWitt: Series A #1, 2, 3, 4, 5, 6, 7, 8, and 9

May 2–27
10 (Los Angeles)

May 31–June 24
Martial Raysse

1967 EXHIBITIONS (DGNY)

January 7–February 1
Scale Models and Drawings

February 4–March 1
Edward Kienholz: Concept Tableaux

March 4–29
Richard Baringer

April 1–28
David Novros: Paintings

April 29–May 24
Anastasi: Six Sites

June 3–28
Language to be looked at and/or things to be read

October 7–November 2
Tom Doyle

November 4–29
Arakawa: Presence or the Third Person

December 2–January 3, 1968
Carl Andre (Periodic Table)

May (DGLA) A Los Angeles *10* show, an iteration of the *10* (New York) show, includes the same ten artists but features entirely different works.

May–June (DGLA) Though Raysse had previously left the Dwan Gallery, a retrospective of the artist's work made between 1960 and 1967 is presented in collaboration with Alexander Iolas Gallery. A catalog is published for the occasion with an essay by critic Otto Hahn and a text by the artist titled "I Have a Thousand Things to Put in Order." The artist and celebrities including Dennis Hopper and his wife, Brooke Hayward, attend the opening. This is the final show held at Dwan Gallery Los Angeles.

June 24 Dwan Gallery Los Angeles closes permanently at the end of the Raysse exhibition. The gallery space is leased to Doug Chrismas of Ace Gallery. William Wilson writes in the *Los Angeles Times*:

> Cheshire-like, Dwan Gallery is disappearing from the scene with a lingering smile. It is the wry French smile of Martial Raysse whose work is being shown in a retrospective for the final exhibition in the Westwood vanguard showplace. . . .The show also has, like a good French film, its poignancy. That comes from the knowledge that Dwan is closing. For seven years it has been a center of delight and controversy, persistently showing risky, unsalable art from Tinguely to Ad Reinhardt, from Kienholz to the Park Place Group. It has been a considerable factor in educating our taste towards sophisticated appreciation. Thanks and adieu.[177]

Summer More than 75,000 young people descend on Haight-Ashbury in San Francisco, drawn by the neighborhood's counterculture image, in a season memorialized as the Summer of Love.

Artforum releases a special issue on American sculpture featuring Dwan artists including LeWitt ("Paragraphs on Conceptual Art"), Smithson ("Towards the Development of an Air Terminal Site"), and Morris ("Notes on Sculpture, Part 3: Notes and Nonsequiturs"), as well as Michael Fried's famous denunciation of minimalism, "Art and Objecthood." The texts include installation shots of Dwan exhibitions.[178]

Dwan Gallery New York

June A show originally titled "Printed Matter" features a range of artworks by both nineteenth- and twentieth-century artists. The gallery publishes a press release written by Smithson under the pseudonym Eton Corrasable (a twist on the brand name of an erasable typing paper of the time). Dwan viewed the show as having "two sides. There were the things that were to be read and there were the language elements that were to just be seen as objects. Both approaches were valid in what we were trying to achieve."[179] The show is the first of four "language" shows to be brought together at Dwan Gallery between 1967 and 1971.

August Dwan travels through Spain and Portugal viewing mosques and Islamic palaces with her daughter, Candace, before heading to her summer house in southern France.[180]

August 30 Ad Reinhardt dies of a massive heart attack at age fifty-three.

October *Sculpture in Environment*, a display of large-scale sculpture by twenty-four artists, is installed throughout Manhattan. The show is sponsored by the city's Administration of Recreation and Cultural Affairs and is intended to bring everyday New Yorkers in contact with works of art.

As part of the *Sculpture in Environment* program, Oldenburg oversees *Placid Civic Monument* (commonly referred to as the "Hole"), a six-foot-long rectangular trench dug into Central Park behind the Metropolitan Museum of Art. Later in the day the hole is refilled with earth. A documentary made by Oldenburg captures the events.

Press conference by E.A.T. (Experiments in Art and Technology Inc.) to gain support from the technical and industrial communities is held at Rauschenberg's studio, 381 Lafayette Street, New York. Dwan is announced as a founding patron of the enterprise.[181]

October/November Doyle's second show at the gallery includes the large-scale multicolored sculpture *The 1st. On the First Day*. It spans the length of the gallery, nearly brushing the ceiling while its deep blue platforms lie close to the ground.

November In Arakawa's best-received show in the States to date, gray canvases filled with graphic symbols and word diagrams line the walls of the gallery. A poster is made in conjunction with the show.

December Smithson publishes his essay "The Monuments of Passaic," a tour of the New Jersey river town, in *Artforum*.

December/January 1968 Andre's second show of the year features three sculptures made of different types of metal—zinc, iron, and aluminum—that visitors are permitted to walk on. Describing these floor pieces and a visitor's encounter with them, Dwan recalled:

DWAN (FOREGROUND) WITH DENNIS HOPPER, BROOKE HAYWARD, AND MARTIAL RAYSSE AT RAYSSE RETROSPECTIVE, DWAN GALLERY LOS ANGELES, SPRING 1967 (27)

ROBERT SMITHSON, DWAN, MARY PEACOCK, AND NANCY HOLT COLLECTING SAND IN THE PINE BARRENS OF NEW JERSEY, WINTER 1968 (28)

27

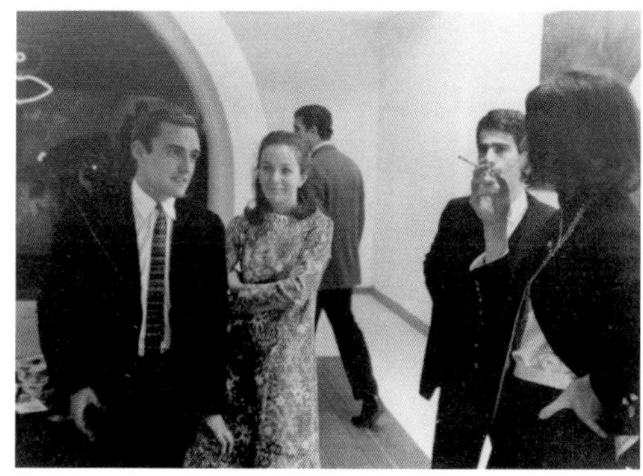

28

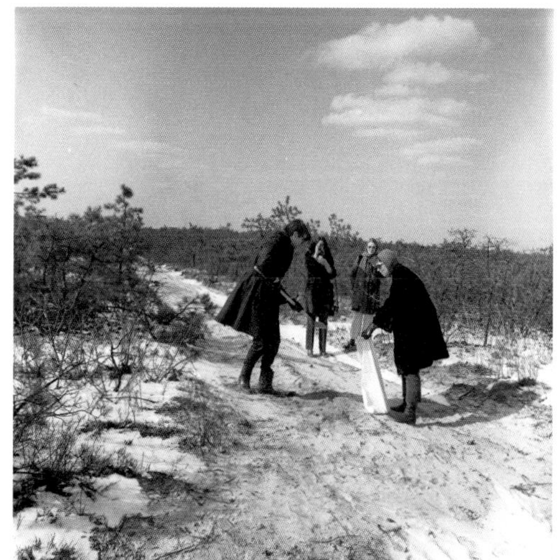

A lot of [people] went out of their way not to stand on them, and then word got around that one could go stand on them, and then word got out that it made a certain sort of sound when you walked across them, if you wore a certain kind of shoes. So there was a whole element of young people coming up from Soho (I took them to be from there) with their babies, who would put their children down very meaningfully and have them go running across them. It got a little bit chaotic at moments, you know, because people were sort of meditating on the sound of it and so forth.[182]

1968

Dwan takes promotional pictures for the duo Silver Apples, a psychedelic electronic band that she also financially backs. The band uses Dwan's photographs as sleeve art for their debut album, *Silver Apples*.

January The third Snelson show is a financial success. Not only do all the works sell out but Snelson also receives several major commissions including one organized by Alfred Barr Jr., founder of the Museum of Modern Art, for Governor Nelson Rockefeller.[183] Here is Dwan's account of the opening day:

[I]t was Saturday morning, and one of my helpers at the gallery was calling and saying, "Virginia, get here immediately, please!" It was something like ten after ten and we opened at ten, and I hadn't come in . . . because usually things start very slowly on a Saturday, even during an opening. People thought it was much more chic to come later in the day. But, "Come here please immediately, because there are people standing around with their checkbooks. They want to buy Snelson." So I rushed on down, only to find that there actually were well-known collectors, who had been influenced by [Hilton Kramer's article in the *New York Times*], and who were in a hurry and feeling [a] certain urgency to buy their Kenneth Snelson. We sold quite a few things . . . that Saturday morning.[184]

Despite its commercial success, and Kramer's enthusiastic preview, critical response to the show is mixed.

January 11 Dwan travels to Washington, DC, to attend a talk by Dan Flavin at the Corcoran Gallery of Art.

February Lucy R. Lippard and John Chandler publish their essay, "The Dematerialization of Art," a classic account of conceptualism, in *Art International*.

Fred Sandback joins the gallery. Dwan discovers the artist when Judd, one of Sandback's teachers at Yale, stages a small exhibition of Sandback's work at his studio. Dwan immediately offers him a show.

In his February show at Dwan, LeWitt once again presents a multipart sculpture (*46 Three-Part Variations on Three Different Kinds of Cubes*) made of white-enameled aluminum that fills the entire space of the gallery. The work represents the finite series of three-part permutations possible using a vocabulary of a solid cube, a cube with one open side, and a cube with two opposite sides removed. A series of sketches and diagrams accompanies the sculpture. The show is remembered for the scathing review by critic Rosalind Krauss, which the confident LeWitt later includes in the catalog for his 1969 retrospective at The Hague's Gemeentemuseum.

Winter Dwan continues her road trips with Smithson and Holt. Accompanied by LeWitt, Morris, and Mary Peacock, they traverse the Pine Barrens in New Jersey. Smithson locates an abandoned airstrip where he digs up sand and pebbles. Smithson incorporates these materials into his first nonsite (*A Nonsite, Pine Barrens, New Jersey*), which he later includes in his 1968 solo show at Dwan. Dwan recollects:

It was in winter, and the ground was really frozen. The reason for the trip was — among other things — to dig up dirt for this "Site / Non-Site" that Bob had in mind. Well, none of us had seen it, of course. We didn't really know for sure what he was doing, but we loved doing the field trip part of it. So I have photographs that I took of all of us standing around in fur coats in this really frigid landscape, with nothing in sight, and Bob digging very important shovelsful of dirt and putting them into gunny sacks, which were then thrown in the back of the car. Some time later, they evolved into this wonderful octagonal piece of sculpture, metal bins and that particular dirt in the metal bins; in these graduating metal bins. Now, these metal bins were like segments on the map. If one were to draw straight lines between the points of these runways at the airport, and then use the longitudinal and latitudinal lines within that, it would break down into these segments. So he had bins made in the shape of these segments, and then dirt from the airport was put into it. So that instead of being an earthwork on the ground, it was an earthwork in the gallery, essentially.[174]

1968 EXHIBITIONS (DGNY)

January 6–31
Kenneth Snelson

February 3–28
Sol LeWitt: 46 Three-Part Variations on Three Different Kinds of Cubes

March 2–27
Robert Smithson

March 30–April 24
Michael Steiner

April 27–May 22
Charles Ross: Prisms

May 25–June 22
Language II

October 5–30
Earthworks

November 2–27
Cool White, etc. from Dan Flavin

November 30–December 21
Erwin Heerich: Cardboard Sculpture

29

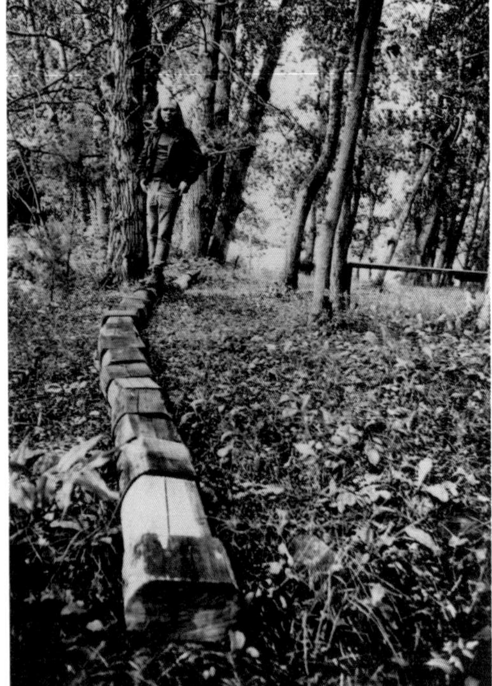

March Flavin joins Dwan Gallery.

For Smithson's second show at Dwan he presents six sculptures executed in fiberglass, painted steel, Plexiglas, and glass. The group includes Smithson's crystalline *Gyrostasis* as well as his first nonsite, *A Nonsite, Pine Barrens, New Jersey*. A teal and blue poster of radiating lines advertises the show.

Andre travels to the Netherlands and Kassel, Germany, to look over proposed sites for his large outdoor sculpture.

March 23 *Minimal Art* opens at the Gemeentemuseum in The Hague. The exhibition also features ten artists and is based on Dwan Gallery's 1966 *10* (New York) show. Weber assists curator Enno Develing in organizing and installing the show. The exhibition of works by American artists travels to several venues in Europe and is met with anti–Vietnam War protests in West Berlin.[185]

March/April Steiner shows four polychromatic sculptures made of polyester resin applied to wood molds for his second show at Dwan Gallery. Moving away from the fabrication processes of the minimalists, he produces irregular chunky shapes painted in bold pastel colors. Some critics respond negatively to his shift in direction.

April Morris publishes "Anti Form," a theory of post-minimal sculpture, in *Artforum*.

De Maria completes his first earthworks, *Two Parallel Lines* and *Mile Long Drawings*, in the Mojave Desert.

April 4 Martin Luther King Jr. is assassinated in Memphis, Tennessee. Riots break out in African American neighborhoods in cities across the country.

April/May For Ross's first show at Dwan Gallery, he shows eight cubic and polygonal forms made of Plexiglas and filled with distilled water. The sculptures are transformed into prisms and refract light along the walls of the gallery, creating spectrums of color. A poster is created for the show.

May Student and worker uprisings take place in Paris and Rome and general strikes spread across Europe.

May/June *Language II* presents a much larger body of contemporary work by younger artists than the inaugural language exhibition in 1967. The *Village Voice* and *Time* magazine single out Joseph Kosuth's photographic blowup, '*Titled (Art as Idea as Idea)*'.

June Accompanied by the artist Dan Graham, Smithson, Holt, and Dwan travel along the East Coast visiting monuments. Each is pursuing his or her own artistic endeavors: Graham scouts tract houses for his photographs, Smithson and Holt search for land for their earthworks, and Dwan tracks down military cemeteries for a photographic series she envisions. Their trip to Arlington Cemetery is sidetracked as they arrive in Washington on June 8, the day of Robert F. Kennedy's funeral.[186] Kennedy was assassinated in Los Angeles on June 6.

De Maria joins Dwan Gallery. Dwan first views his work at a 1966 solo show at Cordier & Ekstrom Gallery. She contacts De Maria right away, but it takes a year before the artist agrees to meet.

June 3 Warhol is shot and critically wounded by Valerie Solanas at his studio, The Factory.

June 27 *Documenta IV* opens in Kassel, Germany. Works by many Dwan artists are on view including Andre, Arakawa, Flavin, Kienholz, LeWitt, and Raysse.

July–August Smithson, Holt, and Heizer make a trip to Mono Lake and Lake Tahoe in California's Sierra Nevada, where they explore and film the landscape. Later, Smithson uses the rocks he gathers in his sculpture *Mono Lake Nonsite*.[187]

Summer The Aspen Institute for Humanistic Study invites Carl Andre to a residency in Colorado. He photographs his "sketching exercises," documenting his creations with materials including logs and rocks at Woody Creek Canyon.

August–September Heizer creates his *Nine Nevada Depressions*, a series featuring nine elements dug into the Nevada desert floor. He receives funding for this project from collector Robert Scull.

August 26–29 The Democratic National Convention is held in Chicago. Antiwar demonstrations and police violence mar the proceedings.

September Dwan, Smithson, and Holt travel to Pennsylvania to visit stone quarries in Bangor and Pen Argyl. Dwan photographs the slate piles. Smithson collects materials that will be used in his *Nonsite (Slate from Bangor, Pa.)*, 1968.

Smithson publishes "A Sedimentation of the Mind: Earth Proposals," a theory of land art, in *Artforum*.

CARL ANDRE WITH *LOG PIECE* IN ASPEN, COLORADO, 1968 (29)

MICHAEL HEIZER AND ROBERT SMITHSON AT DRY LAKE, NEVADA, SUMMER 1968 (30)

ROBERT SMITHSON IN YUCATÁN, MEXICO, APRIL 1969 (31)

30

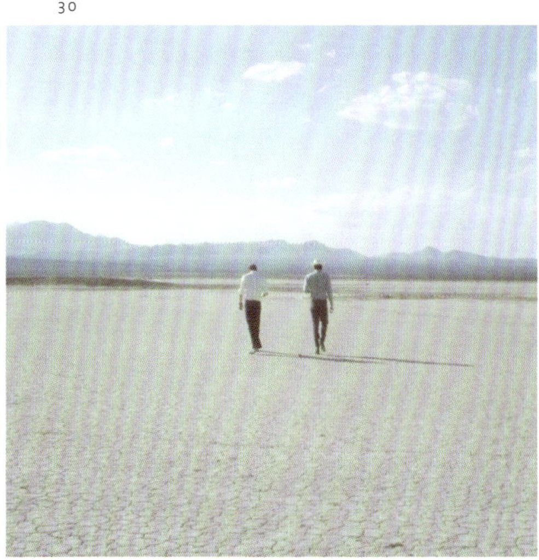

31

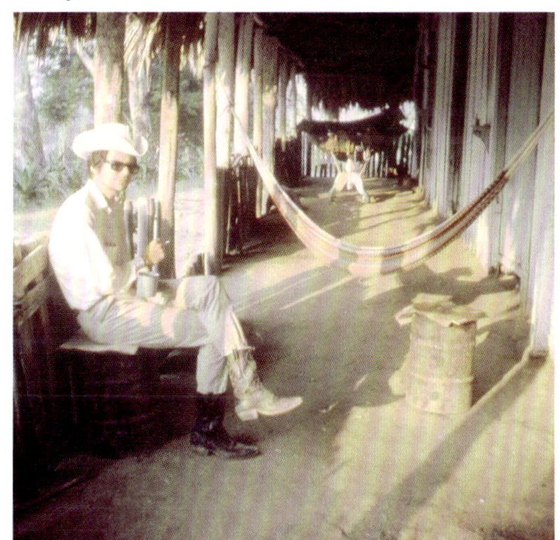

September 20–29 *Prospect 68: An International Preview of the Art in the Galleries of the Avant-garde*, organized by curators Konrad Fischer and Hans Strelow, opens at the Düsseldorf Kunsthalle. Fischer invites sixteen galleries from eight countries to participate. Dwan Gallery is the only American gallery invited. Dwan selects works by Andre, Arakawa, De Maria, Doyle, Flavin, Kienholz, LeWitt, Ross, Sandback, Smithson, Snelson, and Steiner for the show.

September 28–October 10 De Maria builds his first earth room (commonly known as *Munich Earth Room*) at Galerie Heiner Friedrich in Munich, filling the empty gallery with potting soil.

Late September Michael Heizer arrives at Dwan Gallery with a portfolio of 8″ × 10″ photographs documenting his completed earthworks made earlier in the year. Heizer had heard of the gallery from De Maria. After seeing the photographs, Dwan calls De Maria to ask about the artist. She recalls:

> I was astounded. This young person had done these major works without any sort of institutional support. It confused me and set me on edge imagining him working out there in the desert without cultural reinforcement — and not without a real threat of physical annihilation. That kind of integrity and courage is extremely rare.[188]

October *Earthworks* includes ten artists and is the first to treat land art as a genre. Dwan originally looks for open land on which to mount the exhibition. Unable to secure the right location, she instead decides to install at the gallery photo documentation, sketches, and models for works in progress:

> In the late spring of '68, when we still hadn't found land in New Jersey to put these earthworks on, . . . we decided that there was so much energy behind the whole concept — there was so much of a need to get this, to move this out into the world, that [we] wanted to find some vehicle, and the only thing that seemed available was the gallery space, which was very definitely our last choice.[189]

The advertisements for the show feature photographs that Dwan took during her expeditions with Smithson as they searched for sites. The cardboard announcement designed by Dwan with the words "Earth Works" spelled out in sand uses a material not normally found in a gallery. Originally called *Earth Works* (two words) but later condensed by the press, the show receives critical acclaim, though many reviewers speak more broadly about what they herald as a new direction in art.

October 10 Snelson's *Structures* opens in Bryant Park. Dwan sponsors the poster for the show, which is displayed in new kiosks in the park.[190]

November Flavin's first solo show at Dwan Gallery presents sculptures made of fluorescent tubes. One large rectangular work, *untitled (to the "innovator" of Wheeling Peachblow)*, set into the corner of the main gallery, fills the entire space with light. A work consisting of nine vertical lights, *untitled (to Dorothy and Roy Lichtenstein on not seeing anyone in the room)*, bars entrance to the back room while three smaller sculptures are situated in the office.

November/December The first exhibition in the United States of West German artist Erwin Heerich takes place at Dwan Gallery, and the artist travels to New York to attend the opening. Weber arranges the show of more than fifty cardboard constructions with Heerich's European dealer Alfred Schmela. These constructions, wrote one reviewer, gave Heerich "the opportunity to develop independently his own universe of forms, which turned out to be unexpectedly rich and meaningful."[191] A catalog is published for the show.

1969

January Sandback's debut at Dwan Gallery features geometric forms carved in space using elastic cord and steel attached to points on the floor and ceiling.

January 5 While in the Algerian Sahara, De Maria completes *Short Sahara Report, One Mile Line . . . Running North–South* (intended as part of his *Three Continent Project*). A week later, all his files and photographs are confiscated by Algerian police, never to be recovered. De Maria plans to start working on a show for Dwan Gallery when he returns to New York. "The show will center around the relationship between beauty and danger."[192]

February Smithson presents several of his "nonsites," sculptures featuring earth materials placed in containers, stacked in shelves, or dropped on mirrors. Accompanying the sculptures are maps and photographs that reference the source and location of the natural elements. The artist writes the press release for the show, and the exhibition announcement consists of a long folded strip of map that starts at Mono Lake in California and ends in New York City.

1969 EXHIBITIONS (DGNY)

January 4–29
Fred Sandback: Five Situations

February 1–26
Robert Smithson: Mono Lake Site–Nonsite

March 1–28
Charles Ross: Prisms

March 29–April 23
Walter De Maria: Bed of Spikes

April 26–May 21
Carl Andre

May 24–June 18
Language III

October 4–30
Sol LeWitt: Wall Drawings

November 1–27
Arakawa: Decisive Evidence

November 29–December 20
Dwan—Ten Years, Posters

32

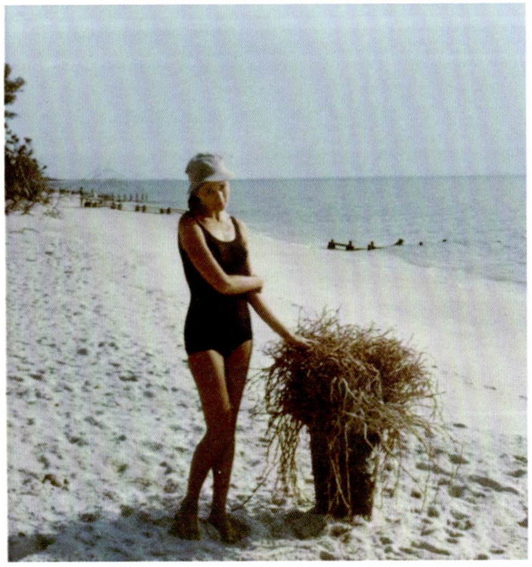

February 11 *Earth Art* opens at the Andrew Dickson White Museum of Art at Cornell University in Ithaca, New York. The show is conceived by independent curator Willoughby Sharp and is the first American museum exhibition to focus on earthworks.

March Ross shows three monumental prism pieces accompanied by photographic enlargements. Ross has shifted to filling the prisms with oil to better refract the light. He includes photographs of the prisms installed in city streets and other locales to underscore the works' existence outside the gallery. Dwan says of the prisms:

> They are exceptional, both in their beauty and geometric precision. But the most profound character of the work is its expansion and compression of space and its implied time. Space is fragmented, warped, reflected, and refracted into endless complex geometric forms, forcing an awareness of our expanding-contracting world and universe.[193]

March 22 *Live in Your Head: When Attitudes Become Form (Works, Concepts, Processes, Situations, Information)* opens at the Kunsthalle Bern curated by Harald Szeemann. Artists represented by Dwan Gallery include Andre, De Maria, Heizer, LeWitt, Sandback, and Smithson; Kienholz, Klein, and Oldenburg are also included.

March/April In his first and only solo show at Dwan Gallery, De Maria presents one work: *Bed of Spikes*. The installation consists of five beds (plates) of steel approximately nine-feet long that feature sharp spikes measuring a foot high. Each bed has a different configuration of spikes. The gallery requires all visitors to sign a waiver in case of injury. A uniformed guard is stationed in the gallery and allows only twenty people in at a time, and no one under the age of eighteen. De Maria records the installation and later creates a film, *Bed of Spikes*, 1968–1969.

April Barbara Reise's "*Untitled 1969*: A Footnote on Art and Minimal Stylehood," a text that argues against the term "minimal art," is published in *Studio International*.

April 15–May 2 Dwan, Smithson, and Holt take a trip to the Yucatán Peninsula in Mexico. They first fly to Fort Myers, Florida, and drive along the Gulf Coast to Sanibel Island and then on to Captiva Island. In Captiva, they show up unannounced to see Rauschenberg, who is living there. Smithson makes *Second Upside-Down Tree*. The travelers then go on to Mérida in the Yucatán Peninsula and during a two-week excursion explore Uxmal, Palenque, Bonampak, Agua Azul, and Yaxchilan. Smithson produces nine *Mirror Displacements* and other works during their journey and writes about the trip in his essay, "Incidents of Mirror-Travel in the Yucatan," published in the September issue of *Artforum*.

April/May For his third show at Dwan Gallery, Andre includes three floor sculptures—one in lead, one in magnesium, and one in copper—each comprising 144 pieces and measuring 144 square feet. Visitors are encouraged to walk on the works.

May/June *Language III* is the largest of the language shows to date and includes contemporary works in a wide range of materials.

June 28 Stonewall riots erupt in Greenwich Village after members of the gay community are involved in an early morning police raid at the Stonewall Inn.

Summer Dwan spends time in France, and Andre visits her at her home there. They discuss upcoming European exhibitions and his recent show at Dwan Gallery.

De Maria completes his *Las Vegas Piece* by cutting four shallow lines into a three-mile-long expanse of the Tula Desert in Nevada. Intended to be an ephemeral work, it is not documented by the artist with photographs or drawings.

Heizer builds his first "object sculpture," *Displaced/Replaced Mass*, using 30-, 52-, and 68-ton boulders in Silver Springs near Reno, Nevada. Scull finances the movement of the boulders from the Sierra Nevada Mountains in California.[194] Dwan visits the site.

July 20 Apollo 11, the first manned mission to reach its destination, lands on the moon, and astronaut Neil Armstrong becomes the first human to step foot on the lunar surface.

August 9 Members of the Manson "family" kill several people including actress Sharon Tate in Los Angeles.

August 15–17 Woodstock music festival takes place in Bethel, New York, with more than 400,000 people in attendance.

September 30–December 10 *Prospect 1969: An International Preview of the World's Galleries* is held in Düsseldorf. Three artists from Dwan Gallery participate—Heizer, Ross, and Smithson.

October Heizer begins construction on *Double Negative*, a site-specific work located on Mormon Mesa about eighty miles northeast of Las Vegas. The square mile of land is located 600 feet above the Virgin River. Dwan purchases the land for Heizer.[195] He continues working on the project through the fall. Dwan later purchases the work from the artist.

DWAN WITH SMITHSON'S *SECOND UPSIDE-DOWN TREE*, CAPTIVA ISLAND, FLORIDA, APRIL 1969 (32)

COVER OF SEPTEMBER 1969 ISSUE OF *ARTFORUM* FEATURING SMITHSON'S *FIRST MIRROR DISPLACEMENT* (33)

33

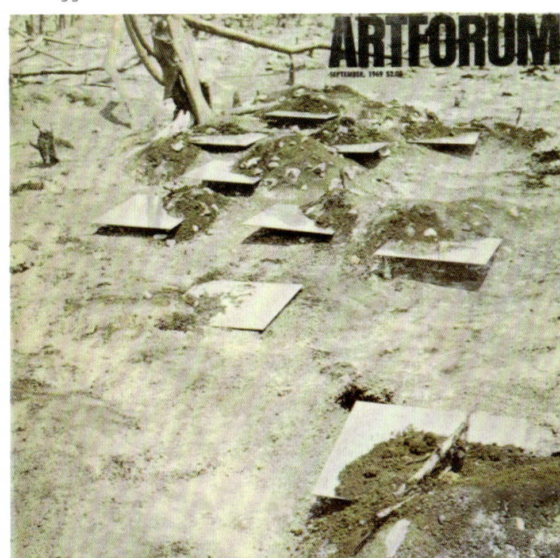

Art Dealer Seth Siegelaub copublishes thirty-six photocopied sets of Andre's *Seven Books of Poetry* with Dwan Gallery.

Smithson creates *Asphalt Rundown* near Rome. He uses a dump truck to pour liquid asphalt down the side of a cliff.

For LeWitt's fall exhibition at Dwan Gallery, he showcases a new direction in his work, conceiving four large drawings that are to be made directly on the walls. Each wall features a different combination of lines, sometimes in different colors. The artist does not execute the works but rather they are installed according to his specific instructions. After the show, the walls of the gallery are painted over. Critic Jean-Louis Bourgeois says of the artist: "LeWitt works with wide expanses of texture so fine, so diaphanous, so unsubstantial that many are close to invisible. They float on their brilliantly lit walls like yard after yard of exquisite gauze. It is no coincidence that what faint patterns there are are really weaves, for LeWitt is interested in that most tantalizing of fabrics, the veil."[196]

November Arakawa's fifth show at Dwan Gallery features paintings, in grays and white with bits of color, that include statements, instructions, messages, and diagrams. The artist states in the poster for his show: "I have not yet decided whether or not to advertise my New York show." On November 13 five students from Rutgers, the State University of New Jersey, visit the exhibition and steal an untitled painting that includes the phrase, "If possible steal any one of these drawings including this sentence." They send a letter of intent in advance, and once they successfully steal the piece, send confirmation via telegram. Though Arakawa believes the "thieves" have misunderstood the work rather than completed it, he offers a resolution and instructs them to donate it to a museum. "Pressed, Arakawa admits that at first he had been angry, but it didn't last. 'That a painting, and particularly a conceptual painting, should generate such passion is beautiful,' he said."[197] Many institutions refuse the painting. The Wadsworth Atheneum is the first to respond with interest, and the work enters its permanent collection. In 1970, Dwan Gallery supports publication of a book documenting the theft of the artwork.

Germano Celant's book *Arte Povera* is published. Dwan Gallery artists that are featured include De Maria, Morris, Smithson, and Heizer.

Dwan's mother passes away.

November 15 A massive antiwar demonstration staged by the Vietnam Moratorium Committee takes place in Washington, DC, with over half a million people in attendance.

November/December A Dwan Gallery "ten year" show features ephemera from the gallery (1959–1969) including exhibition announcements, cards, and posters.

December 3 Dwan hosts a private screening at her apartment of Arakawa's lengthy film, *Why Not: A Serenade of Eschatological Ecology.*

1970

January At Kent State University in Ohio, Smithson builds *Partially Buried Woodshed*, dumping twenty tons of earth on an old woodshed until the central beam cracks.

Dwan first visits *Double Negative*. She meets Heizer at the Las Vegas airport and the next day they drive out to Mormon Mesa to view the sculpture.

Dwan Gallery invites a group of guests to view De Maria's *Las Vegas Piece* and Heizer's *Double Negative*. Dwan, Weber, and the artists lead German curator Hans Strelow, Carlo Huber, director of the Kunstmuseum Basel, and journalist Roy Bongartz on a tour of the earthworks.

Elayne H. Varian's article "New Dealing" is published in *Art in America*. In preparation, Varian interviews Dwan about her gallery and her relationship with her artists.

January/February In advance of Heizer's first exhibition at the gallery, Dwan rents a plane and hires Gianfranco Gorgoni to capture aerial shots of *Double Negative*. The images will eventually constitute the exhibition. As Dwan explains:

> So primarily what we had were just photographs for the exhibition, but the intention was to communicate that the real exhibition was in Nevada. All right, it was under the auspices of the Dwan Gallery; Dwan Gallery's main facility was in New York, but we also had this space out there which was a work of art, and if you really wanted to see the show, you should be out there. And that was revolutionary to my knowledge.[198]

February With support from Dwan Gallery and Ace Gallery in Los Angeles, Smithson takes out a twenty-year lease on ten acres of lakefront land at the northeastern shore of the Great Salt Lake. He spends April constructing the work that will become *Spiral Jetty*, a 1,500-foot-long sculptural coil comprised of rock and earth. Reflecting on *Spiral Jetty*, Dwan states:

I guess I didn't see it until it was completed. That was part of my faith in the artist: they'd sort of wave good-bye and take off and I just assumed that something really worthwhile would come out of it; and it did. But I want to say that *that* is unusual, for the dealer to say, "Now, go do your thing and let me know when it's finished."[199]

February/March Flavin makes an arrangement that he will show simultaneously with Dwan Gallery and Leo Castelli Gallery, resulting in two shows opening at the same time. The main gallery at Dwan features four works, each installed in a corner of the room. Two additional sculptures are included in the rear gallery and office.

March/April *Landing*, a 32-foot-long stainless steel sculpture that sprawls across the entire expanse of the main gallery, is among the five sculptures and four maquettes presented in Snelson's third exhibition at Dwan. A poster featuring the work is published in conjunction with the show.

Spring Dwan flies to Salt Lake City to view Smithson's recently completed *Spiral Jetty*. She photographs the work leaning out of a helicopter.

April In the main gallery, Sandback installs one three-piece trapezoidal sculpture made of white elastic cord that extends from the wall into the viewer's space. The show also includes drawings and a black diagonal made of cord installed corner to corner, bisecting the rectangular space of the rear gallery.

May 4 During antiwar demonstrations at Kent State University in Ohio, four students are shot and killed by the Ohio National Guard.

May Anastasi shows two exhibitions back to back in May at Dwan Gallery. The first features sculptural works made of stacked steel rebar in the main gallery and in the rear gallery a sculpture consisting of a video camera facing into the corner wall and a closed-circuit television displaying an image of the corner. As a visitor approaches the piece, shadows register on the monitor. Dwan reflects on the significance of the video project:

It was really an important piece. What happened later, for instance, [with] Robert Morris and other artists — this kind of information loop . . . minimal information loop — was presaged in this piece and not really pointed out by anyone much. But the artists saw it; the artists definitely saw it.[200]

Anastasi also makes a work—*Issue*—whereby the artist cuts into the wall, removes the layer of plaster from it, and places the debris on the floor in front of the wall where the displacement occurred.

The second installment of Anastasi's May exhibition features the site-specific work *Continuum*, a series of photographs taken of the interior spaces of Dwan Gallery. Each panel is installed on the opposite wall that it depicts, so that the photograph in front of a viewer is an image of the wall located behind the viewer. This effect creates a continuous experience of circuitous looking.

May 17 The Whitney Museum of American Art shutters *Robert Morris: Solo Works* after the artist declares himself on strike and demands that his exhibition close early.

May 22 After artists implore museums to close their doors for one day to show their solidarity against US military involvement in Vietnam and Cambodia, Morris leads a demonstration on the steps of the Metropolitan Museum of Art; the museum does not comply with the protesters.

June The final language show held at Dwan Gallery includes works that have been displayed before, such as Morris's *Card File*, as well as new works in a range of mediums, including Mel Bochner's work *Language Is Not Transparent*, which is painted directly on the wall. Robert Pincus-Witten is one of the few critics to engage the show's premises.

Dwan Gallery participates in the *3e Salon International de Galeries-Pilotes* in Lausanne. They are one of two contemporary galleries from Western Bloc countries invited to participate in the show, which takes place every five years. The gallery shows documentation of artists represented by the gallery in the form of a continuous 35 mm slide show.[201]

June 20–24 Dwan travels to Venice for the biennale and stays at the Excelsior Palace, Lido. The gallery hosts a party at the hotel.[202] Heizer and Flavin represent the United States in the International Pavilion. Arakawa is invited to oversee the Japanese Pavilion.

July 2 *Information*, a major exhibition of conceptual art curated by Kynaston McShine, opens at the Museum of Modern Art.

Fall *Avalanche* magazine published by Willoughby Sharp and Liza Béar debuts. The first issue features the article, "Discussions with Heizer, Oppenheim, Smithson."

1970 EXHIBITIONS (DGNY)

January 10–February 5
Michael Heizer: New York/Nevada

February 7–March 4
Cornered Installations from Dan Flavin, 1963–1970

March 7–April 2
Kenneth Snelson

April 4–30
Fred Sandback

May 2–14
Anastasi: Sculpture

May 16–28
Anastasi: Continuum

June 2–25
Language IV

October 3–29
Richard Long: Sculpture

October 31–November 25
Robert Smithson: Great Salt Lake, Utah

November 28–December 23
Gallery Artists

1971 EXHIBITIONS (DGNY)

January 6–February 4
Charles Ross: Sunlight Dispersion

February 6–March 4
Robert Ryman: Paintings

March 6–31
Dan Flavin: untitleds (to Barnett Newman)

April 3–28
Carl Andre

May 1–26
Sol LeWitt: Prints and Drawings

June 1–25
Final Exhibition: Gallery Artists

DWAN IN DRY LAKE, NEVADA, 1970 (34)

DWAN AT *SPIRAL JETTY*, C. 1970 (35)

34

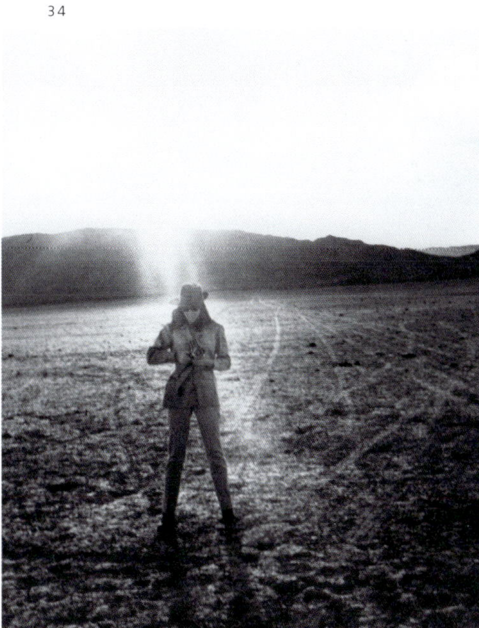

35

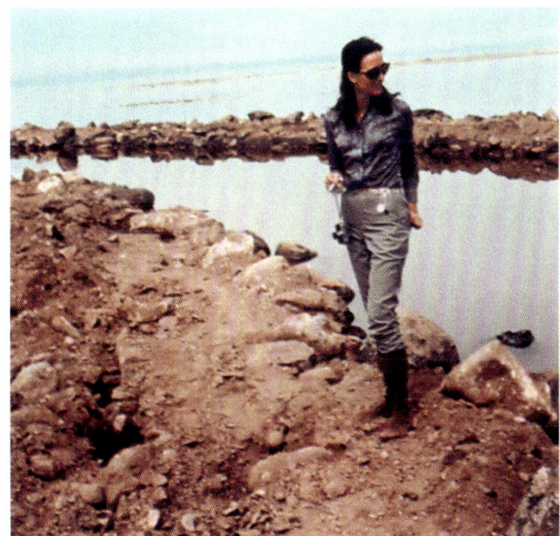

September–October Richard Long arrives on the *Queen Elizabeth II* in September to prepare for the exhibition at Dwan the following month.[203] The gallery arranges for Long to stay with Smithson and Holt at their studio.[204] Long's clay spiral sculpture is made directly on the carpet of the main gallery.

October/November The gallery shows Smithson's 35-minute film, *Spiral Jetty*, which introduces the public to the film's eponymous earthwork and includes aerial and ground images. A poster is produced that features a series of movie treatments for the film.

November/December A show of Dwan Gallery artists features works by Andre, Arakawa, De Maria, Flavin, LeWitt, Long, Ross, Sandback, and Smithson. Five works by the monochrome painter Robert Ryman are included as well, marking the first time the artist has been on view at Dwan Gallery.

1971

January/February The third show of Ross's prisms features a series of three continuous film loop projections capturing sunlight spectrums moving across objects as well as three sculptural works of stacked prisms. Ross describes his work:

> Since 1965 I have been constructing large prisms and prism windows. . . . The pieces are both active and passive in relating to the environment. The size, shape, hue, and position of the projected spectrums change by the minute, hour, day, month, and year with the relative position of the sun in the sky.[205]

February/March Ryman displays twenty-three white paintings, mostly from 1970 to 1971 and utilizing a range of mediums and supports. Ryman has concurrent shows at Dwan and at Fishbach Gallery, located in the same building on 57th Street.

March Flavin shows four rectangular corner pieces at Dwan Gallery dedicated to the abstract expressionist painter Barnett Newman, who had died the previous year. Newman was a strong influence on the minimalist generation and a supporter of Flavin's work. The four works are made of red, yellow, and blue fluorescent light. A photograph of Newman sitting in front of his *Stations of the Cross* is used for the poster and advertisements.

April Andre shows thirty floor sculptures using a range of materials—copper, aluminum, galvanized steel, Plasticine, lead, and silver—in various arrangements. The price of each work is calculated according to the buyer's annual income.

An interview with Weber about Dwan Gallery appears in *Arts Magazine*.[206]

April 20 Dwan circulates a letter to the Dwan Gallery artists confirming rumors that the gallery will close its doors that summer. She asks that they attend a meeting on April 21 at the office of Elliot Hoffman, the gallery's lawyer.

May For LeWitt's last show at Dwan Gallery, a selection of prints and drawings from 1967 through 1971 are on view.

June The final show at Dwan Gallery includes works by the entire roster of artists at the time of its closing.

June–July Dwan Gallery New York closes its doors. Dwan provides three-month stipends to all her artists and puts Paul Toner in charge of selling inventory out of an office in her apartment at the Dakota.

September Weber opens his own gallery, John Weber Gallery. His inaugural show is LeWitt's *Structures and Wall Drawings*. Weber represents several Dwan Gallery artists including Flavin, LeWitt, and Smithson.

Fall Dwan directs and produces artist Elaine Sturtevant's performance piece, *Various Beuys Actions*. The film is based on Dwan's recollections of Joseph Beuys's 1968 film, *Eurasienstab*. The artist dresses like Beuys and follows Dwan's directions as does the cameraman Robert Fiore.

Dwan provides initial support for Ross's large-scale project, *Star Axis*. His search for a site ends in 1975 when he purchases Chupinas Mesa in New Mexico.

Alanna Heiss founds the Institute for Art and Urban Resources Inc., which later becomes MoMA PS1.

Post-Gallery Years

1972

February 5 Calvin Tomkins's article on earthworks, "Onward and Upward with the Arts: Maybe a Quantum Leap," is published in the *New Yorker*; it includes an interview with Dwan and an account of their trip the previous summer to view earthworks by Heizer, De Maria (a foiled attempt), and Smithson.

July Dwan travels with Ross and poet Steve Katz to Nova Scotia, where both she and Ross film the total eclipse of the sun. The resulting 16 mm film, *Arisaig, July 10, 1972*, is in the collection of the Hayden Planetarium.[207] It contains much of Dwan's footage.

DWAN BEING FITTED FOR A BODY CAST FOR KIENHOLZ'S *THE ART SHOW* IN THE ARTIST'S BERLIN STUDIO, FEBRUARY 1975 (36)

DWAN IN GIZA, EGYPT, SPRING 1979 (37)

HEIZER'S *CITY: COMPLEX ONE*, 1997 (38)

DWAN LIGHT SANCTUARY, UNITED WORLD COLLEGE, MONTEZUMA, NEW MEXICO, 1998 (39); DWAN SITTING INSIDE (40)

36

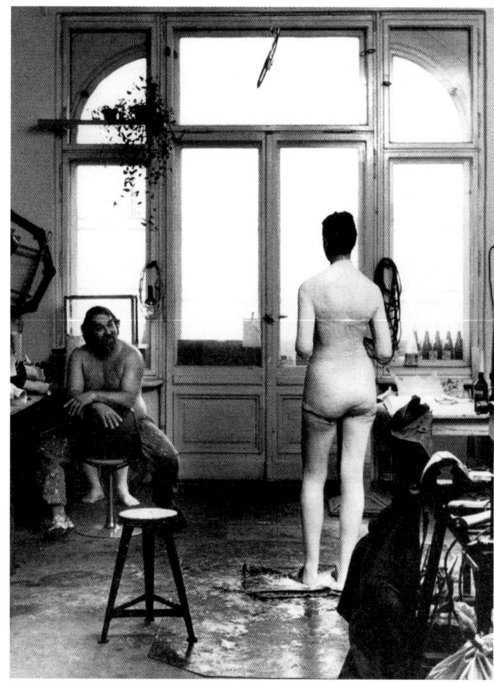

Heizer begins purchasing land for his mile-long *City* located three hours outside of Las Vegas in Garden Valley, Nevada. Dwan funds the first structure, *City: Complex One*, completed in 1974. The project is intended to be built in five phases and to include four additional complexes. As Dwan exclaimed, "For me, this is surely the greatest sculpture of our time." The same summer she travels with Heizer to view the sites of his earlier works in Reno, Virginia City, and Sharon, Nevada.[208]

December The first photograph of Earth in full view, "The Blue Marble," is taken by the Apollo 17 crew.

1973

July 20 Robert Smithson dies in a plane crash while making *Amarillo Ramp* in Amarillo, Texas. Holt and Smithson's mother ask Dwan to join them for the burial at Hillside Cemetery in Lyndhurst, New Jersey.

Holt begins building *Sun Tunnels* in the Utah desert. She completes the work in 1976.

1974

July De Maria completes his *35-Pole Lightning Field*, which is conceived and built for Dwan. The work is located on isolated land with 360-degree visibility between Meteor Crater and Flagstaff, Arizona, loaned by collectors Burton and Emily Tremaine. The work consists of thirty-five polished stainless steel poles with pointed tips, measuring 18 feet high, set up in a grid pattern.

1975

February Kienholz casts Dwan as one of the figures in his tableau *The Art Show*. She flies from New York to Berlin for the body casting process. Kienholz makes a book for her with images and press that document the making of the work.

1976

Dwan films and produces a three-part video portrait of Carl Andre: *Reconfiguration at P.S. 1 (Carl Andre)*, *Carl Andre: A Conversation*, and *The Dinner*.

De Maria escorts Dwan and her daughter, Candace, to view *35-Pole Lightning Field*. The work has to be removed from the site the following year because of an issue securing the land. Dwan eventually donates the work to the Dia Art Foundation.

1977

Dwan travels to New Mexico and makes her first visit to Ross's *Star Axis*.

De Maria builds a larger *Lightning Field* near Quemado, New Mexico, southwest of Albuquerque, with funds from the Dia Art Foundation. The work consists of four hundred steel poles placed 220 feet apart installed over a one-mile-by-one-kilometer grid. De Maria had searched five years for available land, finally locating it in August 1976.

Dwan supports the work of "minimalist" musician La Monte Young and Marian Zazeela, an artist who works with light.

1978

Dwan begins donating works from the Dwan Collection to major institutions. These will include gifts or promised gifts to Dia Art Foundation; Museum of Modern Art; Whitney Museum of American Art; Museum of Contemporary Art, Los Angeles; Art Institute of Chicago; National Gallery of Art; Nelson-Atkins Museum; Walker Art Center; and Weatherspoon Art Museum (the latter in memory of her parents).

June Dwan hears the Gregg Smith Singers on the radio and arranges for Philip Glass to work with them. They perform together at Carnegie Hall in a performance supported by Dwan and Christophe de Menil. This is Glass's first performance at Carnegie Hall.

1979

With camera in hand, Dwan travels to Kenya, France, and the Netherlands. In the spring she travels with Candace to Egypt and Morocco.

1982

September Dwan conceives and produces a two-part film, *John Cage: James Joyce, Marcel Duchamp, Eric Satie, An Alphabet* and *Cage on Cage: An Interview*. Barry Harris serves as director for both projects.

Fall Dwan's "Reflections on Robert Smithson" is published in the College Art Association's *Art Journal*.

1983

Dwan produces a documentary of di Suvero installing his work *Mahatma* in his Long Island City studio.

37

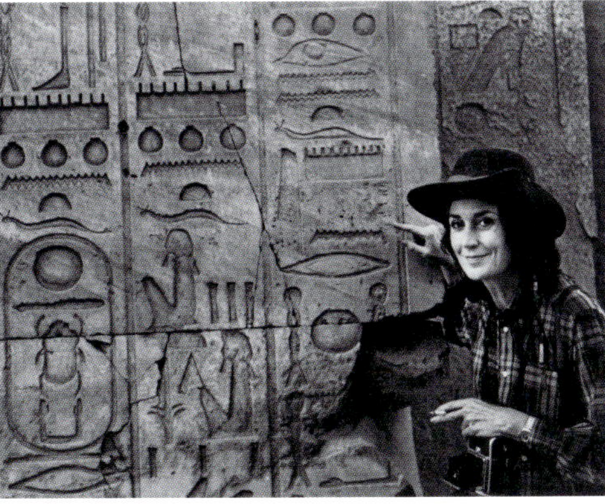

38

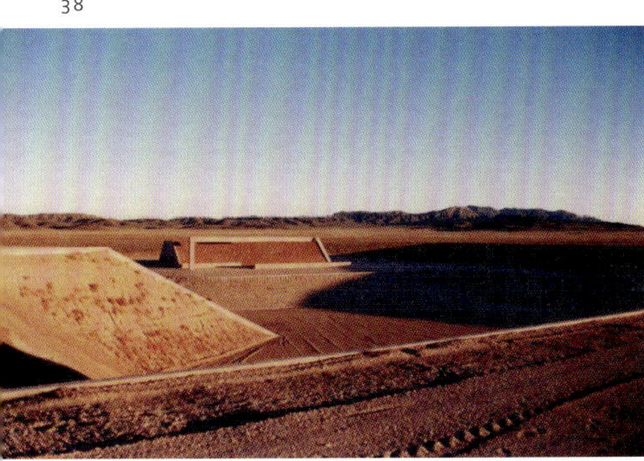

39

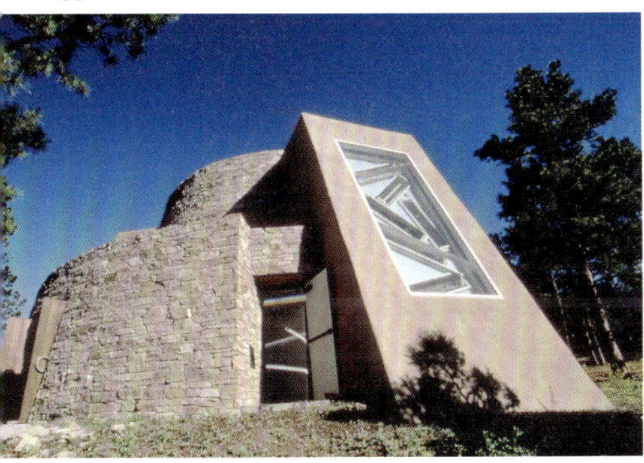

40

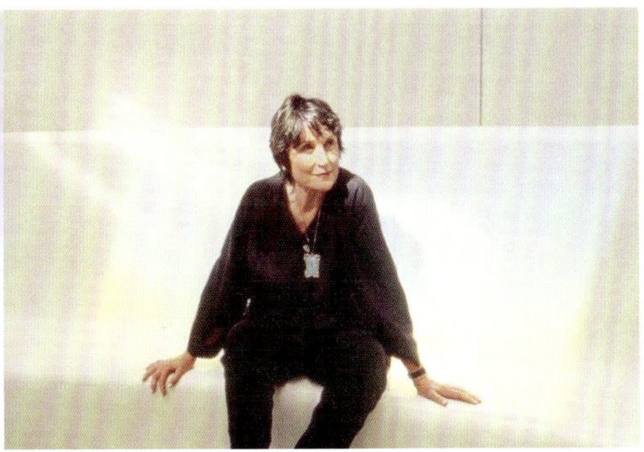

1984

March 21–June 7 Art historian Charles F. Stuckey conducts interviews with Dwan as part of the Archives of American Art Oral History Program.

1985

Dwan is elected as a fellow of the World Academy of Art and Science for her distinguished accomplishments as a gallerist.

December Dwan gifts Heizer's *Double Negative* to the Museum of Contemporary Art, Los Angeles.[209]

1988

A visit to a Pueblo kiva (a walled room for spiritual ceremonies) in the Southwest sparks the idea in Dwan for a light sanctuary based on the universal importance of the number twelve. It will be four years before she initiates the project.

1990

March 5–26 Dwan supports Young and Zazeela's Theatre of Eternal Music big band concert series at Dia Art Foundation in Chelsea, New York.

October 23–December 29 Loïc Malle of Galerie Montaigne, Paris, organizes a two-part tribute exhibition, *Virginia Dwan et Les Nouveaux Réalistes*, followed the next year by *Virginia Dwan: Art Minimal, Art Conceptuel, Earthworks*, October 1–December 14, 1991.

1992

Dwan is awarded the Chevalier de la Légion d'Honneur by the government of France in honor of the Dwan Gallery's support of the nouveaux réalistes.

1996

November After four years of planning and construction, the Dwan Light Sanctuary is completed at the United World College in Montezuma, New Mexico. The light sanctuary is based on Dwan's vision to create a place of quiet and contemplation that is open to all. It is codesigned by Dwan, architect Laban Wingert, and Charles Ross, who installs twelve solar prisms in the apses to optimize the space.

2003

May An article by Michael Kimmelman about Dwan's career is published in the *New York Times* in anticipation of the opening of Dia: Beacon.[210]

2010

July 14–March 21, 2011 Charles F. Stuckey again interviews Dwan as part of the Elizabeth Murray Oral History of Women in the Visual Arts project for the Archives of American Art.

2011

September 12–December 16 *Dwan, Los Angeles/New York: The Ephemera of a Gallery, 1959–1971* opens at David Platzker's Specific Object gallery in New York.

Dwan begins a new series of photographs for a book that will reflect on the human cost of war. She continues photographing military cemeteries throughout the United States. The theme harkens back to the earlier photographs she took of war memorials and cemeteries during her excursions with Smithson and Holt in the 1960s.

2012

May 27–September 3 *Ends of the Earth: Land Art to 1974* opens at the Museum of Contemporary Art, Los Angeles. Dwan writes for the exhibition catalog that receives the Alfred H. Barr Award.[211]

2013

September Dwan bequests 250 works from her personal collection to the National Gallery of Art, Washington. The works, by fifty-two artists, include 34 sculptures, 15 paintings, 159 prints and drawings, 39 photographs, two films, and one set of artists books.

November The Emily Harvey Foundation, New York, presents a week-long screening of films by Dwan, including her films about Andre, Cage, and Sturtevant.

2014

November 8 *Ahead of the Curve: Selections from the Virginia Dwan Collection* opens at the Weatherspoon Art Museum.

2015

July Heizer's *City* becomes part of the Basin and Range National Monument by decree of President Barack Obama.

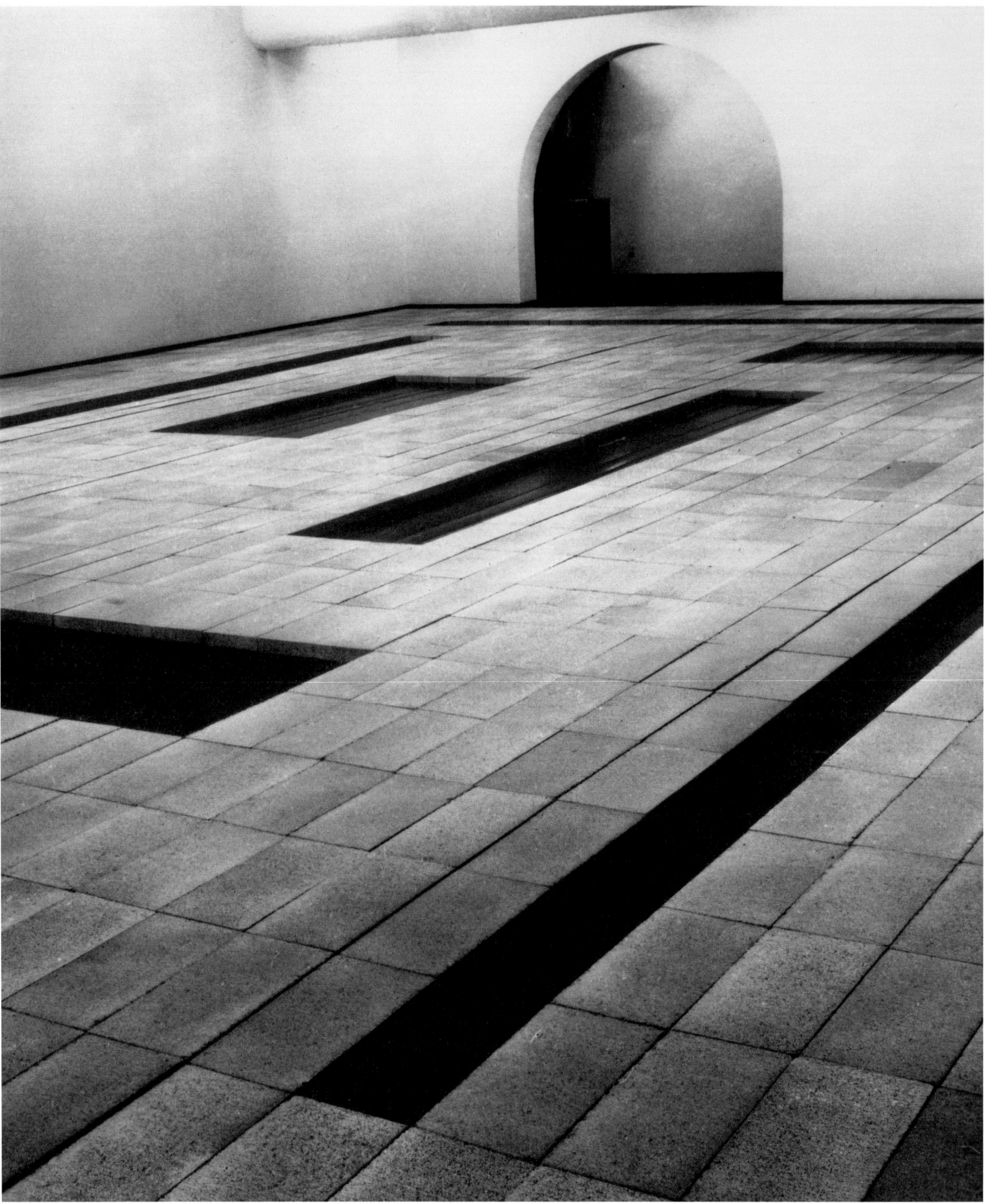

PAIGE ROZANSKI

EXHIBITION HISTORY

DWAN GALLERY, LOS ANGELES AND NEW YORK

STANLEY TWARDOWICZ, ANNOUNCEMENT (1)

REGINALD POLLACK, ANNOUNCEMENT (2)

PAUL BRACH, ANNOUNCEMENT (3)

ROBERT GOODNOUGH, INSTALLATION (4)

1

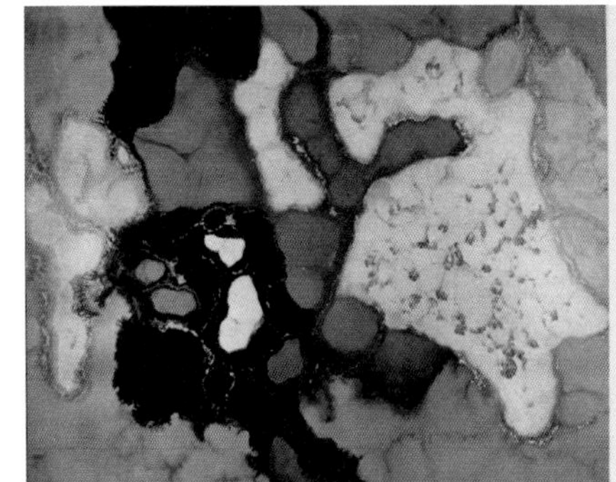

2

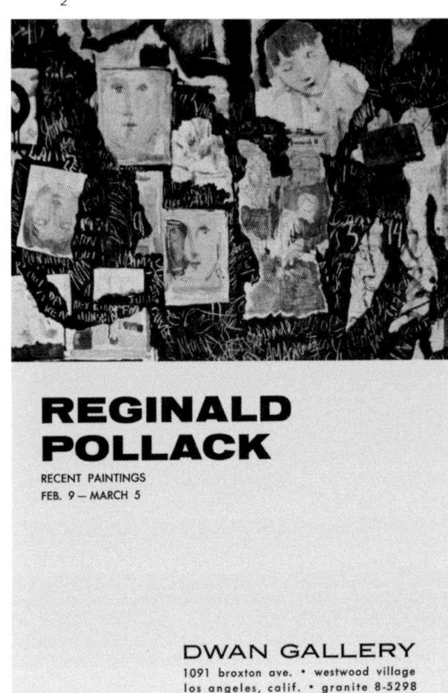

1959–1960 LOS ANGELES

1959

Shim Grudin
September (17)–October 19

Checklist not found

REVIEW / Henry J. Seldis, "In the Galleries: Prints Bring Sample of Masters' Greatness Here," *Los Angeles Times* (September 27, 1959): E9

Stanley Twardowicz
October 19–November 16

CHECKLIST / *#16*, 1959; *#15*, 1959; *#13*, 1957; *#23*, 1958; *#14*, 1959; *#36*, 1957; *#28*, 1958; *#16*, 1957; *#7*, 1957; *#29*, 1958; *#11*, 1958; *#12*, 1958; *#1*, 1959; *#29*, 1957; *#17*, 1959; 5 watercolors, 22″× 30″; 3 watercolors, 19″× 24″; 5 watercolors, 18″× 24″; 2 watercolors, 14½″× 22½″

Jean Rigaud
November (18)–December (14)

Checklist not found

REVIEW / A.M., "In the Galleries: Printmakers, Painters Present Newest Exhibits," *Los Angeles Times* (November 29, 1959): E8

Group Show: Prints
December 7–January 4, 1960

CHECKLIST / Georges Braque, *Les Huitres*; Georges Braque, *L'Oiseau Traversant le Nuage*; Victor Vasarely, *Composition*; Pablo Picasso, *Le Faune*; Marino Marini, *Three Horses*; Alberto Giacometti, *L'Homme debout*; Bernard Buffet, *Empire State Building*; Massimo Campigli, *Soirée d'Octobre*; Massimo Campigli, *Les Amies*; Massimo Campigli, *La Bienvenue*; Isac Friedlander, *Two Horses*; Joan Miró, *Strip Tease in Blue*; Gustave Singier, *Provence-Nuit*; Gustave Singier, *Digue-Espace*; Maurice Estève, *Le Grand Pavois*; Jean Leppien, *Composition*; Jean Le Moal, *Automne*; Stanley William Hayter, *La Noyée*; Marino Marini, *Thomas Mann*; Pablo Picasso, *La Toilette*; Adolf Hirémy-Hirschl, *Gehenna*; Adolf Hirémy-Hirschl, *The Family*; Adolf Hirémy-Hirschl, *The Burial*

MENTION / Henry J. Seldis, "In the Galleries: Robinson Collection on View at Benefit Showing," *Los Angeles Times* (December 20, 1959): D6

1960

Matsumi Kanemitsu
January 9–February 4

CHECKLIST / *Land of Apache*, 1958; *Portrait of an Unknown Poet*, 1959; *Cellar*, 1959; *Untitled*, 1959; *Wes Hardin*, 1958; *Summer Garden*, 1959; *Bourbon*, 1959; *Untitled*, 1959; *Untitled*, 1959; *Untitled #2*, 1959; *Untitled*, 1959; *Untitled*, 1959; *Untitled*, 1959; *D. One*, 1958; *D. Two*, 1959; *D. Three*, 1959; *Untitled*, 1959; *D. Four*, 1959; *D. Five*, 1959; *D. Six*, 1958; *D. Seven*, 1958; *D. Eight*, 1958; *D. Ten*, 1957; *D. Eleven*, 1959; *D. Twelve*, 1958; *Untitled*, 1959; *Untitled*, 1958; *Summer Night*, 1959; *Untitled*, 1959

REVIEWS / Henry J. Seldis, "In the Galleries: Amato's Recent Works Show a New Freedom," *Los Angeles Times* (January 17, 1960): E7 (under "Distinctive Vitality"); Jules Langsner, "Art news from Los Angeles." *Artnews* 59, no. 1 (March 1960): 51 "The affinity between Japanese sensibility and modern American painting can be seen in Kanemitsu at his best."

3

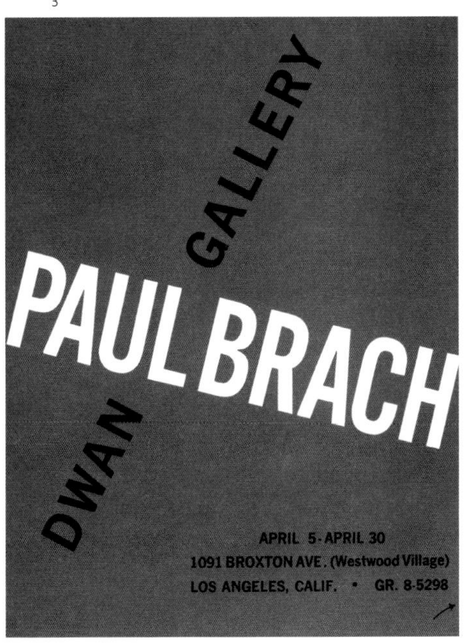

4

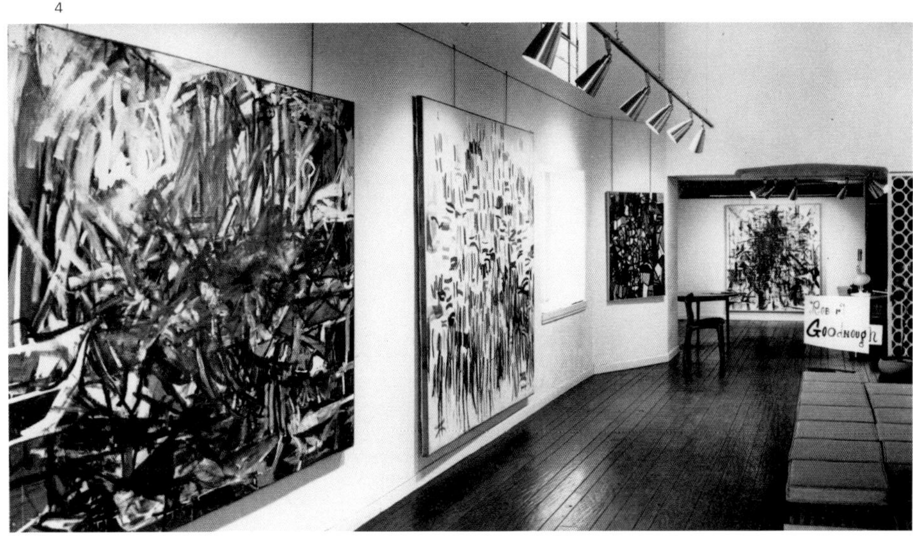

Reginald Pollack: Recent Paintings
February 9–March 5

CHECKLIST / *Oui-Non*; *Ardeche Landscape*; *Corner Painting*; *Renaissance Chair*; *Paintings on Black*; *Roma Antica*; *Studio Wall #1*; *Studio Wall #2*; *Interior #2*; *Green Studio*; *Multiple Painting*; *Roman Faces*; *Homage to Harnett*; *Painting Within a Painting*; *Nude*; *Hang As You Like It*; *After Roman Adventure*; *Labeaume Landscape and Room*; *Parigi* (triptych); *Blue Interior*; *Still Life*; *Reflections in a Roman Eye*; *Nude in Landscape*; *Still Life*; charcoal drawings; pastel drawings

REVIEWS / Charlene Cole, "Art Review," *Westwood Villager/Beverly Hills Times* (n.d.): 9; Henry J. Seldis, "In the Galleries: Thomas Sculpture Shows Maturity, Independence," *Los Angeles Times* (February 14, 1960): G8 (under "Lyrical Talent Shown"); Jules Langsner, "Art news from Los Angeles," *Artnews* 59, no. 1 (March 1960): 48

Friedel Dzubas
March 8–April 2

CHECKLIST / *Lazarus*, 1959; *Jungleskin*, 1959; *Cyclop*, 1959; *Polaris*, 1959; *Silent Sea*, 1959; *Omen*, 1959; *Arena*, 1959; *Kay's Travel*, 1959; *Rush*; *Tomorrow*; *Hidden Treasure*; *Untitled #2*; *Eastern #2*; *Untitled*

REVIEW / Jules Langsner, "Art news from Los Angeles," *Artnews* 59, no. 1 (March 1960): 48

Paul Brach
April 5–30

CHECKLIST / *Phalanx*; *Senacherib*; *Farol*; *Veronica #2*; *Treeburst*; *Pincor*; *Charade*; *Anatomy Lesson*; *Signal #1*; *Signal #2*; *Herald*; *Ozone*; *Observatory*; *Morlin*; *Enfilado*; *Spire*; *Beyond*; *Azimuth #2*; 4 untitled oils on paper

REVIEWS / Charlene Cole, "Art Review," *Westwood Villager/Beverly Hills Times* (April 7, 1960): n.p.; Henry J. Seldis, "In the Galleries: Artists Reflect Early Serenity," *Los Angeles Times* (April 10, 1960): 9 "The best and latest of Paul Brach's abstractions, being show at Westwood's Dwan Gallery to April 30, reflect a serenity rarely achieved by an artist so young." Gerald Nordland, "Art: The Expressionists," *Frontier: The Voice of the New West* 11, no. 7 (May 1960): 20–21 (Nordland also discusses the opening of the gallery and its intentions)

Robert Goodnough
May 2–28

CHECKLIST / *Odysseus I*; *Blue Seated Figure*; *The Survivors*; *The Carnival*; *The Battle*; *The Tree* (small); *Ulysses*; *Gray Seated Figure*; *Pipes*; *Flood II* (small); *Minotaur III*; *Landing "B"*; *Spartan Women II*; *A Man*; *Reclining Figure*; *Struggle, Landscape*; *Seated Figure Abstract #3*

REVIEWS / Henry J. Seldis, "In the Galleries: Jawlensky Role in Modern Art Manifest in Exhibit," *Los Angeles Times* (May 8, 1960): I17 (under "Promising Import") "Though he has not yet solidified a personal vocabulary, his ability to combine a certain exuberance with a great deal of control can be seen in the most successful works here." Jules Langsner, "Art news from Los Angeles," *Artnews* 59, no. 4 (Summer 1960): 56 "Whatever the diversity of Goodnough's influences, he is taking on the appearance of an authentic voice in American painting."

15 OF NEW YORK, ANNOUNCEMENT (5) AND INSTALLATION (6–7)

DRAWINGS, WATERCOLORS, COLLAGES, ANNOUNCEMENT (8)

LARRY RIVERS, GALLERY ENTRANCE DURING EXHIBITION (9) AND ANNOUNCEMENT (10)

5

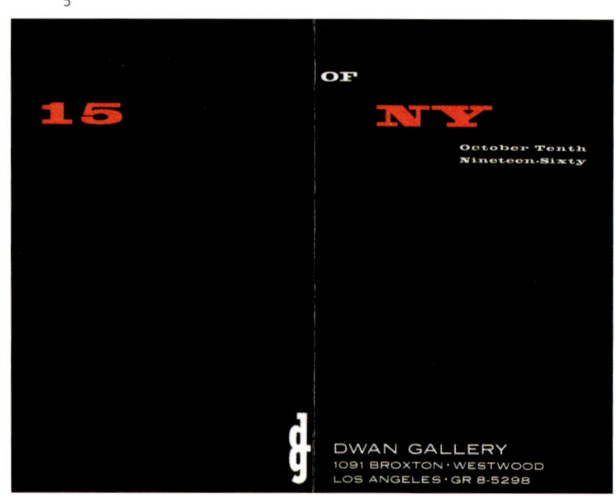

6

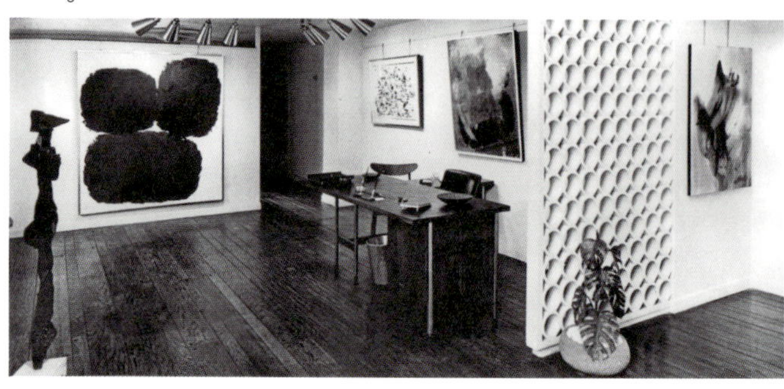

7

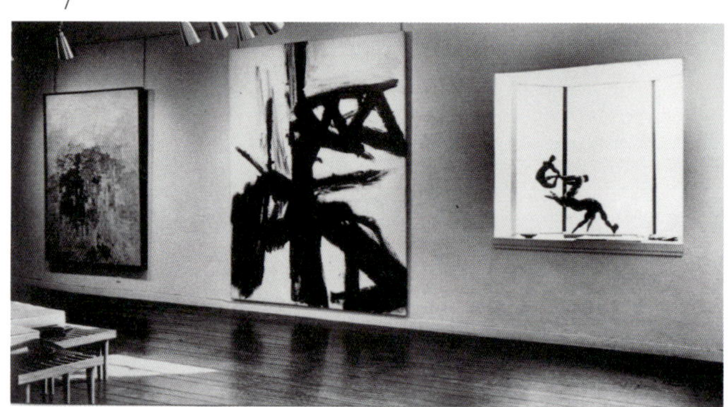

1960–1961 LOS ANGELES

Seymour Boardman: Paintings
May 31–June 25

CHECKLIST / *With Red*, 1959; *The Red and Green*, 1959; *Granada*, 1959; *White #1*, 1959; *Catalan*, 1960; *Backyard*, 1960; *Algonquin*, 1960; *Untitled*, 1959; *March Third*, 1960; *February Fifth*, 1960; *Alhambra*, 1959; *Yellow & Rose*, 1959; *April*, 1959; pencil and wash drawings

REVIEW / Henry J. Seldis, "Kestenbaum Repeat Show Shows Further Maturity," *Los Angeles Times* (June 12, 1960): F6 (under "Glowing Tapestries") "Sumptuous to the point of being exotic, some of the large canvases are decorative in the best sense of the word. They reflect fanciful recollections of nature rather than direct references to it. . . . [A] superior exhibit, both fresh and joyous."

Harry Nadler
June 27–July 23

CHECKLIST / *Castille*; *Landscape Xanadu*; *Golden Striker #2*; *Sun Country*; *Before Noon in the Glen*; *Balbec*; *Blue Hour*; *Golden Striker #3*; *Yerma*; *Golden Striker #4*; *Black Fugue*; *Alba*; *Golden Striker #1*; drawings; pastels

REVIEWS / Gerald Nordland, "Art: In Los Angeles," *Frontier: The Voice of the New West* 11, no. 9 (July 1960): 20; Henry J. Seldis, "In the Galleries: Munter Makes L.A. Debut," *Los Angeles Times* (July 3, 1960): F5 (under "Talented Young Artist")

15 of New York
October 10–November 15

CHECKLIST / Norman Bluhm, *Untitled*, 1958; Paul Brach, *Selene*, 1960; Robert Goodnough, *Standing Figure*, 1960; Philip Guston, *The Room*, 1954–1955; Grace Hartigan, *Untitled*, 1960; Paul Jenkins, *Eyes of the Dove–Astral Indigo*, 1959; Matsumi Kanemitsu, *June Morning*, 1960; Franz Kline, *Garcia*, 1957; Willem de Kooning, *Carole Lombard*, 1947; Raymond Parker, *Untitled*, 1960; Jackson Pollock, *Untitled*, 1951; Robert Richenburg, *Luxuriant Anguish*, 1958–1959; Larry Rivers, *Paul's Flag*, 1960; Stanley Twardowicz, *#28*, 1960; Adja Yunkers, *Untitled #1*, 1960 **In window:** Norman Bluhm, *Untitled*, 1960

REVIEW / Jules Langsner, "Art news from Los Angeles," *Artnews* 59, no. 8 (December 1960): 46 "Fifteen New York painters . . . are at the Dwan Gallery, which merits a citation for assembling such a show, long overdue in this vicinity, and establishing, as it does, the wide diversity of directions blanketed under such loose designations as School of New York or Abstractionism."

MENTION / Gerald Nordland, "Art: The New Yorkers Are Coming!," *Frontier: The Voice of the New West* 12, no. 1 (November 1960): 22

Robert Richenburg
November 14–December 10

CHECKLIST / *Black Rectangles Shot with White*, 1960; *Byzantine Window*, 1959; *Spiraled Rectangles*, 1960; *Twelve Circles, Four Halves*, 1960; *Two Circles*, 1959; *Two Doors*, 1960; *Nine Rounds*, 1959; *Fifteen Circles*, 1960; *Luxuriant Anguish*, 1958–1959; *Syria*, 1960; *Four Closed*, 1960; *Rising Sun*, 1960; *Autumn*, 1960; *Chance Out*, 1960; *The City*, n.d.

REVIEW / Henry J. Seldis, "In Galleries: Paintings by Rose Sparkle," *Los Angeles Times* (November 18, 1960): A5 (under "Large Canvases Are Stunning Decorations") "Robert Richenburg's enormous canvases at Westwood's Dwan Gallery introduce us to the work of a truly ingenious decorator, if one may be allowed to use this word in an affirmative way."

8

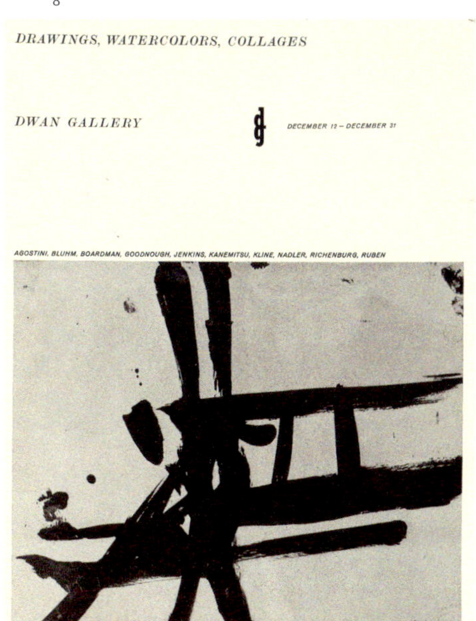

9

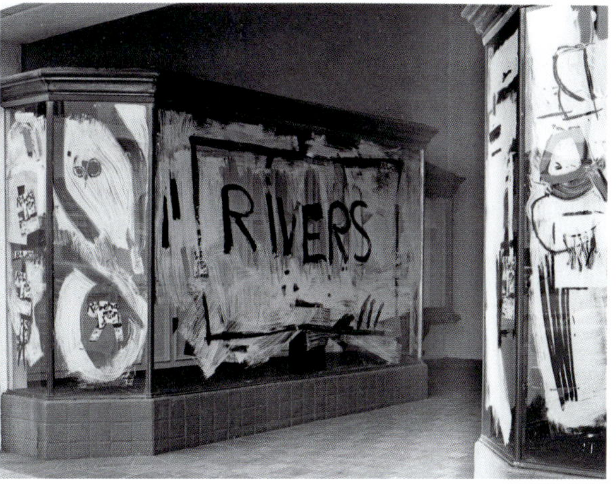

10

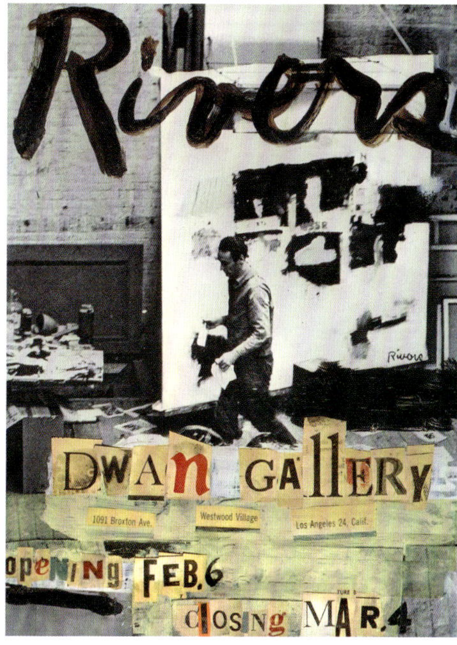

Drawings, Watercolors, Collages
December 12–31

CHECKLIST / Peter Agostini, ink-enamel, 1960; Matsumi Kanemitsu, sumi ink, 1959; Peter Agostini, ink-enamel, 1960; Robert Richenburg, collage, 1960; Norman Bluhm, gouache, 1960; Robert Goodnough, collage, 1957; Peter Agostini, 1958; Peter Agostini, 1957; Peter Agostini, 1957; Peter Agostini, watercolor, 1957; Norman Bluhm, gouache, 1960; Richards Ruben, crayon, 1959; Robert Goodnough, collage, 1957; Matsumi Kanemitsu, crayon, 1960; Franz Kline, oil on paper, 1955; Franz Kline, oil on paper, 1953; Robert Richenburg, collage, 1960; Robert Goodnough, collage, 1957; Matsumi Kanemitsu, sumi, 1960; Richard Ruben, crayon, 1959; Peter Agostini, ink-enamel, 1960; Seymour Boardman, oil wash and pencil, 1960; Matsumi Kanemitsu, sumi ink, 1960; Paul Jenkins, watercolor, 1959; Matsumi Kanemitsu, 1960 **In window:** Harry Nadler, ink, 1959; Paul Jenkins, watercolor, 1959; Robert Richenburg, collage, 1959; Harry Nadler, oil on paper, 1959

MENTIONS / Gerald Nordland, "Art: Exhibition in La Jolla," *Frontier: The New Voice of the West* 12, no. 2 (December 1960): 19 "[T]he general tenor will emphasize the drama of the black line on white surfaces." Henry J. Seldis, "In the Galleries: Gifted Foreign Artist Makes Local Debut," *Los Angeles Times* (December 23, 1960): A2

1961

Stanley Twardowicz
January 9–February 4

CHECKLIST / #26, 1960; #27 *(Arichat)*, 1960; #33 *(Two Tides)*, 1960; #24, 1960; #20, 1960; #22 *(Black Plus Black)*, 1960; #18, 1960; #17, 1960; #11, 1960; #15, 1960; #13, 1960; #30 *(Orange Passage)*, 1960; #28, 1960; #42 *(Black and Grey)*, 1960; #4, 1960; #6 *(Bright or Dark)*, 1960
In window: #12, 1956; #14, 1960; #52, 1960; #51, 1960; #44, 1960; #46, 1960; #49, 1960; #50, 1960; #47, 1960; #48, 1960; #45, 1960

REVIEWS / Henry J. Seldis, "In the Galleries: Show Marks a Departure," *Los Angeles Times* (January 20, 1961): A5 (under "New Yorker's Work Often Mysterious"); Jules Langsner, "Los Angeles Letter," *Art International* 5, no. 2 (March 1, 1961): 30, illustrated

Larry Rivers
February 6–March 4

CHECKLIST / *Summer Nude*, 1960; *Drug Store*, 1959; *U.N. Painting*, 1960; *King of Spades*, 1960; *Jack of Spades*, 1960; *Two of Spades*, 1960; *Jack of Spades*, 1960; *Cozy Cole I*, 1960; *Cozy Cole II*, 1960; *Paul's Flag*, 1960. [*Ford Truck*, *Jazz Drummer*, *Miss New Jersey*, *M*, and *Smoke* are not included in Dwan checklist but are reported as being in the show by Rivers in his autobiography *What Did I Do?*]

REVIEWS / Charlene Cole, *Westwood Villager/Beverly Hills Times* (February 9, 1961): n.p.; Henry J. Seldis, "In the Galleries: Sculpture Exhibit Impresses," *Los Angeles Times* (February 10, 1961): A6 (under "Serious Contribution to American Art?") "This is an exhibit to see since many critics consider Rivers' razzmatazz to be an eminently serious contribution to contemporary American painting." Gerald Nordland, "First Larry Rivers Show on Coast," *Los Angeles Mirror* (February 13, 1961): part 3:3; Gerald Nordland, "Art: The Artist Must Be an Explorer," *Frontier: The Voice of the New West* 12, no. 5 (March 1961): 23–25, illustrated

PHILIP GUSTON, FRANZ KLINE, CATALOG (11)

RAYMOND PARKER, INSTALLATION (12)

YVES KLEIN, INSTALLATION (13) AND POSTER (14)

SALVATORE SCARPITTA, POSTER (15)

SIX SCULPTORS, ANNOUNCEMENT (16)

11

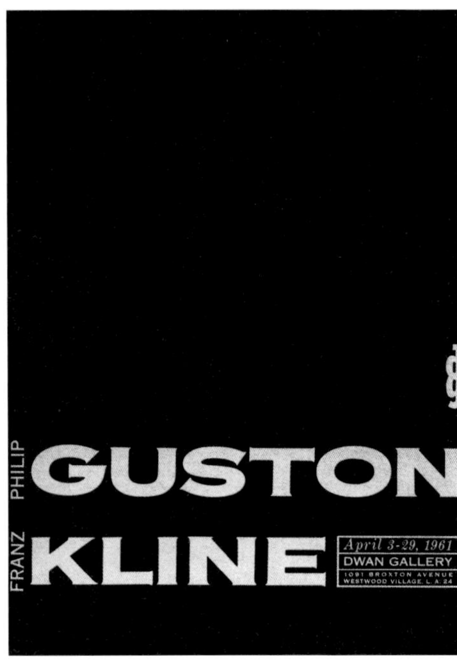

12

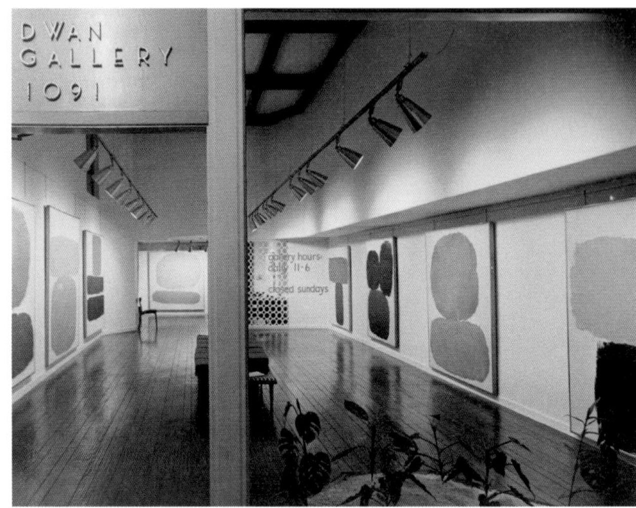

13

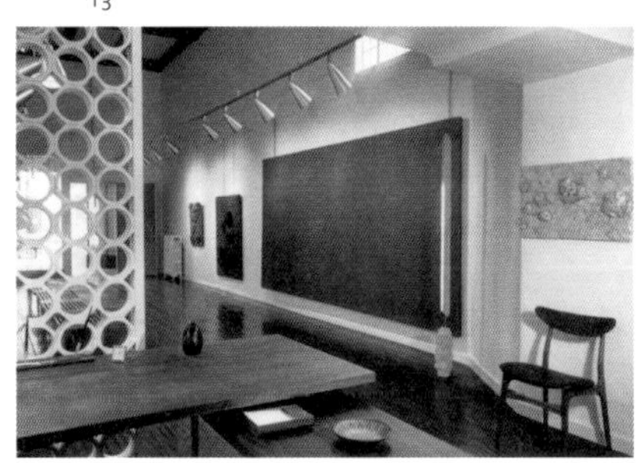

1961 LOS ANGELES

Stephen Pace
March 6–April 1

CHECKLIST / *59-06*, 1959; *57-29*, 1957; *60-06*, 1960; watercolor, 1959; watercolor, 1956; *58-A-4*, 1960; watercolor, 1958; watercolor, 1958; watercolor, 1959; watercolor, 1955 (not hung); *58-A-5*, 1958; *59-A-2*, 1959; *59-A-14*, 1959; *58-A-3*, 1958 **In window:** *60-A-19*, 1960; *57-28*, 1957

Philip Guston, Franz Kline
April 3–29

CHECKLIST / **Franz Kline:** *Black Sienna*, 1960; *Harleman*, 1960; *Garcia*, 1957; *Calumet City*, 1959; *Two Pastels* (diptych), 1958; *Study for August Day*, 1957; *Composition*, 1955; *Composition*, 1953; *Torres*, 1960 **Philip Guston:** *Traveler II*, 1960; *Garden of M*, 1960; *Sleeper II*, 1959; *The Cup*, 1960; *Visit*, 1959; *Wintergreen II*, 1959; *Close Up II*, 1959; *Warwick V*, 1959; *Dover I*, 1958; *The Room*, 1958

REVIEWS / Gerald Nordland, "Art: de Kooning, Kline and Guston," *Frontier: The Voice of the New West* (April 1961): 22–24; Charlene Cole, "Art Review," *Westwood Villager/Beverly Hills Times* (April 6, 1961): 9; Henry J. Seldis, "In the Galleries: Shows Have a N.Y. Flavor," *Los Angeles Times* (April 7, 1961): IIA6 "Franz Kline, whose imposing, stark and poetic exercises in monumental calligraphy are memorable in their directness and architectural strength, can also be persuasive in his smallest drawings. . . . While examination of his canvases leads to the conclusion that Guston has both craftsmanship and inventiveness, this spectator finds them lacking poetry and excitement." "Paintings by Rivers Shown at Art Museum," *Santa Barbara News*, April 9, 1961; Gerald Nordland, "De Kooning, Kline and Guston Shows Attract Great Attention," *Los Angeles Mirror* (April 10, 1961): I9 "While occasional paintings by these artists have been seen on the western slopes, this is the first show which has permitted southlanders to see as many as eight or ten works by each." Jules Langsner, "Los Angeles Letter," *Art International* 5, nos. 5–6 (June–August 1961): 64, illustrated

Raymond Parker
May 1–27

CHECKLIST / *Untitled*, 1960–1961, 80″× 84″; *Untitled*, 1960–1961, 84″× 85″; *Untitled*, 1960–1961, 77″× 85″; *Untitled*, 1960–1961, 73″× 70″; *Untitled*, 1960–1961, 68″× 70″; *Untitled*, 1960–1961, 68″× 70″; *Untitled*, 1960–1961, 68″× 60″; *Untitled*, 1960–1961, 72″× 69″; *Untitled*, 1960–1961, 74″× 69″ **In window:** *Untitled*, 1960–1961, 51″× 60″; *Untitled*, 1960–1961, 68″× 70″

REVIEW / Henry J. Seldis, "Humanity Guerreschi's Forte," *Los Angeles Times* (May 12, 1961): A4 (under "Peter Krohn Exhibit Shows Talent")

Yves Klein — le Monochrome
May 29–June 24

CHECKLIST / *Pink Sponge Relief*; *Blue Sponge Relief*; *Large Blue Monochrome*; *Gold Obelisque*; *Gold Sponge Relief*; *Gold Sponge Sculpture*; *Pink Monochrome*; *"Jonathan Swift," empreinte*; 2 *Fire Paintings*; *Living Brush Painting*; *Blue Obelisque*; *Pink Obelisque*; 4 *Blue Monochromes*; *Blue Rain*

REVIEWS / Henry J. Seldis, "In the Galleries: Octogenarian's Art Abounds in Vigor," *Los Angeles Times* (June 2, 1961): A6 (under "Paris Sensationalist Produces 'Latest'") "It may well be that Klein is trying to provoke us into considering the absurdities of life and art but in doing so he nihilistically destroys even the last shred of the great spiritual nourishment mankind has always found art. He thumbs his nose at the serious spectator and enraptures those to whom 'the latest' is always 'the greatest.' If you don't dig it, you're square, which puts you into some mighty good company." Jules Langsner, "Los Angeles Summer

14

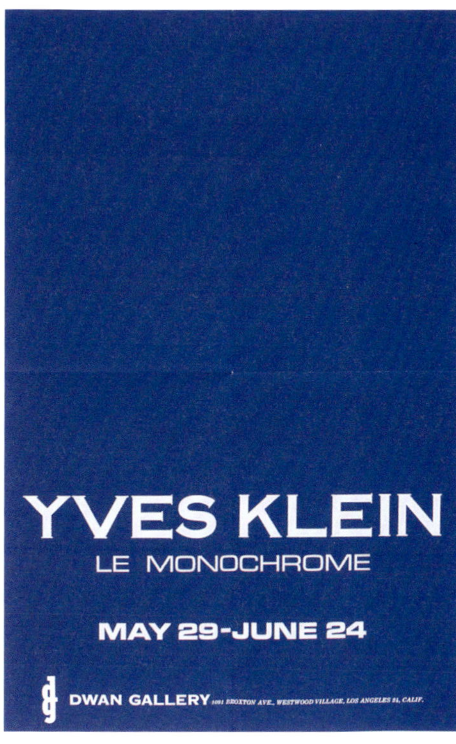

15

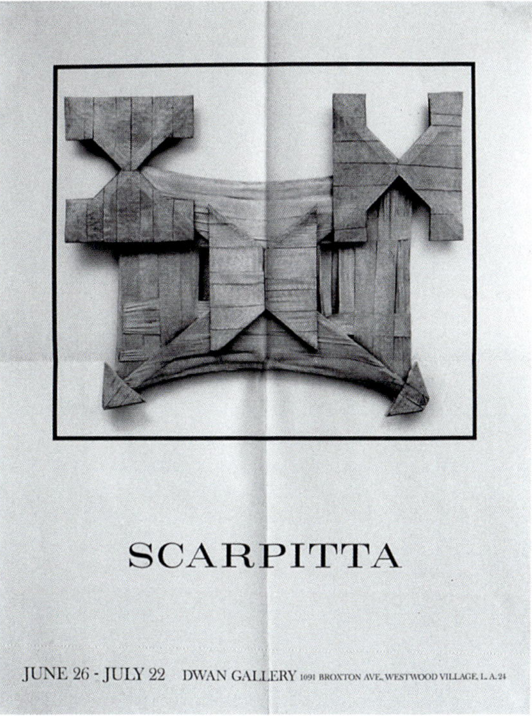

16

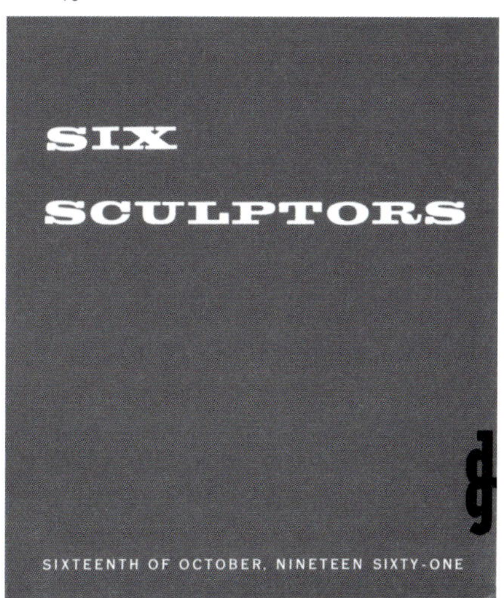

Letter: Klein," *Art International* 5, no. 8 (October 20, 1961): 86, illustrated "The Klein exhibition provoked the expected reaction of outrage, befuddlement and scurrility . . . this spectator, while not subscribing to Klein's metaphysics, enjoyed the show on a purely sensorial level."

Salvatore Scarpitta
June 26–July 22

CHECKLIST / *Little Sphinx*, 1960; *Red Freight*, 1960; *Gunner's Mate*, 1961; *Depart*, 1960; *Diogenes Arriving*, 1961; *Painted Bugle*, 1959; *Helikon*, 1957; *Forager Stalks Plankton*, 1960; *Hollander*, 1958; *Out of Step*, 1960; *Moby Alone*, 1958

REVIEWS / Charlene Cole, "Relief Constructions," *Westwood Villager / Beverly Hills Times*, (June 29, 1961): n.p.; Henry J. Seldis, "In the Galleries: Exhibit Provokes Meditation," *Los Angeles Times* (July 14, 1961): A4 (under "Objects by Scarpitta 'Liberate' Canvas") "Using painted and folded canvas in a sculptural, relief manner, the Italo-American artist evokes a number of personal fantasies and astonishes the viewer by the richness and subtlety he draws from his material."

Joan Mitchell
September 18–October 14

CHECKLIST / *King of Spades*, 1956; *Gentian Violet*, 1960–1961; *The Green Book of Barbara Guest*, 1960; *October Island*, 1956–1957; *Untitled*, 1960; *Untitled*, 1960–1961; *To The Harbourmaster*, 1957–1958; *Untitled*, 1960–1961; *Untitled*, 1960 **In window:** *Untitled*, 1960; *Untitled*, 1960

REVIEWS / Henry J. Seldis, "In the Galleries: Exhibit Illuminates Sweden," *Los Angeles Times* (September 29, 1961): A7 (under "Joan Mitchell Will Make Debut in L.A."); Jules Langsner, "Los Angeles Letter," *Art International* 5, no. 9 (November 20, 1961): 43, illustrated "Mitchell manages to suggest in her pictures involuntary memory traces of the man-made and natural worlds fused in the recesses of the psyche, and then precipitated into visible existence by her meeting with the canvas. . . . It is immediacy of impact that counts in her work, and taken on her own terms, she achieves what she sets out to do."

Six Sculptors
October 16–November 11

CHECKLIST / Peter Agostini, *Summer Cloud*, 1959; Peter Agostini, *Burlesque Queen*, 1950; Peter Agostini, *Woman V*, 1956; Peter Agostini, *Ariel*, 1958; Lee Bontecou, *Untitled*, 1960; Lee Bontecou, *Untitled*, 1959; Lee Bontecou, *Untitled*, 1960; Lee Bontecou, *Untitled*, 1961; César (Baldaccini), *Seul*, 1960; César, *On est trois*, 1961; John Chamberlain, *Ginger*, 1961; John Chamberlain, *Untitled relief*, 1960; Edward Higgins, *Owl*, 1960; Edward Higgins, *Untitled*, 1961; Edward Higgins, *The Hip*, 1960; Louise Nevelson, *Night Garden II*, 1958; Louise Nevelson, *Night Plant II*, 1956; Louise Nevelson, *Royal Organ IV*, 1961

REVIEWS / Henry J. Seldis, "In the Galleries: Sculpture Rises From Junk Heap," *Los Angeles Times* (October 20, 1961): A2; Jules Langsner, "Los Angeles Letter," *Art International* 10 (Christmas 1961): 47, illustrated

MATSUMI KANEMITSU, INSTALLATION (17)

ROBERT GOODNOUGH, CATALOG (18)

AD REINHARDT, INSTALLATION (19)

ROBERT RAUSCHENBERG, INSTALLATION (20)

ARMAN, INSTALLATION (21)

17

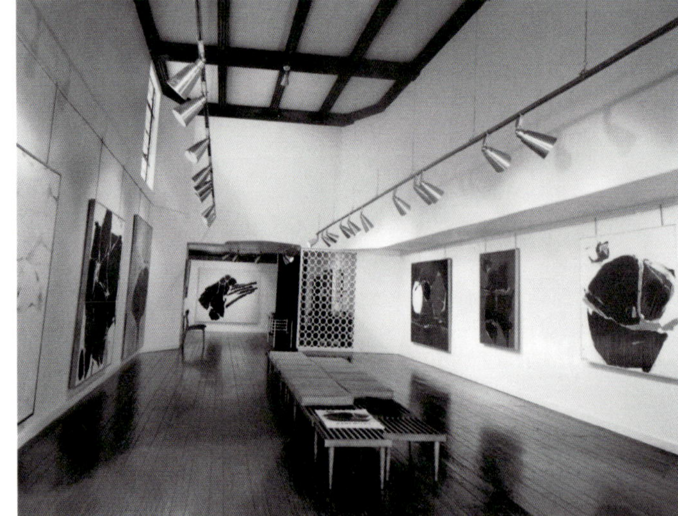

18

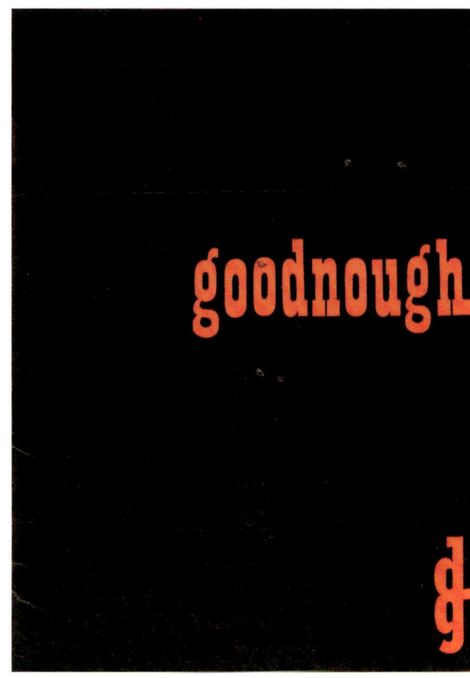

1961–1962 LOS ANGELES

Matsumi Kanemitsu
November 13–December 9

CHECKLIST / *Metamorphosis*, 1960; *Hoe*, 1960; *Friday's Act One*, 1959–1960; *Untitled*, 1960; *Untitled*, 1961; *Northwind*, 1961; *Apocalypse*, 1960; *Untitled*, 1960; *Ko*, 1959; *Blues in the Closet*, 1960; *Sunday*, 1960; *Silent Night*, 1960; *Summer Series*, 1961 **In window:** *Tavern-On-Rod*, 1960; *Malibu Morning*, 1961; *Untitled*, 1961

REVIEW / Henry J. Seldis, "In the Galleries: Kanemitsu Fuses Dynamic Contemplative Elements," *Los Angeles Times* (November 23, 1961): A7 "Elegance of style and subtlety of tonality distinguish the excellent non-objective canvases by Kanemitsu. . . . The talented American Oriental manages to fuse contemplative and dynamic elements in a remarkably successful manner."

MENTION / Jules Langsner, "Los Angeles Letter," *Art International* 10 (Christmas 1961): 47

Group Show
December 11–January 6, 1962

Checklist not found

1962

Robert Goodnough
January 7–February 3

CHECKLIST / *Abstract Horse*, 1961; *Abstract Figure with Letters*, 1961; *Horse and Rider*, 1961; *Seated Horse*, 1961; *Bright Fellow*, 1961; *Two Moving Horses I*, 1961; *Two Moving Horses II*, 1961; *Two Moving Horses IV*, 1961; *Small Seated Horse*, 1961; *Smiling Woman*, 1961; *Movement of Horses*, 1960; *Toreador*, 1958; *The Spartan*, 1960; *Untitled*, 1960; 3 works, *Untitled*, 1961; collages; 2 works, *Untitled*, lithographs; *Landing III*

REVIEW / Henry J. Seldis, "In the Galleries: Canvases Exuberant With Sense of Form," *Los Angeles Times* (January 22, 1962): A4 "One of the few contemporary painters who combines an innate sense of form with a penchant for free painterly expression, Goodnough creates basically joyous expressions as meaningful as they are ingratiating."

Ad Reinhardt
February 4–March 3

CHECKLIST / *A*, 1956; [no title], 1958; *I*, 1954–1958; *M*, 1955; *K*, 1960; *D*, 1952–1954; *B*, 1958; *F*, 1954; *E*, 1953; *G*, 1955; *J* (quadryptic), 1959; [no title], 35″× 17″, 1960 **Over arch:** *C*, 1959 **In window:** *H*, 1954

REVIEWS / Henry J. Seldis, "In the Galleries: Exhibit Boasts Some of Europe's Finest Selections," *Los Angeles Times* (February 9, 1962): C5 (under "Reinhardt Canvases Worth Second Look"); Gerald Nordland, "Art: The Artist as Reinhardt," *Frontier: The Voice of the New West* (March 1962): 23–24 "With these paintings one is forced to make an effort in order to be able to see them at all." Jules Langsner, "Los Angeles Letter," *Art International* 6, no. 3 (April 1962): 65, illustrated "As it happens, Reinhardt's work has not caught the fancy of the chintzy collectors, but all that proves is the all-too-human trait to do as thy neighbor does."

19

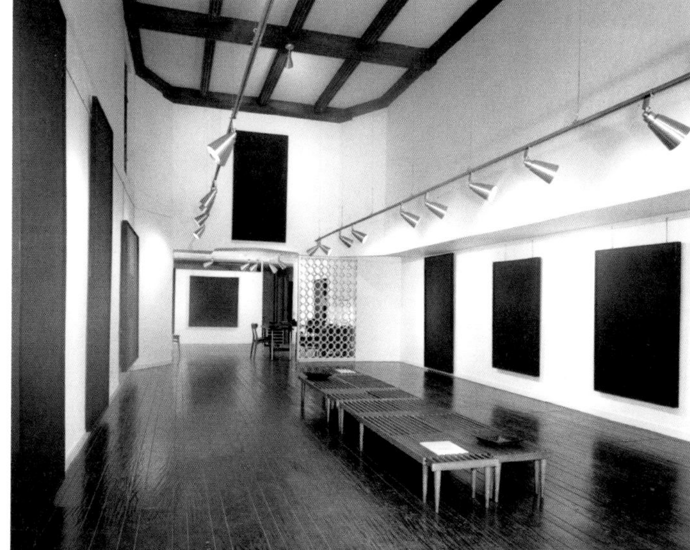

20

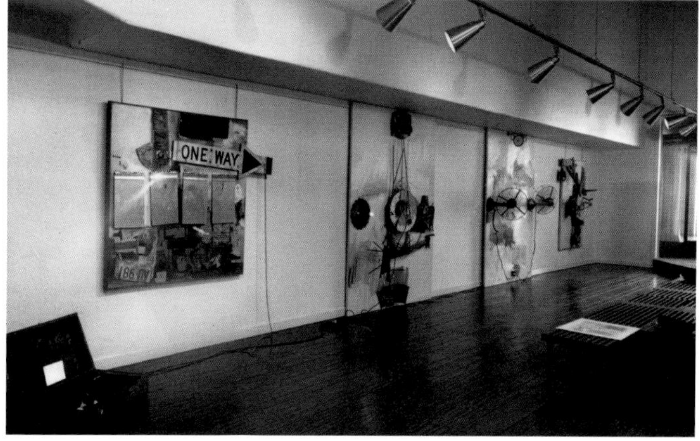

21

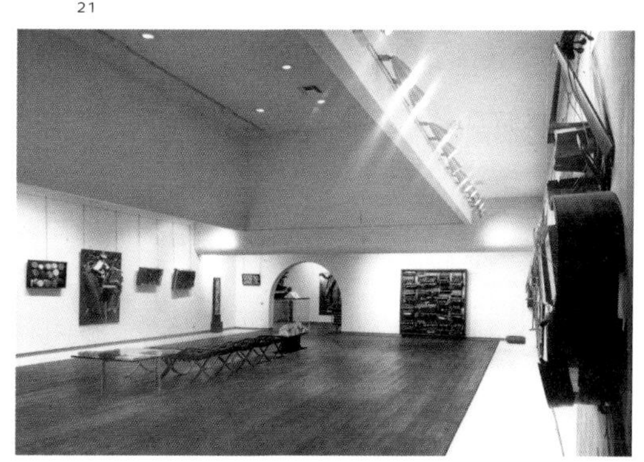

Robert Rauschenberg
March 4–31

CHECKLIST / *Rigger*, 1961; *Blue Exit*, 1961; *First Landing Jump*, 1961; *Blue Eagle*, 1961; *Nettle*, 1960; *Black Market*, 1961; *Navigator*, 1961–1962; *Pantomime*, 1961; *Coexistence*, 1961; *Wooden Gallop*, 1961; drawings

REVIEWS / Henry J. Seldis, "In the Galleries: A Week for Avant-garde," *Los Angeles Times* (March 9, 1962): D7 [Seldis refers to the "raucous" show in Henry J. Seldis, "In the Galleries: Painter Takes Giant Step Into Balanced World," *Los Angeles Times* (April 6, 1962): C8 (under "'Other Art' Objects Mark Waldren Show")]; Arthur Secunda, "Kaleidoscopic Look At Current Exhibits," *Beverly Hills Times* (March 15, 1962): n.p.; Gerald Nordland, "Neo-Dada Goes West," *Arts Magazine* 36, no. 9 (May–June 1962): 102–103 "One cannot help feeling that Rauschenberg is forced to keep working at his shock stock because he is primarily a painter. The paint application has a very special beauty in many of the action-smeared canvases. The appliquéd detritus of flattened cans, light fixtures, TV antennae and broken signs is often no more than that. The objects seldom integrate into the work. The incongruity of the sensuously applied paint and the offensive crushed cans grows continually less shocking."

MENTION / Jules Langsner, "Art news from Los Angeles," *Artnews* 61, no. 3 (May 1962): 46

William Waldren
April 1–28

CHECKLIST / *Edge of Silence*, 1961; *The Opposed*, 1961; *November #4*, 1961; *The X is for Negation*, 1961; *October #10*, 1962; *January #2*, 1962; *Divided by Yesterday*, 1961; *February #1*, 1962; *March #2*, 1962; *June #3*, 1961; *July #1*, 1961; *June #10*, 1961; *February #2*, 1961; *November #12*, 1961; *Sculpture #1*, 1957; *Sculpture #7*, 1957; *Sculpture #9*, 1957; *May*, 1961 (on poster)

REVIEWS / Henry J. Seldis, "In the Galleries: Painter Takes Giant Step Into Balanced World," *Los Angeles Times* (April 6, 1962): C8 (under "'Other Art' Objects Mark Waldren Show"); Jules Langsner, "Los Angeles Letter, May 1962," *Art International* 6, no. 7 (September 25, 1962): 50, 51, illustrated

Arman
May 13–June 9

CHECKLIST / *Reveils* (alarm clocks), 1960; *Moulins à Café* (coffee mills), 1960–1961; *Echeveaux* (spools), 1960; *Les Rouages* (wheels, cogs), 1961; *Poires Sonettes* (doorbells), 1960; *Les Encriers* (ink wells), 1961; *Casseroles en Email* (enameled pots and pans), 1960; *Les Outils* (tools), 1960; *Lampes-Radio* (radio tubes), 1960; *Les Batteurs* (mallets), 1961; *Les Pistons* (pistons), 1960; *Contrebasse*, 1961; *Trompes-Auto* (car horns), 1960; *Les Ampoules* (medicine ampoules), 1960; *Typewriters*, 1962; *Chaussures* (shoes), 1962; *Cartouches* (ink refills), 1962; *Cameras*, 1962; *Brosses* (brushes), 1962; *Pistolets* (pistols), 1962; *Bequilles* (crutches), 1962; *Poubelle-Kit*, 1962; *Violon*, 1962; *Radio*, 1962; *Guitare (Death of Harlequin)*, 1962; *Harpe*, 1962; *Stamps #1*, 1962; *Stamps #2*, 1962; *Stamps #3*, 1961

REVIEWS / Henry J. Seldis, "The Galleries: New Latin Art," *Los Angeles Times* (May 11, 1962): C4 (under "Arman Montages Mark Gallery Debut"); Gerald Nordland, "Reviews: Los Angeles, Arman," *Artforum* 1, no. 2 (July 1962): 7–8, 9, illustrated "The very simple power of repetition found in the massing of these forms works a strange magic, as if of incantation."

GROUP SHOW (JUNE), INSTALLATION (22)

RAYMOND PARKER, ANNOUNCEMENT (23)

MY COUNTRY 'TIS OF THEE, CATALOG (24), INSTALLATION (25), AND ADVERTISEMENT (26)

22

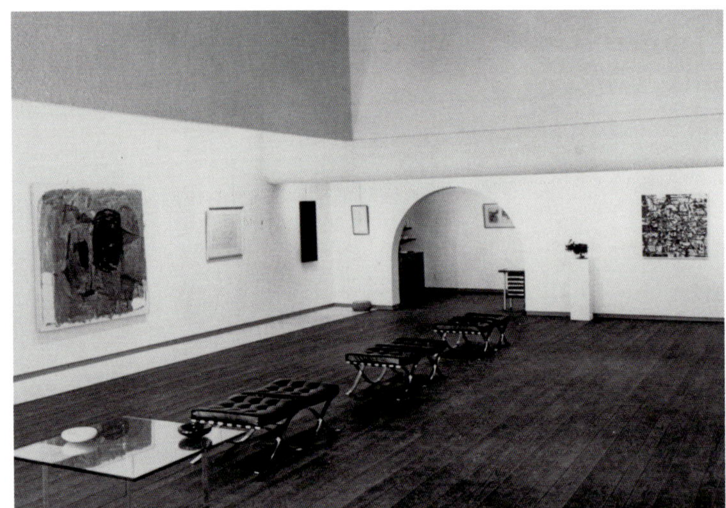

23

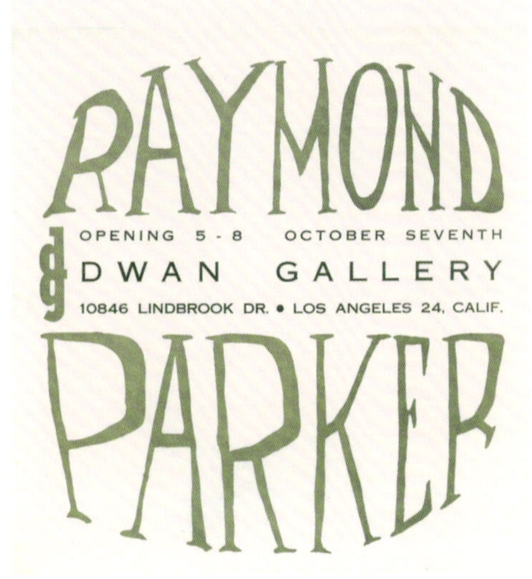

1962 LOS ANGELES

Group Show
June 11–July 7

CHECKLIST / Robert Motherwell, *Monument to Jackson Pollock*, 1956; Jean Tinguely, *Radio & Motor #20*, 1962; Jean Tinguely, *Radio*, 1962; Jackson Pollock, *Untitled*, 1951; Yves Klein, blue sponge sculpture; Willem de Kooning, *Man*, 1947; William Waldren, [no title]; Matsumi Kanemitsu, *Untitled*, 1962; Matsumi Kanemitsu, *Untitled*, 1962; Ad Reinhardt, [no title]; Franz Kline, *Untitled*, 1953; Franz Kline, *Untitled*, 1951; Joan Miró, *Figures et Animaux dans un paysage*, 1942; Raymond Parker, *Untitled P-41*, 1960; Lee Bontecou, *Untitled*; Philip Guston, *Untitled*, 1952; Philip Guston, *Untitled*, 1952

REVIEW / Arthur Secunda, "Reviews: Los Angeles, Group Show: Dwan Galley," *Artforum* 1, no. 4 (September 1962): 8, 9–10, illustrated
"A most serious group show has been hung by the Dwan, providing a lift and a celebration of art whose example other Southern California galleries could hopefully emulate."

Harry Nadler
July 9–28

CHECKLIST / *Encounter #2*, 1962; *Buchenwald Landscape #2*, 1961; *Atalaya*, 1961; *El Portal*, 1962; *Buchenwald Landscape #6*, 1961; *Journey*, 1961–1962; *Encounter #1*, 1962; *Homage to Goya*, 1960; *Catalonia*, 1962; *La Bruja*, 1961; *Encounter #9*, 1962; *Encounter #10*, 1962; *Encounter #11*, 1962; *Encounter #7*, 1962; *Encounter #8*, 1962; *Small Painting #4*, 1962; *Small Painting #10*, 1962; *Small Painting #15*, 1962; *Small Painting #8*, 1962; *Small Painting #3*, 1962; *Small Painting #1*, 1962; *Small Painting #5*, 1962; *Small Painting #14*, 1962; *Small Painting #13*, 1962; *Small Painting #12*, 1962; *Small Painting #6*, 1962; *Small Painting #9*, 1962; *Small Painting #7*, 1962; *Small Painting #2*, 1962; *Small Painting #11*, 1962

REVIEWS / Arthur Millier, "Martyr Portrayed, Woman Worshiped," *Los Angeles Times* (June 17, 1962): N9 (under "A Graduate of UCLA")
"For Nadler's second show at the Dwan Gallery, he includes oils on canvas and paper that place a heavy emphasis on the brush and its ability to capture form, movement, and color." Arthur Secunda, "Reviews: Los Angeles, Harry Nadler," *Artforum* 1, no. 3 (August 1962): 8, 10, illustrated
"As a technical interpreter of formal drama, a stage-setter, he is extraordinarily skilled and cannot be dismissed lightly, for he definitely has something of urgency pending."

Group Show
September 7–October (5)

CHECKLIST / Robert Goodnough, *The Carnival*, 1959; Raymond Parker, *Untitled*, 1959; Larry Rivers, *Jack of Spades*, 1960; Jean Tinguely, *Radio and Motor*, 1962; Ad Reinhardt, *Untitled*, 1954–1958; Edward Higgins, *The Hip*, 1960; Mark Rothko, *Untitled*, 1959; Yves Klein, *Untitled*, 1960; Robert Rauschenberg, *Blue Exit*, 1961; Josef Albers, *Homage to the Square: "Grisaille and Ground,"* 1961

REVIEW / Henry T. Hopkins, "Reviews: Los Angeles, Group Show," *Artforum* 1, no. 6 (November 1962): 48–49, illustrated

24

25

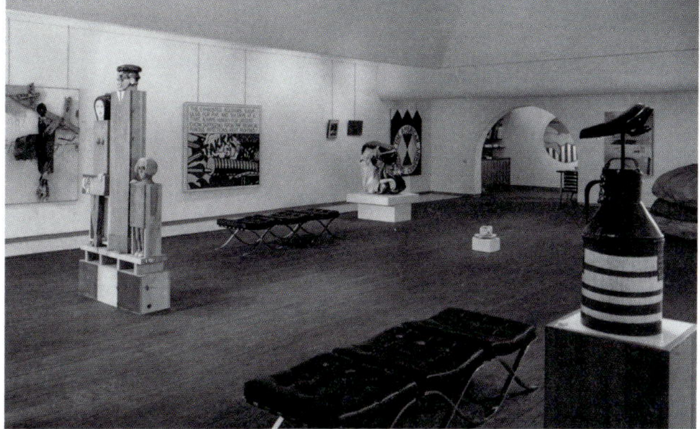

26

by the time this ad is read - not to mention its predecessor - the my country 'tis of thee show will have run its course. it will be followed on december 16 by large oil paintings of matsumi kanemitsu and on december 25 by christmas; at dwan gallery, 10846 lindbrook dr., los angeles 24.

Raymond Parker
October 7–November (3)

CHECKLIST / *Untitled*, 1959–1960; *Untitled*, 1960; *Untitled*, 1960–1961; *Untitled*, 1960; *Untitled*, 1961; seven works titled *Untitled*, 1962

REVIEWS / Henry J. Seldis, "In the Galleries: A First for Balboa," *Los Angeles Times* (October 26, 1962): C4 (under "James McGarrell Canvases Impress"); Jules Langsner, "Los Angeles Letter," *Art International*, 6, no. 10 (December 20, 1962): 39 "He thereby achieves an imagery intrinsic to the existence of pictures instead of reminiscences of things that happen to us in the world outside painting." Don Factor, "Review: Los Angeles, Raymond Parker," *Artforum* 1, no. 7 (January 1963): 12 "But they act as nothing more than well-painted, directionless variations on a theme. In comparing the later paintings with the earlier ones, one finds no sign of refinement or progress."

My Country 'Tis of Thee
November 18–December 15

CHECKLIST / Jasper Johns, *Flag on Orange Field*, 1957; Charles Frazier, *Albion*, 1962; Edward Kienholz, *Untitled American President*, 1962; Andy Warhol, *Marilyn Monroe*, 1962; Claes Oldenburg, *Coffee Cup*, 1962; Claes Oldenburg, *Floorburger*, 1962; Larry Rivers, *Cedar Bar Menu*, 1960; Tom Wesselmann, *Great American Nude #X*, 1961; Robert Indiana, *The American Reaping Company*, 1961; Jasper Johns, *Bronze Flag*, 1962; Larry Rivers, *Small Last Civil War Veteran*, n.d.; John Chamberlain, *Rayvredd*, 1962; Roy Lichtenstein, *Takka Takka*, 1962; Robert Rauschenberg, *Coexistence*, 1961; James Rosenquist, *Hey, Let's Go For A Ride*, 1961; Marisol, *The Kennedys*, 1962

REVIEWS / Henry J. Seldis, "In the Galleries: Jones Show Adds to Artist's Stature," *Los Angeles Times* (November 23, 1962): D14 (under "New Elegance Notes in Sculpture Show"); Henry J. Seldis, "'New Realism' Comes in Humor, Cynicism," *Los Angeles Times* (December 2, 1962): Q2 "There is a humor and irreverence that is fundamentally American in this exhibition but there is also an abundance of cynicism and an overt search for novelty and faddism that does not augur well for the seriousness and future of this new departure." Jules Langsner, "Los Angeles Letter," *Art International* 7, no. 1 (January 25, 1963): 81–82, illustrated "The furor generated by this show stems from two different kinds of provocation: satirical digs at the Stars and Stripes American way of life, and the brash irreverence for canons of art that is found in the works of such participating artists. . . . So far as this reviewer's response is concerned, if there are unpardonable crimes in the show they have nothing to do with jibes at super-patriots or with esthetic blasphemy but rather with the propagation of boredom." Gerald Nordland, "Pop Goes the West," *Arts Magazine* 37, no. 5 (February 1963): 60–61, illustrated; Rosalind G. Wholden, "Reviews: Los Angeles, My Country 'Tis of Thee," *Artforum* 1, no. 8 (February 1963): 20, illustrated "The sweet liberties taken in this show have culminated in the American Dream: advertising at last has been accepted by art!"

Matsumi Kanemitsu: Recent Paintings
December 16–January 4, 1963

CHECKLIST / *Silent*, 1962; *Reflection*, 1962; *62-5*, 1962; *Sorcery*, 1962; *62-4*, 1962; *Mirror*, 1962; *Untitled*, 1962; *The Morning*, 1962; *62-7*, 1962; *Insouciance*, 1962

REVIEW / Henry J. Seldis, "In the Galleries: Kanemitsu Uses Soft Approach in Painting," *Los Angeles Times* (December 21, 1962): D4

MARTIAL RAYSSE, ADVERTISEMENT (27)

DEALER'S CHOICE, ANNOUNCEMENT (28)

FRANZ KLINE, INSTALLATION (29) AND CATALOG (30)

JEAN TINGUELY, INSTALLATION (31, 32)

27

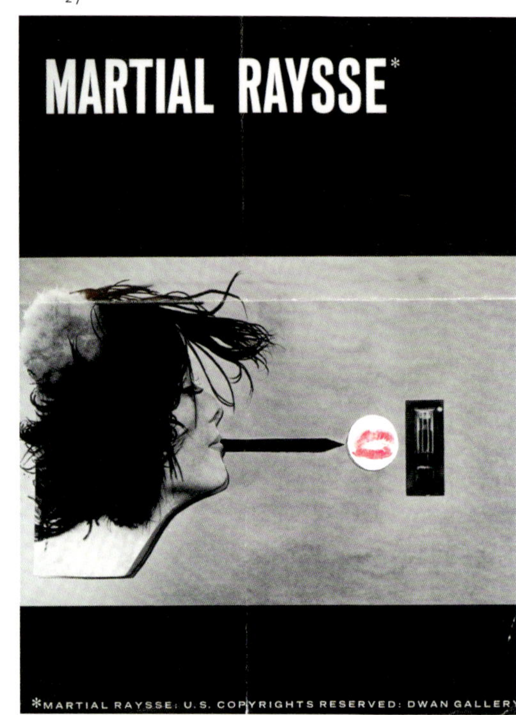

28

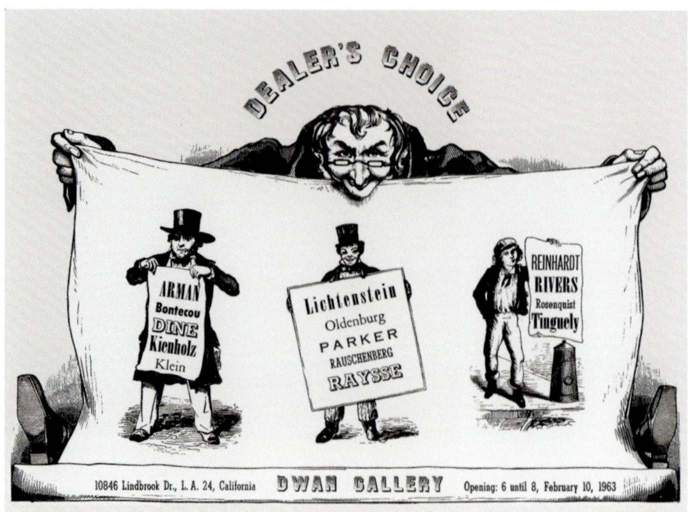

1963

Martial Raysse: Mirrors and Portraits, 1962
January 6–February 2

CHECKLIST / *Seventeen*; *Rose Pour Toujours*; *St. Tropez*; *L'Année Dernière a Capri*; *Rites of Spring*; *Rear View Mirror*; *Sur la Plage*; *Elle*; *Mi-Août*; *Vampirement Votre*; *Lolita*; *Beatrice*; *Kristin*; *Et Dieu Crea la Femme*; *Tahiti Plage*; *Supermarket*; *Portrait of Mme. V.K.*

REVIEWS / Henry J. Seldis, "In the Galleries: Sequin Eyelids, Neon Lips," *Los Angeles Times* (January 18, 1963): D5; Donald Factor, "Reviews: Los Angeles, Martial Raysse," *Artforum* 1, no. 10 (April 1963): 46–47, illustrated "Raysse, in some of these pictures, plays with paint, creating surface effects that have their own inherent interest and crops his photographs in order to control the picture plane. The effect is still too slick and easy, but the hope is raised that he will be able to go beyond the basic joke to an art that is more intrinsically valid."

Dealer's Choice
February 10–March 2

CHECKLIST / Jim Dine, *Colorful Hammer Rack*, 1962; Larry Rivers, *French Money*, 1962; Claes Oldenburg, *Toybox*, 1962; Robert Rauschenberg, *First Landing Jump*, 1961; Roy Lichtenstein, *Mr. Bellamy*, 1961; Martial Raysse, *Portrait of Mme. V.K.*, 1962; Arman, *Fifth Ave.*, 1962; Lee Bontecou, *Untitled*, 1962; Yves Klein, *Monochrome*, 1960; Raymond Parker, *Untitled*, 1959; Jean Tinguely, *Baluba II*, 1962; Edward Kienholz, *The Future as an Afterthought*, 1961; James Rosenquist, *Sight Tssin*, 1962; Ad Reinhardt, *I*, 1954–1958; Lee Bontecou, *Untitled*, 1962; Edward Kienholz, *Bunny Bunny, Your So Funny*, 1962

REVIEWS / Constance Perkins, "In the Galleries: Dada Meaning Reassessed," *Los Angeles Times* (February 18, 1963): C7; Doug McClellan, "Reviews: Los Angeles, Dealers Choice," *Artforum* 1, no. 11 (May 1963): 50–51, illustrated

Franz Kline Memorial: Paintings, 1950–1961
March 3–30 (extended to April 13)

CHECKLIST / *The Clock Face*, 1950; *Poise*, 1952; *Shaft*, 1955; *August Day*, 1957; *Garcia*, 1957; *Pittston*, 1958; *Harleman*, 1960; *Contrada*, 1960; *Black Sienna*, 1960; *Torres*, 1960; *Andrus*, 1961; *Untitled*, 1953; *Composition*, 1955; *Composition*, 1955; *Untitled*, 1955–1956; *Two Pastels*, 1958; *Study for Henry H*, 1959; *Study for Andrus*, 1961

REVIEWS / Constance Perkins, "In the Galleries: Kline's Originality Apparent in Show," *Los Angeles Times* (March 11, 1963): C7; Rosalind G. Wholden, "Kline and Lebrun—A Study in Mastery," *Beverly Hills Times* (March 22, 1963): n.p.; Gerald Nordland, "Art: March in the Galleries," *Frontier: The Voice of the New West* 14, no. 6 (April 1963): 21, 23, illustrated; Jules Langsner, "Arts news from Los Angeles," *Artnews* 62, no. 3 (May 1963): 48 "One thing the exhibition at Dwan establishes beyond a shadow of a doubt is Kline's impregnable position as a major figure in American painting." Donald Factor, "Reviews: Los Angeles, Franz Kline," *Artforum* 1, no. 12 (June 1963): 10, 11, illustrated "The shock and force that once existed is now for the most part gone, and what is left are large very elegant abstractions that permeate the viewer with a nostalgia for the impact they once made on a tired and jaded art world. In effect they have taken on the look of old masters with all that that term implies."

29

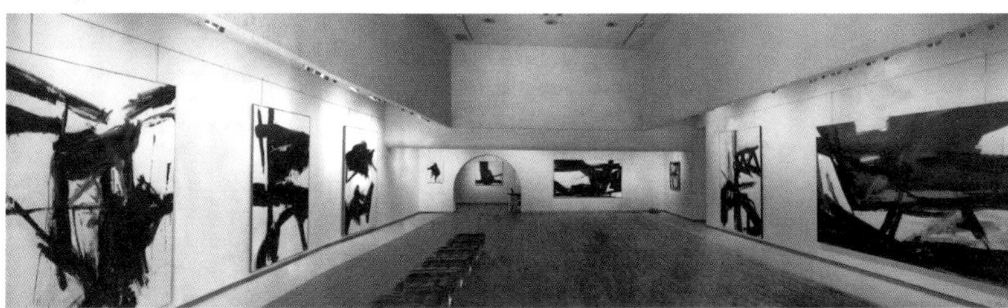

31

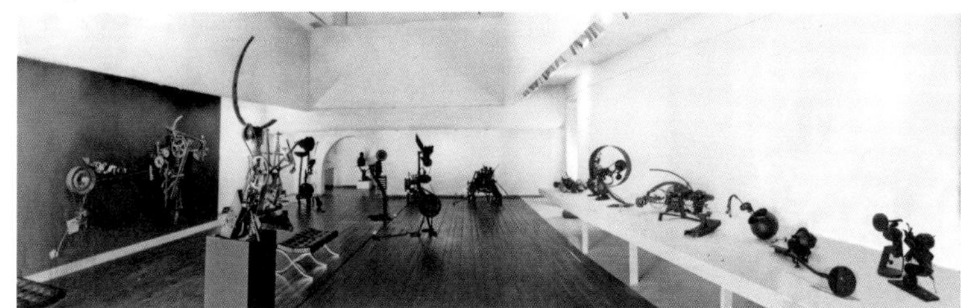

30

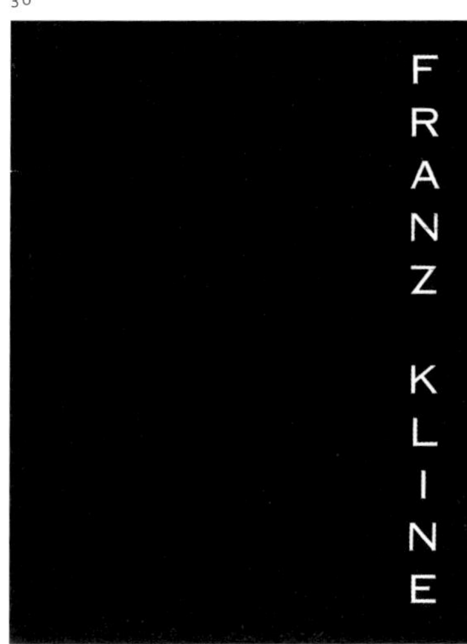

32

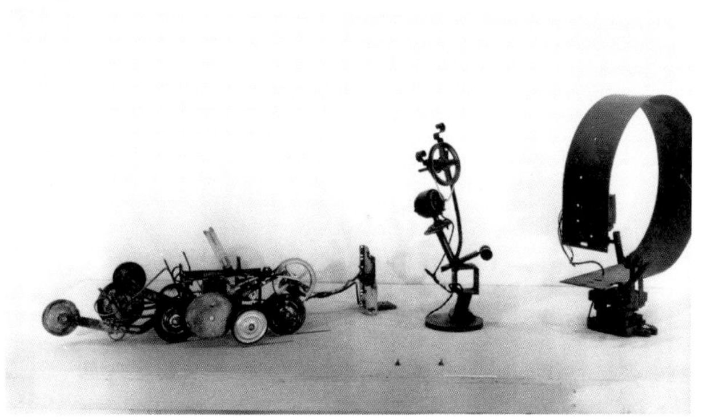

Larry Rivers
April 15–May 11

CHECKLIST / *Dutch Masters II*, 1963; *Tit*, 1963; *Cezanne Stamp*, 1963; *Summer Nude*, 1960; *Dutch Masters I*, 1963; *French Money I*, 1962; *Dutch Masters—Blunts*, 1963; *Parts of the Body*, 1962; *Parts of the Body–Cascading Nude*; *Venus*, 1963; *Parts of the Body–Italian*, 1963; *French Money*, 1962; *Africa*, 1961–1962; *Dutch Masters IV*, 1963; *Small Friendship of America and France*, 1961; *Friendship of America and France*, 1961; *Black Child in a Map of Africa*, 1963; *Double Camel*, 1961; *De Kooning Drawing I*, 1961; *Dutch Masters*, 1963; *De Kooning Drawing II*, 1961; *Webster in a Square*, 1961; *Eye and Ear*, 1963; *Queen of Clubs*, 1960; *Dutch Masters on Paper*, 1963; *Last Civil War Veteran*, 1962; *Yuex*, 1962; *Parts of the Body–Up Side Down Head*, 1962; *Noses*, 1962; *Cedar Bar Menu*, 1960; *Tareton*, 1961; *Double French Money*, 1962; *Small Shoes*, 1961 **In alcove:** *De Kooning Drawing III*, 1963 **In showroom:** *Parts of the Body*, 1962

REVIEWS / Henry J. Seldis, "In the Galleries: Rivers Bridges 2 Modes," *Los Angeles Times* (April 19, 1963): E7 "Larry Rivers is one of the most scintillating young painters in the country and his current Dwan Gallery exhibition is an important one. In a way Rivers seems to be a bridge between the once dominant mode of painting called abstract expressionism and the fashion now in the ascendancy known as 'pop art.'" "Larry Rivers: Best of Anything," *Citizen News* (April 27, 1963): n.p.; Fidel A. Danieli, "A Candid Portrait of Larry Rivers: The World's Greatest Artist—Help!," *UCLA Daily Bruin* (May 3, 1963): 5; Jules Langsner, "Art news from Los Angeles," *Artnews* 62, no. 4 (Summer 1963): 47; Jules Langsner, "Los Angeles Letter," *Art International* 7, no. 6 (June 25, 1963): 79–80, illustrated "Rivers, on the other hand, brings a considerable amount of invention to the presentation of things usually placed at the bottom of the culture totem-pole. That invention is placed in the service of visual wit." H.T.H., "Los Angeles: Larry Rivers, Dwan Gallery," *Artforum* 2, no.1 (July 1963): 43–44, illustrated

RELATED / Robert Breer film screening, April 21, during Larry Rivers exhibition includes *Homage to Jean Tinguely's "Homage to New York,"* 1960; *Pat's Birthday*, 1962; *A Man and His Dog Out for Air*, 1957; *Jamestown Baloos*, 1957; *Eyewash*, 1959; *Horse Over Tea Kettle*, 1962; *Cats*, 1956

Jean Tinguely
May 13–June 8

CHECKLIST / *Cool*; *The Well Tempered Wheel*; *Kropotkin*; *Mrs. Murphy's Chowder*; *Rocker III*; *Peak Production*; *Mautz No. II*; *Wait for Me*; *Viridana*; *Oran*; *Theresina*; *Hanibal*; *Mayfair*; *Odessa*; *Hong Kong*; *Bandini*; *Samurai*; *Atlas*; *Affair of the Heart*; *Spring*; *Attila*; *Fountain II*; *Fountain III*; *Fountain IV*; *Fountain V*; *Fountain VI*; *Fountain VIII*

REVIEW / Don Factor, "Reviews: Los Angeles, Jean Tinguely," *Artforum* 2, no. 3 (September 1963): 14–17, illustrated

Edward Kienholz
June 17–July 13

CHECKLIST / *The Sky Is Falling…Act One*; *The Grave*; *GOD AND HIS PAL*; *The Carnivore*; *Minus the Orange*; *America My Home Town*; *Mother Sterling Revisited*; *Little Boy, Blue Boy*; *Ella Laugh*; *The Four Bears*; *14½ Inches of Cord*; *The Illegal Operation*; *A Star is Birthed*; *The Little Black Heart*; *Untitled Or, I'm Not a Fig-Plucker, Nor A Fig-Plucker's Son, But I'll Pluck Your Figs 'Til A Fig-Plucker Comes*; *The Wedding*; *The Importance of Being A Stuffed Animal*; *The National Banjo on the Knee, Week*;

EDWARD KIENHOLZ, CATALOG COVER (33)

CLAES OLDENBURG, POSTER (34) AND INSTALLATION (35)

SVEN LUKIN, INSTALLATION (36)

AD REINHARDT: RECENT SQUARE PAINTINGS, ANNOUNCEMENT (37) AND INSTALLATION (38)

33

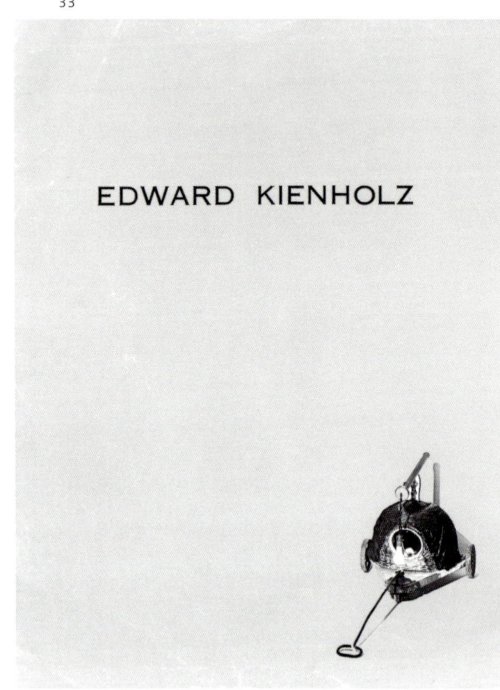

34

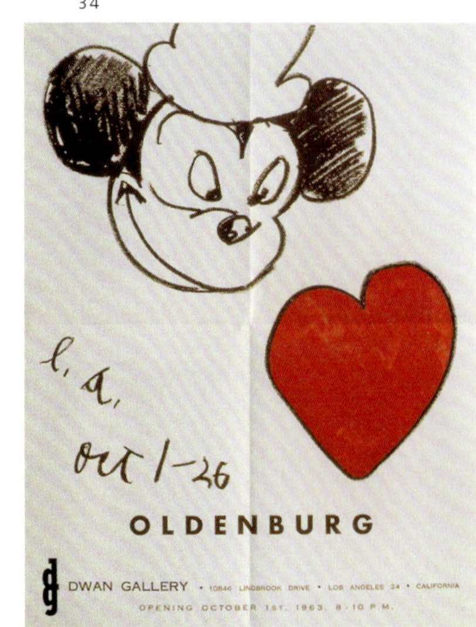

35

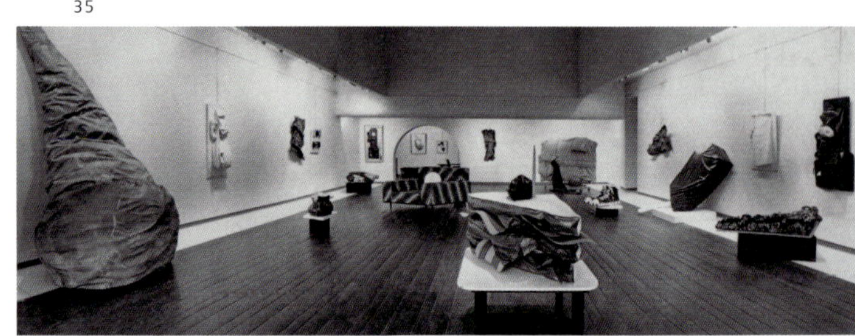

1963 LOS ANGELES

Sleepy's Hollow with Handle and Wheels; *The Blink-Blink Frog*; *Lollypop Goes the Weazel*; *The Casualty*

REVIEWS / Henry J. Seldis, "In the Galleries: Hatred No Spur to Greater Art," *Los Angeles Times* (June 21, 1963): D4 "As if to refute the contention that there is nothing shocking left in art, Kienholz presents us with mad inventions sure to arouse revulsion, close to nausea, from most spectators along with a few hollow laughs." Jules Langsner, "Art news from Los Angeles," *Artnews* 62, no. 5 (September 1963): 16 "No esthete, Kienholz is bent on speaking his piece on the absurdities of man's estate in contemporary America, a predicament he finds both ludicrous and tragic. For Kienholz, the ludicrous and the tragic leave a trail of tangible [evidence] in secondhand stores and junk yards. It is to these repositories that he repairs for the artifacts he glues, nails and wires together, transforming them into visual commentaries with the power to startle the viewer into a 'shock of recognition.'" Clair Wolfe, "The Art of Evil," *Beverly Hills Times* (July 5, 1963): n.p.; Jules Langsner, "Los Angeles Letter," *Art International* 7, no. 8 (November 10, 1963): 80–81, illustrated

MENTION / Donald Factor, "Edward Kienholz," *Artforum* 2, no. 2 (August 1963): 24–25, illustrated "In his more recent work, shown during June at the Dwan Gallery in Los Angeles, [Kienholz] has concentrated more on exploring the metaphysics of juxtaposition. Paint has been used less, having been replaced by surfaces covered in masking tape and coated with fibreglass. His formal problems involve the working with real space close to the floor; in other words, that forgotten area between paintings and in which sculpture stands sit."

Claes Oldenburg
October 1–26

CHECKLIST / **Main Gallery:** *Four Artificial Fur Good Humors*; *Hairpieces, various viewpoints*; *Large Ice Cream Cone*; *Ghost Telephone*; *Big Baked Potato*; *Two Men's Hats*; *Six Ice Cream Bars*; *French Fries with Ketchup*; *Sketch for Telephone*; *Leopard Chair*; *Pea Soup with Frankfurters and Saltines*; *Green Stockings*; *Giant Blue Shirt with Tie*; *Jockeys*; *A Brown Shoe*; *Soft Good Humor*; *Ghost Pocket (Sketch for Pants Pocket)*; *Giant Gym Shoes*; *Bacon, Lettuce and Tomato Sandwich*; *Giant Pecan Slice*; *Pants Pocket with Handkerchief*; *Soft Telephone*; *Sketch of Giant Shirt*; *Two Purses*; *Lingerie Bar* **Office:** *Four Hair Pieces*; *Slice of Birthday Cake*; *Ice Cream Sundae*; *Marshmallow Sundae*; *Banana Split with Loose Slices*; *Good Humor Drawing*; *Mickey Mouse and Heart*; *Zebra Chair Drawing*; *Four Small Flat Pies* **Inter-Office:** *Sponge Powderpuff*; *Frankfurter*; *Plate of Meat*; *Ice Cream Drawing*; *Blue Stockings*; *Stand of Candy Bars*; *Good Humor Relief*; *Pile of Toast*; *Mickey Mouse Drawing*

REVIEWS / Henry J. Seldis, "In the Galleries: Dial $1-0-0-0 for Plastic Pay Phone," *Los Angeles Times* (October 11, 1963): D8; Clair Wolfe, "From Soup to Nuts," *Beverly Hills Times*, (October 25, 1963): n.p.

RELATED / Installation image in Gerald Nordland, "A Succession of Visitors," *Artforum* 2, no. 12 (Summer 1964): 64–68; Arthur M. Berman, "Venice Artist Spotlights Commonplace Objects," *Los Angeles Times* (November 3, 1963): H4.

36

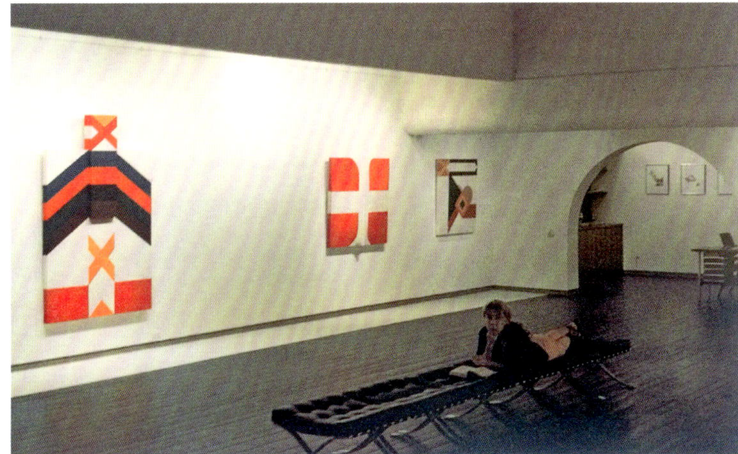

37

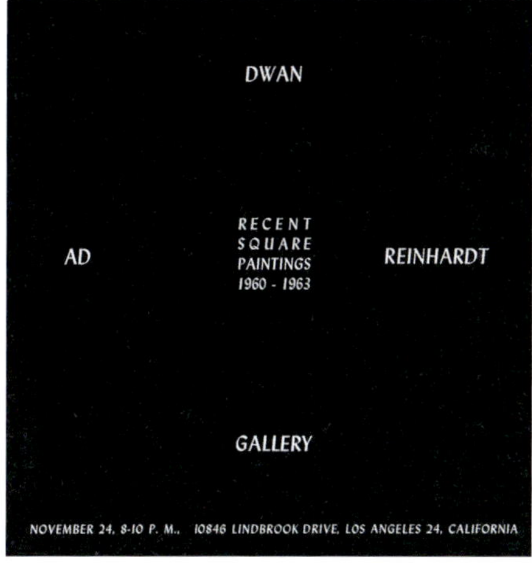

38

Sven Lukin
October 27–November 23

CHECKLIST / *Carolina Pine*; *Dwan Song*; *Crossing*; *Fathers Will Gather*; *Corrida*; *Yes*; *Some Call It A Spear*; *And Daughters With Curls*; *My Hero*; *Libra*; *Eye*; *Dances AA*; drawings—*Untitled*

REVIEWS / Constance Perkins, "In the Galleries: 42 Southland Artists in Impressive Redlands Show," *Los Angeles Times* (November 4, 1963): D8 (under "Whimsical Titles Spark Lukin Show") "Lukin's works are unique in that their geometric forms and their use of a hard-edge style are requisite to the physical construction of their canvases. These he builds with a three-dimensional framework over which the canvas is stretched." Fidel A. Danieli, "Reviews: Los Angeles, Sven Lukin," *Artforum* 2, no. 6 (December 1963): 10, illustrated

Ad Reinhardt: Recent Square Paintings, 1960–1963
November 24–December 28

CHECKLIST / *Abstract Painting, No. 15*, 1960; *Abstract Painting, No. 6*, 1961; *Abstract Painting, No. 11*, 1961; *Abstract Painting, No. 8*, 1962; *Abstract Painting, No. 3*, 1963; *Abstract Painting, No. 10*, 1963; *Abstract Painting, No. 9*, 1962

REVIEWS / Henry J. Seldis, "In the Galleries: Oils Reflect Abject Nihilism," *Los Angeles Times* (December 2, 1963): D17; Don Factor, "Reviews: Los Angeles: Ad Reinhardt," *Artforum* 2, no. 7 (January 1964): 43 "The fact that attention is demanded so quietly, and that the illusion of blankness is only illusion gives the pictures importance. Furthermore, that they are able to raise a number of visual premises or explanations and to deny each of them without denying themselves, is a fact that places them in the forefront of formal abstract painting." Jules Langsner, "Art news from Los Angeles," *Artnews* 62, no. 9 (January 1964): 50

RELATED / Installation images in Irving Sandler, "The New Cool Art," *Art in America* no. 1 (1965): 96–101, and in Ad Reinhardt, "Ad Reinhardt: Three Statements," *Artforum* 5, no. 7 (March 1966): 34–35

Group Show
December 29–January 3, 1964

CHECKLIST / Franz Kline, *Untitled*, 1958; Arakawa, *Untitled*, 1963; Roy Lichtenstein, *Tsing*, 1962; Jim Dine, *Green Shower*, 1962; Charles Frazier, *American Nude #2*, 1963; Tom Wesselmann, *The Great American Nude*, 1961; Jim Dine, *White Bathroom*, 1962; John Chamberlain, *Slauson*, 1963; Robert Rauschenberg, *Trellis*, 1963; Charles Frazier, *Untitled*, 1963; William Waldren, *Untitled*, 1963; Arakawa, *Untitled*, 1963; Charles Frazier, *Untitled*, 1962–1963

NIKI DE SAINT PHALLE, ADVERTISEMENT (39)

BOXES, MAGAZINE COVER (40), ANNOUNCEMENT (41), AND INSTALLATION (42)

ARAKAWA: DIEAGRAMS, INSTALLATION (43)

39

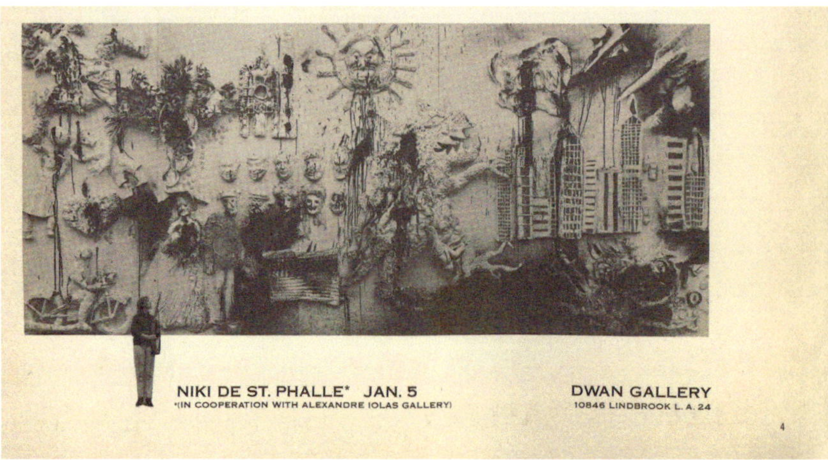

40

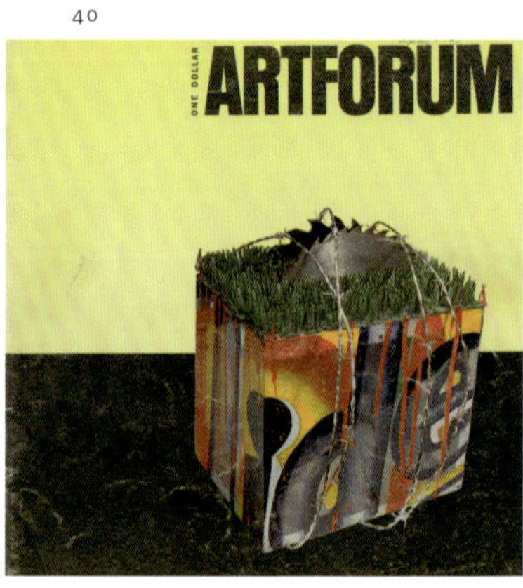

41

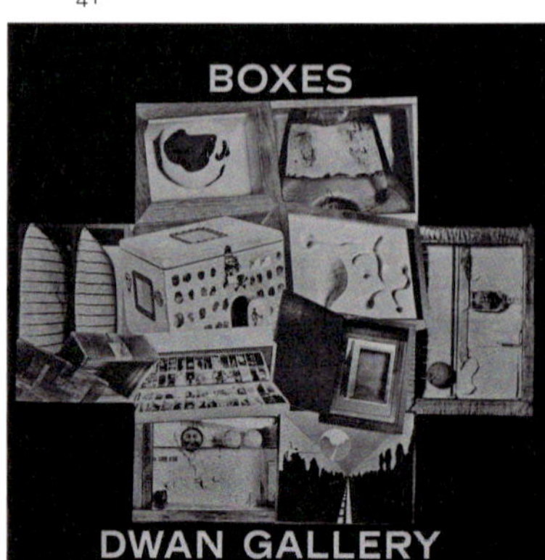

1964

Niki de Saint Phalle
January 5–31

CHECKLIST / *King Kong*, 1963; *Tyrannosaurus Rex*, 1963; *Heart No.1*, 1963; *The Subway*, 1963; *Birth*, 1963; *New England Church*, 1963; *The Monster*, 1963; *The Children*, 1963

REVIEWS / Constance Perkins, "The Galleries: St. Phalle Doubles Paradox," *Los Angeles Times* (January 17, 1964): C7 "It is the world of Bosch re-created in contemporary terms. It is a phantasmagoria filled with dire warnings. Even more frightening is the artist's implied destruction of the creative act itself." Clair Wolfe, "Reviews: Los Angeles, Niki de Saint-Phalle," *Artforum* 2, no. 9 (March 1964): 9, 11, illustrated "Herein lies her genius and the crux of her oeuvre, for she has recreated in the 20th century what may well be one of the most instinctive origins of the art idea. That is, art not necessarily conceived as an object, but as an act."

Boxes
February 2–29

CHECKLIST / Kurt Schwitters, *Untitled*, 1920; Kurt Schwitters, *Lust Murder Box*, 1920; Kurt Schwitters, *Kasten No. 7, Anna Blume*, 1922; Marcel Duchamp, *Boîte-en-valise*, 1938–1942; Louise Nevelson, *Night Plant VI*, 1959; Louise Nevelson, *Skyscape II*, 1963; Joseph Cornell, *Soap Bubble Set*, 1950; Joseph Cornell, *The Smiling Sun*, 1956; Joseph Cornell, *The Sun Series*, 1957; Joseph Cornell, *The Sailing Ship, Objects in Space Series*, 1961; Robert Rauschenberg, *Untitled*, 1962; H.C. Westermann, *Untitled*, 1957; H.C. Westermann, *2063 A.D.*, 1963; H.C. Westermann, *Bullseye*, 1963; Peter Agostini, *Untitled*, 1963; Marisol, *Untitled*, 1959; Jim Dine, *The Black Drill Box*, 1961; Claes Oldenburg, *Boxer Shorts in Box*, 1962; Arman, *Cast Your Ballot Here for a Cleaner Dwan Gallery*, 1962; Martial Raysse, *Supermarket*, 1961; Anthony Berlant, *Coca-Cola Plane Crash*, 1963; Tom Wesselmann, *Great American Still Life with T.V.*, 1963; James Rosenquist, *Toaster*, 1963; Letty Eisenhauer, *Souvenir of New York City*, 1963; Andy Warhol, *Brillo Box*, 1963; Andy Warhol, *Brillo Box*, 1963; Andy Warhol, *Brillo Box*, 1963; Andy Warhol, *Heinz Box*, 1963; Robert Watts, *Guadalcanal*, 1960; Robert Watts, *Checkers*, 1961; Robert Watts, *Safe*, 1961; Robert Watts, *Box of Candy*, 1963; Allan D'Arcangelo, *I Know Where I'm Going*, 1963; Aaron Kuriloff, *Two Pillows*, 1963; Richard Artschwager, *Encyclopedia*, 1963; Gerd Stern, *Turn Ahead No Stopping*, 1962; George Brecht, *The Universal Machine—Derby Epidemic*, n.d.; George Brecht, *Dome*, 1959; George Brecht, *Play Incident*, 1961; John Willenbecher, *Unknown Game #3*, 1963; Robert Morris, *Box with Photo of Door*, 1963; Robert Morris, *Window Box, Ruler and Crystal*, 1963; Arakawa, *The Method of Advancing A Great Distance By Descending*, 1962; Lee Bontecou, *Untitled*, 1959; Lee Bontecou, *Untitled*, 1959; Kenneth Price, *Rosewood Box*, 1962; Kenneth Price, *White and Grey*, 1962; William Waldren, *The Ion*, 1963; Larry Bell, *Lux of the Ferus*, 1963; Kuwayama, *Untitled*, 1963; David Jacobs, *Diamond Box*, 1963; Edward Kienholz, *Lady*, 1960; Boris Lurie, *Immigrant-No-Box*, 1963; Charles Frazier, *Autobiography (1930–)*, 1963; Lucas Samaras, *Wool Box with Pins*, 1963; Lucas Samaras, *Self Portrait*, 1963; Ronald Miyashiro, *Concord #4*, 1963; Ronald Miyashiro, *Concord #9*, 1963; Daniel LaRue Johnson, *The Big N*, 1963; Ben Talbert, *Mnemonic Bisection*, 1960

42

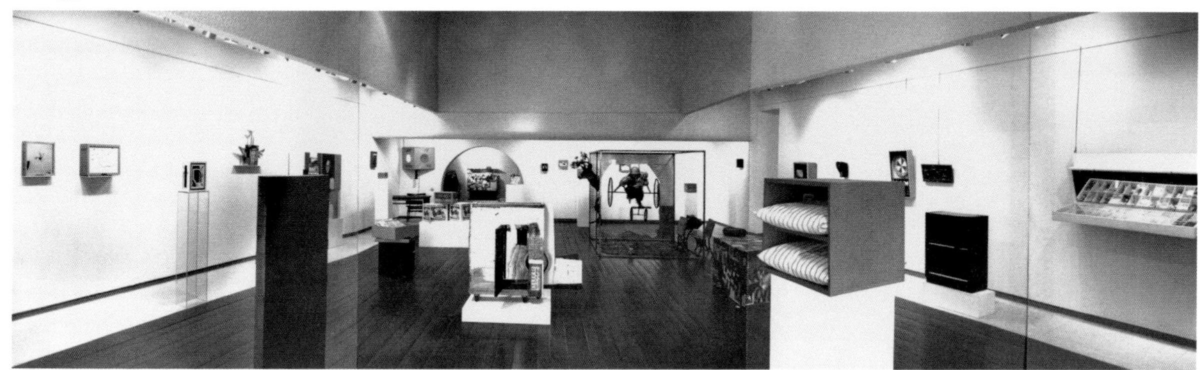

43

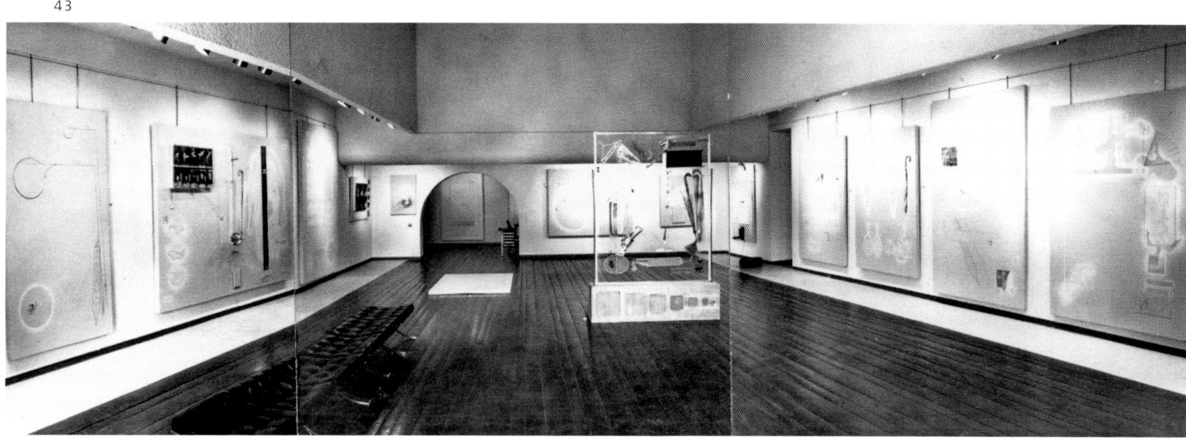

REVIEWS / Henry J. Seldis, "It's Not Completely Square, 'Box Art' Exhibit Proves," *Los Angeles Times* (February 19, 1964): D9; Walter Hopps, "Boxes," *Art International* 8, no. 2 (March 20, 1964): 38–42, illustrated "However arbitrary the format of the exhibition 'Boxes' at first seems, the extraordinary diverse elaboration of its unifying form-idea offers strong counter-argument to those critics who believe there has developed a bland, even homogenous, program characterizing recent art." Donald Factor "Boxes," *Artforum* 2, no. 10 (April 1964): cover, 20–23, illustrated; "Boxes," *Art in America* 52, no. 3 (1964): 98–102, illustrated

RELATED / "Art News: Houston Curator to Lecture at Occidental," *Los Angeles Times* (February 2, 1964): D31, D34 (under "Dwan Gallery")

William Waldren
March 1–26

CHECKLIST / *Untitled Triptych*, 1964; seven works titled *Untitled*, 1964; *Untitled Diptych*, 1964

REVIEWS / Constance Perkins, "In the Galleries: Artist Silva Gives Mundane Reality an Air of Fantasy," *Los Angeles Times* (March 16, 1964): C11 (under "Waldren Artistry Tremendously Moving") "William Waldren's recent works at the Dwan Gallery afford an unforgettable experience. To define these large white relief paintings is to destroy the metaphysical nature of their symbolism. To describe them is even difficult. Built out of a mixture of polyester sand and plaster, these tremendously moving, deeply modeled, colorless expanses are peculiarly organic yet wholly unreal. They seem to be parts of an unknown anatomy of the earth." Clair Wolfe, "William Waldren, Dwan Gallery," *Artforum* 2, no. 10 (April 1964): 49–50, illustrated

Arakawa: Dieagrams
March 29–April 25

CHECKLIST / *The Double Image of the Cosine Graph*; *The Hangar is Under the Ground. How Can It M-O-V-E*; *The Spectrum of Time Discovered*; *As He Was Somersaulting Through The Air, He Stopped In Mid-Air And He Caught A Glimpse Of The Umbrella And The Funnel Having Intercourse*; *He Saw the Umbrella Falling Down Onto The Hook Which Was Looking At The Comb In The Funnel-Shaped Garden.*; *The Officially Recognized S.A. Equation*; *The Method of Advancing A Great Distance By Descending*; *The Ocean Has Been Cut Into Equal Parts; And One of These Parts Has Been Taken Out Of It.*; *Face of Masturbation*; *Mass Multiplied By Speed Equals The Spectrum*; *The Time Within The Refrigerator Has Color*; *About The Ellipse*; *In the Cross-Section Of The Hangar We Can See A Different Blood For Every Color Of The Spectrum*; *If You Want, You Can Make Everything By Accelerating The Mixer To The Speed of Light*; *If You Cannot Believe This Please Hang Your Hat on the Double Hook*; *The Hook and the Comb Marry And Their Child Can Shit Seven Colors*; *I Looked Between The Umbrella And The Ceiling*; *Without The Water The Ship Moves Upside Down Through The Solid Rock*; *The Discovery Of The Second Law Of Perspective*; *The Hook Lives Near The Ocean*; *The Comb Is So Attracted To The Hook That It Runs To Meet It. They Touch—and the Butterfly Appears.*; *The S.A. Balance*; *Three Combs*; *Dia-Gram with Duchamp's Glass As A Minor Detail*; *From The Mixer To The Feather*; *Hammock Swinging*; *A Small Funnel On The Step Ladder Without Steps*; *About Fading Away*; *About The Pillow*; *Chair*; *Nine Swings With A Double Hangar*; *The Comb Cuts Into The Jump*; *Light Shines Through The Net Making Half An Umbrella*; *Inside A Brightly Shining Wall*,

MARTIAL RAYSSE, POSTER (44), ADVERTISEMENT (45), AND INSTALLATION (46)

EDWARD KIENHOLZ: THREE TABLEAUX, INSTALLATION (47) AND ANNOUNCEMENT (48)

JAMES ROSENQUIST, ANNOUNCEMENT (49)

LUCAS SAMARAS, POSTER (50)

44

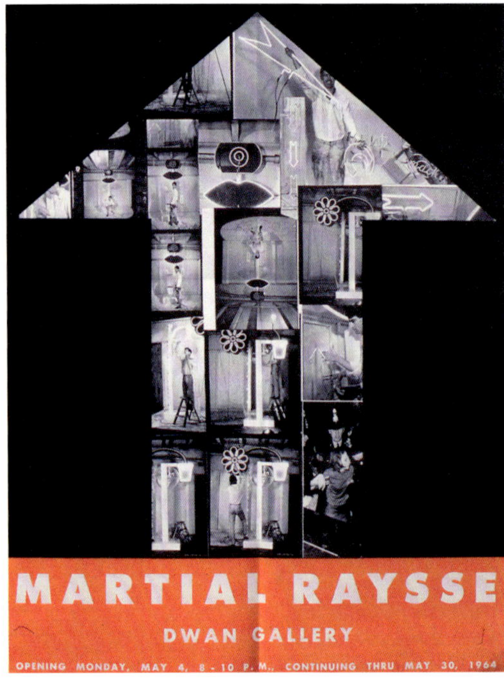

45

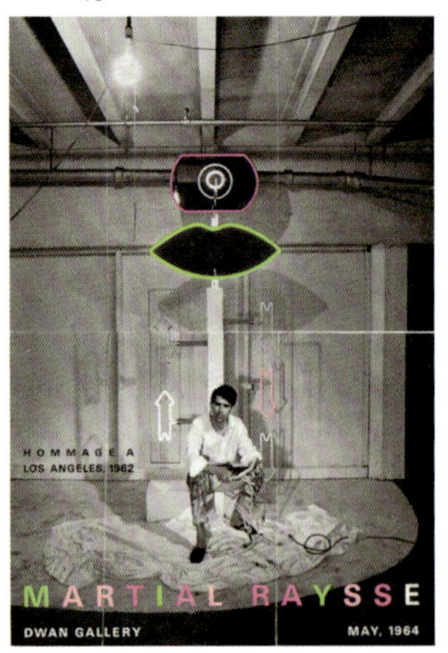

46

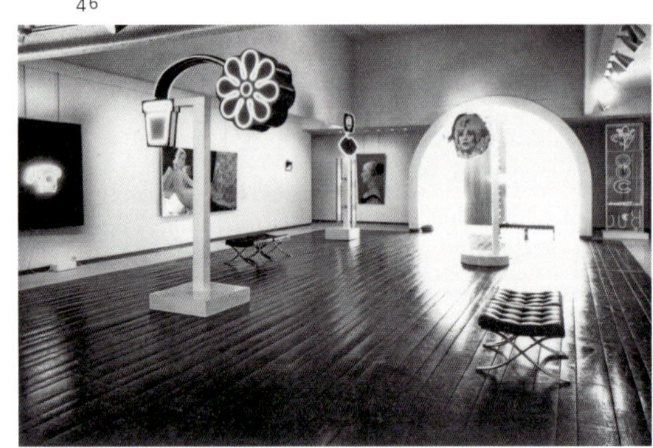

Three Different Size Umbrellas; *From Masturbation An Earthquake Begins*; *The Last S.A. Dieagram*

REVIEWS / Constance Perkins, "Fusion of Paint, Sculpture," *Los Angeles Times* (April 13, 1964): E18 (under "Anonymous Artist Exhibits Precision") "Although the refinement of the works takes precedence over subject matter, it is obvious that every element employed has symbolic meaning to the artist and that most important of all are the stroboscopic renderings given various items." Clair Wolfe, "Reviews: Los Angeles, Arakawa," *Artforum* 2, no. 11 (May 1964): 12, 14, 15, illustrated

Martial Raysse
May 4–30

CHECKLIST / *Obelisk*, 1964; *Venice–Venice*, 1964; *Oasis*, 1964; *Conversation Printaniere*, 1963; *Spring Morning*, 1964; *Foliage Cans*, 1964; *Tableau Decoupe*, 1963; *Yellow Nude*, 1964; *Breakfrest*, 1964; *Spring*, 1964; *Journal*, 1963; *Flowering Bulb*, 1964; *The Pot and the Flower*, 1964; *Hello–Hello*, 1964; *Made in Japan*, 1964; *Homage to Los Angeles*, 1962; *The Apple*, 1963; *Portrait of an Old Friend*, 1963

REVIEW / Henry J. Seldis, "In the Galleries: Altoon Expands Pop Art Horizons," *Los Angeles Times* (May 18, 1964): C6 (under "Whimsy May Find Hollywood Market")

Gallery Artists
June 1–27

CHECKLIST / Charles Frazier, *Object of Affection*, 1964; Charles Frazier, *Viva Sweet Love*, 1964; Charles Frazier, *Box of Sky*, 1964; Charles Frazier, *Quarter Moon*, 1964; Arakawa, *Untitled*, 1963; Arakawa, *Untitled*, 1963; Edward Kienholz, *Walter Hopps, Hopps, Hopps*, 1959; Arakawa, *Untitled*, 1963; Edward Kienholz, *We'll Catch the Boss and Put Him On the Cross*, 1961; Edward Kienholz, *The Black Widow*, 1964; Edward Kienholz, *Untitled Or, I'm Not a Fig-Plucker Nor A Fig-Plucker's Son, But I'll Pluck Your Figs 'Til A Fig-Plucker Comes*, 1963; Martial Raysse, *Gordon Cooper*, 1964; Martial Raysse, *Snack*, 1964; Jean Tinguely, *Totem II (Wild Man)*, 1960; Martial Raysse, *Askew Painting*, 1964; Jean Tinguely, *Wait for Me*, 1963; Martial Raysse, *A.M.*, 1964; Jean Tinguely, *Spring*, 1963

New York, New York
June 29–July 25

CHECKLIST / Louise Nevelson, *Night Gardens II*, 1958; Larry Rivers, *Dutch Masters I*, 1963; Franz Kline, *Contrada*, 1960; David Smith, *Circles and Angles*, 1959; Roy Lichtenstein, *Takka Takka*, 1962; Robert Rauschenberg, *Straw-Boss*, 1962; Jim Dine, *Pink Bathroom*, 1962; Josef Albers, *Grisaille and Ground*, 1961; Alfred Jensen, *Image and After Image*, 1962; Edward Higgins, *Untitled*, 1963; Willem de Kooning, *Untitled*, 1961; Sven Lukin, *Untitled #1*, 1961; Roy Lichtenstein, *Ha Ha Ha*, 1962; Andy Warhol, *Brillo Boxes*, 1963; Lee Bontecou, *Untitled*, 1961; Tom Wesselmann, *Great American Nude #16*, 1961; Mark Rothko, *Untitled*, 1959; Philip Guston, *Garden of M*, 1960

Edward Kienholz: Three Tableaux
September 29–October 24

CHECKLIST / *Backseat Dodge-38*, 1964; *Bucket of Tar with Speaker*, 1964; *Army and Soul*, 1964; *While Visions of Sugar Plums Danced in Their Heads*, 1964; *The Birthday*, 1964

REVIEWS / John Reuschel, "Reviews: Los Angeles: Edward Kienholz, Three Tableaux," *Artforum* 3, no. 1 (September 1964): 14–15, illustrated "These

47

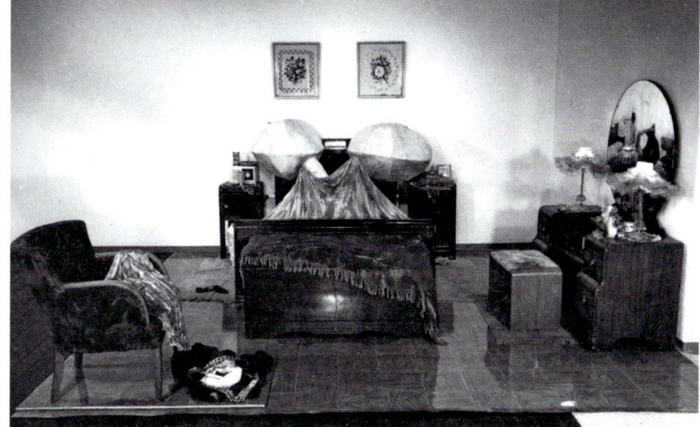

49

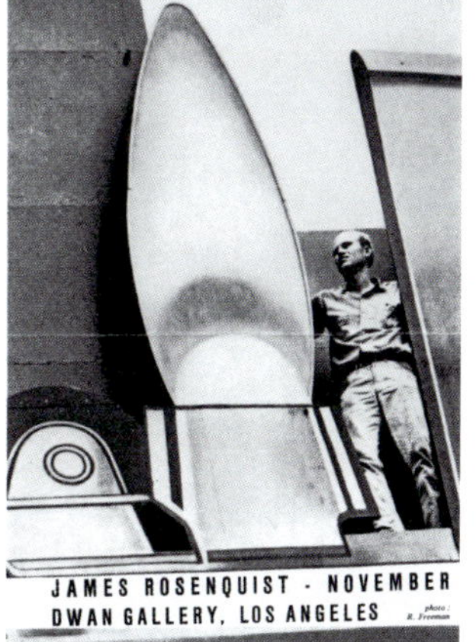

50

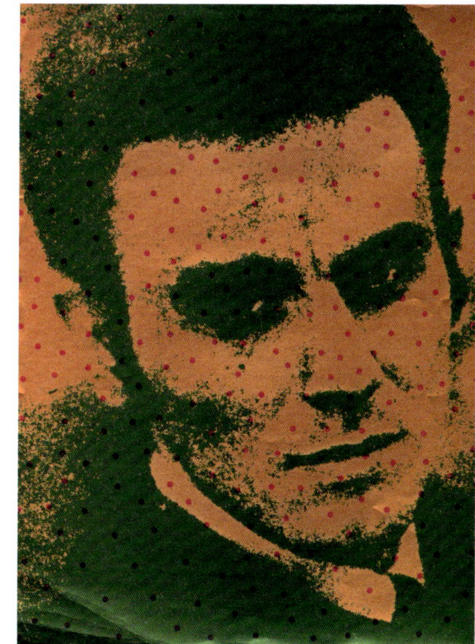

48

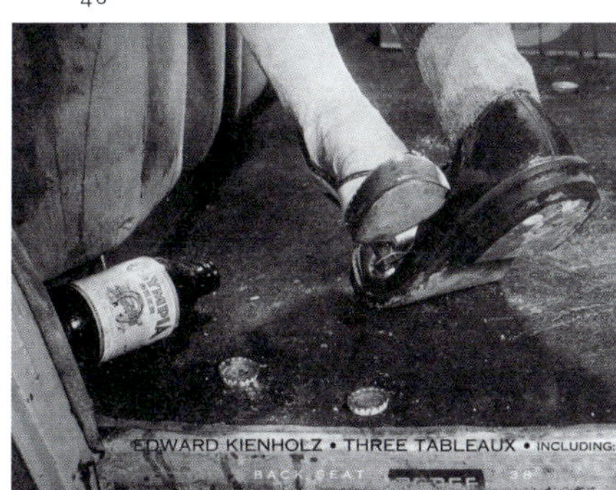

works are truly delightful in a nerve-wrecking sort of way, and Kienholz's control of a tremendous vocabulary of beat-up cars, electricity, luggage, chairs, Pall Malls, Olympia beer cans, cast-off or torn up garments, linoleum, mangled bedclothes, plaster, screen, paint, and plastic is just simply amazing." Henry J. Seldis, "In the Galleries: Mullican Artistry Triumph of Talent," *Los Angeles Times* (October 2, 1964): C9 (under "Kienholz Artistry Deeply Pessimistic") "Out of a psychotic anger this artist has created images that reflect the hate and horror he finds in fundamental areas of life in our time and place. There is a blind fury here that leads Kienholz to enforce his vile images with mechanical contraptions and a re-creation of stenches. In a torment of self-criticism and guilt that he extends to every man, Kienholz mines his considerable ingenuity in the large and intricate assemblages. . . . The snicker, the leer, the meretricious admiration and the success de scandal that may well make this show a favorite with the cool purveyors of 'the latest' will not be able to hide the fact of Keinholz' total rejection of all that might be affirmative in the human condition." Paul Rivas, "Art Forum," *Beverly Hills Times* (October 2, 1964): n.p.; Philip Leider, "Kienholz," *Frontier: The Voice of the New West* (November 1964): 25 "It is art made for no one's living room, and hurrah for that. It is an art which it would be quite pointless to understand in terms of the standard categories of art history. It comes out of the compulsive cataloguing of the details of our days and ways that begins innocently enough with Whitman, and within a century, spirals insanely to the relentless lists of horrors compiled by the Beat poets and the obsessive, obscene humor of Lenny Bruce." John Coplans, "Art news from Los Angeles," *Artnews* 63, no. 10 (February 1965): 51, illustrated "At the Dwan Gallery — in a series of three tableaux — Edward Kienholz continued not only to violate all standards of esthetic propriety, but also to project a stream of art that is a blunt affront to the public. The unusualness of his format, the vulgarity and virulence of his imagination and a whole series of new skills that he brings into assemblage combine to make him an artist not only extremely difficult to adjust to, but also hard to place. . . . At the same time he brings to assemblage an astonishing facility with electricity, carpentry, joining, etc., a whole inventory of skills that can be as important to art as modeling and drawing used to be."

MENTION / Rosalind G. Wholden, "Los Angeles," *Arts Magazine* 39, no. 3 (November 1964): 14

James Rosenquist
October 27–November 24

CHECKLIST / *3 Peanuts*, 1964; *Orange Field*, 1964; *Silo*, 1963–1964; *Joan Crawford*, 1964; *Wrap II*, 1964; *Conveyer Belt*, 1964; *Fruit Salad*, 1964; *Discs*, 1964; *Dishes*, 1964; *Director*, 1964; *Silhouette*, 1964

REVIEWS / Henry J. Seldis, "In the Galleries: Pop Artist Will Survive Trend," *Los Angeles Times* (November 2, 1964): D6 "As the tide turns, James Rosenquist will no doubt emerge as the most gifted of a handful of pop painters who will be able to devote their artistic and painterly gifts to other less shallow modes of expression." William Wilson, "Reviews: Los Angeles, James Rosenquist, Dwan Gallery," *Artforum* 3, no. 3 (December 1964): 12–13, illustrated

Lucas Samaras
November 24–January 3, 1965

CHECKLIST / *"S" Box with Stairway, Fish, Combs*, 1964; *Smaller Brown Bat with Book and Objects Inside*, 1964; *Wall Piece–4 Squares within a Square, All Pins*, 1964; *Pyramidal Box with Yarn on Face: Foot, Broken Glass in Glass, and "C,"* 1964; *Green and Red Yarn with*

THE ARENA OF LOVE,
POSTER (51)
AND INSTALLATION (52)

DAKOTA DALEY & NICHOLAS QUENNELL,
INSTALLATION (53)

51

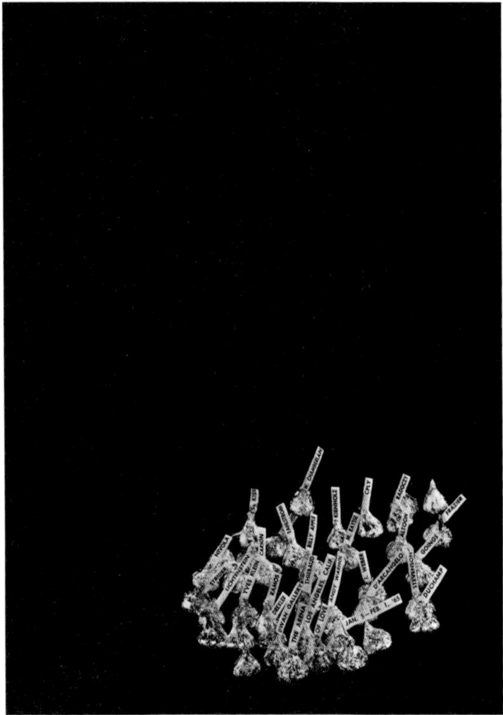

52

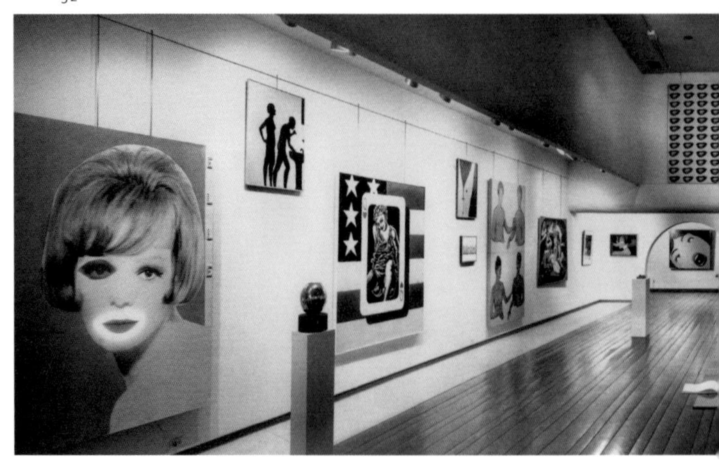

Pins, 1963; *Bag with Paintings*, 1964; *Wool and Combs on Plate, with Tree Shape within Plexi-Glass Box*, 1964; *Semicircular Box with Scull's Apartment Inside*, 1964; *Box with "L," Finger, Ear, Eyeballs, Etc.*, 1964; *Wall Piece–Colored Yarn with Pins Not Covering Entire Surface, Rectangular Aperture in Center*, 1964; *Self Portrait with Pins*, 1964; *Floor Piece–Pin Box*, 1964; *Wall Piece–Target of Colored Yarn*, 1964; *Wall Piece–4 Forks at Corners with Tacks and Instrument Protruding From Center*, 1964; *Box with Forks, and Jewels Strewn on Bottom with Hair Coming From Center: And "A,"* 1964; *Book No. 8*, 1962; *Box with Opening Doors and Whirlpool Waterglass*, 1964; *Accordion Box with Mirrors and Tacks*, 1964; *Wall Piece–2 Pyramids within a Square, Pins, and Colored Yarn*, 1964

REVIEWS / Constance Perkins, "In the Galleries: Sense of Human Warmth in Pat Berger's Imagery," *Los Angeles Times* (December 7, 1964): D15 (under "Samaras' Art Both Dull, Exciting"); Nancy Marmer, "Reviews: Los Angeles, Lucas Samaras," *Artforum* 3, no. 4 (January 1965): 11–12, illustrated; Nancy Marmer, "Los Angeles Letter," *Art International* 9, no. 1 (February 1965): 31, illustrated

1965

The Arena of Love
DGLA / January 5–February 6

CHECKLIST / Marcel Duchamp, *The Laundress' Apron*, 1959; Martial Raysse, *Rose Pour Toujours*, 1962; Idelle Weber, *Geometric Painter at Home with His Wife*, 1963; Charles Frazier, *Object of Affection*, 1964; Ben Talbert, *The Queen of Hearts*, 1964; Albert Radoczy, *The Smiles*, 1964; Wayne Thiebaud, *Lipstick Row*, 1964; Dakota Daley and Nicholas Quennell, *Gabrielle d'Estreés, Holding a Sapphire Ring in Her Left Hand While Her Sister Touches Her Breast, Signifying the Birth of the Duc de Vendôme*, 1964; Constantino Nivola, *Two Reclining Figures*, 1962; Ralph Goings, *Harem*, 1964; Öyvind Fahlström, *Triptych*, 1963; Lew Carson, *Too Many Kisses*, 1964; Richard Hamilton, *Just What Is It That Makes Today's Homes So Different . . .*, 1954; Marjorie Strider, *Mouth*, 1963; Öyvind Fahlström, *Study for Lithograph to Poem by Walasse Ting*, 1963; Andy Warhol, *Marilyn Monroe's Lips*, 1962; Sandra Daley, *Narcissus*, 1964; Allan D'Arcangelo, *Smoke Dream #1*, 1963; Roy Lichtenstein, *The Kiss III*, 1962; Mel Ramos, *Kiss Me*, 1964; Mel Ramos, *Love*, 1964; Allan D'Arcangelo, *Marilyn*, 1962; Constantino Nivola, *Two Figures*, 1962; Ralph Goings, *Monroe Doctrine*, 1964; Yves Klein, *Untitled*, 1962; Wynne Chamberlain, *Three Nudes*, 1963; Billy Apple, *Revlon's Low Down Pink*, 1963; Wayne Thiebaud, *Bikini*, 1964; Idelle Weber, *Happy Valentine's Day*, 1962; John Altoon, *Angel Face*, 1964; Harold Stevenson, *Untitled*, 1961; William Copley (CPLY), *Untitled*, 1964; Charles Frazier, *Untitled #1*, 1964; Edward Kienholz, *Mother Sterling*, 1961

REVIEW / Henry J. Seldis, "In the Galleries: The Pop Art Pot Boiling Briskly," *Los Angeles Times* (January 11, 1965): C7 "The fermentation of pop art continues to bubble on the local exhibition scene. Perhaps the most refreshing hi-jinx in this direction is a show currently at the Dwan Gallery named 'The Arena of Love.' Frankly erotic in many of its manifestations, the show has produced the first 'Adults Only' sign I have ever seen on an art gallery's door."

MENTION / Philip Leider, "Small but Select," *Frontier: The Voice of the New West* 16, no. 5 (March 1965): 21–22

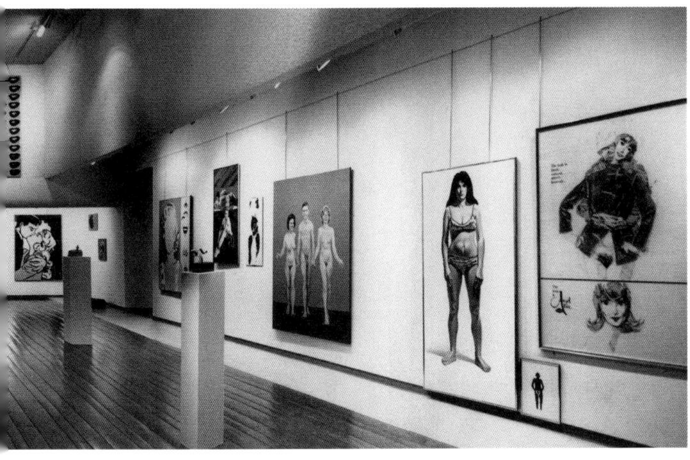

53

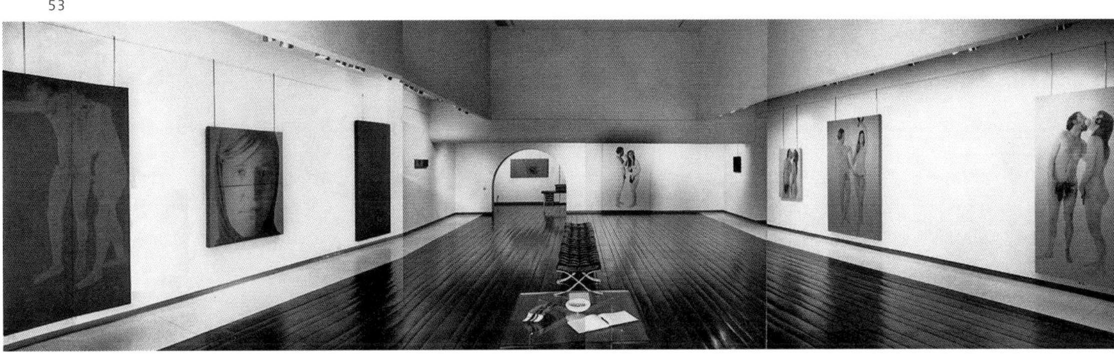

Drawings: Oldenburg, Dine, Whitman, Talbert
DGLA / February 9–March 13

CHECKLIST / Jim Dine, *Palette (Joan) 5*, 1964; Jim Dine, *Double Toothbrush Holder*, 1962; Jim Dine, *Study for Child's Room*, 1962; Jim Dine, *Toothbrush and Tumbler Holder #6*, 1962; Jim Dine, *Toothbrush and Tumbler Holder #8*, 1962; Jim Dine, *Toothbrush and Tumbler Holder #10*, 1962; Jim Dine, *Toothbrush and Tumbler with Metal Screw*, 1962; Jim Dine, *Four Ties*, 1961; Jim Dine, *Ties*, 1961; Jim Dine, *A Tie*, 1961; Jim Dine, *Lips*, 1960; Jim Dine, *(4) Four Chairs #9*, 1962; Jim Dine, *Double Palettes*, 1963; Ben Talbert, *Poster for "Ubu Roi"*, 1964; Ben Talbert, *Drawings for the 1964 Production of "Ubu Roi"*, 1964; Claes Oldenburg, *Two Sided Drawing: a. Fat Overalls-Dance Costume, b. Female Dancer, Looking Down*, 1961; Claes Oldenburg, *Cartoon Strip: Yes and No*, 1960; Claes Oldenburg, *Ray Gun Poster: Two Men, One with Balloon*, 1959; Claes Oldenburg, *Sketch of Dance Prop: Junk-wagon*, 1961; Claes Oldenburg, *Sketch for Telephone*, 1963; Claes Oldenburg, *Espressor Cup*, 1964; Claes Oldenburg, *Sketch of a Refrigerator*, 1963; Claes Oldenburg, *Chantilly Dessert, While Eating*, 1964; Claes Oldenburg, *Sketch for Giant Shirt and Tie*, 1963; Claes Oldenburg, *Sketch of a Typewriter*, 1963; Claes Oldenburg, *Plan for Outlet and Plug*, 1964; Claes Oldenburg, *Study for Vacuum Cleaner*, 1964; Claes Oldenburg, *Two Figures and Marquee ("Wee-")*, 1961; Claes Oldenburg, *Stuffed Numbers, Irregular Shape*, 1963; Claes Oldenburg, *Figure of Girl, Bending Forward with Black Knee Length Stockings*, 1960; Claes Oldenburg, *Entrance to an Estate, Lenox, Mass.*, 1959; Robert Whitman, *Sun Spots*, 1964; Robert Whitman, *Camera Putting Out Meat & Plants*, 1964; Robert Whitman, *The Camera as a Meat Grinder*, 1964; Robert Whitman, *Full Black Moon*, 1964; Robert Whitman, *Toilet with a Woman on It*, 1964; Robert Whitman, *Toilet*, 1964; Robert Whitman, *What the Toilet Sees*, 1964; Robert Whitman, *Corn Cob*, 1964; Robert Whitman, *Saturn*, 1964; Robert Whitman, *Untitled Drawing*, 1964; Robert Whitman, *Eggplant*, 1964; Robert Whitman, *Potato*, 1964

REVIEWS / Don Factor, "Reviews: Los Angeles, Drawings by Dine, Oldenburg, Talbert and Whitman," *Artforum* 3, no. 7 (April 1965): 9, illustrated; Nancy Marmer, "Los Angeles Letter," *Art International* 9, no. 4 (May 1965): 45, illustrated

Dakota Daley & Nicholas Quennell
DGLA / March 16–April 10

CHECKLIST / *Adam and Eve #4*, 1965; *Eve #2*, 1965; *Adam and Eve #6*, 1965; *Eve #4*, 1965; *Eve #3*, 1965; *Adam and Eve #2*, 1965; *Adam #1*, 1965; *Adam and Eve #3*, 1965; *Adam and Eve #5*, 1965; *Adam and Eve #1*, 1965; *Adam and Eve #7*, 1965; *Adam #2*, 1965; *Adam #3*, 1965

REVIEWS / William Wilson, "In the Galleries: Dole, a Second-Generation Dadaist, Outdoes the First," *Los Angeles Times* (March 26, 1965): D8 (under "Collaborative Show at Dwan Gallery") "Their satire is funny. The idea that Adam and Eve were just a couple of nice kids in love is mildly touching. So much is enough for a *Playboy* magazine spread, too little for a gallery that has shown important avant-garde performers." Irving B. Petlin, "Los Angeles: Dakota [Daley] and Nicholas [Quennell], Dwan Gallery," *Artforum* 3, no. 8 (May 1965): 16–17, illustrated; Fidel Danieli, "Reviews: Los Angeles," *Artnews* 64, no. 3 (May 1965): 65

ROBERT RAUSCHENBERG: DRAWINGS, INSTALLATION (54)

MARK DI SUVERO (TWO LARGE WORKS), INSTALLATION (55, 56)

LARRY RIVERS: RECENT WORK, POSTER (57)

EDWARD KIENHOLZ: THE BEANERY, POSTER (58)

ARAKAWA: FOR INSTANCE, INSTANT, POSTER (59)

54

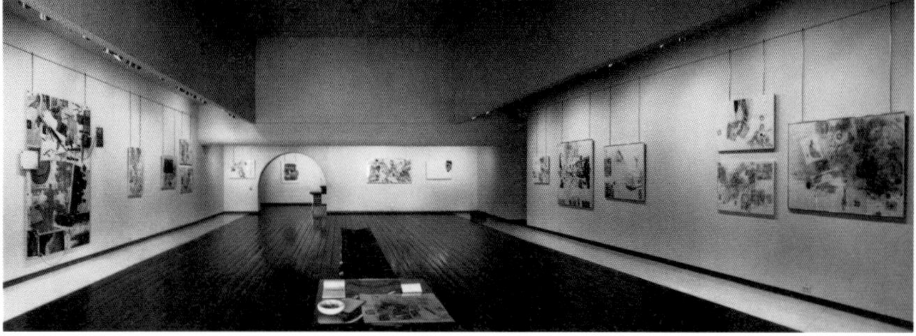

55

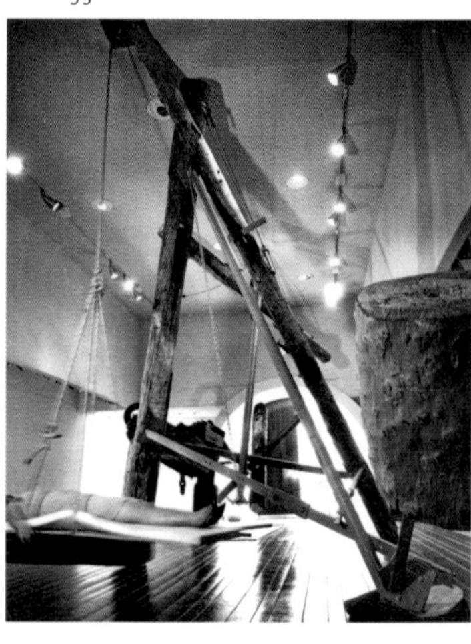

56

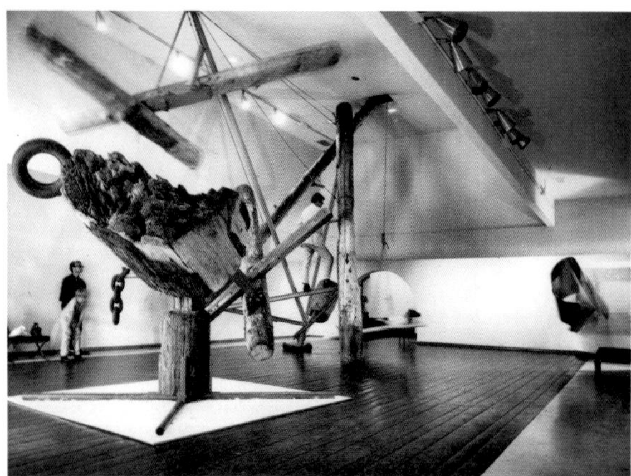

1965–1966 LOS ANGELES AND NEW YORK

Robert Rauschenberg: Drawings
DGLA / April 13–May 8

CHECKLIST / *Lead Envelope*, 1965; *New York Bird Calls for Öyvind Fahlström*, 1965; *House Warming*, 1965; *Omen*, 1965; *Decoder III*, 1965; *Decoder I*, 1965; *Decoder II*, 1965; *Umpire*, 1965; *Mainspring*, 1965; *Proverb*, 1965; *Paraphrase*, 1965; *Prowler*, 1965; *Escort*, 1965; *Backer*, 1965; *Battery*, 1965; *Quicksand*, 1965; *Shell*, 1965; *Promise*, 1965

REVIEWS / William Wilson, "In the Galleries: Exhibition That Instructs," *Los Angeles Times* (April 23, 1965): C9; Nancy Marmer, "Reviews: Los Angeles, Robert Rauschenberg," *Artforum* 3, no. 9 (June 1965): 10–11, illustrated; Nancy Marmer, "Los Angeles Letter," *Art International* 9, no. 5 (June 1965): 41, illustrated

Charles Frazier
DGLA / May 11–June 5

CHECKLIST / Fourteen works titled *Untitled*, 1964

REVIEW / William Wilson, "In the Galleries: Sculpture Exhibit Impresses," *Los Angeles Times* (May 17, 1965): C11 "In Frazier's case the final impressions are a fixture of sentimentality, hedonism and because of the golden polish of the pieces, a love of the superficially luxurious. Regarded simply as forms, they are rich if occasionally overgenerous visual delights."

Group Show
DGLA / June 8–July 3

CHECKLIST / Martial Raysse, *The Pot and the Flower*, 1964; Ad Reinhardt, *A*, 1956; Larry Rivers, *Africa*, 1961–1962; Robert Watts, *Guadalcanal*, 1960; Franz Kline, *Black Sienna*, 1960; Edward Kienholz, *Army and Soul*, 1964; Lucas Samaras, *Book No. 8*, 1962; Lee Bontecou, *Untitled #38*, 1961; Arman, *Cartouches*, 1962; Jean Tinguely, *Vehicule Stable*, 1961–1962; Martial Raysse, *Gordon Cooper*, 1963; Arakawa, *Untitled*, 1963; Lucas Samaras, *Floor Piece–Pin Box*, 1964; Jean Tinguely, *Meta Kandinsky*, 1958; Philip Guston, *Garden of M*, 1960; Sven Lukin, *Dwan Song*, 1963

Mark di Suvero
DGLA / September 29–November 13

CHECKLIST / *Pre-Columbian*, 1965; *Nova Albion*, 1964–1965

REVIEWS / Henry J. Seldis, "A Tour de Force of Sculptor's Art," *Los Angeles Times* (October 4, 1965): D9 "A smaller piece — though monumental by ordinary standards — is titled 'Pre-Columbian' after the estimated age of a tree trunk that is part of its construction. The entire superstructure of this work moves freely and easily though it is enormously heavy. On the California beach where Di Suvero assembled his distinctive constructions, the winds kept part of them moving at all times." Nancy Marmer, "Reviews: Los Angeles, Mark Di Suvero," *Artforum* 4, no. 4 (December 1965): 12–13, illustrated

RELATED / Images of works on the beach featured in "Mark Di Suvero: Three New Sculptures," *Artforum* 3, no. 8 (May 1965): 36–38, illustrated

57

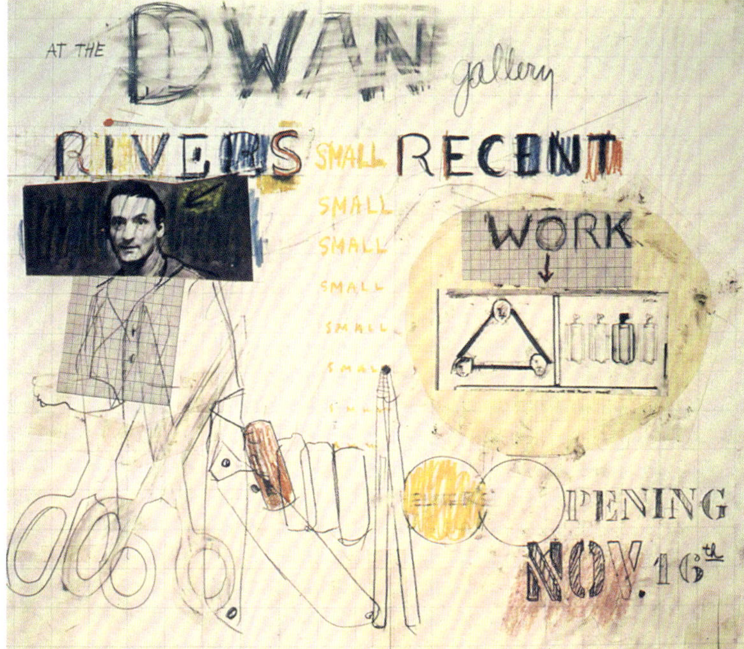

58

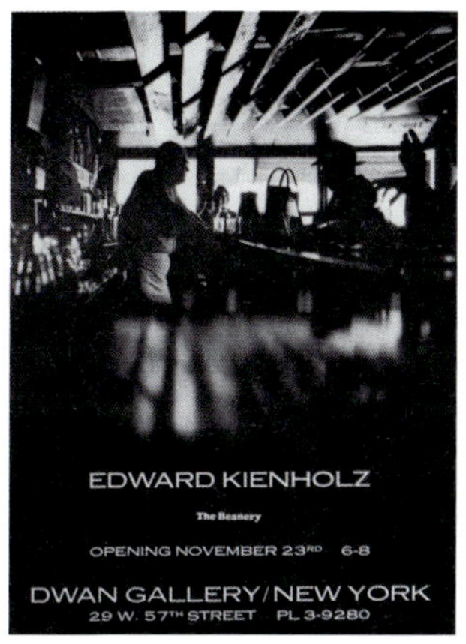

59

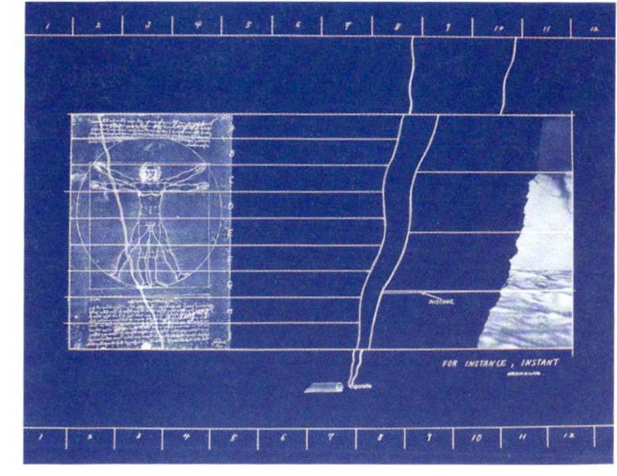

Larry Rivers: Recent Work
DGLA / November 16–December 11

CHECKLIST / *Announcement for 1965 Exhibition*, 1965; *Bulls-Eye Flowers Cut Out*, 1965; *5 Flowers Cut Out*, 1965; *The Daily Screw*, 1963; *Film Festival Sketch*, 1963; *Parts of the Body–French* (cut-out), 1964; *Hyacinths*, 1965; *Announcement for 1965 Exhibition*, 1965; *Dutch Masters* (drawing for a banner), 1964; *6 Flowers Cut Out*, 1965; *Freya*, 1959; *Parts of the Face–French*; *Narcissus Cut Outs*, 1965; *Models and Shoes Cut Outs* 1965; *Webster and Cigars*, 1965; *Discards from the "Toilet" I*, n.d.; *Sunday Screw*, 1963; *Two of Spades*, 1961; *Clarice*, 1964

REVIEWS / Henry J. Seldis, "In the Galleries: Larry Rivers Fans Get Short-Changed," *Los Angeles Times* (November 29, 1965): C13 "The present exhibition at the Dwan Gallery is an illustration of how every scrap from the hand of today's celebrity artist is readily elevated in the market to be presented as a significant work of art." Irving S. Petlin, "Los Angeles: Larry Rivers," *Artforum* 4, no. 5 (January 1966): 14–15, illustrated

Edward Kienholz: The Beanery
DGNY / November 23–December 31

CHECKLIST / *The Beanery*, 1965

REVIEWS / Suzi Gablik, "Crossing the Bar," *Artnews* 64, no. 6 (October 1965): 22–25, illustrated; Grace Glueck, "New Place to Go: Ersatz Beanery," *New York Times* (November 25, 1965): 45; "Kienholz Tableau at the Dwan...," *Women's Wear Daily* (November 26, 1965): n.p.; Emily Genauer, "Edward Kienholz," *New York Herald Tribune* (November 27, 1965): 6; "Art: Greasy Verisimilitude," *Time* (December 17, 1965): 68; "The Beanery," *Newsweek* (December 20, 1965): 103–104; "Beanery Built for Art," *Life* 60, no. 2 (January 14, 1966): 78–83; Dore Ashton, "Commentary from Washington and New York," *Studio International* 171, no. 874 (February 1966): 80–81; William Berkson, "In the Galleries: Ed Kienholz," *Arts Magazine* 40, no. 4 (February 1966): 63; Michael Blankfort, "Ed Kienholz: A Very Private Report," *Los Angeles Magazine* (April 1966): 48–50, 52; Sidney Tillim, "Edward Kienholz's 'Barney's Beanery'–The Underground Pre-Raphaelitism of Edward Kienholz," *Artforum* 4, no. 8 (April 1966): 38–40

Group Show
DGLA / December 21–January 15, 1966

CHECKLIST / Forrest Myers, *Kun A Mon*, 1965; Allan D'Arcangelo, *Untitled #7*, 1965; Anthony Magar, *Untitled*, 1965; Arakawa, *Unknown (Seven Color) Blood*, 1965; Robert Grosvenor, *Untitled*, 1965; Neil Williams, *Baby Baumblatt*, 1964; Mark di Suvero, *Knight's Gambit*, 1965

1966

Arakawa: For instance, instant
DGNY / January 4–29

CHECKLIST / *Diagram of Meeting*, 1964; *Ignore the Compass*, 1964; *Separated Continuums*, 1965; *Tubes*, 1965; *Bottomless*, 1965; *Enigmatic Convergence & Transformation*, 1965; *Webster's Dictionary, Page I*, 1965; *Unknown Blood–As you walk by Look*, 1965; *Diagram of Imagination*, 1965; *Untitled (House Diagram)*, 1965

REVIEWS / Suzi Gablik, "Reviews and Previews," *Artnews* 64, no. 8 (December 1965): 10 "He literally seems to pivot his mind on the frontier of visibility and invisibility, presence and absence,

ANASTASI: SOUND OBJECTS, ANNOUNCEMENT (60) AND INSTALLATION (61)

ALLAN D'ARCANGELO, ANNOUNCEMENT (62)

TOM DOYLE, POSTER (63)

ROBERT MORRIS: SCULPTURE, POSTER (64)

ARAKAWA, INSTALLATION (65)

60

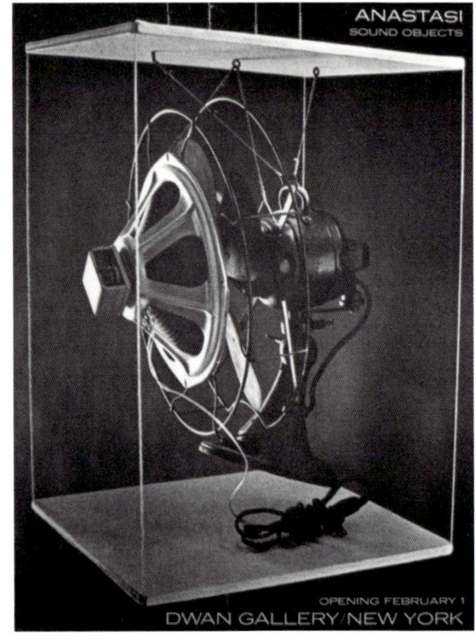

61

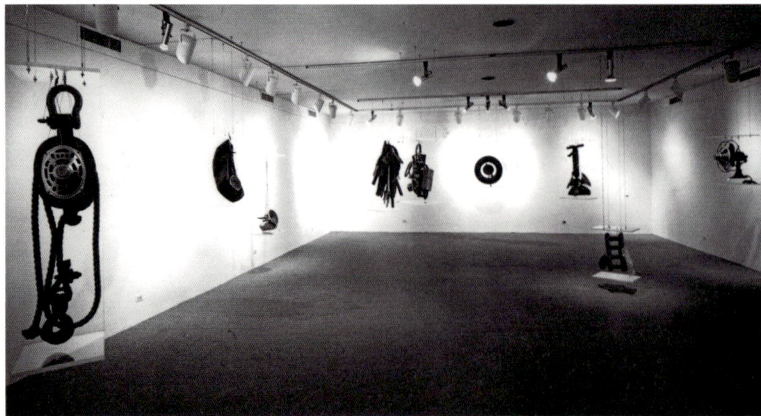

62

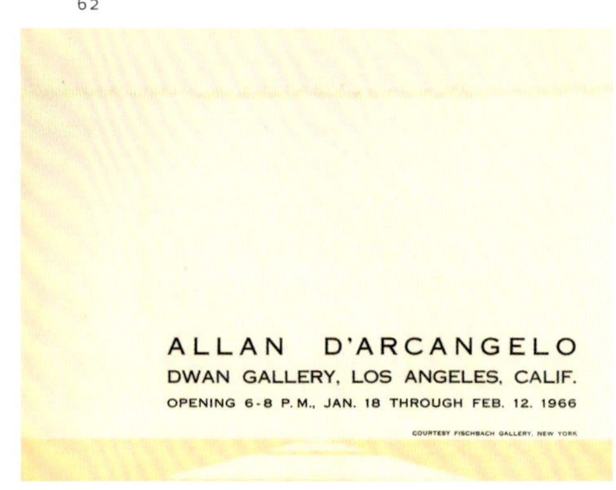

the metaphysical and the material. His work vibrates with extrasensorial perceptions and eidetic charges, and the strange luminosity of dematerializing shapes implies things are happening which are not seen." Nan R. Piene, "New York: Gallery Notes," *Art in America* 54, no. 1 (January–February 1966): 120–121, illustrated "Arakawa's paintings look a little bit like what might happen if a contemplative poet were let loose to chart his life's and afterlife's progression with visual symbols on a linear diagram from a page out of *Scientific American*." John Canady, "Arakawa," *New York Times* (January 15, 1966): 23; Dennis Adrian, "New York: Arakawa, Dwan Gallery," *Artforum* 5, no. 7 (March 1966): 49, 51, illustrated; Amy Goldin, "In the Galleries," *Arts Magazine* 40, no. 3 (March 1966): 6

MENTION / Annette Michelson, "New York Letter," *Art International* 10, no. 3 (March 20, 1966): 71

Allan D'Arcangelo
DGLA / January 18–February 12

CHECKLIST / *Untitled #4*, 1965; *Untitled #6*, 1965; *Untitled #9*, 1965; *Untitled #1*, 1965; *Untitled #15*, 1965; *Untitled #3*, 1965; *Untitled #5*, 1965; *Untitled #2*, 1965

REVIEWS / William Wilson, "In the Galleries: Oversimplification Mars Dwan Exhibit," *Los Angeles Times* (January 28, 1966): C4; Don Factor, "Los Angeles: Allan D'Arcangelo," *Artforum* 4, no. 8 (April 1966): 15, 17, illustrated; Kurt von Meier, "Los Angeles Letter," *Art International* 10, no. 5 (May 20, 1966): 58, illustrated

Anastasi: Sound Objects
DGNY / February 1–26

CHECKLIST / *Untitled–Oil Can & Sledge*, 1965; *Untitled–Pneumatic Drill & Asp*, 1965; *Untitled–Phone Book*, 1965; *Untitled–Salt Box*, 1965; *Untitled–Brown Paper & Wire*, 1965; *Untitled–Electric Fan*, 1966; *Untitled–Inflated Inner Tube*, 1966; *Untitled–Cinder Block & Destroyed Jug*, n.d.; *Untitled–Shovel*, 1966; *Untitled–Deflated Inner Tube*, 1966; *Untitled–Pick*, 1966; *Untitled–Bucket of Water & Faucet*, 1966; *Untitled–Window*, 1966; *Untitled–Pulley*, 1966; *Destroyed Barrel*, 1966; *Untitled–Power Saw*, 1966; *Untitled–Radiator*, 1966

REVIEWS / John Gruen, "William Anastasi," *New York Herald Tribune* (February 5, 1966): 8; Douglas M. Davis, "Galleries Festooned with Odd Shapes, Sounds, and Motions," *The National Observer* (February 28, 1966): 20, illustrated; Suzi Gablik, "Reviews and Previews," *Artnews* 65, no. 1 (March 1966): 10; Mel Bochner, "In the Galleries: Anastasi," *Arts Magazine* 40, no. 6 (April 1966): 63; Lucy Lippard, "New York Letter," *Art International* 10, no. 4 (April 20, 1966): 78, illustrated "They are, in essence, ready-mades with congruent Cageian sound effects. Anastasi plays a factually intellectual game, the fascination lying in the strong literal quality rather than in any associative impedimenta. Instead of exploiting the appearance of the common object or our opinions on the urban scenes evoked, he presents the pieces as events, and their singular clarity thus takes on the purity of experience — not dreamed, nor in any way distorted, but kept in context by the sound and merely heightened by the visual exactitude."

Neil Williams
DGLA / February 15–March 12

CHECKLIST / *Dapper Dan*, 1965; *Tubby in Love*, 1965; *Untitled*, 1965; *Variations on "64" Series Show*, 1963–1964; *Drawing for Neil William's One-Man Exhibition*, 1965; *Untitled*, 1964; *Untitled*, 1964; *Green Gallery '64 Show Series*, 1963–1964; *Untitled*, 1965; *Announcement for One-Man Exhibition*, 1965; *Untitled*, 1963; *Blue Mijanau*, 1964; *My Sweet Drollop*, 1965; *Baby Baumblatt*, 1964

63

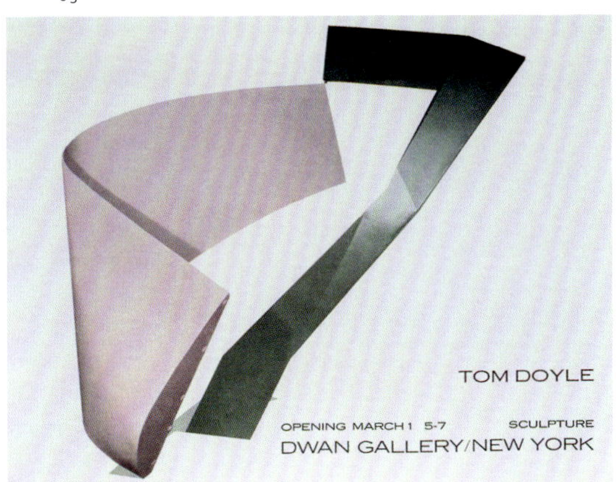

64

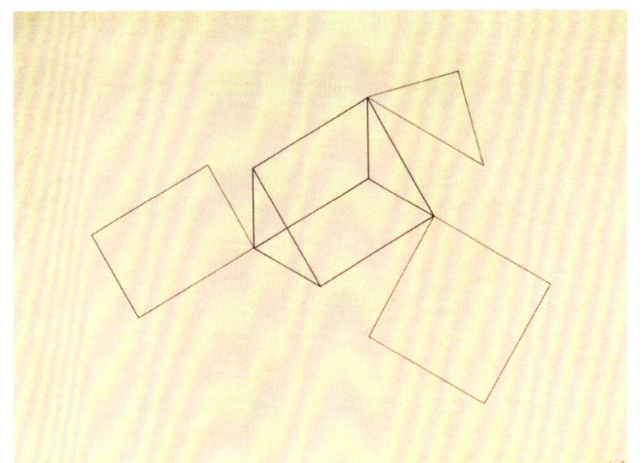

65

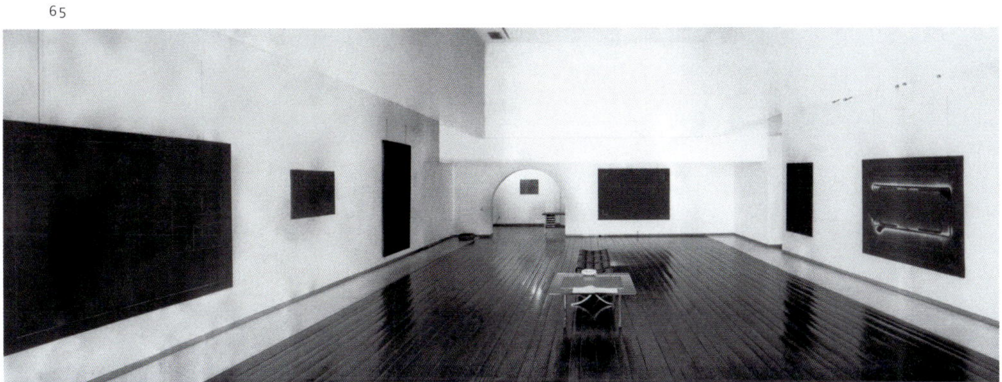

REVIEWS / William Wilson, "In the Galleries: Infinite Visual Suggestions in Art Work of Hans Arp," *Los Angeles Times* (February 21, 1966): C11; Don Factor, "Los Angeles: Neil Williams, Dwan Gallery," *Artforum* (April 1966): 14, 17, illustrated; Kurt von Meier, "Los Angeles Letter," *Art International* 10, no. 5 (May 20, 1966): 58, illustrated

Tom Doyle
DGNY / March 1–March 26

CHECKLIST / *LaVergne*, 1966; *Over Owl's Creek*, 1966

REVIEWS / Hilton Kramer, "Art: There's Nothing Like Thinking Big, Sometimes," *New York Times* (March 12, 1966): L23; Ted Berrigan, "Reviews and Previews," *Art News* 65, no. 2 (April 1966): 15 "Seeing this work is a process rather than an act: it makes you move around it in perpetual search of a finish line which is somehow not there." Dennis Adrian, "New York: Tom Doyle," *Artforum* 4, no. 9 (May 1966): 51–52, 54, illustrated

Robert Morris: Sculpture
DGLA / March 15–April 9

CHECKLIST / Six works titled *Untitled*, 1966, and seven works titled *Untitled*, 1965

REVIEWS / Don Factor, "Los Angeles: Robert Morris, Dwan Gallery," *Artforum* 4, no. 9 (May 1966): 13 "The prime significance of these sculptures is the effect of forcing the viewer into a kind of gestalt showdown. These non-reducible, closed forms sit uncomfortably in the gallery space, or, in gestalt terms, the 'visual field,' and permit of no direct analysis. Thus, they force the viewer into analyzing the field itself and disrupting his organizational habits. Morris has here accomplished an important break with past sculpture, which has tended to serve as a free-standing, three-dimensional pictorial or iconographical device, by creating a sculpture that serves to redirect the entire environmental experience." Kurt von Meier, "Los Angeles Letter," *Art International* 10, no. 5 (May 1966): 58–59, illustrated; William Wilson, "In the Galleries: Horiuchi Works Possess Unwavering Good Taste," *Los Angeles Times* (May 28, 1966): C7

Arakawa
DGLA / April 12–May 7

CHECKLIST / *The Diagram of Imagination*, 1965–1966; *Separated Continuums*, December 18, 1965; *Appearance of Cup and Bottle*, 1965–1966; *Announcement for One-Man Exhibition*, 1966; *The Diagram of Dream*, December 2, 1965; *My Name*, January 28, 1966; *Separated Continuums*, January 11, 1966; *Untitled*, 1966; *This Canvas is a Perfect Rectangle*, March 5, 1966

REVIEWS / William Wilson, "In the Galleries: Tom Arakawa's Blueprints Rely on Word Association," *Los Angeles Times* (April 15, 1966): C6 "A blueprint is both specific and ambiguous. Arakawa uses words visually to create various interpretations. . . . We cease to think of the universal reduced to the commonplace and think of the commonplace in large mystical terms." Don Factor, "Los Angeles: Arakawa, Dwan Gallery," *Artforum* 4, no. 10 (June 1966): 15–16, illustrated

KENNETH SNELSON, INSTALLATION (66)

SOL LEWITT, ANNOUNCEMENT (67) AND ILLUSTRATED CHECKLIST FOR THE EXHIBITION (68)

ROBERT GROSVENOR, INSTALLATION (69)

A SUMMER SHOW, INSTALLATION (70)

10 (NEW YORK), INSTALLATION (71)

66

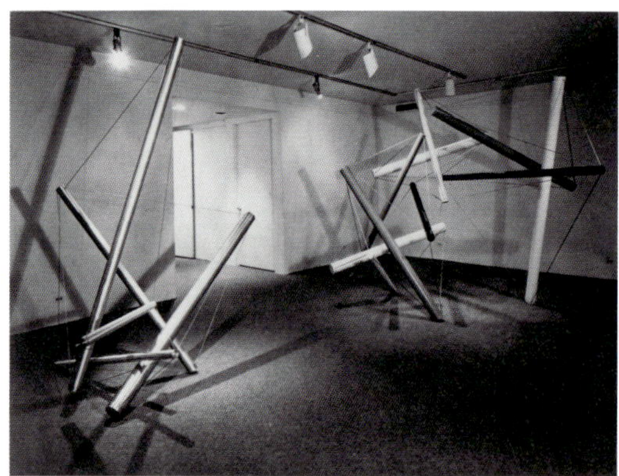

68

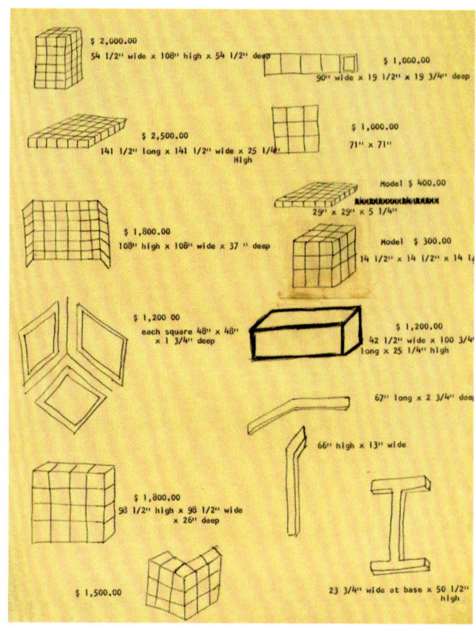

69

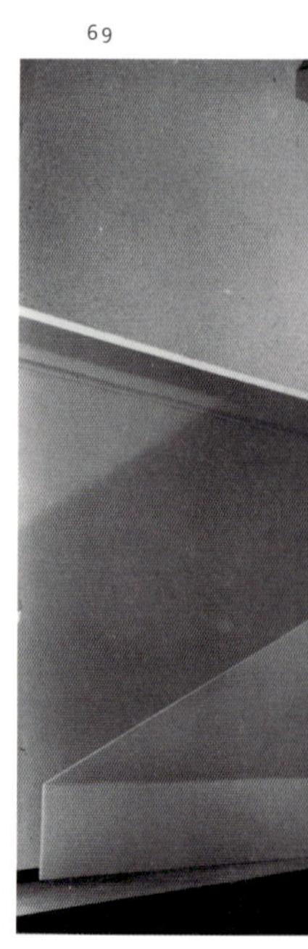

67

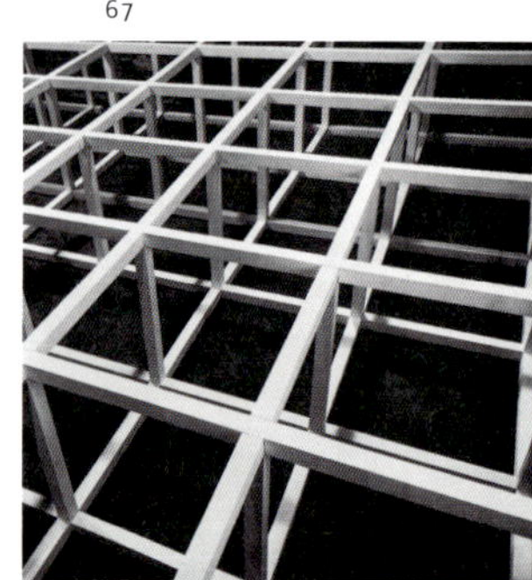

1966 LOS ANGELES AND NEW YORK

Kenneth Snelson
DGNY / April 12–May 7

CHECKLIST / *Audrey I*, 1965; *Audrey II*, 1966; *Sagg Main Street*, 1966; *Sag Harbor II*, 1965; *X-Piece (Blue and Orange)*, 1962; *Atom*, 1964; *Ico-Circle*, 1962; *Face-Centered Cubic Spheres*, 1962; *Trigonal Tower*, 1963; *Spring Street*, 1964; *Tower (Cantilever)*, 1962; *Sag Harbor I*, 1965; *Circle Group I*, 1964; *Circle Group II*, 1965; *Circle Group III*, 1965

REVIEWS / John Canaday, "Constructions on the 'Tensegrity' Principle," *New York Times* (April 16, 1966): L29 "Works of art these constructions certainly are, and an artist Mr. Snelson certainly is. But he is at the same time an engineer, and his sculptures are exercises in structural theory that have the special beauty of bridges, radio transmission towers, the skeletons of skyscrapers under construction and other projects." Peter Schjeldahl, "Reviews and Previews," *Artnews* 65, no. 3 (May 1966): 21; Dore Ashton, "Historicism and respect for tradition: New York commentary," *Studio International* 171, no. 878 (June 1966): 277, illustrated; William Berkson, "In the Galleries," *Arts Magazine* 40, no. 8 (June 1966): 52, illustrated; James R. Mellow, "New York Letter," *Art International* 10, no. 7 (September 15, 1966): 57

Group Show
DGLA / May 10–28

CHECKLIST / Edward Kienholz, *Lieutenant Carter (The Bad Cop)*, 1961; Sven Lukin, *Dwan Song*, 1963; Mark di Suvero, *Untitled*, 1962; Robert Rauschenberg, *Fossil for Bob Morris*, 1965; John Chamberlain, *Nanny*, 1966; James Rosenquist, *Silhouette*, 1964; Mark di Suvero, *Washington's Bong*, 1965; Ad Reinhardt, *F Abstract Painting No. 10*, 1963; John Chamberlain, *Cat-Bird Seat*, 1966; Robert Rauschenberg, *Whale*, 1964

Sol LeWitt
DGNY / May 10–June 3

CHECKLIST / *Serial Project #1 Sets A, B, C, D*, 1966; *Standing Modular Structure ("Double Modular Cube")*, 1966; *Modular Floor Structure*, 1966; *Standing Modular Structure ("Floor-Wall Grid")*, 1966; *Hanging Modular Wall Piece with Cube*; *Wall Grid*; *For Model Floor Structure*; *Model for Structure Wood/Block*; *Modular Structure (Standing)*, 1966; *Wall Piece "Bent Stick,"* 1965; *55"× 55"× 55"*; *Wall Piece I (Hockey Stick)*, 1965

REVIEWS / Hilton Kramer, "Sol LeWitt," *New York Times* (May 21, 1966): 20; Mel Bochner, "In the Galleries," *Arts Magazine* 40, no. 9 (September/October 1966): 61

Robert Grosvenor
DGLA / June 7–July 2

Checklist / *Still No Title*, 1966; *Tenerife*, 1966; *Model for Ceiling Piece*, 1966

REVIEW / William Wilson, "In the Galleries: Exhibit Offers Sure Cure for Pavlov–Raoul Dufy Syndrome," *Los Angeles Times* (June 10, 1966): D9 "Working together the pieces set the gallery space in motion, warping and slicing it until the rectangular room is transformed into an arena of moving space."

RELATED / Installation images in David Bourdon, "The Cantilevered Rainbow," *Artnews* 66, no. 4 (Summer 1967): 28–31

A Summer Show
DGLA / July 5–30

CHECKLIST / DeWain Valentine, *Candy Cones*, 1966; Richard Matthews, *Troglodytidae*, 1966; David Crum, *Nauvoo*, 1966; David Crum, *La Harpe*, 1966; Richard Matthews, *O.A.*, 1966; David Crum, *Macomb*, 1966; James Massey,

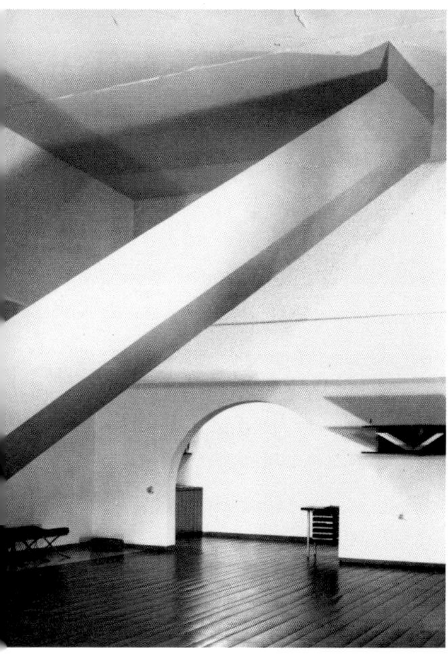

70

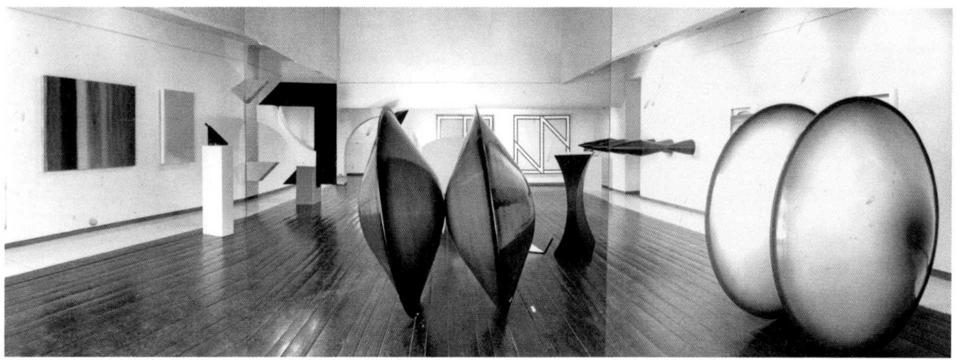

71

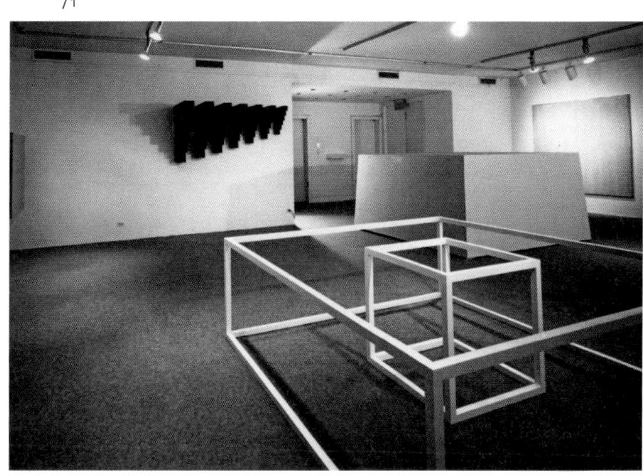

Jitney, 1966; James Massey, *Bas-Besa*, 1966; James Massey, *Strikly*, 1966; Richard Matthews, *Hummer* 1966; John Carruthers, *Untitled #1*, 1966; John Carruthers, *Untitled #2*, 1966; John Carruthers, *Untitled #3*, 1966; John Carruthers, *Untitled #4*, 1966; John Carruthers, *Untitled #5*, 1966; John Carruthers, *Al Baker Series #2*, 1966; John Carruthers, *Al Baker Series #1*, 1966; Richard Matthews, *Paceminterris*, 1966; DeWain Valentine, *3 Red*, 1966; James Massey, *Cliffords Bird (King)*, 1966; Nancy Gowans, *Untitled #1*, 1966; Nancy Gowans, *Untitled #2*, 1966; DeWain Valentine, *Blue Tandem*, 1966; Nancy Gowans, *Untitled #2*, 1966; DeWain Valentine, *Yo-Yo*, 1966; Richard Matthews, *The Blue Max*, 1966; John Carruthers, *Untitled #6*, 1966; John Carruthers, *Untitled #7*, 1966; John Carruthers, *Untitled #8*, 1966; John Carruthers, *Untitled #9*, 1966; Jessie Jacobs, *Light #3*, 1966; Jessie Jacobs, *Light #4*, 1966; Jessie Jacobs, *Light #1*, 1966; Jessie Jacobs, *Light #2*, 1966

REVIEWS / Fidel A. Danieli, "Two Showings of Younger Los Angeles Artists," *Artforum* 5, no. 2 (October 1966): 24–26, illustrated; Kurt von Meier, "Los Angeles Letter," *Art International* 10, no. 10 (December 20, 1966): 54, illustrated

Anthony Magar–Forrest Myers
DGLA / October 4–29

CHECKLIST / Forrest Myers, *Zigaratt & W. & W. W. W.*, 1966; Anthony Magar, *For Liz*, 1966; Forrest Myers, *Laser's Daze*, 1966; Anthony Magar, *Rake's Progress*, 1966; Anthony Magar, *Plexus*, 1966; Forrest Myers, *Sando's Pipeline*, 1966; Forrest Myers, *Timothy's Time Truck*, 1966; Forrest Myers, *Sa! J. A.*, 1966

REVIEWS / William Wilson, "In the Galleries: Talent in Anonymous Style," *Los Angeles Times* (October 10, 1966): C18; Donald Factor, "Anthony Magar, Forrest Myers at Dwan," *Artforum* 5, no. 4 (December 1966): 54–55, illustrated

10 (New York)
DGNY / October 4–29

CHECKLIST / Carl Andre, *Field*, 1966; Jo Baer, *Horizontal Flanking: large scale*, 1966; Dan Flavin, *Daylight and Cool Light*, 1964; Donald Judd, *Untitled*, 1966; Sol LeWitt, *A5*, 1966; Agnes Martin, *Leaves*, 1966; Robert Morris, *Untitled*, 1966; Ad Reinhardt, *Ultimate Painting #39*; Robert Smithson, *Alogon*, 1966; Michael Steiner, *Untitled*, 1965

REVIEWS / Annette Michelson, "10 x 10: 'concrete reasonableness,'" *Artforum* 5, no. 5 (January 1967): 30–31, illustrated "It is the series of patent but equivocal relationships obtaining between or among these works which is compelling. For what they share, they also dispute. A common accord is a basis for contention." Lucy R. Lippard, "After A Fashion–The Group Show," *The Hudson Review* 19, no. 4 (Winter 1966–1967): 620–626; Emily Genauer, "Friday Tour of Art," *World Journal Tribune* (October 14, 1966): 50 (under "10 x 10")

David Novros (five paintings)
DGLA / November 1–26

CHECKLIST / *6:36*, 1966; *6:32*, 1966; *3:18*, 1964; *4:20*, 1966; *6:59*, 1966

REVIEWS / Henry J. Seldis, "In the Galleries: David Novros Artistry Impresses," *Los Angeles Times* (November 7, 1966): C23; John Coplans, "David Novros in L.A.," *Artforum* 5, no. 5 (January 1967): 27, illustrated "1964 is a very surprising date for the earliest work in the exhibition, quite radical and advanced for so young a painter."

MICHAEL STEINER, POSTER (72)

JOHN CHAMBERLAIN: NEW WORKS, INSTALLATION (73) AND POSTER (74)

ROBERT SMITHSON, INSTALLATION (75)

SCALE MODELS AND DRAWINGS, INSTALLATION (76)

KENNETH SNELSON, INSTALLATION (77)

72

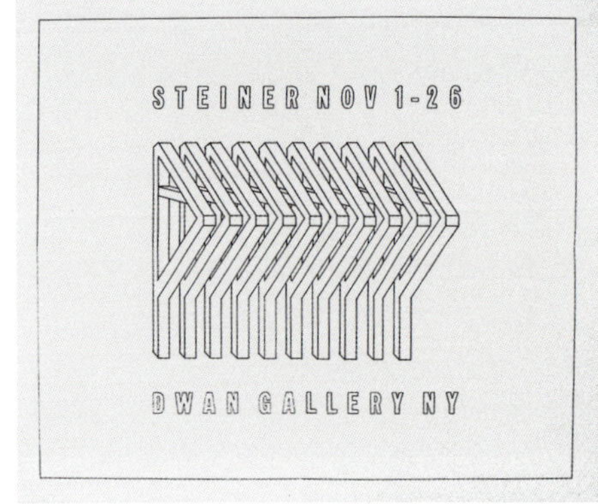

73

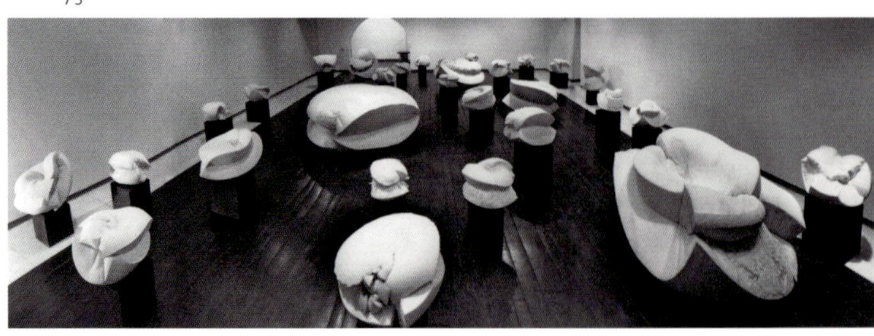

74

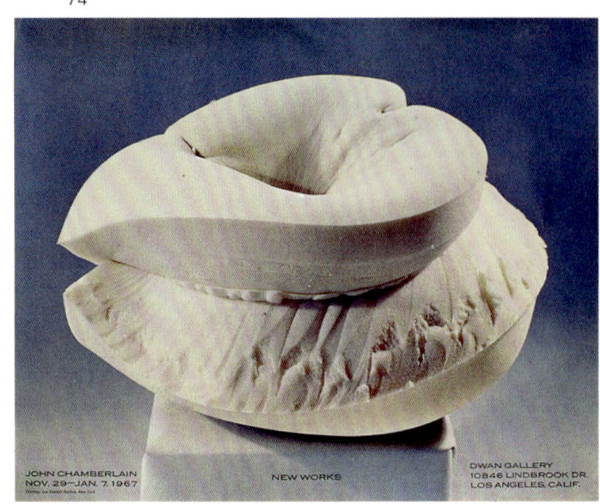

1966–1967 LOS ANGELES AND NEW YORK

Michael Steiner
DGNY / November 1–26

CHECKLIST / *Untitled* (2 cubes, 3 V's), 1965; *Untitled*, 1965; *Untitled* (2 U's), 1966; *Untitled* (3 blocks, 3 rods), 1966; *Untitled* (4's), 1966

REVIEWS / Ted Berrigan, "Reviews and Previews: Michael Steiner," *Artnews* 65, no. 7 (November 1966): 68; Michael Benedikt, "New York Letter," *Art International* 11, no. 1 (January 20, 1967): 57–58, illustrated; Max Kozloff, "Michael Steiner, Dwan Gallery," *Artforum* 5, no. 5 (January 1967): 56–57, illustrated

John Chamberlain: New Works (foam)
DGLA / November 29–January 1, 1967

CHECKLIST / *Untitled*, 1966; *Chefoo*, 1966; *Yunnan*, 1966; *Nanfeng*, 1966; *Nanchang*, 1966; *Fukien*, 1966; *Yin Yang*, 1966; *Taiping*, 1966; *Lolos*, 1966; *Yungfeng*, 1966; *Chingkanshan*, 1966; *Liu Ting*, 1966; *Yutu*, 1966; *Sian*, 1966; *Tungku*, 1966; *Kian*, 1966; *Manabend Ra*, 1966; *Sining*, 1966; *Whampoa*, 1966; *Kiangsi*, 1966; *Lo Man*, 1966; *Changsha*, 1966; *Ma An-Shan*, 1966; *Ta Tung*, 1966; *Lo An*, 1966; *Toupi*, 1966; *Szechuan*, 1966

REVIEWS / William Wilson, "In the Galleries: Rubbery Sculpture Softly Appealing," *Los Angeles Times* (December 5, 1966): D24 "Viewed together, these works constitute easily the most eccentric visual assault in some months. Their effect is not really visual but tactile and oral." Jules Langsner, "Los Angeles," *Artnews* 65, no. 9 (January 1967): 63; Philip Leider, "A New Medium for John Chamberlain," *Artforum* 5, no. 6 (February 1967): 48–49, illustrated

Robert Smithson
DGNY / November 29–January 5, 1967

CHECKLIST / *Terminal*, 1966; *Doubles*, 1966; *Plunge*, 1966; *Alogon #2*, 1966; *Three Vortices (Black Vortex, White Vortex, Mirror Vortex)*; *Ziggurat (Ziggurat Mirror)*; *Little Vortex*

REVIEWS / Scott Burton, "Reviews and Previews: Robert Smithson," *Artnews* 65, no. 8 (December 1966): 18; "Robert Smithson," *57th Street Review* 1, no. 2 (December 15, 1966): n.p.; Jeanne Siegel, "In the Galleries," *Arts Magazine* 41, no. 3 (December 1966/January 1967): 60–61, illustrated "What is unique in his work is the use of separate units, and what is new in this exhibition in the major work called *Plunge* is the actual manipulation by hand of the units to denote time." Dore Ashton, "New York commentary," *Studio International* 173, no. 886 (February 1967): 100–101, illustrated; Robert Pincus-Witten, "New York: Robert Smithson," *Artforum* 5, no. 6 (February 1967): 60–61, illustrated; James R. Mellow, "New York," *Art International* 11, no. 2 (February 20, 1967): 66–67, illustrated

RELATED / Installation view in Sol LeWitt, "Paragraphs on Conceptual Art," *Artforum* 5, no. 10 (Summer 1967): 81

1967

Scale Models and Drawings
DGNY / January 7–February 1

CHECKLIST / Carl Andre, drawing; Carl Andre, three drawings; Richard Baringer, model for dark bronze anodized aluminum arch; Richard Baringer, model for black anodized aluminum sculpture 40′ high; Ronald Bladen, pencil drawing: sketch of wind tunnel and sound volume; Mel Bochner, 36 dry-mounted photographs and 12 drawings; Christo, model and collage, *42390 Cubic Feet Empaquetage*, for Minneapolis School of Art, cosponsored [by] contemporary art group, Walker Art Center, October 24–29,

75

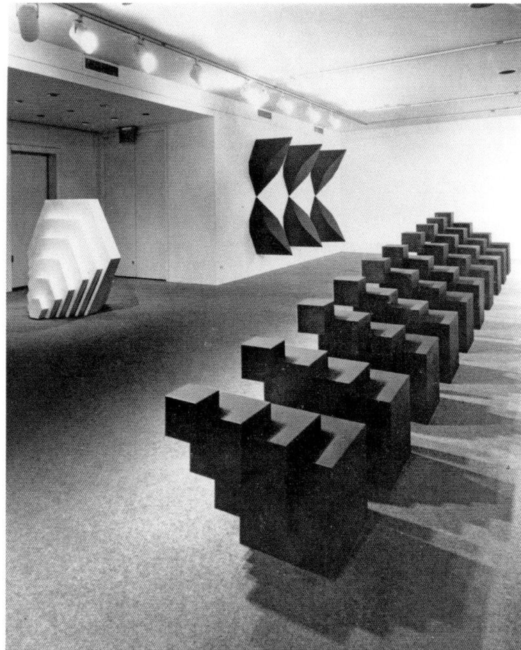

76

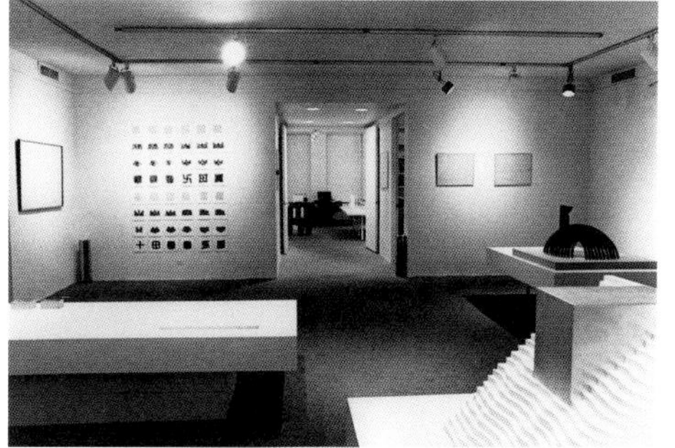

77

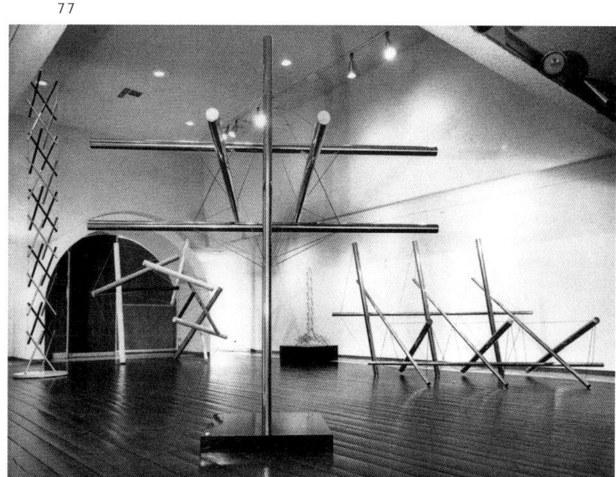

1966; Walter De Maria, Desert Walk–walls in the desert; Walter De Maria, View of person in the walls as seen by a helicopter; Walter De Maria, View of walls from 2 miles (?) in the distance; Walter De Maria, The entrance and/or the exit; Walter De Maria, Views of walls from an airplane; Walter De Maria, Imaginary view of the last 40 feet; Mark di Suvero, model; Dan Flavin, four drawings; Dan Flavin, drawing; Robert Grosvenor, Project for Existing Building with at least one glass wall; Donald Judd, drawing, 11″× 14″ (Pipe piece); Donald Judd, two drawings, 17½″× 22″; Sol LeWitt, Each Table; Robert Morris, plaster model; Tony Smith, drawing of F.D.R. Memorial; Tony Smith, cardboard model, Made in Steel; Robert Smithson, Model and drawing for Tar Pool and Gravel Pit; Robert Smithson, untitled model; Kenneth Snelson, Model for 30' Cantilever Tower; Michael Steiner, Scale Model for Pool Project; Michael Steiner, Mountain piece; Peter Hutchinson, Project for One-Man Show—Design for Gallery, Step I: Drawing; Peter Hutchinson, Step II: Model of Gallery; Peter Hutchinson, Step III: One Wall of Gallery

REVIEWS / David Bourdon, "Immodest Proposals For Monuments," *New York/World Journal Tribune* (January 8, 1967): 22–23; Charlotte Willard, "Color Study," *New York Post* (January 28, 1967): 45; H.R., "Reviews and Previews," *Artnews* 65, no. 10 (February 1967): 11, 60, illustrated; Patricia Sloane, "In the Galleries," *Arts Magazine* 41, no. 4 (February 1967): 57, illustrated; Dan Graham, "Models & Monuments: The Plague of Architecture," *Arts Magazine* 41, no. 5 (March 1967): 32–34; Robert Pincus-Witten, "New York: Scale Models and Drawings," *Artforum* 5, no. 7 (March 1967): 52, illustrated

Kenneth Snelson
DGLA / January 9–February 4

CHECKLIST / *Trigonal Tower*, 1963; *Audrey I*, 1965; *Vine Street*, 1966; *Untitled Study*, 1965; *Study for Vine Street*, 1966; *Study for Six I*, 1966; *Untitled Study*, 1966; *Untitled Study*, 1966; *Six I*, 1966; *Column*, 1961–1967; *Revolver*, 1966

REVIEWS / Henry Seldis, "In the Galleries: Snelson's Sculptures Imaginative," *Los Angeles Times* (January 16, 1967): D10 "Snelson has managed to combine artistic sensitivity and engineering discovery to create a unique kind of sculpture in which voids and invisible physical forces become integral parts of the work that demonstrate so clearly what kind of space can result from pure structure." Jules Langsner, "Los Angeles," *Artnews* 66, no. 1 (March 1967): 58, illustrated; Kurt von Meier, "Los Angeles," *Art International* 11, no. 9 (April 20, 1967): 54–55, illustrated

RELATED / Installation view in John Coplans, "An Interview with Kenneth Snelson," *Artforum* 5, no. 7 (March 1967): 46–49, illustrated

Edward Kienholz: Concept Tableaux
DGNY / February 4–March 1

CHECKLIST / **Tableau:** *The State Hospital*, 1965 **Concepts:** *The Black Leather Chair*, 1966; *The Office Building*, 1964; *The Art Show*, 1963; *The God Box #3*, 1963; *The Commercial 2*, 1965; *After the Ball is Over #2*, 1963; *The American Trip*, 1966; *The World*, 1967; *The God Box #1*, 1963; *Mayor Sam Edsel*, 1965; *After the Ball is Over #1*, 1964; *The God Box #2*, 1963; *The Cement Store #1*, 1965; *The Cement Store #2*, 1965; *The State Hospital*, 1965

DWAN GALLERY NEW YORK AT DWAN GALLERY LOS ANGELES, ANNOUNCEMENT (78) AND INSTALLATION (79)

CARL ANDRE (CUTS), INSTALLATION (80)

DAVID NOVROS: PAINTINGS, INSTALLATION (81)

SOL LEWITT: SERIES A, INSTALLATION (82)

ANASTASI: SIX SITES, POSTER (83)

10 (LOS ANGELES), INSTALLATION (84)

78

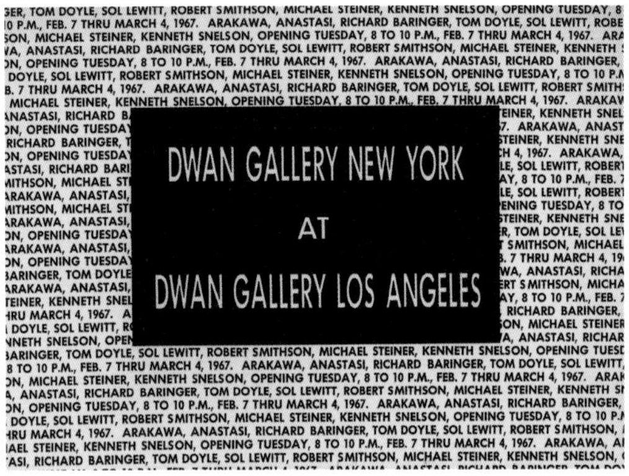

80

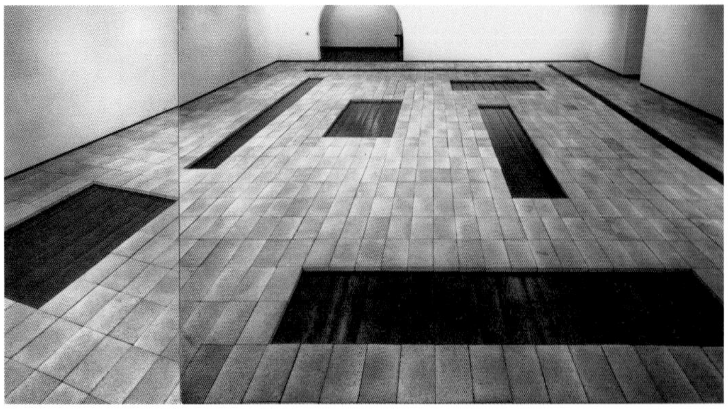

79

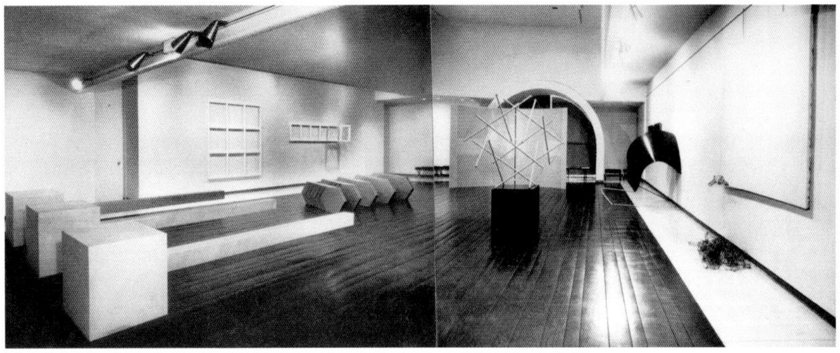

REVIEWS / Grace Glueck, "Bringing Back Beardsley," *New York Times* (February 19, 1967): 115 (under "Conceptually Yours"); Charlotte Willard, "All Around the Town," *New York Post* (February 25, 1967): 46; John Perreault, "Reviews and Previews," *Artnews* 66, no. 1 (March 1967): 14; Felice T. Ross, "Gallery Previews in New York," *Pictures on Exhibit* 30, no. 6 (March 1967): 10–11, illustrated; Dennis Adrian, "New York: Edward Kienholz," *Artforum* 5, no. 8 (April 1967): 56–58, illustrated; Jill Johnston, "New York," *Arts/Canada* no. 107 (April 1967): n.p.; Michael Benedikt, "New York," *Art International* 11, no. 9 (April 20, 1967): 79, illustrated

Dwan Gallery New York at Dwan Gallery Los Angeles
DGLA / February 7–March 4

CHECKLIST / Richard Baringer, *Untitled*, 1966; Arakawa, *Separated Continuums*; Arakawa, *The Diagram of Alphabet Skin 1966*, 1966; Tom Doyle, *I-U-KA*, 1965; Kenneth Snelson, *Tetrakaidecahedron*, 1963; Anastasi, *Situation Monumental*, 1966; Kenneth Snelson, *Planar*, 1963; Michael Snelson, *Untitled*, 1966; Sol LeWitt, *Hanging Modular Structure*, 1966; Sol LeWitt, *Hanging Modular Structure*, 1966; Robert Smithson, *Discontinuous Aggregates (Second Version)*, 1966–1967

REVIEW / Fidel A. Danieli, "New York Group, Dwan Gallery," *Artforum* 5, no. 8 (April 1967): 61–62, illustrated

Richard Baringer
DGNY / March 4–29

CHECKLIST / Six works titled *Untitled*, 1966

REVIEWS / Grace Glueck, "New York Gallery Notes," *Art in America* 55, no. 2 (March–April 1967): 106 (under "Dwan Gallery"); Kim Levin, "Reviews and Previews," *Artnews* 66, no. 2 (April 1967): 8, illustrated "These paintings on curved surfaces become architectural, space-enclosing, experimental objects." Felice T. Ross, "Gallery Previews in New York," *Pictures on Exhibit* 30, no. 7 (April 1967): 23; James R. Mellow, "New York," *Art International* 11, no. 5 (May 20, 1967): 58–59, illustrated

Carl Andre (Cuts)
DGLA / March 8–April 1

CHECKLIST / *Cuts*, 1967; *16 Pieces of Slate*, 1967; *16 Pieces of Aluminum*, 1967; *49 Pieces of Steel*, 1967; *21 Pieces of Aluminum*, 1967

REVIEWS / William Wilson, "In the Galleries: Frankenthaler Art Enters New Phase," *Los Angeles Times* (March 26, 1967): D2 (under "Carl Andre Exhibits at Dwan Gallery") "Its importance has partly to do with the fact that the viewer is aware of the specific things that happen to him on that floor. Does one walk on art? If you don't, you stand in the holes and you're shorter than everybody. In other words the work, whether formal or psychological in interpretation, sets up a complex thought process with minimal means." Kurt von Meier, "Los Angeles," *Art International* 11, no. 4 (April 20, 1967): 51; Jane Livingston, "Los Angeles: Carl Andre," *Artforum* 5, no. 9 (May 1967): 62–63, illustrated

RELATED / Installation view in Barbara Rose, "The Value of Didactic Art," *Artforum* 5, no. 8 (April 1967): 34; Dan Graham, "Carl Andre," *Arts Magazine* (December 1967/January 1968): 34–35

81

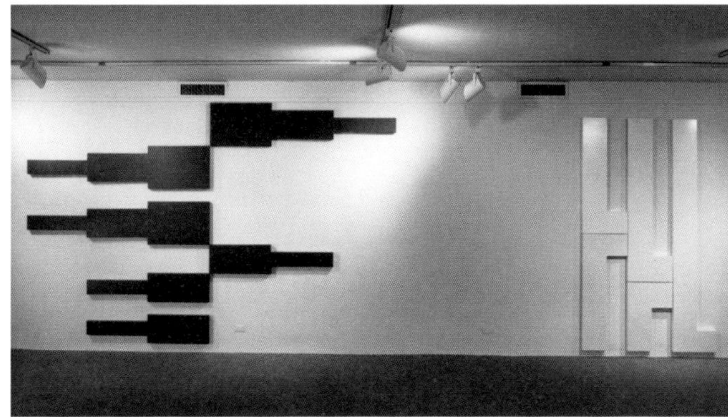

82

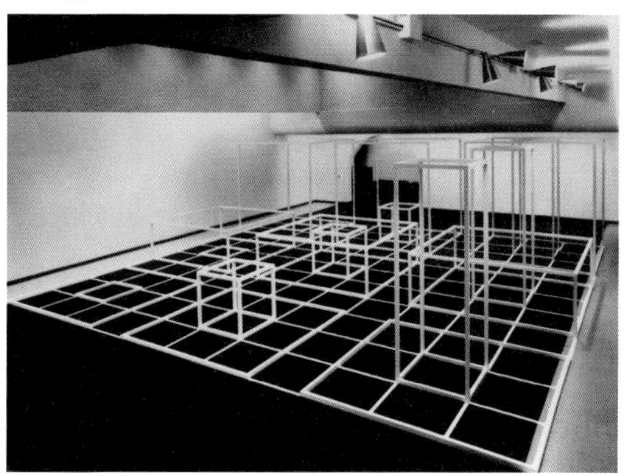

83

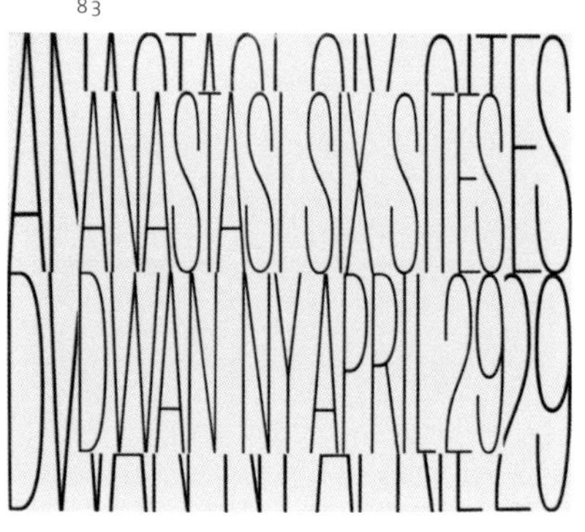

84

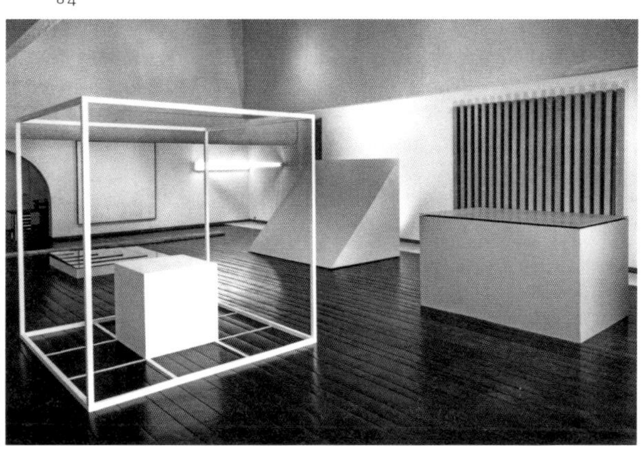

David Novros: Paintings
DGNY / April 1–28

CHECKLIST / *8′6″× 13′*, 1967; *8′6″× 6′*, 1967; *4′6″× 14′6″*, 1967; *7′× 9′*, 1967; *6′× 8′*, 1967

REVIEWS / "Rotor Reflector Review: David Novros Paintings, Dwan Gallery…," *57th Street Review* 1, no. 6 (April 20, 1967): n.p.; Pat Sloane, "In the Galleries: David Novros," *Arts Magazine* 41, no. 7 (May 1967): 57 "He teeters between commitment to the overt wall decoration, and commitment to the non-canvas canvas." Felice T. Ross, "Gallery Previews in New York," *Pictures on Exhibit* 30, no. 8 (May 1967): 18; Harris Rosenstein, "Total and Complex," *Artnews* 66, no. 3 (May 1967): cover, 54, illustrated

Sol LeWitt: Series A #1, 2, 3, 4, 5, 6, 7, 8, and 9
DGLA / April 4–29

CHECKLIST / *Series A #1*, 1967; *Series A #2*, 1967; *Series A #3*, 1967; *Series A #4*, 1967; *Series A #5*, 1967; *Series A #6*, 1967; *Series A #7*, 1967; *Series A #8*, 1967; *Series A #9*, 1967

REVIEW / William Wilson, "In the Galleries: LeWitt Grid Work on Display," *Los Angeles Times* (April 7, 1967): D11 "One seems to be able to define only what LeWitt's work is not. It seems to me that it is precisely absence that lends the frame its most positive quality, which is a heightened sense of opened-up air."

RELATED / Installation view in Mel Bochner, "The Serial Attitude," *Artforum* 6, no. 4 (December 1967): 28

Anastasi: Six Sites
DGNY / April 29–May 24

CHECKLIST / **Main Gallery:** *East Wall*; *North Wall (right)*; *North Wall (left)*; *West Wall (right)*; *West Wall (left)*; *South Wall*, 1967

REVIEWS / L. George, "Anastasi," *57th Street Review* 1, no. 6 (May 18, 1967): n.p.; H.R., "Reviews and Previews," *Artnews* 66, no. 4 (Summer 1967): 12; Gregory Battcock, "In the Galleries: Anastasti," *Arts Magazine* 41, no. 8 (Summer 1967): 57, illustrated "Anastasi's new works are both an affront and a travesty. At the same time, the observer can regard them as approbation, eulogy and homage. . . . It's a very good show. Cerebral integrity of this magnitude is rare. These works reflect the incisive logic also found in the candid observations of Bob Dylan, Stokely Carmichael and in the films of Warhol. There is no credibility gap here."

10 (Los Angeles)
DGLA / May 2–27

CHECKLIST / Ad Reinhardt, *Ultimate Painting #6*, 1960; Sol LeWitt, *Series B #8*, 1967; Jo Baer, *Untitled*, 1966; Robert Smithson, *Untitled*, 1967; Carl Andre, *Untitled*, 1967; Agnes Martin, *Leaf in the Wind*, 1963; Dan Flavin, *Untitled*, 1966; Robert Morris, *Untitled*, 1966; Michael Steiner, *Untitled*, 1966; Donald Judd, *Untitled*, 1966

MARTIAL RAYSSE, INSTALLATION (85)

LANGUAGE TO BE LOOKED AT AND/OR THINGS TO BE READ, POSTER (86) AND INSTALLATION (87)

TOM DOYLE, ANNOUNCEMENT (88)

CARL ANDRE (PERIODIC TABLE), POSTER (89)

KENNETH SNELSON, ADVERTISEMENT (90)

85

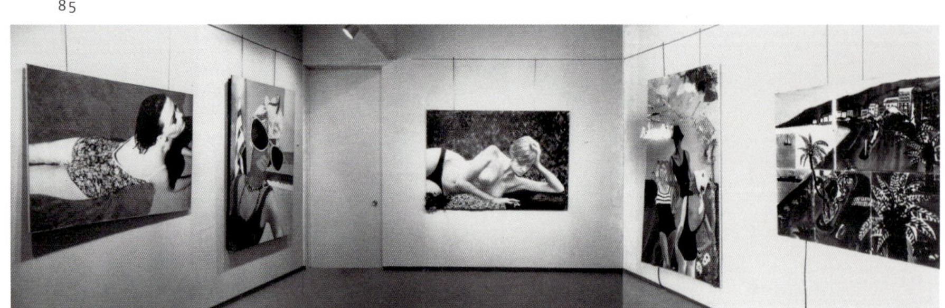

86

Language to be looked at and/or things to be read Carl Andre Arakawa Walter De Maria Marcel Duchamp Dan Flavin Dan Graham Robert Indiana Jasper Johns On Kawara Edward Kienholz Sol LeWitt Roy Lichtenstein René Magritte Filippo Marinetti Robert Morris Claes Oldenburg Francis Picabia Ad Reinhardt Robert Smithson Kenneth Snelson Dwan Gallery 29 West 57 Street, New York City Opening Saturday June 3 1967

87

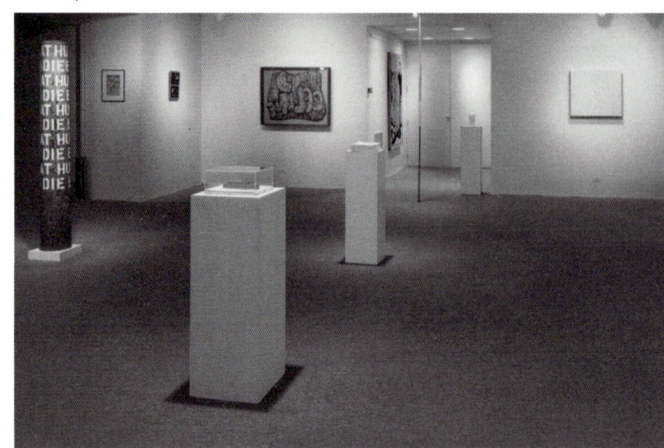

1967–1968 LOS ANGELES AND NEW YORK

Martial Raysse
DGLA / May 31–June 24

CHECKLIST / *Express Certain Psychological Definitions And So What About The Chicken*, 1966; *The Pot and the Flower*, 1964; *Kristin*, 1962; *Noon: Mediterranean Landscape*, 1966; *Switzerland Eyes Susy Creamcheese*, 1967; *Rear View Mirror*, 1962; *Made in Japan*, 1964; *Tri-Colore Moderne Painting*, 1964; *Puerto Rico Eyes Neon Style*, 1967; *Cela S'appelle L'Aurore*, 1964; *Transfusion*, 1960; *Elle*, 1962; *Supermarket*, 1961; *Girl on the Beach*, 1965; *Sur La Plage–Titre Intelligent*, 1962; *Simple and Quiet Painting*, 1965; *Snack*, 1964; *La Vision Est Un Phenomene Sentimental*, 1966; *High-Tension-Candies*, 1966

REVIEWS / Gregory Battcock, "In the Galleries: Martial Raysse," *Arts Magazine* 41, no. 7 (May 1967): 59; William Wilson, "Raysse Exhibit Lights Up Slowly Fading Dwan Gallery," *Los Angeles Times* (June 2, 1967): D9; Jane Livingston, "Los Angeles," *Artforum* 6, no. 1 (September 1967): 62–63, illustrated "Stepping into the gallery from the insolent, high-pitched commercial atmosphere of Los Angeles, one is stimulated to a fascinating sequence of speculation about the culture just outside in contrast with the distilled view of popular French culture within. The striking distinction is between Raysse's febrile, exacerbated ultra-preciosity and the American Pop culture's untrammeled innocence in vulgarity. The ascendant example is *Made in Japan* (1964) in which a poisonous green Ingres nude languishes upon variously colored cushions, holding a fan made of real peacock feathers. The technique is a combination of collage and a sort of photo-serigraphic method which Raysse uses repeatedly. The colors have that special hideousness which is singular to cheap color reproduction."

Language to be looked at and/or things to be read
DGNY / June 3–28

CHECKLIST / F.T. Marinetti, *I Paroliberi Futuristi*, 1913; Rene Magritte, *Key of Dreams*, 1932; Claes Oldenburg, *Celine*, 1959; Carl Andre, *Word Tube*, 1967; Barry Bryant, *Abstract Calendar*, 1967; Roy Lichtenstein, *Girl with Piano*, 1963; Dan Flavin, *I'm Still, I suppose alone (to Marilyn Monroe)*; Marcel Duchamp, *The*, 1915; On Kawara, *Today Series No. 110*, 1966; On Kawara, *Today Series No. 111*, 1966; On Kawara, *Today Series No. 112*, 1966; Ad Reinhardt, *Portend of the Artist as a Yhung Mandala*, 1955; Carl Andre, *Flags (An Opera for Three Voices)*, 1964; Marcel Duchamp, *Anagramme*, 1961; Robert Morris, *Swift Night Ruler*, 1963; Robert Morris, *The Card File*, 1961; Arakawa, *Webster's Dictionary, Page I*, 1965; Arakawa, *Still Life*, 1967; Edward Kienholz, *The Black Leather Chair*, 1966; Robert Smithson, *Pulverizations*, 1967; Walter De Maria, *Drug Talk*, 1964; Kenneth Snelson, *Model for Atomic Forms*, 1966; Carl Andre, *Quincy Island*, 1964; Dan Graham, *Untitled Poem*, 1966; Sol LeWitt, *Dwan Gallery Los Angeles Announcement*, 1967; Francis Picabia, *Untitled*, c. 1917; Robert Indiana, *EAT-HUG-DIE Column*, 1964; Jasper Johns, *The Critic Smiles*, 1959; Robert Smithson, *Proposal for the Detection of Approximate Period Quantity*, 1966

REVIEWS / John Perreault, "Legibility," *Village Voice* (June 15, 1967): 13; Dennis Adrian, "New York: Language to Be Looked At and/or Things to Be Read," *Artforum* 6, no. 1 (September 1967): 59, illustrated; Scott Burton, "Reviews and Previews," *Artnews* 66, no. 5 (September 1967): 15

88

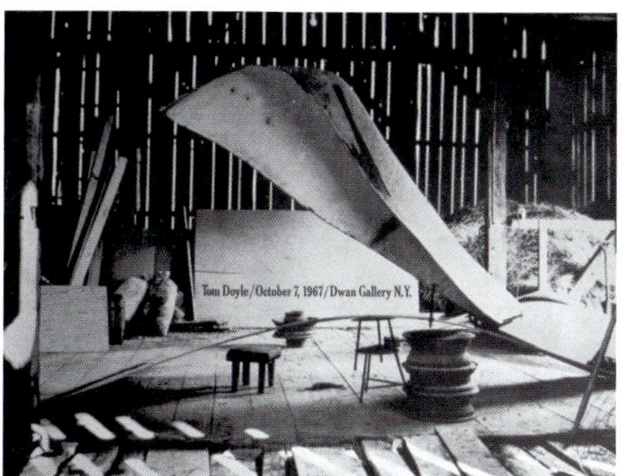

89

	1 H HYDROGEN									
2 He HELIUM	3 Li LITHIUM	4 Be BERYLLIUM	5 B BORON	6 C CARBON	7 N NITROGEN	8 O OXYGEN	9 F FLUORINE			
10 Ne NEON	11 Na SODIUM	12 Mg MAGNESIUM	13 Al ALUMINUM	14 Si SILICON	15 P PHOSPHORUS	16 S SULFUR	17 Cl CHLORINE			
18 A ARGON	19 K POTASSIUM	20 Ca CALCIUM	21 Sc SCANDIUM	22 Ti TITANIUM	23 V VANADIUM	24 Cr CHROMIUM	25 Mn MANGANESE	26 Fe IRON	27 Co COBALT	28 Ni NICKEL
	29 Cu COPPER	30 Zn ZINC	31 Ga GALLIUM	32 Ge GERMANIUM	33 As ARSENIC	34 Se SELENIUM	35 Br BROMINE			
36 Kr KRYPTON	37 Rb RUBIDIUM	38 Sr STRONTIUM	39 Y YTTRIUM	40 Zr ZIRCONIUM	41 Nb NIOBIUM	42 Mo MOLYBDENUM	43 Tc TECHNETIUM	44 Ru RUBIDIUM	45 Rh RHODIUM	46 Pd PALLADIUM
	47 Ag SILVER	48 Cd CADMIUM	49 In INDIUM	50 Sn TIN	51 Sb ANTIMONY	52 Te TELLURIUM	53 I IODINE			
54 Xe XENON	55 Cs CESIUM	56 Ba BARIUM	57-71 La-Lu RARE-EARTH METALS	72 Hf HAFNIUM	73 Ta TANTALUM	74 W TUNGSTEN	75 Re RHENIUM	76 Os OSMIUM	77 Ir IRIDIUM	78 Pt PLATINUM
	79 Au GOLD	80 Hg MERCURY	81 Tl THALLIUM	82 Pb LEAD	83 Bi BISMUTH	84 Po POLONIUM	85 At ASTATINE			
	86 Rn RADON	87 Fr FRANCIUM	88 Ac ACTINIUM	90 Th THORIUM	91 Pa PROTACTINIUM	92 U URANIUM				

90

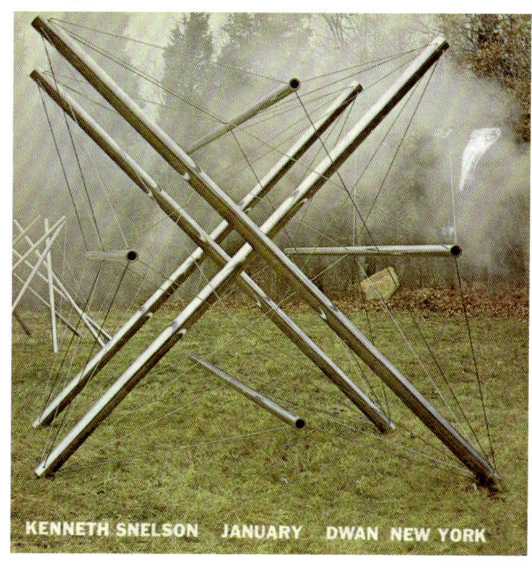

Tom Doyle
DGNY / October 7–November 2

CHECKLIST / *The 1st. On The First Day*, 1967; *Snicker's Gap*, 1967; *Bermuda Hundred*, 1967

REVIEWS / Felice T. Ross, "Gallery Previews in New York," *Pictures on Exhibit* 31, no. 2 (November 1967): 18; Emily Wasserman, "New York: Tom Doyle, Dwan Gallery" *Artforum* 6, no. 4 (December 1967): 60–61; John Fischer, "Tom Doyle," *Arts Magazine* 42, no. 3 (December 1967/January 1968): 57

Arakawa: Presence or the Third Person
DGNY / November 4–29

CHECKLIST / *Vacation #1*, 1967; *Self Portrait*, 1967; *Self Portrait*, 1967; *Separate Continuums #2*, 1966; *Names Birthday (A Couple)*, 1967; *The Diagram of a Meeting (A Conversation)*, 1967; *Fifty Two (52)*, 1966; *Untitled*, 1967; *Still Life*, 1967; *Alphabet Skin #3*, 1966–1967; *Still Life*, 1967 **Office:** *Still Life*, 1967; *Arakawa And I*, 1967; *Explosion*, 1967; *Still Life*, 1967; *Untitled*, 1967

REVIEWS / H. R., "Reviews and Previews," *Artnews* 66, no. 7 (November 1967): 11; Felice T. Ross, "Gallery Previews in New York," *Pictures on Exhibit* 31, no. 3 (December 1967): 18; Jacqueline Barnitz, "Arakawa," *Arts Magazine* 42, no. 3 (December 1967/January 1968): 53, illustrated; Dore Ashton, "New York commentary," *Studio International* 175, no. 896 (January 1968): 41, illustrated; James R. Mellow, "New York Letter," *Art International* 12, no. 1 (January 20, 1968): 62–63, illustrated "What Arakawa's show raises is the difficult problem in painting of what is purely visual and what is 'literary.' He has reduced the literary elements down to the nouns-which-are-the-names-for-things and reproduced them as pictorial elements. In a brilliantly perverse way, he has reduced painting to a literary genre. One can already see the implications of this disturbing trend."

Carl Andre (Periodic Table)
DGNY / December 2–January 3, 1968

CHECKLIST / *144 Pieces of Aluminum*, 1967; *144 Pieces of Iron*, 1967; *144 Pieces of Zinc*, 1967; *Names, An Opera for Three Voices*

REVIEWS / Dan Graham, "Carl Andre," *Arts Magazine* 42, no. 3 (December 1967/January 1968): 35; Al Brunelle, "Reviews and Previews," *Artnews* 66, no. 9 (January 1968): 11; Felice T. Ross, "Gallery Previews in New York," *Pictures on Exhibit* 31, no. 4 (January 1968): 18; Philip Leider, "Carl Andre, Dwan Gallery," *Artforum* 6, no. 6 (February 1968): 46–47; James R. Mellow, "New York Letter," *Art International* 12, no. 2 (February 20, 1968): 73, illustrated

1968 NEW YORK

Kenneth Snelson
January 6–31

CHECKLIST / *Double City Boots*, 1967; *V. X.*, 1967; *Untitled*, 1967; *Untitled*, 1967; *Six #2*, 1967; *Wiggins Fork*, 1967; *City Boots*, 1967; *Untitled Study*, 1967

REVIEWS / Charlotte Willard, "The Third Dimension," *New York Post* (January 13, 1968): 14, illustrated, 46; Hilton Kramer, "Kenneth Snelson," *New York Times* (January 20, 1968): L25; Al Brunelle, "Reviews and views," *Artnews* 66, no. 9 (January 1968): 10, 55, illustrated; Mary Zucker, "Gallery Previews in New York," *Pictures on Exhibit* 30, no. 5 (February 1968): 13–14; Emily Wasserman, "New York: Kenneth Snelson, Dwan Gallery," *Artforum* 6, no. 7 (March 1968): 57–58, illustrated "Despite all the costly looking sleekness, and the real attempts at structured complexity, Snelson's work for the most part runs itself out into nothing more than a rather vapid elegance."

SOL LEWITT: 46 THREE-PART VARIATIONS ON THREE DIFFERENT KINDS OF CUBES, INSTALLATION (91) AND POSTER (92)

ROBERT SMITHSON, POSTER (93)

CHARLES ROSS: PRISMS, INSTALLATION (94)

LANGUAGE II, ANNOUNCEMENT (95)

DWAN GALLERY ADVERTISEMENT (96)

91

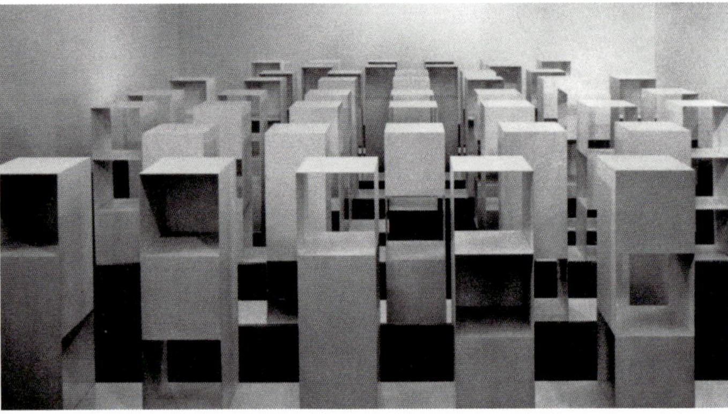

92

46 Three-Part
Variations
On 3 Different
Kinds Of Cubes
Sol LeWitt
Dwan Gallery
29 W 57 St NYC
Opens Saturday
Feb 3, 1968

93

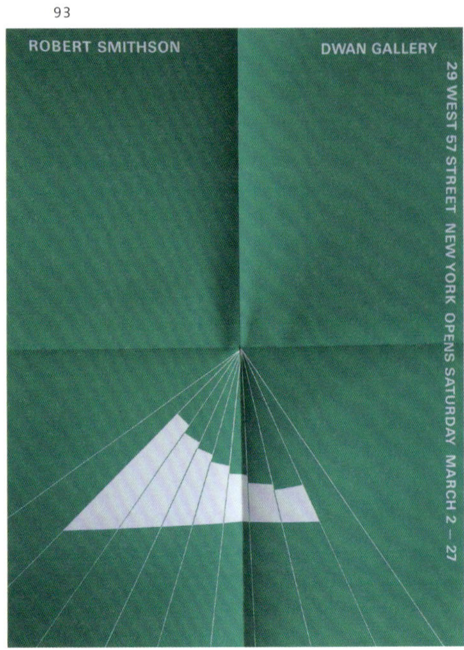

1968 NEW YORK

RELATED / Gregory Battcock, "Kenneth Snelson," *Arts Magazine* 42, no. 4 (February 1968): cover (*City Boots*), 27–29

Sol LeWitt: 46 Three-Part Variations on Three Different Kinds of Cubes
February 3–28

CHECKLIST / *Untitled (1–2FB; 6 units)*, 1968; *Untitled (1–1; 5 units)*, 1968; *Untitled (2FB–2FB; 3 units)*, 1968; *Untitled (2FB–3R; 4 units)*, 1968; *Untitled (2FB–2RL; 3 units)*, 1968; *Untitled (2FB–2FB; 2 units)*, 1968; *Untitled (2FB–1; 2 units)*, 1968; *Untitled (3F–3B; 7 units)*, 1968; *Untitled (3F–2RL; 5 units)*, 1968; *Untitled (3F–3F; 4 units)*, 1968; *Untitled (3F–3B; 3 units)*, 1968; *Untitled (3F–1; 3 units)*, 1968; *Layout* drawing, 1968; 47 *Three-Part Variations* drawing, 1968; *Model for 46 Three-Part Variations*, 1968; 15 drawings of *Variations*

REVIEWS / Peter Schjeldahl, "By Lonely, Difficult Evolutions . . . ," *New York Times* (February 8, 1968): D27; Jeanne Siegel, "In the Galleries," *Arts Magazine* 42, no. 4 (February 1968): 57, illustrated; Marcia Tucker, "Reviews and Previews," *Artnews* 66, no. 10 (February 1968): 14; John Perreault, *Village Voice* (February 15, 1968): 15; Felice T. Ross, "Gallery Previews in New York," *Pictures on Exhibit* 30, no. 6 (March 1968): 24; "Exhibitions: Mystical & Magical," *Time Magazine* (March 22, 1968): 54–55, illustrated; James R. Mellow, "New York Letter," *Art International* 12, no. 4 (April 20, 1968): 65–66, illustrated; Rosalind Krauss, "New York: Sol LeWitt, Dwan Gallery," *Artforum* 6, no. 8 (April 1968): 57–58, illustrated "But there is really only one question that is finally relevant and that is: what does this cumbrous, mechanical joining or filling of content with form have to do with the enterprise of art?"

Robert Smithson
March 2–27

CHECKLIST / *Pointless Vanishing Point*, 1968; *Gyrostasis*, 1968; *Leaning Strata*, 1968; *Sinistral Spiral*, 1968; *Shift*, 1968; *A Non-Site (Indoor Earthwork)*, 1968

REVIEWS / H.R., "Reviews and Previews," *Artnews* 67, no. 1 (March 1968): 14, 24, 54, illustrated "There is an uncanny thrust, a sense of encroachment on the unknown in Smithson's work which proves that this is no child's play." Cindy Nemser, "In the Galleries," *Arts Magazine* 42, no. 6 (April 1968): 59; Felice T. Ross, "Gallery Previews in New York," *Pictures on Exhibit* 30, no. 7 (April 1968): 18; James R. Mellow, "New York Letter," *Art International* 12, no. 5 (May 15, 1968): 67–68, illustrated; Emily Wasserman, "New York: Robert Smithson, Dwan Gallery," *Artforum* 6, no. 9 (May 1968): 62, illustrated "Elaborate conceptualizing about non-sites and pointless vanishing points, that in view of the poverty of sculptural achievement or invention, seems marginal to the issue of the work itself."

Michael Steiner
March 30–April 24

CHECKLIST / *Wind Rose*, 1968; *Iberia*, 1968; *Cameron*, 1968; *Ifigenia #1*, 1968

REVIEWS / Michael Benedikt, "Reviews and Previews," *Artnews* 67, no. 2 (April 1968): 57 "Michael Steiner, whose last exhibition was one of the better minimalist shows of the year, has abandoned minimalism with startling explicitness." Felice T. Ross, "Gallery Previews in New York," *Pictures on Exhibit* 30, no. 8 (May 1968): 19 "The new trend of the work is laudatory; it has become dynamic and more complete. Each piece contains more interesting relationships between shapes and colors. Yet each work remains often

94

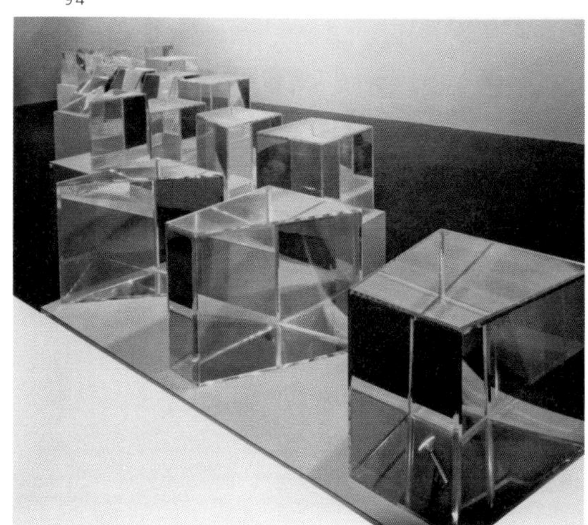

95

ADAM
BOUGHT
COLD
DOOM
ENTERED
FROST
GOT
HOARY
IN
JUST
KNOWLEDGE
LIKE MORALITY
NUMBER
OLD
PERDITIONS
QUICKLY
RECOUNT
SINS
WHEN
X-RAYING
YESTERDAYS
ZEAL

96

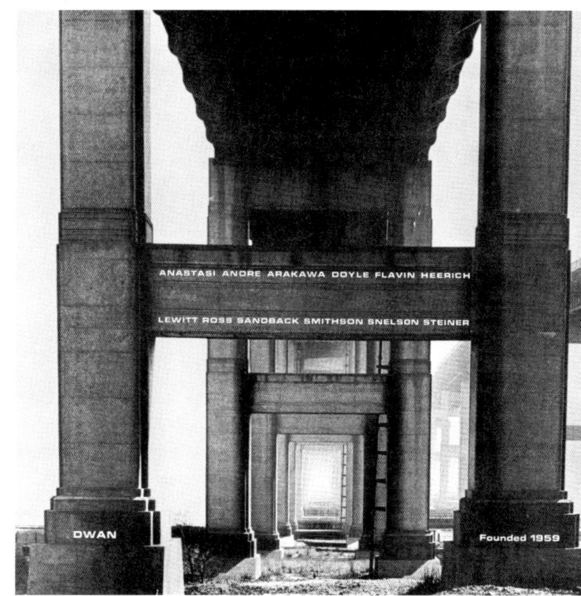

disconcertingly disjointed; and in the sense that these isolated relationships between the pairs seem more expressive than the totality, the work is unresolved." Emily Wasserman, "New York: Michael Steiner, Dwan Gallery," *Artforum* 7, no. 10 (Summer 1968): 56–57, illustrated "Notwithstanding, there is an impressive confidence to his show at the Dwan Gallery, as Steiner attempts to balance complex interlocking forms which have, aside from their lyrical coloration, a ponderous chunkiness." James R. Mellow, "New York Letter," *Art International* 12, no. 6 (Summer 1968): 107–108, illustrated

RELATED / John Samuel Margolies, "Michael Steiner," *Arts Magazine* 42, no. 6 (April 1968): 42–43, illustrated

Charles Ross: Prisms
April 27–May 22

CHECKLIST / Eight works titled *Untitled*, 1968

REVIEWS / Grace Glueck, "Art: Lila Katzen's Floors," *New York Times* (May 4, 1968): 34 (under "Charles Ross"); Gregory Battcock, "In the Galleries," *Arts Magazine* 42, no. 7 (May 1968): 58, illustrated; Scott Burton, "Reviews and Previews," *Artnews* 67, no. 3 (May 1968): 17, 58, illustrated; Lucy Lippard, *New York* (May 6, 1968): 46–47, illustrated; John Perreault, "Telstars," *Village Voice* (May 9, 1968): 15; Felice T. Ross, "Gallery Previews in New York," *Pictures on Exhibit* 31, no. 9 (June 1968): 16; Emily Wasserman, "Richard Van Buren, David Novros, Charles Ross," *Artforum* 6, no. 10 (Summer 1968): 36–38, illustrated

Language II
May 25–June 22

CHECKLIST / **Main Gallery:** William Copley, *Think*, 1961; Carl Frederick Renterswärd, *Remembrant. F.*, 1965; Hanne Darboven, *Untitled Drawing*, 1968; Robert Indiana, *Coenties Slip*, 1962; Arakawa, *Untitled*, 1968; Robert Morris, *Document*, 1963; Dan Graham, *Poem: Discrete Scheme Without*, 1965; Dan Graham, *"One" Concrete Poem*, 1967; Dan Flavin, *To James Joyce and James Johnson Sweeney*, 1960; Dennis Oppenheim, *Map of New York*, 1968; On Kawara, *Lat. 31° 25′N; Long. 8° 41′E*, 1966; Lawrence Weiner, *Untitled*, 1968; Carl Andre, *Structure White Consciousness*, 1965; Joseph Kosuth, *Titled: (Art As Idea As Idea)*, 1968; Robert Rauschenberg, *Rome*, 1952; Michael Heizer, *Untitled*, 1968; Robert Smithson, *Non-Site #2*, 1967; Ray Johnson, *Letter*, 1966; Sol LeWitt, *Untitled*, 1963; Marcel Duchamp, *Discs Inscribed with Puns* (8 pieces), 1926; Edward Kienholz, *The Commercial #2*, 1965; Walter De Maria, *Untitled*, 1967; Allan Kaprow, *Untitled*, 1967 **Rear Gallery:** Hannah Weiner, *When Does It or You Begin?*, 1968; Anastasi, *200.00*, 1967; Bernar Venet, *Flow About a Triangular Wing for Large Values of M*, 1968; James Lee Byars, *A White Paper Will Blow Through the Streets*, 1966; Peter Hutchinson, *Witch-Hazel*, 1963; R. Denis Dunn, *All of These Poetry*, 1967; Freifeld, *Untitled*, 1967; Steve Katz, *Page from Book "The Exaggerations of Peter Prince,"* 1968; Jackson Mac Low, *5.2.3.6.5., The 3rd Biblical Poem*, 1955; William Wiley, *Mexican Autumn Turns Copper*, 1967; Christine Kozlov, *Practice Project*, 1966; Elaine Sturtevant, *Dada*, 1968; Bici Hendricks, *Word Work*, 1966; Walter De Maria, *Invisible Word Drawing*, 1965; Rosemarie Castoro, *Untitled Working Drawing*, 1968; Dick Higgins, *Graphis #143 & 144*, 1967; H.C. Westermann, *Untitled*, 1968; Lila Katzen, *Language*, 1967; Ed Meeneley, *Village Voice Classified*, 1967; Mel Bochner, *Letter*, 1968

EATHWORKS, INSTALLATION (97–98) AND ANNOUNCEMENT (99)

COOL WHITE, ETC. FROM DAN FLAVIN, ANNOUNCEMENT (100)

ERWIN HEERICH: CARDBOARD SCULPTURE, INSTALLATION (101)

FRED SANDBACK: FIVE SITUATIONS, POSTER (102)

97

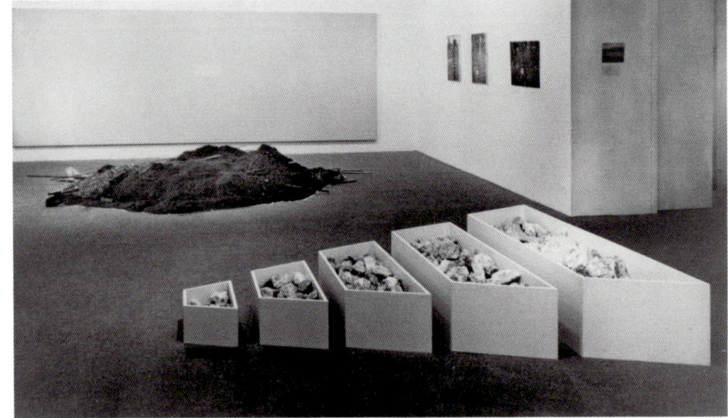

99

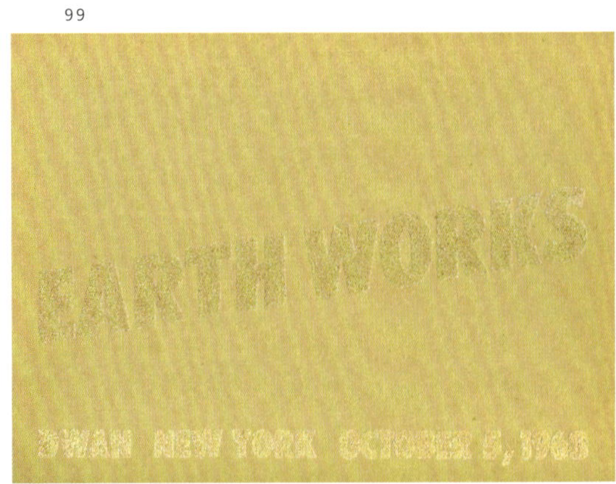

98

1968–1969 NEW YORK

REVIEWS / John Perreault, "Word Works," *Village Voice* (June 13, 1968): 15; "Exhibitions: Poetic Package," *Time* (June 14, 1968): 85; "Images: Language II at Dwan," *Arts Magazine* 42, no. 8 (June/Summer 1968): 21

RELATED / John Chandler, "The Last Word in Graphic Art," *Art International* 12, no. 9 (November 20, 1968): 25–28

Earthworks
October 5–30

CHECKLIST / Carl Andre, 3 photo blowups of two works executed in Aspen, CO, summer 1968; Carl Andre, Rock pile and long sectional log piece; Herbert Bayer, Earth mound, Sculptured Garden Project, 1955; Walter De Maria, Painting (inscribed The Color Men Choose When They Attack the Earth), 1968; Michael Heizer, Abstraction of Dissipate #2, 1968; Michael Heizer, Robert Morris, Earthwork, 1968; Robert Morris, Drawing of Evanston, Illinois, earth project, 1968; Robert Morris, Drawing of Crushed Rock, Graded Sizes, 1968; Claes Oldenburg, Project for asphalt field 30′ × 30′; Claes Oldenburg, Project to bury studio-objects in 30′ × 30′ plot; Claes Oldenburg, Film of grave-size hole commissioned and executed behind the Metropolitan Museum, October 1967; Claes Oldenburg, Plexiglas box [filled with earth and earthworms], 1968; Dennis Oppenheim, Model, Cotopaxi Volcano, Ecuador, 1968; Dennis Oppenheim, Photograph of spiral work executed in New Haven, CT; Sol LeWitt, Book of Photographs showing *Buried Cube*, Bergeyk, Holland, 1968; Robert Smithson, A Non-Site (Franklin, NJ), 1968; Robert Smithson, Aerial photo of Non-Site and sites, Franklin, NJ, 1968; Robert Smithson, 20 Instamatic snapshots of the 5 sites of Franklin, NJ, Non-Site, 1968; Stephen Kaltenbach, Blueprint Project, 1967

REVIEWS / Grace Glueck, "Moving Mother Earth," *New York Times* (October 6, 1968): D38; David Bourdon, "The Earth Movers," *Time* (October 11, 1968): 84, illustrated "'Our original idea,' explains the gallery's earth mother, Virginia Dwan, 'was just to show earth as a medium, but it's difficult to know where to draw the line.'" John Perreault, "Long Live Earth!" *Village Voice* 14, no. 1 (October 12, 1968): 17; Felice T. Ross, "Gallery Previews in New York," *Pictures on Exhibit* 32, no. 2 (November 1968): 15, 23–24, illustrated; Don McDonagh, "Art's new earthmen," *Financial Times, London* (November 14, 1968): 3; Douglas Davis, "A Trend Out of the Galleries: Outsize Works in the Open," *National Observer* no. 47 (November 18, 1968): 22; James R. Mellow, "New York Letter," *Art International* 12, no. 9 (November 20, 1968): 64 "What the radical Earthworks show did illustrate quite graphically were the pressures which contemporary works of art — by their demanding scale, physical requirements and general inclination to go elsewhere — are bringing to bear upon the normal methods and structures of museums and galleries." Sidney Tillim, "Earthworks and the New Picturesque," *Artforum* 7, no. 4 (December 1968): 42–45, illustrated "Never has it been clearer that anything can be an artistic medium, as long as it is used literally rather than symbolically. At the same time, in the light of all this, rarely has the future of modernism seemed more problematic."

RELATED / Grace Glueck, "Multiplicity Is Key Word in City's Art Galleries This Fall," *New York Times* (July 30, 1968): 32; Grace Glueck, "New York Gallery Notes: Circa 1825–2000," *Art in America* 56, no. 5 (September/October 1968): 110, illustrated; David L. Shirey, "What Is It," *Art in America* 57, no. 3 (May/June 1969): 32–47 (under "Earthworks," 33–34)

100

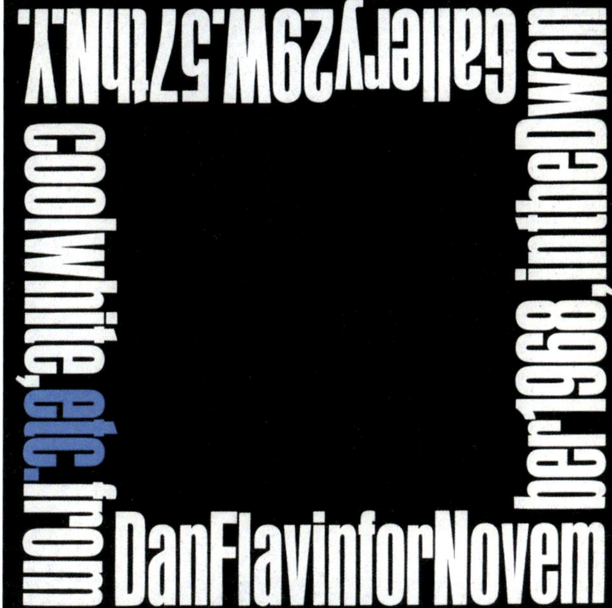

101

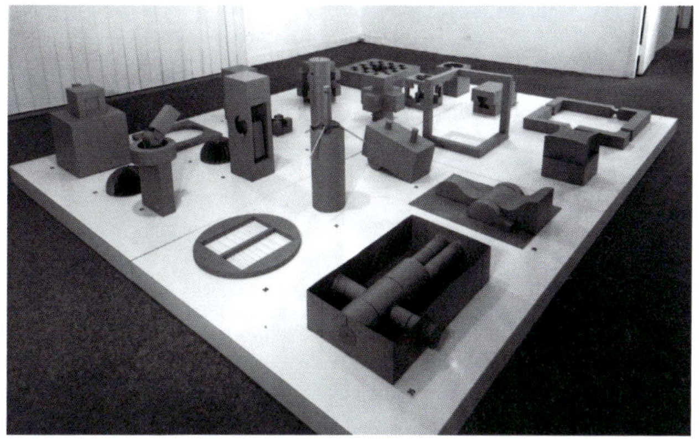

102

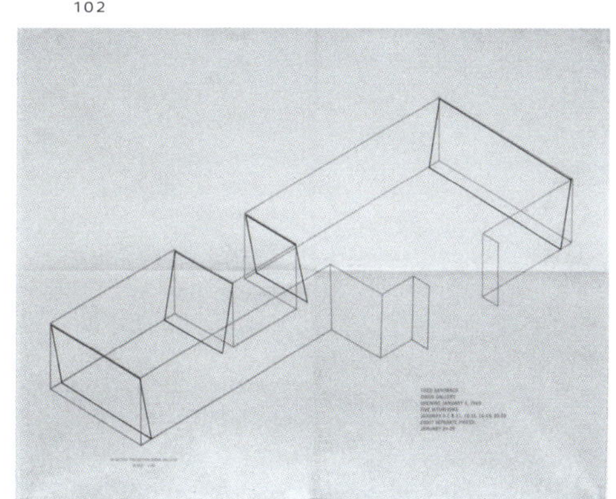

Cool White, etc. from Dan Flavin
November 2–27

CHECKLIST / **Main Gallery:** *Untitled (to the "innovator" of Wheeling Peachblow)*, 1968; *Untitled (to Dorothy & Roy Lichtenstein on not seeing anyone in the room)*, 1968 **Office:** *Untitled*, 1966; *Untitled*, 1964; *Untitled*, 1965; *Untitled*, 1963

REVIEWS / John Perreault, "Dump, Drop, Drape," *Village Voice* (November 14, 1968): 18; Philip Leider, "The Flavin Case," *New York Times* (November 24, 1968): D27; Stephen A. Kurtz, "Reviews and Previews," *Artnews* 67, no. 8 (December 1968): 17; Felice T. Ross, "Gallery Previews in New York," *Pictures on Exhibit* 32, no. 3 (December 1968): 22 (under "[Don] Flavin"); Miriam Brumer, "In the Galleries: Dan Flavin," *Arts Magazine* 43, no. 3 (December 1968/January 1969): 60; Rosalind Krauss, "New York: Dan Flavin, Dwan Gallery," *Artforum* 7, no. 5 (January 1969): 53–54, illustrated "As Flavin deploys it, the fluorescent tube is clearly a graphic device. It possesses both the figurative density of a line, and the inherent ambiguity of its position in space. It can build images, the interiors of which are different in quality from the space outside them; it can differentiate or divide space either along a frontal surface or in depth. Finally, it can produce stable illusions, as when corners of rooms are eradicated by even lighting, or skewed by contradictory shadows." Dore Ashton, "New York commentary," *Studio International* 177, no. 907 (January 1969): 45; James R. Mellow, "New York Letter," *Art International* 13, no. 1 (January 20, 1969): 53, illustrated

Erwin Heerich: Cardboard Sculpture
November 30–December 21

CHECKLIST / Nine works titled *Untitled*, 1968, and three works titled *Untitled*, 1967; ten drawings, 1958–1960; ten working drawings **Corridor:** *Untitled*, 1957; *Untitled*, 1966 **Rear Gallery:** *Untitled*, 1966; *Untitled*, 1967; *Untitled*, 1966; *Untitled*, 1967; *Untitled*, 1966; *Untitled*, 1963; *Untitled*, 1963; *Untitled*, 1963; *Untitled*, 1963; *Untitled*, 1963; *Untitled*, 1963; *Untitled*, 1963; 7 paintings, 1967; *Untitled*, 1966; *Untitled*, 1966; *Untitled*, 1961; *Untitled*, 1967; *Untitled*, 1965; *Untitled*, 1961; *Untitled*, 1963; *Untitled*, 1963; *Untitled*, 1964; *Untitled*, 1961; *Untitled*, 1965; *Untitled*, 1961; *Untitled*, 1964; *Untitled*, 1963; *Untitled*, 1962; *Untitled*, 1962; *Untitled*, 1962; *Untitled*, 1962; *Untitled*, 1962; *Untitled*, 1963; *Untitled*, 1963; *Untitled*, 1965; *Untitled*, 1962; *Untitled*, 1962

REVIEWS / Jean Leering, "Erwin Heerich," *Arts Magazine* 43, no. 3 (December 1968/January 1969): cover, 28–29, illustrated; Henry J. Seldis, "Brilliant Francis Bacon Display in N.Y.," *Los Angeles Times* (December 6, 1968): H1; Gerald E. Scofield, "Gallery Previews in New York," *Pictures on Exhibit* 32, no. 4 (January 1969): 18; Lawrence Campbell, "Reviews and Previews," *Artnews* 67, no. 9 (January 1969): 21 "He is a master of the vocabulary of Minimal sculpture and offers a seemingly endless repertory of ideas and possibilities. He is also an impeccable craftsman."

1969

Fred Sandback: Five Situations
January 4–29

CHECKLIST / **Main Gallery:** 5 Drawings, 1969; *Untitled*, 1967; *Untitled*, 1968; *4 Unit Horizontal*, 1969; *Trapezoid*, 1968; *Untitled* (2 units), 1968; *Untitled*, 1969 **Rear Gallery:** *Untitled*, 1968; *Untitled (in series of 8)*, 1968

REVIEWS / Stephen A. Kurtz, "Reviews and Previews: Fred Sandback," *Artnews* 67, no. 10 (February 1969): 22, 68, illustrated; Gerald E. Scofield, "Gallery Previews in New York," *Pictures on Exhibit* 32, no. 5 (February 1969):

ROBERT SMITHSON: MONO LAKE SITE–NONSITE, INSTALLATION (103)

CHARLES ROSS: PRISMS, INSTALLATION (104)

WALTER DE MARIA: BED OF SPIKES, RELEASE FORM (105), ADVERTISEMENT (106), AND INSTALLATION (107)

CARL ANDRE, INSTALLATION (108)

103

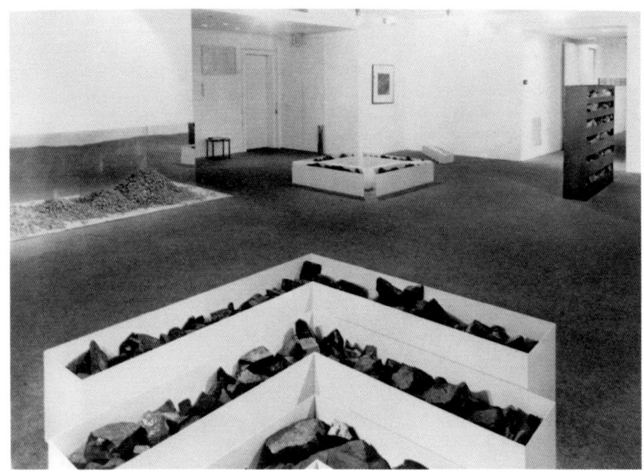

104

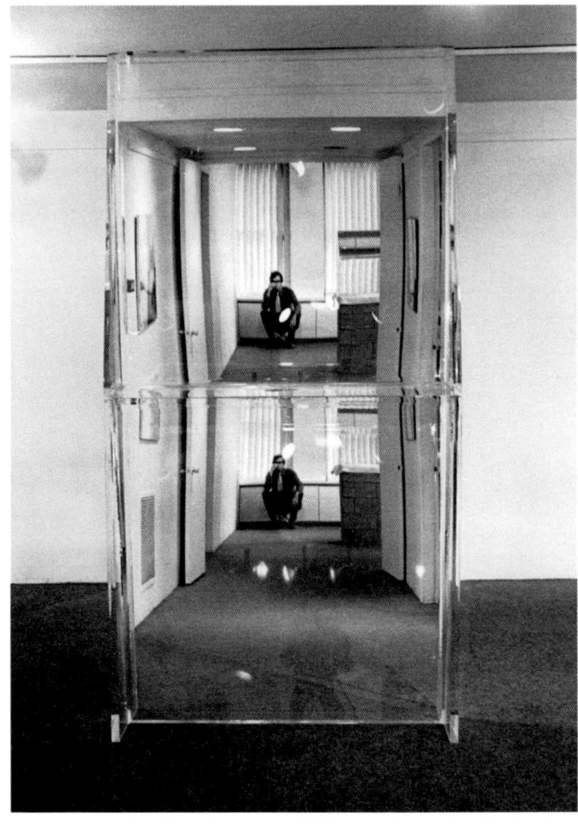

13; James R. Mellow, "New York Letter," *Art International* 13, no. 3 (March 1969): 59–60, illustrated; Don McDonagh, "Sculpture on the move," *Financial Times, London* (March 7, 1969): 3

Robert Smithson: Mono Lake Site–Nonsite
February 1–26

CHECKLIST / **Main Gallery:** *Gravel Mirror with Cracks and Dust* (gravel from Bergen), 1969; *Nonsite–Site Uncertain*, 1968; *Double Nonsite–California & Nevada*, 1968; *Nonsite–Death Valley*, 1968; *Nonsite–"Line of Wreckage," Bayonne, NJ*, 1968. **Rear Gallery:** *Six Stops on a Station*, 1968; *Nonsite–Mono Lake*, 1968

REVIEWS / Anthony Robbin, "Smithson's Non-Site Sights," *Artnews* 67, no. 10 (February 1969): cover, 50–53, illustrated; Felice T. Ross, "Gallery Previews in New York," *Pictures on Exhibit* 32, no. 6 (March 1969): 26–27; Cindy Nemser, "In the Galleries: Robert Smithson," *Arts Magazine* 43, no. 5 (March 1969): 59 "In our time, Smithson and his fellow earth movers are reshaping our attitudes towards an environment we have been conditioned to disdain. . . . Through their abstraction and generalization [his non-sites] reveal the macrocosm through the microcosm." Robert Pincus-Witten, "New York: Robert Smithson, Dwan Gallery," *Artforum* 7, no. 8 (April 1969): 69, 71, illustrated "The spatial contractions and expansions which Smithson's work encapsulates — and which are of an intellectual order rather than a physical fact — are all didactically and admirably clear." Peter Schjeldahl, "New York Letter," *Art International* 13, no. 4 (April 1969): 62–63, illustrated "These *Non-Sites*, as they are called, are evidently intended to provoke thought, drawing the mind away from the desultory spectacle of the gallery rocks to the huge, the timeless presence of all those other rocks 'out there,' as well as into the fly-swarm of aesthetic casuistry that magically surrounds any ripe corpse of an idea these days to give it an appearance of life. . . . But, in general, there is a discouraging air about this work, these indistinct, rhetorical ideas carried out in a lugubrious manner."

Charles Ross: Prisms
March 1–28

CHECKLIST / *Prism Window Double Wedge*, 1968; *Split Level*, 1969; *Prism Coffin*, 1969

REVIEWS / Felice T. Ross, "Gallery Previews in New York," *Pictures on Exhibit* 32, no. 7 (April 1969): 16–17; Peter Schjeldahl, "New York Letter," *Art International* 13, no. 5 (May 20, 1969): 37

Walter De Maria: Bed of Spikes
March 29–April 23

CHECKLIST / *Bed of Spikes #1*, 1969; *Bed of Spikes #2* (3 rows), 1969; *Bed of Spikes #3* (5 rows), 1969; *Bed of Spikes #4* (7 rows), 1969; *Bed of Spikes #5* (9 rows)

REVIEWS / Grace Glueck, "New York Gallery Notes: Trends Down, Sales Up," *Art in America* 57, no. 2 (March–April 1969): 119, illustrated "'Sure there's a certain amount of danger,' De Maria says. 'But people can use their eyes to ascertain it. If there's no danger, then the meaning of the piece isn't there.'" Grace Glueck, "Danger on Fifty-Seventh Street," *New York Times* (April 13, 1969): D33 "The cool, Minimal form of the beds, as elegantly austere as Don Judd's boxes, is contradicted by the romance of the death threat they pose. The viewer, standing too close, can thrill to the realization that one unfriendly shove could lethally impale him." Alfred Frankenstein, "Domes, Girls & Spikes," *San Francisco Examiner and Chronicle* (April 27, 1969): 35–36, illustrated "The precision of their setting is one of their most extraordinary qualities. Their combination of extremely precise craftsmanship with extremely perilous aggressiveness is, of

105

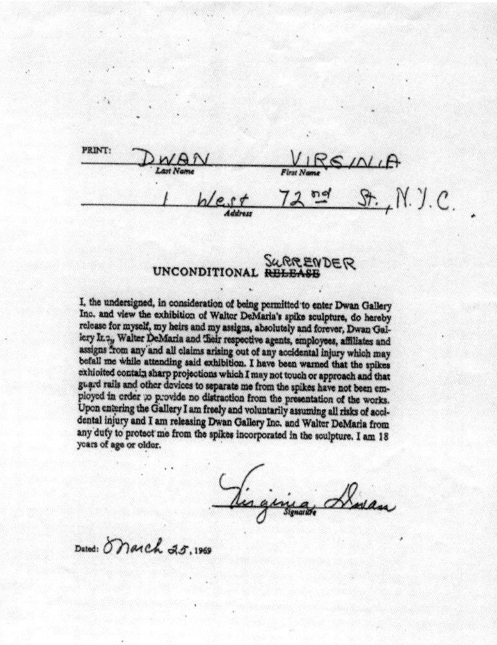

PRINT: DWAN VIRGINIA
Last Name First Name
1 West 72nd St., N.Y.C.
Address

UNCONDITIONAL ~~RELEASE~~ SURRENDER

I, the undersigned, in consideration of being permitted to enter Dwan Gallery Inc. and view the exhibition of Walter DeMaria's spike sculpture, do hereby release for myself, my heirs and my assigns, absolutely and forever, Dwan Gallery Inc., Walter DeMaria and their respective agents, employees, affiliates and assigns from any and all claims arising out of any accidental injury which may befall me while attending said exhibition. I have been warned that the spikes exhibited contain sharp projections which I may not touch or approach and that guard rails and other devices to separate me from the spikes have not been employed in order to provide no distraction from the presentation of the works. Upon entering the Gallery I am freely and voluntarily assuming all risks of accidental injury and I am releasing Dwan Gallery Inc. and Walter DeMaria from any duty to protect me from the spikes incorporated in the sculpture. I am 18 years of age or older.

Virginia Dwan
Signature

Dated: March 25, 1969

106

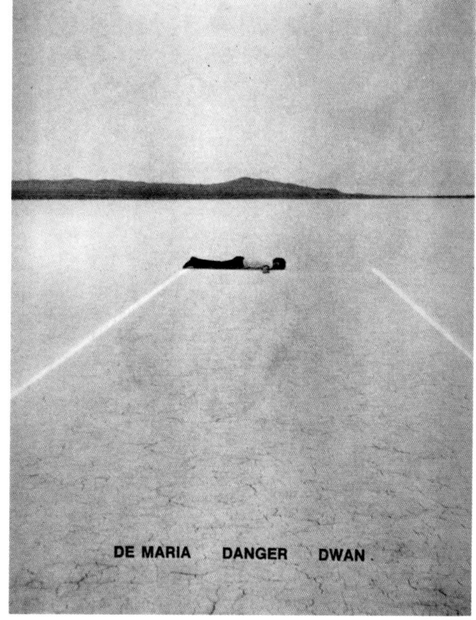

107

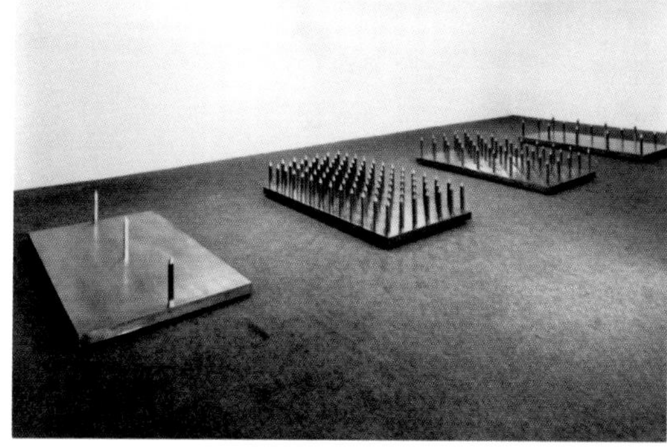

108

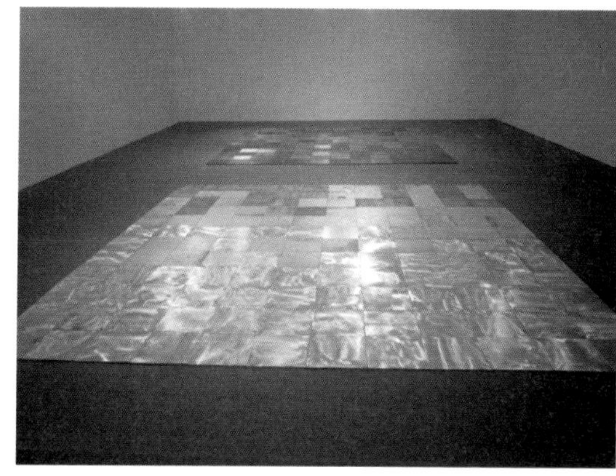

course, a social metaphor of no mean irony. De Maria means it that way or not." Frank Farniolis, "Gallery Previews in New York," *Pictures on Exhibit* 32, no. 8 (May 1969): 25; Noel Frackman, "In the Galleries: Walter de Maria," *Arts Magazine* 43, no. 7 (May 1969): 60, illustrated; Katherine G. Kline, "Reviews and Previews," *Artnews* 68, no. 3 (May 1969): 15, 16–17, illustrated; "Sculpture: High Priest of Danger," *Time*, Latin American edition (May 2, 1969): 36 "[M]ore than 2,500 visitors came to titter nervously or gaze in horrified wonder at De Maria's five Indian fakir-like steel beds. . . . Still the most distressing aspect of *The Beds of Spikes* lies not in the abstract danger that they symbolize but in their creator's evident delight in endowing them with all the murderous loveliness of a well-made gun, knife or racing car." Dore Ashton, "New York commentary," *Studio International* 177, no. 912 (June 1969): 289; Peter Schjeldahl, "New York Letter," *Art International* 13, no. 6 (Summer 1969): 68, illustrated

RELATED / "Hot-bed of modern art," *Sunday Times London* (March 30, 1969): 8

Carl Andre
April 26–May 21

CHECKLIST / *144 Pieces of Magnesium*, 1969; *144 Pieces of Lead*, 1969; *144 Pieces of Copper*, 1969

REVIEWS / Philip Leider, "'To Introduce a New Kind of Truth,'" *New York Times* (May 25, 1969): D41 "It will be a hard show to understand without coming to grips with Andre's germinative importance, for the themes which have concerned him — the truth of materials, the victory of gravity, the rigor of the literal — are there everywhere being explored. The exhibition makes clear that if criticism has been slow to acknowledge Andre's stature, his fellow sculptors have not." Felice T. Ross, "Gallery Previews in New York," *Pictures on Exhibit* 32, no. 9 (June 1969): 16; Kathleen G. Kline, "Reviews and Previews," *Artnews* 68, no. 4 (Summer 1969): 12

Language III
May 24–June 18

CHECKLIST / Anastasi, *This piece becomes the subject for repeated forgeries*, 1969; Rosemarie Castoro, *Sharp Changes*, 1968–1969; Rosemarie Castoro, *A Day in the Life of a Conscientious Objector*, 1969; Douglas Huebler, *No Title*, 1969; Carl Andre, *Untitled*, 1965; Paul Pechter, *Untitled–floor piece*, 1969; Carl Fernbach-Flarsheim, *Canvas in Three Minutes*, 1969; Robert Smithson, *The Hypothetical Continent of Lemuria*, 1969; Vito Acconci, *Untitled Sound Tape Location Poem*, 1969; Lawrence Weiner, *Structure Poem*, 1968; Roger Cutforth, *Time Piece in April*, 1969; Roger Cutforth, *Noon Heat*, 1969; Luis Camnitzer, *Door*, 1969; Charles Frazier in collaboration with Michael Benedikt, *BOX*, 1969; Marcel Duchamp, *La Jaconde 6/35*, 1964; Kurt Schwitters, *Luftig (gay)*, 1921; Edward Kienholz, *The Commercial #2*, 1965; Robert Morris, *Card File*, 1962; Madeline Gins, *Blanks*, 1969; John Seery, *Untitled*, 1969; Charles Ross, *Incident Impregnates from the Katz' Prism*, 1968–1969; Les Packer, *Elements Toward an Infinite Language*, 1969; Ken Snelson, *Untitled*, 1969; Walter De Maria, *Saint Sebastian*, 1968; Arakawa, *Untitled–Letter to John Weber*,

LANGUAGE III, INSTALLATION (109) AND ANNOUNCEMENT (110)

SOL LEWITT: WALL DRAWINGS, ANNOUNCEMENT (111)

ARAKAWA: DECISIVE EVIDENCE, POSTER (112) AND INSTALLATION (113)

109

110

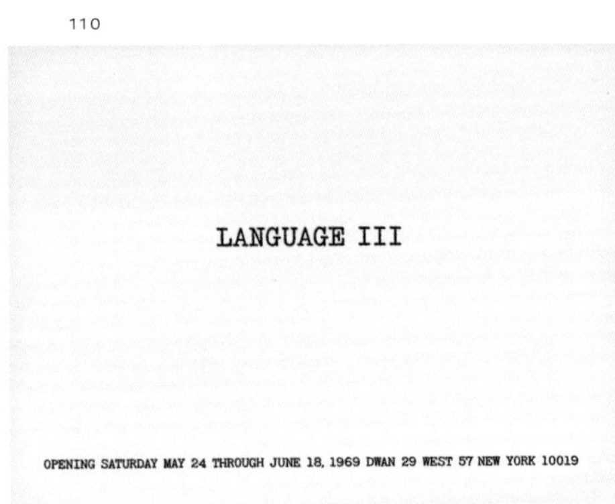

1969 NEW YORK

1966; Arakawa, *Statement*, 1968; Arakawa, *Untitled*, 1969; Sol LeWitt, *Plan for Wall Drawing*, 1969; Hanne Darboven, *Untitled*, 1968; Joseph Kosuth, *(Class Four: Matter) lil Organic Matter (Art As idea As Idea)*, 1969; Joseph Kosuth, *(Class One: Abstract Relations)–(One Part) 1X Causation (Art As Idea As Idea)*, 1968–1969; Joseph Kosuth, *Titled (Art As Idea As Idea)*, 1966; On Kawara, *I got up at 12:38 PM–May 11, 1969*, 1969; On Kawara, *I got up at 2:05 PM–May 12, 1969*, 1969; On Kawara, *I got up at 12:44 PM–May 13, 1969*, 1969; On Kawara, *I got up at 3:06 PM–May 14, 1969*, 1969; On Kawara, *I got up at 10:03 AM–May 15, 1969*, 1969; Bernar Venet, *N.Y. Stock Exchange, April 10, 1969*, 1969; R. Barthelme, *Determinization System 1*, 1969; Ad Reinhardt, *No War Postcard*, 1968; Robert Bruce Newman, *Directions to Make Mirror Magic*, 1969; Robert Bruce Newman, *Signs*, 1968–1969; Michael Heizer, *Art Before Life*, 1968; Michael Heizer, *Triple Landscape*, 1969; Sol LeWitt, *Beckett Play*, 1969; Terry Atkinson, and Michael Baldwin, *22 sentences: The French Army*, 1969; Christine Kozlov, *Eating Piece*, 1969; Dan Graham, *Proposition*, 1968; Charles Ross, *Portrait*, 1964; Iain Baxter, *N.E. Thing Co.*, 1968; John Perreault, *Edible Poem (Alphabet Series)*, 1968; Naomi Dash, *Object Poem*, 1969; Schuldt, *Ivory Textbody (an edition)*, 1965; Schuldt, *Glass Textbody (Edition 10)*, 1965; Ronald Gross, *Letter Cage*, 1968; John Giorno, *Matchbook*, 1969; Gene Berry, *Sorry This Painting is Temporarily Out of Style*, 1961; Lee Lozano, *Investment Piece*, 1969; Lee Lozano, *Cash Piece*, 1969; Ted Glass, *Bochner (One of a series: Archipenko, Bochner, Da Vinci, De Kooning, Ernst, Flavin, Poussin, Resnick, Rousseau, Tatlin)*, 1968; Ted Glass, *Ernst (One of a series: Archipenko, Bochner, Da Vinci, De Kooning, Ernst, Flavin, Poussin, Resnick, Rousseau, Tatlin)*, 1968; Bici Hendricks, *Word Work 2...Shadows*, 1969; Hannah Weiner, *3 × 27 for Sol LeWitt*, 1968; Jim Richmond, *Words On Rock*, 1969; Stephen Kaltenbach, *BLOOD, SKIN, FLESH, EARTH, AIR, FIRE, WATER, BONE*, 1968; Vito Acconci, *"The location of the contents of Page 1, Rogets Thesaurus . . ."* 1969; Naomi Dash, *Shadow Poem*, 1969; Schuldt, *tenir au courant*, 1968–1969; Terence Anderson, *Trash Poem*, 1969; Donald Burgy, *Birth Documentation*, 1969; Adrian Piper, *Untitled*, 1969; Rosemarie Castoro, *A Day in the Life of a Conscientious Objector*, ink on paper, 1969; Rosemarie Castoro, *Sharp Changes*, ink on paper, 1969; Mel Ramsden, *Six Negatives*, 1968–1969; Fred Sandback, *Eight-part Sculpture for the Dwan Gallery*, 1969; David Nelson, *An eight-page drawing*, 1969; Marcel Broodthaers, *Le Corbeau et Le Renard*, 1968; Eleanor Antin, *Blood of the Poet*, 1967–1968; John Baldessari, *"Solving Each Problem As It Arises,"* 1967; John Giorno, *"I'm tired of being scared,"* 1969; Ruth Jacoby, *From Beginning to End*, 1969; Nancy Holt, *Detach Here*, 1967

REVIEW / Peter Schjeldahl, "New York Letter," *Art International* 13, no. 8 (October 1969): 75–76, illustrated "I must say first off that the show was mostly pretty miasmal. It accidentally served to distinguish the theatrical and temporal aspects of Events as the keys to that movement's relative success. . . . [T]he artists, when they start playing with language, unless they stay on familiar ground (as do Arakawa and Luis Camnitzer in their 'naming' paintings), tend to create more mess than message or even 'massage' (cf. McLuhan). However, in a show of 79 works by nearly half as many creators there are bound to be exceptions and incidental pleasures, and in fact there were, many of them (as well as many of the clinkers) made possible by the fact that the selection of works had been made with a happy disregard for formal or ideological boundaries."

111

112

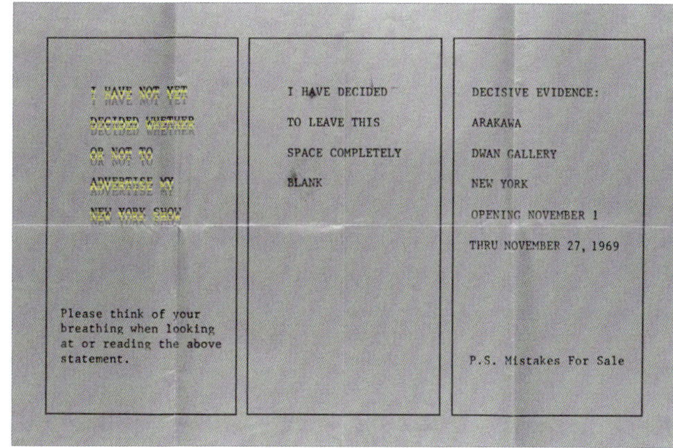
I HAVE NOT YET
DECIDED WHETHER
OR NOT TO
ADVERTISE MY
NEW YORK SHOW

Please think of your breathing when looking at or reading the above statement.

I HAVE DECIDED
TO LEAVE THIS
SPACE COMPLETELY
BLANK

DECISIVE EVIDENCE:
ARAKAWA
DWAN GALLERY
NEW YORK
OPENING NOVEMBER 1
THRU NOVEMBER 27, 1969

P.S. Mistakes For Sale

113

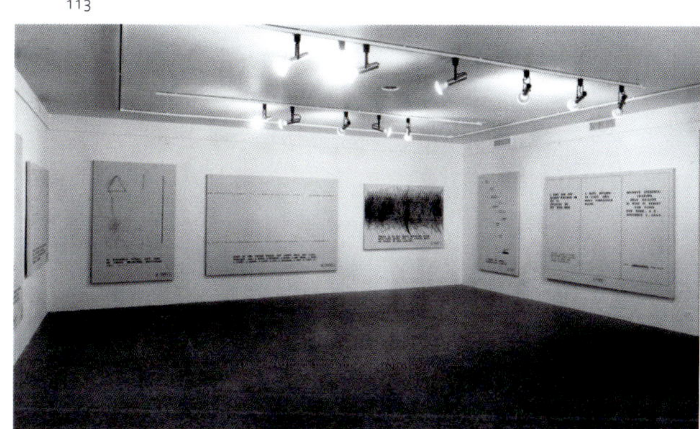

Sol LeWitt: Wall Drawings
October 4–30

CHECKLIST / **Main Gallery:** Wall drawings **Corridor:** *Plan for Drawing on East Wall of the Dwan Gallery*, 1969; *Plan for Drawing on the West Wall of the Dwan Gallery*, 1969; *Plan for Drawing on the North Wall of the Dwan Gallery*, 1969; *Plan for Drawing on the South Wall Dwan Gallery*, 1969 **Rear Gallery:** *Box #1 with Drawing Series 1, 2, 3, 4 A*, 1969; *Box #2 with Drawing Series 1, 2, 3, 4 B*, 1969; *Book of Drawings–Sets 1, 2, 3, 4 A & B*, 1969

REVIEWS / John Perreault, "The Monet of Minimalism," *Village Voice* (October 23, 1969): 18 "LeWitt changes our conception of what a drawing is. . . . [his] 'wall drawings' are tough and delicate simultaneously." Stephen A. Kurtz, "Reviews and Previews," *Artnews* 68, no. 7 (November 1969): 84; Cindy Nemser, "In the Galleries," *Arts Magazine* 44, no. 22 (November 1969): 63 "In the case of the wall works, his results have not been terribly successful. Perhaps due to the artificial lighting in the gallery or to the irregularities of the specific surfaces, the pencil marks are difficult to see and seem to be little more than innocuous mural decorations." Felice T. Ross, "Gallery Previews in New York," *Pictures on Exhibit* 33, no. 2 (November 1969): 21; Carter Ratcliff, "New York Letter," *Art International* 13, no. 10 (December 1969): 75; Jean-Louis Bourgeois, "New York: Sol LeWitt, Dwan Gallery," *Artforum* 8, no. 4 (December 1969): 71, illustrated; Kenneth Baker, "The Home Forum," *Christian Science Monitor* (February 11, 1970): 8, illustrated

Arakawa: Decisive Evidence
November 1–27

CHECKLIST / **Main Gallery:** *Name and Compose it. My advertisement*, 1969; *Talking or Walking*, 1969; *Shadow Boxing*, 1969; *Moving picture*, 1969; *(Sculpture)? Use this*, 1969; *Untitled*, 1969; *Hard or Soft*, 1969; *Shape*, 1969; *Untitled*, 1969; *Detail of...*, 1969; *Exercise*, 1969; *Portrait of a civilization*, 1969; *Paintings*, 1969 **Corridor:** *Untitled*, 1969; *Poster* (signed); *Blank*, 1969 **Rear Gallery:** *Look at it #1*, 1969; *Look at it #2*, 1969; *Mistake*, 1967/1968

REVIEWS / Lawrence Alloway, "Arakawa's Paintings: A Reading," *Arts Magazine* 44, no. 22 (November 1969): cover, 26–28, illustrated "These paintings, by taking the situation of the spectator as an opportunity to request a specific action or thought, are spectator-traps. That is to say, they act as lessons in self-awareness, converting one's (presumed) inclinations towards mediation and reverie into flashes of self-consciousness." Grace Glueck, "A Sort of Distant Star," *New York Times* (November 23, 1969): D27 (under "Challenge"); Stephen A. Kurt, "Reviews and Previews," *Artnews* 68, no. 8 (December 1969): 8; Felice T. Ross, "Gallery Previews in New York," *Pictures on Exhibit* 33, no. 3 (December 1969): 20; Jean-Louis Bourgeois, "New York: Arakawa, Dwan Gallery," *Artforum* 8, no. 5 (January 1970): 71, illustrated; Carter Ratcliff, "New York Letter," *Art International* 14, no. 1 (January 20, 1970): 94; Hans Strelow, "An das Atmen denken, Arakawa in der New Yorker Dwan Gallery," *Frankfurter Allgemeine Zeitung* (January 1970): n.p.

RELATED / Arakawa, "Notes on My Paintings," *Arts Magazine* 44, no. 22 (November 1969): 29; Lawrence Alloway, "Arakawa Annexed," *Arts Magazine* 44, no. 4 (February 1970): 46–47, illustrated

MICHAEL HEIZER: NEW YORK / NEVADA, POSTER (114)

CORNERED INSTALLATIONS FROM DAN FLAVIN, 1963–1970, INSTALLATION (115) AND ANNOUNCEMENT (116)

KENNETH SNELSON, INSTALLATION (117)

114

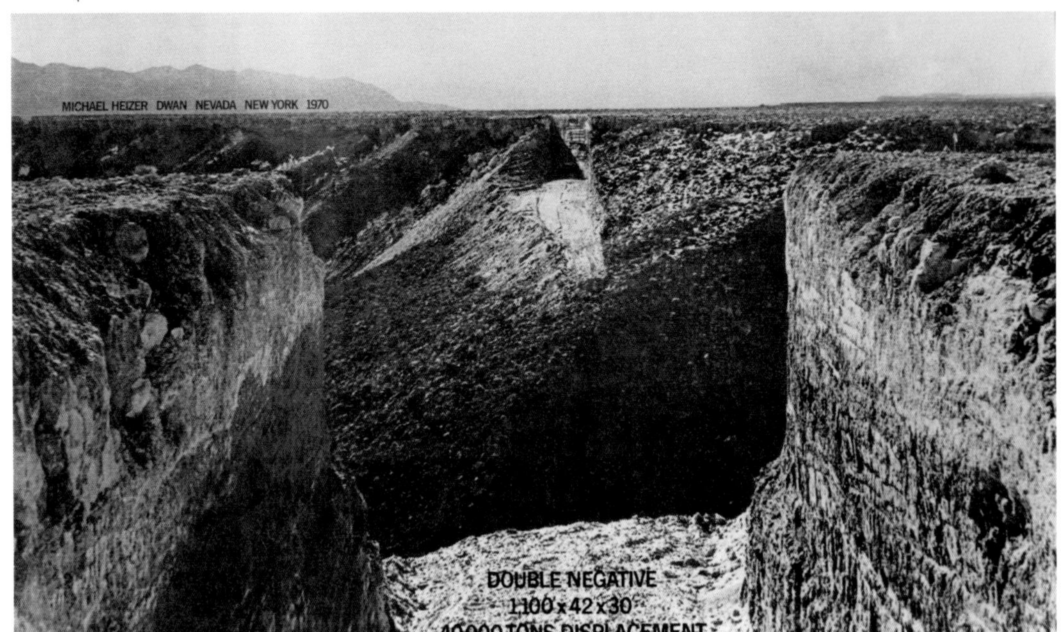

Dwan — Ten Years, Posters
November 29–December 20

CHECKLIST / **Main Gallery:** Posters and other documentation from *My Country 'Tis of Thee* (1962), *Boxes* (1964), *Neil Williams* (1966), *Allan D'Arcangelo* (1966), *Robert Morris* (1966), *Arakawa* (1966), *Robert Grosvenor* (1966), *A Summer Show* (1966), *Anthony Magar–Forrest Myers* (1966), *David Novros* (1966), *John Chamberlain* (1967), *Kenneth Snelson* (1967), *Dwan Gallery New York at Dwan Gallery Los Angeles* (1967), *Carl Andre* (1967), *Ten* (1967), *Sol LeWitt* (1967), *Edward Kienholz* (1966), *Anastasi* (1966), *Michael Steiner* (1968), *Tom Doyle* (1966), *Kenneth Snelson* (1966), *Sol LeWitt* (1966), *Arakawa* (1966), *Robert Smithson* (1966), *Scale Models and Drawings* (1967), *Edward Kienholz: Concept Tableaux* (1967), *Richard Baringer* (1967), *Anastasi* (1967), *Arakawa* (1967), *David Novros* (1967), *Language to be looked at and/or things to be read* (1967), *Tom Doyle* (1967), *Michael Steiner* (1967), *Carl Andre* (1967), *Kenneth Snelson* (1968), *Sol LeWitt* (1968), *Robert Smithson* (1968), *Charles Ross: Prisms* (1968), *Language II* (1968), *Earthworks* (1968), *Cool, White, etc. from Dan Flavin* (1968), *Fred Sandback–Five Situations* (1969), *Robert Smithson* (1969), *Charles Ross* (1969), *Walter De Maria* (1969), *Carl Andre* (1969), *Language III* (1969), *Sol LeWitt–Wall Drawings*(1969), *Arakawa* (1969) **Corridor:** *Larry Rivers* (1965), *Mark di Suvero* (1965), *Charles Frazier* (1965), *The Arena of Love* (1965), *Dakota Daley & Nicholas Quennell* (1965), *Robert Rauschenberg* (1965), *Group Show* (1966)

REVIEWS / Cindy Nemser, "In the Galleries," *Arts Magazine* 44, no. 3 (December 1969/January 1970): 60 "'The art that the Dwan gallery shows today will be the establishment art five or ten years from now.' This candid declaration was made by Virginia Dwan, when, on the occasion of the gallery's tenth anniversary, she attempted to define the role it has played in the art world over the past ten years. . . . According to Virginia Dwan the secret is in knowing just when to allow the avant-garde fruit to fall into one's lap. . . . By judiciously keeping an ear to the artistic underground, its directors have seized upon the right moment to package and publicize many of the most advanced ideas and outrageous objects around." Carter Ratcliff, "New York Letter," *Art International* 14, no. 2 (February 20, 1970): 77

1970

Michael Heizer: New York / Nevada
January 10–February 5

CHECKLIST / **Main Gallery:** *30 ton granite mass,* 1969; *Displaced Mass, Double Negative Rotary Interior (360°) From Center Base of Avalanche Cut (42′) 1100′ × 42′ × 30′, 40,000 tons displaced, Virgin River Mesa, Nevada,* 1969; *Displaced Mass, View from north cut linking 600′ across 300′ depth open canyon space to avalanche cut and south wall cut, 1100′ × 42′ × 30′* **Corridor:** *Levitated Mass/Cement block in ground,* 1969 **Rear Gallery:** *Munich Depression Optical Diagrams,* 1969; *Sunset–Nevada* **Office:** *Sunset–Nevada*

REVIEWS / Lawrence Alloway, "Art," *The Nation* (January 26, 1970): 92 "The original looks marvelous, but the information in the exhibition could be put on a postcard. Blown-up photographs and captions do not an exhibition make." Harris Rosenstein, "Reviews and Previews," *Artnews* 69, no. 1 (March 1970): 16 "All of this, it seems, points to the difficulty of relating a gallery show to work that is not only antithetic to the gallery situation, but attempts to engage the different mode of

115

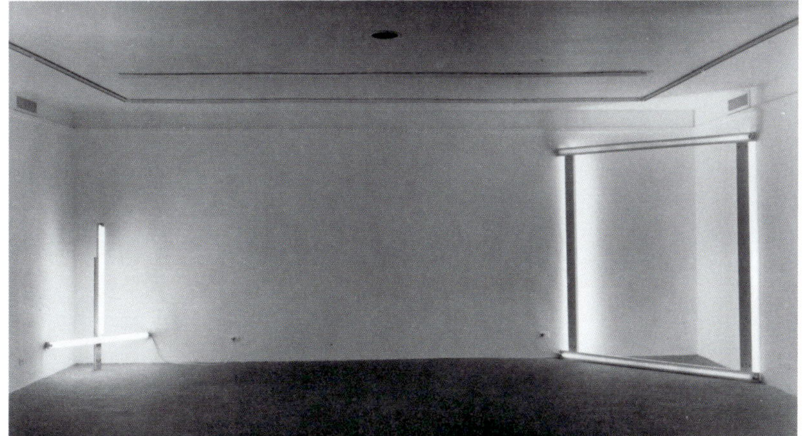

116

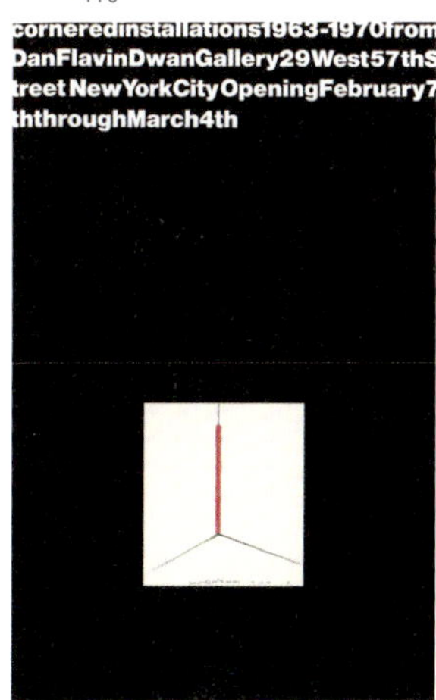

117

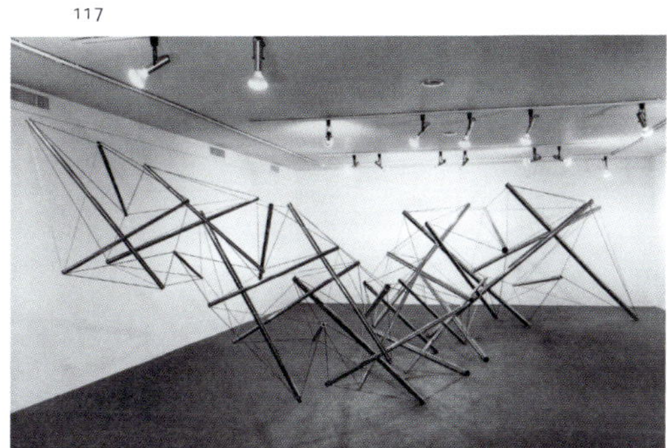

apprehension we have for physical entities beyond human scale. Photographs à la *National Geographic* are merely evidence and cannot stand in for the work, so it seems that Heizer has developed parallel means for gallery work that [are] adequately self-referential to measure up to the circumstances while still carrying, in a remote and eerie way, reference to work in another domain of experience." Bitite Vinklers, "New York," *Art International* 14, no. 3 (March 20, 1970): 91, illustrated "[H]is gesture is at the same time a very romantic one. It is a rejection of the city and of civilization and a reincarnation of the American frontier spirit in seeking out and grappling with virgin territory on a grandiose scale. Heizer's earth projects, ultimately preserved only in photographs or other records, remain extremely remote geographically and experientially for most of their viewers, and are therefore easily surrounded with an air of mystery and grandeur." Dore Ashton, "New York commentary," *Studio International* 179, no. 920 (March 1970): 119; Kenneth Baker, "The Home Forum," *Christian Science Monitor* (December 1, 1970): 12, illustrated, 43; Felice T. Ross, "Gallery Previews in New York," *Pictures on Exhibit* 33, no. 6 (March 1970): 18

RELATED / William Wilson, "Don't Know Trenches, but We Know What We Like," *Los Angeles Times* (July 27, 1969): N16; Roy Bongartz, "It's Called Earth Art—And Boulderdash," *New York Times Sunday Magazine* (February 1, 1970): 16–17, 22–30, illustrated; Philip Leider, "How I Spent My Summer Vacation on Art and Politics in Nevada, San Francisco and Utah," *Artforum* 9, no. 1 (September 1970): 40–49, illustrated; Grégoire Müller, "Michael Heizer," *Arts Magazine* 44, no. 3 (December 1969 / January 1970): 42–45, illustrated; Bill Vincent, "Stalking the Double Negative on Mormon Mesa," *The Nevadan* (July 15, 1973): 6

Cornered Installations from Dan Flavin, 1963–1970
February 7–March 4

CHECKLIST / **Main Gallery:** *Untitled (to Pat and Bob Rohm) 1/5*, 1969; *Untitled (to Heiner Friedrich) 1/3*, 1968–1969; *Untitled (to Shirley) 1/3*, 1965–1969; *Red out of a corner (to Annina)*, 1963 **Rear Gallery:** *Untitled (to Mr. & Mrs. Richard Fraenkel)*, 1968 **Office:** *Untitled (to Ira Licht)*, 1969–1970

REVIEWS / Jean-Louis Bourgeois, "New York: Dan Flavin, Dwan, Castelli," *Artforum* 8, no. 4 (April 1970): 81, 82, illustrated; Katherine G. Kline, "Reviews and Previews," *Artnews* 69, 2 (April 1970): 20

Kenneth Snelson
March 7–April 2

CHECKLIST / **Main Gallery:** *Osaka II*, 1969; *Landing*, 1970 **Corridor:** *Kroller-Muller Tower Maquette*, 1969 **Rear Gallery:** *Easy K* (maquette), 1970; *Northwood II*, 1970 **Office:** *Untitled*, n.d.; *Osaka* (maquette), 1969; *Northwood II* (maquette), 1970 **Back Room:** *Easy K* (small maquette), 1970

REVIEWS / Felice T. Ross, "Gallery Previews in New York," *Pictures on Exhibit* 33, no. 7 (April 1970): 17, 29, illustrated; Carter Ratcliff, "Reviews and Previews," *Artnews* 69, no. 3 (May 1970): 73 "He has so mastered the intricacies of his method that a piece containing dozens of segments and stretching for yards over the floor will, in fact, touch the floor in only three or four places." Bitite Vinklers, "New York," *Art International* 14, no. 3 (May 20, 1970): 84

FRED SANDBACK, INSTALLATION (118)

ANASTASI: SCULPTURE, INSTALLATION (119)

ANASTASI: CONTINUUM, INSTALLATION (120)

LANGUAGE IV, ANNOUNCEMENT (121) AND INSTALLATION (122)

RICHARD LONG: SCULPTURE, INSTALLATION (123)

ROBERT SMITHSON: GREAT SALT LAKE, UTAH, POSTER (124)

118

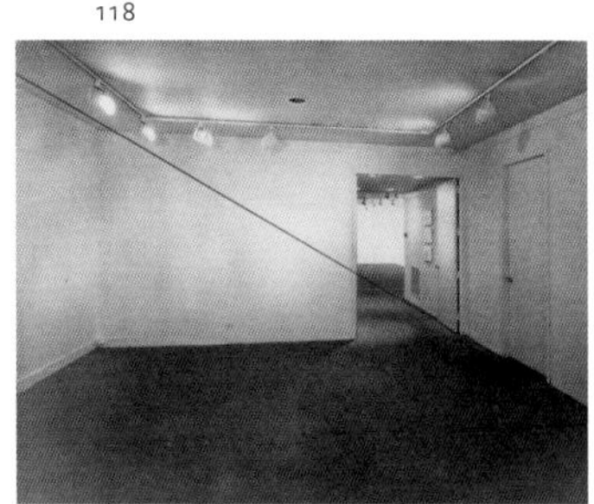

119

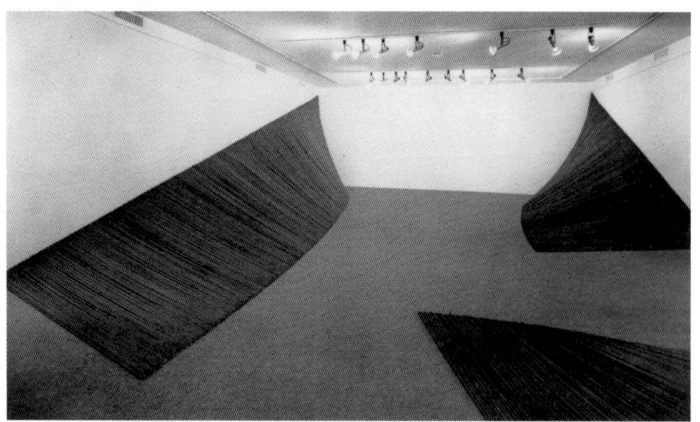

120

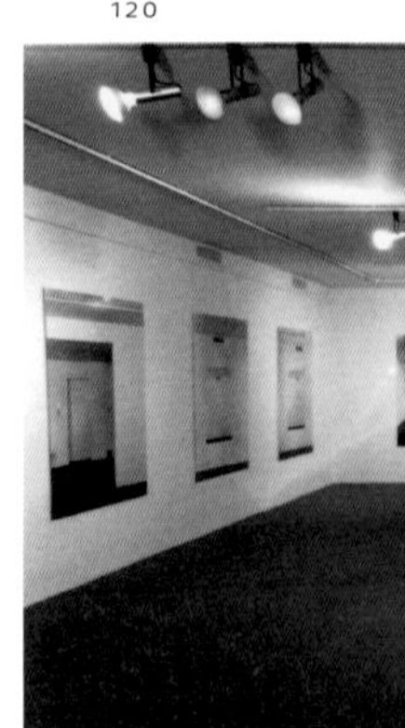

121

LANGUAGE IV

OPENING TUESDAY JUNE 2 THROUGH JUNE 25, 1970 DWAN 29 WEST 57 NEW YORK 10019

122

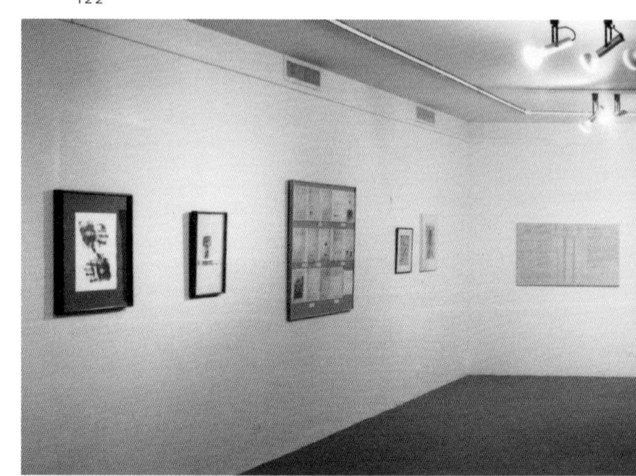

Fred Sandback
April 4–30

CHECKLIST / **Main Gallery:** *Untitled*, 1970 **Corridor:** *First Project for Sonsbeek 70 (Burnt Grass)*, 1970; *Second Project for Sonsbeek 70 (Dead Grass)*, 1970; *Third Project for Sonsbeek 70 (Poppies)*, 1970 **Rear Gallery:** *Untitled (One of Four Diagonals)*, 1970

REVIEWS / Cindy Nemser, "In the Galleries," *Arts Magazine* 44, 7 (May 1970): 65; Carter Ratcliff, "New York," *Art International* 14, no. 6 (Summer 1970): 139

Anastasi: Sculpture
May 2–14

CHECKLIST / **Main Gallery:** *Untitled*, 1969; *Untitled*, 1969; *Untitled*, 1969 **Corridor:** *Untitled*, 1962 **Rear Gallery:** *Untitled*, 1967; *Untitled (wall rearrangement)*, 1966; *Untitled*, 1965; *Untitled*, 1965

REVIEWS / Miriam Brumer, "In the Galleries," *Arts Magazine* 44, no. 8 (Summer 1970): 64; Carter Ratcliff, "Reviews and Previews," *Artnews* 69, no. 4 (Summer 1970): 12

Anastasi: Continuum
May 16–28

CHECKLIST / Objects #1, #2, #3, #4, #5, #6, #7, #8, #9, #10, #11, and #12 from *Continuum (A Souvenir)*, 1968–1970

REVIEW / Miriam Brumer, "In the Galleries," *Arts Magazine* 44, no. 8 (Summer 1970): 64

Language IV
June 2–25

CHECKLIST / **Main Gallery:** Arakawa, *X-Ray of a diagram 2/5*, 1969; Arakawa, *X-Ray of a diagram 99/100*, 1969; Joseph Kosuth, *Special Investigation (Proposition One) (Art As Idea As Idea)*, 1969; Kenneth Snelson, *End Plugs Diagram*, 1968; Robert Morris, *Card File*, 1961; Anastasi, *Untitled*, 1970; Mel Bochner, *#1: Language Is Not Transparent*, 1970; Bernar Venet, *The Mathematics of Computation*, 1968–1969; Francis Picabia, Number 19 of Picabia's *review 391 (Portrait de Rrose Sélavy par Francois Picabia), date*; F. T. Marinetti, *I Paroliberi Futuristi*, 1913; Arakawa, *Mechanism of Meaning*, 1969 (unfinished); Ray Johnson, *Interview*, 1967; Jasper Johns, *Untitled*, 1963; Marcel Duchamp, *Apolinére Enameled 1/8*, 1916–1917; Marcel Duchamp, *Rrose Sélavy*, 1967; Walter De Maria, *Telegram*, April 6, 1968; Robert Smithson, *Drawing for Tar Pool & Gravel Pit*, 1967; Robert Smithson, *Map of broken clear glass*, 1969; Charles Ross, *Solar Burn*, 1970; Claes Oldenburg, *Poster for the Happening titled Auto Bodys*, December 1963; Michael Heizer, *Galerie Heiner Friedrich*; Terry Fugate-Wilcox, *Untitled*, 1969; Ian Wilson, *Language IV* **Rear Gallery:** Ad Reinhardt, *No War Postcard*, 1968; Barry Bryant, *XNIXONX 10017, #3*, 1970; Agnes Denes, *Dialectic Triangulation: A Visual Philosophy*, 1970; Madeline Gins, *Word Rain*, 1969; Edward Kienholz, *The Office Building*, 1965; Carl Andre, *Set of 7 books*, 1969; Giora Novak, *16" globe covered with newspaper*, 1968; Adrian Piper, *Context #8: Written Information Voluntarily Supplied To Me During The Period of April 30 To May 30, 1970*, 1970; Hannah Weiner, *Excerpt from "Harry and Banana,"* 1970; Hojo, *Jung Shin (mind)*; Dorothea Rockburne, *Set*, 1970; Jonathan Borofsky, *Xerox copy of my thought process–illustrated from April, 1969 through Feb. 1970*, 1969–1970; Art-Language, *American Editor–Joseph Kosuth*, February 1970; Arakawa, *Stolen by Kathe Gregory, Marilyn Landis, Russell F. Lewis, David Crane, Scott R. Kahn*, 1970

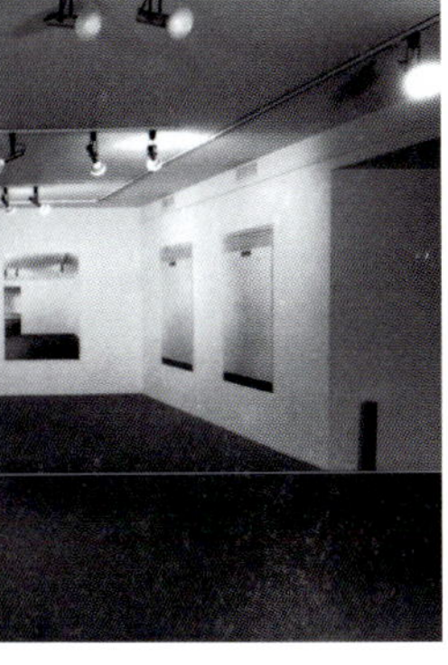

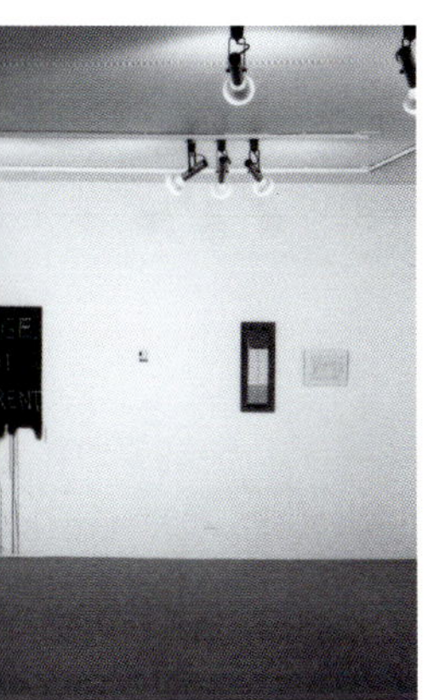

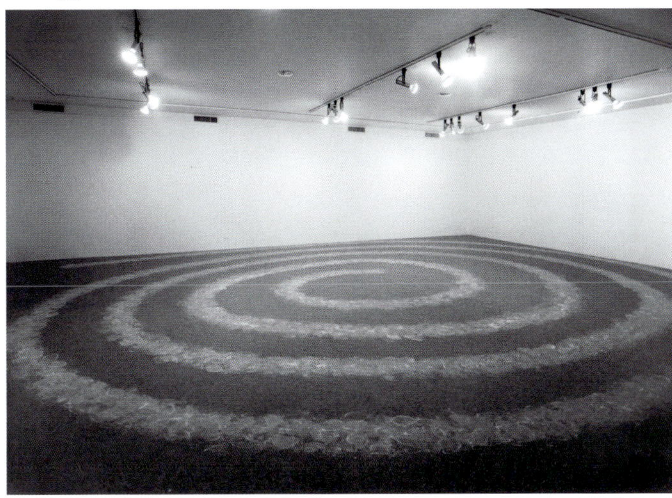

124

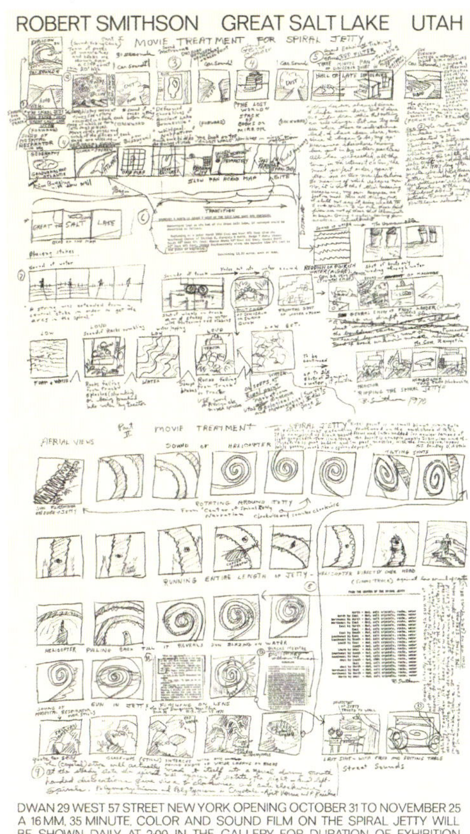

REVIEW / Robert Pincus-Witten, "New York: Language, Dwan Gallery," *Artforum* 9, no. 1 (September 1970): 75, illustrated "Rumor has it that the 'LANGUAGE' exhibition, held annually these past four years at the Dwan Gallery, will be discontinued. Since these exhibitions have been so difficult, crowded and divorced from familiar pictorial issues — *belle facture*, say, or sensuous impasto — and because of their historical sprawl, they have been overlooked, ignored even, by the critical reviews. Yet their relationship to the recent development of an art seemingly based on linguistic principles has been profound and abiding. . . . What the four 'Language' exhibitions suggest is that our vaunted Cartesian limpidity leads to experiences which are by no means clear. This lesson was codified by Mel Bochner who, on a hand dropped blackboard, chalked 'LANGUAGE IS NOT TRANSPARENT.'"

Richard Long: Sculpture
October 3–29

CHECKLIST / **Main Gallery:** *Sculpture*, 1970
Rear Gallery: *Sculpture*, 1970

REVIEWS / Elizabeth C. Baker, "Reviews and Previews," *Artnews* 69, no. 7 (November 1970): 22 "The concept of duration, of distance, of walking, of traces of the artist's presence in a specific locale are all important factors in Long's thinking." Willis Domingo, "Gallery Reviews, Richard Long," *Arts Magazine* 45, no. 2 (November 1970): 63, 64, illustrated; Joseph Masheck, "New York: Richard Long, Dwan Gallery," *Artforum* 9, no. 4 (December 1970): 78–79, illustrated "It is impossible not to think of Smithson's *Spiral Jetty* at the Great Salt Lake. . . . Long's work, which almost asks to be compared with it, because formally it is simply a large spiral, and because it is a very literary, even satirical, intrusion of landscape into a city room and onto the very carpet, is but a meager shadow." Gerrit Henry, "New York," *Art International* 14, no. 10 (Christmas 1970): 76, illustrated

Robert Smithson: Great Salt Lake, Utah
October 31–November 25

CHECKLIST / *Spiral Jetty*, 1970

REVIEWS / John Ashbery, "Reviews and Previews," *Artnews* 69, no. 8 (December 1970): 62 "By using a film as a medium for telling about his experiment he has successfully avoided the boredom overkill that up until now has been one of the chief bugs in Conceptual Art, including Smithson's own previous pseudo-scientific 'exhibits' of geological ephemera. . . . My anxiety on viewing such work stemmed not from boredom — on the contrary, I found it fascinating — but from concern that tributary ennui would get to the spectator before the ultimate apotheosis of *emmerdement* has been reached. . . . By surreptitiously re-introducing romance in the guise of cinematic narrative, Smithson has played a very mean trick on the other Conceptual artists and has also produced the first masterpiece in a new form that has been fretfully awaiting one for some time." Willis Domingo, "Gallery Reviews, Robert Smithson," *Arts Magazine* 45, no. 3 (December 1970/January 1971): 56–57, illustrated "Not only does the jetty leave its trace on individual frames as would any object on

GALLERY ARTISTS, ANNOUNCEMENT (125)

CHARLES ROSS: SUNLIGHT DISPERSION, ANNOUNCEMENT (126)

ROBERT RYMAN, ANNOUNCEMENT (127) AND INSTALLATION (128)

DAN FLAVIN: UNTITLEDS (TO BARNETT NEWMAN), ANNOUNCEMENT (129) AND INSTALLATION (130)

CARL ANDRE, INSTALLATION (131)

125

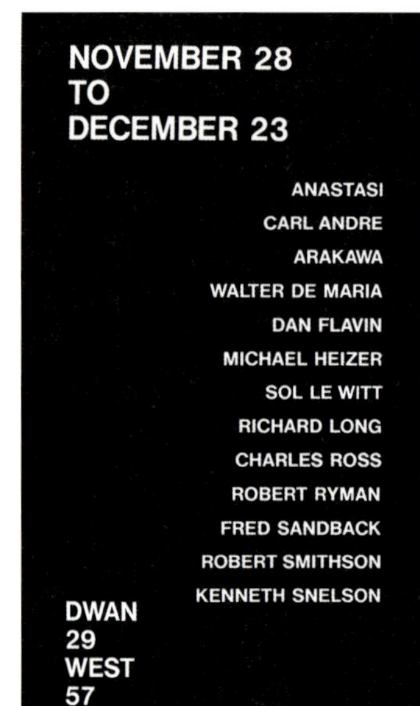

126

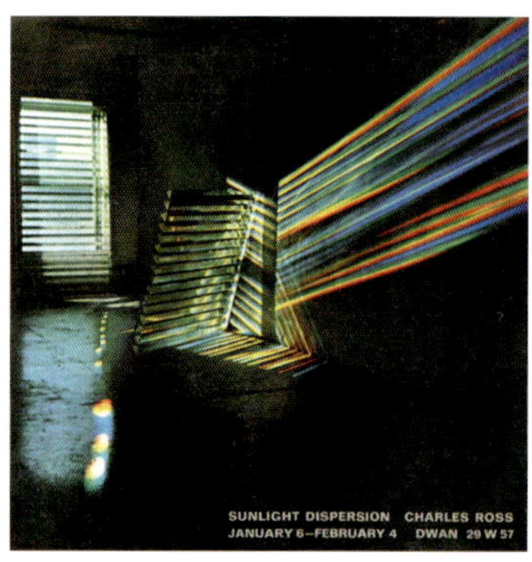

127

FEBRUARY 6–MARCH 4

ROBERT RYMAN

PAINTINGS

DWAN GALLERY

29 WEST 57TH ST. NEW YORK

128

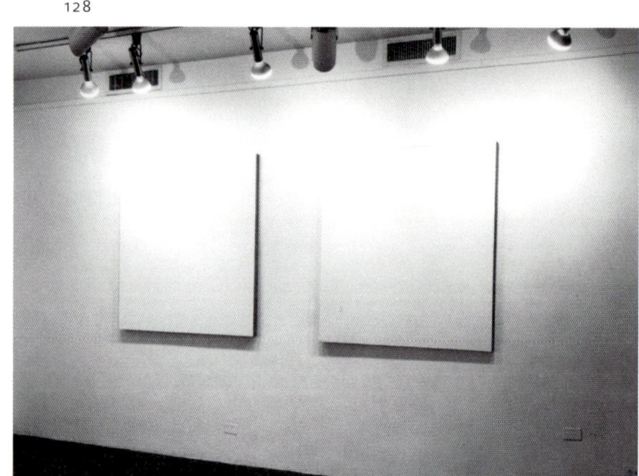

any photograph, the form of the continuous film is weaved out of the loops of the jetty. It is as if the celluloid had somehow been wrapped around this circular figure." Joseph Masheck, "New York: Robert Smithson, Dwan Gallery," *Artforum* 9, no. 5 (January 1971): 73–74 "It is possible, even likely, that we were not ready for the art of Robert Smithson until we had seen the earth from outer space. . . . As yet only Smithson's art has sufficient sweep and enough contemplative calm to deal with matters of such immensity as they enter the sphere of our real experience for the first time." Gerrit Henry, "New York Letter," *Art International* 15, no. 1 (January 20, 1971): 42, illustrated

RELATED / Philip Leider, "How I Spent My Summer Vacation on Art and Politics in Nevada, San Francisco and Utah," *Artforum* 9, no. 1 (September 1970): 40–49, illustrated

Gallery Artists
November 28–December 23

CHECKLIST / Carl Andre, *Lintel*, proposed 1960, executed 1970; Robert Ryman, *Untitled*, 1959; Robert Ryman, *Untitled*, 1960; Robert Ryman, *Untitled*, 1961; Robert Ryman, *Untitled*, 1961; Robert Ryman, *Twelve*, 1961; Dan Flavin, *Untitled, 1/5*, 1963; Sol LeWitt, Five Silkscreen Prints, 1970; Arakawa, *Mapping of Meaning*, Detail from *Mechanism of Meaning*, 1969–1970; Anastasi, *Untitled*, 1969; Robert Smithson, *Gyrostasis*, 1967; Walter De Maria, *Walk Around The Box*, 1961; Walter De Maria, *Calendar*, 1961; Charles Ross, *Model for Prism Wall Muybridge Window*, 1969; Fred Sandback, *Pink Corner Piece*, 1970; Sol LeWitt, *9 Part Set C*, 1966–1969; Sol LeWitt, *9 Part Set D*, 1966–1969; Kenneth Snelson, *Microfiche I*, 1970; Richard Long, *Reflections in the Little Pigeon River, Great Smoky Mountains, Tennessee*, 1970

REVIEW / Kenneth Baker, "New York: Group Show, Dwan Gallery," *Artforum* 9, no. 6 (February 1971): 80–81

1971

Charles Ross: Sunlight Dispersion
January 6–February 4

CHECKLIST / **Main Gallery:** *Sunlight Film Loops*, 1970: *Loop 1 (Cup, September 3, 2:15 p.m. / Table Corner, July 5, 3:00 p.m. / Hand, October 12, 1:00 p.m.)*; *Loop 2 (Wall Sunlight, January 8, 10:00 a.m. / To Floor, January 21, 10:45 a.m. / Creeping Dots, March 24, 12:30 p.m. Long Dots with Chair, November 6, 11:00 a.m.)*; *Loop 3 (Table, June 18, 2:45 p.m. / Chair, May 20, 1:30 p.m. / Plants, May 11, 1:30 p.m.)* **Corridor:** *Untitled (stack of 3)*, 1970 **Rear Gallery:** *Untitled (2 units)*, 1970 **Office:** *Untitled (stack of 6)*, 1970

REVIEWS / Willis Domingo, "Gallery Reviews, Charles Ross," *Arts Magazine* 45, no. 4 (February 1971): 55; Carter Ratcliff, "Reviews and Previews," *Artnews* 69, no. 10 (February 1971): 24; Kenneth Baker, "New York: Charles Ross, Dwan Gallery," *Artforum* 9, no. 7 (March 1971): 63–64; Gerrit Henry, "New York Letter," *Art International* 15, no. 3 (March 20, 1971): 52

129

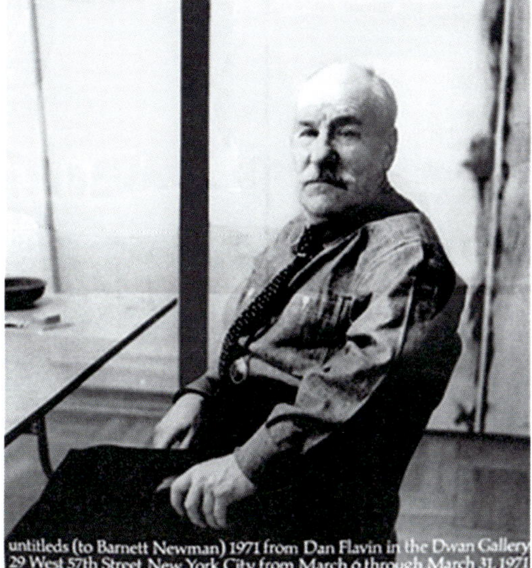

130

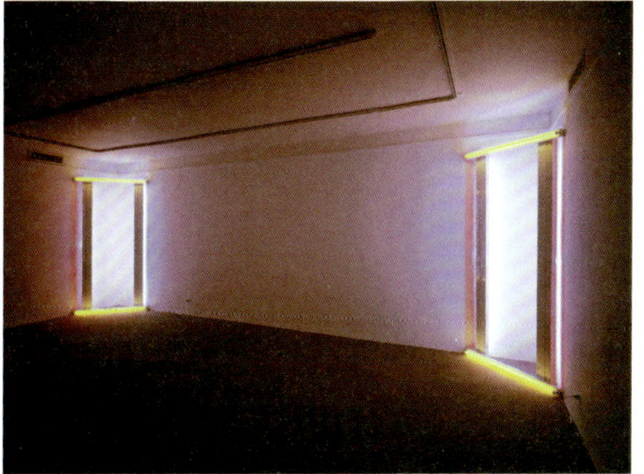

131

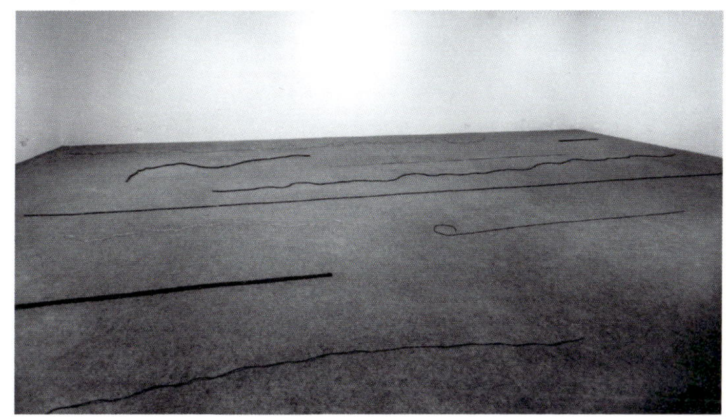

Robert Ryman: Paintings
February 6–March 4

CHECKLIST / **Main Gallery, West Wall:** *Finished Painting III*, 1970; *Unfinished Painting II*, 1970 **South Wall:** *"Untitled" (New York)*, 1971 **East Wall:** *Surface Veil #1*, 1970; *Untitled*, 1970; *Untitled*, 1971; *Untitled*, 1970; *Surface Veil #2*, 1970; *Untitled*, 1970; *Untitled*, 1970; *Untitled*, 1970; *Unfinished Painting I*, 1970; *Untitled*, 1970; *Untitled*, 1971; *Untitled*, 1970 **North Wall:** *Untitled*, 1970; *Untitled*, 1971; *Surface Veil #3*, 1970; *Untitled*, 1970; *Surface Veil #4*, 1970 **West Wall:** *Untitled*, 1970; *Untitled*, 1970 **Rear Gallery:** *Delta*, 1966

REVIEWS / Peter Schjeldahl, "The Ice Palace That Robert Ryman Built," *New York Times* (February 7, 1971): D21; Carter Ratcliff, "Robert Ryman's Double Positive," *Artnews* 70, no. 1 (March 1971): 54–57, 71, illustrated; Kenneth Baker, "New York: Robert Ryman, Fishbach Gallery and Dwan Gallery," *Artforum* 9, no. 8 (April 1971): 78–79

Dan Flavin: untitleds (to Barnett Newman)
March 6–31

CHECKLIST / **Main Gallery:** *untitled (to Barnett Newman) one*, 1971; *untitled (to Barnett Newman) two*, 1971; *untitled (to Barnett Newman) three*, 1971; *untitled (to Barnett Newman) four*, 1971 **Corridor:** *(to Barnett Newman) one, 1971 for Dwan Gallery*, 1971; *(to Barnett Newman) two, 1971 for Dwan Gallery*, 1971; *(to Barnett Newman) three, 1971 for Dwan Gallery*, 1971; *(to Barnett Newman) four, 1971 for Dwan Gallery*, 1971; *(to Barnett Newman) pairings, 1971 for Dwan Gallery*, 1971 **Rear Gallery:** *untitled (to Annalee fondly)*, 1971 **Office:** *untitled (to Paolina)*, 1971; *untitled (to Paul Toner)*, 1971

REVIEWS / Joseph Perreault, "Snotty remarks," *Village Voice* (March 23, 1971): 17; Willis Domingo, "New York Galleries, Dan Flavin," *Arts Magazine* 45, no. 6 (April 1971): 82–83, illustrated; Carter Ratcliff, "Reviews and Previews," *Artnews* 70, no. 2 (April 1971): 12

Carl Andre
April 3–28

CHECKLIST / **Main Gallery:** *32 Pieces of Plasticine Bricks*, 1970; *7 Pieces of Lead Plated Copper Wire*, 1970; *16 Pieces of Steel Reinforcement Rods*, 1970; *12 Pieces of Galvanized Steel*, 1970; *26 Pieces of Steel Rod*, 1970; *11 Pieces of Aluminum Wire*, 1970; *57 Pieces of Steel Reinforcement Rods*, 1970; *28 Pieces of Solid Plastic Rods*, 1970; *8 Pieces of Galvanized Steel*, 1970; *5 Pieces of Steel Square Rod*, 1970; *14 Pieces of Steel Wire*, 1970; *7 Pieces of Steel Plate*, 1970 **Rear Gallery:** *8 Pieces of Steel Sheet*, 1970; *71 Pieces of Steel Sheet*, 1970; *13 Pieces of Lead*, 1970; *9 Pieces of Aluminum Strip*, 1970; *37 Pieces of Steel Sheet*, 1970; *15 Pieces of Stainless Steel*, 1970; *18 Pieces of Steel*, 1970; *10 Pieces of Lead Plated Cooper*, 1970; *6 Pieces of Stainless Steel Wire*, 1970; *82 Pieces of Steel Magnets*, 1970; *41 Pieces of Copper Foil*, 1970; *24 Pieces of Galvanized Steel*, 1970; *15 Pieces of Lead Wire*, 1970; *6 Pieces of Graphite*, 1970; *42 Pieces of Aluminum*, 1970; *9 Pieces of Lead*, 1970; *12 Pieces of Silver*, 1970; *7 Pieces of Steel Sheet*, 1970

SOL LEWITT: PRINTS AND DRAWINGS, ANNOUNCEMENT (132) AND INSTALLATION (133–134)

FINAL EXHIBITION: GALLERY ARTISTS, ANNOUNCEMENT (135–136) (FRONT AND BACK)

POSTCARD TO VIRGINIA FROM CARL ANDRE (137)

LETTER TO VIRGINIA FROM SOL LEWITT (138)

132

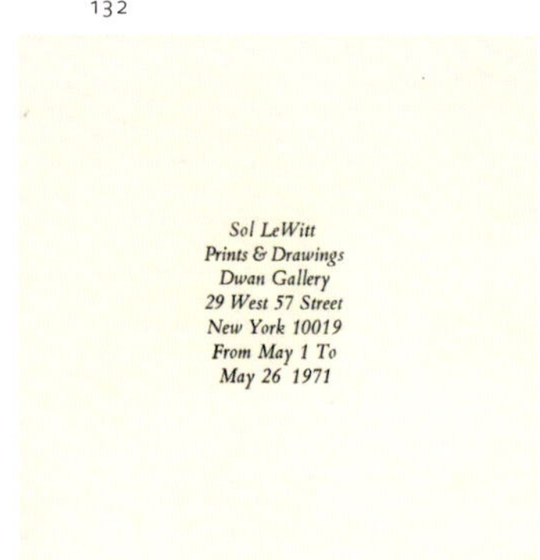

133

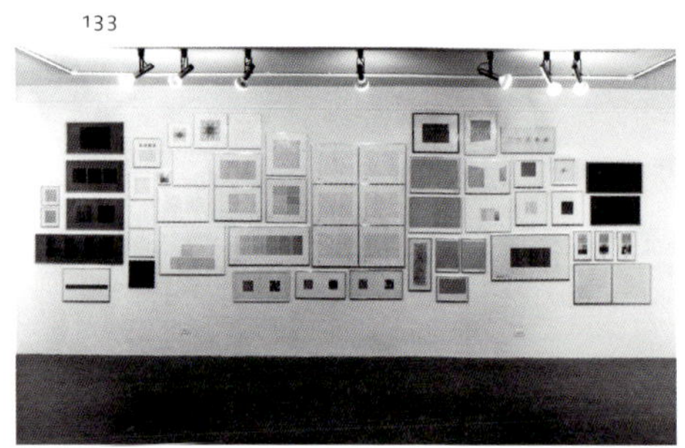

134

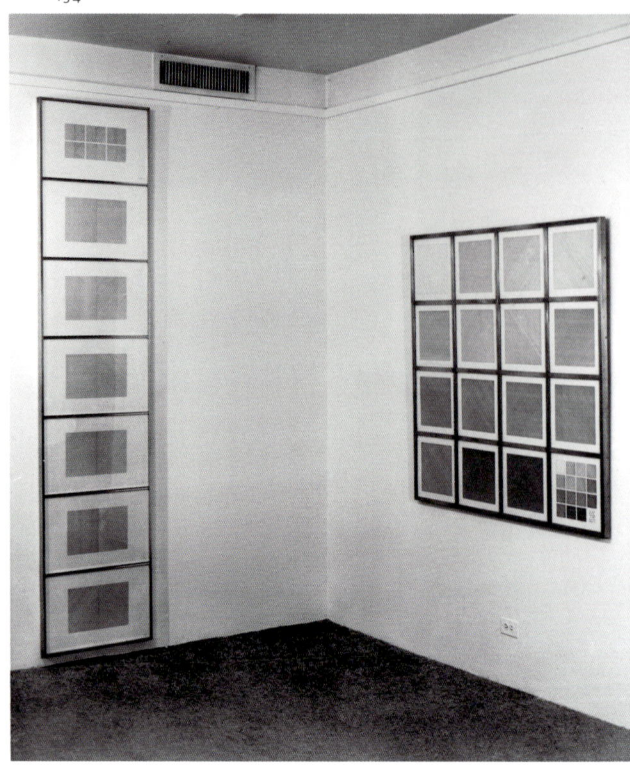

1971 NEW YORK

REVIEWS / Grace Glueck, "No Bones in Their Noses," *New York Times* (April 18, 1971): D21 (under "Cash Flow") "With income-reporting on the honor system, the show has already sold out." Willis Domingo, "New York Galleries, Carl Andre," *Arts Magazine* 45, no. 7 (May 1971): 55, 56, illustrated; Harris Rosenstein, "Reviews and Previews," *Artnews* 70, no. 3 (May 1971): 10 "A new wrinkle here, which for Andre may be an effort to unthwart himself politically, is the imposition of an egalitarian pricing system on collectors: 1 per cent of the purchaser's gross annual income per linear yard of the work." Kenneth Baker, "New York: Carl Andre, Dwan Gallery," *Artforum* 9, no. 10 (June 1971): 80–81, illustrated; Gregory Battcock, "New York," *Art and Artists* 6, no. 3 (June 1971): 59

Sol LeWitt: Prints and Drawings
May 1–26

CHECKLIST / **Foyer:** *Folded Piece*, 1971 **Main Gallery:** *Silkscreen Print–Four Colors*, 1970; *Silkscreen Print–Black and White*, 1971; *Silkscreen Prints–Black and White*, 1971; *Silkscreen Prints–Yellow*, 1971; *Silkscreen Prints–4 Colors*, 1970; *Drawing*, 1969; *Drawing*, 1969; *I, II, III*, 1969; *1" Line Diagonal Horizontal*, 1970; *Drawing for Five Cubes with Hidden Cubes*, 1968; *Drawing for Cube with Hidden Cubes*; *Straight Lines Drawn in 4 Directions*, 1971; *Plan for Wall Drawing/Dwan Gallery*, 1969; *Drawing*, 1970; *Short Straight Lines, Etc.*, 1971; *Plan for Wall Drawing*, 1970; *Plan for Wall Drawing*, 1970; *Plan for Wall Drawing*, 1970; *Drawing 124/123*, 1969; *Four Colored Drawing*, 1970; *Four Colored Drawing*, 1970; *Drawing*, 1970; *Four Colored Drawing*, 1970; *Four Colored Drawing*, 1970; *Four Colored Drawing*, 1970; *6 Part Drawing With 1" Lines*, 1970; *III 2314 A&B*, 1969; *II 1234*, 1968; *Yellow Drawing*, 1971; *Four Colored Drawing*, 1970; *Composite Drawing*, 1970; *I 13 (3412) A&B*, 1968; *Yellow X*, 1971; *2 Part Drawing*, 1970; *Black X*, 1971; *Yellow Short Lines Not Touching*, 1971; *Double Yellow Drawing*, 1971; *Three Kinds of Progressions*, 1971; *Four Color X*, 1971; *Number Drawing*, 1968; *Small Drawing*, 1971; *Yellow Drawing*, 1971; *Yellow Lines Not Touching*, 1971; *Yellow 1,2,3,4*, 1971; *IV 12B*, 1969; *A1 Drawing/Gray Paper*; *Drawing With 3 Square, Gray Paper*, 1969; *Double Drawing/Gray Paper*, 1969; *Joanne's Drawing/Gray Paper*, 1969; *Flavin's Drawing*, 1970; *Yellow, Blue and Black/Small Drawing*, 1970; *Red, Black and Blue/Small Drawing*, 1970; *16 Etchings–4 Colors*, 1971; *Refer to Wall Label reading: Lithographs With Lines Approximately 1" Long*, 1970; *Refer to Wall Label reading: 16 Lithographs With Lines Approximately 1" Long*, 1970; *6 2-Part Drawings/Color*, 1970; *3 Part Color Drawing*, 1970; *3 Part Color Drawing*, 1970; *3 Part Color Drawing*, 1970; *3 Part Color Drawing*, 1970; *3 Part Color Drawing*, 1970; *16 Part Color Drawing*, 1970; *7 Part Drawing–Black & White*, 1970 **Corridor:** *4 Etchings*, 1971 **Rear Gallery:** *14 Pieces in Five Sets*, 1969; *123 (6 3-Part Variations)*, 1968; *333/7 3-Part Variations*, 1968; *333/7 3-Part Variations*, 1968; *7 2-Part Variations*, 1968; *Work Drawing*, *3 Cube Drawing*, 1971; *Wall Piece 1965*, 1971;

135

136

138

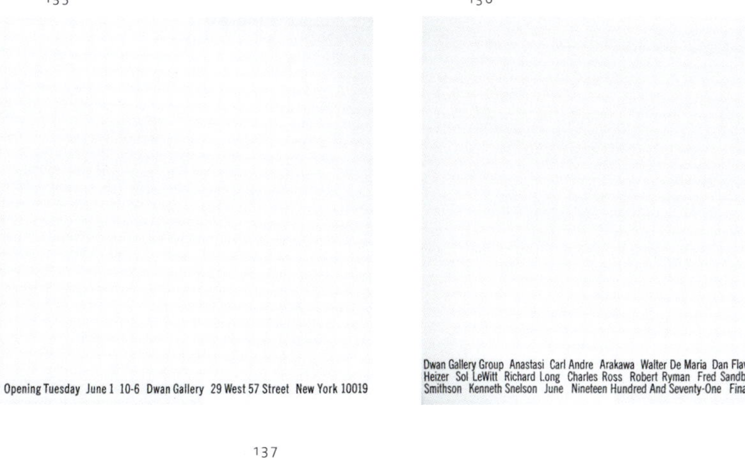

April 22, 1971

Dear Virginia

It's so hard to believe that there will be no Dwan Gallery any more. It had played so important a part of my life that it is difficult to get accustomed to the idea that it will not exist.

I owe so much to you and I would like to thank you for your confidence in me and my art. As far as I am concerned we will always be friends,

love

Sol

137

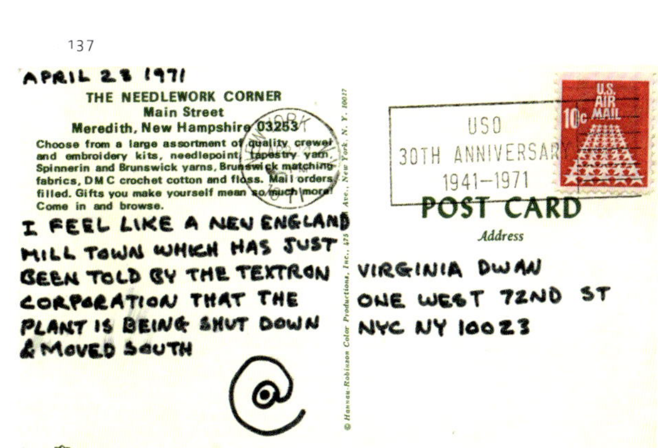

Drawing with Errors, 1971; seventeen works titled *Work Drawing*, 1967; *Work Drawing*, 1968; *Plan and Elevation*, 1967; six works titled *Work Drawing*, 1965; *Paste-up*, 1967; *Standing Piece Drawing*, 1965; *Work Drawing–Layout*, 1967; *Lithograph–Black and White, Lines Not Long, Etc.*, 1970; *Lithograph–Four Colors*, 1970; *Lithograph–Vertical Lines, Not Touching*, 1970; *Set A*, 1967; *Set B*, 1967; *Set C*, 1967; *Set D*, 1967; 10 Lithographs–*Black and White and Four Colors*, 1971
Office: 4 *Color Wall Drawing*, 1969

REVIEWS / Harris Rosenstein, "Reviews and Previews," *Artnews* 70, no. 4 (Summer 1971): 16 "His move to drawing directly on the wall, as he does once in this show, is a clarification in that it brings us closer to a pure regard of the operations and weakens the distracting concept of pictorial space. While his axiom-system approach is severe, it is not defeating. At least for him it is a liberating initiative and does not preclude strong, lovely improvisation, entirely within its limits." Willis Domingo, "New York Gallery Reviews, Sol LeWitt," *Arts Magazine* 45, no. 8 (Summer 1971): 52; Herbert Raymond, "New York," *Art and Artists* 6, no. 5 (August 1971): 54, illustrated.

Final Exhibition: Gallery Artists
June 1–25

CHECKLIST / **Main Gallery:** Richard Long, *Square Dance*, October 1969; Fred Sandback, *Untitled*, 1971; Arakawa, *10 Reassembling (from Mechanism of Meaning Series)*, 1970; Michael Heizer, *Bolivia/Nevada*, 1970; Michael Heizer, *Nevada/Texas*, 1970; Charles Ross, *Solar Burn–The condition of Sunlight daily*, 1971; Robert Smithson, *Spiral Jetty Film Documentation #1*, 1971; Robert Smithson, *Spiral Jetty Film Documentation #2*, 1971; Robert Smithson, *Spiral Jetty Film Documentation #3*, 1971; Sol LeWitt, *4 Part Silkscreen Print 30/30*, 1971; Robert Ryman, *Black and White*, 1965; Robert Ryman, *Black and White*, 1965; Anastasi, *Untitled*, 1969 **Corridor:** Walter De Maria, *Death Concept Drawing*, 1964; Walter De Maria, 1970
Rear Gallery: Dan Flavin, *Untitled (to Virginia Dwan)*, 1971; Kenneth Snelson, slides of various works

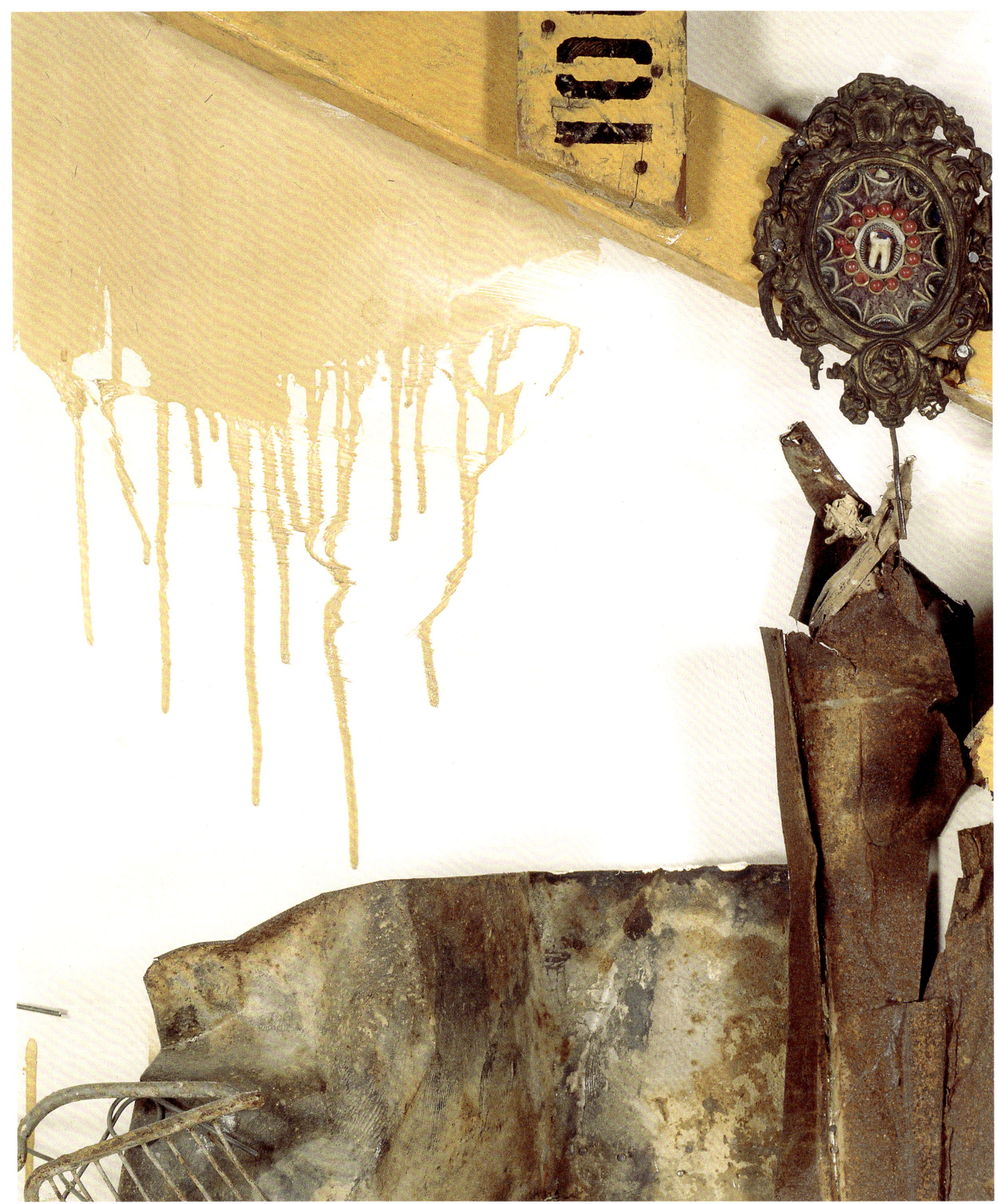

CHECKLIST OF WORKS IN THE EXHIBITION

CAT. 1

Larry Rivers, *Virginia Dwan*, 1963, graphite on paper, sheet: $14\frac{15}{16} \times 17\frac{15}{16}$ in. (38 × 45.5 cm), Collection of Virginia Dwan

CAT. 2

Larry Rivers, *Maquette for Larry Rivers Exhibition at Dwan Gallery*, 1961, collage of cut-out text, paint, and tape on gelatin silver print mounted on paper board, mount (irregular): $14\frac{1}{16} \times 12\frac{3}{16}$ in. (35.7 × 31 cm), Collection of Virginia Dwan

CAT. 3

Larry Rivers, *Maquette for Larry Rivers Exhibition at Dwan Gallery*, 1963, collage of gelatin silver prints, paint, graphite, ink, charcoal, cut-out text, and tape on paper, sheet: 14 × 14 in. (35.6 × 35.6 cm), Collection of Virginia Dwan

CAT. 4

Matsumi Kanemitsu, *Wes Hardin*, 1958, oil on canvas, 50 × 60 in. (127 × 152.4 cm), Los Angeles County Museum of Art, Gift of Mr. and Mrs. Vadim Kondratief (Los Angeles only)

CAT. 5

Robert Goodnough, *Abstract No. 4 "Pipes,"* 1956, oil on canvas, $44\frac{5}{16} \times 46$ in. (112.6 × 116.8 cm), Los Angeles County Museum of Art, Gift from the Michael and Dorothy Blankfort Collection (Los Angeles only)

CAT. 6

Philip Guston, *The Room*, 1954–1955, oil on canvas, $71\frac{7}{8} \times 60$ in. (182.6 × 152.4 cm), Los Angeles County Museum of Art, Museum Purchase, Contemporary Art Council Fund (Los Angeles only)

CAT. 7

Philip Guston, *Sleeper II*, 1959, oil on canvas, 68 × 65 in. (172.7 × 165.1 cm), Jeanne and Richard Levitt, Des Moines, Iowa (Washington only)

CAT. 8

Franz Kline, *Torres*, 1959–1960, oil on canvas, $40\frac{3}{4} \times 47$ in. (103.5 × 119.4 cm), Susan and David Gersh, Los Angeles, California (Los Angeles only)

CAT. 9

Franz Kline, *Pittston*, 1958, oil on canvas, $77\frac{3}{4} \times 71$ in. (197.5 × 180.3 cm), Collection of Lynn and Allen Turner (Washington only)

CAT. 10

Ad Reinhardt, *Abstract Painting (A)*, 1954, oil on canvas, 108 × 40 in. (274.3 × 101.6 cm), Collection of Virginia Dwan (Washington only)

CAT. 11

Lee Bontecou, *Untitled*, 1960, welded metal, canvas, and wire relief, $7\frac{3}{4} \times 7 \times 3$ in. (19.7 × 17.8 × 7.6 cm), Los Angeles County Museum of Art, Gift of Robert H. Halff through the Modern and Contemporary Art Council (Los Angeles only)

CAT. 12

Yves Klein, *Untitled Blue Monochrome* (IKB 187), 1960, dry pigment and synthetic resin on canvas mounted on board, $15\frac{3}{4} \times 14$ in. (40 × 35.6 cm), Collection of Virginia Dwan

CAT. 13

Yves Klein, *Untitled Pink Monochrome* (MP 21), 1961, dry pigment and synthetic resin on gauze mounted on panel, $18\frac{7}{8} \times 14\frac{15}{16}$ in. (48 × 38 cm), Collection of Virginia Dwan

CAT. 14

Yves Klein, *L'eau et le Feu* (F 113), 1961, burnt cardboard on panel, $13\frac{9}{16} \times 22\frac{1}{2}$ in. (34.5 × 57.2 cm), Collection of Virginia Dwan

CAT. 15

Yves Klein, *Untitled Monogold* (MG 31), 1961, gold leaves on panel, $14\frac{3}{16} \times 10\frac{13}{16}$ in. (36 × 27.5 cm), Collection of Virginia Dwan

CAT. 16

Yves Klein, *Transfer of "Zone de sensibilité picturale immaterielle" to Michael Blankfort, Pont au Double, Paris, February 10, 1962*, 1962, gelatin silver prints, 16a image: $19\frac{1}{2} \times 15\frac{1}{2}$ in. (49.6 × 39.3 cm), 16b image: $15\frac{7}{16} \times 19\frac{1}{2}$ in. (39.2 × 49.5 cm), 16c image: $15\frac{1}{2} \times 19\frac{1}{2}$ in. (39.4 × 49.5 cm), 16d image: $15\frac{9}{16} \times 19\frac{1}{2}$ in. (39.5 × 49.5 cm), Los Angeles County Museum of Art, Michael and Dorothy Blankfort Bequest

CAT. 17

Yves Klein, *Untitled Blue Monochrome* (IKB 186), 1960, dry pigment and synthetic resin on gauze mounted on panel, $17\frac{15}{16} \times 39$ in. (45.5 × 99 cm), Collection of Virginia Dwan

CAT. 18

Edward Kienholz, *Traveling Art Show Kit*, 1961, valise, mixed media with various elements, $7\frac{13}{16} \times 14\frac{1}{8} \times 10\frac{5}{8}$ in. (19.8 × 35.8 × 26.9 cm), Private Collection

CAT. 19

Robert Rauschenberg, *Coexistence*, 1961, oil, fabric, wood, and other found materials on canvas, $66\frac{3}{4} \times 49\frac{7}{8} \times 14\frac{1}{4}$ in. (169.6 × 126.7 × 36.2 cm), Virginia Museum of Fine Arts, Gift of the Sydney and Frances Lewis Foundation (Washington only)

CAT. 20

Robert Rauschenberg, *Wooden Gallop*, 1962, oil, wood, paper, metal, fragment of yellow rubber life raft, and cola can on plywood, $48 \times 49\frac{1}{2} \times 10\frac{3}{4}$ in. (121.9 × 125.7 × 27.3 cm), Chrysler Museum of Art, Norfolk, Virginia, Gift of Walter P. Chrysler, Jr. (Los Angeles only)

CAT. 21

Robert Rauschenberg, *Maquette for Robert Rauschenberg Exhibition at Dwan Gallery*, 1962, collage of newspaper cut-out, envelope with telegram, offset printing, paint, graphite, and tape on paper, 20 × 17 in. (50.8 × 43.2 cm), Collection of Virginia Dwan

CAT. 22

Robert Rauschenberg, *Untitled (For Virginia with Hook)*, 1965, printed paper, staples, Plexiglas, screws, washers, and hook, 9¼ × 10 in. (23.5 × 25.4 cm), Collection of Virginia Dwan

CAT. 23

Arman, *Alarm Clocks (Reveils)*, 1960, alarm clocks in painted wood box, 23½ × 47⁵⁄₁₆ × 5 in. (59.7 × 120.2 × 12.7 cm), Collection Museum of Contemporary Art Chicago, gift of Debra and Robert N. Mayer from the Robert B. Mayer Memorial Loan Collection

CAT. 24

Jean Tinguely, *Maquette for Jean Tinguely Exhibition at Dwan Gallery*, 1963, collage of silver diffusion transfer prints (Polaroids), red-pencil drawing, ballpoint pen, brown marker, red felt, wire, and tape on paper, sheet: 30⁹⁄₁₆ × 25½ in. (77.7 × 64.7 cm), Collection of Virginia Dwan

CAT. 25

Jean Tinguely, *Odessa*, 1963, scrap, forged iron, wheel, electronic motor, and black paint, 51 × 31 × 26 in. (129.5 × 78.7 × 66 cm), Collection of Virginia Dwan

CAT. 26

Jean Tinguely, *Portrait of Virginia*, 1963, mixed media construction with radio, circuit board, andiron, speaker, and motor, 40½ × 10½ × 16 in. (102.9 × 26.7 × 40.6 cm), Collection of Virginia Dwan

CAT. 27

Jean Tinguely, *Untitled (Motor Sculpture)*, 1963, ballpoint pen on paper, sheet: 10⁷⁄₁₆ × 7³⁄₁₆ in. (26.5 × 18.3 cm), Collection of Virginia Dwan

CAT. 28

Jean Tinguely, *Untitled (Motor Sculpture)*, 1963, ballpoint pen on paper, sheet: 11 × 6⅞ in. (27.9 × 17.4 cm), Collection of Virginia Dwan

CAT. 29

Jean Tinguely with Niki de Saint Phalle, *Dear Virginia: à bientôt*, undated, colored ink with collage on card, sheet: 8¼ × 11⅝ in. (21 × 29.5 cm), Collection of Virginia Dwan

CAT. 30

Jean Tinguely with Niki de Saint Phalle, *Chère Virginia: come sta?*, October 3, 1978, colored ink with collage on paper, sheet: 8¼ × 11⅝ in. (21 × 29.5 cm), Collection of Virginia Dwan

CAT. 31

Niki de Saint Phalle, *Tyrannousaurus Rex etranglé par un cobra*, c. 1963, colored markers, ballpoint pen, and graphite on paper, sheet: 14³⁄₁₆ × 19⁵⁄₁₆ in. (36 × 49.1 cm), Collection of Virginia Dwan

CAT. 32

Martial Raysse, *C'est Moi*, 1964, transfer, paint, and sunglasses on canvas, 13 × 16 in. (33 × 40.6 cm), Collection of Virginia Dwan

CAT. 33

Martial Raysse, *Pablo*, 1965, gouache and photocopy collage on canvas with aluminum frame and plastic letters, 8¾ × 7¼ in. (22.2 × 18.4 cm), Collection of Virginia Dwan

CAT. 34

Martial Raysse, *Made in Japan*, 1964, photomechanical reproductions and wallpaper with airbrush ink, gouache, ink, tacks, peacock feathers, and plastic flies on paper mounted on fiberboard, 51⅛ × 96¼ in. (129.9 × 244.5 cm), Hirshhorn Museum and Sculpture Garden, Smithsonian Institution, Washington, DC, Gift of Joseph H. Hirshhorn, 1972 (Washington only)

CAT. 35

John Chamberlain, *Rayvredd*, 1962, painted and chromium-plated steel, 34 × 34 × 38 in. (86.4 × 86.4 × 96.5 cm), The Museum of Contemporary Art, Los Angeles, Gift of Robert H. Halff (Los Angeles only)

CAT. 36

Charles Frazier, *Albion*, 1962, wood and canvas, 81 × 36 × 4½ in. (205.7 × 91.4 × 11.4 cm), Los Angeles County Museum of Art, Anonymous Gift (Los Angeles only)

CAT. 37

Claes Oldenburg, *Study for Announcement for One-Man Show at Dwan Gallery—Mickey Mouse with Red Heart*, 1963, wax crayon and watercolor on paper, sheet: 16⅝ × 13¾ in. (42.2 × 34.9 cm), Whitney Museum of American Art, New York, Gift of The American Contemporary Art Foundation, Inc., Leonard A. Lauder, President

CAT. 38

Claes Oldenburg, *Baked Potato #1*, 1963, burlap soaked in plaster over wire frame, painted with enamel; jersey filled with kapok, 15 × 25 × 15 in. (38.1 × 63.5 × 38.1 cm), Los Angeles County Museum of Art, Gift of Robert H. Halff through the Modern and Contemporary Art Council (Los Angeles only)

CAT. 39

Claes Oldenburg, *Coffee Cup*, 1962, muslin soaked in plaster over wire frame, painted with enamel, 6 × 11 × 10 in. (15.2 × 27.9 × 25.4 cm), Susan and David Gersh, Los Angeles, California (Los Angeles only)

CAT. 40

Claes Oldenburg, *Giant Wedge of Pecan Pie*, 1963, muslin soaked in plaster over wire frame, wood, painted with enamel, 14⅜ × 50½ × 20¾ in. (36.5 × 128.3 × 52.7 cm), Seattle Art Museum, Gift of the Virginia and Bagley Wright Collection, in honor of the 75th Anniversary of the Seattle Art Museum

CAT. 41

Claes Oldenburg, *Autobodys*, 1963, 16 mm film, black-and-white, silent, 20 minutes, Whitney Museum of American Art, New York, Gift of Claes Oldenburg (Los Angeles only)

CAT. 42

Tom Wesselmann, *Still Life #2*, 1962, oil and collage on board, 48 × 48⅛ in. (121.9 × 122.2 cm), Norton Simon Museum, Pasadena, California, Gift of Mr. Fred Heim (Los Angeles only)

CAT. 43

Marcel Duchamp, *From or by Marcel Duchamp or Rrose Sélavy (The Box in a Valise)*, 1935–1941, paper, board, and mixed media, 16⅛ × 14⅞ × 4⅛ in. (41 × 37.8 × 10.5 cm), Los Angeles County Museum of Art, Gift of The Grinstein Family (Los Angeles only)

CAT. 44

Lucas Samaras, *Untitled*, 1963, box, photographs, pins, and colored yarn, 10¼ × 14⅜ × 8 in. (26 × 36.5 × 20.3 cm), Los Angeles County Museum of Art, Michael and Dorothy Blankfort Bequest

CAT. 45

James Rosenquist, *Toaster*, 1963, oil on vinyl, chromed barbed wire, metal saw blades, plastic, and wood, with dripped paint, 11¾ × 9¼ × 12½ in. (29.9 × 23.5 × 31.8 cm), Frederick R. Weisman Art Foundation, Los Angeles

CAT. 46

Andy Warhol, *Brillo Box*, c. 1964, house paint and silkscreen ink on plywood, 13⅛ × 16 × 11½ in. (33.3 × 40.6 × 29.2 cm), Whitney Museum of American Art, New York, Gift of The American Contemporary Art Foundation, Inc., Leonard A. Lauder, President

CAT. 47

Andy Warhol, *Brillo Box*, c. 1964, house paint and silkscreen ink on plywood, 13⅛ × 16 × 11½ in. (33.3 × 40.6 × 29.2 cm), Whitney Museum of American Art, New York, Gift of The American Contemporary Art Foundation, Inc., Leonard A. Lauder, President

CAT. 48

Andy Warhol, *Brillo Box*, c. 1964, house paint and silkscreen ink on plywood, 13⅛ × 16 × 11½ in. (33.3 × 40.6 × 29.2 cm), Whitney Museum of American Art, New York, Gift of The American Contemporary Art Foundation, Inc., Leonard A. Lauder, President

CAT. 49

Larry Bell, *Lux at the Ferus*, 1961–1962, glass, household mirror, wood, and paint, 13 × 11¾ × 4⅞ in. (33 × 29.9 × 12.4 cm), The Museum of Contemporary Art, Los Angeles, Gift of Michael Asher (Los Angeles only)

CAT. 50

Ken Price, *White and Grey*, 1962, enclosed fired and painted clay, 8¼ × 10¼ × 6 in. (21 × 26 × 15.2 cm), The Museum of Contemporary Art, Los Angeles, Gift of Michael Asher (Los Angeles only)

CAT. 51

Ronald Miyashiro, *Concord #9*, 1963, wood, cardboard, and acrylic, 10⅝ × 15¹⁄₁₆ × 8¼ in. (27 × 38.3 × 21 cm), Collection of the artist (Los Angeles only)

CAT. 52

Daniel LaRue Johnson, *The Big N*, 1963, painted wood and mixed media, 8¼ × 6¾ × 3⅜ in. (21 × 17.2 × 8.6 cm), Gift of Allison Banks Herbert, Collection of the California African American Museum (Los Angeles only)

CAT. 53

Edward Kienholz, *Portrait of Virginia*, 1963, metal, wood, glass, bottle, lightbulb, battery, plaster, and polyester resin, 43½ × 19½ × 11½ in. (110.5 × 49.5 × 29.2 cm), Collection of Virginia Dwan

CAT. 54

Edward Kienholz, *Back Seat Dodge '38*, 1964, paint, fiberglass and flock, 1938 Dodge, recorded music and player, chicken wire, beer bottles, artificial grass, and cast plaster figures, 66 × 120 × 156 in. (167.6 × 304.8 × 396.2 cm), Los Angeles County Museum of Art, Purchased with funds provided by the Art Museum Council Fund

CAT. 55

Edward Kienholz, *After the Ball Is Over #1*, 1965, concept tableau, plaque: 9¼ × 11¾ in. (23.5 × 29.8 cm), framed concept: 13⅜ × 9¼ in. (33.7 × 23.5 cm), Collection of Nancy Reddin Kienholz, Courtesy of L.A. Louver, Venice, California

CAT. 56

Edward Kienholz and Jean Tinguely, *The American Trip*, 1966, concept tableau, plaque: 9¼ × 11¾ in. (23.5 × 29.9 cm), framed concept: 13⅜ × 9¼ in. (34 × 23.5 cm), Collection of Nancy Reddin Kienholz, Courtesy of L.A. Louver, Venice, California

CAT. 57

Mark di Suvero, *Pre-Columbian*, 1965/2004, wood, steel, iron, tire, and paint, 98 × 171 × 110½ in. (248.9 × 434.3 × 280.7 cm), Fine Arts Museums of San Francisco, Gift of Mr. and Mrs. Lowell McKegney (Washington only)

CAT. 58

Sol LeWitt, *Modular Wall Structure*, 1968, baked enamel on aluminum, 88½ × 88½ × 10 in. (224.8 × 224.8 × 25.4 cm), Collection of Virginia Dwan

CAT. 59

Robert Morris, *Untitled (Battered Cubes)*, 1966, painted fiberglass, 4 units: each 24 × 36 × 36 in. (61 × 91.4 × 91.4 cm), overall installed: 108 × 108 in. (274.3 × 274.3 cm), Collection of Virginia Dwan

CAT. 60

Ad Reinhardt, *Ultimate Painting*, 1963, oil on canvas, 60 × 60 in. (152.4 × 152.4 cm), Collection of Virginia Dwan

CAT. 61

Agnes Martin, *The Cliff*, 1967, acrylic and graphite on canvas, 72 × 72 in. (182.9 × 182.9 cm), Collection of Virginia Dwan

CAT. 62

Jo Baer, *Horizontals Flanking (Small, Thalo-Green Line)*, 1968, oil on canvas (diptych), each panel: 34 × 48 in. (86.4 × 121.9 cm), both panels installed: 34 × 99⅛ in. (86.4 × 251.8 cm), National Gallery of Art, Washington, The Dorothy and Herbert Vogel Collection

CAT. 63

Donald Judd, *Untitled*, 1965, galvanized iron and green Plexiglas, 6 × 27 × 24 in. (15.2 × 68.6 × 61 cm), National Gallery of Art, Washington, The Dorothy and Herbert Vogel Collection, Ailsa Mellon Bruce Fund, Patrons' Permanent Fund, and Gift of Dorothy and Herbert Vogel

CAT. 64

Dan Flavin, *"monument" for V. Tatlin*, 1966, cool white fluorescent light, height: 144 in. (365.8 cm), National Gallery of Art, Washington, Gift of Virginia Dwan (Washington only)

CAT. 65

Dan Flavin, *"monument" on the survival of Mrs. Reppin*, 1966, warm white and red fluorescent light, 6¾ × 84¼ in. (17.2 × 214 cm), Norton Simon Museum, Pasadena, California, Museum Purchase, Fellows Acquisition Fund (Los Angeles only)

CAT. 66

Carl Andre, *64 Steel Square*, 1967, hot rolled steel (64 units), ⅜ × 64 × 64 in. (1 × 162.6 × 162.6 cm), National Gallery of Art, Washington, Gift of Edward R. Broida

CAT. 67

Robert Smithson, *Glass Stratum*, 1967, glass, 17½ × 84 × 12 in. (44.5 × 213.4 × 30.5 cm), National Gallery of Art, Washington, Gift of Virginia Dwan

CAT. 68

Fred Sandback, *Blue Corner Piece*, 1970, blue elastic cord, 72 × 72 in. (182.9 × 182.9 cm), Collection of Virginia Dwan

CAT. 69

Kenneth Snelson, *V–X*, 1968, stainless steel and wire cable, height: 72 in. (182.9 cm); diameter: 120 in. (304.8 cm), National Gallery of Art, Washington, Gift of the artist (Washington only)

CAT. 70

Sol LeWitt, *Serial Project, 1 (ABCD)*, 1966, baked enamel on steel units over baked enamel on aluminum, 20 × 163 × 163 in. (50.8 × 414 × 414 cm), The Museum of Modern Art, New York, Gift of Agnes Gund and purchase (by exchange), 1978 (Washington only)

CAT. 71

Sol LeWitt, *Sol LeWitt, Dwan Gallery, Los Angeles*, April 1967, offset print on light brown paper, 14 × 14 in. (35.5 × 35.5 cm), Collection of Virginia Dwan (Washington only) / Los Angeles County Museum of Art, Balch Art Research Library (Los Angeles only)

CAT. 72

Sol LeWitt, *B 2-5-8 (s)*, 1967, painted aluminum, 13½ × 48¾ × 13½ in. (34.3 × 123.8 × 34.3 cm), The Museum of Contemporary Art, Los Angeles, Gift of Lannan Foundation (Los Angeles only)

CAT. 73

Sol LeWitt, *I, II, III, IV*, 1969, ink and pencil on paper, framed: 17¾ × 17¾ × 1⅛ in. (45.1 × 45.1 × 2.9 cm), Los Angeles County Museum of Art, Gift of Robert H. Halff through the Modern and Contemporary Art Council (Los Angeles only)

CAT. 74

William Anastasi, *Issue*, 1966/2016, wall removal, variable height × 4½ × approximately ¼ in. (variable height × 11.4 × approximately .6 cm), Collection of Virginia Dwan (Washington only)

CAT. 75

Robert Morris, *Card File*, 1962, metal, wood, and paper, 26 15/16 × 10⅝ × 1 9/16 in. (68.5 × 27 × 4 cm), Centre Pompidou, Paris, Collection du Musée national d'art moderne/Centre de création industrielle

CAT. 76

Eleanor Antin, *Blood of a Poet Box*, 1965–1968, wood box containing ninety-four glass slides of blood specimens and specimen list, 11½ × 7¾ × 1½ in. (29.2 × 19.7 × 3.8 cm), Lent by the American Fund for the Tate Gallery 2009

CAT. 77

Carl Andre, *Passport*, 1963, typewritten text in red on paper, sheet: 10 15/16 × 8½ in. (27.8 × 21.6 cm), Collection of Virginia Dwan

CAT. 78

Carl Andre, *Passport*, 1963, typewritten text in red on two sheets of paper, each sheet: 10 15/16 × 8½ in. (27.8 × 21.6 cm), Collection of Virginia Dwan

CAT. 79

Carl Andre, *Passport*, 1963, typewritten text in black on two sheets of paper, each sheet: 10 15/16 × 8½ in. (27.8 × 21.6 cm), Collection of Virginia Dwan

CAT. 80

Rosemarie Castoro, *A Day in the Life of a Conscientious Objector*, 1969, digital projection, 11 × 8½ in. (27.9 × 21.6 cm), Courtesy of the Estate of Rosemarie Castoro and Broadway 1602 Uptown & Harlem

CAT. 81

Robert Smithson, *Pulverizations*, 1966, gelatin silver print (Photostat), sheet: 11 × 8½ in. (27.9 × 21.6 cm), Collection of Virginia Dwan

CAT. 82

Lawrence Weiner, *Structure Poem*, 1968, pen and black ink on graph paper, sheet: 11 × 8½ in. (27.9 × 21.6 cm), National Gallery of Art, Washington, The Dorothy and Herbert Vogel Collection

CAT. 83

Joseph Kosuth, *'Titled (Art as Idea as Idea)' [real]*, 1968, mounted photograph, 48 × 48 in. (121.9 × 121.9 cm), Courtesy of the artist and Sean Kelly Gallery

CAT. 84

Mel Bochner, *Language Is Not Transparent*, 1970, chalk on paint and wall, template: 36 × 48¼ in. (91.4 × 122.6 cm), overall installation: 72 × 48¼ in. (182.9 × 122.6 cm), Los Angeles County Museum of Art, Modern and Contemporary Art Council Fund

CAT. 85

Nancy Holt, *Detach Here*, 1967, ink on paper, 8 × 8½ in. (20.3 × 21.6 cm), Estate of the artist

CAT. 86

Shusaku Arakawa, *Untitled ('Stolen')*, 1969, oil on canvas, 72 × 48 in. (182.9 × 121.9 cm), Wadsworth Atheneum Museum of Art, Hartford, Connecticut, Gift of "The Thieves": Gregory, Landis, Lewis, Crane and Kahn

CAT. 87

Lee Lozano, *Untitled (Party/Paranoia, Painting, Real Money)*, Vol. 2, pages 32, 33, 33A, #s 394, 395, 396, March 15, 1969–July 9, 1969, graphite and ink on paper, each sheet: 11 × 9 in. (27.9 × 22.9 cm), framed: 12⅜ × 28⅞ in. (31.4 × 73.3 cm), Wadsworth Atheneum Museum of Art, Hartford, Connecticut. Alexander A. Goldfarb Contemporary Art Acquisition Fund

CAT. 88

Edward Kienholz, *For Reducing Virginia's Account to Zero*, 1972, aquarelle and ink on paper, framed: 12 × 14 in. (30.5 × 35.6 cm), Collection of Virginia Dwan (Washington only)

CAT. 89

Robert Smithson, *Gyrostasis*, 1967, painted steel, 41½ × 30 × 24 in. (105.4 × 76.2 × 61 cm), Collection of Virginia Dwan

CAT. 90

Robert Smithson, *Aerial Map: Proposal for Dallas–Fort Worth Regional Airport*, 1967, gelatin silver print collage, sheet: 14 × 10¹¹⁄₁₆ in. (35.5 × 27.2 cm), Collection of Virginia Dwan

CAT. 91

Robert Morris, *Model and Cross-Section for Project in Earth and Sod*, 1966, plaster model, 20 × 24 in. (50.8 × 61 cm), Collection of the artist, courtesy of Castelli Gallery

CAT. 92

Carl Andre, *Proposal for Airport Sculpture*, 1968, graphite on lined notebook paper, sheet (irregular): 7⅝ × 5 in. (19.4 × 12.7 cm), Collection of Virginia Dwan

CAT. 93

Sol LeWitt, *Buried Cube (layout for book page)*, undated, black-and-white photographs, ink, and graphite on graph paper, framed: 13⅝ × 19⅝ × 1½ in. (34.6 × 49.9 × 3.8 cm), LeWitt Collection, Chester, Connecticut

CAT. 94

Robert Smithson, *A Nonsite, Pine Barrens, New Jersey*, 1967 (map), Photostat with typed text, 12⅝ × 10⅝ in. (32 × 27 cm); 1968 (nonsite), painted aluminum, sand, and painted wood, 12 × 65½ × 65½ in. (30.5 × 166.4 × 166.4 cm), National Gallery of Art, Washington, Gift of Virginia Dwan

CAT. 95

Robert Smithson, *Nonsite #2*, 1967, cut-out map and text on paper, sheet: 27⅜ × 21³⁄₁₆ in. (69.5 × 53.8 cm), Collection of Virginia Dwan (Washington only)

CAT. 96

Dennis Oppenheim, *2-Dimensional Information (Contour Lines) / Transferred from Point A to Location B / Lines scribed on swamp grid with sickle-mower / Cuts filled with aluminum filings / (residue from aluminum borings) / Piece completely submerged in water / at high tide 12:00 noon / Size: 175′ × 200′ Photo: Infrared aero-film*, 1969, chromogenic color prints, map, typewritten text on paper, 28¼ × 22⅜ × ¹⁵⁄₁₆ in. (71.8 × 56.8 × 2.4 cm), The Museum of Modern Art, New York. Partial gift of the Daled Collection and partial purchase through the generosity of Maja Oeri and Hans Bodenmann, Sue and Edgar Wachenheim III, Marlene Hess and James D. Zirin, Agnes Gund, Marie-Josée and Henry R. Kravis, and Jerry I. Speyer and Katherine G. Farley

CAT. 97

Carl Andre, *Log Piece*, 1968, chromogenic print, 20⅜₁₆ × 30 in. (51.7 × 76.2 cm), Collection of Virginia Dwan

CAT. 98

Robert Smithson, *Inverted Tree*, 1969, ink on paper, sheet: 17⅛ × 14¹⁄₁₆ in. (43.5 × 35.7 cm), Collection of Virginia Dwan

CAT. 99

Michael Heizer, *Displaced/Replaced Mass (1/3)*, 1969, 30-ton granite block in concrete depression, 22 feet 7⅝ in. × 5 feet 11⅝ in. × 4 feet 11¾ in. (6.9 × 1.8 × 1.5 m), Silver Springs, Nevada. No longer extant. Represented in the exhibition by a documentary photograph taken in 1969 by Michael Heizer.

Michael Heizer, *Displaced/Replaced Mass (2/3)*, 1969, 52-ton granite block in concrete depression, 50 feet 2⅜ in. × 15 feet 9 in. × 9 feet 2¼ in. (15.3 × 4.8 × 2.8 m), Silver Springs, Nevada. No longer extant. Represented in the exhibition by a documentary photograph taken in 1969 by Michael Heizer.

Michael Heizer, *Displaced/Replaced Mass (3/3)*, 1969, 68-ton granite block in concrete depression, 41 feet 4 in. × 10 feet 11½ in. × 9 feet 2¼ in. (12.6 × 3.3 × 2.8 m), Silver Springs, Nevada. No longer extant. Represented in the exhibition by a documentary photograph taken in 1969 by Michael Heizer.

CAT. 100

Michael Heizer, *Bolivia/Nevada*, 1970, photo offset on aluminum plate, framed: 36½ × 44⅝ in. (92.7 × 113.4 cm), Collection of Virginia Dwan

CAT. 101

Michael Heizer, *Scientific American*, 1970, photo offset on aluminum plate, framed: 36½ × 44½ in. (92.7 × 113 cm), Collection of Virginia Dwan

CAT. 102

Michael Heizer, *Double Negative*, 1969, 240,000-ton displacement of rhyolite and sandstone, 1,500 × 50 × 30 feet (457.2 × 15.2 × 9.1 m), Mormon Mesa, Overton, Nevada. Museum of Contemporary Art, Los Angeles. Represented in the exhibition by a photomural of a documentary photograph taken in 1969 by Tom Vinetz.

CAT. 103

Walter De Maria, *High Energy Bar*, 1966, stainless steel, 1½ × 14 × 1½ in. (3.8 × 35.6 × 3.8 cm), engraved: "No. 54 HIGH ENERGY BAR ©WALTER DE MARIA 1966," Collection of Virginia Dwan

CAT. 104

Walter De Maria, *35-Pole Lightning Field*, 1974, 35 stainless-steel poles spaced 200 feet apart, height: 18 feet (5.5 m), overall: rectangular grid array (seven poles long × five poles wide). Original installation on flat, isolated land in northern Arizona. Removed from site and donated to Dia Art Foundation, New York. As of 2016, the work has not been reinstalled. Represented in the exhibition by a photomural of a photograph taken in 1974 by Helen Winkler-Fosdick.

CAT. 105

Walter De Maria, *Lightning Field*, 1977, 400 stainless-steel poles spaced 220 feet apart, average height: 20⅔ feet (6.3 m), overall dimensions: 1 mile × 1 kilometer. Long-term installation in Quemado, New Mexico. Commissioned and maintained by the Dia Art Foundation, New York.

CAT. 106

Charles Ross, *Stack of Two Prisms*, 1970, Plexiglas and fluid, 18 × 43½ × 8 in. (45.7 × 110.5 × 20.3 cm), Collection of Virginia Dwan (Washington only)

CAT. 107

Charles Ross, *Solar Burn 1/29/77*, 1977, painted wooden panel burned by the sun, 14¼ × 16¼ in. (36.2 × 41.3 cm), Collection of Virginia Dwan

CAT. 108

Charles Ross, *Star Axis*, 1971–ongoing, granite, sandstone, bronze, stainless steel, and earth, 11 stories high by one-tenth of a mile long, Chupinas Mesa, New Mexico. Represented in the exhibition by a photomural of a photograph taken in 2015 by Kerry Loewen.

CAT. 109

Robert Smithson, *Spiral Jetty*, 1970, black basalt rocks and earth, 1,500 × 15 feet (457.2 × 4.6 m), Great Salt Lake, Utah. Dia Art Foundation, New York. Represented in the exhibition by a photomural of a photograph taken in 1970 by Gianfranco Gorgoni

CAT. 110

Robert Smithson, *Spiral Jetty*, 1970, graphite on paper, sheet: 9 × 11$\frac{15}{16}$ in. (22.8 × 30.3 cm), Collection of Virginia Dwan

CAT. 111

Robert Smithson, *Spiral Island with Curved Jetty*, 1970, graphite on paper, sheet: 14$\frac{1}{16}$ × 17$\frac{1}{16}$ in. (35.7 × 43.4 cm), Collection of Virginia Dwan

CAT. 112

Robert Smithson, *Green Island–Spiral Island*, 1970, graphite and crayon on paper, sheet: 17¾ × 19 in. (45.1 × 48.3 cm), Collection of Virginia Dwan

CAT. 113

Robert Smithson, *Pierced Spiral*, 1971, graphite on paper, sheet: 18$\frac{13}{16}$ × 23$\frac{15}{16}$ in. (47.8 × 59.2 cm), Collection of Virginia Dwan

CAT. 114

Robert Smithson, *Untitled*, 1970, ink on paper, sheet: 11⅞ × 9 in. (30.2 × 22.9 cm), Collection of Virginia Dwan

CAT. 115

Robert Smithson, *Movie Treatment for Spiral Jetty (part I)*, 1971, photographic enlargement, graphite touch-ups, sheet: 38$\frac{3}{16}$ × 47¾ in. (97 × 121.3 cm), Collection of Virginia Dwan

CAT. 116

Robert Smithson, *Movie Treatment for Spiral Jetty (part II)*, 1971, photographic enlargement, graphite touch-ups, sheet: 38⅛ × 47⅛ in. (96.8 × 119.7 cm), Collection of Virginia Dwan

CAT. 117

Robert Smithson, *Movie Treatment 3, Spiral Jetty*, 1970, graphite on paper, sheet: 12 × 9 in. (30.5 × 22.9 cm), Collection of Virginia Dwan

CAT. 118

Robert Smithson, *The Earth's History*, 1970, graphite on paper, sheet (irregular): 19 × 24 in. (48.2 × 60.9 cm), Collection of Virginia Dwan

CAT. 119

Robert Smithson, *Movie Treatment 8, Spiral Jetty*, 1970, graphite on paper, sheet: 11⅞ × 9 1/16 in. (30.2 × 23 cm), Collection of Virginia Dwan

CAT. 120

Robert Smithson, *Movie Treatment 9, Spiral Jetty*, 1970, graphite on paper, sheet: 11⅞ × 9 1/16 in. (30.2 × 23 cm), Collection of Virginia Dwan

CAT. 121

Robert Smithson, *Clockwise & Counterclockwise Revolution Shot from Copter*, 1970, graphite on paper, sheet (irregular): 19 × 24 in. (48.2 × 60.9 cm), Collection of Virginia Dwan

CAT. 122

Robert Smithson, *The Spiral Jetty, Great Salt Lake, Utah*, 1970, graphite on paper, sheet: 19 × 23 13/16 in. (48.2 × 60.5 cm), Collection of Virginia Dwan

CAT. 123

Robert Smithson, *The Spiral Jetty, Great Salt Lake, Utah*, 1970, graphite on paper, sheet: 19 × 24 in. (48.2 × 60.9 cm), Collection of Virginia Dwan

CAT. 124

Robert Smithson, *Spiral Jetty*, 1970, 16 mm film, Collection of Virginia Dwan

CAT. 125

Robert Ryman, *untitled, Surface Veil 26″ × 26″*, 1970, oil on fiberglass on foamcore, 26 × 26 × ⅛ in. (66 × 66 × .32 cm), The Museum of Contemporary Art, Los Angeles, The Barry Lowen Collection (Los Angeles only)

CAT. 126

Robert Ryman, *Surface Veil #3*, 1970, oil on fiberglass panel mounted on featherboard, 39 × 39 in. (99.1 × 99.1 cm), Private Collection, New York (Washington only)

FIG. 21, PAGE 61

Edward Kienholz, *The Illegal Operation*, 1962, polyester resin, pigment, shopping cart, wooden stool, concrete, lamp, fabric, basin, metal pots, blanket, hooked rug, and medical equipment, 59 × 48 × 54 in. (149.9 × 121.9 × 137.2 cm), Los Angeles County Museum of Art, Partial gift of Betty and Monte Factor and purchased with funds provided by the Art Museum Council, Daniel Greenberg and Susan Steinhauser, the Modern and Contemporary Art Council, Dallas Price-Van Breda and Bob Van Breda, the Robert H. Halff Fund, David G. Booth and Suzanne Deal Booth, Virginia Dwan, Elaine and Bram Goldsmith, The Grinstein Family, Ric and Suzanne Kayne, Alice and Nahum Lainer, Frederick R. Weisman Art Foundation, Mrs. Harry Lenart, The Robert Gore Rifkind Foundation, Philippa Calnan and Laura Lee Woods (Los Angeles only)

NOT ILLUSTRATED

Charles Ross, *Six Prisms from the Origin of Colors*, 1970, Plexiglas and liquid-filled acrylic, six units, each: 98 × 18 × 18 in. (248.9 × 45.7 × 45.7 cm), Los Angeles County Museum of Art, Gift of Virginia Dwan (Los Angeles only)

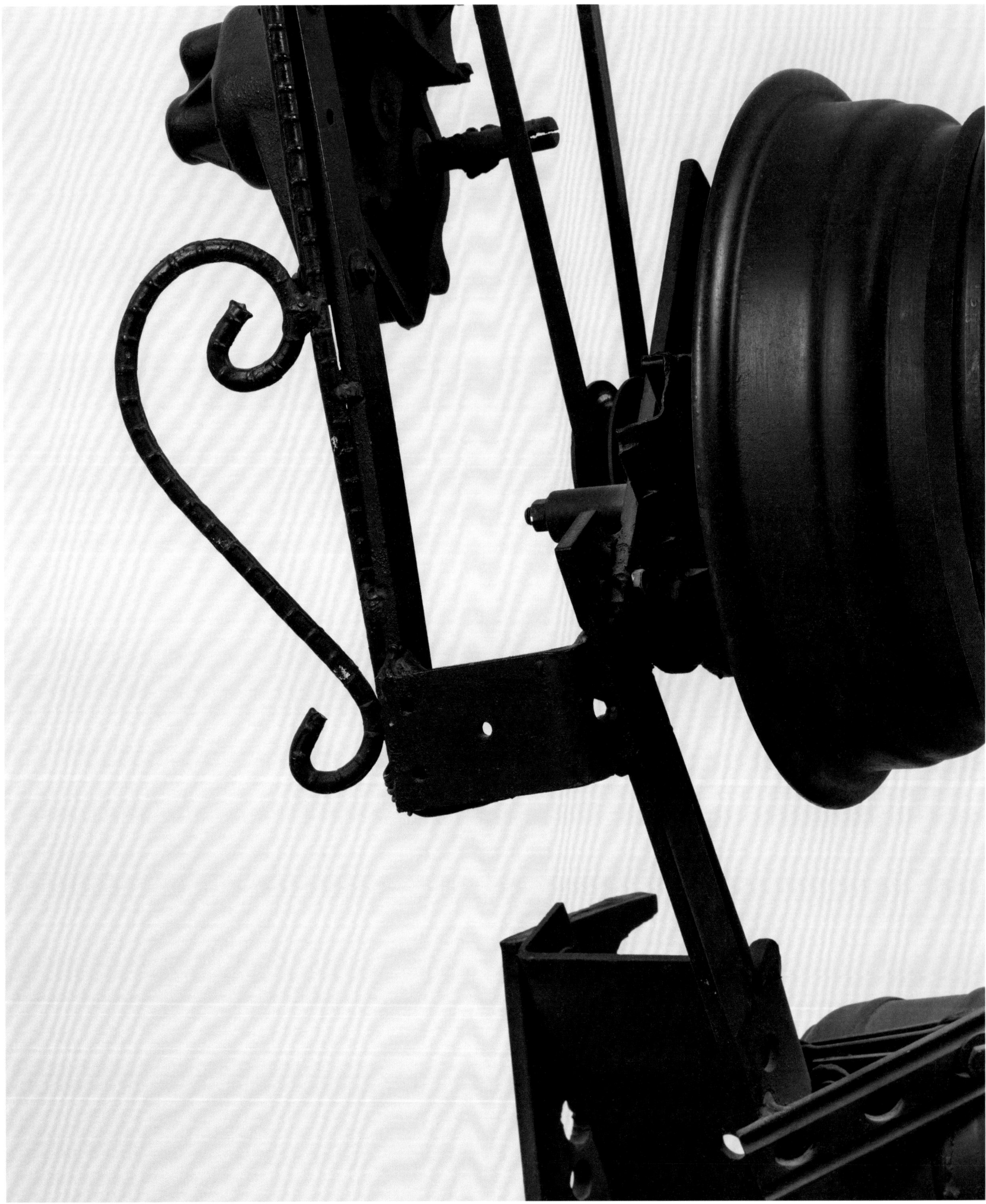

NOTES

The Art Gallery in an Era of Mobility

1 Charles F. Stuckey, "Interview with Virginia Dwan," Archives of American Art, Smithsonian Institution, Washington (hereafter "Interview," AAA), March 21–June 7, 1984, tape 8.

2 The Kinks, "This Time Tomorrow" (1970).

3 The trip lasted two-and-a-half weeks. Smithson's calendar indicates that he returned from Mérida on May 2, and Holt on May 4. Datebook of Robert Smithson, Robert Smithson Papers, AAA, microfilm roll #3822.

4 Robert Hobbs, *Robert Smithson: Sculpture* (Ithaca, 1981), 231.

5 During the Sanibel trip shells were gathered for a third work, *Nonsite Mirror with Crushed Shells (Sanibel Island)*, 1969, that Smithson completed in New York.

6 Smithson planned the Yucatán itinerary. Holt made the arrangements for the trip and shopped with Dwan for backpacks, hammocks, and other supplies before they left. (E-mail, Anne Kovach, Dwan Gallery Archive, October 27, 2015.) Dwan's interest in Mexico preceded the Yucatán trip. She had traveled with Jean Tinguely and Niki de Saint Phalle to Cabo San Lucas in the Baja in 1963 and visited Mexico again in 1968, in part with the idea of "blazing a trail to the Yucatan" to gather "ideas for our trip." (Postcard from Dwan to Robert Smithson, February 20, 1968, Robert Smithson Papers, AAA.) Dwan's interest in Mesoamerican sites was initially triggered by Sibylle Cles-Reden, *The Realm of the Great Goddess: The Story of the Megalith Builders* (London, 1961), a book that was given to her by Carl Andre. A word of thanks to Mary Miller for inspiring my interest in Mesoamerican art and for discussing the Yucatán journey with me.

7 "They were both so terribly bright and brilliant. It was Bob and Bob." (Stuckey, "Interview," AAA, tape 10.) Smithson's first *Upside-Down Tree* was made in Alfred, New York; the third at Yaxchilan the week after they left Sanibel. Hobbs, *Robert Smithson*, 149, 164.

8 See the Dantesque interpretation of Smithson's trees in Suzaan Boettger, "In the Yucatan: Mirroring Presence and Absence" in Eugenie Tsai and Cornelia Butler, eds. *Robert Smithson* (Museum of Contemporary Art, Los Angeles, 2004), 204–205.

9 Smithson's attack on biological conceptions of growth and time in favor of geological metaphors of "inorganic time" is advanced in his essays "Entropy and the New Monuments" (1966) and "Quasi-Infinities and the Waning of Space" (1966) reprinted in *Robert Smithson: The Collected Writings* (Berkeley, 1996), 10–23, 34–37.

10 Hobbs, *Robert Smithson*, 146.

11 In his first published travelogue, "The Crystal Land" (1966), Smithson mentions four travelers by name (himself, Holt, Donald Judd, and Julie Finch Judd). In "A Tour of the Monuments of Passaic, New Jersey" (1967) we encounter a first-person narrator. "Incidents of Mirror-Travel in the Yucatan" (1969) is devoid of human travelers. The impersonal third-person ("one") and second-person ("you") appear sporadically.

12 Dwan also took exposures of a cemetery, a major theme of her later photographic practice. Charles F. Stuckey, unpublished chronology, Virginia Dwan private archives, New York.

13 Smithson, "Incidents of Mirror-Travel in the Yucatan," *Artforum* 8, no. 1 (September 1969): 30.

14 Smithson, "Incidents of Mirror-Travel in the Yucatan," 30.

15 Another section of film, poorly exposed, depicts the jungle, and another the Usumacinta River and its shore shot from the moving dugout discussed below.

16 Dwan recalled to Ann Reynolds that Smithson assigned godlike identities to each of the travelers. Smithson was Tezcatlipoca, Aztec god of the night sky, ancestral memory, and time; Dwan was Coatlicue, Serpent Lady/Earth Mother. Dwan did not recall the god assigned to Holt. Reynolds, *Robert Smithson: Learning from New Jersey and Elsewhere* (Cambridge, MA, 2003), 280, n. 106.

17 Stuckey, "Interview," AAA, tape 9.

18 Smithson, "Incidents of Mirror-Travel in the Yucatan," 32.

19 As argued in Jennifer Roberts, *Mirror-Travels: Robert Smithson and History* (New Haven, 2004), 98–103.

20 See Anton Ehrenzweig, *The Hidden Order of Art: A Study in the Psychology of Artistic Imagination* (Berkeley, 1967). Smithson's absorption of Ehrenzweig's model is discussed in Roberts, *Mirror-Travels*, 98–103, and in Reynolds, *Robert Smithson*, 206–207.

21 Author's telephone conversation with Dwan, October 22, 2015.

22 On the emergence of site-specificity and related notions of "space" and "place" during the late 1960s, see Emily Taub Webb, "On Site-Specificity: A Genealogy," PhD dissertation, Emory University, 2010, and Miwon Kwon, *One Place After Another: Site-Specific Art and Locational Identity* (Cambridge, MA, 2014).

23 The classic account of this space is Brian O'Doherty, *Inside the White Cube: The Ideology of the Gallery Space* (Santa Monica, 1976).

24 Such as the works of William Anastasi discussed below and the Institutional Critique practices of artists like Michael Asher and Daniel Buren.

25 Daniel Buren, "The Function of the Studio," in *October: The First Decade* (Cambridge, MA, 1987), 201. On the transition from portable sculptural objects to site-specific endeavors, see Rosalind E. Krauss, "Sculpture in the Expanded Field," in *The Originality of the Avant-Garde and Other Modernist Myths* (Cambridge, MA, 1985), 276–290.

26 A storage facility for works of fine art and other precious objects. Artworks held in freeports escape import taxes or duties, and are not taxed when sold. See David Segal, "Swiss Freeports Are Home for a Growing Treasury of Art," *New York Times* (July 21, 2012).

27 Smithson, "Incidents of Mirror-Travel in the Yucatan," 32–33.

28 Stuckey, "Interview," AAA, tape 8.

29 My description of the two sites as "dialectical" is a modification of an earlier discussion that construed these models as oppositional. See author's "The Functional Site; Or, The Transformation of Site-Specificity" (1995) in Erika Suderburg, ed., *Space/Site/Intervention: Situating Installation Art* (Minneapolis, 2000), 23–37.

30 Douglas George Karsner,"'Leaving on a Jet Plane': Commercial Aviation, Airports and Post-Industrial American Society," PhD dissertation, Temple University, 1993, 288–289.

31 The Eisenhower plan followed the passage of the Collier-Burns Highway Act of 1947, which funded highway construction in California. Eric Avila, "All Freeways Lead to East Los Angeles: Rethinking the L.A. Freeway and Its Meanings," in Wim de Wit and Christopher James Alexander, eds., *Overdrive: L.A. Constructs the Future, 1940–1990* (J. Paul Getty Museum, Los Angeles, 2013), 38.

32 Tom Lewis, *Divided Highways: Building the Interstate Highways, Transforming American Life* (New York, 1997), ix.

33 On the military origins and nationalistic implications of jet propulsion technology in the US, see Jenifer Leigh Van Vleck, "No Distant Places: Aviation and the Global American Century," PhD dissertation, Yale University, 2009. My thanks to Martin Collins, curator, Smithsonian National Air and Space Museum, for this reference.

34 Karsner,"'Leaving on a Jet Plane,'" 288, and Vanessa R. Schwartz, "LAX: Designing for the Jet Age," in de Wit and Alexander, eds., *Overdrive*, 165–166.

35 Led by the ambitious CEO Juan Trippe, Pan American Airways offered the first intercontinental jet flight from New York to Paris on October 26, 1958. National Airlines offered the first domestic flight from New York to Miami on December 10, 1958. Karsner, "'Leaving on a Jet Plane,'" 176, and Schwartz, "LAX: Designing for the Jet Age," 165. The aviation firms Douglas Aircraft, Lockheed Corporation, Northrop Aircraft, and North American Aviation maintained their headquarters in Los Angeles.

36 Between 1955 and 1970 the annual number of domestic flyers grew from 38 to 153 million. The volume of international flyers to the US increased from a few thousand after World War II to approximately 16.2 million by 1970, also a direct result of jet travel. Schwartz, "LAX: Designing for the Jet Age," 166.

37 Karsner, "'Leaving on a Jet Plane,'" 180, 188.

38 Schwartz, "LAX: Designing for the Jet Age," 163–164.

39 See, e.g., Philip Leider, "The Cool School," *Artforum* 2, no. 12 (1964): 47–52, and Bar bara Rose, "Los Angeles: The Second City," *Art in America* 54, no. 1 (January/February 1966): 110–115. The East Coast/West Coast binary has proved to be extremely durable in discussions of minimal and pop formats in particular. Exchanges between practitioners on the two coasts are unexamined, and style and artistic identity are rendered transparent to locality. See Ken D. Allan, Lucy Bradnock, and Lisa Turvey, "For People Who Know the Difference: Defining the Pop Art Sixties," in Rebecca Peabody et al., eds., *Pacific Standard Time: Los Angeles Art 1945–1980* (J. Paul Getty Museum, Los Angeles, 2011), 124–182.

40 Needless to say, glossy art periodicals—the New York–based *Arts Magazine*, *Artnews*, and *Art in America*, the Lugano-based *Studio International*, and the California-based *Artforum*—were extremely influential during this period, circulating images of works and exhibitions and critical ideas.

41 The "long sixties"—a popular term for the period stretching roughly from the late fifties to the mid-to-late seventies—is at once the conclusion of high modernity and the instantiation of the "contemporary" (postmodernity, globalism: the era in which we now find ourselves broadly limned). On the pivotal nature of the sixties in accounts of contemporaneity, see the seminal essay by Fredric Jameson, "Periodizing the Sixties," in Sohnya Sayres et al., eds., *The Sixties without Apology* (Minneapolis, 1984), 178–220.

42 Elayne Varian, "Interview with Virginia Dwan of the Dwan Gallery," 1969, Exhibition Records of the Contemporary Wing of the Finch College Museum of Art, 1943–1975, Archives of American Art, Smithsonian Institution, Washington, unpaginated.

43 Stuckey, "Interview," AAA, tape 6.

44 Recent studies of the contemporary gallery include Christophe Cherix, *In and Out of Amsterdam: Travels in Conceptual Art, 1960–1976* (Museum of Modern Art, New York, 2009), which traces the transnational affiliations of artists based in Amsterdam, Los Angeles, and London associated with the Amsterdam-based gallery Art & Project, and Brigitte Kölle, ed., *Konrad Fischer: Okey Dokey* (Köln, 2008). Significant studies of modernist galleries include Rebecca A. Rabinow, ed., *Cézanne to Picasso: Ambroise Vollard, Patron of the Avant-Garde* (Metropolitan Museum of Art, New York, 2006) and Sylvie Patry, ed., *Inventing Impressionism: Paul Durand-Ruel and the Modern Art Market* (National Gallery, London, 2015).

45 The history of Dwan Gallery is deemphasized or omitted in many accounts of the sixties Los Angeles art scene. One exception is Hunter Drohojowska-Philp, *Rebels in Paradise: The Los Angeles Art Scene and the 1960s* (New York, 2011), 100–114. A scholarly volume forthcoming from MIT Press, edited by Anne Kovach, will do much to redress this lack.

46 Stuckey, "Interview," AAA, tape 1.

47 Stuckey, "Interview," AAA, tape 1.

48 Dwan spoke of the importance of promoting her artists' works through loans of works to university museums as "an educational matter rather than a selling situation.... We are more interested in getting the works out to be seen and let people know what is happening in the visual arts." Varian, "Interview with Virginia Dwan of the Dwan Gallery," unpaginated.

49 Stuckey, "Interview." AAA, tape 1.

50 Blum reduced the number of artists Ferus represented by Hopps and Kienholz from "seventy-odd to a dozen or so" West Coast artists, and shifted the focus of its program as discussed here. See Roberta Bernstein, "An Interview with Irving Blum" in *Ferus* (Gagosian Gallery, New York, 2002), 24.

51 Other notable spaces included the galleries of Felix Landau, Everett Ellin, Rolf Nelson, Nicholas Wilder, Huysman Gallery (the short-lived venture of art historian Henry Hopkins), Brockman Gallery (the venture of Dale and Alonzo Davis, a center of the Black Arts Movement), and the galleries of Eugenia Butler (who had previously worked at Dwan) and Riko Mizuno, among others. See Lucy Bradnock and Rani Singh, "Papa's Got a Brand New Bag: Crafting an Art Scene," 110–117; Allan, Bradnock, and Turvey, "For People Who Know the Difference," 128–143; and John Tain, "Riko Mizuno," 180, all in Peabody et al., *Pacific Standard Time*. On Brockman Gallery see Kellie Jones, *Now Dig This! Art and Black Los Angeles: 1960–1980* (Hammer Museum, Los Angeles, 2011). William Hackman, *Out of Sight: The Los Angeles Art Scene of the Sixties* (New York, 2015), mentions several of these spaces.

52 Blum quoted in Drohojowska-Philp, *Rebels in Paradise*, 101.

53 Coplans, "Circles of Style on the West Coast," *Art in America* 52, no. 3 (June 1964): 40.

54 Bereal quoted in Kristine McKenna, *The Ferus Gallery: A Place to Begin* (Göttingen, 2009), 155. Lawrence Weschler, "Edward Kienholz: Oral History Transcript," 1977, Oral History Program, University of California, Los Angeles, 277–278.

55 Shirley Nielson Blum quoted in McKenna, *The Ferus Gallery*, 206.

56 As does the fact that Ferus was also backed by a woman patron. Sadye Moss bought a one-third interest in Ferus in 1958 and underwrote its activities for five years. See Drohojowska-Philp, *Rebels in Paradise*, 38.

57 Stuckey, "Interview," AAA, tape 1.

58 Recalling his efforts to show Rauschenberg, Blum remarked: "That territory was already occupied" by Dwan. Bernstein, "An Interview with Irving Blum," 35.

59 Blum staged the first West Coast exhibitions of Jasper Johns, Frank Stella, Roy Lichtenstein, Ellsworth Kelly, and Andy Warhol (Warhol's first gallery show of *Campbell's Soup Cans* anywhere). The New York gallery careers of Larry Bell and Ruscha were launched by Blum.

60 Among the New York galleries Dwan collaborated with during the gallery's Los Angeles years were Stephen Radich, Tibor de Nagy, Green, Castelli, Stable, Alexander Iolas, and Sidney Janis.

61 Completed by the Janss Investment Company in 1929, the building is located across the street from the company's headquarters, the former Janss Dome Building.

62 The gallery was approximately fifty-feet long by nearly twenty-three-feet wide.

63 The clerestory window was often covered to favor the even, artificial light of the track lamps.

64 Hamner & Son Collegemen's Shop was the original tenant of the space. See Mark Wanamaker, *Westwood (Images of America)* (Mount Pleasant, SC, 2010), 91.

65 An exhibition of the lyrical abstract painter Stanley Twardowicz occurred in the months preceding Kanemitsu's show.

66 Organized by the museum's International Council, the exhibition traveled to eight European venues in 1958–1959.

67 Brata, Hansa, and Tanager were the best-known 10th Street spaces. Dwan worked with 57th Street and Upper East Side galleries during this period. For a critical account of 10th Street style see Clement Greenberg, "Post-Painterly Abstraction" (1964), in *Clement Greenberg: The Collected Essays and Criticism*, ed. John O'Brian (Chicago, 1993), 4:192–197.

68 Jules Langsner, "Art News from Los Angeles," *Artnews* 59, no. 1 (March 1960): 51. Kanemitsu's Asian American identity is a recurring theme in discussions of his work. Born in Ogden, UT, in 1922 and a resident of Japan in childhood, Kanemitsu returned to the US in 1940 and was placed in a Japanese-American internment camp in 1941. Studying with Fernand Léger and Yasuo Kuniyoshi after the war, he settled in New York before relocating to Los Angeles in the sixties after having spent time there preparing his exhibitions at Dwan and making prints at June Wayne's Tamarind Lithography Workshop in 1961. For a thoughtful discussion of the artist and his work, see John Yau, "Kanemitsu in Los Angeles During the Sixties and Seventies," *Brooklyn Rail* (May 6, 2008).

69 Henry Seldis, "Promising Import," *Los Angeles Times* (May 8, 1960): E17.

70 The Goodnough show was "the most successful" of 1960, according to a letter of November 4, 1960, from Eugenie K. Thompson to Samuel M. Kootz, Dwan Gallery Archive.

71 Robert Richenburg, Paul Brach, Raymond Parker, Larry Rivers, and Stanley Twardowicz had one-person shows at Dwan Gallery. *15 of New York* also included works by Norman Bluhm, Grace Hartigan, Paul Jenkins, and Adja Yunkers.

72 *Fourteen from New York*, January 18–February 13, 1960. The artists included James Brooks, Arshile Gorky, Philip Guston, Hans Hoffman, Franz Kline, Willem de Kooning, Joan Mitchell, Robert Motherwell, Barnett Newman, Louise Nevelson, Jackson Pollock, Milton Resnick, Mark Rothko, and Jack Tworkov. McKenna, *The Ferus Gallery*, 201.

73 Dwan had wanted solo shows of both artists, but there were not enough works available to her from their New York dealer, Sidney Janis. Stuckey, "Interview," AAA, tape 2. As it turned out, the double format caused for unflattering comparisons. Henry Seldis praised the "directness and architectural strength" of Kline's work and acknowledged Guston's "craftsmanship," yet found Guston's paintings "lacking poetry and excitement." Seldis, "In the Galleries: Shows Have a N.Y. Flavor," *Los Angeles Times* (April 7, 1961): IIA6.

74 In an early account of Guston's mid-1950s' works H.H. Arnason spoke of their "sense of order, of structure" coupled with "rougher, more violent" textures and brushstrokes: *Philip Guston* (New York, 1962), 27.

75 I owe this detail to David McKee, who recalled a remark by Guston that the black shape in *Sleeper II* was inspired by Rothko's hat.

76 On Dwan's checklist for the show, the title *Torres* is written by hand, implying that the work was a late addition. One of the few works in the exhibition to sell, it would join *Black Sienna*, *Garcia*, and another work, *Harleman*, in the Kline memorial show that Dwan organized in March 1963.

77 Larry Rivers with Arnold Weinstein, *What Did I Do?: The Unauthorized Autobiography* (New York, 1992), 372.

78 Harold Rosenberg, "The American Action Painters" (1952), in David Shapiro and Cecile Shapiro, eds., *Abstract Expressionism: A Critical Record* (Cambridge, 1990), 75–85.

79 For example, *Drugstore* (1959) blended the thick gestural brushwork of de Kooning and Kline with mimetic depictions of a pharmacist and customers along with stenciled references to medications and Kodak film. Several works, including *King of Spades* and *Jack of Spades* (both 1960) alluded to playing cards.

80 In his third of several visits to Paris, Rivers took a French conversation class and befriended two neighbors, the couple Jean Tinguely and Niki de Saint Phalle, leading to a collaborative work by Rivers and Tinguely, *The Friendship of America and France* (1962).

81 Reinhardt had been omitted from the Museum of Modern Art's *New American Painting* exhibition (1958). The influential critic Clement Greenberg was hostile to his work.

82 Reinhardt had long been represented by the well-established Betty Parsons Gallery, a space associated with New York School painting. Along with Iris Clert Gallery in Paris, Dwan provided a fresh context for Reinhardt's work during the sixties. On the positive turn in Reinhardt's critical fortunes during this period see Lynn Zelevansky, "Ad Reinhardt and the Younger Artists of the Sixties," in *American Art of the 1960s: Museum of Modern Art*, Studies in Modern Art (New York, 1991), 1:16–38.

83 A single square format work, *Abstract Painting (D)* (54″ × 54″), hung in the office.

84 Reinhardt, "Art-as-Art," in Barbara Rose, ed., *The Selected Writings of Ad Reinhardt* (New York, 1975), 53.

85 Stuckey, "Interview," AAA, tape 2.

86 Gerald Nordland, "Art: The Artist as Reinhardt," *Frontier: The Voice of the New West* (March 1962): 23–24.

87 I refer to Yve-Alain Bois's remarkable account of the painter's project, "The Limit of Almost," in *Ad Reinhardt* (Museum of Modern Art, New York, 1991), 11–34.

88 As Klein observed: "But each painting's blue world, although of the same blue and identical in execution, revealed an entirely other essence and atmosphere; none resembled the other." Yves Klein, "Selections from 'The Monochrome Adventure'" in *Yves Klein 1928–1962: A Retrospective* (Institute for the Arts, Rice University, Houston, 1982), 221.

89 The balloons were released in the courtyard of the nearby Saint-Germain-des-Prés. The Clert presentation was called *Propositions Monochromes*; the Allendy exhibit, *Pigment Pur*. The shows occurred in May 1957. My account of this phase of Klein's activity and his project as a whole is indebted to the important essay by Nan Rosenthal, "Assisted Levitation: The Art of Yves Klein," in *Yves Klein 1928–1962*, 89–135.

90 At the opening two Republican Guards in military dress and helmets "guarded" the entrance, as Clert's small space became crowded with visitors.

91 Castelli had already included Klein in a group show of new sculpture, *Works in Three Dimensions*, October 20–November 7, 1959.

92 It may be that Klein did not pair the Castelli and Dwan shows as deliberately as the Clert/Allendy installations, which occurred coincidentally in the French capital (see n. 89). But the two American shows nevertheless betray a Kleinian logic of repetition coupled with comparison, with difference, as I argue here.

93 *Yves Klein—le Monochrome* alluded both to the monochrome canvases that Klein exhibited and to his self-ascribed identity *as* a (or "the") monochrome.

94 The Castelli show also included several sponge sculptures, now in the collection of the Albright-Knox Gallery.

95 In a thoughtful account of Klein's visit to the US, Robert Pincus-Witten attributes the monochromatic focus of the show to Castelli, who sought to "carefully avoi[d] the theatrical aspects of Klein's work" that would be "seen as too outré for the prevailing New York taste." He also suggests that in restraining Klein's endeavor Castelli may have sought to prevent the Frenchman from overshadowing his New York artists. Robert Pincus-Witten, "Yves Klein," in Robert Pincus-Witten and Rotraut Klein-Moquay, *Yves Klein USA* (Paris, 2009), 43.

96 *Artnews* quoted in Thomas McEvilley, "Yves Klein: Conquistador of the Void," in *Yves Klein 1928–1962*, 73.

97 Klein did not live long enough to see the most damaging response, a dismissive and influential review by Donald Judd of a posthumous show at Iolas Gallery. See "In the Galleries: Yves Klein," *Arts Magazine* (January 1963), in Donald Judd, *Complete Writings 1959–1975* (Halifax, 1975), 69. The lackluster reception of the Castelli show precipitated Klein's most famous text, "The Chelsea Manifesto," a defense of his work named for the New York hotel where he and his fiancée stayed.

98 "He [Klein] adored California!" Stuckey, "Interview," AAA, tape 1. See also the account in Sidra Stich, *Yves Klein* (Museum Ludwig, Köln, 1994), 135–136.

99 "I chose to show all of the work that was possible to get into the gallery." Stuckey, "Interview," AAA, tape 1.

100 Klein had up to this point purged these relational aspects from his art in an effort to rid his project of the gestural mannerisms of *Art Informel*, the French version of action painting. Instead he decided *where* to affix the sponges on the support. Nan Rosenthal compares the relational aspect of the sponge reliefs to the disposition of boulders in the famous Zen Ryoan-Ji garden in Kyoto, which Klein had seen during a trip to Japan in 1952–1953. Rosenthal, "Assisted Levitation," 112.

101 See Exhibition History, pp. 324–325, for other works shown.

102 Jules Langsner, "Los Angeles Summer Lettter: Klein," *Art International* 5, no. 8 (October 20, 1961): 86.

103 Henry Seldis disliked the show enough to find two occasions to attack it in the *Los Angeles Times*. See Seldis, "In the Galleries: Octogenarian's Art Abounds in Vigor" (June 2, 1961): A6, and "Exhibit Boasts Some of Europe's Finest Selections" (February 9, 1962): C5.

104 Stuckey, "Interview," AAA, tape 1.

105 Stuckey, "Interview," AAA, tape 1.

106 The small network included Castelli Gallery, Galerie Rive Droite, Sonnabend Gallery Paris, and Alexander Iolas Gallery in New York, among others. Gallery Rive Droite refused to pay any of the shipping charges of Klein's works to California (Georges Marci to Dwan, March 20, 1961, Dwan Gallery Archive). A list of "Paintings on Consignment at Dwan Gallery" dated October 26, 1961, shows four works as damaged upon arrival from Castelli.

107 Klein and Rotraut Uecker were warmly received by Dwan and Kondratief, by Kienholz, Moses, and Hopps, and by collectors Fred and Marcia Weisman. See Chronology, p. 290. In an interview years later about their American trip, Rotraut Klein-Moquay fondly recalled Dwan's beach house and the white Bristol convertible that the dealer and her husband loaned to their guests. She recalls that Klein brought "a lot" of artist's materials over from Paris to make smaller works to exchange with other artists or to present as gifts. "Interview with Rotraut Klein-Moquay" and the archival materials collected in Pincus-Witten and Klein-Moquay, *Yves Klein USA*. The feeling was mutual with Dwan: "It was totally intoxicating to be able to have contact with [them]. They were extraordinary people; conversations with Yves Klein, who also stayed with his wife at our home in California, were cosmic" (Stuckey, "Interview," AAA, tape 1).

108 *Untitled Blue Monochrome*, 1960, is inscribed "IKB Pour Philippe et Pour Virginia... Toute l'amitié de Yves Klein le Monochrome 1960." The dedication to Dwan and Kondratief on the verso of *Untitled Monogold*, 1961, has faded.

109 Robert Pincus-Witten has described Klein as "our first 'post-studio' artist who, rather like a medieval cathedral builder, journeyed from city to city to make works of art." In Pincus-Witten and Klein-Moquay, *Yves Klein USA*, 36.

110 The Blankforts were among the Dwan Gallery's earliest supporters, acquiring Goodnough's *Abstract No. 4 "Pipes,"* a work they donated with the rest of their collection, including Klein's *Anthropometry* (1959), to the Los Angeles County Museum of Art. Dwan recalled that the Blankforts traveled to Paris to attend a family wedding. The witnesses included François Mathey of the Musée des arts décoratifs at the Louvre, Madame Bordeaux Le Pecq, president of the Salon des Comparaisons, the art critic Pierre Descargues, and the gallerists Virginia Dwan, Jeannine de Goldschmidt, Jean Larcade, and Dorothy Blankfort.

111 "Testimonial from Michael Blankfort" (1982), in Pincus-Witten and Klein-Moquay, *Yves Klein USA*, 181.

112 Both Scarpitta and Bontecou were represented by Castelli. Dwan's efforts to give Bontecou, an artist of great interest to her, a one-person show in Los Angeles did not come to pass.

113 See Judd, "Specific Objects" (1965), in Judd, *Complete Writings 1959–1975*, 184.

114 *Blue Exit* (1961), a work in oil and graphite on canvas, was the only conventional painting in the show.

115 For more detailed discussions of *Black Market* see Joshua Shannon, *The Disappearance of Objects: New York Art and the Rise of the Postmodern City* (New Haven, 2009), 134–144, 211, nn. 73, 74, 75, and Branden Joseph, "Rauschenberg's Refusal," in Paul Schimmel, ed., *Robert Rauschenberg: Combines* (Museum of Contemporary Art, Los Angeles, 2005), 257–282.

116 Rauschenberg's inversions of the vertical and horizontal axes of perception and cognition, most famously embodied in works like *Bed* and *Monogram*, have inspired a vast literature beginning with Leo Steinberg, *Other Criteria: Confrontations with Twentieth Century Art* (Oxford, 1972), 55–92.

117 Shannon argues that many of the objects in these combines allude to the remaking of Lower Manhattan in *The Disappearance of Objects*, 93–148.

118 Indicated by the fact that the title of the work was penciled in on the show's checklist.

119 That autumn, the photo silkscreen became the artist's medium of choice. Dwan's second and final show of Rauschenberg (April 1965) included two late combines, transfer drawings, and silkscreen paintings.

120 An additional message on the envelope reads: "Try studio upstairs."

121 See Chronology, p. 292. Dwan recalled with amusement Rauschenberg's arrival at Malibu with Cage, Cunningham, and the Cunningham's dance troupe in a VW minibus, along with the company's costumes and sets that Rauschenberg had designed.

122 On the various *tirs* performed by Saint Phalle in Los Angeles see *Niki de Saint Phalle: Monograph* (Lausanne, 2001), 244–253; Sarah Wilson, "*Tirs, Tears, Ricochets,*" in *Niki de Saint Phalle: 1930–2002* (Grand Palais, Paris, 2015), 95–96; and Chronology, pp. 289, 292.

123 Gerald Nordland was not persuaded by Rauschenberg's conjunctions of painting and refuse. Conceding that Rauschenberg's paint application "has a very special beauty," he objected that the "appliquéd detritus... seldom integrate[d] into the work." Nordland, "Neo-Dada Goes Hollywood," *Arts Magazine* 36, no. 9 (May–June 1962): 102.

124 Dwan recounted with some vexation her efforts to sell *First Landing Jump* (Stuckey, "Interview," AAA, tape 1). Twenty years later the market for the artist changed dramatically, and *Coexistence* sold at Christie's for $190,000 on May 13, 1981, a world record for the artist (Collection Files, Virginia Museum of Fine Arts, Richmond).

125 "I wanted a certain informality and yet a feeling, hopefully, would be given that the prospective client was being treated in a special way; [the client] was separated, set apart, and given special attention and an opportunity to see the works that I felt were important for [the client] to see." (Stuckey, "Interview," AAA, tape 2.) It was precisely this arrangement that the artist Michael Asher exposed in his 1974 exhibition at Claire Copley Gallery in Los Angeles, which involved the removal of the barrier wall between Copley's office and the exhibition space.

126 Reinhardt enlisted this format in several shows during this period. See Reinhardt, "The Black (Square) Painting Shows, 1963, 1964, 1965," *Artforum* 4, no. 7 (March 1966): 35.

127 "He knew they would make it there, the new world would recognize their talent." "Interview with Rotraut Klein-Moquay," in Pincus-Witten and Klein-Moquay, *Yves Klein USA*, 10. On Dwan's introductions to Arman and Raysse in summer 1961, see Chronology, p. 291.

128 Stuckey, "Interview," AAA, tape 2. Dwan has noted that during the 1960s Arman's accumulations more pointedly evoked the piles of human possessions stolen from concentration camp victims and discovered after the end of World War II.

129 Jean-Michel Bouhours, *Arman* (Centre Georges Pompidou, Paris, 2010), 302, and Stuckey, "Interview," AAA, tape 2. At Dwan's request Kienholz built a number of boxes for these works to Arman's specifications. See Chronology, p. 293.

130 Stuckey, "Interview," AAA, tape 2.

131 The Arman catalogue raisonné lists another title: *La Hora de Todos* (*All the Time*). Denyse Durand-Ruel, *Arman: Catalogue Raisonné, Vol.* 2 (Paris, 1991), 28–29.

132 E. & J. Bonetto, Milan; Fratelli Borletti, Milan; Forestier, Nice; JAZ (Compagnie Industrielle de Mécanique Horlogère, Paris); SMI (Société Meridionale d'Industrie, Marseilles).

133 Franz Kafka, "The Metamorphosis," *The Complete Stories* (New York, 1971), 90.

134 Tinguely and Saint Phalle arrived in Los Angeles, where Tinguely had opened a show at the Minama Gallery. Pontus Hultén, *Jean Tinguely: "Méta"* (Boston, 1975), 246–257.

135 See Dwan's recollection of her visit to a hardware store with these artists in Writings, p. 245.

136 Hultén, *Jean Tinguely*, 257.

137 Tinguely's titles were as varied as his presentations: from ancient warriors (*Attila*, *Hannibal*) and places (*Odessa*, *Mayfair*) to films (Bunuel's *Viridiana*, Roy's *Bandini*) to a brand of paint (*Mautz II*).

138 The work is one of the artist's *Radio Sculptures* developed in response to Cage's compositions incorporating mundane sounds and to Rauschenberg's combine *Broadcast* (1959). See Andres Pardey, "Among the Sculptures in the Museum Tinguely Collection," in *Museum Tinguely Basel: The Collection* (Basel, 2012), 86.

139 See Writings, p. 245, and Chronology, pp. 297–298, for a description of this event. The fountain became Tinguely's favored form of public sculpture, resulting in major commissions including his collaboration with Saint Phalle, *La Fontaine Stravinsky* (1983) at the Centre Pompidou, Paris.

140 "It was a whole half-year later that Niki had her show, after Jean Tinguely's. But they worked in what had formerly been a welding factory that we were able to rent.... They built whole shows in there, the two of them." Stuckey, "Interview," AAA, tape 3.

141 As suggested in Annja Müller-Alsbach's rigorous investigation of Tinguely's graphic art, "The Medium of Drawing in the Oeuvre of Jean Tinguely" in *Museum Tinguely Basel: The Collection*, 247–375.

142 *Tyrannosaurus Rex/The Monster/Tir Dragon (Study for King Kong)*, 1963. The work is reproduced in *Niki de Saint Phalle*, 135. In this study for the larger work, Saint Phalle rotated the direction of the monster 180 degrees.

143 The exhibition occurred in the same season as Hopps's *The New Painting of Common Objects* held at the Pasadena Art Museum and Sidney Janis's *International Exhibition of the New Realists* at Sidney Janis Gallery in New York. Ferus Gallery had exhibited Andy Warhol's *Thirty-Two Campbell's Soup Cans* from July 9 through August 4, 1962.

144 Dwan visited the studios of Larry Rivers, Robert Indiana, Andy Warhol, Roy Lichtenstein, Tom Wesselmann, and Claes Oldenburg to scout out works for the show. Stuckey, "Interview," AAA, tape 3.

145 Dwan recalled: "I think maybe John Chamberlain wasn't quite certain that his work—which has no particular American imagery—was fitting with the exhibition. However, in my mind, the fact that he was doing mangled American cars was enough." Stuckey, "Interview," AAA, tape 3.

146 Langsner, "Los Angeles Letter," *Art International* 7, no. 1 (January 25, 1963): 81, and Seldis, "In the Galleries: 'New Realism' Comes in Humor, Cynicism," *Los Angeles Times* (December 2, 1962): Q2.

147 "The exhibition has been wonderfully well-received here on the coast.... Both the Wesselmann and Oldenburg Cup [cat. 39] have been sold, as have most of the works which were available for sale." Weber to Richard Bellamy, December 7, 1962, Dwan Gallery Archive.

148 The representation of gender in pop and the gendering of mass culture are vast subjects. See, for example, Cécile Whiting, *A Taste for Pop: Pop Art, Gender and Consumer Culture* (Cambridge, 1997), and Andreas Huyssen, *After the Great Divide: Modernism, Mass Culture, Post-Modernism* (Bloomington, 1986).

149 "Neon lights and fluorescent-like colors bring art as entertainment to one of its peaks of absurdity as French 'artist' Martial Raysse adds the mannequin touch of the 'new realism' at the Dwan Gallery. One lucky collector is now in possession of a bigger-than-life photographic blowup of a leggy model applying suntan lotion to herself. Raysse's contributions to this 'work of art' include sequin eyelids, some garish poster paint, thinly applied, and a giant pair of sunglasses that dangle from the panel." Seldis, "In the Galleries: Sequin Eyelids, Neon Lips," *Los Angeles Times* (January 18, 1963): D5.

150 "It's all fun and games with Martial Raysse, who is having his second exhibition at the Dwan Gallery. . . . He apparently has a very good time performing his various tricks and the viewer is in for some lively entertainment." Seldis, "In the Galleries: 'Altoon Expands Pop Art,'" *Los Angeles Times* (May 18, 1964): C6.

151 Kanemitsu to Dwan, December 24, 1962, Dwan Gallery Archive. Similarly, Adolph Gottlieb, Philip Guston, Robert Motherwell, and Mark Rothko protested against Sidney Janis's *International Exhibition of the New Realists* at this time, ultimately leaving the gallery. On Kanemitsu's correspondence with Dwan see Chronology, p. 295.

152 Weber wrote approvingly to Richard Bellamy "that [Bellamy] and Virginia had settled the question of Oldenburg and Rosenquist exhibiting at the Dwan." Weber to Bellamy, December 7, 1962, Dwan Gallery Archive. Rosenquist's show opened in 1964, the year the artist completed his major multipanel works *F-111* and *World's Fair Mural.*

153 Oldenburg made several studies for the poster, including some of Mickey Mouse with varying expressions in different settings and at least one depicting a hot-dog in a roll. It was the first time the artist worked with the mouse, a recurring motif in his oeuvre. See Maartje Oldenburg, "Chronology," in Achim Hochdörfer, *Claes Oldenburg: The Sixties* (New York, 2012), 288–289.

154 Hochdörfer, *Claes Oldenburg*, 58.

155 Thomas Crow, *The Long March of Pop: Art, Music, and Design, 1930–1995* (New Haven, 2014), 242.

156 I attribute this to the enlarged scale of the works exhibited at Green by artists like Oldenburg, Judd, Morris, and Flavin, an impression reinforced in the fine installation shots by photographer Rudy Burckhardt.

157 "Claes's show was very handsome and I am proud to have had it. I think, however, that he was a bit disappointed in the 'results.' I'm afraid that Los Angeles is still not New York in terms of collectors and that it will be awhile before they reach the point of sophistication and enthusiasm for the true avant-garde that is found in New York." Weber to Sidney Janis, November 2, 1963, Dwan Gallery Archive.

158 Hochdörfer, *Claes Oldenburg*, 60. Hochdörfer traces the perfection of this syntagmatic form of display to the artist's three exhibitions at Janis in 1964, 1966, and 1967, where drawing plays an increasingly important role, "by way of" his shows at Green and Dwan.

159 On the influence of Freud's theory of dreams on Oldenburg's early work, see Lisa Freiman, "Claes Oldenburg's 'Psychoaesthetics,'" PhD dissertation, Emory University, 2001.

160 An allusion to a drive-in theater at night, as noted in Cécile Whiting's meticulous account of the event in *Pop L.A.: Art and the City in the 1960s* (Berkeley, 2006), 170–171.

161 Claes Oldenburg, script for *Autobodys*, quoted in Whiting, *Pop L.A.*, 176.

162 As curator, then director, of the Pasadena Art Museum, Hopps organized groundbreaking shows of Schwitters (1962), Duchamp (1963), and Cornell (1966–1967). Weber had also hoped to include works by Francis Picabia and Salvador Dali; the Picabia loan fell through. Weber to Walter Hopps, December 19, 1963, Dwan Gallery Archive.

163 Hopps, *Boxes* (Dwan Gallery, Los Angeles, 1964), unpaginated.

164 Stuckey, "Interview," AAA, tape 4. *Boxes* preceded Warhol's famous show in New York in April and May, when he filled the Stable Gallery with ersatz Brillo, Heinz, Campbell's Soup, and Del Monte Peach Halves boxes. Warhol showed yellow, red, and blue "3¢ Off" *Brillo*s at Dwan. At Stable he exhibited white, red, and blue *Brillo*s.

165 Weber spoke of his pride at showing these works. "You should know that these were the first three Brillo Boxes created by Andy Warhol. The circumstances for this creation was that in early 1964, in January of 1964 to be exact, I organized a box exhibition. As Andy Warhol was at that time, and still is, a very close friend of mine, I asked him if he would possibly consider constructing a box for this exhibition. Much to my surprise and pleasure, the three Brillo Boxes plus a Heinz Box, which was subsequently sold, arrived in California. . . . It is no small amount of pleasure and ego satisfaction on my part that my box exhibition helped issue this very important phase of Warhol's artistic career into existence." John Weber, Letter to Mrs. A. Main, Academy for Educational Development, New York, April 5, 1969, Dwan Gallery Archive.

166 "With the *Brillo Box*, the true philosophical question of the nature of art had been attained." Arthur C. Danto, *Beyond the Brillo Box: The Visual Arts in Post-Historical Perspective* (New York, 1992), 6.

167 On the morning of September 15, 1963, Ku Klux Klan members Robert Edward Chambliss, Bobby Frank Cherry, and Thomas Blanton, Jr. placed fifteen sticks of dynamite in the basement stairwell of the 16th Street Baptist Church. Four children—Addie Mae Collins, Denise McNair, Carole Robertson, and Cynthia Wesley—died in the explosion.

168 See Donald Factor, "Boxes," *Artforum* 2, no. 10 (April 1964): 20–23. The gallery received catalog requests from Joseph Cornell, Lawrence Alloway, Brian O'Doherty, and Lucy Lippard.

169 Henry Seldis, "In the Galleries: Mullican Artistry Triumph of Talent," *Los Angeles Times* (October 2, 1964): C9.

170 See Chronology, p. 301.

171 Leider, "Art: Kienholz," *Frontier* 16, no. 1 (November 1964): 25.

172 The explorer assigned this name after allegedly landing at Drake's Beach near Point Reyes.

173 Seldis, "In the Galleries: A Tour de Force of Sculptor's Art," *Los Angeles Times* (October 4, 1965): D9.

174 Judd, "Specific Objects," 183.

175 "New York was the center of the art world, and I wanted to see the gallery in that situation." Dwan quoted in Christopher Bollen, "Land Art," *Interview Magazine*, August 11, 2015.

176 Stuckey, "Interview," AAA, tape 5.

177 Dwan hired collector and architect David Whitney to make these improvements. Whitney, the partner of Philip Johnson, was then affiliated with the Green Gallery. Stuckey, "Interview," AAA, tape 5.

178 On this and other details of *The Beanery* see the discussion in Alex Potts, *Experiments in Modern Realism: World Making, Politics, and the Everyday in Postwar European and American Art* (New Haven, 2013), 64–65.

179 Stuckey, "Interview," AAA, tape 5. Articles on the show appeared in mass circulation publications such as *Life*, *Time*, and *Newsweek*, and in numerous art magazines.

180 Carl Andre, *Equivalents I–VIII*, Tibor de Nagy Gallery, March 1966.

181 Dwan saw Doyle's and LeWitt's works for the first time in the exhibition *Sculpture from All Directions*, World House Galleries, November 3–27, 1965. In addition to *Wall Piece (Hockey Stick)* LeWitt showed a second *Bent Stick* and a black floor structure. LeWitt fabricated the works in wood. The example in the Dwan collection, *Modular Wall Structure*, from 1968 (cat. 58), was fabricated in painted metal.

182 See Exhibition History, p. 344 and Mel Bochner's review of the show, "Sol LeWitt" (1966), in Bochner, *Solar Systems and Rest Rooms: Writings and Interviews, 1965–2007* (Cambridge, MA, 2008), 6.

183 Robert Morris, "Notes on Sculpture" (1966), in Battcock, ed., *Minimal Art*, 232.

184 See Chronology, p. 304.

185 James Meyer, *Minimalism: Art and Polemics in the Sixties* (New Haven, 2001). The theory of minimalism as a field reflects a structuralist understanding of an aesthetic movement as a field of difference: Morris is Morris, LeWitt is LeWitt; but "Morris" is meaningful *in relation to* LeWitt, Judd, Andre, and so on.

186 Stuckey, "Interview," AAA, tape 5. Morris had studied with Reinhardt at Hunter College, where he completed his MA thesis on Brancusi's sculpture in 1966.

187 Stuckey, "Interview," AAA, tape 5. Michael Steiner was the tenth participant.

188 Michelson, "10 x 10: 'Concrete Reasonableness,'" *Artforum* 5, no. 5 (January 1967): 31.

189 Michael Govan and Tiffany Bell, *Dan Flavin: The Complete Lights 1961–1996* (Dia Art Foundation, New York, 2004), 250–251. Flavin's *"monument" on the survival of Mrs. Reppin* was dedicated to a half-Englishwoman who was married to a German soldier and interned by the Allies after World War II.

190 The "cuts" pointed to Andre's installation *Equivalents I–VIII* at Tibor de Nagy Gallery in New York in March 1966.

191 See Morris's critique of complex regular forms in "Notes on Sculpture," in Battcock, ed., *Minimal* Art, 227–228.

192 Dwan described *10* as an antidote to the "high energy" and violence of the sixties. Stuckey, "Interview," AAA, tape 5.

193 Dwan also mounted a dual showing of Forrest Myers and Anthony Magar at the Westwood gallery in October 1966. On the history of Park Place see Linda Dalrymple Henderson, *Reimagining Space: The Park Place Gallery Group in 1960s New York* (Blanton Museum of Art, Austin, TX, 2009).

194 John Coplans, "David Novros in L.A.," *Artforum* 5, no. 5 (January 1967): 27.

195 For a discussion of Snelson's "tensegrity" and its constructivist precedence see Maria Gough, *The Artist as Producer: Russian Constructivism in Revolution* (Berkeley, 2005).

196 On the salability of Snelson's work at Dwan, see Chronology, pp. 304, 309. *Snelson Structures*, Bryant Park, New York, October 6–November 6, 1968. *Needle Tower* is now in the collection of the Hirshhorn Museum and Sculpture Garden.

197 "It seemed to me reductive Minimalism was self-defeating (as the work of Robert Morris proved), and once the least means was achieved one had to go another way." Sol LeWitt to the author, December 4, 1995.

198 Sol LeWitt, "Paragraphs on Conceptual Art," in Alicia Legg, ed., *Sol LeWitt* (Museum of Modern Art, New York, 1978), 166.

199 The show *Scale Models and Drawings* in January–February 1967 featured Mel Bochner's important *Thirty Six Photographs and Twelve Diagrams* (1966), a photo-documentation of mathematically determined arrangements of blocks on a grid. Unlike the permutations of LeWitt's *Serial Project*, which exhausts itself with Set D, Bochner's work is open-ended: a viewer can imagine countless arrangements of blocks in addition to the twelve that Bochner made.

200 The tripartite pricing structure of these works challenged conventional models of ownership. First the buyer acquired the concept, then she paid the artist to execute the work, and then she covered the cost of the materials. With the exception of *The State Hospital* (1965), the concept tableaux were never executed.

201 O'Doherty, *Inside the White Cube*, 34, and Webb, "On Site-Specificity: A Genealogy," 140.

202 *Language II* (1968), *Language III* (1969), *Language IV* (1970). See Exhibition History for details.

203 The works included a 1913 "Liberated Word" poem by Marinetti; Duchamp's *The* (1915), a sheet of illogical sentences in which the article "the" has been replaced by an asterisk, and *Anagram for Pierre de Massot* (1961), a collage depicting a public facility inscribed with Massot's name and its anagrammatic inversion (*Pissot/iere*: Urinal); Picabia's *Untitled* (c. 1917); and Magritte's *Key of Dreams* (1932).

204 The show also included a work by Barry Bryant, a Western interpreter of Buddhism, inspired by the Tibetan calendar.

205 There were twenty-two artists in the first language show, thirty-nine in the second, sixty-one in the third, and thirty-two in *Language IV*.

206 With the exception of Joan Mitchell and Niki de Saint Phalle, and the artist couple Dakota Daley/Nicholas Quennell, the roster of one-person shows at Dwan was overwhelmingly male and white. Dwan was no different from her peers at Castelli, Ferus, Janis, and Green in this regard. Women did figure prominently in the major group shows: *15 of New York* (Grace Hartigan, Adja Yunkers), *Six Sculptors* (Lee Bontecou), *My Country 'Tis of Thee* (Marisol), *Boxes* (Bontecou, Marisol, Letty Eisenhauer, Louise Nevelson), *10* (Jo Baer and Agnes Martin). Following the all-male composition of *Language to be looked at and/or things to be read*, *Language II* included Hanne Darboven, Hannah Weiner, Elaine Sturtevant, Christine Kozlov, Rosemarie Castoro, and Lila Katzen; *Language III*, Castoro, Darboven, Dash, Kozlov, Weiner, Eleanor Antin, Naomi Dash, Madeline Gins, Bici Hendricks, Ruth Jacoby, Lee Lozano, Nancy Holt, and Adrian Piper; *Language IV*, Gins, Piper, Weiner, Agnes Denes, and Dorothea Rockburne.

207 *Card File* was included in *Language to be looked at and/or things to be read*, *Language III*, and *Language IV*. The entry for this work in Jeffrey Weiss, *Robert Morris: Object Sculpture, 1960–1965* (New Haven, 2014), 106, indicates the work was also included in *Language II*, although it does not appear as *Card File* on the show's checklist. My discussion of Morris's work is indebted to Weiss's perceptive account.

208 Quoted in Weiss, *Robert Morris*, 109. The pseudo-bureaucratic formats of historical conceptualism are discussed in Benjamin H.D. Buchloh, "Conceptual Art 1962–1969: From the Aesthetic of Administration to the Critique of Institutions," *October* 55 (Winter 1990): 105–143.

209 "Tlön, Uqbar, Orbis Tertius" and "The Library of Babel" in Jorge Luis Borges, *Labyrinths: Selected Stories and Other Writings* (New York, 1962), 3–18, 51–58.

210 Eleanor Antin in Cindy Nemser, *Art Talk: Conversations with 12 Women Artists* (New York, 1975), 278.

211 Castoro's poem was indeed prescient: the Weather Underground (aka the Weathermen) announced its formation at the Students for a Democratic Society convention in Chicago on June 18, 1969.

212 February 1969 witnessed Operation Menu, the extensive bombing of North Vietnamese and Viet Cong targets in Cambodia by order of President Richard Nixon, and the second Tet Offensive in South Vietnam, which led to more than 1,000 US casualties.

213 This point was communicated by Castoro in conversation with the author.

214 Castoro showed a second poem and slide work, *Sharp Charges*, in *Language III*. The slide projection was heralded in the show *Projected Art* curated by Elayne Varian at the Contemporary Study Wing, Finch College of Art, New York, December 8, 1966–January 8, 1967, which included a slide work by Dan Graham. See Eric de Bruyn, "The Filmic Anomaly: Moments in Post-Minimalism (1966–1970)," PhD dissertation, City University of New York, 2002.

215 "Language to Be Looked At and/or Things to be Read," in *Robert Smithson: The Collected Writings*, 61.

216 Andre and Castoro married in 1963. His tenure as a freight brakeman lasted from 1960 to 1964 and involved arranging lines of freight wagons into particular sequences. Andre noted the influence of that activity on his sculpture and poetry, which also involve the arrangement of individual elements. See "My sculptural finishing school..." (1972) in Carl Andre, *Cuts: Texts 1959–2004*, ed. James Meyer (Cambridge, MA, 2005), 222.

217 For a discussion of the "list" or inventory in sixties practice see Briony Fer, *The Infinite Line: Remaking Art after Modernism* (New Haven, 2004), 145–162.

218 "A Museum of Language in the Vicinity of Art" in *Robert Smithson: The Collected Writings*, 79–80.

219 Smithson never executed the works envisioned in *Pulverizations* but did complete the related model, *Tar Pool and Gravel Pit* (1966). (See Hobbs, *Robert Smithson: Sculpture*, 74.) The nested square format of these proposals—examined by Sol LeWitt in *Serial Project #1* and in his relief *Wall Stucture, Blue* (1962)—suggests the influence of LeWitt's thinking on the younger artist in 1966–1967.

220 Weiner enacted ONE STANDARD AIR FORCE DIE MARKER THROWN INTO THE SEA and other "statements" during a visit to the Nova Scotia College of Art and Design in Halifax in 1969.

221 Alexander Alberro and Alice Zimmerman, "NOT HOW IT SHOULD BE WERE IT TO BE BUILT BUT HOW IT COULD BE WERE IT TO BE BUILT," in *Lawrence Weiner* (London, 1998), 50.

222 Lucy R. Lippard and John Chandler, "The Dematerialization of Art," *Art International* 2, no. 22 (February 1968): 31–36.

223 Joseph Kosuth, "Art After Philosophy, I and II," in Gregory Battcock, ed., *Idea Art* (New York, 1973), 83.

224 Kosuth in Battcock, *Idea Art*, 95.

225 E.C. Goossen, *The Art of the Real: USA 1948–1968* (New York, 1968).

226 "Excerpts from Speculation (1967–1970)," in Bochner, *Solar Systems and Rest Rooms*, 72.

227 See Jessica Prinz, "Language Is Not Transparent," in Richard S. Field, *Mel Bochner: Thought Made Visible 1966–1973* (New Haven, 1995), 192–199.

228 Bochner, "Excerpts from Speculation (1967–1970)," 75.

229 See Holt's remarks on this work in James Meyer, "Interview with Nancy Holt," in Alena Williams, *Nancy Holt: Sightlines* (Berkeley, 2011), 222. Although *Detach Here* does not appear on the checklists of the language shows, Holt recalled to the author that the work was in *Language III*.

230 The Wadsworth Atheneum, Hartford, finally accessioned the work. The project is documented in Kathe Gregory et al., *Stolen* (New York, 1970).

231 The version in this exhibition is the original extract from Lozano's journals.

232 Smithson was offered the consultancy by Walther Prokosch, a partner in Tippetts-Abbett-McCarthy-Stratton, among the designers of John F. Kennedy Airport, after Prokosch heard Smithson lecture at a panel at Yale in June 1966. The firm did not secure the commission, and Smithson's association with the project ended in June 1967. On the Dallas–Fort Worth Regional Airport project and the formation of land art see Suzaan Boettger, *Earthworks: Art and the Landscape of the Sixties* (Berkeley, 2002) and Reynolds, *Robert Smithson: Learning from New Jersey and Elsewhere*, 133–143.

233 "Towards the Development of an Air Terminal Site," in *Robert Smithson: The Collected Writings*, 56. Originally published in *Artforum* 5, no. 10 (Summer 1967): 36–40.

234 Smithson died in a plane crash surveying the site of his earthwork *Amarillo Ramp* on July 20, 1973. His major statements on land art include "The Monuments of Passaic" (1967), "A Sedimentation of Mind: Earth Projects" (1968), "The Spiral Jetty" (1972), and "Frederick Law Olmsted and the Dialectical Landscape" (1973). "Towards the Development of an Air Terminal Site" is his first attempt to theorize this form.

235 *Robert Smithson: The Collected Writings*, 54. "Our whole notion of airflight is casting off the old meaning of speed through space, and developing a new meaning based on instantaneous time [52–53]."

236 "Aerial Art" in *Robert Smithson: The Collected Writings*, 117.

237 Andre's third proposal did not make it into the published version of Smithson's essay.

238 "Aerial Art" in *Robert Smithson: The Collected Writings*, 117. Smithson made a maquette of the work in mirrors. The Dwan Gallery records do not confirm whether this project was exhibited. The maquette is reproduced in Boettger, *Earthworks*, 57.

239 See Smithson's statement describing these connections in Hobbs, *Robert Smithson: Sculpture*, 96, and Hobbs's own fine analysis of *Gyrostasis*, 95–98. Smithson completed a third spiral work, *Spiral Hill*, in Emmen, Netherlands, in 1971.

240 This theory was argued by such nineteenth-century physicists as William Thomson (Lord Kelvin) and Hermann von Helmholtz and was popularized during the sixties in such works as J.G. Ballard's novel *The Crystal World* (1966), the inspiration for Smithson's article "The Crystal Land" (1966).

241 Smithson had the sculptural component of *Nonsite #2* destroyed. See Hobbs, *Robert Smithson: Sculpture*, 104, n. 32.

242 I allude to Mel Bochner's critique of minimalism's tautological aspiration, "Serial Art Systems: Solipsism," in Bochner, *Solar Systems and Rest Rooms*, 37–41.

243 Stuckey, "Interview," AAA, tape 7.

244 Although *Earth Mound* was represented photographically in *Earthworks*, correspondence in the Dwan Archive suggests that Dwan would have preferred to show a model of Bayer's work.

245 The Franklin nonsite staged an exaggeratedly false one-point perspective. Viewed from one end, the trapezoidal containers appeared to recede into a fictive space, as Renaissance paintings do, even though Smithson's sculpture was little more than nine feet long. See the description of this work in Hobbs, *Robert Smithson: Sculpture*, 105–108.

246 *Placid Civic Monument* was Oldenburg's contribution to the *Sculpture in Environment* show organized by the New York City Administration of Recreation and Cultural Affairs in October 1967. Oldenburg also showed proposals for two other works, *Project for Asphalt Field 30′ × 30′* and *Project to Bury Studio Objects in 30′ × 30′ Plot*.

247 "Essay on Sculpture for E.C. Goossen" in Andre, *Cuts*, 233. I interpret *Rock Pile* as the "cairn" and *Log Piece* as the "log" or "line" cited in Andre's prescient poem.

248 See Morris's account of "undifferentiated" perception, or "scanning," inspired by the writings of Anton Ehrenzweig in "Notes on Sculpture, Part 4: Beyond Objects," *Artforum* 7, no. 8 (April 1969): 50–54.

249 Checklist, *Earthworks*, Dwan Gallery Archive. The work remained in Morris's possession until it was acquired by the Dia Art Foundation in May 2016.

250 In addition to the New Haven *2-Dimensional Information (Contour Lines)* work in the current exhibition, the Dwan Archive checklist included Oppenheim's scale model of a work transposing the cartographical lines of the volcanic Mount Cotopaxi in Ecuador to a wheat field in Smith Center, KS, the geographical center of the US. The model was a cocoa mat incised with the irregular concentric circles of the mountain's elevation installed on a low plinth.

163 John Weber to David Novros, December 6, 1966.

164 Max Kozloff, "Michael Steiner, Dwan Gallery," *Artforum* 5, no. 5 (January 1967): 56–57, illustrated.

165 John Weber to Leo Castelli, November 12, 1966.

166 Leider, "A New Medium for John Chamberlain," *Artforum* 5, no. 6 (February 1967): 48–49, illustrated.

167 Stuckey, "Interview," AAA, tape 5.

168 Dwan Archives, account book, no. 576, September 22, 1966.

169 Pincus-Witten, "New York: Robert Smithson," *Artforum* 5, no. 6 (February 1967): 61.

170 Michael Benedikt, "New York: Notes on the Whitney Annual 1966," *Art International* 11, no. 2 (February 20, 1967): 57–58, illustrated.

171 Stuckey, "Interview," AAA, tape 7.

172 Stuckey, "Interview," AAA, tape 6.

173 Langsner, "Los Angeles," *Artnews* 66, no. 1 (March 1967): 58, illustrated.

174 Stuckey, "Interview," AAA, tape 7.

175 Loïc Malle, "Charles Ross," in Klaus Ottmann, *Charles Ross: The Substance of Light* (Santa Fe, 2012), 300.

176 John Weber to Patrick J. Lannan, April 22, 1967.

177 William Wilson, "Raysse Exhibit Lights Up Slowly Fading Dwan Gallery," *Los Angeles Times* (June 2, 1967).

178 *Artforum* 5, no. 10 (Summer 1967): 79–83 (LeWitt), 36–40 (Smithson), 24–29 (Morris), 12–23 (Fried). Includes installation views of Dwan Gallery featuring works by Judd, Smithson, and Morris.

179 Stuckey, "Interview," AAA, tape 6.

180 Dwan to James Fitzsimmons, October 21, 1967.

181 Letter from Robert Rauschenberg, September 19, 1967.

182 Stuckey, "Interview," AAA, tape 7.

183 John Weber to John Powers, January 16, 1968: the show makes $28,000 on opening day.

184 Stuckey, "Interview," AAA, tape 7.

185 C. Blok, "Minimal Art at The Hague," *Art International* 12, no. 5 (May 15, 1968): 18–24, illustrated; Anita Feldman, "In the Museums: Minimal Art," *Arts Magazine* 42, no. 8 (June/Summer 1968): 57.

186 See Writings, p. 257.

187 Suzaan Boettger, *Earthworks: Art and the Landscape of the Sixties* (Oakland, 2004), 131.

188 Jed Horner, "A New Stone Age in Nevada," *Quest* (September 1980): 75.

189 Stuckey, "Interview," AAA, tape 7.

190 Doris Freedman (director, department of cultural affairs, New York) to Dwan, September 24, 1968.

191 Jean Leering, "Erwin Heerich," *Arts Magazine* 43, no. 3 (December 1968/January 1969): 29.

192 Walter De Maria to Dwan and John Weber, January 25, 1969.

193 Dwan to collector Ward Bennett, March 13, 1969.

194 Boettger, *Earthworks*, 193.

195 Horner, "A New Stone Age in Nevada," 77.

196 Bourgeois, "New York: Sol LeWitt, Dwan Gallery," *Artforum* 8, no. 4 (December 1969): 71, illustrated.

197 Grace Glueck, "A Sort of Distant Star," *New York Times* (November 23, 1969).

198 Stuckey, "Interview," AAA, tape 9.

199 Stuckey, "Interview," AAA, tape 9.

200 Stuckey, "Interview," AAA, tape 9.

201 John Weber to Richard Long, April 15, 1970.

202 Kay Epstein to Richard Long, June 12, 1970.

203 Richard Long to Kay Epstein, undated.

204 Kay Epstein to Richard Long, July 8, 1970.

205 Charles Ross to Moshe Safdie, January 13, 1971.

206 "Statements by Gallery Directors," *Arts Magazine* 45, no. 6 (April 1971): 60.

207 *http://charlesrossstudio.com/biography/biography.html* (accessed March 8, 2016).

208 See Writings, pp. 269–270.

209 Douglas C. McGill, "Coast Museum Acquires 'Earthwork,'" *New York Times* (December 12, 1985); William Wilson, "New MOCA Acquisition Is a Hole in the Ground," *Los Angeles Times* (December 10, 1985).

210 Michael Kimmelman, "The Forgotten Godmother of Dia's Artists," *New York Times* (May 11, 2003): "But art dealing, at its best, is not just a business, and what made her a poor businesswoman made her a legendary dealer, the grande dame of the avant-garde, or a part of it, briefly."

211 Philipp Kaiser and Miwon Kwon, eds., *Ends of the Earth: Land Art to 1974* (Munich, 2012), 93–95.

Books

Alberro, Alexander. *Lawrence Weiner* London, 1998.

Andre, Carl. *Cuts: Texts 1959–2004*, edited by James Meyer. Cambridge, MA, 2005.

Anfam, David. *Franz Kline: Black and White, 1950–1961*. Menil Collection, Houston, 1994.

The Art Show 1963–1977: Edward Kienholz. Galerie Folker Skulima and Centre Georges Pompidou, Musée national d'art moderne, Berlin and Paris, 1977.

Axsom, Richard H., and David Platzker. *Printed Stuff: Prints, Posters, and Ephemera by Claes Oldenburg: A Catalogue Raisonné 1958–1996*. New York, 1997.

Baker, Kenneth. *The Lightning Field*. New Haven, 2008.

Barron, Stephanie. *Ken Price Sculpture: A Retrospective*. Los Angeles County Museum of Art, 2012.

Battcock, Gregory, ed. *Idea Art*. New York, 1973.

Battcock, Gregory, ed. *Minimal Art: A Critical Anthology*. New York, 1968.

Beardsley, John. *Earthworks and Beyond: Contemporary Art in the Landscape*. New York, 1984.

Berger, Maurice. *Labyrinths: Robert Morris, Minimalism, and the 1960s*. New York, 1989.

Bernstein, Roberta. "An Interview with Irving Blum" In *Ferus*, edited by Ealan Wingate, Lisa Kim, and Erin Wright, 22–30. Gagosian Gallery, New York, 2002.

Bochner, Mel. *Solar Systems and Rest Rooms: Writings and Interviews, 1965–2007*. Cambridge, MA, 2008.

Boettger, Suzaan. *Earthworks: Art and the Landscape of the Sixties*. Oakland, 2004.

Bois, Yve-Alain. "The Limit of Almost." In *Ad Reinhardt*. Museum of Modern Art, New York, 1991.

Borges, Jorge Luis. *Labyrinths: Selected Stories and Other Writings*. New York, 1962.

Bouhours, Jean-Michel. *Arman*. Centre Georges Pompidou, Paris, 2010.

Brown, Julia, ed. *Michael Heizer: Sculpture in Reverse*. Museum of Contemporary Art, Los Angeles, 1984.

Buren, Daniel. "The Function of the Studio." In *October: The First Decade*, edited by Annette Michelson, Rosalind E. Krauss, Douglas Crimp, and Joan Copjec, 201–207. Cambridge, MA, 1987.

Celant, Germano, ed. *Claes Oldenburg: An Anthology*. Solomon R. Guggenheim Museum and the National Gallery of Art, New York and Washington, 1995.

Celant, Germano, ed. *Dennis Oppenheim: Explorations*. Milan, 2001.

Celant, Germano. *Michael Heizer*. Milan, 1996.

Cherix, Christophe. *In and Out of Amsterdam: Travels in Conceptual Art, 1960–1976*. Museum of Modern Art, New York, 2009.

Cles-Reden, Sibylle. *The Realm of the Great Goddess: The Story of the Megalith Builders*. London, 1961.

Crow, Thomas. *The Long March of Pop: Art, Music, and Design, 1930–1995*. New Haven, 2014.

Danto, Arthur C. *Beyond the Brillo Box: The Visual Arts in Post-Historical Perspective*. New York, 1992.

de Wit, Wim, and Christopher James Alexander, eds. *Overdrive: L.A. Constructs the Future, 1940–1990*. J. Paul Getty Museum, Los Angeles, 2013.

Drohojowska-Philp, Hunter. *Rebels in Paradise: The Los Angeles Art Scene and the 1960s*. New York, 2011.

Durand-Ruel, Denyse. *Arman: Catalogue Raisonné. Vol. 2*. Paris, 1991.

Edward Kienholz. Los Angeles County Museum of Art, 1966.

Ehrenzweig, Anton. *The Hidden Order of Art: A Study in the Psychology of Artist Imagination*. Berkeley, 1967.

Fer, Briony. *The Infinite Line: Remaking Art after Modernism*. New Haven, 2004.

Field, Richard S. *Mel Bochner: Thought Made Visible 1966–1973*. New Haven, 1995.

Franz Kline 1910–1962. Castello di Rivoli, 2004.

Garrels, Gary, ed. *Sol LeWitt: A Retrospective*. San Francisco Museum of Modern Art, 2000.

Goldstein, Ann, and Anne Rorimer. *Reconsidering the Object of Art: 1965–1975*. Museum of Contemporary Art, Los Angeles, 1995.

Goossen, E.C. *The Art of the Real: USA 1948–1968*. New York, 1968.

Gough, Maria. *The Artist as Producer: Russian Constructivism in Revolution*. Berkeley, 2005.

Govan, Michael, and Tiffany Bell. *Dan Flavin: The Complete Lights, 1961–1996*. Dia Art Foundation, New York, 2004.

Gregory, Kathe, Marilyn Landis, Russell F. Lewis, David Crane, and Scott R. Kahn. *Stolen*. New York, 1970.

Hackman, William. *Out of Sight: The Los Angeles Art Scene of the Sixties*. New York, 2015.

Henderson, Linda Dalrymple. *Reimagining Space: The Park Place Gallery Group in 1960s New York*. Blanton Museum of Art, Austin, 2009.

Hobbs, Robert. *Robert Smithson: Sculpture.* Ithaca, 1981.

Hochdörfer, Achim, ed. *Claes Oldenburg: The Sixties.* Munich, 2012.

Hopps, Walter. *James Rosenquist: A Retrospective.* Solomon R. Guggenheim Museum, New York, 2003.

Hopps, Walter. *Kienholz: A Retrospective: Edward and Nancy Reddin Kienholz.* Whitney Museum of American Art, New York, 1996.

Hultén, Pontus. *Edward Kienholz.* Kunsthaus Zürich, 1971.

Hultén, Pontus. *Jean Tinguely: "Méta."* Boston, 1975.

Hultén, Pontus. *Tinguely.* Centre Georges Pompidou, Musée national d'art moderne, Paris, 1989.

Humblet, Claudine. *La nouvelle abstraction américaine, 1950–1970.* 3 vols. Milan, 2003.

Huyssen, Andreas. *After the Great Divide: Modernism, Mass Culture, Post-Modernism.* Bloomington, 1986.

Jameson, Fredric. "Periodizing the Sixties." In *The Sixties without Apology*, edited by Sohnya Sayres et al., 178–220. Minneapolis, 1984.

Jones, Kellie. *Now Dig This! Art and Black Los Angeles: 1960–1980.* Hammer Museum, Los Angeles, 2011.

Judd, Donald. *Complete Writings 1959–1975.* Halifax, 1975.

Kafka, Franz. "The Metamorphosis." In *The Complete Stories.* New York, 1971.

Kaiser, Philipp, and Miwon Kwon, eds. *Ends of the Earth: Land Art to 1974.* Museum of Contemporary Art, Los Angeles, 2012.

Kelley, Jeff. *Childsplay: The Art of Allan Kaprow.* Berkeley, 2004.

Kölle, Brigitte, ed. *Konrad Fischer: Okey Dokey.* Köln, 2008.

Koshinka, Katerina. *Lucas Samaras: A Retrospective.* National Gallery—Alexandros Soutzos Museum, Athens, 2005.

Krauss, Rosalind E. *The Originality of the Avant-Garde and Other Modernist Myths.* Cambridge, MA, 1985.

Krauss, Rosalind E. *Robert Morris: The Mind/Body Problem.* Solomon R. Guggenheim Museum, New York, 1994.

Kubler, George. *The Shape of Time: Remarks on the History of Things.* New Haven, 2008.

Kwon, Miwon. *One Place After Another: Site-Specific Art and Locational Identity.* Cambridge, MA, 2014.

Legg, Alicia, ed. *Sol LeWitt.* Museum of Modern Art, New York, 1978.

Lehrer-Graiwer, Sarah. *Lee Lozano: Dropout Piece.* London, 2014.

Lewis, Tom. *Divided Highways: Building the Interstate Highways, Transforming American Life.* New York, 1997.

Lippard, Lucy R. *Overlay: Contemporary Art and the Art of Prehistory.* New York, 1995.

Lozano, Lee. *Lee Lozano: Notebooks 1967–70.* New York, 2009.

Martial Raysse. Centre Georges Pompidou, Musée national d'art moderne, Paris, 2014.

Martial Raysse. Galerie nationale du Jeu de Paume and Carré d'art, Musée d'art, contemporain, Paris and Nîmes, 1992.

McKenna, Kristine. *The Ferus Gallery: A Place to Begin.* Göttingen, 2009.

McShine, Kynaston. *Primary Structures: Younger American and British Sculptors.* Jewish Museum, 1966.

Meyer, James. "The Functional Site: Or, The Transformation of Site-Specificity." In *Space/Site/Intervention: Situating Installation Art*, edited by Erika Suderburg, 23–37. Minneapolis, 2000.

Meyer, James. *Minimalism: Art and Polemics in the Sixties.* New Haven, 2001.

Minimal Art. Haags Gemeentemuseum, The Hague, 1968.

Museum of Contemporary Art. *Michael Heizer: Double Negative.* Museum of Contemporary Art, Los Angeles, 1991.

Museum Tinguely Basel: The Collection. Basel, 2012.

Nemser, Cindy. *Art Talk: Conversations with 12 Women Artists.* New York, 1975.

Niki de Saint Phalle: Monograph: Paintings, Tirs, Assemblages, Reliefs, 1949–2000. Lausanne, 2001.

Niki de Saint Phalle: 1930–2002. Grand Palais, Galeries nationales, and Guggenheim Museum, Paris and Bilbao, 2015.

Nisbet, James. *Ecologies, Environments, and Energy Systems in Art of the 1960s and 1970s.* Cambridge, MA, 2014.

Nittve, Lars, and Helle Crenzien, eds. *Sunshine and Noir: Art in L.A. 1960–1997.* Louisiana Museum for moderne kunst, Humlebaek, 1997.

O'Doherty, Brian. *Inside the White Cube: The Ideology of the Gallery Space.* Santa Monica, 1976.

O'Neill, Rosemary. *Art and Visual Culture on the French Riviera, 1959–1971.* Farnham, Surrey, 2012.

Ottmann, Klaus, Thomas McEvilley, et al. *Charles Ross: The Substance of Light.* Santa Fe, 2012.

Peabody, Rebecca, Andrew Perchuk, Glenn Phillips, and Rani Singh, eds. *Pacific Standard Time: Los Angeles Art 1945–1980*, J. Paul Getty Museum, Los Angeles, 2011.

Pincus, Robert L. *On a Scale that Competes with the World: The Art of Edward and Nancy Reddin Kienholz*. Berkeley, 1990.

Pincus-Witten, Robert, and Rotraut Klein-Moquay, eds. *Yves Klein USA*. Paris, 2009.

Potts, Alex. *Experiments in Modern Realism: World Making, Politics and the Everyday in Postwar European and American Art*. New Haven, 2013.

Primary Structures: Younger American and British Sculptors. Jewish Museum, New York, 1966.

Reinhardt, Ad. "Art-as-Art." In *Art-as-Art: The Selected Writings of Ad Reinhardt*, edited by Barbara Rose. New York, 1975.

Reversible Destiny: Arakawa/Gins. Guggenheim Museum Soho, New York, 1997.

Reynolds, Ann. *Robert Smithson: Learning from New Jersey and Elsewhere*. Cambridge, MA, 2003.

Rivers, Larry, with Arnold Weinstein. *What Did I Do?: The Unauthorized Autobiography*. New York, 1992.

Robert Morris, the Mind/Body Problem. Solomon R. Guggenheim Museum, New York, 1994.

Robert Rauschenberg–Jean Tinguely: Collaborations. Museum Jean Tinguely Basel, 2009.

Robert Ryman. InK, Halle für Internationale neue Kunst, Zürich, 1980.

Robert Smithson Retrospective: Works 1955–1973. Museet for Samtidskunst, Oslo, 1999.

Roberts, Jennifer. *Mirror-Travels: Robert Smithson and History*. New Haven, 2004.

Romantischer Konzeptualismus = Romantic Conceptualism. Kunsthalle Nürnberg, 2007.

Rorimer, Anne. *New Art in the Sixties and Seventies: Redefining Reality*. London, 2001.

Rose, Barbara. *Claes Oldenburg*. Museum of Modern Art, New York, 1969.

Rosenberg, Harold. "The American Action Painters." In *Abstract Expressionism: A Critical Record*, edited by David Shapiro and Cecile Shapiro, 75–85. Cambridge, 1990.

Salvatore Scarpitta: Catalogue Raisonné. Milan, 2005.

Schimmel, Paul. *Robert Rauschenberg: Combines*. Museum of Contemporary Art, Los Angeles, 2005.

Selz, Peter. *Art of Engagement: Visual Politics in California and Beyond*. Berkeley, 2005.

Shannon, Joshua. *The Disappearance of Objects: New York Art and the Rise of the Postmodern City*. New Haven, 2009.

Smith, Brydon. *Donald Judd: Catalogue Raisonné of Paintings, Objects, and Wood Blocks, 1960–1974*. National Gallery of Canada, Ottawa, 1975.

Smithson, Robert. *Robert Smithson: The Collected Writings*, edited by Jack Flam, Berkeley, 1996.

Smithson, Robert. "The Spiral Jetty." In *Arts of the Environment*, edited by Gyorgy Kepes, 222–232. New York, 1972.

Steinberg, Leo. *Other Criteria: Confrontations with Twentieth Century Art*. Oxford, 1972.

Stich, Sidra. *Yves Klein*. Museum Ludwig, Köln, 1994.

Storr, Robert. *Robert Ryman*. Tate Gallery and Museum of Modern Art, London and New York, 1993.

Tiberghien, Gilles A. *Land Art*. Paris, 1993; New York, 1995.

Tsai, Eugenie, and Cornelia Butler, eds. *Robert Smithson*. Museum of Contemporary Art, Los Angeles, 2004.

Violand-Hobi, Heidi E. *Jean Tinguely: Life and Work*. New York, 1995.

Virginia Dwan: Art Minimal, Art Conceptuel, Earthworks, New York, Les Anées 60–70: Ad Reinhardt, Anastasi, Carl André, Arawaka. Galerie Montaigne, Paris, 1991.

Virginia Dwan Collection. UCLA Art Galleries, Los Angeles, 1965.

Virginia Dwan et les nouveaux réalistes: Los Angeles, les années 60: Arman, Klein, Raysse, Niki de Saint-Phalle, Tinguely. Galerie Montaigne, Paris, 1990.

Wanamaker, Mark. *Westwood (Images of America)*. Mount Pleasant, SC, 2010.

Weiss, Jeffrey. *Robert Morris: Object Sculpture 1960–1965*. New Haven, 2013.

Whiting, Cécile. *Pop L.A.: Art and the City in the 1960s*. Berkeley, 2006.

Whiting, Cécile. *A Taste for Pop: Pop Art, Gender and Consumer Culture*. Cambridge, 1997.

William Anastasi: A Retrospective. Nikolaj, Copenhagen Contemporary Art Center, Copenhagen, 2001.

William Anastasi: A Selection of Works from 1960 to 1989. Scott Hanson Gallery, New York, 1989.

Williams, Alena. *Nancy Holt: Sightlines*. Berkeley, 2011.

Yves Klein 1928–1962: A Retrospective. Rice University, Houston, 1982.

Zelevansky, Lynn. "Ad Reinhardt and the Younger Artists of the Sixties." In *American Art of the 1960s*. Museum of Modern Art, Studies in Modern Art, vol. 1, 16–38. New York, 1991.

Articles

Bochner, Mel. "Excerpts from Speculation (1967–1970)." *Artforum* 8, no. 9 (May 1970): 70–73.

Bollen, Christopher. "Land Art." *Interview Magazine* (August 11, 2015).

Buchloh, Benjamin H.D. "Conceptual Art 1962–1969: From the Aesthetic of Administration to the Critique of Institutions." *October* 55 (Winter 1990): 105–143.

Buchloh, Benjamin H.D. "Figures of Authority, Ciphers of Regression: Notes on the Return of Representation in European Paintings." *October* 16 (Spring 1981): 36–68.

Coplans, John. "Circles of Style on the West Coast." *Art in America* 52, no. 3 (June 1964): 40.

Danto, Arthur C. "The Artworld." *Journal of Philosophy* 61, no. 19 (October 15, 1964): 571–584.

"Discussions with Heizer, Oppenheim, Smithson." *Avalanche*, no. 1 (Fall 1970): 48–71.

Dwan, Virginia. "Reflections on Robert Smithson." *College Art Association Art Journal* 42, no. 3 (Autumn 1982): 233.

Fried, Michael. "Art and Objecthood." *Artforum* 5, no. 10 (Summer 1967): 12–23.

Horne, Jed. "A New Stonehenge in Nevada." *Quest/80* 4, no. 7 (September 1980): 77.

Judd, Donald. "Specific Objects." *Arts Yearbook* 8 (1965): 74–82.

Kimmelman, Michael. "The Forgotten Godmother of Dia's Artists." *New York Times*. May 11, 2003.

Kimmelman, Michael. "A Sculptor's Colossus of the Desert." *New York Times*. December 12, 1999.

Kosuth, Joseph. "Art after Philosophy." *Studio International* 178, nos. 915, 916, 917 (October–December 1969): Part 1 (134–137), Part 2 (160–161), Part 3 (212–213).

Leider, Philip. "The Cool School." *Artforum* 2, no. 12 (1964): 47–52.

LeWitt, Sol. "Paragraphs on Conceptual Art." *Artforum* 5, no. 10 (Summer 1967): 79–83.

Lippard, Lucy R., and John Chandler. "The Dematerialization of Art." *Art International* 2, no. 22 (February 1968): 31–36.

Morris, Robert. "Anti Form." *Artforum* 6, no. 8 (April 1968): 33–35.

Morris, Robert. "Notes on Sculpture, Part 1." *Artforum* 4, no. 6 (February 1966): 42–44.

Morris, Robert. "Notes on Sculpture, Part 3." *Artforum* 5, no. 10 (Summer 1967): 24–29.

Morris, Robert. "Notes on Sculpture, Part 4: Beyond Objects." *Artforum* 7, no. 8 (April 1969): 50–54.

Nordland, Gerald. "Art: The Artist as Reinhardt." *Frontier: The Voice of the New West* (March 1962): 23–24.

Owens, Craig. "Earthwords," *October* 10 (Autumn 1979): 120–130.

"Rebuilding Three Galleries." *Architectural Forum* 120, no. 3 (March 1964): 114–115.

Reinhardt, Ad. "Art-as-Art." *Art International* 6, no. 10 (December 20, 1962): 36–37.

Reinhardt, Ad. "Art vs. History." *Artnews* 64, no. 9 (January 1966): 19.

Reinhardt, Ad. "The Black (Square) Painting Shows, 1963, 1964, 1965." *Artforum* 4, no. 7 (March 1966): 35.

Reise, Barbara. "*Untitled 1969*: A Footnote on Art and Minimal Stylehood." *Studio International* 177, no. 910 (April 1969): 166–172.

Rose, Barbara. "ABC Art." *Art in America* 53, no. 5 (October/November 1965): 57–69.

Rose, Barbara. "Los Angeles: The Second City." *Art in America* 54, no. 1 (January/February 1966): 110–115.

Smithson, Robert. "Aerial Art." *Studio International* 12, no. 5 (April 1969): 180–181.

Smithson, Robert. "The Crystal Land." *Harper's Bazaar*, no. 3054 (May 1966): 72–73.

Smithson, Robert. "Entropy and the New Monuments." *Artforum* 4, no. 10 (June 1966): 26–31.

Smithson, Robert. "Incidents of Mirror-Travel in the Yucatan." *Artforum* 8, no. 1 (September 1969): 28–33.

Smithson, Robert. "The Monuments of Passaic." *Artforum* 6, no. 4 (December 1967): 48–51.

Smithson, Robert. "A Sedimentation of the Mind: Earth Proposals." *Artforum* 7, no. 1 (September 1968): 44–50.

Smithson, Robert. "Towards the Development of an Air Terminal Site." *Artforum* 5, no. 10 (Summer 1967): 36–40.

"Statements by Gallery Directors." *Arts Magazine* 45, no. 6 (April 1971): 60.

Tomkins, Calvin. "Onward and Upward with the Arts: Maybe a Quantum Leap." *New Yorker*, no. 51 (February 5, 1972): 42–67.

Vincent, Bill. "Stalking the Double Negative on Mormon Mesa." *The Nevadan*. July 15, 1973.

Yau, John. "Kanemitsu in Los Angeles During the Sixties and Seventies." *Brooklyn Rail*. May 6, 2008.

Unpublished Sources

de Bruyn, Eric. "The Filmic Anomaly: Moments in Post-Minimalism (1966–1970)." PhD dissertation, City University of New York, 2002.

Freiman, Lisa. "Claes Oldenburg's 'Psychoaesthetics.'" PhD dissertation, Emory University, 2001.

Karsner, Douglas George. "'Leaving on a Jet Plane': Commercial Aviation, Airports and Post-Industrial American Society." PhD dissertation, Temple University, 1993.

Smithson, Robert, and Nancy Holt Papers. Archives of American Art, Smithsonian Institution, Washington.

Stuckey, Charles F. "Interview with Virginia Dwan." March 21–June 7, 1984. Archives of American Art, Smithsonian Institution, Washington.

Stuckey, Charles F. "Interview with Virginia Dwan." July 14, 2010–March 21, 2011. Elizabeth Murray Oral History of Women in the Visual Arts Project. Archives of American Art, Smithsonian Institution, Washington.

Van Vleck, Jenifer Leigh. "No Distant Places: Aviation and the Global American Century." PhD dissertation, Yale University, 2009.

Varian, Elayne. "Interview with Virginia Dwan of the Dwan Gallery." Exhibition Records of the Contemporary Wing of the Finch College Museum of Art. 1969, Archives of American Art, Smithsonian Institution, Washington.

Webb, Emily Taub. "On Site-Specificity: A Genealogy." PhD dissertation, Emory University, 2010.

Weschler, Lawrence. "Edward Kienholz: Oral History Transcript." 1977. Oral History Program. University of California, Los Angeles.

Weschler, Lawrence. "Interview with Virginia Dwan (Concerning Ed Kienholz)." March 1979. Dwan Archives, New York.

Publications by the Dwan Gallery

Edward Kienholz. Los Angeles, 1963.

Erwin Heerich: Cardboard Sculpture 1956–1958. New York, 1968.

Franz Kline Paintings 1950–1961. Los Angeles, 1963.

Martial Raysse. Los Angeles, 1967.

My Country 'Tis of Thee. Los Angeles, 1962.

Philip Guston, Franz Kline. Los Angeles, 1961.

10. New York, 1966.

Films by Virginia Dwan

Carl Andre: A Portrait (in three parts). 1976. Digital–video transfer. Filmed and directed by Virginia Dwan. Total running time 2:40:28. Part one: *Reconfiguration: Carl Andre at P.S. 1*. (39:57). Part two: *A Conversation* (1:01:12). Part three: *The Dinner* (54:45).

John Cage: A Portrait (in two parts). 1982. Digital–video transfer. Conceived and produced by Virginia Dwan; directed by Barry Harris. Total running time 2:18:23. Part one: *James Joyce, Marcel Duchamp, Eric Satie, An Alphabet* (1:10:45), reading by John Cage. Part two: *An Interview* (1:07:38), written and conducted by Virginia Dwan.

Sturtevant. *Study for Various Beuys Actions*. c. 1971. Digital–16 mm film transfer. All moving segments directed by Virginia Dwan. *Fat Meditation* directed by Sturtevant. Filmed by Robert Fiore. Performed by Sturtevant. Total running time: 26:33.

ACKNOWLEDGMENTS

An exhibition of this scale is made possible by many supporters and collaborators. I want first to thank Virginia Dwan for agreeing to the idea of the exhibition, for lending many treasured works from her collection, for opening up her archive for our research, and for sharing her writings with the readers of this book. I have appreciated her thoughtful guidance in the preparation of the show and trust that she feels we have told her story well.

That story—encompassing the art scenes of both coasts, Paris, and several aesthetic tendencies—is intricate and complex, and it could not have been told without the generous loans from many museums and private collectors listed separately in this volume; I offer them my sincere thanks. Numerous works came from our institutional partner, the Los Angeles County Museum of Art. My thanks to the museum's director Michael Govan and senior curator Stephanie Barron for their assistance with these and other loans. Barron's contribution and expertise have been invaluable. The selection of works has expanded, and the narrative has been enriched.

Several of the Dwan Gallery artists were actively involved in refabricating works, providing photographs, or even donating their artworks in the show to the National Gallery of Art. I am extremely grateful to William Anastasi, Mel Bochner, Michael Heizer, Joseph Kosuth, Robert Morris, Charles Ross, and Kenneth Snelson.

From the outset, Earl A. Powell III, director of the National Gallery of Art, and deputy director and chief curator Franklin Kelly have been unflagging in their enthusiasm. My friend and colleague Harry Cooper, curator of modern art, and D. Dodge Thompson, chief of exhibitions, have been immensely supportive of the show and ensured the integrity of its concept. Judith Brodie, curator of modern prints and drawings, and Sarah Greenough, senior curator of photographs, brought their estimable expertise to this project. Curatorial assistant Paige Rozanski helped coordinate the show; her meticulous research is represented in her impressive contributions to this catalog.

Funding for the exhibition was secured by Christine Myers, chief development officer, and deputy corporate relations officer Cristina Del Sesto. Wendy Battaglino, exhibition officer, and registrars Theresa Beall and Lehua Fisher oversaw the show's detailed arrangements with their usual professionalism. Our conservators—Jay Krueger, Katy May, Kimberly Schenck, Connie McCabe, Ronel Namde, Bethann Heinbaugh, and James Gleason—ensured that fragile artworks would be shown to best advantage, with Caroline Danforth attending to matting and framing. The show has been brilliantly installed by Mark Leithauser, senior curator and chief of design, and his colleagues Jamé

Anderson, Donna Kirk, Andrea D'Amato, and Lisa Farrell. Working with Susan Arensberg, head of exhibition programs, Lynn Matheny coordinated the information materials and the superb exhibition film directed by Carroll Moore, edited by David Hammer, and produced by Elizabeth Laitman Hughes. Chief of media productions Vicki Toye and her talented colleagues Brian Dooda and Adam Enatsky produced the wonderful audio, video, and cinematic components. Barbara Wood, Peter Dueker, Lorene Emerson, Ricardo Blanc, Tricia Zigmund, and John Schwartz provided the show's photographic materials—an enormous effort in itself.

This catalog has been lovingly produced by Judy Metro, editor in chief and head of publishing, who edited it personally; I am grateful for her hard work and the outstanding result. It was beautifully designed by Margaret Bauer. Its production was managed by deputy publisher Chris Vogel and production associate John Long, with the able editorial assistance of Katie Brennan. Sara Sanders-Buell oversaw the arduous but necessary task of re-photographing many of the works. I am delighted to acknowledge Susan Bielstein and Alan Thomas of the University of Chicago Press, our copublisher.

The display of Dwan ephemera and archival materials in the library was organized by Yuri Long with the support of Neal Turtell. The film program was curated by Peggy Parsons and Joanna Raczynska; the musical program was selected by Danielle Hahn. Faya Causey and Ali Peil organized the scholarly symposium with the assistance of Sarah Battle. I thank them and the Gallery's chief of communications Anabeth Guthrie; our present and former general counsels, Nancy Breuer and Elizabeth Croog, and attorneys Julian Saenz and Isabelle Raval; and in the Gallery Shops, chief of retail operations David Krol and his colleagues Don Henderson, Christine DerDerian, and Noriko Bell.

A number of individuals provided essential advice and assistance. I wish to thank David McKee, James Demetrion, David Gray, Caroline Collier, Jill O'Bryan, Sarah Eckhardt, Elyse Goldberg, Don Menveg, Lisa Jann, Tiffany Daneshgar, Jamin An, Ann Temkin, Cora Rosevear, Loïc Malle, Charlotte Ménard, Philippe Siauve, Billie Milam Weisman, Mary-Ellen Powell, Elizabeth Childress, Michael Childress, Hannah Kerr, Doug Munson, Dove Bradshaw, Amy Plumb Oppenheim, Alexandra Magnuson, Catherine Manchada, Lauren Mellon, Dana Miller, Gretta Johnson, Carey Ascenzo, Douglas Dreishpoon, Tom Martinelli, Richard Shebairo, Tim Burgard, Anke Kempkes, Sofia LeWitt, Janet Passehl, Didier Ottinger, Patricia Hickson, Eileen Doyle, Madeleine Grynsztejn, Michael Darling, Liz Rudnick, Katy Rodgers, Gina Guy, Stephen Jones, and Ellen Swieskowski. The exhibition and catalog have been enriched by the photography of Virginia Dwan, EPW Studio, Gianfranco Gorgoni, Michael Heizer, Kerry Loewen, Tom Vinetz, Julian Wasser, and Helen Winkler-Fosdick, among others. Our research benefited from the resources of the Library of Congress, the Archives of American Art, Smithsonian Institution, UCLA Library Special Collections, and the National Gallery of Art Library.

I wish to acknowledge Candace Dwan, who witnessed the extraordinary history recorded in these pages; I hope that she feels we have done justice to her mother's legacy. Anne Kovach of the Dwan Archive was instrumental in the show's conception and realization and did much to facilitate our research. I offer her my deepest thanks. Last but not least, I thank Chris Boutlier, whose encouragement was essential to this effort.

JAMES MEYER, *Deputy Director and Chief Curator, Dia Art Foundation*

Page numbers in italic type indicate illustrations. Dwan Gallery exhibitions are followed by DGLA or DGNY and the year.

Every effort has been made to locate the copyright holders for the reproductions used in this book. Any omissions will be corrected in subsequent editions.

Display images

P. 4: Photographer Leland Y. Lee; p. 14: Photo © Julian Wasser, Courtesy of Craig Krull Gallery, Santa Monica, California; p. 16: Photographer Virginia Dwan. Courtesy of Virginia Dwan Archives; p. 240: Photographer John D. Schiff. Courtesy Dwan Gallery Archives; p. 284: Photograph by Carl Andre. Courtesy of Virginia Dwan Archives; p. 318: Courtesy Dwan Gallery Archives

The Art Gallery in an Era of Mobility

Fig. 1: Photographer Nancy Holt. Courtesy Holt Archives; fig. 2: Photographer Robert Smithson. Courtesy Smithson Estate/VAGA; fig. 3: © Holt-Smithson Foundation/Licensed by VAGA, New York, NY; figs. 4–6, 9: Photographer Virginia Dwan. Courtesy of Virginia Dwan Archives; fig. 7: Stockbyte/Getty Images; fig. 8: Cooper Hewitt, New York, Museum purchase from General Acquisitions Endowment and Smithsonian Institution Collections Acquisition Program Funds, 1999.45.1. Cooper Hewitt, Smithsonian Design Museum/Art Resource, NY; figs. 10, 13–15: Photographer I. Serisawa. Courtesy Dwan Gallery Archives; fig. 11: Collection Stedelijk Museum Amsterdam; fig. 12: © All Rights Reserved. © Yves Klein/Artists Rights Society (ARS), New York/ADAGP, Paris 2016; fig. 16: Collection Moderna Museet, Stockholm. Photo: Moderna Museet/Stockholm; fig. 17: © James Rosenquist/Licensed by VAGA, New York, NY. Used by permission. All rights reserved; fig. 18: © Dennis Hopper, Courtesy of The Hopper Art Trust. Photo courtesy of the Oldenburg van Bruggen Studio; fig. 19: Hessisches Landesmuseum Darmstadt. Photographer Wolfgang Fuhrmannek; fig. 21: © Nancy Reddin Kienholz. Photo © Museum Associates/LACMA. © Kienholz. Courtesy of L.A. Louver, Venice, California; fig. 22: Nova Albion, François Pinault Collection. Knight's Gambit, destroyed. Pre-Columbian, Fine Arts Museum of San Francisco at the Palace of the Legion of Honor, Gift of Mr. and Mrs. Lowell McKegney. Photograph by Barbara Willa Brown; figs. 23, 25: Courtesy Dwan Gallery Archives; fig. 24: Collection Stedelijk Museum Amsterdam. © Kienholz. © Courtesy of L.A. Louver, Venice, California. Photo courtesy Stedelijk Museum Amsterdam; fig. 26: Photographer John D. Schiff. Courtesy Dwan Gallery Archives; figs. 27, 28, 30: Photographer Walter Russell. Courtesy Dwan Gallery Archives; figs. 29: Photographer Herbert Beyer. Courtesy Dwan Gallery Archives; fig. 31: © Michael Heizer/Triple Aught Foundation. Photograph by Michael Heizer. Courtesy of the artist and Gagosian Gallery; fig. 32: © Michael Heizer/Triple Aught Foundation. Photographer Virginia Dwan. Courtesy of the artist and Gagosian Gallery and Dwan Gallery Archives

Plates

Cats. 1–3, 21, 22, 27, 71, 77–79, 92: Photographer Tricia Zigmund; cats. 2, 10, 12–15, 17, 22, 25, 26, 29–31, 33, 53, 58 (cover), 59–61, 66, 68, 88–90, 95, 98, 100, 103, 106, 110–114, 124: EPW Studio; cat. 7: © Estate of Philip Guston, courtesy Hauser & Wirth; cats. 12–15, 17: © Yves Klein, ADAGP, Paris/ARS, New York, 2016; cat. 16: © Yves Klein, ADAGP, Paris/ARS, New York, 2016. Photo © Giancarlo Botti; cats. 18, 53, 55, 56: © Kienholz. Courtesy of L.A. Louver, Venice, California; cat. 19: Photographer Katherine Wetzel © Virginia Museum of Fine Arts; cat. 23: Photographer Nathan Keay © Museum of Contemporary Art Chicago; cats. 24, 31, 97: Photographer Ric Blanc; cats. 32, 107: Photographer Greg Williams; cat. 34: Photography by Lee Stalsworth; cat. 35: © 2016 Fairweather LTD/Artists Rights Society (ARS), New York; cat. 37: Digital image © Whitney Museum, NY. © 1963 Claes Oldenburg; cats. 38, 40: © 1963 Claes Oldenburg; cat. 41: Photo courtesy of the Oldenburg van Bruggen Studio © 1963 Claes Oldenburg. Photographer Julian Wasser; cat. 42: Art © Estate of Tom Wesselmann/Licensed by VAGA, New York, NY; cat. 44: © Lucas Samaras, courtesy Pace Gallery; cat. 45: Art © James Rosenquist/Licensed by VAGA, New York, NY; cats. 46–48: © 2016 The Andy Warhol Foundation for the Visual Arts, Inc./Artists Rights Society (ARS), New York. Digital image © Whitney Museum, NY. Photography by Jerry L. Thompson; cat. 54: © Kienholz. Courtesy of L.A. Louver, Venice, California. Digital image © 2016 Museum Associates/LACMA, Licensed by Art Resource, NY; cat. 57: © Mark di Suvero, courtesy of the artist and Spacetime C.C.; cats. 59, 91: © 2016 Robert Morris/Artists Rights Society (ARS), New York; cats. 62, 63, 69: Image courtesy of the Board of Trustees, National Gallery of Art, Washington; cats. 64, 66: Image courtesy of the Board of Trustees, National Gallery of Art, Washington. Photographer Lee Ewing; cat. 65: © 2016 Stephen Flavin/Artists Rights Society (ARS), New York; cat. 67: Art © Holt-Smithson Foundation/Licensed by VAGA, New York, NY. Image courtesy of the Board of Trustees, National Gallery of Art, Washington. Photographer Lee Ewing; cat. 70: Digital image © The Museum of Modern Art/Licensed by SCALA/Art Resource, NY. © 2016 The LeWitt Estate/Artists Rights Society (ARS), New York; cat. 72: © 2016 The LeWitt Estate/Artists Rights Society (ARS), New York; cat. 75: © 2016 Robert Morris/Artists Rights Society (ARS), New York. Photo © CNAC/MNAM/Dist. RMN-Grand Palais/Art Resource, NY; cat. 76: © Tate, London 2016; cats. 81, 90, 110, 111, 117–120, 123: Art © Holt-Smithson Foundation/Licensed by VAGA, New York, NY. Photographer Tricia Zigmund; cat. 82: Image courtesy of the Board of Trustees, National Gallery of Art, Washington. Photographer Erica Abbey; cat. 88: © Kienholz. Courtesy of L.A. Louver, Venice, California. Photographer Tricia Zigmund; cats. 89, 95, 98, 112–116: Art © Holt-Smithson Foundation/Licensed by VAGA, New York, NY; cat. 94: Art © Holt-Smithson Foundation/Licensed by VAGA, New York, NY. Photographer Lee Ewing; cats. 99, 102 (pp. 211, 212): © Michael Heizer/Triple Aught Foundation. Photograph by Michael Heizer. Courtesy of the artist and Gagosian Gallery; cats. 100, 101: © Michael Heizer/Triple Aught Foundation. Courtesy of the artist and Gagosian Gallery; cat. 102 (p. 213): © Michael Heizer/Triple Aught Foundation. Photograph by John Weber. Courtesy of the artist and Gagosian Gallery; cat. 103: © Estate of Walter De Maria. Photographer David Lubarsky; cat. 104: © Estate of Walter De Maria. Photographer Helen Winkler-Fosdick; cat. 105: © Estate of Walter De Maria. Photographer John Client; cat. 108: Photographer Kerry Loewen; cat. 109 (p. 224): Art © Holt-Smithson Foundation/Licensed by VAGA, New York, NY. Photo © Aerographics, Salt Lake City, 2016. Courtesy Dia Art Foundation, New York; cat. 109 (p. 225, top): Art © Holt-Smithson Foundation/Licensed by VAGA, New York, NY. Photo © Gianfranco Gorgoni; cat. 109 (p. 225, bottom): Art © Holt-Smithson Foundation/Licensed by VAGA, New York, NY. Photo by George Steinmetz, Courtesy Dia Art Foundation, New York; cats. 121, 122: Art © Holt-Smithson Foundation/Licensed by VAGA, New York, NY. Photographer Ric Blanc

Writings

P. 243: © All Rights Reserved. © Yves Klein/Artists Rights Society (ARS), New York/ADAGP, Paris 2016; 246: Photograph by William Claxton/Courtesy Demont Photo Management; pp. 248, 251: Photographer Walter Russell. Courtesy Dwan Gallery Archives; p. 255 (top and bottom), pp. 256, 260 (top and bottom), p. 281: Photographer Virginia Dwan. Courtesy of Virginia Dwan Archives; p 261: Photographer Anne Kovach. Courtesy Dwan Gallery Archives; p. 273: Photographer Robert Smithson. Courtesy Smithson Estate/VAGA; p. 274: Photographer Nancy Holt. Courtesy Holt Archives; p. 283: © Michael Heizer/Triple Aught Foundation. Photograph by Michael Heizer. Courtesy of the artist and Gagosian Gallery and Dwan Gallery Archives; p. 264: Hans Strelow Archive

Virginia Dwan Chronology

Figs. 1–5, 8, 9, 13, 17, 28, 29, 40: Courtesy of Virginia Dwan Archives; figs. 6, 7, 12, 14–16, 19, 21–24, 27: Courtesy Dwan Gallery Archives; fig. 10: Photograph by Giancarlo Botti. Los Angeles County Museum of Art Balch Art Research Library, Papers of Michael and Dorothy Blankfort, 1961–1995, BLA.001.001. © Yves Klein/Artists Rights Society (ARS), New York/ADAGP, Paris 2016. © All rights reserved; fig. 11: Photograph by William Claxton/Courtesy Demont Photo Management; fig. 18: Photo courtesy of the Oldenburg van Bruggen Studio; fig. 20: © Kienholz. Courtesy of L.A. Louver, Venice, California; fig. 25: Photographer John D. Schiff. Courtesy Dwan Gallery Archives; figs. 26, 30, 31: Photographer Virginia Dwan. Courtesy of Virginia Dwan Archives; figs. 32, 35: Photographer Nancy Holt. Courtesy Holt Archives; fig. 33: Art © Holt-Smithson Foundation/Licensed by VAGA, New York, NY; fig. 34: © Michael Heizer/Triple Aught Foundation. Photograph by Michael Heizer. Courtesy of the artist and Gagosian Gallery and Virginia Dwan Archives; fig. 36: Photographer Nancy Reddin Kienholz/© Kienholz. Courtesy of L.A. Louver, Venice, California; fig. 37: Photographer Candace Dwan. Courtesy of Virginia Dwan Archives; fig. 38: © Michael Heizer/Triple Aught Foundation. Photographer Virginia Dwan. Courtesy of the artist and Gagosian Gallery and Virginia Dwan Archives; fig. 39: Photographer Dan Budnick. Courtesy Dwan Gallery Archives

Exhibition History: Dwan Gallery, Los Angeles and New York

All images Courtesy Dwan Gallery Archives.

Figs. 12, 17, 19, 20, 29, 31, 32: Photographer I. Serisawa, Los Angeles, CA; fig. 13: Yves Klein/Artists Rights Society (ARS), New York/ADAGP, Paris 2016; figs. 14, 15, 44, 57–60, 64, 74, 88, 89, 92, 112, 129: Photographer Joshua Nefsky; fig. 42: ©Julian Wasser; figs. 43, 65, 87, 91, 103, 107–109, 113, 115, 117–119, 121–123, 131–134: Photographer Walter Russell; figs. 61, 71, 75: Photographer John D. Schiff; figs. 63, 72, 83, 93, 98, 102: Photographer Anne Kovach; fig. 84: Photographer Virginia Dwan; fig. 120: Photographer Eric Pollitzer; fig. 128: Photographers Robert Mates and Paul Katz

Epigraph (p. 18)

The Kinks, "This Time Tomorrow." Written by Raymond Davies. Published by ABKCO Music, Inc. Used by permission. All rights reserved.

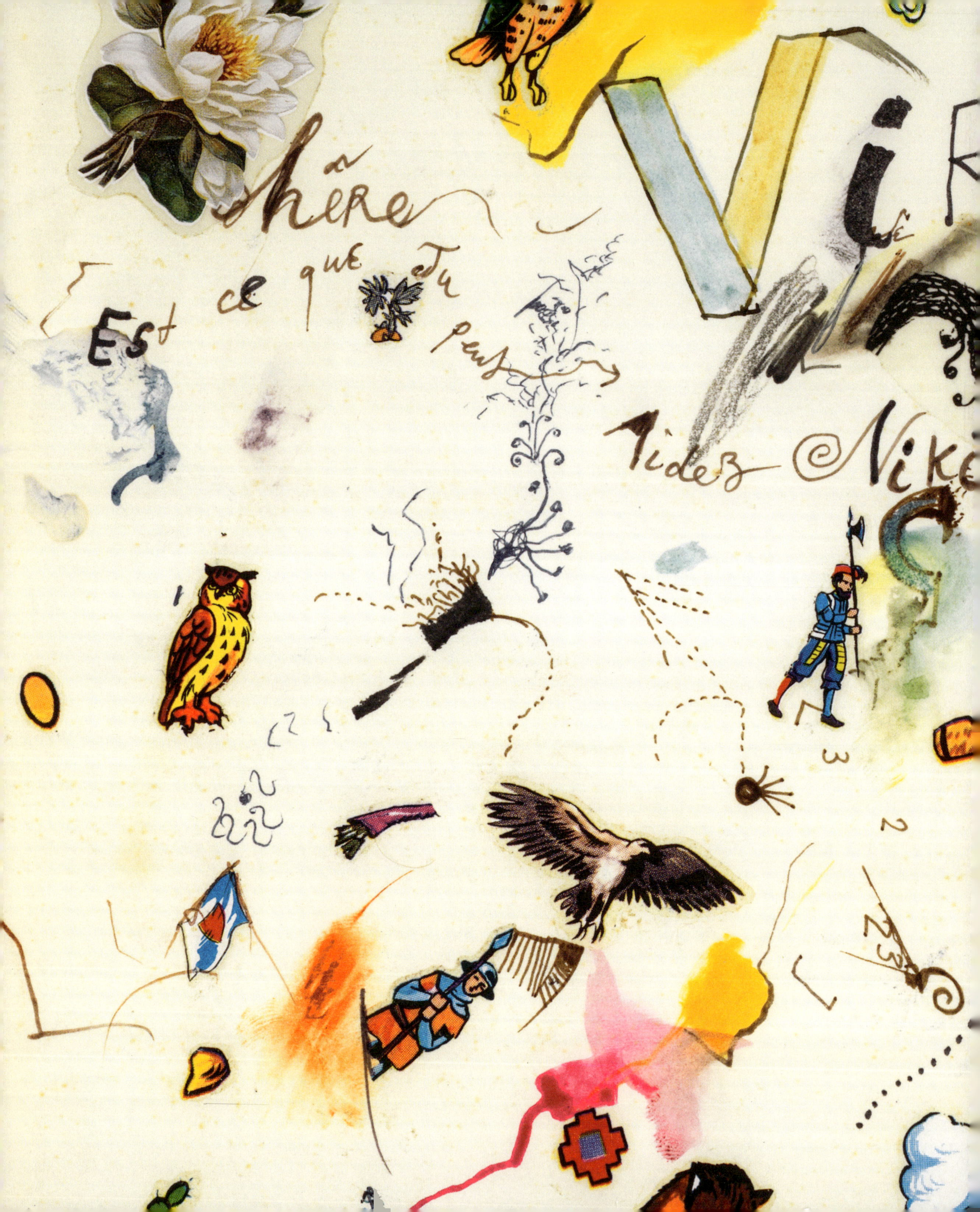
Est ce que tu peux